CHILTON'S
REPAIR MANUAL

MW00606631

CHEVROLET CAMARO 1982–92

All U.S. and Canadian models of the Chevrolet Camaro

Senior Vice President	Ronald A. Hoxter
Publisher and Editor-In-Chief	Kerry A. Freeman, S.A.E.
Executive Editors	Dean F. Morgantini, S.A.E., W. Calvin Settle, Jr., S.A.E.
Managing Editor	Nick D'Andrea
Special Products Manager	Ken Grabowski, A.S.E., S.A.E.
Senior Editors	Jacques Gordon, Michael L. Grady, Debra McCall, Kevin M. G. Maher, Richard J. Rivele, S.A.E., Richard T. Smith, Jim Taylor, Ron Webb
Project Managers	Martin J. Gunther, Will Kessler, A.S.E., Richard Schwartz
Production Manager	Andrea Steiger
Product Systems Manager	Robert Maxey
Director of Manufacturing	Mike D'Imperio
Editor	Don Schnell

CHILTON BOOK COMPANY

ONE OF THE DIVERSIFIED PUBLISHING COMPANIES,
A PART OF CAPITAL CITIES/ABC, INC.

CONTENTS

GENERAL INFORMATION and MAINTENANCE

1 How to use this book
2 Tools and Equipment
13 Routine Maintenance

ENGINE PERFORMANCE and TUNE-UP

39 Tune-Up Performance
40 Tune-Up Specifications

ENGINE and ENGINE OVERHAUL

86 Engine Electrical System
94 Engine Service
97 Engine Specifications

EMISSION CONTROLS

162 Emission Controls System and Service

FUEL SYSTEM

191 Carbureted Fuel System
226 Carburetor Specifications
225 TBI Fuel Injection System
234 MFI and TPI Fuel Injection

CHASSIS ELECTRICAL

258 Heating and Air Conditioning
266 Windshield Wipers and Washers
268 Instruments and Switches
272 Lighting
273 Circuit Protection

7 DRIVE TRAIN

276 Manual Transmission
279 Clutch
285 Automatic Transmission
293 Drive Line
295 Rear Axle

8 SUSPENSION and STEERING

303 Front Suspension
312 Rear Suspension
316 Steering

9 BRAKES

331 Brake Systems
341 Front Disc Brakes
345 Rear Drum Brakes
348 Rear Disc Brakes

10 BODY

360 Exterior
367 Interior

11 MECHANIC'S DATA

382 Mechanic's Data
384 Glossary
390 Abbreviations
392 Index

**221 Chilton's Fuel Economy
and Tune-Up Tips**

373 Chilton's Body Repair Tips

SAFETY NOTICE

Proper service and repair procedures are vital to the safe, reliable operation of all motor vehicles, as well as the safety of those performing repairs. This book outlines procedures for servicing and repairing vehicles using safe effective methods. The procedures contain many NOTES, CAUTIONS and WARNINGS which should be followed along with standard safety procedures to eliminate the possibility of personal injury or improper service which could damage the vehicle or compromise its safety.

It is important to note that repair procedures and techniques, tools and parts for servicing motor vehicles, as well as the skill and experience of the individual performing the work vary widely. It is not possible to anticipate all of the conceivable ways or conditions under which vehicles may be serviced, or to provide cautions as to all of the possible hazards that may result. Standard and accepted safety precautions and equipment should be used during cutting, grinding, chiseling, prying, or any other process that can cause material removal or projectiles.

Some procedures require the use of tools specially designed for a specific purpose. Before substituting another tool or procedure, you must be completely satisfied that neither your personal safety, nor the performance of the vehicle will be endangered.

Although the information in this guide is based on industry sources and is as complete as possible at the time of publication, the possibility exists that the manufacturer made later changes which could not be included here. While striving for total accuracy, Chilton Book Company cannot assume responsibility for any errors, changes, or omissions that may occur in the compilation of this data.

PART NUMBERS

Part numbers listed in the reference are not recommendations by Chilton for any product by brand name. They are references that can be used with interchange manuals and aftermarket supplier catalogs to locate each brand supplier's discrete part number.

SPECIAL TOOLS

Special tools are recommended by the vehicle manufacturer to perform their specific job. Use has been kept to a minimum, but where absolutely necessary, they are referred to in the text by the part number of the tool manufacturer. These tools can be purchased, under the appropriate part number, from the Service Tool Division, Kent-Moore Corporation, 1501 South Jackson Street, Jackson, MI 49203 or an equivalent tool can be purchased locally from a tool supplier or parts outlet. Before substituting any tool for the one recommended, read the SAFETY NOTICE at the top of this page.

ACKNOWLEDGEMENTS

Chilton Book Company expresses appreciation to Chevrolet Motor Division, General Motors Corporation for their generous assistance.

Copyright © 1992 by Chilton Book Company
All Rights Reserved
Published in Radnor, Pennsylvania 19089 by Chilton Book Company
ONE OF THE DIVERSIFIED PUBLISHING COMPANIES, A PART OF CAPITAL CITIES/ABC, INC.

Manufactured in the United States of America
    67890   109876

Chilton's Repair Manual: Camaro 1982–92
ISBN 0-8019-8306-1 pbk.
Library of Congress Catalog Card No. 91-058843

General Information and Maintenance

HOW TO USE THIS BOOK

Chilton's Repair Manual for Camaro covers all models from 1982 through 1992.

The first two Chapters will be the most used, since they contain maintenance and tune-up information and procedures. Studies have shown that a properly tuned and maintained Camaro can get at least 10% better gas mileage (which translates into lower operating costs) and periodic maintenance will catch minor problems before they turn into major repair bills. The other Chapters deal with the more complex systems of your Camaro. Operating systems from engine through brakes are covered to the extent that the average do-it-yourselfer becomes mechanically involved.

A secondary purpose of this book is a reference guide for owners who want to understand their Camaro and/or their mechanics better. In this case, no tools at all are required. Knowing just what a particular repair job requires in parts and labor time will allow you to evaluate whether or not you're getting a fair price quote and help decipher itemized bills from a repair shop.

Before attempting any repairs or service on your Camaro, read through the entire procedure outlined in the appropriate Chapter. This will give you the overall view of what tools and supplies will be required. There is nothing more frustrating than having to walk to the bus stop on Monday morning because you were short one gasket on Sunday afternoon. So read ahead and plan ahead. Each operation should be approached logically and all procedures thoroughly understood before attempting any work. Some special tools that may be required can often be rented from local automotive jobbers or places specializing in renting tools and equipment. Check the yellow pages of your phone book.

All Chapters contain adjustments, maintenance, removal and installation procedures, and overhaul procedures. When overhaul is not considered practical, we tell you how to remove the failed part and then how to install the new or reconditioned replacement. In this way, you at least save the labor costs. Backyard overhaul of some components (such as the alternator or water pump) is just not practical, but the removal and installation procedure is often simple and well within the capabilities of the average Camaro owner.

Two basic mechanic's rules should be mentioned here. First, whenever the LEFT side of the Camaro or engine is referred to, it is meant to specify the DRIVER'S side of the Camaro. Conversely, the RIGHT side of the Camaro means the PASSENGER'S side. Second, all screws and bolts are removed by turning counterclockwise, and tightened by turning clockwise.

Safety is always the most important rule. Constantly be aware of the dangers involved in working on or around an automobile and take proper precautions to avoid the risk of personal injury or damage to the vehicle. See the Chapter in this Chapter, Servicing Your Vehicle Safely, and the SAFETY NOTICE on the acknowledgment page before attempting any service procedures and pay attention to the instructions provided. There are 3 common mistakes in mechanical work:

1. Incorrect order of assembly, disassembly or adjustment. When taking something apart or putting it together, doing things in the wrong order usually just costs you extra time; however it CAN break something. Read the entire procedure before beginning disassembly. Do everything in the order in which the instructions say you should do it, even if you can't immediately see a reason for it. When you're taking apart something that is very intricate (for example a carburetor), you might want to draw a picture of how it looks when assembled at one point in order to make sure you get everything back in

its proper position. We will supply exploded views whenever possible, but sometimes the job requires more attention to detail than an illustration provides. When making adjustments (especially tune-up adjustments), do them in order. One adjustment often affects another and you cannot expect satisfactory results unless each adjustment is made only when it cannot be changed by any other.

2. Overtorquing (or undertorquing) nuts and bolts. While it is more common for overtorquing to cause damage, undertorquing can cause a fastener to vibrate loose and cause serious damage, especially when dealing with aluminum parts. Pay attention to torque specifications and utilize a torque wrench in assembly. If a torque figure is not available remember that, if you are using the right tool to do the job, you will probably not have to strain yourself to get a fastener tight enough. The pitch of most threads is so slight that the tension you put on the wrench will be multiplied many times in actual force on what you are tightening. A good example of how critical torque is can be seen in the case of spark plug installation, especially where you are putting the plug into an aluminum cylinder head. Too little torque can fail to crush the gasket, causing leakage of combustion gases and consequent overheating of the plug and engine parts. Too much torque can damage the threads or distort the plug, which changes the spark gap at the electrode. Since more and more manufacturers are using aluminum in their engine and chassis parts to save weight, a torque wrench should be in any serious do-it-yourselfer's tool box.

There are many commercial chemical products available for ensuring that fasteners won't come loose, even if they are not torqued just right (a very common brand is Loctite®). If you're worried about getting something together tight enough to hold, but loose enough to avoid mechanical damage during assembly, one of these products might offer substantial insurance. Read the label on the package and make sure the product is compatible with the materials, fluids, etc. involved before choosing one.

3. Crossthreading. This occurs when a part such as a bolt is screwed into a nut or casting at the wrong angle and forced, causing the threads to become damaged. Crossthreading is more likely to occur if access is difficult. It helps to clean and lubricate fasteners, and to start threading with the part to be installed going straight in, using your fingers. If you encounter resistance, unscrew the part and start over again at a different angle until it can be inserted and turned several times without much effort. Keep in mind that many parts, especially spark plugs, use tapered threads so that gentle turning will automatically bring the part you're threading to the proper angle if you don't force it or resist a change in angle. Don't put a wrench on the part until it's been turned in a couple of times by hand. If you suddenly encounter resistance and the part has not seated fully, don't force it. Pull it back out and make sure it's clean and threading properly.

Always take your time and be patient; once you have some experience, working on your Camaro will become an enjoyable hobby.

TOOLS AND EQUIPMENT

Naturally, without the proper tools and equipment, it is impossible to properly service your vehicle. It would be impossible to catalog each tool that you would need to perform each or every operation in this book. It would also be unwise for the amateur to rush out and buy an expensive set of tools an the theory that he may need one or more of them at sometime.

The best approach is to proceed slowly, gathering together a good quality set of those tools that are used most frequently. Don't be misled by the low cost of bargain tools. It is far better to spend a little more for better quality. Forged wrenches, 6- or 12-point sockets and fine tooth ratchets are by far preferable to their less expensive counterparts. As any good mechanic can tell you, there are few worse experiences than trying to work on a Camaro with bad tools. Your monetary savings will be far outweighed by frustration and mangled knuckles.

Certain tools, plus a basic ability to handle tools, are required to get started. A basic mechanics tool set, a torque wrench, and a Torx® bits set. Torx® bits are hexlobular drivers which fit both inside and outside on special Torx® head fasteners used in various places on Camaro vehicles.

Begin accumulating those tools that are used most frequently; those associated with routine maintenance and tune-up.

In addition to the normal assortment of screwdrivers and pliers you should have the following tools for routine maintenance jobs:

1. SAE/Metric wrenches, sockets and combination open end/box end wrenches in sizes from ⅛ in. (3mm) to ¾ in. (19mm); and a spark plug socket (⅝ in.)

If possible, buy various length socket drive extensions. One break in this department is that the metric sockets available in the U.S. will all fit the ratchet handles and extensions you may already have (¼, ⅜ and ½ in. drive).

2. Jackstands for support
3. Oil filter wrench
4. Oil filter spout for pouring oil

5. Grease gun for chassis lubrication

6. A container for draining oil

7. Many rags for wiping up the inevitable mess.

In addition to the above items, there are several others that are not absolutely necessary, but handy to have around. These include oil-dry (cat box gravel will work just as well), a transmission funnel and the usual supply of lubricants, antifreeze and fluids, although these can be purchased as needed. This is a basic list for routine maintenance, but only your personal needs and desires can accurately determine your list of necessary tools.

The second list of tools is for tune-ups. While the tools involved here are slightly more sophisticated, they need not be outrageously expensive. There are several inexpensive tach/dwell meters on the market that are every bit as good for the average mechanic as a professional model. Just be sure that it goes to at least 1,200–1,500 rpm on the tach scale and that it works on 4-, 6- and 8-cylinder engines. A basic list of tune-up equipment could include:

1. Tach-dwell meter

2. Spark plug wrench

3. Inductive timing light

4. Spark plug gauge/adjusting tools

Here again, be guided by your own needs. In addition to these basic tools, there are several other tools and gauges you may find useful. These include:

1. A compression gauge. The screw-in type is slower to use, but eliminates the possibility of a faulty reading due to escaping pressure

2. A manifold vacuum gauge

3. A test light

4. An induction meter. This is used for determining whether or not there is current in a wire. These are handy for use if a wire is broken somewhere in a wiring harness.

As a final note, you will probably find a torque wrench necessary for all but the most basic work. The beam type models are perfectly adequate, although the click (breakaway) type are more precise, and you don't have to crane your neck to see a torque reading in awkward situations. The breakaway torque wrenches are more expensive and should be recalibrated periodically.

Torque specification for each fastener will be given in the procedure in any case that a specific torque value is required. If no torque specifications are given, use the following values as a guide, based upon fastener size:

6mm bolt/nut – 4 ft. lbs. (0.4 Nm)
8mm bolt/nut – 7 ft. lbs. (0.8 Nm)
10mm bolt/nut – 12 ft. lbs. (1.4 Nm)
12mm bolt/nut – 18 ft. lbs. (2.2 Nm)
14mm bolt/nut – 25 ft. lbs. (3.0 Nm)
16mm bolt/nut – 35 ft. lbs. (4.2 Nm)
20mm bolt/nut – 57 ft. lbs. (7.0 Nm)

Special Tools

NOTE: *Special tools are occasionally necessary to perform a specific job or are recommended to make a job easier. Their use has been kept to a minimum. When a special tool is indicated, it will be referred to by manufacturer's part number, and where possible, an illustration of the tool will by provided so that an equivalent tool may be used. A list of tool manufacturers and their addresses follows:*

General Motors
Service Tool Division
Kent-Moore
29784 Little Mack
Roseville, MI 48066-2298

Normally, the use of special factory tools is avoided for repair procedures, since these are not readily available for the do-it-yourself mechanic. When it is possible to perform the job with more commonly available tools, it will be pointed out, but occasionally, a special tool was designed to perform a specific function and should be used. Before substituting another tool, you should be convinced that neither your safety nor the performance of the vehicle will be compromised.

SERVICING YOUR VEHICLE SAFELY

It is virtually impossible to anticipate all of the hazards involved with automotive maintenance and service, but care and common sense will prevent most accidents.

The rules of safety for mechanics range from "don't smoke around gasoline," to "use the proper tool for the job." The trick to avoiding injuries is to develop safe work habits and take every possible precaution.

Dos

• Do keep a fire extinguisher and first aid kit within easy reach.

• Do wear safety glasses or goggles when cutting, drilling or prying, even if you have 20-20 vision. If you wear glasses for the sake of vision, they should be made of hardened glass that can also serve as safety glasses, or wear safety goggles over your regular glasses.

• Do shield your eyes whenever you work around the battery. Batteries contain sulphuric acid; in case of contact with the eyes or skin, flush the area with water or a mixture of water and baking soda and get medical attention immediately.

• Do use safety stands for any under Camaro

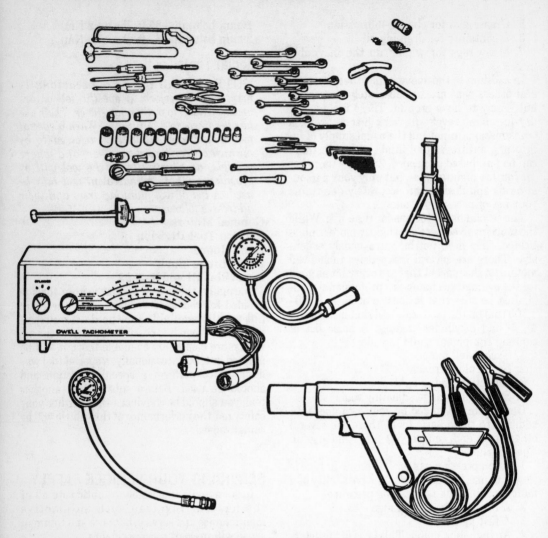

A basic assortment of hand tools needed for automotive service

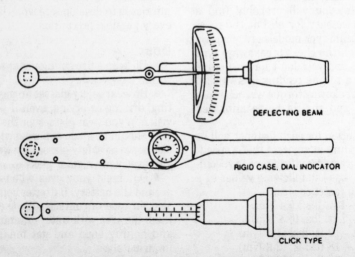

DEFLECTING BEAM

RIGID CASE, DIAL INDICATOR

CLICK TYPE

Three different style torque wrenches available

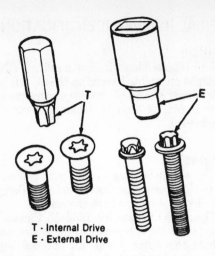

T - Internal Drive
E - External Drive

Special Torx® and inverted Torx® sockets

service. Jacks are for raising vehicles; safety stands are for making sure the vehicle stays raised until you want it to come down. Whenever the vehicle is raised, block the wheels remaining on the ground and set the parking brake.

• Do use adequate ventilation when working with any chemicals. Like carbon monoxide, the asbestos dust resulting from brake lining wear can be poisonous in sufficient quantities.

• Do disconnect the negative battery cable when working on the electrical system. The secondary ignition system can contain more than 40,000 volts.

• Do follow manufacturer's directions whenever working with potentially hazardous materials. Both brake fluid and antifreeze are poisonous if taken internally.

• Do properly maintain your tools. Loose hammerheads, mushroomed punches and chisels, frayed or poorly grounded electrical cords, excessively worn screwdrivers, spread wrenches (open end), cracked sockets, slipping ratchets, or faulty droplight sockets can cause accidents.

• Do use the proper size and type of tool for the job being done.

• Do when possible, pull on a wrench handle rather than push on it, and adjust your stance to prevent a fall. If you must push on a wrench, try to keep your hand open.

• Do be sure that adjustable wrenches are tightly adjusted on the nut or bolt and pulled so that the face is on the side of the fixed jaw.

• Do select a wrench or socket that fits the nut or bolt. The wrench or socket should sit straight, not cocked.

• Do strike squarely with a hammer; avoid glancing blows.

• Do set the parking brake and block the

drive wheels if the work requires that the engine be running.

Don'ts

• Don't run an engine in a garage or anywhere else without proper ventilation — EVER! Carbon monoxide is poisonous; it takes a long time to leave the human body and you can build up a deadly supply of it in your system by simply breathing in a little every day. You may not realize you are slowly poisoning yourself. Always use power vents, windows, fans or open the garage doors.

• Don't work around moving parts while wearing a necktie or other loose clothing. Short sleeves are much safer than long, loose sleeves and hard-toed shoes with neoprene soles protect your toes and give a better grip on slippery surfaces. Jewelry such as watches, fancy belt buckles, beads or body adornment of any kind is not safe working around a Camaro. Long hair should be hidden under a hat or cap.

• Don't use pockets for toolboxes. A fall or bump can drive a screwdriver deep into your body. Even a wiping cloth hanging from the back pocket can wrap around a spinning shaft or fan.

• Don't smoke when working around gasoline, cleaning solvent or other flammable material.

• Don't smoke when working around the battery. When the battery is being charged, it gives off explosive hydrogen gas.

• Don't use gasoline to wash your hands; there are excellent soaps available. Gasoline may contain lead, and lead can enter the body through a cut, accumulating in the body until you are very ill. Gasoline also removes all the natural oils from the skin so that bone-dry hands will suck up oil and grease.

• Don't service the air conditioning system unless you are equipped with the necessary tools and training. The refrigerant, R-12, is extremely cold and when exposed to the air, will instantly freeze any surface it comes in contact with, including your eyes. Although the refrigerant is normally non-toxic, R-12 becomes a deadly poisonous gas in the presence of an open flame. One good whiff of the vapors from burning refrigerant can be fatal.

• Don't use screwdrivers for anything other than driving screws! A screwdriver used as a prying tool can snap when you least expect it, causing injuries. At the very least, you'll ruin a good screwdriver.

• Don't use a bumper jack (that little ratchet, scissors, or pantograph jack supplied with the car) for anything other than changing a flat! These jacks are only intended for emergency use out on the road; they are NOT designed as a

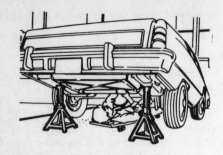

Always safely support the vehicle

maintenance tool. If you are serious about maintaining your car yourself, invest in a hydraulic floor jack of at least 1½ ton (1361kg) capacity, and at least two sturdy jackstands.

HISTORY

In 1967, Chevrolet entered the "pony car" market with an all new car, the Camaro. Available in two body styles, a convertible and a 2-door sports coupe. The 1968 Camaro changed little in appearance while the 302 Z28 increased in popularity and production. The 1969 model showed minor styling changes. Due to a complete restyling, the 1970 Camaro didn't appear in the showrooms until February of that year. The convertible was killed by lagging public demand and high insurance rates.

As the muscle car field diminished, it was felt that the Camaro would either have to change radically or vanish altogether from the field. It did neither; instead gradually losing the fire-breathing, street racer image and V8s larger than 5.7L to become a sporty grand touring car. While the engines gradually lessened in size and performance, the rest of the Camaro has been upgraded to form a responsive handling car.

The 1982 and later Camaro is a completely redesigned body style. It has shed a few hundred excess pounds thereby becoming more fuel efficient than previous models. This new body style has greatly enhanced Camaro's appeal to buyers of all ages.

MODEL IDENTIFICATION

The Camaro, the "F-body" carline of General Motors, carries only two series, the Sport Coupe and the Berlinetta. Within the Sport Coupe series, Camaro branches out into the Z28 Camaro and the International Race Of Champions, IROC Z Camaro. The Berlinetta has the more sophisticated interior, with more electronic instrumentation and controls.

SERIAL NUMBER IDENTIFICATION

Vehicle

The vehicle identification number (VIN) is stamped on a plate located on the top left hand side (driver's side) of the instrument panel so that it can be seen by looking through the windshield.

Engine

The 4-cylinder engine VIN code is stamped on the left side transmission mounting flange of the engine, directly above the starter.

The V6 VIN code for 1982–83 Camaros is stamped at the top center of the engine block, behind the water pump. An optional engine VIN code is location in front of the engine block, right side, below the cylinder head.

The V6 VIN code for 1984–88 Camaros is stamped on the left side transmission mounting flange of the engine. An optional engine VIN code location is also on the transmission mounting flange, directly above the main VIN code number.

The V8 engine VIN codes are on the front of the engine block, directly below the right cylinder head.

Transmission

A transmission VIN number is stamped on each transmission. The location of the

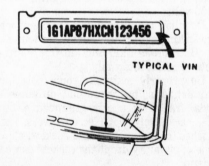

TYPICAL VIN

Vehicle Identification Number location

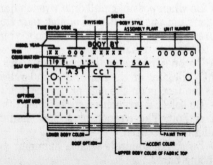

Body identification plate—1982

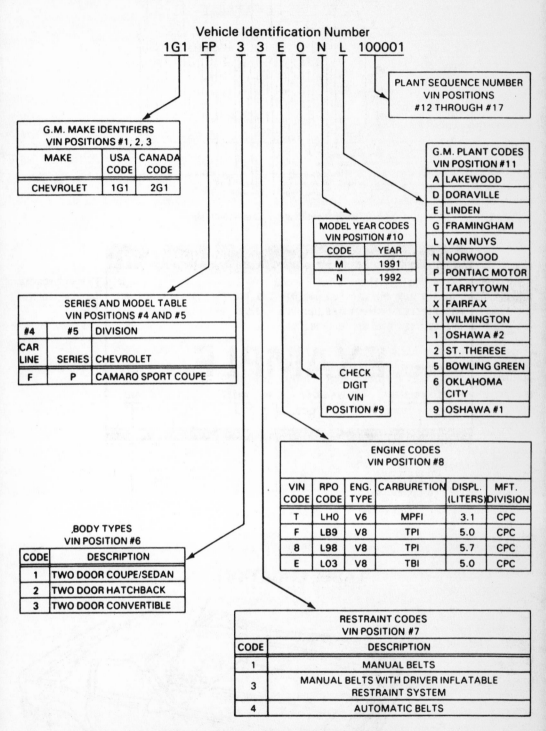

Vehicle Identification Number

1G1 FP 3 3 E 0 N L 100001

PLANT SEQUENCE NUMBER
VIN POSITIONS
#12 THROUGH #17

G.M. MAKE IDENTIFIERS
VIN POSITIONS #1, 2, 3

MAKE	USA CODE	CANADA CODE
CHEVROLET	1G1	2G1

G.M. PLANT CODES
VIN POSITION #11

A	LAKEWOOD
D	DORAVILLE
E	LINDEN
G	FRAMINGHAM
L	VAN NUYS
N	NORWOOD
P	PONTIAC MOTOR
T	TARRYTOWN
X	FAIRFAX
Y	WILMINGTON
1	OSHAWA #2
2	ST. THERESE
5	BOWLING GREEN
6	OKLAHOMA CITY
9	OSHAWA #1

MODEL YEAR CODES
VIN POSITION #10

CODE	YEAR
M	1991
N	1992

SERIES AND MODEL TABLE
VIN POSITIONS #4 AND #5

#4	#5	DIVISION
CAR LINE	SERIES	CHEVROLET
F	P	CAMARO SPORT COUPE

CHECK DIGIT VIN POSITION #9

ENGINE CODES
VIN POSITION #8

VIN CODE	RPO CODE	ENG. TYPE	CARBURETION	DISPL. (LITERS)	MFT. DIVISION
T	LHO	V6	MPFI	3.1	CPC
F	LB9	V8	TPI	5.0	CPC
8	L98	V8	TPI	5.7	CPC
E	LO3	V8	TBI	5.0	CPC

BODY TYPES
VIN POSITION #6

CODE	DESCRIPTION
1	TWO DOOR COUPE/SEDAN
2	TWO DOOR HATCHBACK
3	TWO DOOR CONVERTIBLE

RESTRAINT CODES
VIN POSITION #7

CODE	DESCRIPTION
1	MANUAL BELTS
3	MANUAL BELTS WITH DRIVER INFLATABLE RESTRAINT SYSTEM
4	AUTOMATIC BELTS

Vehicle Identification Number location—1990–92

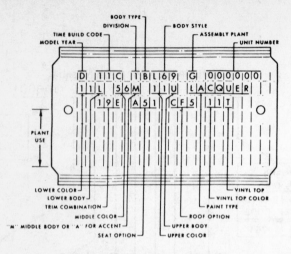

Body identification plate—1983–90

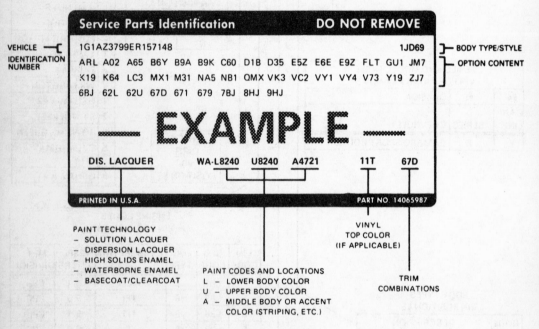

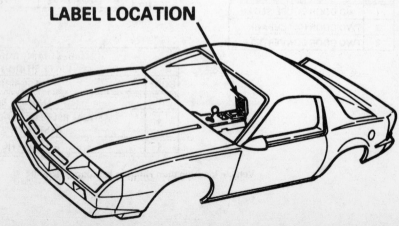

LABEL LOCATION

Service parts identification label—1991–92

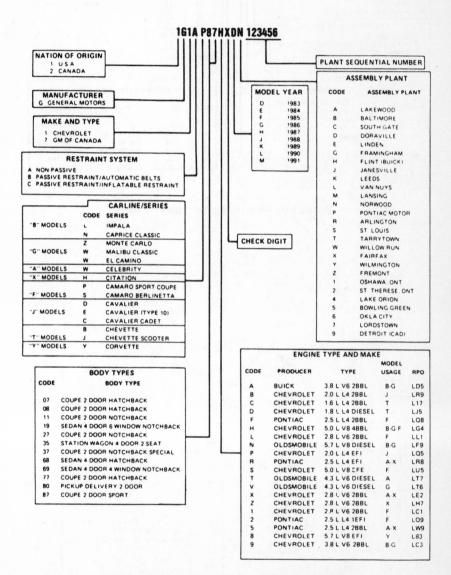

1G1A P87HXDN 123456

NATION OF ORIGIN
1 U S A
2 CANADA

MANUFACTURER
G GENERAL MOTORS

MAKE AND TYPE
1 CHEVROLET
7 GM OF CANADA

RESTRAINT SYSTEM
A NON-PASSIVE
B PASSIVE RESTRAINT/AUTOMATIC BELTS
C PASSIVE RESTRAINT/INFLATABLE RESTRAINT

PLANT SEQUENTIAL NUMBER

MODEL YEAR

CODE	YEAR
D	1983
E	1984
F	1985
G	1986
H	1987
J	1988
K	1989
L	1990
M	1991

CHECK DIGIT

ASSEMBLY PLANT

CODE	ASSEMBLY PLANT
A	LAKEWOOD
B	BALTIMORE
C	SOUTH GATE
D	DORAVILLE
E	LINDEN
G	FRAMINGHAM
H	FLINT (BUICK)
J	JANESVILLE
K	LEEDS
L	VAN NUYS
M	LANSING
N	NORWOOD
P	PONTIAC MOTOR
R	ARLINGTON
S	ST LOUIS
T	TARRYTOWN
W	WILLOW RUN
X	FAIRFAX
Y	WILMINGTON
Z	FREMONT
1	OSHAWA, ONT
2	ST THERESE, ONT
4	LAKE ORION
5	BOWLING GREEN
6	OKLA CITY
7	LORDSTOWN
9	DETROIT (CAD)

CARLINE/SERIES

	CODE	SERIES
"B" MODELS	L	IMPALA
	N	CAPRICE CLASSIC
	Z	MONTE CARLO
"G" MODELS	W	MALIBU CLASSIC
	W	EL CAMINO
"A" MODELS	W	CELEBRITY
"X" MODELS	H	CITATION
	P	CAMARO SPORT COUPE
"F" MODELS	S	CAMARO BERLINETTA
	D	CAVALIER
"J" MODELS	E	CAVALIER (TYPE 10)
	C	CAVALIER CADET
	B	CHEVETTE
"T" MODELS	J	CHEVETTE SCOOTER
"Y" MODELS	Y	CORVETTE

BODY TYPES

CODE	BODY TYPE
07	COUPE 2 DOOR HATCHBACK
08	COUPE 2 DOOR HATCHBACK
11	COUPE 2 DOOR NOTCHBACK
19	SEDAN 4 DOOR 6 WINDOW NOTCHBACK
27	COUPE 2 DOOR NOTCHBACK
35	STATION WAGON 4 DOOR 2 SEAT
37	COUPE 2 DOOR NOTCHBACK SPECIAL
68	SEDAN 4 DOOR HATCHBACK
69	SEDAN 4 DOOR 4 WINDOW NOTCHBACK
77	COUPE 2 DOOR HATCHBACK
80	PICKUP DELIVERY 2 DOOR
87	COUPE 2 DOOR SPORT

ENGINE TYPE AND MAKE

CODE	PRODUCER	TYPE	MODEL USAGE	RPO
A	BUICK	3.8 L V6 2BBL	B-G	LD5
B	CHEVROLET	2.0 L L4 2BBL	J	LR9
C	CHEVROLET	1.6 L L4 2BBL	T	L17
D	CHEVROLET	1.8 L L4 DIESEL	T	LJ5
F	PONTIAC	2.5 L L4 2BBL	F	LQ8
H	CHEVROLET	5.0 L V8 4BBL	B-G-F	LG4
L	CHEVROLET	2.8 L V6 2BBL	F	LL1
N	OLDSMOBILE	5.7 L V8 DIESEL	B-G	LF9
P	CHEVROLET	2.0 L L4 EFI	J	LQ5
R	PONTIAC	2.5 L L4 EFI	A-X	LR8
S	CHEVROLET	5.0 L V8 CFE	F	LU5
T	OLDSMOBILE	4.3 L V6 DIESEL	A	LT7
V	OLDSMOBILE	4.3 L V6 DIESEL	G	LT6
X	CHEVROLET	2.8 L V6 2BBL	A-X	LE2
Z	CHEVROLET	2.8 L V6 2BBL	X	LH7
1	CHEVROLET	2.8 L V6 2BBL	F	LC1
2	PONTIAC	2.5 L L4 1EFI	F	LQ9
5	PONTIAC	2.5 L L4 2BBL	A-X	LW9
8	CHEVROLET	5.7 L V8 EFI	Y	L83
9	CHEVROLET	3.8 L V6 2BBL	B-G	LC3

Vehicle Identification Number location—1983–88

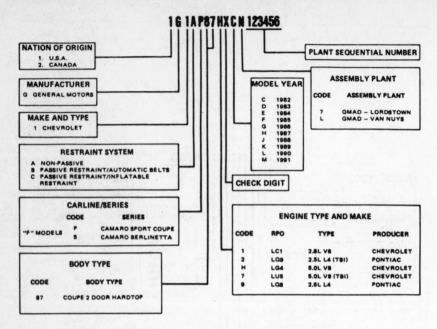

1 G 1 A P 87 H X C N 123456

NATION OF ORIGIN
1. U.S.A.
2. CANADA

MANUFACTURER
G GENERAL MOTORS

MAKE AND TYPE
1 CHEVROLET

RESTRAINT SYSTEM
A NON-PASSIVE
B PASSIVE RESTRAINT/AUTOMATIC BELTS
C PASSIVE RESTRAINT/INFLATABLE RESTRAINT

CARLINE/SERIES

	CODE	SERIES
"F" MODELS	P	CAMARO SPORT COUPE
	S	CAMARO BERLINETTA

BODY TYPE

CODE	BODY TYPE
87	COUPE 2 DOOR HARDTOP

PLANT SEQUENTIAL NUMBER

MODEL YEAR

C	1982
D	1983
E	1984
F	1985
G	1986
H	1987
J	1988
K	1989
L	1990
M	1991

ASSEMBLY PLANT

CODE	ASSEMBLY PLANT
7	GMAD – LORDSTOWN
L	GMAD – VAN NUYS

CHECK DIGIT

ENGINE TYPE AND MAKE

CODE	RPO	TYPE	PRODUCER
1	LC1	2.8L V6	CHEVROLET
2	LQ9	2.5L L4 (TBI)	PONTIAC
H	LG4	5.0L V8	CHEVROLET
7	LU5	5.0L V8 (TBI)	CHEVROLET
9	LQ8	2.5L L4	PONTIAC

Vehicle Identification Number codes—1982

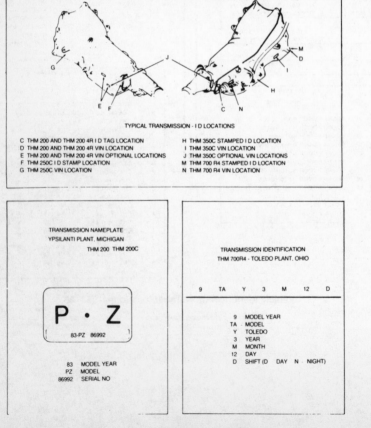

TYPICAL TRANSMISSION - I D LOCATIONS

C THM 200 AND THM 200 4R I D TAG LOCATION
D THM 200 AND THM 200 4R VIN LOCATION
E THM 200 AND THM 200 4R VIN OPTIONAL LOCATIONS
F THM 250C I D STAMP LOCATION
G THM 250C VIN LOCATION

H THM 350C STAMPED I D LOCATION
I THM 350C VIN LOCATION
J THM 350C OPTIONAL VIN LOCATIONS
M THM 700 R4 STAMPED I D LOCATION
N THM 700 R4 VIN LOCATION

TRANSMISSION NAMEPLATE
YPSILANTI PLANT, MICHIGAN
THM 200 THM 200C

P · Z

83-PZ 86992

83   MODEL YEAR
PZ   MODEL
86992 SERIAL NO

TRANSMISSION IDENTIFICATION
THM 700R4 - TOLEDO PLANT, OHIO

9   TA   Y   3   M   12   D

9   MODEL YEAR
TA   MODEL
Y   TOLEDO
3   YEAR
M   MONTH
12   DAY
D   SHIFT (D   DAY   N · NIGHT)

Transmission VIN location—1982–84

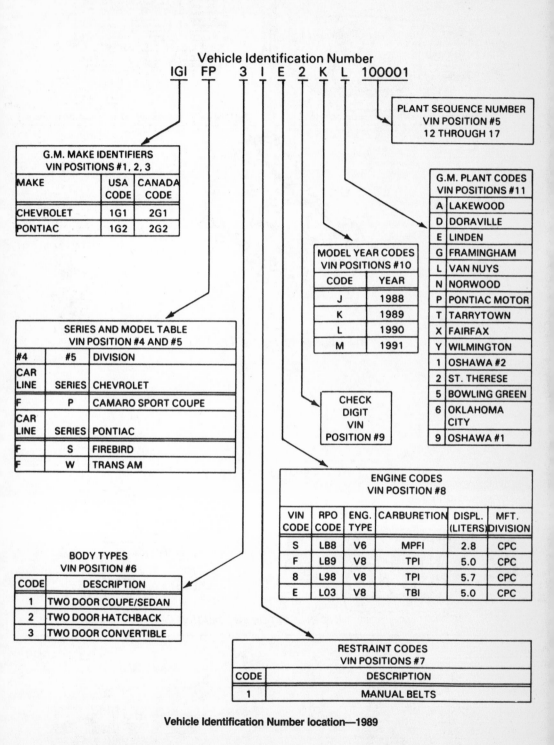

Vehicle Identification Number

IGI FP 3 I E 2 K L 100001

PLANT SEQUENCE NUMBER
VIN POSITION #5
12 THROUGH 17

G.M. MAKE IDENTIFIERS
VIN POSITIONS #1, 2, 3

MAKE	USA CODE	CANADA CODE
CHEVROLET	1G1	2G1
PONTIAC	1G2	2G2

G.M. PLANT CODES
VIN POSITIONS #11

A	LAKEWOOD
D	DORAVILLE
E	LINDEN
G	FRAMINGHAM
L	VAN NUYS
N	NORWOOD
P	PONTIAC MOTOR
T	TARRYTOWN
X	FAIRFAX
Y	WILMINGTON
1	OSHAWA #2
2	ST. THERESE
5	BOWLING GREEN
6	OKLAHOMA CITY
9	OSHAWA #1

MODEL YEAR CODES
VIN POSITIONS #10

CODE	YEAR
J	1988
K	1989
L	1990
M	1991

SERIES AND MODEL TABLE
VIN POSITION #4 AND #5

#4	#5	DIVISION
		CHEVROLET
CAR LINE	SERIES	
F	P	CAMARO SPORT COUPE
		PONTIAC
CAR LINE	SERIES	
F	S	FIREBIRD
F	W	TRANS AM

CHECK DIGIT
VIN POSITION #9

ENGINE CODES
VIN POSITION #8

VIN CODE	RPO CODE	ENG. TYPE	CARBURETION	DISPL. (LITERS)	MFT. DIVISION
S	LB8	V6	MPFI	2.8	CPC
F	LB9	V8	TPI	5.0	CPC
8	L98	V8	TPI	5.7	CPC
E	L03	V8	TBI	5.0	CPC

BODY TYPES
VIN POSITION #6

CODE	DESCRIPTION
1	TWO DOOR COUPE/SEDAN
2	TWO DOOR HATCHBACK
3	TWO DOOR CONVERTIBLE

RESTRAINT CODES
VIN POSITIONS #7

CODE	DESCRIPTION
1	MANUAL BELTS

Vehicle Identification Number location—1989

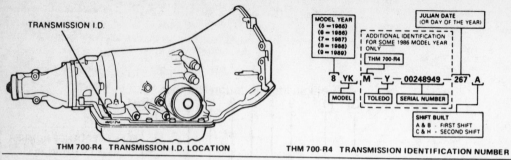

THM 700-R4   TRANSMISSION I.D. LOCATION

THM 700-R4   TRANSMISSION IDENTIFICATION NUMBER

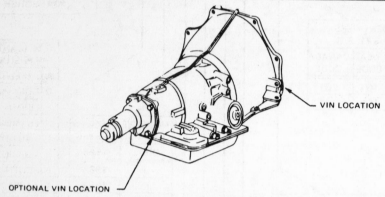

Transmission VIN location—1985–89

HYDRA-MATIC 4L60

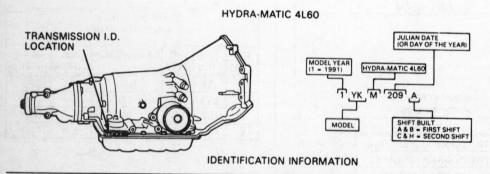

IDENTIFICATION INFORMATION

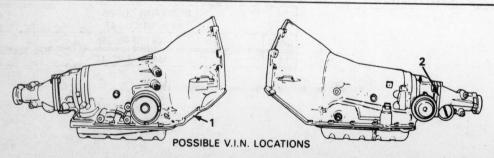

POSSIBLE V.I.N. LOCATIONS

Transmission VIN location—1990–92

transmission serial number on each transmission is shown in the illustration.

Rear Axle

Rear axle ratio, differential type, manufacturer and build date are stamped on the right axle tube on the foward side and on a metal tag attached to the axle cover.

ROUTINE MAINTENANCE

Air Cleaner

The air cleaner has a dual purpose. It not only filters the inducted air going into the engine, but also acts as a flame arrester if the engine should backfire. If an engine maintenance procedure requires the temporary removal of the air cleaner, remove it; otherwise, never run the engine without it.

REMOVAL AND INSTALLATION

NOTE: *The air cleaner assembly on Camaros with port fuel injection are mounted remotely near the radiator. It is connected to the intake manifold by flexible air intake ducting. The air cleaner element may be replace easily.*

1. Remove the nut(s) or screw clamp at the top of the air cleaner.
2. Remove the air filter.
3. To install, replace the filter and install the air cleaner cover.

Fuel Filter

There are three different types of fuel filters that may be used on Camaro: internal filter, inline filter and in-tank filter.

The internal filter is used on all carburetors and is located in the inlet fitting. A spring is installed behind the filter to hold the filter outward, sealing it against the inlet fitting. A check valve is also built into the fuel filter element.

The inline fuel filter is just that, installed in the fuel tank-to-engine fuel line, usually mounted on the rear crossmember of the Camaro.

The in-tank fuel filter is located on the lower end of the fuel pickup tube in the fuel tank. The filter is made of woven plastic and prevents dirt from entering the fuel line and also stops water unless the filter becomes completely submerged in water. This filter is self-cleaning and normally requires no maintenance.

REMOVAL AND INSTALLATION

CAUTION: *Never smoke when working around gasoline! Avoid all sources of sparks*

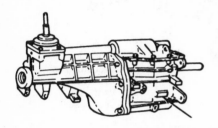

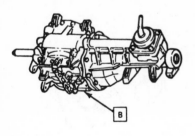

A.   VIN derivative location
B.   VIN derivative optional location

Manual transmission VIN location

REAR AXLE IDENTIFICATION

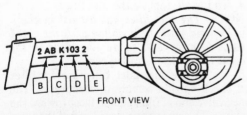

FRONT VIEW

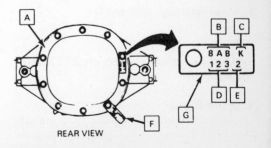

REAR VIEW

A.   Axle cover   E.   Shift
B.   Axle code   F.   Limited slip tag
C.   Manufacturer   G.   Axle code tag
D.   Day built

Rear axle identification

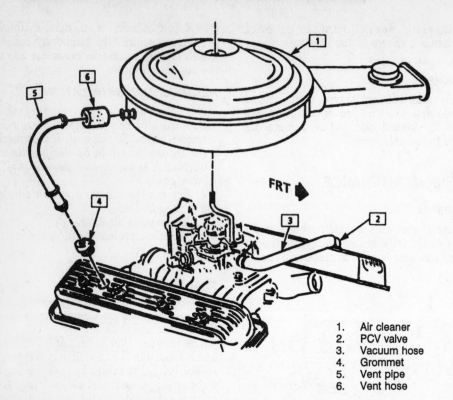

1. Air cleaner
2. PCV valve
3. Vacuum hose
4. Grommet
5. Vent pipe
6. Vent hose

Air cleaner assembly—carbureted and TBI engines

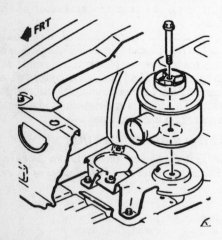

Air cleaner assembly—MPFI and TPI

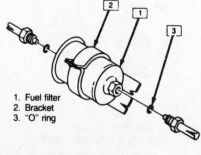

1. Fuel filter
2. Bracket
3. "O" ring

Fuel Injected in-line filter assembly

or ignition. Gasoline vapors are EXTREME-
LY volatile!

Carbureted Engine

1. Remove the air cleaner assembly. Disconnect the fuel line connection at the fuel inlet filter nut.

2. Remove the fuel inlet nut from the
carburetor.

3. Remove the fuel filter and spring.

4. To install, replace the fuel filter.
NOTE: *The fuel filter has a built in check
valve; and must be installed with the check
valve to meet with safety standards in the
event the vehicle is rolled over.*

5. Install the fuel inlet filter spring, filter
and check valve assembly in carburetor. The
check valve end of filter should faces toward the
fuel line. The ribs on the closed end of the filter
element will prevent the filter from being installed incorrectly unless it is forced.

6. Install the nut in the carburetor and tight-
en nut to 46 ft. lbs. (62 Nm).

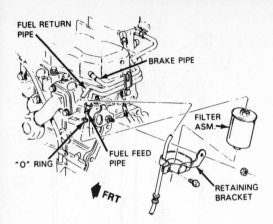

Fuel Injected in-line filter assembly—2.5L engine

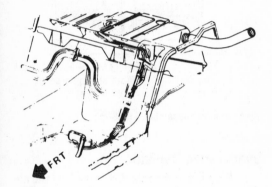

Fuel Injected in-line filter assembly—except 2.5L engine

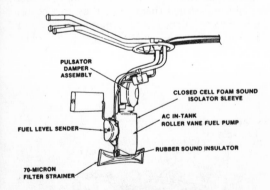

In-tank fuel filter assembly—fuel injected engines

7. Install the fuel line and tighten connection.

8. Start the engine and check for leaks. Install the air cleaner assembly.

Inline Filter

CAUTION: *To reduce the risk of fire and personal injury, it is necessary to relieve the fuel pressure before servicing the fuel system.*

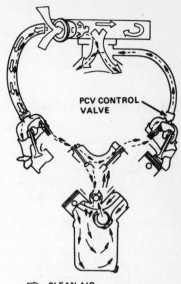

⇨ CLEAN AIR

→ VOLATILE OIL FUMES

- - → MIXTURE OF AIR AND FUMES

Positive Crankcase Ventilation (PCV) System

Positive Crankcase Ventilation (PCV) system

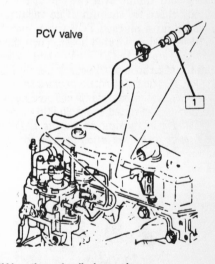

PCV location—4 cylinder engines

1. Using two wrenches, hold the wrench on the fuel filter stationary while loosening the fuel line nut with the other wrench.

2. Repeat Step 1 on the other side of the fuel filter.

3. Loosen the fuel filter bracket screw and remove the fuel filter and O-rings.

4. To install, make sure that the O-rings are good. If not, replace them.

5. Slide the fuel filter into the bracket making sure of the filter fuel flow direction is correct.

6. Install O-rings and the fuel lines.

7. Using two wrenches, torque the fittings to 22 ft. lbs. (30 Nm).

8. Turn the ignition switch ON to prime the fuel system and check for leaks.

Positive Crankcase Ventilation (PCV)

The crankcase ventilation system (PCV) must be operating correctly to provide complete removal of the crankcase vapors. Fresh air is supplied to the crankcase from the air filter, mixed with the internal exhaust gases, passed through the PCV valve and into the intake manifold.

The PCV valve meters the flow at a rate depending upon the manifold vacuum. If the manifold vacuum is high, the PCV restricts the flow to the intake manifold. If abnormal, operating conditions occur, excessive amounts of internal exhaust gases back flow through the crankcase vent tube into the air filter to be burned by normal combustion.

If the engine is idling roughly, a quick check of the PCV valve can be made. While the engine is idling, pull the PCV valve from the valve cover, place your thumb over the end of the PCV valve and check for vacuum. If no vacuum exists, check for a plugged PCV valve, manifold port, hoses or deteriorated hoses. Turn the engine **OFF**, remove the PCV valve and shake it. Listen for the rattle of the check needle inside the valve. If it does not rattle, replace the valve.

The PCV system should be checked at every oil change and serviced every 30,000 miles.

NOTE: *Never operate an engine without a PCV valve or a ventilation system, for it can become damaged.*

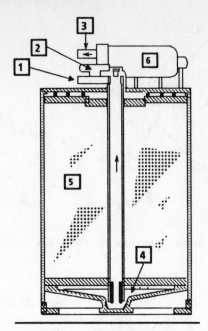

1. Tank tube
2. Inlet air
3. Purge tube
4. Liquid fuel area
5. Vapor storage area
6. Purge solenoid

Vapor canister assembly—1985–92

Evaporative Canister

To limit gasoline vapor discharge into the air this system is designed to trap fuel vapors, which normally escape from the fuel system. Vapor arrest is accomplished through the use of the charcoal canister. This canister absorbs fuel vapors and stores them until they can be removed to be burned in the engine. Removal of the vapors from the canister is accomplished by

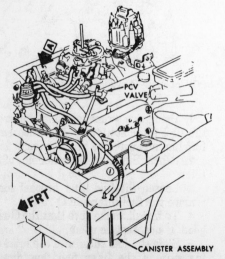

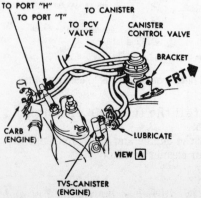

PCV and vapor canister location—most 6 and 8 cylinder engines

a solenoid operated bowl vent or vacuum operated purge valve mounted on the canister. In addition to the fuel system modifications and the canister, the fuel tank requires a non-vented gas cap. The domed fuel tank positions a vent high enough above the fuel to keep the vent pipe in the vapor at all times. The single vent pipe is routed directly to the canister. From the canister, the vapors are routed to the PCV system, where they will be burned during normal combustion.

REPLACEMENT

1. Tag and disconnect all hoses connected to the charcoal canister.
2. Loosen the retaining clamps and then lift out the canister.
3. Grasp the filter in the bottom of the canister with your fingers and pull it out. Replace it with a new one.
4. Install canister and tighten retaining clamps.
5. Install all hoses to canister.
NOTE: *Some models do not have replaceable filters.*

Battery

All General Motors vehicles have a "maintenance free" battery as standard equipment, eliminating the need for fluid level checks and the possibility of specific gravity tests. Nevertheless, the battery does require some attention.

Once a year, the battery terminals and the cable clamps should be cleaned. Remove the side terminal bolts and the cables, negative cable

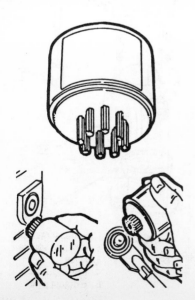

Battery terminal cleaning tool

first. Clean the cable clamps and the battery terminals with a wire brush until all corrosion, grease, etc. is removed and the metal is shiny. It is especially important to clean the inside of the clamp thoroughly, since a small deposit of foreign material or oxidation there will prevent a sound electrical connection and inhibit either starting or charging. Special tools are available for cleaning the side terminal clamps and terminals.

Before installing the cables, loosen the battery holddown clamp, remove the battery, and check the battery tray. Clear it of any debris and check it for corrosion. Rust should be wire-brushed away, and the metal given a coat of anti-rust paint. Install the battery and tighten the holddown clamp securely, but be careful not to overtighten, which will crack the battery case.

After the clamps and terminals are clean, reinstall the cables, negative cable last. Give the clamps and terminals a thin external coat of grease after installation, to retard corrosion.

Check the cables at the same time that the terminals are cleaned. If the cable insulation is cracked or broken, or if the ends are frayed, the cable should be replaced with a new cable of the same length and gauge.

CAUTION: *Keep flames or sparks away from the battery; it gives off explosive hydrogen gas! Battery electrolyte contains sulphuric acid. If you should get any on your skin or in your eyes, flush the affected areas with plenty of clear water; if it lands in your eyes, get medical help immediately!*

TESTING THE MAINTENANCE FREE BATTERY

Maintenance free batteries do not require normal attention as far as fluid level checks are concerned. However, the terminals require periodic cleaning, which should be performed at least once a year.

The sealed top battery cannot be checked for charge in the normal manner, since there is no provision for access to the electrolyte. To check the condition of the battery:

1. Check the built in hydrometer on top of the battery:
   a. If a green dot appears in the middle of the indicator eye on top of the battery, the battery is sufficiently charged.
   b. If the indicator eye is clear or light yellow, the electrolyte fluid is too low and the battery must be replaced.
   c. If the indicator eye is dark, the battery has a low charge and should be charged.
2. Load test the battery:
   a. Connect a battery load tester and a voltmeter across the battery terminals (the bat-

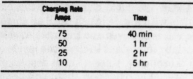

Charging Rate	
Amps	Time
75	40 min
50	1 hr
25	2 hr
10	5 hr

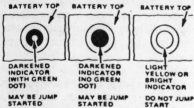

BATTERY TOP	BATTERY TOP	BATTERY TOP
DARKENED INDICATOR (WITH GREEN DOT)	DARKENED INDICATOR (NO GREEN DOT)	LIGHT YELLOW OR BRIGHT INDICATOR
MAY BE JUMP STARTED	MAY BE JUMP STARTED	DO NOT JUMP START

ESTIMATED TEMPERATURE	MINIMUM VOLTAGE
70° F. (21° C.)	9.6
50° F. (10° C.)	9.4
30° F. (0° C.)	9.1
15° F. (−10° C.)	8.8
0° F. (−18° C.)	8.5
0° F. (BELOW: −18° C.)	8.0

Maintenance-free batteries contain their own built-in hydrometer

tery cables should be disconnected from the battery).

b. Apply a 300 ampere load to the battery for 15 seconds to remove the surface charge. Remove the load.

c. Wait 15 seconds to allow the battery to recover. Apply the appropriate test load, as specified:

• 692, 83–50 Battery — Test load: 150 amperes
• 693, 83–60 Battery — Test load: 180 amperes
• 695, 87A–60 Battery — Test load: 230 amperes
• 70–315 Battery — Test load: 150 amperes
• 70–355 Battery — Test load: 170 amperes
• 75–500 Battery — Test load: 250 amperes
• 75–630 Battery — Test load: 310 amperes
• 730 Battery — Test load: 260 amperes
• 731 Battery — Test load: 280 amperes
• 600 Battery — Test load: 260 amperes
• 601 Battery — Test load: 310 amperes

Take a voltage reading at the end of 15 seconds of load. Disconnect the load.

d. Check the results against the following chart. If the battery voltage is at or above the specified voltage for the temperature listed, the battery is good. If the voltage falls below what's listed, the battery should be replaced.

CHARGING THE BATTERY

NOTE: *Do not charge a battery if the indicator eye is clear or light yellow. The battery should be replaced. If the battery feels hot (125°F) or if violent gassing or spewing of the*

electrolyte through the vent hole(s) occurs, discontinue charging or reduce the charging rate. Always follow the battery charger manufacturer's information for charging the battery.

1. To charge a sealed terminal battery out of the car, install adapter kit ST–1201 or 1846855 or equivalent.

2. Make sure that all charger connections are clean and tight.

NOTE: *For best results, the battery should be charged while the battery electrolyte and plates are at room temperature. A battery that is extremely cold may not accept the charging current for several hours after starting the charger.*

3. Charge the battery until the indicator eye shows a green dot. (It may be necessary to tip the battery from side to side to get the green dot to appear after charging.) The battery should be checked every half hour while charging.

Early Fuel Evaporation System EFE

The EFE system is used on some engines to provide a source of quick heat to the engine induction system during cold driveaway. There are two types of EFE systems: the vacuum servo type (located in the exhaust manifold) and the electric grid type (located under the carburetor).

The vacuum servo type consists of a valve in the exhaust manifold and a EFE control solenoid valve which is controlled by the ECM.

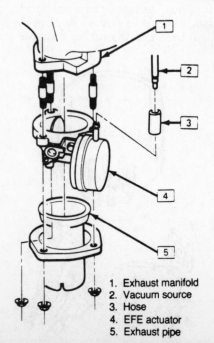

1. Exhaust manifold
2. Vacuum source
3. Hose
4. EFE actuator
5. Exhaust pipe

EFE vacuum servo valve

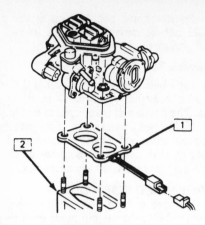

1. EFE heater
2. Intake manifold

EFE electrically heated grid

The electrical type consists of an electrical grid plate, mounted directly under the carburetor. The ECM controls the grid plate voltage by way of an EFE relay.

Both types are designed to produce rapid heating of the intake manifold, providing quick fuel evaporation and a more even distribution of fuel to aid in cold engine operation.

Every 30,000 miles, check the EFE valve (make sure it is free, not sticking) and the hoses for cracking or deterioration. If necessary, replace or lubricate. Check the electrically heated grid for meltdown and replace as necessary.

Belts

INSPECTION

The belts which drive the engine accessories such as the alternator or generator, the air pump, power steering pump, air conditioning compressor and water pump are of either the V-

belt design or flat, serpentine design. Older belts show wear and damage readily, since their basic design was a belt with a rubber casing. As the casing wore, cracks and fibers were readily apparent. Newer design, caseless belts do not show wear as readily, and an untrained eyes cannot distinguish between a good, serviceable belt and one that is worn to the point of failure.

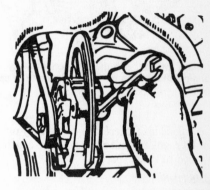

Loosening the component mounting and adjusting bolts slightly

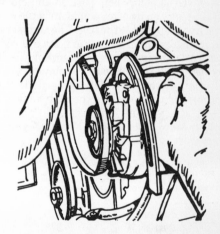

Remove the belt by pushing the component toward the engine

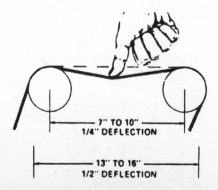

7" TO 10"
1/4" DEFLECTION

13" TO 16"
1/2" DEFLECTION

A gauge is recommended, but the belt deflection may be checked using light thumb pressure

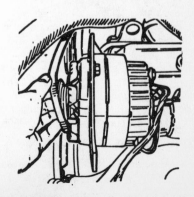

Remove the belt

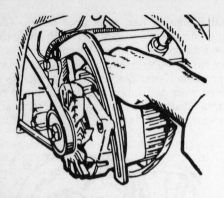

To tighten the belt, pull the component away from the engine and tighten the mounting bolts to specification

It is a good idea, therefore, to visually inspect the belts regularly and replace them, routinely, every two to three years.

ADJUSTING

V-Belts

Belts are normally adjusted by loosening the bolts of the accessory being driven and moving that accessory on its pivot points until the proper tension is applied to the belt. The accessory is held in this position while the bolts are tightened. To determine proper belt tension, you can purchase a belt tension gauge or simply use the deflection method. To determine deflection, press inward on the belt at the mid-point of its longest straight run. The belt should deflect (move inward) ⅜–½ in. (10–13mm). A general

rule for alternator belt tension is the pulley should not be capable of being turned with hand pressure.

Serpentine Belt

A single belt is used to drive all of the engine accessories formerly driven by multiple drive belts. The single belt is referred to a serpentine belt. All the belt driven accessories are ridgedly mounted with belt tension maintained by a spring loaded tensioner. Because of the belt tensioner, no adjustment is necessary.

REMOVAL AND INSTALLATION

To remove a drive belt, simply loosen the accessory being driven and move it on its pivot point to free the belt. Then, remove the belt. If a belt tensioner is used, push (rotate) the

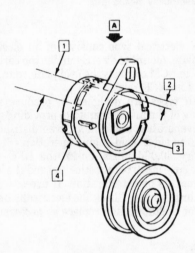

THE INDICATOR MARK ON THE MOVEABLE PORTION OF THE TENSIONER MUST BE WITHIN THE LIMITS OF THE SLOTTED AREA ON THE STATIONARY PORTION OF THE TENSIONER ANY READING OUTSIDE THESE LIMITS INDICATES EITHER A DEFECTIVE BELT OR TENSIONER

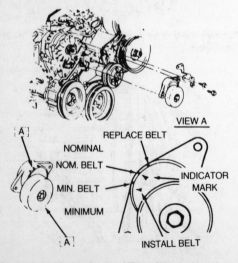

Serpentine belt tensioner—V6 engine

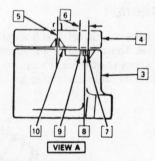

1. Used belt acceptable wear range
2. New belt range
3. Arm
4. Spindle
5. Fixed belt length indicator
6. With new belt installed, fixed pointer must fall within this range
7. Minimum length—new belt
8. Nominal length—new belt
9. Maximum length—new belt
10. Replace belt position

Serpentine belt tensioner—V8 engine

tensioner using a 15mm socket, and remove the belt.

NOTE: *Take care as not to bend the tensioner when applying torque. Damage to the tensioner will occur. Maximum torque to load belt should not exceed 30 ft. lbs.*

It is important to note, however, that on engines with many driven accessories, several or all of the belts may have to be removed to get at the one to be replaced.

Hoses

REMOVAL AND INSTALLATION

Radiator hoses are generally of two constructions, the preformed (molded) type, which is custom made for a particular application, and the spring-loaded type, which is made to fit several different applications. Heater hoses are all of the same general construction.

Hoses are retained by clamps. To replace a hose, loosen the clamp and slide it down the hose, away from the attaching point. Twist the hose from side to side carefully until it is free, then pull it off. Before installing the new hose, make sure that the outlet fitting is as clean as possible. Coat the fitting with non-hardening sealer and slip the hose into place. Install the clamp and tighten it. Fill and bleed the cooling system.

NOTE: *Remember to position the hoses and clamps in their original location to avoid rubbing against other moving components; ensure the hoses and clamps are beyond the pipe lip.*

Air Conditioning System

The Cycling Clutch Orifice Tube (CCOT) system includes the compressor, condenser, evaporator, an accumulator/drier with fixed orifice tube, a clutch cycling switch with or without a temperature probing capillary tube to maintain a selected comfortable temperature within the vehicle, while preventing evaporator freeze-up. Full control of the system is maintained through the use of a selector control, mounted in the dash assembly. The selector control makes use of a vacuum supply and electrical switches to operate mode doors and the blower motor. A sight glass is not used in this system and one should not be installed. The correct quantity of refrigerant must be maintained to obtain maximum system performance.

NOTE: *All air conditioning system charging and discharging requires the use of special refrigerant recycling/recovery equipment and should only be attempted by a certified professional techinician.*

GENERAL SERVICING PROCEDURES

The most important aspect of air conditioning service is the maintenance of pure and adequate charge of refrigerant in the system; likewise, the systems greatest enemy is moisture and therefor a system cannot function properly and will be damaged if leaks are not repaired in a timely manor. A refrigeration system cannot function properly if a significant percentage of the charge is lost. Refrigerant leaks can occur because of oil contamination on the hoses and lines or vibration can cause a cracking or loosening of the air conditioning fittings. As a result, the extreme operating pressures of the system force refrigerant out.

SAFETY WARNINGS

A list of general precautions that should be observed while working around the air conditioning system is as follows:

1. Always wear safety goggles when performing any work around the refrigerant system.

2. If refrigerant should contact the eyes or skin, flush the exposed area with cold water and seek medical assistance immediately.

3. Wrap a towel around the fitting valves when connecting or disconnecting the lines.

4. Thoroughly purge the service gauges and hoses of air and moisture before connecting them to the system. Keep them capped when not in use.

5. Thoroughly clean any refrigerant fitting before disconnecting it, in order to minimize the entrance of dirt into the system.

6. Plan any operation that requires opening the system beforehand in order to minimize the length of time it will be exposed to open air. Cap or seal the open ends to minimize the entrance of foreign material.

7. Never disconnect the air conditioning gauge service line at the gauges, always disconnect the line at the service fiting, otherewise the schraeder valve in the fitting will remain open and completely discharge the system, causing possible injury or system damage.

8. When adding oil, ensure the system has been properly discharged and pour the oil through an extremely clean and dry tube or funnel. Keep the oil capped whenever possible. Do not use oil that has not been kept tightly sealed.

9. Use only refrigerant 12, which is intended for use in only automotive air conditioning systems. Avoid the use of refrigerant 12 that may be packaged for another use, such as cleaning, or powering a horn, as it is impure.

10. Completely evacuate any system that has been opened to replace a component, other than when isolating the compressor, or that has leaked sufficiently to draw in moisture and air.

HOW TO SPOT BAD HOSES

Both the upper and lower radiator hoses are called upon to perform difficult jobs in an inhospitable environment. They are subject to nearly 18 psi at under hood temperatures often over 280°F., and must circulate nearly 7500 gallons of coolant an hour—3 good reasons to have good hoses.

A good test for any hose is to feel it for soft or spongy spots. Frequently these will appear as swollen areas of the hose. The most likely cause is oil soaking. This hose could burst at any time, when hot or under pressure.

Swollen hose

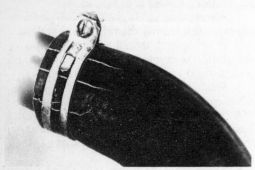

Cracked hoses can usually be seen but feel the hoses to be sure they have not hardened; a prime cause of cracking. This hose has cracked down to the reinforcing cords and could split at any of the cracks.

Cracked hose

Weakened clamps frequently are the cause of hose and cooling system failure. The connection between the pipe and hose has deteriorated enough to allow coolant to escape when the engine is hot.

Frayed hose end (due to weak clamp)

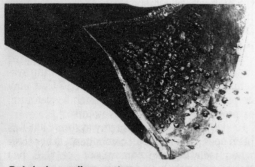

Debris, rust and scale in the cooling system can cause the inside of a hose to weaken. This can usually be felt on the outside of the hose as soft or thinner areas.

Debris in cooling system

This requires evacuating air and moisture with a good vacuum pump for at least one hour.

11. Use a wrench on both halves of a fitting that is to be disconnected, so as to avoid placing torque on any of the refrigerant lines.

12. The above procedures should only be attempted by a professional certified technician.

SYSTEM INSPECTION

CAUTION: *Refrigerant will freeze any surface, including your eyes, that it contacts. In addition, the refrigerant changes into a poisonous gas in the presence of a flame.*

1. Operation of the air conditioning blower at all four speeds with the mode button in any position except OFF and engagement of the compressor clutch would indicate that the electrical circuit are functioning properly. (The blower will not operate in any speed with the mode button in the OFF position.)

2. Operation of the air conditioning control selector (mode) button to distribute air from designed outlets would indicate proper functioning.

Oil Leaks

System leaks can usually be identified as oily areas around the hoses or components. If a hoses is thought to be leaking, simply grasp the hose with one hand and the line with the other and attempt to turn the hose, if the hose turns it is defective and must be replaced.

NOTE: *If it is determined that the system has a leak, it should be corrected as soon as possible by a professional certified technician. Leaks may allow moisture to enter and cause expensive repairs.*

Cooling System

The air conditioning system depends on the cooling system to lower the condenser tempera-

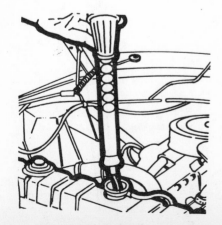

Use of an inexpensive antifreeze tester is recommended to check protection level

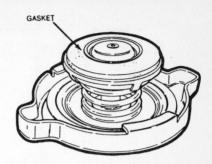

GASKET

Check the condition of the radiator cap and gasket

ture and change the vapors into a liquid; therefor the cooling system must be in proper working order. The cooling system quantity and protection factor must be satisfactory. The cooling fan/s must also be operating properly.

Radiator Cap

For efficient operation of an air conditioned car's cooling system, the radiator cap should hold pressure which meets the manufacturer's specifications. A cap which fails to hold pressure should be replaced.

Condenser

Any obstruction of or damage to the condenser fin configuration will restrict the air flow which is essential to its efficient operation. It is therefore, a good rule to keep this unit clean and in proper physical shape.

NOTE: *Bug screens are regarded as obstructions.*

Condensation Drain Tube

A molded drain tube allows the condensation which accumulates in the bottom of the evaporator housing to drain outside of the vehicle. Occasionally over time, this tube, which is generally located on the engine firewall below the evaporator housing will become obstructed and allow the evaporator housing to fill up with water (condensation). Simply unclog any obstruction in the drain tube and allow the water to drain. Be careful not to damage the evaporator core.

If this tube is obstructed, the air conditioning performance can be restricted and condensation buildup can spill over onto the vehicle's floor.

REFRIGERANT LEVEL CHECKS

The same hand-felt temperature of the evaporator inlet pipe and the accumulator surface of an operating system would indicate a properly charged system. The system contains NO sightglass.

RELATIVE HUMIDITY (%)	AMBIENT AIR TEMP		LOW SIDE		ENGINE SPEED (rpm)	CENTER DUCT AIR TEMPERATURE		HIGH SIDE	
	°F	°C	kPa	PSIG		°F	°C	kPa	PSIG
20	70	21	200	29	2000	40	4	1034	150
	80	27	200	29		44	7	1310	190
	90	32	207	30		48	9	1689	245
	100	38	214	31		57	14	2103	305
30	70	21	200	29	2000	42	6	1034	150
	80	27	207	30		47	8	1413	205
	90	32	214	31		51	11	1827	265
	100	38	221	32		61	16	2241	325
40	70	21	200	29	2000	45	7	1138	165
	80	27	207	30		49	9	1482	215
	90	32	221	32		55	13	1931	280
	100	38	269	39		65	18	2379	345
50	70	21	207	30	2000	47	8	1241	180
	80	27	221	32		53	12	1620	235
	90	32	234	34		59	15	2034	295
	100	38	276	40		69	21	2413	350
60	70	21	207	30	2000	48	9	1241	180
	80	27	228	33		56	13	1655	240
	90	32	249	36		63	17	2069	300
	100	38	296	43		73	23	2482	360
70	70	21	207	30	2000	50	10	1276	185
	80	27	234	34		58	14	1689	245
	90	32	262	38		65	18	2103	305
	100	38	303	44		75	24	2517	365
80	70	21	207	30	2000	50	10	1310	190
	80	27	234	34		59	15	1724	250
	90	32	269	39		67	19	2137	310
90	70	21	207	30	2000	50	10	1379	200
	80	27	249	36		62	17	1827	265
	90	32	290	42		71	22	2275	330

Air conditioning performance test

Windshield Wipers

For maximum effectiveness and longest element life, the windshield and wiper blades should be kept clean. Dirt, tree sap, road tar and so on will cause streaking, smearing and blade deterioration if left on the windshield. It is advisable to wash the windshield carefully with a commercial glass cleaner at least once a month. Wipe off the rubber blades with a wet rag afterwards. Do not attempt to move the wipers back and forth by hand; damage to the motor and drive mechanism will result.

If the blades are found to be cracked, broken or torn, they should be replaced immediately. Replacement intervals will vary with usage, although ozone deterioration usually limits blade lift to about one year. If the wiper pattern is smeared or streaked, or if the blade chatters across the glass, the blades should be replaced. It is easiest and most sensible to replace them in pairs.

There are basically three different types of wiper blade refills, which differ in their method of replacement. One type has two release buttons, approximately ⅓ of the way up from the ends of the blade frame. Pushing the buttons down releases a lock and allows the rubber blade to be removed from the frame. The new blade slides back into the frame and locks in place.

The second type of refill has two metal tabs which are unlocked by squeezing them

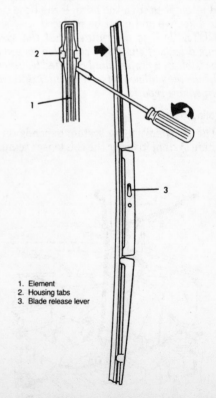

1. Element
2. Housing tabs
3. Blade release lever

The rubber element may be changed without replacing the entire assembly

together. The rubber blade can then be withdrawn from the frame jaws. A new one is installed by inserting it into the front frame jaws and sliding it rearward to engage the remaining frame jaws. There are usually four jaws; be certain when installing that the refill is engaged in all of them. At the end of its travel, the tabs will lock into place on the front jaws of the wiper blade frame.

The third type is a refill made from polycarbonate. The refill has a simple locking device at one end which flexes downward out of the groove into which the jaws of the holder fit, allowing easy release. By sliding the new refill through all the jaws and pushing through the slight resistance when it reaches the end of its travel, the refill will lock into position.

Regardless of the type of refill used, make sure that all of the frame jaws are engaged as the refill is pushed into place and locked. The metal blade holder and frame will scratch the glass if allowed to touch it.

Tires and Wheels

The tires should be rotated as specified in the Maintenance Intervals Chart. Refer to the accompanying illustrations for the recommended rotation patterns.

The tires on your car should have built-in tread wear indicators, which appear as ½ in. (12.7mm) bands when the tread depth gets as low as $\frac{1}{16}$ in. (1.6mm). When the indicators appear in 2 or more adjacent grooves, it's time for new tires.

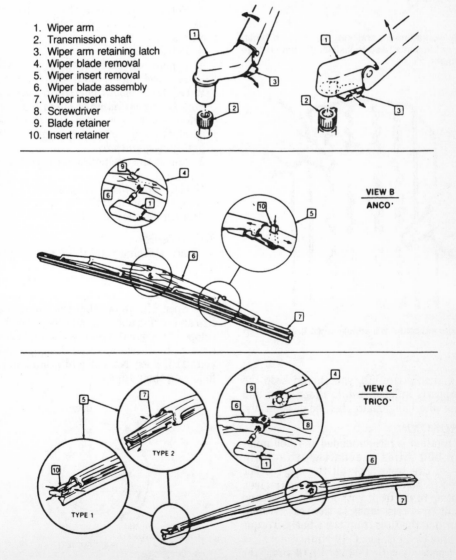

1. Wiper arm
2. Transmission shaft
3. Wiper arm retaining latch
4. Wiper blade removal
5. Wiper insert removal
6. Wiper blade assembly
7. Wiper insert
8. Screwdriver
9. Blade retainer
10. Insert retainer

VIEW B
ANCO·

VIEW C
TRICO·

TYPE 2

TYPE 1

Wiper arm, blade and insert servicing

Tread depth can be checked using an inexpensive gauge

Recommended tire rotation patterns

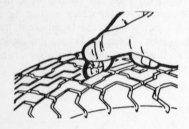

A penny works fine for checking tread depth, when the top of Lincoln's head is visible, it's time for tire replacement.

Tread wear indicators will appear when tires are worn out

For optimum tire life, you should keep the tires properly inflated, rotate them often and have the wheel alignment checked periodically.

TIRE ROTATION

Tire rotation is recommended at 7,500 miles and 15,000 miles thereafter, to obtain maximum tire wear. For all tire sizes other than P245/50VR16, rotate the rear tires straight up to the front without criss-cross and the front tires criss-cross to the rear without dismounting the tires from the wheels. Torque wheel nuts to 80 ft. lbs. (110 Nm).

For Camaro's with P245/50VR16 tires, the tires must be dismounted from the wheels

because of different wheel offset and directional tires. They should be rotated in the following manner:

1. Dismount the tires from the wheels. (Mark the tires rotation direction on the side wall.)

2. Rotate the tires (not the wheels) front-to-back and the back-to-front without criss-crossing tires.

3. Rebalance tires.

4. Replace wheels in their original position. Torque wheel nuts to 80 ft. lbs. (110 Nm).

WARNING: *Avoid overtightening the lug nuts to prevent damage to the brake disc or drum. Alloy wheels can also be cracked by overtightening. Use of a torque wrench is highly recommended.*

5. Adjust the tire pressures according to the tire placard.

NOTE: *Mark the wheel position or direction of rotation on radial tires or studded snow tires before removing them.*

TIRE DESIGN

When replacing your tires, you should take note of the Tire Performance Criteria Specification Number (TPC Spec. No.) molded into the tire sidewall near the tire size marking. The TPC Spec. No. shows that the tire meets rigid size and performance standards which were developed for your Camaro. When replacing your tires with all-season tread design, make sure your TPC Spec. No. has a MS (mud and snow) following the number.

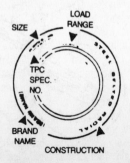

Tire information location

If a replacement tire does not have a TPC Spec. No., you should use the same size, load range, speed rating and construction type (bias, bias-belted, or radial) as the original tires on your car. A different size or type of tire may affect such things as ride, handling, maximum speed capability, speedometer/odometer calibration, vehicle ground clearance, and tire or tire chain clearance to the body or chassis.

The tires on your car were selected to provide the best all around performance for normal operation when inflated as specified. Oversize tires will not increase the maximum carrying capacity of the vehicle, although they will provide an extra margin of tread life. Be sure to check overall height before using larger size tires which may cause interference with suspension components or wheel wells. When replacing conventional tire sizes with other tire size designations, be sure to check the manufacturer's recommendations. Interchangeability is not always possible because of differences in load ratings, tire dimensions, wheel well clearances, and rim size. Also due to differences in handling characteristics, 70 Series and 60 Series tires should be used only in pairs on the same axle; radial tires should be used only in sets of four.

The wheels must be the correct width for the tire. Tire dealers have charts of tire and rim compatibility. A mismatch can cause sloppy handling and rapid tread wear. The old rule of thumb is that the tread width should match the rim width (inside bead to inside bead) within an inch. For radial tires, the rim width should be 80% or less of the tire (not tread) width.

The height (mounted diameter) of the new tires can greatly change speedometer accuracy, engine speed at a given road speed, fuel mileage, acceleration, and ground clearance. Tire manufacturers furnish full measurement specifications. Speedometer drive gears are available for correction.

NOTE: *Dimensions of tires marked the same size may vary significantly, even among tires from the same manufacturer.*

The spare tire should be usable, at least for low speed operation, with the new tires.

For maximum satisfaction, tires should be used in sets of five. Mixing or different types (radial, bias-belted, fiberglass belted) should be avoided. Conventional bias tires are constructed so that the cords run bead-to-bead at an angle. Alternate plies run at an opposite angle. This type of construction gives rigidity to both tread and sidewall. Bias-belted tires are similar in construction to conventional bias ply tires. Belts run at an angle and also at a 90° angle to the bead, as in the radial tire. Tread life is improved considerably over the conventional bias

tire. The radial tire differs in construction, but instead of the carcass plies running at an angle of 90° to each other, they run at an angle of 90° to the bead. This gives the tread a great deal of rigidity and the sidewall a great deal of flexibility and accounts for the characteristic bulge associated with radial tires.

Radial tires are recommended for use on all models. If they are used, tire sizes and wheel diameters should be selected to maintain ground clearance and tire load capacity equivalent to the minimum specified tire. Radial tires should always be used in sets of five, but in an emergency radial tires can be used with caution on the rear axle only. If this is done, both tires on the rear should be of radial design.

NOTE: *Radial tires should never be used on only the front axle.*

TIRE STORAGE

Store the tires at the proper inflation pressure if they are mounted on wheels. Keep them in a cool dry place, laid on their sides. If the tires are stored in the garage or basement, do not let them stand on a concrete floor; set them on strips of wood.

TIRE INFLATION

The tire pressure is the most often ignored item of automotive maintenance. Gasoline mileage can drop as much as 0.8 percent for every 1 pound/square inch (psi) of under inflation.

Pressures should be checked before driving, since pressure can increase as much as 6 psi due to heat. It is a good idea to have an accurate gauge and to check pressures weekly. Not all gauges on service station air pumps are accurate.

CARE OF SPECIAL WHEELS

A protective coating is applied to all aluminum wheels to prevent degradation. Avoid prolonged use of automatic car washes which will wear off the protective coating. When using cleaners, read the label on the package and make sure it will not damage or remove the protective coating.

FLUIDS AND LUBRICANTS

Fuel Recommendations

The engine is designed to operate on unleaded gasoline ONLY and is essential for the proper operation of the emission control system. The use of unleaded fuel will reduce spark plug fouling, exhaust system corrosion and engine oil deterioration.

In most parts of the United States, fuel with

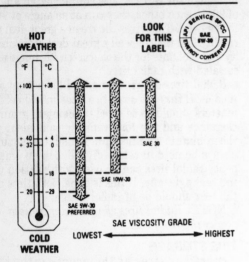

Recommended SAE viscosity grade engine oils

an octane rating of 87 should be used; in high altitude areas, fuel with an octane rating as low as 85 may be used.

In some areas, fuel consisting of a blend of alcohol may be used; this blend of gasoline and alcohol is known as gasohol. When using gasohol, never use blends exceeding 10% ethanol (ethyl or grain alcohol) or 5% methanol (methyl or wood alcohol).

NOTE: *The use of fuel with excessive amounts of alcohol may jeopardize the new car and emission control system warranties.*

Oil Recommendations

Use only oil which has the API (American Petroleum Institute) designation **SG, CC, CD, SG/CC** or **SG/CD**.

Since fuel economy is effected by the viscosity (thickness) of the engine oil, it is recommended to select an oil with reference to the outside temperature. For satisfactory lubrication, use a lower viscosity oil for colder temperatures and a higher viscosity oil for warmer temperatures.

Recommended Lubricants

Lubricant	Classification
Engine Oil	SF, SF/CC or SF/CD
Engine Coolant	Mixture of water and a good quality Ethylene Glycol base anti freeze
Brake System and Master Cylinder	DOT 3
Parking Brake Cables	Chassis grease meeting requirements of GM 6031-M
Power Steering System & Pump Reservoir	GM Power Steering Fluid, Part No. 1050017 or equivalent
Automatic Transmission	DEXRON® II Automatic Transmission Fluid
Automatic Transmission Shift Linkage	Engine Oil
Manual Transmission Shift Linkage	Chassis grease
Manual Transmission	SAE 80-90W GL5 lubricant
Clutch Linkage Pivot Points	Engine oil
Front Wheel Bearings	GM Part #1051344 wheel bearing grease or equivalent
Chassis Lubrication	Chassis grease meeting requirements of GM 6031-M
Windshield Washer Solvent	GM Optikleen Washer Solvent, Part No. 1051515 or equivalent
Hood Latch Assembly a. pivots and spring anchor b. release pawl	a. Engine oil b. Chassis grease meeting requirements of GM 6031-M
Hood and Door Hinges	Engine oil
Body door hinge pins, station wagon tailgate hinge and linkage, station wagon folding seat, fuel door hinge, rear compartment hinges	Engine oil
Key Lock Cylinders	WD-40 Spray lubricant or equivalent

The oil level should be between the "ADD" and "FULL" marks on the dipstick

Oil level is checked using the dipstick

Engine

OIL LEVEL CHECK

Your engine oil should be checked at regular interval (such as every fuel stop), check the engine oil as follows:

1. Make sure the car is parked on level ground.

2. When checking the oil level it is best for the engine to be at normal operating temperature, although checking the oil immediately after stopping will lead to a false reading. Wait a few minutes after turning off the engine to allow the oil to drain back into the crankcase.

3. Open the hood and locate the dipstick which will be on either the passenger's side for the V8 engine or driver's side for the L4 and V6 engines. Pull the dipstick from its tube, wipe it clean and then reinsert it.

4. Pull the dipstick out again and, holding it horizontally, read the oil level. The oil should be between the **FULL** and **ADD** marks on the dipstick. If the oil is below the **ADD** mark, add oil of the proper viscosity through the capped opening in the top of the cylinder head cover.

5. Replace the dipstick and check the oil level again after adding any oil. Be careful not to overfill the crankcase. Approximately 1 quart (0.9L) of oil will raise the level from the **ADD** mark to the **FULL** mark. Excess oil will generally be consumed at an accelerated rate.

OIL AND FILTER CHANGE

Under normal operating conditions, the oil is to be changed every 7,500 miles (12,000km) or 12 months, which ever occurs first. Change the filter at first oil change and then at every other oil change, unless 12 months pass between changes. Although, for best protection against premature engine wear, a new filter should be installed with every oil change.

If driving under such conditions, such as: dusty areas, trailer towing, idling for long periods of time, low speed operation, or when operating with temperatures below freezing and driving short distances — under 4 miles (6.4km) — change the oil and filter every 3,000 miles (1361km) or 3 months.

The oil should be disposed of properly after it is drained from the vehicle. Store the oil in a suitable container and take the container to an official oil recycling station. Most gas stations or oil and lube facilities will take the used oil for little or no expense to you.

Removal and Installation

1. Raise the car and support on jackstands. Remove the oil pan drain plug and drain oil into a suitable pan.
CAUTION: *The engine oil will be hot. Keep your arms, face and hands away from the oil as it drains out.*

2. Using an oil filter wrench, remove the oil filter and place it in the oil catch pan. Using a clean rag, wipe oil filter mounting surface.

3. When installing the oil filter, place a small amount of oil on the sealing gasket and tighten the filter only hand tight or ¾ of a turn past gasket contact. Do not overtighen the filter.

4. Install the oil pan drain plug and torque to 18 ft. lbs. (25 Nm).

5. Using a funnel, add oil through the oil fill cap. Lower car, start the engine and inspect for oil leaks.
CAUTION: *The EPA warns that prolonged contact with used engine oil may cause a number of skin disorders, including cancer! You should make every effort to minimize your exposure to used engine oil. Protective gloves should be worn when changing the oil. Wash your hands and any other exposed skin areas as soon as possible after exposure to used engine oil. Soap and water, or waterless hand cleaner should be used.*

Manual Transmission

FLUID RECOMMENDATIONS

All 4-speed and 1982–84 5-speed manual transmissions, use only SAE 80W or SAE 80W/90 GL-5 gear lubricant (SAE 80W GL-5 in Canada).

• 1985–86 and 1988–92 5-speed manual transmissions use Dexron®II automatic transmission fluid.

• 1987 5-speed manual transmissions use SAE 5W-30 manual transaxle oil (GM #1052931 or equivalent).

LEVEL CHECK

The oil in the manual transmission should be checked every 12 months or 15,000 miles.

1. Raise the car and support on jackstands as close to level as possible.

2. Remove the filler plug from the side of the transmission housing.

3. If lubricant begins to trickle out of the hole, there is enough and you need not go any further. Otherwise, carefully insert your finger (watch out for sharp threads) and check to see if the oil is up to the edge of the hole.

4. If not, add oil through the hole until the level is at the edge of the hole. Most gear lubricants come in a plastic squeeze bottle with a nozzle; making additions simple.

5. Install and tighten the filler plug.

DRAIN AND REFILL

The fluid in the manual transmission does not require changing. If you do choose to change the transmission fluid, the fluid can be drained out through the lower drain plug hole on the side of the transmission. Fill the transmission with the recommended gear lubricant to the bottom of the filler plug hole and install the filler plug.

Automatic Transmission

FLUID RECOMMENDATIONS

Use only Dexron®II Automatic Transmission Fluid.

LEVEL CHECK

Check the automatic transmission fluid level at each oil change. Driving with too much or too little transmission fluid can damage the transmission. The dipstick can be found in the rear of the engine compartment. The fluid level should be checked only when the transmission is at normal operating temperature. If your Camaro has been driven at highway speeds for a long time, or in city traffic in hot weather, or pulling a trailer, wait for about 30 minutes for the fluid to cool down so a correct reading can be read.

1. Park the car on a level surface, with the parking brake on. Start the engine and let it idle for about 15 minutes. Move the transmission through all the gears and then back to **P**.

2. Remove the dipstick and carefully touch the wet end of the dipstick to see if the fluid is cool, warm, or hot. Wipe it clean and then reinsert it firmly. Be sure that it has been pushed all the way in. Remove the dipstick again and check the fluid level while holding it horizontally.

　　a. Fluid is cool (room temperature), the level should be about ⅛–⅜ in. (3–10mm) below the ADD mark.

　　b. Fluid is warm, the level should be close to the **ADD** mark, either above or below.

　　c. Fluid is too hot to hold, the level should be at the **FULL** mark.

3. If the fluid level is low, add Dexron®II automatic transmission fluid (ATF) through the dipstick tube. This is easily done with the aid of a funnel. Check the level often as you are filling the transmission. Be extremely careful not to overfill it. Overfilling will cause slippage, seal damage and overheating. Approximately 1 pint (0.473L) of ATF will raise the fluid level from one notch/line to the other.

NOTE: *If the fluid on the dipstick appears discolored (brown or black), or smells burnt, serious transmission troubles, probably due to overheating, should be suspected. The transmission should be inspected by a qualified technician to locate the cause of the burnt fluid.*

DRAIN AND REFILL

Refer to the PAN AND FILTER SERVICE procedure.

PAN AND FILTER SERVICE

The automatic transmission fluid and filter should be changed every 15,000 miles (24,000km) if your Camaro is driven in heavy city traffic in hot weather, in hilly or mountainous terrain, frequent trailer pulling, or uses such as found in taxi, police car or delivery service. If your Camaro is driven under other than listed above conditions, change the fluid and filter every 30,000 miles (48,300km).

1. Raise and support the car on jackstands. Place an oil catch pan under the transmission.

2. Remove the oil pan bolts from the front and sides only.

3. Loosen rear oil pan bolts approximately 4 turns.

WARNING: *Do not damage the transmission case or oil pan sealing surfaces.*

4. Lightly tap the oil pan with a rubber mallet or a pry it to allow fluid to drain.

5. Remove the remaining oil pan bolts, then remove the oil pan and pan gasket.

6. Remove the filter and O-ring.

7. Clean the transmission case and oil pan gasket surfaces with suitable solvent and air dry. Make sure to remove all traces of the old gasket.

8. To install, coat the O-ring seal with a small amount of oil.

9. Install the new O-ring onto the filter.

10. Install the new filter into the case.

11. Install the oil pan and new gasket.

12. Install the oil pan bolts and tighten them to 15 ft. lbs. (20 Nm).

13. Lower the car.

14. Fill the transmission to proper level with Dexron®II fluid.

15. Check cold fluid level reading for initial fill. Do not overfill the transmission.

16. Follow the fluid level check procedure described before.

17. Check the oil pan gasket for leaks.

Drive Axle

FLUID RECOMMENDATIONS

SAE 80W or SAE 80W-90 GL-5 (SAE 80W GL-5 in Canada) gear lubricant.

LEVEL CHECK

The gear lubricant in the drive axle should be checked every 12 months or 15,000 miles (24,000km).

1. Raise the car and support on jackstands as close to level as possible.

2. Remove the filler plug from the side of the drive axle housing.

3. If lubricant begins to trickle out of the hole, there is enough and you need not go any further. Otherwise, carefully insert your finger (watch out for sharp threads) and check to see if the lubricant is up to the edge of the hole.

4. If not, add oil through the hole until the level is at the edge of the hole. Most gear lubricants come in a plastic squeeze bottle with a nozzle; making additions simple.

5. Install and tighten the filler plug.

DRAIN AND REFILL

The rear axle should have the gear lubricant changed every 7,500 miles (12,000km). If equipped with a limited slip differential, be sure to add 4 oz. (118ml) of GM limited slip additive part No. 1052358.

1. Raise the car and support on jackstands. Place a container under the differential to catch the fluid.

2. Remove the bolts retaining the cover to the housing. Pry the cover from the differential housing and allow the fluid to drain into the catch pan.

3. Clean and inspect the differential. With the cover and housing washed free of oil, apply sealer to the mating surfaces.

4. Using a new gasket, install the cover and torque the bolts to 20 ft. lbs. (27 Nm) in a clockwise pattern to insure uniform draw on the gasket. Fill the differential with fluid through the fill plug and add limited slip additive, as required.

5. The fluid level should reached a level within ⅜ in. (10mm) of the filler plug hole. Replace the filler plug. Lower the car and inspect for leaks.

Cooling System

CAUTION: *When draining the coolant, keep in mind that cats and dogs are attracted by* the ethylene glycol antifreeze, and are quite likely to drink any that is left in an uncovered container or in puddles on the ground. This will prove fatal in sufficient quantity. Always drain the coolant into a sealable container. Coolant should be reused unless it is contaminated or several years old or taken to a recycling facility such as a service station.

FLUID RECOMMENDATIONS

When adding or changing the fluid in the system, create a 50/50 mixture of high quality ethylene glycol antifreeze and water.

LEVEL CHECK

The fluid level may be checked by observing the fluid level marks of the recovery tank. The level should be below the **ADD** mark when the system is cold. At normal operating temperatures, the level should be between the **ADD** and the **FULL** marks. Only add coolant to bring the level to the **FULL** mark.

CAUTION: *Should it be necessary to remove the radiator cap, make sure that the system has had time to cool, reducing the internal pressure.*

DRAINING AND REFILLING

CAUTION: *Do not remove a radiator cap while the engine and radiator are still hot. Danger of burns by scalding fluid and steam under pressure may result!*

1. With a cool engine, slowly rotate the radiator cap counterclockwise to the detent without pressing down on the cap.

2. Wait until any remaining pressure is relieved by listening for a hissing sound.

3. After all the pressure is relieved, press down on the cap and continue to rotate the radiator cap counterclockwise.

4. With a suitable container to catch the fluid under the radiator, open the radiator drain cock. If equipped, remove the engine block drain plugs to drain the coolant from the block.

5. Loosen or slide the recovery tank hose clamp at the radiator filler neck overflow tube and remove the hose. Holding the hose down to the drain pan, drain the recovery tank. Attach the hose to the filler neck overflow and tighten the clamp.

6. Close the radiator drain cock and install the engine block drain plug.

7. With the engine idling, add coolant until the level reaches the bottom of the filler neck. Install the radiator cap, making sure that the arrows on the cap line up with the overflow tube.

NOTE: *Never add cold water to an overheated engine while the engine is not running.*

8. Add coolant to the recovery tank.

9. After filling the radiator and recovery

tank, run the engine until it reaches normal operating temperature, to make sure that the thermostat has opened and all the air is bled from the system.

FLUSHING AND CLEANING THE SYSTEM

The cooling system should be drained, thoroughly flushed and refilled at least every 30,000 miles or 24 months. These operations should be done with the engine cold.

CAUTION: *To drain the cooling system, allow the engine to cool down BEFORE ATTEMPTING TO REMOVE THE RADIATOR CAP. Then turn the cap until it hisses. Wait until all pressure is off the cap before removing it completely. To avoid burns and scalding, always handle a warm radiator cap with a heavy rag.*

1. Remove the radiator and recovery tank caps. Run the engine until the upper radiator hose gets hot. This means that the thermostat is open and the coolant is flowing through the system.

2. Turn the engine **OFF** and place a large container under the radiator. Open the drain cock at the bottom of the radiator. Remove the block drain plugs to speed up the draining process.

3. At the dash, set the heater **TEMP** control lever to the fully **HOT** position. Close the drain valve, install the block drain plug and add water until the system is full. Repeat the draining and filling process several times, until the liquid is nearly colorless.

4. Remove the recovery tank and rinse it out with clean water. Install the recovery tank.

5. After the last draining, fill the system with a 50/50 mixture of ethylene glycol and water. Run the engine until the system is hot and add coolant, if necessary. Replace the caps and check for any leaks.

Master Cylinder (Clutch and Brake)

FLUID RECOMMENDATIONS

When adding or replacing the brake fluid, always use a top quality fluid, such as Delco Supreme II or DOT-3. DO NOT allow the brake fluid container or master cylinder reservoir to remain open for long periods of time; brake fluid absorbs moisture from the air, reducing its effectiveness and causing corrosion in the lines.

LEVEL CHECK

The master cylinders are located in the left rear Chapter of the engine compartment. The brake master cylinder consists of an aluminum body and a translucent nylon reservoir with minimum fill indicators. The clutch master cylinder is located below the brake master cylinder. The reservoir for it is located right beside the brake master cylinder and is made of translucent nylon. The fluid level of the reservoirs should be kept near the top of the observation windows.

WARNING: *Any sudden decrease in the fluid level indicates a possible leak in the system and should be checked out immediately. Do not allow brake fluid to spill on the vehicle's finish; it will remove the paint. In case of a spill, flush the area with water and mild soap.*

Power Steering Pump

FLUID RECOMMENDATIONS

When filling or replacing the fluid of the power steering pump reservoir, use GM power steering fluid, part #1050017 or equivalent.

LEVEL CHECK

Power steering fluid level should be checked at least twice a year. To prevent possible overfilling, check the fluid level only when the fluid has warmed to operating temperatures and the wheels are turned straight ahead. If the level is low, fill the pump reservoir until the fluid level measures between the COLD and HOT marks on the reservoir dipstick. Low fluid level usually produces a moaning sound as the wheels are turned (especially when standing still or parking) and increases steering wheel effort.

Steering Gear

FLUID RECOMMENDATIONS

Use lubricant meeting GM-4673M (GM part number 1052182)

Chassis Greasing

Chassis lubrication can be performed with a pressurized grease gun or it can be performed at home by using a hand-operated grease gun. Wipe the grease fittings clean before greasing in order to prevent the possibility of forcing any dirt into the component.

Body Lubrication

HOOD LATCH AND HINGES

Clean the latch surfaces and apply clean engine oil to the latch pilot bolts and the spring anchor. Use the engine oil to lubricate the hood hinges as well. Use a chassis grease to lubricate all the pivot points in the latch release mechanism.

DOOR HINGES

The gas tank filler door, car door, and rear hatch or trunk lid hinges should be wiped clean and lubricated with clean engine oil. Silicone spray also works well on seals, but must be

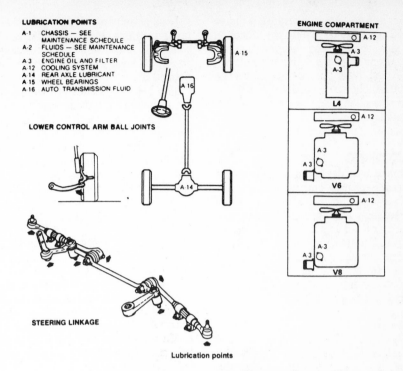

LUBRICATION POINTS

A-1   CHASSIS — SEE
        MAINTENANCE SCHEDULE
A-2   FLUIDS — SEE MAINTENANCE
        SCHEDULE
A-3   ENGINE OIL AND FILTER
A-12 COOLING SYSTEM
A-14 REAR AXLE LUBRICANT
A-15 WHEEL BEARINGS
A-16 AUTO TRANSMISSION FLUID

ENGINE COMPARTMENT

LOWER CONTROL ARM BALL JOINTS

STEERING LINKAGE

Lubrication points

Chassis lubrication points

applied more often. Use engine oil to lubricate the trunk or hatch lock mechanism and the lock bolt and striker. The door lock cylinders can be lubricated easily with a shot silicone spray or one of the many dry penetrating lubricants commercially available.

PARKING BRAKE LINKAGE

Use chassis grease on the parking brake cable where it contacts the guides, links, levers, and pulleys. The grease should be water resistant for durability under the car.

ACCELERATOR LINKAGE

Lubricate the throttle lever, and the accelerator pedal lever at the support inside the car with clean engine oil.

TRANSMISSION SHIFT LINKAGE

Lubricate the shift linkage with water resistant chassis grease which meets GM Specification 6031M or its equal.

Wheel Bearings

Once every 30,000 miles, clean and repack wheel bearings with a wheel bearing packer. Remove any excess grease from the exposed surface of the hub and seal.

WARNING: *It is important that wheel bearings be properly adjusted after installation. Improperly adjusted wheel bearings can cause steering instability, front end shimmy and wander, and increased tire wear.*

REMOVAL, REPACKING, INSTALLATION AND ADJUSTMENT

1. Raise the car and support it at the lower arm. Remove the wheel. Remove the brake caliper and support it on a wire.

2. Remove the dust cap, cotter pin, castle nut, thrust washer and outside wheel bearing. Pull the disc/hub assembly from the steering knuckle.

3. Pry out the inner seal and remove the inner bearing.

4. Wipe out the grease from inside the hub.

5. Clean the wheel bearings thoroughly with solvent and check their condition before installation. After cleaning, check parts for excessive wear and replace damaged parts.

WARNING: *Do not allow the bearing to spin when blowing dry with compressed air, as this would allow the bearing to turn without lubrication.*

6. Apply a sizable amount of lubricant to the palm of one hand. Using your other hand, work the bearing into the lubricant so that the grease is pushed through the rollers and out the other side. Keep rotating the bearing while continuing to push the lubricant through it.

7. Apply grease to the inside of the hub and install the inner bearing in the hub. Install a new grease seal, be careful not to damage the seal.

8. Install the disc/hub assembly onto the steering knuckle. Install the outer bearing,

thrust washer and castle nut. Torque the nut to 16 ft. lbs. (22 Nm) while turning the wheel.

9. Back the nut off and retighten until nearest slot aligns with the cotter pin hole.

10. Insert a new cotter pin. Endplay should be between 0.001–0.005 in. (0.025–0.127mm). If play exceeds this tolerance, the wheel bearings should be replaced.

TRAILER TOWING

Your Camaro was designed and intended primarily to carry people. Towing a trailer may affect some characteristic of the car, like handling, durability and economy. Proper use of the correct equipment is highly recommended for your safety and satisfaction.

Factory trailer towing packages are available on most cars. However, if you are installing a trailer hitch and wiring on your car, there are a few thing that you ought to know.

Trailer Weight

Trailer weight is the first, and most important, factor in determining whether or not your vehicle is suitable for towing the trailer you have in mind. The horsepower-to-weight ratio should be calculated. The basic standard is a ratio of 35:1. That is, 35 pounds of GVW for every horsepower.

To calculate this ratio, multiply you engine's rated horsepower by 35, then subtract the weight of the vehicle, including passengers and luggage. The resulting figure is the ideal maximum trailer weight that you can tow. One point to consider: a numerically higher axle ratio can offset what appears to be a low trailer weight. If the weight of the trailer that you have in mind is somewhat higher than the weight you just calculated, you might consider changing your rear axle ratio to compensate.

Hitch Weight

There are three kinds of hitches: bumper mounted, frame mounted, and load equalizing.

Bumper mounted hitches are those which attach solely to the vehicle's bumper. Many states prohibit towing with this type of hitch, when it attaches to the vehicle's stock bumper, since it subjects the bumper to stresses for which it was not designed. Aftermarket rear step bumpers, designed for trailer towing, are acceptable for use with bumper mounted hitches.

Frame mounted hitches can be of the type which bolts to two or more points on the frame, plus the bumper, or just to several points on the frame. Frame mounted hitches can also be of the tongue type, for Class I towing, or, of the receiver type, for Classes II and III.

Load equalizing hitches are usually used for large trailers. Most equalizing hitches are welded in place and use equalizing bars and chains to level the vehicle after the trailer is hooked up.

The bolt-on hitches are the most common, since they are relatively easy to install.

Check the gross weight rating of your trailer. Tongue weight is usually figured as 10% of gross trailer weight. Therefore, a trailer with a maximum gross weight of 2,000 lb. (907kg) will have a maximum tongue weight of 200 lb. (90.7kg). Class I trailers fall into this category. Class II trailers are those with a gross weight rating of 2,000–3,500 lb. (907–1588kg), while Class III trailers fall into the 3,500–6,000 lb. (1588–2722kg) category. Class IV trailers are those over 6,000 lb. (2722kg) and are for use with fifth wheel trucks, only.

When you've determined the hitch that you'll need, follow the manufacturer's installation instructions, exactly, especially when it comes to fastener torques. The hitch will be subjected to a lot of stress and good hitches come with hardened bolts. Never substitute an inferior bolt for a hardened bolt.

Wiring

Wiring the car for towing is fairly easy. There are a number of good wiring kits available and these should be used, rather than trying to design your own. All trailers will need brake lights and turn signals as well as tail lights and side marker lights. Most states require extra marker lights for overly wide trailers. Also, most states have recently required back-up lights for trailers, and most trailer manufacturers have been building trailers with back-up lights for several years.

Additionally, some Class I, most Class II and just about all Class III trailers will have electric brakes.

Add to this number an accessories wire, to operate trailer internal equipment or to charge the trailer's battery, and you can have as many as seven wires in the harness.

Determine the equipment on your trailer and buy the wiring kit necessary. The kit will contain all the wires needed, plus a plug adapter set which included the female plug, mounted on the bumper or hitch, and the male plug, wired into, or plugged into the trailer harness.

When installing the kit, follow the manufacturer's instructions. The color coding of the wires is standard throughout the industry.

One point to note, some domestic vehicles, and most imported vehicles, have separate turn signals. On most domestic vehicles, the brake lights and rear turn signals operate with the same bulb. For those vehicles with separate turn signals, you can purchase an isolation unit so that the brake lights won't blink whenever the turn signals are operated, or, you can go to your local electronics supply house and buy four diodes to wire in series with the brake and turn signal bulbs. Diodes will isolate the brake and turn signals. The choice is yours. The isolation units are simple and quick to install, but far more expensive than the diodes. The diodes, however, require more work to install properly, since they require the cutting of each bulb's wire and soldering in place of the diode.

One final point, the best kits are those with a spring loaded cover on the vehicle mounted socket. This cover prevents dirt and moisture from corroding the terminals. Never let the vehicle socket hang loosely. Always mount it securely to the bumper or hitch.

Cooling

ENGINE

One of the most common, if not THE most common, problem associated with trailer towing is engine overheating.

With factory installed trailer towing packages, a heavy duty cooling system is usually included. Heavy duty cooling systems are available as optional equipment on most cars, with or without a trailer package. If you have one of these extra-capacity systems, you shouldn't have any overheating problems.

If you have a standard cooling system, without an expansion tank, you'll definitely need to get an Aftermarket expansion tank kit, preferably one with at least a 2 quart (1.8L) capacity. These kits are easily installed on the radiator's overflow hose, and come with a pressure cap designed for expansion tanks.

Another helpful accessory is a Flex Fan. These fan are large diameter units are designed to provide more airflow at low speeds, with blades that have deeply cupped surfaces. The blades then flex, or flatten out, at high speed, when less cooling air is needed. These fans are far lighter in weight than stock fans, requiring less horsepower to drive them. Also, they are far quieter than stock fans.

If you do decide to replace your stock fan with a flex fan, note that if your car has a fan clutch, a spacer between the flex fan and water pump hub will be needed.

Aftermarket engine oil coolers are helpful for prolonging engine oil life and reducing overall engine temperatures. Both of these factors increase engine life.

While not absolutely necessary in towing Class I and some Class II trailers, they are recommended for heavier Class II and all Class III towing.

Engine oil cooler systems consist of an adapter, screwed on in place of the oil filter, a remote filter mounting and a multi-tube, finned heat exchanger, which is mounted in front of the radiator or air conditioning condenser.

TRANSMISSION

An automatic transmission is usually recommended for trailer towing. Modern automatics have proven reliable and, of course, easy to operate, in trailer towing.

The increased load of a trailer, however, causes an increase in the temperature of the automatic transmission fluid. Heat is the worst enemy of an automatic transmission. As the temperature of the fluid increases, the life of the fluid decreases.

It is essential, therefore, that you install an automatic transmission cooler.

The cooler, which consists of a multi-tube, finned heat exchanger, is usually installed in front of the radiator or air conditioning compressor, and hooked inline with the transmission cooler tank inlet line. Follow the cooler manufacturer's installation instructions.

Select a cooler of at least adequate capacity, based upon the combined gross weights of the car and trailer.

Cooler manufacturers recommend that you use an Aftermarket cooler in addition to, and not instead of, the present cooling tank in your car's radiator. If you do want to use it in place of the radiator cooling tank, get a cooler at least two sizes larger than normally necessary.

NOTE: *A transmission cooler can, sometimes, cause slow or harsh shifting in the transmission during cold weather, until the fluid has a chance to come up to normal operating temperature. Some coolers can be purchased with or retrofitted with a temperature bypass valve which will allow fluid flow through the cooler only when the fluid has reached operating temperature, or above.*

PUSHING AND TOWING

Push Starting

Your Camaro should not be push started or tow started. This may damage the catalytic converter or other parts of the car, under some conditions.

Towing

NOTE: *Proper equipment and towing methods must be used to tow your Camaro, so that personal injury or property damage can be avoided. When the vehicle is towed, the steering must be unlocked, the transmission is in neutral, and the parking brake released. Do not tow your Camaro on all four wheels.*

Camaros with an automatic transmission may be towed on the drive wheels at speeds up to 35 mph (56km/h) for distances not exceeding 50 miles (80km). Severe damage to the automatic transmission may result if the speed or distance limits are exceeded.

JUMP STARTING

The chemical reaction in a battery produces explosive hydrogen gas. This is the safe way to jump start a dead battery, reducing the chances of an accidental spark that could cause an explosion.

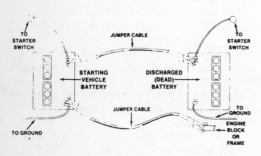

Negative ground battery cable connections for jump starting

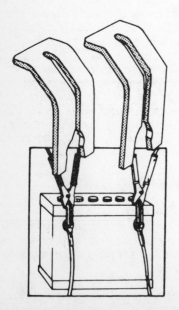

Side terminal battery adapters for charging or jump starting

Precautions

1. Be sure both batteries are of the same voltage.
2. Be sure both batteries are of the same polarity (have the same grounded terminal).
3. Be sure the vehicles are not touching.
4. Be sure the vent cap holes are not obstructed.
5. Do not smoke or allow sparks around the battery.
6. In cold weather, check for frozen electrolyte in the battery.
7. Do not allow electrolyte on your skin or clothing.

Procedure

1. Bring the starting vehicle close (they must not touch) so that the batteries can be reached easily.
2. Turn the ignition OFF and all accessories must be off (except for hazard light, if required).
3. Put both cars in **P** or **N** and set the parking brake.
4. If the terminals on the run down battery are heavily corroded, clean them.
5. Identify the positive and negative posts on both batteries and connect the cables in the order shown.
6. Start the engine of the starting vehicle and run it at fast idle. Try to start the car with the dead battery. Crank it for no more than 10

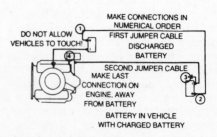

Recommended battery jumper connection

Alternator bracket location for negative jumper cable connection

seconds at a time and let it cool off for 20 seconds in between tries.

7. If it doesn't start in 3 tries, there is something else wrong.

8. Disconnect the cables in the reverse order.

JACKING

The standard jack utilizes slots in the bumper to raise the car. The jack supplied with the car should never be used for any service operation other than tire changing. Never get under the car while it is supported by only a jack. Always block the wheels when changing tires.

The service operations in this book often require that one end or the other, or both, of the car be raised and safely supported. The ideal method, of course, would be a hydraulic hoist. Since this is beyond both the resource and requirement of the do-it-yourselfer, a small hydraulic, screw or scissors jack will suffice for the procedures in this guide. Two sturdy Jackstands should be acquired if you intend to work under the car at any time. An alternate method of raising the car would be drive-on ramps. These are available commercially or can be fabricated from steel. Be sure to block the wheels when using ramps. Never use concrete blocks to support the car. They may break if the load is not evenly distributed.

Regardless of the method of jacking or hoisting the car, there are only certain areas of the undercarriage and suspension you can safely use to support it. See the illustration and make sure that only the shaded areas are used. In addition, be especially careful that you do not damage the catalytic converter. Remember that various cross braces and supports on a lift can sometimes contact low hanging parts of the car.

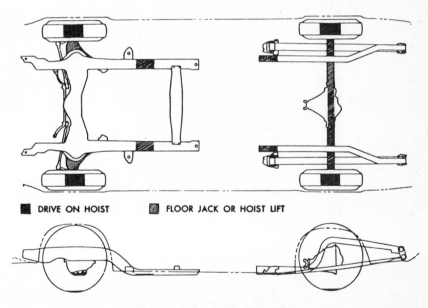

■ DRIVE ON HOIST   ▨ FLOOR JACK OR HOIST LIFT

Vehicle hoisting and jacking points

CAPACITIES

Year	VIN	Engine No. Cyl. Liters	Crankcase Includes Filter (qts.)	Transmission (pts.)			Drive Axle (pts.)	Fuel Tank (gal.)	Cooling System (qt.)	
				4-Sp	5-Sp	Auto.			w/AC	wo/AC
1982	2	4-2.5L	3	3.5	—	7	3.5	16	9.1	8.8
	1	6-2.8L	4	3.5	—	7	3.5	16	9.1	8.8
	H	8-5.0L	5	3.5	—	7	3.5	16	9.1	8.8
	7	8-5.0L	5	3.5	—	7	3.5	16	9.1	8.8

CAPACITIES

Year	VIN	Engine No. Cyl. Liters	Crankcase Includes Filter (qts.)	Transmission (pts.)			Drive Axle (pts.)	Fuel Tank (gal.)	Cooling System (qt.)	
				4-Sp	5-Sp	Auto.			w/AC	wo/AC
1983	2	4-2.5L	3	3.5	3.5	7	3.5	16	9.1	8.8
	1	6-2.8L	4	3.5	3.5	7	3.5	16	9.1	8.8
	H	8-5.0L	5	3.5	3.5	7	3.5	16	9.1	8.8
	7	8-5.0L	5	3.5	3.5	7	3.5	16	9.1	8.8
1984	2	4-2.5L	3	3.5	3.5	7	3.5	16	9.1	8.8
	1	6-2.8L	4	3.5	3.5	7	3.5	16	9.1	8.8
	H	8-5.0L	5	3.5	3.5	7	3.5	16	9.1	8.8
	G	8-5.0L	5	3.5	3.5	7	3.5	16	9.1	8.8
1985	2	4-2.5L	3	—	4.0	10	3.5	15.5	13.0	12.75
	S	6-2.8L	4	—	4.0	10	3.5	15.5	12.5	12.5
	H	8-5.0L	5	—	4.0	10	3.5	16.2	17.0	15.5
	G	8-5.0L	5	—	4.0	10	3.5	16.2	17.0	17.0
	F	8-5.0L	5	—	4.0	10	3.5	15.5	17.0	17.0
1986	2	4-2.5L	3	—	6.6	10	3.5	15.5	9.8	9.8
	S	6-2.8L	4	—	6.6	10	3.5	15.5	12.5	12.5
	H	8-5.0L	5	—	6.6	10	3.5	16.2	15.6	15.3
	G	8-5.0L	5	—	6.6	10	3.5	16.2	17.0	17.0
	F	8-5.0L	5	—	6.6	10	3.5	15.5	17.0	17.0
	8	8-5.7L	5	—	6.6	10	3.5	15.5	17.0	17.0
1987	S	6-2.8L	4	—	6.6	10	3.5	15.5	12.5	12.5
	H	8-5.0L	5	—	6.6	10	3.5	16.2	15.6	15.3
	F	8-5.0L	5	—	6.6	10	3.5	15.5	17.0	17.0
	8	8-5.7L	5	—	6.6	10	3.5	15.5	17.0	17.0
1988	S	6-2.8L	4	—	5.8	10	3.5	15.9	12.5	12.5
	E	8-5.0L	5	—	5.8	10	3.5	15.9	15.6	15.3
	F	8-5.0L	5	—	5.8	10	3.5	15.9	17.0	17.0
	8	8-5.7L	5	—	5.8	10	3.5	15.9	17.0	17.0
1989	S	6-2.8L	4	—	5.9	10	3.5	15.5	12.4	12.4
	E	8-5.0L	5	—	5.9	10	3.5	15.5	15.6	15.6
	F	8-5.0L	5	—	5.9	10	3.5	15.5	17.0	17.0
	8	8-5.7L	5	—	5.9	10	3.5	15.5	17.0	17.0
1990	T	6-3.1L	4	—	5.9	10	4.0	15.5	14.5	14.5
	E	8-5.0L	5	—	5.9	10	4.0	15.5	18.0	17.5
	F	8-5.0L	5	—	5.9	10	4.0	15.5	17.4	17.3
	8	8-5.7L	5	—	5.9	10	4.0	15.5	16.3	16.1
1991	T	6-3.1L	4	—	5.9	10	4.0	15.5	14.8	14.7
	E	8-5.0L	5	—	5.9	10	4.0	15.5	18.0	17.4
	F	8-5.0L	5	—	5.9	10	4.0	15.5	18.0	17.9
	8	8-5.7L	5	—	5.9	10	4.0	15.5	16.7	16.6
1992	T	6-3.1L	4	—	5.9	10	4.0	15.5	14.7	14.7
	E	8-5.0L	5	—	5.9	6.3	4.0	15.5	18.0	17.3
	F	8-5.0L	5	—	5.9	10	4.0	15.5	17.3	17.1
	8	8-5.7L	5	—	5.9	10	4.0	15.5	16.4	16.4

Engine Performance and Tphone-Up

Tune-Up

2

TUNE-UP PROCEDURES

In order to extract the full measure of performance and economy from your engine, it is essential that it is properly tuned at regular intervals. A regular tune-up will keep your Camaro's engine running smoothly and will prevent the annoying breakdowns and poor performance associated with an untuned engine.

A complete tune-up should be performed every 30,000 miles (48,300km). This interval should be halved if the car is operated under severe conditions such as trailer towing, prolonged idling, start-and-stop driving, or if starting or running problems are noticed. It is assumed that the routine maintenance described in Chapter 1 has been kept up, as this will have a decided effect on the results of a tune-up. All of the applicable steps of a tune-up should be followed in order, as the result is a cumulative one.

If the specifications on the underhood tune-up sticker in the engine compartment of your car disagree with the Tune-Up Specifications chart in this Chapter, the figures on the sticker must be used. The sticker often reflects changes made during the production run.

Spark Plugs

A typical spark plug consists of a metal shell surrounding a ceramic insulator. A metal electrode extends downward through the center of the insulator and protrudes a small distance. Located at the end of the plug and attached to the side of the outer metal shell is the side electrode. The side electrode bends in at a 90° angle so that its tip is even with, and parallel to, the tip of the center electrode. The distance between these two electrodes (measured in thousandths of an inch or milimeters) is called the spark plug gap. The spark plug in no way produces a spark but merely provides a gap across which the current

can arc. The coil produces anywhere from 20,000 to 40,000 volts or more, which travels to the distributor where it is distributed through the spark plug wires to the spark plugs. The current passes along the center electrode and jumps the gap to the side electrode, and, in so doing, ignites the air/fuel mixture in the combustion chamber.

SPARK PLUG HEAT RANGE

Spark plug heat range is the ability of the plug to dissipate heat. The longer the insulator (or the farther it extends into the engine), the hotter the plug will operate; the shorter the insulator the cooler it will operate. A plug that absorbs little heat and remains too cool will quickly accumulate deposits of oil and carbon since it is not hot enough to burn them off. This leads to plug fouling and consequently to misfiring. A plug that absorbs too much heat will have deposits to, but due to the excessive heat the electrodes will burn them away quickly and in some instances, pre-ignition may result. Pre-ignition takes place when the combustion chamber temperature is to high and the air/fuel mixture explodes before the actual spark occurs. This early ignition will usually cause a pinging during low speeds and heavy loads.

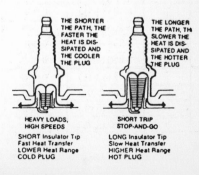

Spark plug heat range

GASOLINE ENGINE TUNE-UP SPECIFICATIONS

Year	Engine VIN	Engine Displacement Liters (cc)	Spark Plugs Gap (in.)	Ignition Timing (deg.) MT	AT	Fuel Pump (psi) ②	Idle Speed (rpm) MT	AT	Valve Clearance In.	Ex.
1982	2	4-151 (2.5L)	0.060	8B	8B	9–13	775	500	Hyd.	Hyd.
	1	6-173 (2.8L)	0.045	10B	10B	4–6.5	850	700	Hyd.	Hyd.
	H	8-305 (5.0L)	0.045	6B	6B	4–6.5	750	575	Hyd.	Hyd.
	7	8-305 (5.0L)	0.045	—	6B	9–13	—	500	Hyd.	Hyd.
1983	2	4-151 (2.5L)	0.060	8B	8B	9–13	775	500	Hyd.	Hyd.
	1	6-173 (2.8L)	0.045	10B	10B	4–6.5	850	700	Hyd.	Hyd.
	H	8-305 (5.0L)	0.045	6B	6B	4–6.5	750	575	Hyd.	Hyd.
	7	8-305 (5.0L)	0.045	—	6B	9–13	—	500	Hyd.	Hyd.
1984	2	4-151 (2.5L)	0.060	8B	8B	9–13	775	500	Hyd.	Hyd.
	1	6-173 (2.8L)	0.045	10B	10B	4–6.5	850	700	Hyd.	Hyd.
	H	8-305 (5.0L)	0.045	6B	6B	4–6.5	750	575	Hyd.	Hyd.
	G	8-305 (5.0L)	0.045	6B	6B	4–6.5	750	500	Hyd.	Hyd.
1985	2	4-151 (2.5L)	0.060	8B	8B	9–13	775	500	Hyd.	Hyd.
	S	6-173 (2.8L)	0.045	10B	10B	40–47	600	500	Hyd.	Hyd.
	H	8-305 (5.0L)	0.045	6B	6B	4–6.5	750	550	Hyd.	Hyd.
	G	8-305 (5.0L)	0.045	6B	6B	4–6.5	750	500	Hyd.	Hyd.
	F	8-305 (5.0L)	0.045	—	8B	40–47	—	500	Hyd.	Hyd.
1986	2	4-151 (2.5L)	0.060	8B	8B	9–13	775	500	Hyd.	Hyd.
	S	6-173 (2.8L)	0.045	10B	10B	40–47	600	500	Hyd.	Hyd.
	H	8-305 (5.0L)	0.045	6B	6B	4–6.5	750	550	Hyd.	Hyd.
	G	8-305 (5.0L)	0.045	6B	6B	4–6.5	750	550	Hyd.	Hyd.
	F	8-305 (5.0L)	0.045	—	8B	40–47	—	500	Hyd.	Hyd.
	8	8-350 (5.7L)	0.035	6B	6B	40–47	450	400	Hyd.	Hyd.
1987	S	6-173 (2.8L)	0.045	10B	10B	40–47	600	500	Hyd.	Hyd.
	H	8-305 (5.0L)	0.035	6B	6B	4–6.5	700	500	Hyd.	Hyd.
	F	8-305 (5.0L)	0.035	6B	6B	40–47	500	500	Hyd.	Hyd.
	8	8-350 (5.7L)	0.035	6B	6B	40–47	450	400	Hyd.	Hyd.
1988	S	6-173 (2.8L)	0.045	10B	10B	40–47	450	400	Hyd.	Hyd.
	E	8-305 (5.0L)	0.035	6B	6B	9–13	450	400	Hyd.	Hyd.
	F	8-305 (5.0L)	0.035	6B	6B	40–47	500	500	Hyd.	Hyd.
	8	8-350 (5.7L)	0.035	6B	6B	40–47	450	400	Hyd.	Hyd.
1989	S	6-173 (2.8L)	0.045	10B	10B	40–47	450	400	Hyd.	Hyd.
	E	8-305 (5.0L)	0.035	6B	6B	9–13	450	400	Hyd.	Hyd.
	F	8-305 (5.0L)	0.035	6B	6B	40–47	500	500	Hyd.	Hyd.
	8	8-350 (5.7L)	0.035	6B	6B	40–47	450	400	Hyd.	Hyd.
1990	T	6-191 (3.1L)	0.045	10B	10B	40–47	①	①	Hyd.	Hyd.
	E	8-305 (5.0L)	0.035	0	0	9–13	①	①	Hyd.	Hyd.
	F	8-305 (5.0L)	0.035	6B	6B	40–47	①	①	Hyd.	Hyd.
	8	8-350 (5.7L)	0.035	6B	6B	40–47	①	①	Hyd.	Hyd.
1991	T	6-191 (3.1L)	0.045	10B	10B	40–47	①	①	Hyd.	Hyd.
	E	8-305 (5.0L)	0.035	0	0	9–13	①	①	Hyd.	Hyd.
	F	8-305 (5.0L)	0.035	6B	6B	40–47	①	①	Hyd.	Hyd.
	8	8-350 (5.7L)	0.035	6B	6B	40–47	①	①	Hyd.	Hyd.

GASOLINE ENGINE TUNE-UP SPECIFICATIONS

Year	Engine VIN	Engine Displacement Liters (cc)	Spark Plugs Gap (in.)	Ignition Timing (deg.) MT	AT	Fuel Pump (psi) ②	Idle Speed (rpm) MT	AT	Valve Clearance In.	Ex.
1992	T	6-191 (3.1L)	0.045	10B	10B	40–47	①	①	Hyd.	Hyd.
	E	8-305 (5.0L)	0.035	0	0	9–13	①	①	Hyd.	Hyd.
	F	8-305 (5.0L)	0.035	6B	6B	40–47	①	①	Hyd.	Hyd.
	8	8-350 (5.7L)	0.035	6B	6B	40–47	①	①	Hyd.	Hyd.

NOTE: The lowest cylinder pressure should be within 75% of the highest cylinder pressure reading. For example, if the highest cylinder is 134 psi, the lowest should be 101 psi. The engine should be at normal operating temperature with throttle valve in the wide open position.

The underhood specifications sticker often reflects tune-up specification changes in production. Sticker figures must be used if they disagree with those in this chart.

① See underhood emission decal for specification
② Key on, engine off

The general rule of thumb for choosing the correct heat range when picking a spark plug is: if most of your driving is long distance, high speed travel, use a colder plug; if most of your driving is stop and go, use a hotter plug. Original equipment plugs are your best choice, but most people never have occasion to change their plugs from the factory recommended heat range. It is first recommended that the cause of the fouled plug be diagnosed instead of temporarily fixing the problem by increasing or decreasing the spark plug heat range.

REMOVAL

Spark plug replacement is recommended every 30,000 miles (48,300km).

When you're removing spark plugs, you should work on one at a time. Don't start by removing the plug wires all at once, because, unless you number them, they're going to get mixed up. On some models though, it will be more convenient for you to remove all the wires before you start to work on the plugs. If this is necessary, take a minute before you begin and number the wires with tape before you take them off. The time you spend here will pay off later.

1. Twist the spark plug boot and remove the boot from the plug. You may also use a plug wire removal tool designed especially for this purpose. Do not pull on the wire itself. When the wire has been removed, take a wire brush and clean the area around the plug. Make sure that all the grime is removed so that none will enter the cylinder after the plug has been removed.

2. Remove the plug using the proper size socket, extensions, and universals as necessary.

3. If removing the plug is difficult, apply some penetrating oil near the plug threads, allow it to work in, then remove the plug. Also, be sure that the socket is straight on the plug, especially on those hard to reach plugs.

INSPECTION

Check the plugs for deposits and wear. If they are not going to be replaced, clean the plugs thoroughly. Remember that any kind of deposit will decrease the efficiency of the plug. Plugs can be cleaned on a spark plug cleaning machine, which can sometimes be found in service stations, or you can do an acceptable job of cleaning with a stiff brush. If the plugs are cleaned, the electrodes must be filed flat. Use

Twist the boot and pull the wire off the spark plug; never pull on the wire itself

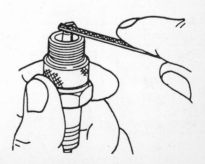

Used spark plugs in good condition may be filled and re-used

an ignition points file, not an emery board or the like, which will leave deposits. The electrodes must be filed perfectly flat with sharp edges; rounded edges reduce the spark plug voltage by as much as 50%.

Check spark plug gap before installation. The ground electrode (the L-shaped one connected to the body of the plug) must be parallel to the center electrode and the specified size wire/blade gauge (see Tune-Up Specifications) should pass through the lap with a slight drag. Always check the gap on new plugs, they are not always set correctly at the factory. Do not use a flat feeler gauge when measuring the gap, because the reading will be inaccurate.

Wire gapping tools usually have a bending tool attached. Use that to adjust the side electrode until the proper distance is obtained. Absolutely never bend the center electrode. Also, be careful not to bend the side electrode too far or too often; it may weaken and break off with-

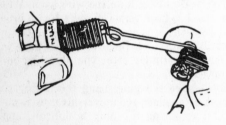

Adjust the plug gap by bending the side electrode

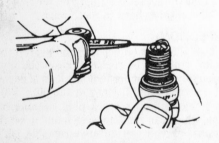

Spark plug gap may also be set using a wire gauge

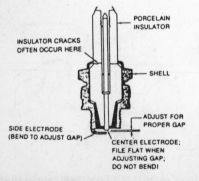

Cross section of a spark plug

in the engine, requiring removal of the cylinder head to retrieve it.

INSTALLATION

1. Lubricate the threads of the spark plugs with a drop of oil. Install the plugs and tighten them hand-tight. Take care not to cross-thread them.

2. Tighten the spark plugs with the socket. Do not apply the same amount of force you would use for a bolt; just snug them in. If a torque wrench is available, tighten to 11–15 ft. lbs.

3. Install the wires on their respective plugs. Make sure the wires are firmly connected. You will be able to feel them click into place.

Spark Plug Wires

CHECKING AND REPLACING

Every 15,000 miles (24,100km), inspect the spark plug wires for burns, cuts, or breaks in the insulation. Check the boots and the nipples on the distributor cap. Replace any damaged wiring.

Every 30,000 miles (48,300km) or so, the resistance of the wires should be checked with an ohmmeter. Wires with excessive resistance will cause misfiring, and may make the engine difficult to start in damp weather. Generally, the useful life of the cables is 40,000–60,000 miles (64,400–96,600km).

To check resistance, remove the distributor cap, leaving the wires in place. Connect one lead of an ohmmeter to an electrode within the cap; connect the other lead to the corresponding spark plug terminal (remove it from the spark plug for this test). Replace any wire which shows a resistance over 30,000Ω. Generally speaking, however, resistance should not be over 25,000Ω, and 30,000Ω must be considered the outer limit of acceptability.

It should be remembered that resistance is also a function of length; the longer the wire, the greater the resistance. Thus, if the wires on your car are longer than the factory originals, resistance will be higher, quite possibly outside these limits.

When installing new wires, replace them one at a time to avoid mixups. Start by replacing the longest one first. Install the boot firmly over the spark plug. Route the wire over the same

HEI Plug Wire Resistance Chart

Wire Length	Minimum	Maximum
0–15 inches	3000 ohms	10,000 ohms
15–25 inches	4000 ohms	15,000 ohms
25–35 inches	6000 ohms	20,000 ohms
Over 35 inches		25,000 ohms

HEI Plug Wire Resistance Chart

path as the original. Insert the nipple firmly onto the tower on the distributor cap, then install the cap cover and latches to secure the wires.

FIRING ORDERS

NOTE: *To avoid confusion always remove and tag the spark plug wires one at a time, for replacement.*

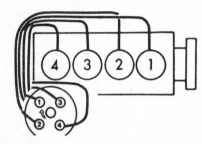

2.5L Engine
Engine Firing Order: 1-3-4-2
Distributor Rotation: Clockwise

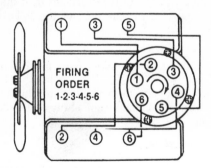

FIRING ORDER 1-2-3-4-5-6

2.8L and 3.1L Engines
Engine Firing Order:1-2-3-4-5-6
Distributor Rotation: Clockwise

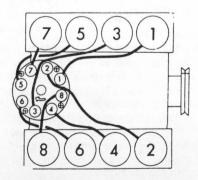

5.0L and 5.7L Engines
Engine Firing Order: 1-8-4-3-6-5-7-2
Distributor Rotation: Clockwise

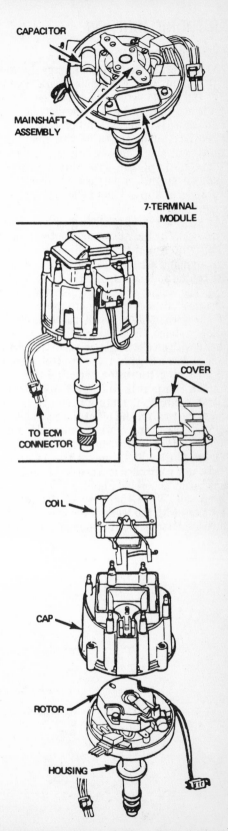

CAPACITOR

MAINSHAFT ASSEMBLY

7-TERMINAL MODULE

COVER

TO ECM CONNECTOR

COIL

CAP

ROTOR

HOUSING

HEI/(EST) distributor with internally mounted ignition coil

ELECTRONIC IGNITION

Description and Operation

The Camaro uses a High Energy Ignition (HEI) system with Electronic Spark Timing (EST) and is completely self-contained unit — all parts are contained within the distributor or has an external mounted ignition coil.

The distributor contains the electronic module, and the magnetic triggering device. The magnetic pickup assembly contains a permanent magnet, a pole piece with internal teeth, and a pickup coil (not to be confused with the ignition coil).

All spark timing changes are done electronically by the Electronic Control Module (ECM) which monitors information from various engine sensors, computes the desired spark timing and then signals the distributor to change the timing accordingly. No vacuum or mechanical advance systems are used.

In the HEI system, as in other electronic ignition systems, the breaker points have been replaced with an electronic switch (a transistor) which is located within the control module. This switching transistor performs the same function the points did in a conventional ignition system; it simply turns the coil's primary current on and off at the correct time. Essentially electronic and conventional ignition systems operate on the same principle.

The module which houses the switching transistor is controlled (turned on and off) by a magnetically generated impulse induced in the pick-up coil. When the teeth of the rotating timer align with the teeth of the pole piece, the induced voltage in the pickup coil signals the electronic module to open the coil primary circuit. The primary current then decreases, and a high voltage is induced in the ignition coil secondary windings which is then directed through the rotor and high voltage leads (spark plug wires) to fire the spark plugs.

In essence, the pickup coil/module system simply replaces the conventional breaker points and condenser. The condenser found within the distributor is for radio suppression purposes only and has nothing to do with the ignition process. The module automatically controls the dwell period, increasing it with increasing engine speed. Since dwell is automatically controlled, it cannot be adjusted. The module itself is non-adjustable and non-repairable and must be replaced if found defective.

Some engines are also equipped with Electronic Spark Control (ESC). The ESC system is used in conjunction with the EST system to reduce spark knock by retarding the ignition timing. A knock sensor, which is installed in the cylinder block, sends a signal to the ESC control module and then in turn to the ECM, which then adjusts the timing accordingly.

HEI SYSTEM PRECAUTIONS

Before going on to troubleshooting, it might be a good idea to take note of the following precautions:

Timing Light Use

Inductive pickup timing lights are the best kind to use with HEI. Timing lights which connect between the spark plug and the spark plug wire occasionally (not always) give false readings.

Spark Plug Wires

The plug wires used with HEI systems are of a different construction than conventional wires. When replacing them, make sure you get the correct wires, since conventional wires won't carry the voltage. Also, handle them carefully to avoid cracking or splitting. Never pierce the HEI ignition wires.

Tachometer Use

Not all tachometers will operate or indicate correctly when used on a HEI system. While some tachometers may give a reading, this does not necessarily mean the reading is correct. In addition, some tachometers hook up differently from others. If you can't figure out whether or not your tachometer will work on your car, check with the tachometer manufacturer. Dwell readings, of course, have no significance at all with the HEI system.

1. Distributor cap
2. Clamp
3. Bolt
4. Distributor

HEI/(EST) distributor with externally mounted ignition coil

HEI System Testers

Instruments designed specifically for testing HEI systems are available from several tool manufacturers. Some of these will even test the module itself. All testing and diagnosis of the system should only be performed by a proffesioanl technician.

Diagnosis and Testing

The symptoms of a defective component within the HEI system are exactly the same as those you would encounter in a conventional system. Some of these symptoms are:
- Hard start or no start
- Rough Idle
- Poor Fuel Economy
- Engine misses under load or while accelerating.

If you suspect a problem in your ignition system, there are certain preliminary checks which you should carry out before you begin to check the electronic portions of the system. First, it is extremely important to make sure the vehicle battery is in good state of charge. A defective or poorly charged battery will cause the various components of the ignition system to read incorrectly when they are being tested. Second, make sure all wiring connections are clean and tight, not only at the battery, but also at the distributor cap, ignition coil, and at the electronic control module.

Since the only change between electronic and conventional ignition systems is in the distributor component area, it is imperative to check the secondary ignition circuit first. If the secondary circuit checks out properly, then the engine condition is probably not the fault of the ignition system. To check the secondary ignition system, perform a simple spark test. Remove one of the plug wires and insert some sort of extension in the plug socket. An old spark plug with the ground electrode removed makes a good extension. Hold the wire and extension about ¼ in. (6mm) away from the block and crank the engine. If a normal spark occurs, then the problem is most likely not in the ignition system. Check for fuel system problems, or fouled spark plugs.

If, however, there is no spark or a weak spark, then further ignition system testing will have to be done. Troubleshooting techniques fall into two categories, depending on the nature of the problem. The categories are (1) Engine cranks, but won't start or (2) Engine runs, but runs rough or cuts out. To begin with, let's consider the first case.

Engine Falls to Start

If the engine won't start, perform a spark test as described earlier. This will narrow the problem area down considerably. If no spark occurs, check for the presence of normal battery voltage at the battery (BAT) terminal on the ignition coil. The ignition switch must be in the **ON** position for this test. Either a voltmeter or a test light may be used for this test. Connect the test light wire to ground and the probe end to the BAT terminal at the coil. If the light comes on, you have voltage to the distributor. If the light fails to come on, this indicates an open circuit in the ignition primary wiring leading to

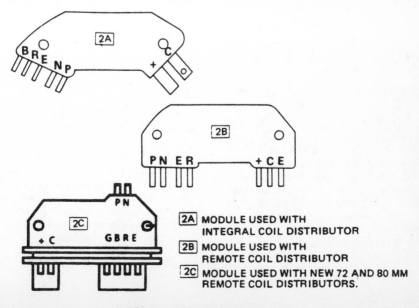

2A MODULE USED WITH INTEGRAL COIL DISTRIBUTOR

2B MODULE USED WITH REMOTE COIL DISTRIBUTOR

2C MODULE USED WITH NEW 72 AND 80 MM REMOTE COIL DISTRIBUTORS.

Ignition coil and module identification

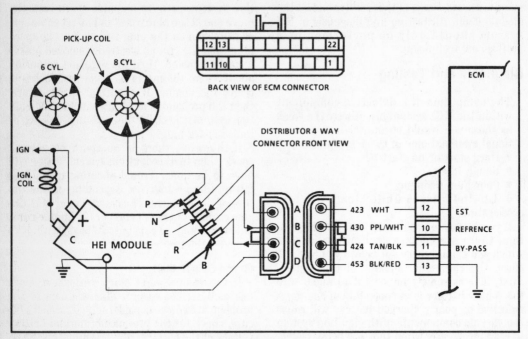

CHART C-4A
IGNITION SYSTEM CHECK
5.0L
CARBURETED

1. Checks for proper output from the ignition system. The spark tester requires a minimum of 25,000 volts to fire. This check can be used in case of an ignition miss because the system may provide enough voltage to run the engine but not enough to fire a spark plug under heavy load.

1A. If spark occurs with EST connector disconnected, pick-up coil output is too low for EST operation.

2. Normal reading during cranking is about 8-10 volts.

3. Checks for a shorted module or grounded circuit from the ignition coil to the module. The distributor module should be turned off so normal voltage should be about 12 volts. If the module is turned "ON", the voltage would be low but above 1 volt. This could cause the ignition coil to fail from excessive heat. With an open ignition coil primary winding, a small mount of voltage will leak through the module from the "Bat." to the tach. terminal.

4. Checks the voltage output with the pick-up coil triggering the module. A spark indicates that the ignition system has sufficient output, however intermittent no-starts or poor performance could be the result of incorrect polarity between the ignition coil and the pick-up coil.
    The color of the pick-up coil connector has to be yellow if one of the ignition coil leads is yellow. If the ignition coil has a white lead, any pick-up coil connector color except yellow is OK.

5. Checks for an open module or circuit to it. 12 volts applied to the module "P" terminal should turn the module "ON" and the voltage should drop to about 7-9 volts.

6. This should turn off the module and cause a spark. If no spark occurs, the fault is most likely in the ignition coil because most module problems would have been found before this point in the procedure. A module tester could determine which is at fault.

Ignition system diagnostic procedure with integral coil—1982–8/

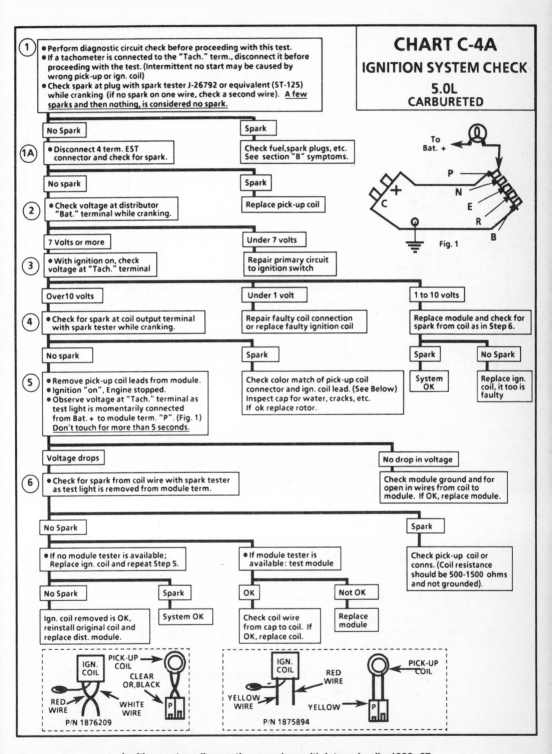

1
- Perform diagnostic circuit check before proceeding with this test.
- If a tachometer is connected to the "Tach." term., disconnect it before proceeding with the test. (Intermittent no start may be caused by wrong pick-up or ign. coil)
- Check spark at plug with spark tester J-26792 or equivalent (ST-125) while cranking (if no spark on one wire, check a second wire). A few sparks and then nothing, is considered no spark.

CHART C-4A
IGNITION SYSTEM CHECK
5.0L
CARBURETED

To Bat. +

P
N
E
R
B
C

Fig. 1

No Spark

1A
- Disconnect 4 term. EST connector and check for spark.

Spark
Check fuel, spark plugs, etc. See section "B" symptoms.

No spark

2
- Check voltage at distributor "Bat." terminal while cranking.

Spark
Replace pick-up coil

7 Volts or more

3
- With ignition on, check voltage at "Tach." terminal

Under 7 volts
Repair primary circuit to ignition switch

Over 10 volts

4
- Check for spark at coil output terminal with spark tester while cranking.

Under 1 volt
Repair faulty coil connection or replace faulty ignition coil

1 to 10 volts
Replace module and check for spark from coil as in Step 6.

No spark

5
- Remove pick-up coil leads from module.
- Ignition "on", Engine stopped.
- Observe voltage at "Tach." terminal as test light is momentarily connected from Bat. + to module term. "P". (Fig. 1) Don't touch for more than 5 seconds.

Spark
Check color match of pick-up coil connector and ign. coil lead. (See Below) Inspect cap for water, cracks, etc. If ok replace rotor.

Spark
System OK

No Spark
Replace ign. coil, it too is faulty

Voltage drops

6
- Check for spark from coil wire with spark tester as test light is removed from module term.

No drop in voltage
Check module ground and for open in wires from coil to module. If OK, replace module.

No Spark

- If no module tester is available; Replace ign. coil and repeat Step 5.

- If module tester is available: test module

Spark
Check pick-up coil or conns. (Coil resistance should be 500-1500 ohms and not grounded).

No Spark
Ign. coil removed is OK, reinstall original coil and replace dist. module.

Spark
System OK

OK
Check coil wire from cap to coil. If OK, replace coil.

Not OK
Replace module

IGN. COIL — PICK-UP COIL — CLEAR OR, BLACK
RED WIRE — WHITE WIRE — P
P/N 1876209

IGN. COIL — PICK-UP COIL — RED WIRE
YELLOW WIRE — YELLOW — P
P/N 1875894

Ignition system diagnostic procedure with integral coil—1982–87

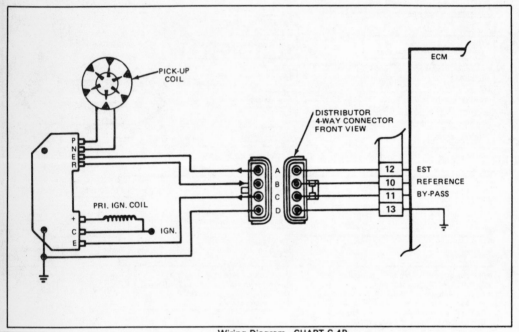

Wiring Diagram - CHART C-4B

CHART C-4B, IGNITION SYSTEM CHECK (REMOTE COIL) (2.8L)

1. Two wires are checked if there is not spark, because one may be a bad wire.

2. A spark says the problem must be distributor cap or rotor.

3. Normally, there should be battery voltage at the + terminal. Low voltage would indicate an open or high resistance circuit from distributor to coil or ignition switch.

4. Checks for a shorted module or grounded circuit from the ignition coil to the module. The distributor module should be turned "OFF", so normal voltage should be about 12 volts. If the module is turned "ON", the voltage would be low, but above 1 volt. This could cause the ignition coil to fail from excessive heat.
   With an open ignition coil primary winding, a small amount of voltage will leak through the module from the "Bat." to the tach terminal.

5. Checks for an open module, or circuit to it. 12 volts applied to the module "P" terminal should turn the module "ON" and the voltage should drop to about 7-9 volts.

6. This should turn "OFF" the module and cause a spark. If no spark occurs, the fault is most likely in the ignition coil because most module problems would have been found before this point in the procedure. A module tester could determine which is at fault.

Ignition system diagnostic procedure with remote coil—1982–84

1984 CCC
CHART C-4B
IGNITION SYSTEM CHECK
(REMOTE COIL)

Perform diagnostic circuit check before proceeding with this test.
If a tachometer is connected to the tachometer terminal, disconnect it before proceeding with the test.

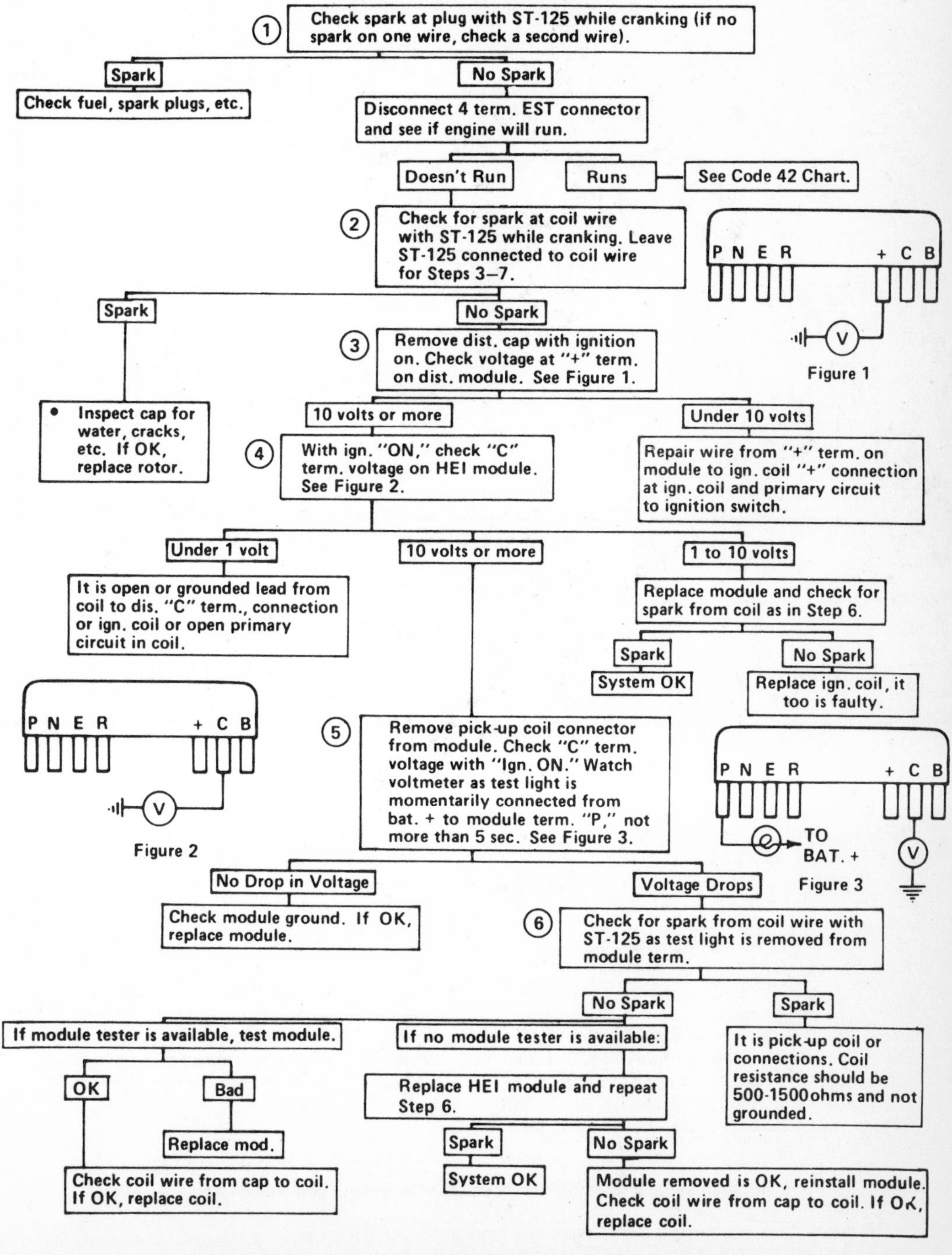

① Check spark at plug with ST-125 while cranking (if no spark on one wire, check a second wire).

Spark
Check fuel, spark plugs, etc.

No Spark
Disconnect 4 term. EST connector and see if engine will run.

Doesn't Run   **Runs** — See Code 42 Chart.

② Check for spark at coil wire with ST-125 while cranking. Leave ST-125 connected to coil wire for Steps 3–7.

P N E R   + C B

Figure 1

Spark
• Inspect cap for water, cracks, etc. If OK, replace rotor.

No Spark
③ Remove dist. cap with ignition on. Check voltage at "+" term. on dist. module. See Figure 1.

10 volts or more
④ With ign. "ON," check "C" term. voltage on HEI module. See Figure 2.

Under 10 volts
Repair wire from "+" term. on module to ign. coil "+" connection at ign. coil and primary circuit to ignition switch.

Under 1 volt
It is open or grounded lead from coil to dis. "C" term., connection or ign. coil or open primary circuit in coil.

10 volts or more

1 to 10 volts
Replace module and check for spark from coil as in Step 6.

Spark
System OK

No Spark
Replace ign. coil, it too is faulty.

P N E R   + C B

Figure 2

⑤ Remove pick-up coil connector from module. Check "C" term. voltage with "Ign. ON." Watch voltmeter as test light is momentarily connected from bat. + to module term. "P," not more than 5 sec. See Figure 3.

P N E R   + C B

TO BAT. +   Figure 3

No Drop in Voltage
Check module ground. If OK, replace module.

Voltage Drops
⑥ Check for spark from coil wire with ST-125 as test light is removed from module term.

No Spark

Spark
It is pick-up coil or connections. Coil resistance should be 500-1500 ohms and not grounded.

If module tester is available, test module.

OK   Bad
      Replace mod.

Check coil wire from cap to coil. If OK, replace coil.

If no module tester is available:
Replace HEI module and repeat Step 6.

Spark
System OK

No Spark
Module removed is OK, reinstall module. Check coil wire from cap to coil. If OK, replace coil.

Ignition system diagnostic procedure with remote coil—1982–84

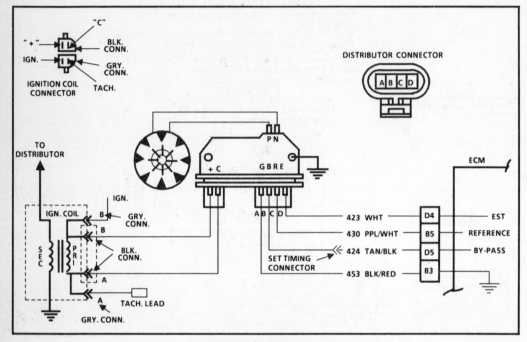

CHART C-4A

IGNITION SYSTEM CHECK
5.0L & 5.7L "F" SERIES
FUEL INJECTION (PORT)

Test Description: Step numbers refer to step numbers on diagnostic chart.

1. Checks for proper output from the ignition system. The spark tester requires a minimum of 25,000 volts to fire. This check can be used in case of an ignition miss because the system may provide enough voltage to run the engine but not enough to fire a spark plug under heavy load.

1A. If spark occurs with EST connector disconnected, pick-up coil output is too low for EST operation.

2. Normal reading during cranking is about 8-10 volts.

3. Checks for a shorted module or grounded circuit from the ignition coil to the module. The distributor module should be turned off so normal voltage should be about 12 volts. If the module is turned "ON", the voltage would be low but above 1 volt. This could cause the ignition coil to fail from excessive heat. With an open ignition coil primary winding, a small mount of voltage will leak through the module from the "Bat." to the tach. terminal.

4. Checks the voltage output with the pick-up coil triggering the module. A spark indicates that the ignition system has sufficient output, however intermittent no-starts or poor performance could be the result of incorrect polarity between the ignition coil and the pick-up coil.

   The color of the pick-up coil connector has to be yellow if one of the ignition coil leads is yellow. If the ignition coil has a white lead, any pick-up coil connector color except yellow is OK.

5. Checks for an open module or circuit to it. 12 volts applied to the module "P" terminal should turn the module "ON" and the voltage should drop to about 7-9 volts.

6. This should turn off the module and cause a spark. If no spark occurs, the fault is most likely in the ignition coil because most module problems would have been found before this point in the procedure. A module tester could determine which is at fault.

Ignition system diagnostic procedure with remote coil—1985–92

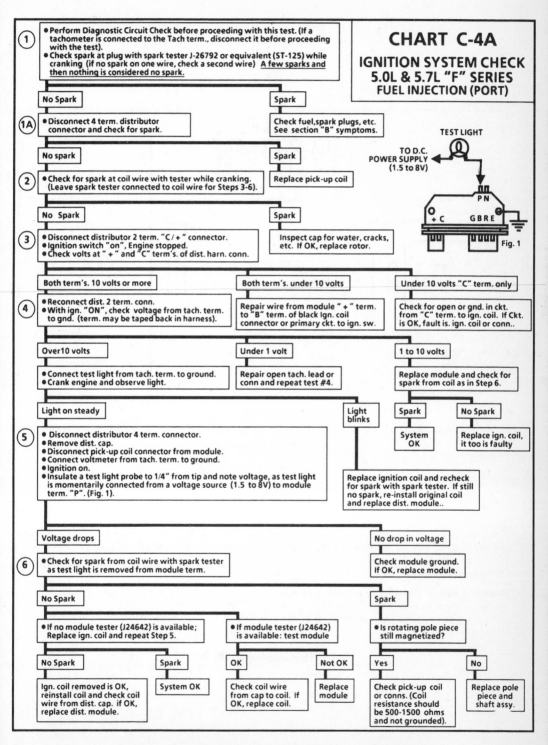

CHART C-4A

IGNITION SYSTEM CHECK 5.0L & 5.7L "F" SERIES FUEL INJECTION (PORT)

(1) • Perform Diagnostic Circuit Check before proceeding with this test. (If a tachometer is connected to the Tach term., disconnect it before proceeding with the test).
• Check spark at plug with spark tester J-26792 or equivalent (ST-125) while cranking (if no spark on one wire, check a second wire) A few sparks and then nothing is considered no spark.

| No Spark | Spark |

(1A) • Disconnect 4 term. distributor connector and check for spark.

Check fuel, spark plugs, etc. See section "B" symptoms.

TEST LIGHT
TO D.C. POWER SUPPLY (1.5 to 8V)

| No spark | Spark |

(2) • Check for spark at coil wire with tester while cranking. (Leave spark tester connected to coil wire for Steps 3-6).

Replace pick-up coil

P N
+ C   G B R E
Fig. 1

| No Spark | Spark |

(3) • Disconnect distributor 2 term. "C / + " connector.
• Ignition switch "on", Engine stopped.
• Check volts at " + " and "C" term's. of dist. harn. conn.

Inspect cap for water, cracks, etc. If OK, replace rotor.

| Both term's. 10 volts or more | Both term's. under 10 volts | Under 10 volts "C" term. only |

(4) • Reconnect dist. 2 term. conn.
• With ign. "ON", check voltage from tach. term. to gnd. (term. may be taped back in harness).

Repair wire from module " + " term. to "B" term. of black Ign. coil connector or primary ckt. to ign. sw.

Check for open or gnd. in ckt. from "C" term. to ign. coil. If Ckt. is OK, fault is. ign. coil or conn..

| Over10 volts | Under 1 volt | 1 to 10 volts |

• Connect test light from tach. term. to ground.
• Crank engine and observe light.

Repair open tach. lead or conn and repeat test #4.

Replace module and check for spark from coil as in Step 6.

| Light on steady | | Light blinks | Spark | No Spark |

(5) • Disconnect distributor 4 term. connector.
• Remove dist. cap.
• Disconnect pick-up coil connector from module.
• Connect voltmeter from tach. term. to ground.
• Ignition on.
• Insulate a test light probe to 1/4" from tip and note voltage, as test light is momentarily connected from a voltage source (1.5 to 8V) to module term. "P". (Fig. 1).

System OK

Replace ign. coil, it too is faulty

Replace ignition coil and recheck for spark with spark tester. If still no spark, re-install original coil and replace dist. module..

| Voltage drops | | No drop in voltage |

(6) • Check for spark from coil wire with spark tester as test light is removed from module term.

Check module ground. If OK, replace module.

| No Spark | | Spark |

• If no module tester (J24642) is available; Replace ign. coil and repeat Step 5.

• If module tester (J24642) is available: test module

• Is rotating pole piece still magnetized?

| No Spark | Spark | OK | Not OK | Yes | No |

Ign. coil removed is OK, reinstall coil and check coil wire from dist. cap. if OK, replace dist. module.

System OK

Check coil wire from cap to coil. If OK, replace coil.

Replace module

Check pick-up coil or conns. (Coil resistance should be 500-1500 ohms and not grounded).

Replace pole piece and shaft assy.

Ignition system diagnostic procedure with remote coil—1985–92

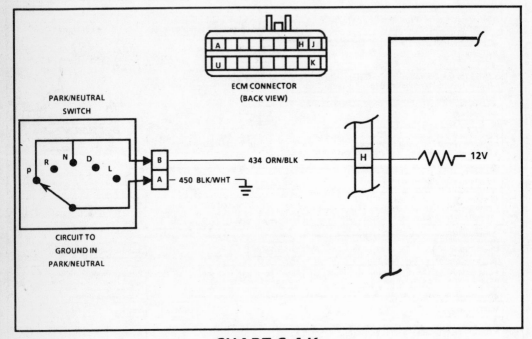

CHART C-4 K

EST PERFORMANCE CHECK
5.0L
CARBURETED

1. Grounding the "test" terminal causes the system to go to a fixed spark advance which should be different from that obtained with EST operating.

   Engine is run at fast idle to get more spark advance. Usually the change is enough so it can be heard in RPM change. If so, it is not necessary to check timing.

2. The check in drive is made because some engines will not have EST operating in P/N.

3. Checks to see if fault is in MAP/VAC system.

EST performance test—1982–85

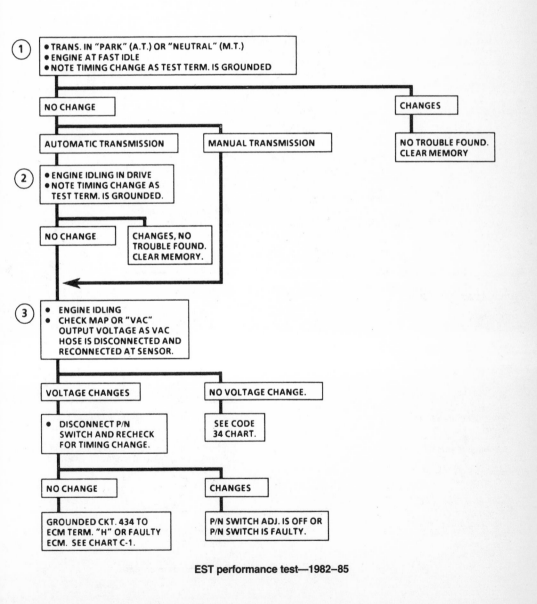

CHART C-4 K
EST PERFORMANCE CHECK
5.0L
CARBURETED

1
- TRANS. IN "PARK" (A.T.) OR "NEUTRAL" (M.T.)
- ENGINE AT FAST IDLE
- NOTE TIMING CHANGE AS TEST TERM. IS GROUNDED

NO CHANGE

CHANGES

AUTOMATIC TRANSMISSION   MANUAL TRANSMISSION

NO TROUBLE FOUND.
CLEAR MEMORY

2
- ENGINE IDLING IN DRIVE
- NOTE TIMING CHANGE AS
  TEST TERM. IS GROUNDED.

NO CHANGE

CHANGES, NO
TROUBLE FOUND.
CLEAR MEMORY.

3
- ENGINE IDLING
- CHECK MAP OR "VAC"
  OUTPUT VOLTAGE AS VAC
  HOSE IS DISCONNECTED AND
  RECONNECTED AT SENSOR.

VOLTAGE CHANGES

NO VOLTAGE CHANGE.

- DISCONNECT P/N
  SWITCH AND RECHECK
  FOR TIMING CHANGE.

SEE CODE
34 CHART.

NO CHANGE

CHANGES

GROUNDED CKT. 434 TO
ECM TERM. "H" OR FAULTY
ECM. SEE CHART C-1.

P/N SWITCH ADJ. IS OFF OR
P/N SWITCH IS FAULTY.

EST performance test—1982–85

ESC DIAGNOSTIC PROCEDURES

| ENGINE DETONATION |

Check engine coolant for proper level and concentration.

Check detonation sensor connector for proper installation.

Check initial timing per emissions label specifications. Reconnect vacuum advance hose after completing timing check.

If trouble remains

Check ESC system performance as follows:

Operate engine until top radiator hose is warm.

Turn air conditioner off, install tachometer to engine.

Set throttle fast idle CAM on high step of CAM. Engine RPM must be above 1800 RPM.

Use a steel rod, such as a socket wrench breaker bar, to tap the front area of the intake manifold. Tap the manifold rapidly with medium to havey taps.

Observe RPM drop of 200 or more RPM. Engine RPM should return to original RPM within 20 seconds after tapping stops.

RPM DROPS AS NOTED ABOVE.

Disconnect 4 pin connector to distributor.

On the distributor side of the connector, jumper together pin A and pin C.

Check distributor per H.E.I. diagnostic procedure in section 6D of the service manual.

Distributor checks OK.

Reconnect distributor to ESC controller.

Check carburetor, turbocharger, and other diagnostics under "engine detonation" in the car service manual.

RPM DOES NOT DROP AS NOTED ABOVE.

Check detonation sensor for any type of physical damage. Detonation sensor is sensitive to physical damage.

Check detonation sensor for proper installation. Note torque valve.

Check polarity of ohmmeter leads before proceeding

Disconnect detonation sensor connector at cowl. On the sensor side of the harness, connect the positive lead of the ohmmeter to the connector terminal attached to the center conductor of the sensor lead. Connect the negative lead to ground. Resistance: 175 to 375 OHMS.

CONTINUED ON NEXT PAGE

ESC system diagnostic procedure—1982 5.0L carbureted engine

ESC DIAGNOSTIC PROCEDURES (Cont'd)

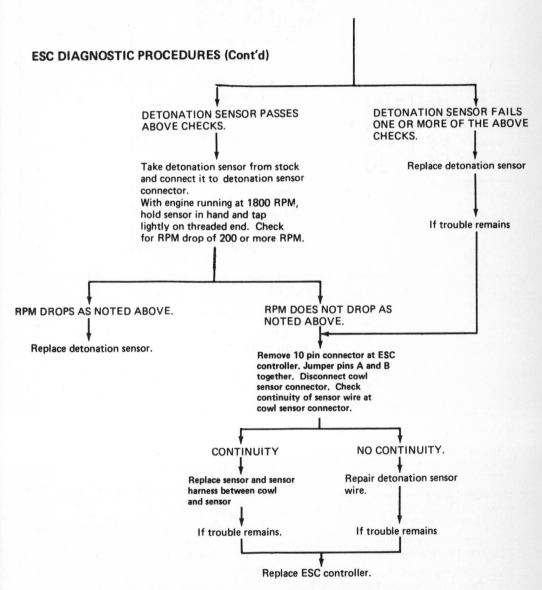

DETONATION SENSOR PASSES ABOVE CHECKS.

Take detonation sensor from stock and connect it to detonation sensor connector.
With engine running at 1800 RPM, hold sensor in hand and tap lightly on threaded end. Check for RPM drop of 200 or more RPM.

DETONATION SENSOR FAILS ONE OR MORE OF THE ABOVE CHECKS.

Replace detonation sensor

If trouble remains

RPM DROPS AS NOTED ABOVE.

Replace detonation sensor.

RPM DOES NOT DROP AS NOTED ABOVE.

Remove 10 pin connector at ESC controller. Jumper pins A and B together. Disconnect cowl sensor connector. Check continuity of sensor wire at cowl sensor connector.

CONTINUITY

Replace sensor and sensor harness between cowl and sensor

If trouble remains.

NO CONTINUITY.

Repair detonation sensor wire.

If trouble remains

Replace ESC controller.

ESC system diagnostic procedure—1982 5.0L carbureted engine

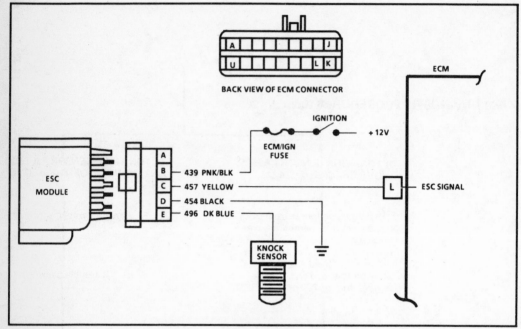

CHART C-5
ELECTRONIC SPARK CONTROL
5.0L
CARBURETED

If the timing is retarded at idle, it may be due to ESC operating.
ESC should not operate unless a knock is present.

1. This is the ESC functional check. Simulating an engine knock by tapping the engine block should normally cause an RPM drop (decrease timing). If it doesn't drop, either the timing is not retarding or is retarded all the time.

2. This should cause full retard by dropping the voltage at ECM term. "L." Retarded timing should cause an RPM drop.

3. Normally, voltage should be .08V AC or higher for a good knock sensor circuit.

4. "Service Engine Soon" light should be "on" and a Code 43 set because ESC system would be retarded too long. If no light comes on, the ECM is not retarding the spark because of a voltage on CKT. 457 to terminal "L" or the ECM is faulty.

5. Checks to see if knock sensor is reason for retard signal. If engine knock is not present, and timing increases when knock sensor is disconnected, fault is an over sensitive knock sensor. Timing should not normally increase.

6. Checks to see if retard signal is due to "noise" on signal wire or faulty controller. If timing increases when wire is disconnected from controller, fault is due to knock sensor signal wire running too close to an ignition or charging system wire. Reroute wire to correct.

ESC system diagnostic procedure—1983–87 5.0L carbureted engine

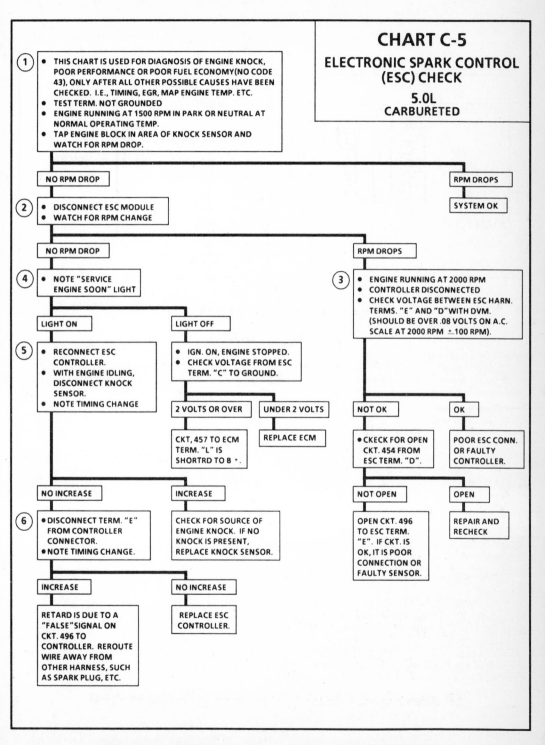

CHART C-5
ELECTRONIC SPARK CONTROL (ESC) CHECK
5.0L
CARBURETED

(1)
- THIS CHART IS USED FOR DIAGNOSIS OF ENGINE KNOCK, POOR PERFORMANCE OR POOR FUEL ECONOMY(NO CODE 43), ONLY AFTER ALL OTHER POSSIBLE CAUSES HAVE BEEN CHECKED. I.E., TIMING, EGR, MAP ENGINE TEMP. ETC.
- TEST TERM. NOT GROUNDED
- ENGINE RUNNING AT 1500 RPM IN PARK OR NEUTRAL AT NORMAL OPERATING TEMP.
- TAP ENGINE BLOCK IN AREA OF KNOCK SENSOR AND WATCH FOR RPM DROP.

NO RPM DROP

RPM DROPS

SYSTEM OK

(2)
- DISCONNECT ESC MODULE
- WATCH FOR RPM CHANGE

NO RPM DROP

RPM DROPS

(4)
- NOTE "SERVICE ENGINE SOON" LIGHT

(3)
- ENGINE RUNNING AT 2000 RPM
- CONTROLLER DISCONNECTED
- CHECK VOLTAGE BETWEEN ESC HARN. TERMS. "E" AND "D" WITH DVM. (SHOULD BE OVER .08 VOLTS ON A.C. SCALE AT 2000 RPM ±100 RPM).

LIGHT ON

LIGHT OFF

(5)
- RECONNECT ESC CONTROLLER.
- WITH ENGINE IDLING, DISCONNECT KNOCK SENSOR.
- NOTE TIMING CHANGE

- IGN. ON, ENGINE STOPPED.
- CHECK VOLTAGE FROM ESC TERM. "C" TO GROUND.

NOT OK

OK

2 VOLTS OR OVER

UNDER 2 VOLTS

CKT, 457 TO ECM TERM. "L" IS SHORTRD TO B +.

REPLACE ECM

- CKECK FOR OPEN CKT. 454 FROM ESC TERM. "D".

POOR ESC CONN. OR FAULTY CONTROLLER.

NO INCREASE

INCREASE

(6)
- DISCONNECT TERM. "E" FROM CONTROLLER CONNECTOR.
- NOTE TIMING CHANGE.

CHECK FOR SOURCE OF ENGINE KNOCK. IF NO KNOCK IS PRESENT, REPLACE KNOCK SENSOR.

NOT OPEN

OPEN

OPEN CKT. 496 TO ESC TERM. "E". IF CKT. IS OK, IT IS POOR CONNECTION OR FAULTY SENSOR.

REPAIR AND RECHECK

INCREASE

NO INCREASE

RETARD IS DUE TO A "FALSE"SIGNAL ON CKT. 496 TO CONTROLLER. REROUTE WIRE AWAY FROM OTHER HARNESS, SUCH AS SPARK PLUG, ETC.

REPLACE ESC CONTROLLER.

ESC system diagnostic procedure—1983–87 5.0L carbureted engine

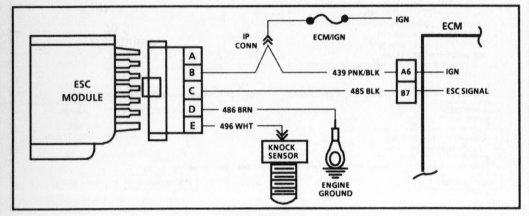

CHART C-5

ELECTRONIC SPARK CONTROL
5.0L & 5.7L "F" SERIES
FUEL INJECTION (PORT)

Circuit Description:

Electronic spark control is accomplished with a module that sends a voltage signal to the ECM. As the knock sensor detects engine knock, the voltage from the ESC module to the ECM is shut off and this signals the ECM to retard timing, if engine rpm is over about 900.

Test Description: Step numbers refer to step numbers on diagnostic chart.

1. If a Code 43 is not set, but a knock signal is indicated while running at 1500 rpm, listen for an internal engine noise. Under a no load condition, there should not be any detonation, and if knock is indicated, an internal engine problem may exist.
2. Usually a knock signal can be generated by tapping on the right exhaust manifold. This test can also be performed at idle. Test number 1 was run at 1500 rpm to determine if a constant knock signal was present, which would affect engine performance.
3. This tests whether the knock signal is due to the sensor, a basic engine problem, or the ESC module.
4. If the module gorund circuit is faulty, the ESC module will not function correctly. The test light should light indicating the ground circuit is OK.
5. Contacting CKT 496, with a test light to 12 volts, should generate a knock signal to determine whether the knock sensor is faulty, or the ESC module can't recognize a knock signal.

Diagnostic Aids:

"Scan" tools have two positions to diagnose the ESC system. The knock signal can be monitored to see if the knock sensor is detecting a knock condition and if the ESC module is functioning, knock signal should display "yes", whenever detonation is present. The knock retard position on the "Scan" displays the amount of spark retard the ECM is commanding. The ECM can retard the timing up to 20 degrees.

If the ESC system checks OK, but detonation is the complaint, refer to Detonation/Spark knock in Section B.

ESC system diagnostic procedure—1986–89 5.0L and 5.7L fuel injected engines

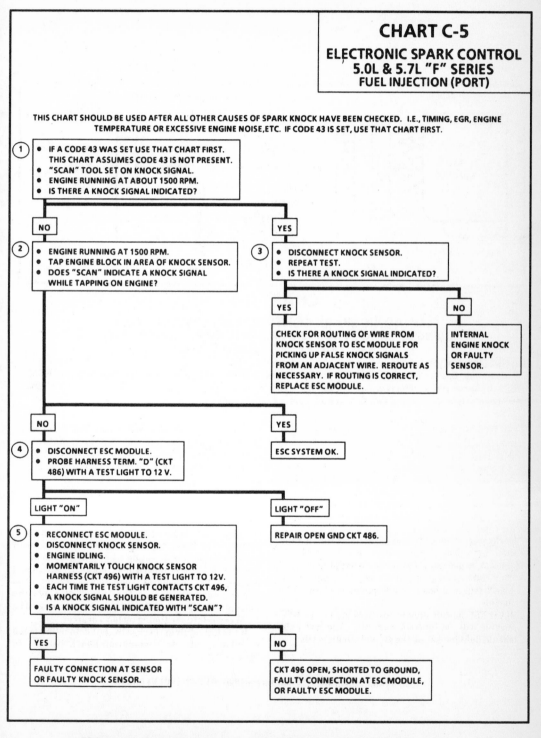

CHART C-5
ELECTRONIC SPARK CONTROL
5.0L & 5.7L "F" SERIES
FUEL INJECTION (PORT)

THIS CHART SHOULD BE USED AFTER ALL OTHER CAUSES OF SPARK KNOCK HAVE BEEN CHECKED. I.E., TIMING, EGR, ENGINE TEMPERATURE OR EXCESSIVE ENGINE NOISE,ETC. IF CODE 43 IS SET, USE THAT CHART FIRST.

(1)
- IF A CODE 43 WAS SET USE THAT CHART FIRST. THIS CHART ASSUMES CODE 43 IS NOT PRESENT.
- "SCAN" TOOL SET ON KNOCK SIGNAL.
- ENGINE RUNNING AT ABOUT 1500 RPM.
- IS THERE A KNOCK SIGNAL INDICATED?

NO

YES

(2)
- ENGINE RUNNING AT 1500 RPM.
- TAP ENGINE BLOCK IN AREA OF KNOCK SENSOR.
- DOES "SCAN" INDICATE A KNOCK SIGNAL WHILE TAPPING ON ENGINE?

(3)
- DISCONNECT KNOCK SENSOR.
- REPEAT TEST.
- IS THERE A KNOCK SIGNAL INDICATED?

YES

NO

CHECK FOR ROUTING OF WIRE FROM KNOCK SENSOR TO ESC MODULE FOR PICKING UP FALSE KNOCK SIGNALS FROM AN ADJACENT WIRE. REROUTE AS NECESSARY. IF ROUTING IS CORRECT, REPLACE ESC MODULE.

INTERNAL ENGINE KNOCK OR FAULTY SENSOR.

NO

YES

(4)
- DISCONNECT ESC MODULE.
- PROBE HARNESS TERM. "D" (CKT 486) WITH A TEST LIGHT TO 12 V.

ESC SYSTEM OK.

LIGHT "ON"

LIGHT "OFF"

(5)
- RECONNECT ESC MODULE.
- DISCONNECT KNOCK SENSOR.
- ENGINE IDLING.
- MOMENTARILY TOUCH KNOCK SENSOR HARNESS (CKT 496) WITH A TEST LIGHT TO 12V.
- EACH TIME THE TEST LIGHT CONTACTS CKT 496, A KNOCK SIGNAL SHOULD BE GENERATED.
- IS A KNOCK SIGNAL INDICATED WITH "SCAN"?

REPAIR OPEN GND CKT 486.

YES

NO

FAULTY CONNECTION AT SENSOR OR FAULTY KNOCK SENSOR.

CKT 496 OPEN, SHORTED TO GROUND, FAULTY CONNECTION AT ESC MODULE, OR FAULTY ESC MODULE.

ESC system diagnostic procedure—1986–89 5.0L and 5.7L fuel injected engines

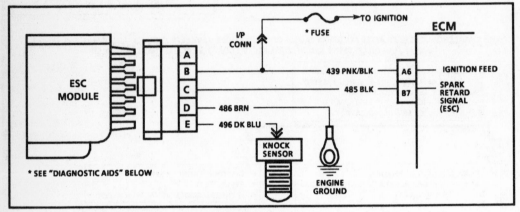

CHART C-5

ELECTRONIC SPARK CONTROL (ESC) SYSTEM CHECK
(ENGINE KNOCK, POOR PERFORMANCE, OR POOR ECONOMY)
5.0L (VIN E) "F" CARLINE (TBI)

Circuit Description:

Electronic Spark Control (ESC) is accomplished with a module that sends a voltage signal to the ECM. When the knock sensor detects engine knock, the voltage from the ESC module to the ECM is shut "OFF" and this signals the ECM to retard timing, if engine rpm is over about 900.

Test Description: Numbers below refer to circled numbers on the diagnostic chart.

1. If a Code 43 is not set, but a knock signal is indicated while running at 1500 rpm, listen for an internal engine noise. Under a no load condition, there should not be any detonation, and if knock is indicated, an internal engine problem may exist.
2. Usually a knock signal can be generated by tapping on the exhaust manifold. This test can also be performed at idle. Test number 1 was run at 1500 rpm, to determine if a constant knock signal was present, which would affect engine performance.
3. This tests whether the knock signal is due to the knock sensor, a basic engine problem, or the ESC module.
4. If the ESC module ground circuit is faulty, the ESC module will not function correctly. The test light should light indicating the ground circuit is OK.

5. Contacting CKT 496, with a test light to 12 volts, should generate a knock signal to determine whether the knock sensor is faulty, or the ESC module can't recognize a knock signal.

Diagnostic Aids:

* ECM Fuse

"Scan" tools have two positions to diagnose the ESC system. The knock signal can be monitored to see if the knock sensor is detecting a knock condition and if the ESC module is functioning, knock signal should display "YES", whenever detonation is present. The knock retard position on the "Scan" displays the amount of spark retard the ECM is commanding. The ECM can retard the timing up to 20 degrees.

If the ESC system checks OK, but detonation is the complaint, refer to "Detonation/Spark Knock" in Section "B".

ESC system diagnostic procedure—1990–91 5.0L (VIN E) engine

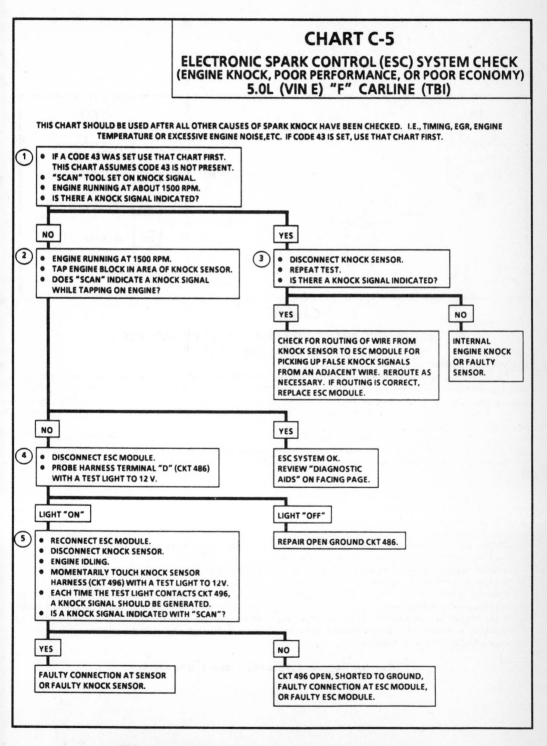

CHART C-5

ELECTRONIC SPARK CONTROL (ESC) SYSTEM CHECK
(ENGINE KNOCK, POOR PERFORMANCE, OR POOR ECONOMY)
5.0L (VIN E) "F" CARLINE (TBI)

THIS CHART SHOULD BE USED AFTER ALL OTHER CAUSES OF SPARK KNOCK HAVE BEEN CHECKED. I.E., TIMING, EGR, ENGINE TEMPERATURE OR EXCESSIVE ENGINE NOISE,ETC. IF CODE 43 IS SET, USE THAT CHART FIRST.

(1)
- IF A CODE 43 WAS SET USE THAT CHART FIRST. THIS CHART ASSUMES CODE 43 IS NOT PRESENT.
- "SCAN" TOOL SET ON KNOCK SIGNAL.
- ENGINE RUNNING AT ABOUT 1500 RPM.
- IS THERE A KNOCK SIGNAL INDICATED?

NO

YES

(2)
- ENGINE RUNNING AT 1500 RPM.
- TAP ENGINE BLOCK IN AREA OF KNOCK SENSOR.
- DOES "SCAN" INDICATE A KNOCK SIGNAL WHILE TAPPING ON ENGINE?

(3)
- DISCONNECT KNOCK SENSOR.
- REPEAT TEST.
- IS THERE A KNOCK SIGNAL INDICATED?

YES

NO

CHECK FOR ROUTING OF WIRE FROM KNOCK SENSOR TO ESC MODULE FOR PICKING UP FALSE KNOCK SIGNALS FROM AN ADJACENT WIRE. REROUTE AS NECESSARY. IF ROUTING IS CORRECT, REPLACE ESC MODULE.

INTERNAL ENGINE KNOCK OR FAULTY SENSOR.

NO

YES

(4)
- DISCONNECT ESC MODULE.
- PROBE HARNESS TERMINAL "D" (CKT 486) WITH A TEST LIGHT TO 12 V.

ESC SYSTEM OK. REVIEW "DIAGNOSTIC AIDS" ON FACING PAGE.

LIGHT "ON"

LIGHT "OFF"

(5)
- RECONNECT ESC MODULE.
- DISCONNECT KNOCK SENSOR.
- ENGINE IDLING.
- MOMENTARILY TOUCH KNOCK SENSOR HARNESS (CKT 496) WITH A TEST LIGHT TO 12V.
- EACH TIME THE TEST LIGHT CONTACTS CKT 496, A KNOCK SIGNAL SHOULD BE GENERATED.
- IS A KNOCK SIGNAL INDICATED WITH "SCAN"?

REPAIR OPEN GROUND CKT 486.

YES

NO

FAULTY CONNECTION AT SENSOR OR FAULTY KNOCK SENSOR.

CKT 496 OPEN, SHORTED TO GROUND, FAULTY CONNECTION AT ESC MODULE, OR FAULTY ESC MODULE.

ESC system diagnostic procedure—1990–91 5.0L (VIN E) engine

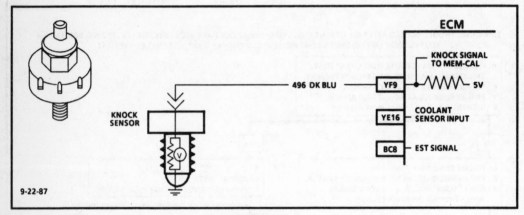

CHART C-5

ELECTRONIC SPARK CONTROL (ESC) SYSTEM CHECK
3.1L (VIN T) "F" CARLINE (PORT)

Circuit Description:

    The knock sensor is used to detect engine detonation and the ECM will retard the electronic spark timing based on the signal being received. The circuitry within the knock sensor causes the ECM's 5 volts to be pulled down so that under a no knock condition, CKT 496 would measure about 2.5 volts. The knock sensor produces an A/C signal which rides on the 2.5 volt DC voltage. The amplitude and frequency are dependent upon the knock level.

    The Mem-Cal used with this engine, contains the functions which were part of remotely mounted ESC modules used on other GM vehicles. The ESC portion of the Mem-Cal then sends a signal to other parts of the ECM which adjusts the spark timing to retard the spark and reduce the detonation.

Test Description: Numbers below refer to circled numbers on the diagnostic chart.

1. With engine idling, there should not be a knock signal present at the ECM because detonation is not likely under a no load condition.
2. Tapping on the engine lift hood bracket should simulate a knock signal to determine if the sensor is capable of detecting detonation. If no knock is detected, try tapping on engine block closer to sensor before replacing sensor.
3. If the engine has an internal problem which is creating a knock, the knock sensor may be responding to the internal failure.

4. This test determines if the knock sensor is faulty or if the ESC portion of the Mem-Cal is faulty. If it is determined that the Mem-Cal is faulty, be sure that is is properly installed and latched into place. If not properly installed, repair and retest.

Diagnostic Aids:

    While observing knock signal on the "Scan," there should be an indication that knock is present when detonation can be heard. Detonation is most likely to occur under high engine load conditions.

ESC system diagnostic procedure—1990–91 3.1L engine

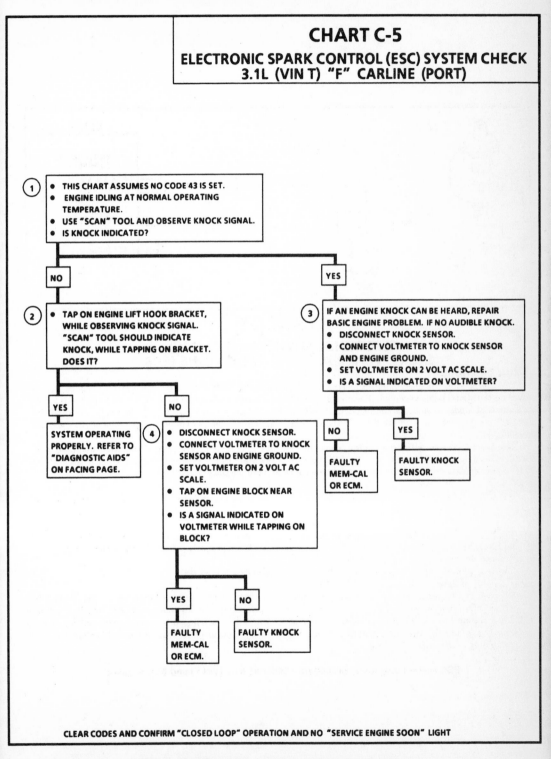

CHART C-5
ELECTRONIC SPARK CONTROL (ESC) SYSTEM CHECK
3.1L (VIN T) "F" CARLINE (PORT)

1
- THIS CHART ASSUMES NO CODE 43 IS SET.
- ENGINE IDLING AT NORMAL OPERATING TEMPERATURE.
- USE "SCAN" TOOL AND OBSERVE KNOCK SIGNAL.
- IS KNOCK INDICATED?

NO

YES

2
- TAP ON ENGINE LIFT HOOK BRACKET, WHILE OBSERVING KNOCK SIGNAL. "SCAN" TOOL SHOULD INDICATE KNOCK, WHILE TAPPING ON BRACKET. DOES IT?

3
- IF AN ENGINE KNOCK CAN BE HEARD, REPAIR BASIC ENGINE PROBLEM. IF NO AUDIBLE KNOCK.
- DISCONNECT KNOCK SENSOR.
- CONNECT VOLTMETER TO KNOCK SENSOR AND ENGINE GROUND.
- SET VOLTMETER ON 2 VOLT AC SCALE.
- IS A SIGNAL INDICATED ON VOLTMETER?

YES

NO

SYSTEM OPERATING PROPERLY. REFER TO "DIAGNOSTIC AIDS" ON FACING PAGE.

4
- DISCONNECT KNOCK SENSOR.
- CONNECT VOLTMETER TO KNOCK SENSOR AND ENGINE GROUND.
- SET VOLTMETER ON 2 VOLT AC SCALE.
- TAP ON ENGINE BLOCK NEAR SENSOR.
- IS A SIGNAL INDICATED ON VOLTMETER WHILE TAPPING ON BLOCK?

NO

FAULTY MEM-CAL OR ECM.

YES

FAULTY KNOCK SENSOR.

YES

FAULTY MEM-CAL OR ECM.

NO

FAULTY KNOCK SENSOR.

CLEAR CODES AND CONFIRM "CLOSED LOOP" OPERATION AND NO "SERVICE ENGINE SOON" LIGHT

ESC system diagnostic procedure—1990–91 3.1L engine

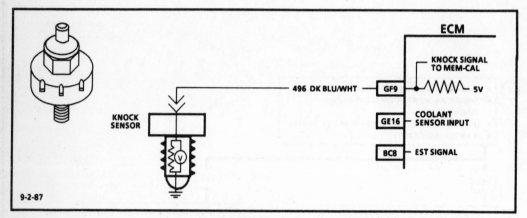

KNOCK SENSOR

ECM

KNOCK SIGNAL TO MEM-CAL

496 DK BLU/WHT | GF9 | 5V

GE16 | COOLANT SENSOR INPUT

BC8 | EST SIGNAL

9-2-87

CHART C-5
ELECTRONIC SPARK CONTROL (ESC)
5.0L (VIN F) & 5.7L (VIN 8) "F" CARLINE (PORT)

Circuit Description:

The knock sensor is used to detect engine detonation and the ECM will retard the electronic spark timing based on the signal being received. The circuitry within the knock sensor causes the ECM's 5 volts to be pulled down so that under a no knock condition, CKT 496 would measure about 2.5 volts. The knock sensor produces an A/C signal which rides on the 2.5 volt DC voltage. The amplitude and frequency are dependent upon the knock level.

The Mem-Cal used with this engine, contains the functions which were part of remotely mounted ESC modules used on other GM vehicles. The ESC portion of the Mem-Cal then sends a signal to other parts of the ECM which adjusts the spark timing to retard the spark and reduce the detonation.

Test Description: Numbers below refer to circled numbers on the diagnostic chart.

1. With engine idling, there should not be a knock signal present at the ECM because detonation is not likely under a no load condition.
2. Tapping on the engine lift hood bracket should simulate a knock signal to determine if the sensor is capable of detecting detonation. If no knock is detected, try tapping on engine block closer to sensor before replacing sensor.
3. If the engine has an internal problem which is creating a knock, the knock sensor may be responding to the internal failure.

4. This test determines if the knock sensor is faulty or if the ESC portion of the Mem-Cal is faulty. If it is determined that the Mem-Cal is faulty, be sure that it is properly installed and latched into place. If not properly installed, repair and retest.

Diagnostic Aids:

While observing knock signal on the "Scan," tool there should be an indication that knock is present when detonation can be heard. Detonation is most likely to occur under high engine load conditions.

ESC system diagnostic procedure—1990–91 5.0L (VIN F) and 5.7L engines

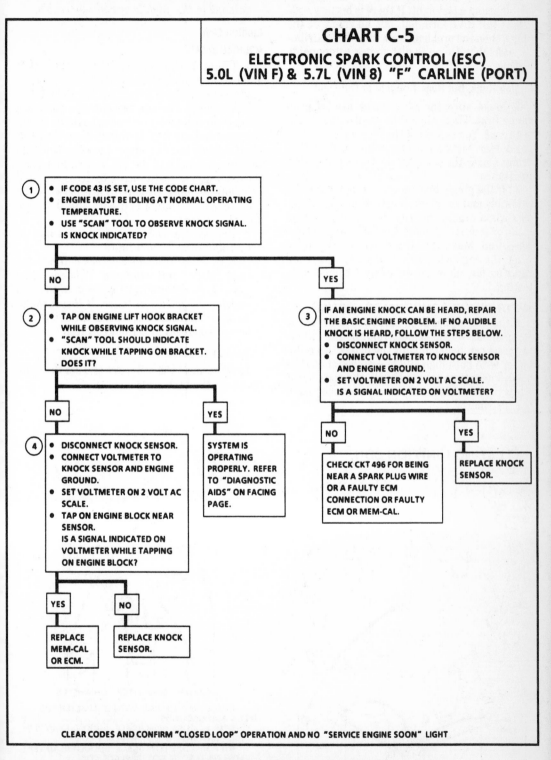

CHART C-5

ELECTRONIC SPARK CONTROL (ESC)
5.0L (VIN F) & 5.7L (VIN 8) "F" CARLINE (PORT)

1
- IF CODE 43 IS SET, USE THE CODE CHART.
- ENGINE MUST BE IDLING AT NORMAL OPERATING TEMPERATURE.
- USE "SCAN" TOOL TO OBSERVE KNOCK SIGNAL. IS KNOCK INDICATED?

NO

YES

2
- TAP ON ENGINE LIFT HOOK BRACKET WHILE OBSERVING KNOCK SIGNAL.
- "SCAN" TOOL SHOULD INDICATE KNOCK WHILE TAPPING ON BRACKET. DOES IT?

3
IF AN ENGINE KNOCK CAN BE HEARD, REPAIR THE BASIC ENGINE PROBLEM. IF NO AUDIBLE KNOCK IS HEARD, FOLLOW THE STEPS BELOW.
- DISCONNECT KNOCK SENSOR.
- CONNECT VOLTMETER TO KNOCK SENSOR AND ENGINE GROUND.
- SET VOLTMETER ON 2 VOLT AC SCALE. IS A SIGNAL INDICATED ON VOLTMETER?

NO

YES

NO

YES

4
- DISCONNECT KNOCK SENSOR.
- CONNECT VOLTMETER TO KNOCK SENSOR AND ENGINE GROUND.
- SET VOLTMETER ON 2 VOLT AC SCALE.
- TAP ON ENGINE BLOCK NEAR SENSOR.
  IS A SIGNAL INDICATED ON VOLTMETER WHILE TAPPING ON ENGINE BLOCK?

SYSTEM IS OPERATING PROPERLY. REFER TO "DIAGNOSTIC AIDS" ON FACING PAGE.

CHECK CKT 496 FOR BEING NEAR A SPARK PLUG WIRE OR A FAULTY ECM CONNECTION OR FAULTY ECM OR MEM-CAL.

REPLACE KNOCK SENSOR.

YES

NO

REPLACE MEM-CAL OR ECM.

REPLACE KNOCK SENSOR.

CLEAR CODES AND CONFIRM "CLOSED LOOP" OPERATION AND NO "SERVICE ENGINE SOON" LIGHT

ESC system diagnostic procedure—1990–91 5.0L (VIN F) and 5.7L engines

the distributor. In this case, you will have to check wiring continuity back to the ignition switch using a test light. If there is battery voltage at the BAT terminal, but no spark at the plugs, then the problem lies within the distributor assembly. Go on to distributor components testing.

Engine Runs, But Runs Roughly or Cuts Out

1. Make sure the plug wires are in good shape first. There should be no obvious cracks or breaks. You can check the plug wires with an ohmmeter, but do not pierce the wires with a probe. Check the chart for the correct plug wire resistance.

2. If the plug wires are good, remove the cap assembly and check for moisture, cracks, chips, or carbon tracks, or any other high voltage leaks or failures. Replace the cap if any defects are found. Make sure the timer wheel rotates when the engine is cranked. If everything is all right so far, go on to distributor components testing.

DISTRIBUTOR COMPONENTS TESTING

If the trouble has been narrowed down to the components within the distributor, the following tests can help pinpoint the defect. An ohmmeter with both high and low ranges should be used. These tests are made with the distributor wires disconnected and the cap removed from the distributor.

WARNING: *The tachometer terminals must never be allowed to touch ground, otherwise damage to the module or coil is possible.*

Ignition Coil

MOUNTED IN CAP

1. Connect an ohmmeter between the TACH and BAT terminals on the ignition coil. The primary coil resistance should be less than 1Ω.

2. To check the coil secondary resistance, connect an ohmmeter between the high tension terminal and the BAT terminal. Note the reading. Connect the ohmmeter between the high tension terminal and the TACH terminal. Note the reading. The resistance in both cases should be 6,000–30,000Ω. Be sure to test between the high tension terminal and both the BAT and TACH terminals.

3. Replace the coil only if the readings in Step 1 and Step 2 are infinite.

NOTE: *These resistance checks will not disclose shorted coil windings. This condition can only be detected with scope analysis or a suitably designed coil tester. If these instruments are unavailable, replace the coil with a known good coil as a final coil test.*

EXTERNALLY MOUNTED

1. Disconnect the coil wires and set the ohmmeter on the high scale.

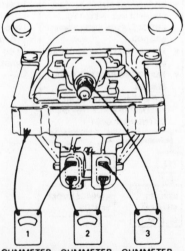

TESTING IGNITION COIL

```
1                    2
OHMMETER            OHMMETER
```

Testing internally mounted ignition coil

TESTING IGNITION COIL

```
1        2        3
OHMMETER OHMMETER OHMMETER
```

CHECK IGNITION COIL WITH OHMMETER FOR OPENS AND GROUNDS:
   STEP 1. — USE HIGH SCALE. SHOULD READ VERY HIGH (INFINITE). IF NOT, REPLACE COIL.
   STEP 2. — USE LOW SCALE. SHOULD READ VERY LOW OR ZERO. IF NOT, REPLACE COIL.
   STEP 3. — USE HIGH SCALE. SHOULD NOT READ INFINITE. IF IT DOES, REPLACE COIL.

Testing externally mounted ignition coil

2. Connect the ohmmeter as illustrated in test No. 1.

3. The ohmmeter should read near infinite or very high.

4. Next, set the ohmmeter to the low scale.

5. Connect the ohmmeter as illustrated in test No. 2.

6. The ohmmeter should read zero or very low.

7. Next, set the ohmmeter on the high scale again.

8. Connect the ohmmeter as illustrated in test No. 3.

9. The ohmmeter should NOT read infinite.

10. If the reading are not as specified, replace the coil.

Pickup Coil

1. Remove the distributor cap and rotor.

2. Disconnect the pickup coil lead.

3. Set the ohmmeter on the high scale and connect it as illustrated in test No. 1.

4. The ohmmeter should read infinity at all times.

5. Next, set the ohmmeter on the low scale and connect it as illustrated in test No. 2.

6. The ohmmeter should read a steady value between 500–1500Ω.

7. If the readings are not as specified, replace the pickup coil.

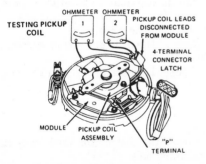

Testing the pick-up coil—with ignition coil mounted in cap

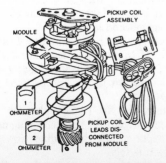

Testing the pick-up coil—with ignition coil externally mounted

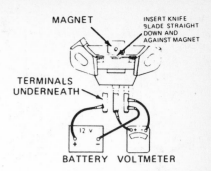

Testing the Hall Effect switch

8. If no defects have been found at this time, and you still have a problem, then the module will have to be checked. If you do not have access to a module tester, the only possible alternative is a substitution test.

Hall Effect Switch

1. With the hall effect switch removed from the distributor, connect a 12 volt battery source and voltmeter as illustrated, being careful not to cross connections.

2. The voltmeter should read less than 0.5 volts.

3. Next, insert a knife blade straight down and against the magnet.

4. The voltmeter should read within a ½ volt of battery voltage.

5. If the readings are not as specified, the switch is defective.

HEI System Maintenance

Except for periodic checks on the spark plug wires, and an occasional check of the distributor cap for cracks (see Steps 1 and 2 under Engine Runs, But Runs Rough or Cuts Out for details), no maintenance is required on the HEI system. No periodic lubrication is necessary; engine oil lubricates the lower bushing, and an oil-filled reservoir lubricates the upper bushing.

Component Replacement

CAPACITOR

The capacitor, if equipped, is part of the coil wire harness assembly. The capacitor is used only for radio noise suppression, it will seldom need replacement.

ESC KNOCK SENSOR

The knock sensor is located on the passenger side of the block above the oil pan.

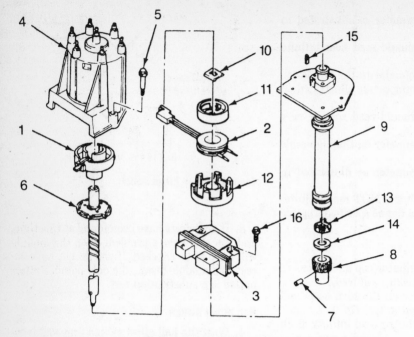

Exploded view of the sealed module HEI distributor

1. Rotor
2. Pickup coil
3. Module
4. Cap
5. Screw
6. Shaft
7. Pin
8. Gear
9. Housing
10. Retainer
11. Housing
12. Pole piece
13. Tang washer
14. Washer
15. Pin
16. Screw

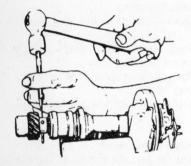

Removing distributor shaft and roll pin

ESC MODULE

The module is located on a bracket in the left rear engine compartment, next to the fuel pump relay.

HEI DISTRIBUTOR

NOTE: *The distributor will have to be removed from the engine and disassembled if the pickup coil or distributor shaft need to be replaced.*

1. Disconnect the negative battery cable.
2. Remove the air cleaner assembly.
3. Disconnect the electrical connectors from the side of the distributor.
4. Remove the distributor cover and wire retainer, if equipped. Turn the retaining screws counterclockwise and remove the cap.
5. Mark the relationship of the rotor to the distributor housing and the housing relationship to the engine.
6. Remove the distributor retaining bolt and hold-down clamp.
7. Pull the distributor up until the rotor just stops turning counterclockwise and again note the position of the rotor.
8. Remove the distributor from the engine.

To install:

9. Insert the distributor into the engine, with the rotor aligned to the last mark made, then slowly install the distributor the rest of the way until all marks previously made are aligned.
10. Install the distributor hold-down clamp and retaining bolt.
11. If removed, install the wiring harness retainer and secondary wires.
12. Install the distributor cap.
13. Reconnect the wire connectors to the side of the distributor. Make certain the connectors are fully seated and latched.
14. Reconnect the negative battery cable.

NOTE: *If the engine was accidentally cranked after the distributor was removed, the following procedure can be used during installation.*

15. Remove the No. 1 spark plug.
16. Place a finger over the spark plug hole and have a helper crank the engine slowly until compression is felt.
17. Align the timing mark on the pulley to **0** on the engine timing indicator.

18. Turn the rotor to point between No. 1 spark plug tower on the distributor cap.

19. Install the distributor assembly in the engine and ensure the rotor is pointing toward the No. 1 spark plug tower.

20. Install the cap and spark plug wires.

21. Check and adjust engine timing.

DISTRIBUTOR CAP

1. Disconnect the ignition switch wire from the distributor cap. Also disconnect the tachometer wire, if so equipped.

2. Release the coil wire connectors from the cap.

3. Remove the distributor cap by turning the four latches (the L4 distributor has 2 latches) counterclockwise.

4. Remove the cap.

5. To install, position the cap into place, matching the notch in the cap with the distributor housing and secure it by turning the latches.

6. Connect the coil connectors.

7. Connect the tachometer wire, if so equipped, and connect the ignition wire to the distributor cap.

ROTOR

1. Disconnect the negative battery cable.

2. Remove the distributor cap.

3. Unscrew the two rotor attaching screws, if equipped and then lift off the rotor.

4. To install, position the cap into place and secure the cap with the 2 rotor attaching screws, if equipped.

5. Install the distributor cap.

6. Connect the negative battery cable.

HEI MODULE

1. Disconnect the negative battery cable.

2. Remove the air cleaner assembly, as required.

3. Remove the distributor cap and rotor.

4. Remove the module retaining screws, then lift the stamped sheet metal shield and module upwards.

5. Disconnect the module leads. Note the col-

or code on the leads, as these cannot be interchanged.

NOTE: *Do not wipe the grease from the module or distributor base, if the same module is to be replaced.*

To install:

6. Spread the silicone grease, included in package, on the metal face of the module and on the distributor base where the module seats.

7. Fit the module leads to the module. Make certain the leads are fully seated and latched. Seat the module and metal shield into the distributor and install the retaining screws.

8. Install the rotor and cap.

9. Install the air cleaner assembly.

10. Reconnect the negative battery cable.

PICKUP COIL

1. Disconnect the negative battery cable.

2. Remove the distributor assembly.

3. Support the distributor assembly in a vice and drive the roll pin from the gear. Remove the shaft assembly.

4. To remove the pickup coil, remove the retainer and shield.

5. Lift the pickup coil assembly straight up to remove it from the distributor.

To install:

6. Assembly the pickup coil, shield and retainer.

7. Install the shaft.

8. Install the gear and roll pin to the shaft. Make certain the matchmarks are aligned.

9. Spin the shaft and verify that the teeth do not touch the pole piece.

10. Reinstall the distributor.

11. Reconnect the negative battery cable.

IGNITION COIL

External Type

1. Disconnect the negative battery cable.

2. Remove the secondary coil lead. Pull on the boot while twisting it.

3. Disconnect the harness connectors from the coil.

4. Remove the coil mounting screws.

5. Remove the ignition coil. If necessary, drill and punch out the rivets holding the coil to the bracket.

To install:

6. Place the ignition coil into position and install the mounting screws.

7. Reconnect the harness connector to the coil. Make certain the connectors are fully seated and latched.

8. Install the secondary lead to the coil tower.

9. Reconnect the negative battery cable.

Integral Type

1. Disconnect the negative battery cable.

2. Remove the cover and wire retainer.

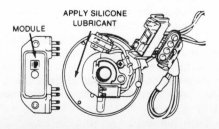

Module replacement; ensure the mating surfaces are coated with silicone lubricant

3. Disconnect the battery feed wire and coil connections from the cap.

4. Remove the coil cover attaching screws and cover.

5. Remove the coil attaching screws and lift the coil and leads from the cap.

To install:

6. Position the ignition coil and leads into the cap. Be certain the resistor brush, seal and coil grounds are properly positioned.

7. Install the mounting screws.

8. Install the coil cover and retaining screws.

9. Reconnect the feed wire and coil connection to the cap.

10. Install the cover and wire retainer.

11. Reconnect the negative battery cable.

Ignition Timing

DESCRIPTION

Ignition timing is the measurement, in degrees of crankshaft rotation, of the point at which the spark plugs fire in each of the cylinders. It is measured in degrees before or after Top Dead Center (TDC) of the compression stroke.

Because it takes a fraction of a second for the spark plug to ignite the mixture in the cylinder, the spark plug must fire a little before the piston reaches TDC. Otherwise, the mixture will not be completely ignited as the piston passes TDC and the full power of the explosion will not be utilized by the engine.

The timing measurement is given in degrees of crankshaft rotation before the piston reaches TDC (BTDC). If the base setting (at idle), for the ignition timing is 5°BTDC, the spark plug must fire 5° before each piston reaches TDC.

As the engine speed increases, the pistons go faster. The spark plugs have to ignite the fuel even sooner if it is to be completely ignited when the piston reaches TDC.

If the ignition is set too far advanced (BTDC), the ignition and expansion of the fuel in the cylinder will occur too soon and tend to force the piston down while it is still traveling up. This causes engine ping. If the ignition spark is set too far retarded, after TDC (ATDC), the piston will have already passed TDC and started on its way down when the fuel is ignited. This will cause the piston to be forced down for only a portion of its travel. This will result in poor engine performance and lack of power.

When timing the engine, the No. 1 plug wire should be used to trigger the timing light. The notch for the No. 1 cylinder is scribed across the pulley.

The basic timing light operates from the car's battery. Two alligator clips connect to the battery terminals, while a third wire connects to the spark plug with an adapter or to the spark plug wire with an inductive pickup. This type of light is more expensive, but the xenon bulb provides a nice bright flash which can even be seen in sunlight. Some timing lights have other functions built into them, such as dwell meters, tachometers, or remote starting switches. These are convenient, in that they reduce the tangle of wires under the hood, but may duplicate the functions of tools you already have.

Because the car has electronic ignition, you should use a timing light with an inductive pickup. This pickup simply clamps around the Number 1 spark plug wire, eliminating the adapter. It is not susceptible to crossfiring or false triggering, which may occur with a conventional light due to the greater voltages produced by HEI.

ADJUSTMENT

NOTE: *When adjusting the timing, refer to the instructions on the emission control label located in the engine compartment. Follow all instructions on the label.*

1. Locate the timing marks on the crankshaft pulley and the front of the engine.

2. Clean off the marks and coat them with white paint or chalk, so that they may be easily identified.

3. Warm the engine to normal operating temperatures and stop the engine. Connect a tachometer to the distributor.

4. Install a timing light with an inductive pick-lead to the No. 1 spark plug wire; front cyl. of 2.5L engine, front right cyl. of 2.8L engine and front left cyl. of 5.0L and 5.7L engine.

5. To set the base timing, the ECM EST must be bypassed. To do this, do the following:

• For all feedback carburetor systems — disconnect the 4-wire connector at the distributor

• For all fuel injected engines (except 5.0L TPI engine) — ground diagnostic terminal (terminals A and B) in the ALDL diagnostic connector

• For 5.0L and 5.7L TPI engine — disconnect the single connector tan/black wire at the right rear valve cover

6. Turn off all accessories, place the transmission in **N** for manual and **PARK** for auto. Set the parking brake.

7. Loosen the distributor bolt so that the distributor may be turned.

8. Start the engine and aim the timing light at the timing marks. With the engine idling, adjust the timing marks.

9. Turn the engine off and tighten the distributor bolt. Turn the engine on and recheck the timing marks.

10. Turn the engine off and disconnect the timing light and tachometer. Reconnect the distributor connectors.

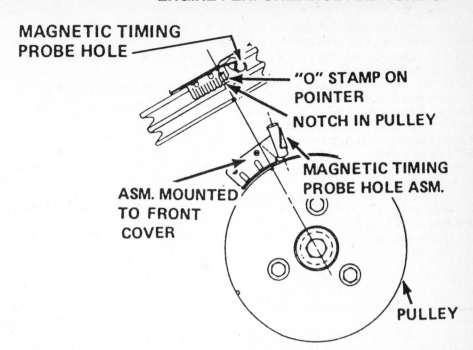

MAGNETIC TIMING
PROBE HOLE

"O" STAMP ON
POINTER

NOTCH IN PULLEY

MAGNETIC TIMING
PROBE HOLE ASM.

ASM. MOUNTED
TO FRONT
COVER

PULLEY

View of the timing marks on the front crankshaft pulley

VALVE LASH

All models utilize a hydraulic valve lifter system to obtain zero lash. No adjustment is necessary. An initial adjustment is required anytime that the lifters are removed or the valve train is disturbed.

ADJUSTMENT
4-Cylinder Engines
The 2.5L engine uses a shoulder type rocker arm bolt which provides a fixed centering of the plunger in the lifter, the bolts should be torqued to 20 ft. lbs. (27 Nm) and no further adjustment is necessary.

V6 and V8 Engines
The valves may be adjusted with the engine idling or shut off. If you choose to adjust the valves with the engine idling, the use of oil stop-

Valve adjustment—V8 engines

per clips, which prevent oil splatter is recommended and the valves may be adjusted in any sequence.

If you adjust the valves with the engine shut off it will be a much cleaner process, but you will need to follow a cylinder and valve adjustment procedure.

To adjust the valves with the engine running proceed as follows:

Establish normal operating temperature by running the engine for several minutes. Shut the engine off and remove the valve cover(s). After valve cover removal, torque the cylinder heads to specification. Plug all open vacuum lines.

Restart the engine. Valve lash is set with the engine warm and idling. Turn the rocker arm nut counterclockwise until the rocker arm begins to clatter. Reverse the direction and turn the rocker arm down slowly until the clatter just stops. This is the zero lash position. Turn the nut down an additional ¼ turn and wait ten seconds until the engine runs smoothly. Continue with additional ¼ turns, waiting ten seconds each time, until the nut has been turned down 1 full turn from the zero lash position. This 1 turn, pre-load adjustment must be performed to allow the lifter to adjust itself and prevents possible interference between the valves and pistons. Noisy lifters should be cleaned or replaced.

To adjust the valves with the engine **OFF** proceed as follows:

1. Crank the engine until the mark on the damper aligns with the TDC or 0° mark on the timing tab and the engine is in No. 1 firing position. This can be determined by placing the fingers on the No. 1 cylinder valves as the marks align. If the valves do not move, it is in No. 1 firing position. If the valves move, it is in No. 4 (V6) or No. 6 (V8) firing position and the crankshaft should be rotated one more revolution to the No. 1 firing position.

2. The adjustment is made in the same manner on both engines.

3. With the engine in No. 1 firing position, the following valves can be adjusted:
- V8 Exhaust — 1,3,4,8
- V8 Intake — 1,2,5,7
- V6 Exhaust — 1,2,3
- V6 Intake — 1,5,6

NOTE: *Distinguishing the exhaust from intake valves is easy, simply look for the intake or exhaust runner directly inline with the valve.*

4. Back the adjusting nut out until lash can be felt at the push rod, then turn the nut until all lash is removed (this can be determined by rotating the push rod while turning the adjusting nut). When all lash has been removed, turn the nut in 1½ additional turns, this will center the lifter plunger.

5. Crank the engine 1 full revolution until the marks are again in alignment. This is No. 4 (V6) or No. 6 (V8) firing position. The following valves can now be adjusted:
- V8 Exhaust — 2,5,6,7
- V8 Intake — 3,4,6,8
- V6 Exhaust — 2,3,4
- V6 Intake — 4,5,6

6. Reinstall the rocker arm covers using new gaskets or sealer.

7. Install the distributor cap and wire assembly.

8. Adjust the carburetor idle speed.

IDLE SPEED AND MIXTURE ADJUSTMENTS

Carbureted Engines

NOTE: *Idle speed and mixture settings are factory set and sealed; adjustment of the idle mixture requires special tools including an exhaust gas analyzer and should not be attempted by the do-it-yourselfer, but only by an authorized GM dealer.*

A cover is in place over the idle air bleed valve, and the access holes to the idle mixture needles are sealed with hardened plugs to prevent the factory settings from being tampered with. These items are NOT to be removed unless required for cleaning, part replacement, improper dwell readings or if the System Performance Check indicates the carburetor is the cause of the trouble.

2.8L Engine

MIXTURE PLUG REMOVAL

1. Remove the carburetor from the engine, following normal service procedures to gain access to the plugs covering the idle mixture needles.

2. Invert carburetor and drain fuel into a suitable container.

CAUTION: *Take precautions to avoid the risk of fire.*

3. Place carburetor on a suitable holding fixture, with the intake manifold side up. Use care to avoid damaging linkage, tubes and parts protruding from air horn.

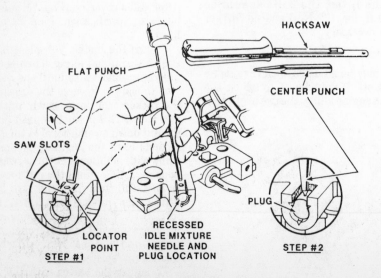

Idle mixture needle plug removal

4. Make 2 parallel cuts in the throttle body, 1 on each side of the locator points beneath the idle mixture needle plug (manifold side), with a hacksaw.

NOTE: *The cuts should reach down to the steel plug, but should not extend more than ⅛ in. (3mm) beyond the locator points. The distance between the saw cuts depends on the size of the punch to be used.*

5. Place a flat punch near the ends of the saw marks in the throttle body. Hold the punch at a 45° angle and drive it into the throttle body until the casting breaks away, exposing the steel plug. The hardened plug will break, rather than remaining intact. It is not necessary to remove the plug in a whole piece, but do remove the loose pieces.

6. Reinstall the carburetor using a new gasket.

PRE-ADJUSTMENT PROCEDURE

1. Remove the idle mixture needle plugs and turn the idle mixture screw in until lightly seated, then back out 4 turns using tool J–29030 or equivalent.

2. Ensure the plug covering the idle air bleed is in place and no dirt has entered.

3. Remove the vent stack screen to gain access to the lean mixture screw. Turn the screw in until lightly bottomed and then back out 2½ turns using tool J–2869–10 or equivalent.

4. Reinstall the carburetor, if previously removed.

5. Do not install the air cleaner.

6. Disconnect the bowl vent line at the carburetor.

7. Disconnect the EGR valve and canister purge hose at the carburetor; plug the carburetor ports.

8. Refer to the Vehicle Emission Control Information Label and observe the hose coming from carburetor port "D" to the temperature sensor and secondary vacuum break TVS; disconnect and plug the hose at the temperature sensor on the air cleaner.

9. Connect the positive lead of a dwell meter to the mixture control solenoid test lead (green connector generally located on right fenderwell) and connect the other lead to ground. Set the dwell meter to the 6-cylinder position.

10. Connect a tachometer to the distributor brown lead. The tachometer should be connected to the distributor side of the tach filter if the vehicle is equipped with a factory tachometer.

11. Block the drive wheels, set the parking brake and place the transmission in **P** for vehicles equipped with an automatic transmission or neutral for manual transmissions.

MIXTURE ADJUSTMENT PROCEDURE

1. Perform the carburetor pre-adjustment procedure.

THESE ADJUSTMENTS SHOULD BE PERFORMED ONLY IF INDICATED BY SYSTEM PERFORMANCE CHECK.

LEAN MIXTURE SCREW:

① WITH VENT SCREEN (OR ENTIRE AIR HORN) OFF, USE TOOL J-28696-10 OR BT-7928 OR EQUIVALENT, TO LIGHTLY BOTTOM LEAN MIXTURE SCREW.

② BACK OUT NUMBER OF TURNS INDICATED IN SPECIFICATIONS.

③ REFER TO VEHICLE MANUFACTURER'S SERVICE MANUAL SECTION 6C FOR "LEAN MIXTURE ADJUSTMENT".

IDLE MIXTURE SCREW:

④ WITH IDLE MIXTURE SCREW PLUG REMOVED, USE TOOL J-29030 OR BT-7610B OR EQUIVALENT TO LIGHTLY BOTTOM SCREW.

⑤ BACK OUT NUMBER OF TURNS INDICATED IN SPECIFICATIONS.

⑥ REFER TO SERVICE MANUAL SECTION 6C FOR "IDLE MIXTURE ADJUSTMENT".

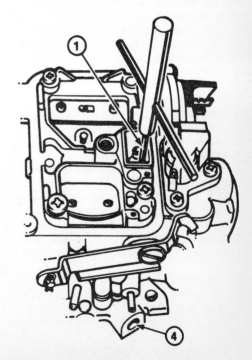

Lean mixture and idle mixture adjustment—2.8L engine

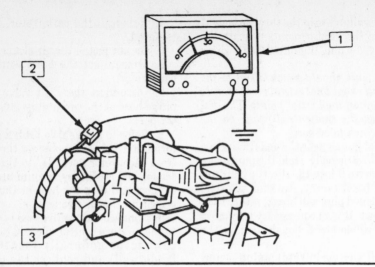

1	DWELL METER (SET ON 6-CYL SCALE)
2	M/C SOLENOID DWELL CONNECTOR
3	CARBURETOR

Dwell meter connection

2. Run the engine on the high step of the fast idle cam until the engine is thoroughly warmed up and in closed-loop operation (the dwell begins to vary).

3. Run the engine at 3,000 rpm and adjust the lean mixture screw slowly in small increments, allowing the dwell to stabilize. The dwell reading should be approximately 35°. If the reading is too low, back the screw out; too high, turn the screw in. If you are unable to achieve the specification, inspect the main metering circuit of the carburetor for leaks, restrictions, etc.

NOTE: *It is normal for the dwell reading to constantly vary ±5° while idling and occasionally as much as 10–15° momentarily, due to temporary mixture changes.*

4. Allow the engine to idle.

5. Adjust the idle mixture screw to obtain an average dwell reading of 25° with the cooling fan **OFF**. If the reading is too low, back the screw out; too high, turn the screw in. Allow the reading to stabilize after each adjustment.

6. If unable to adjust to specification, inspect the idle system for vacuum leaks, restrictions, etc.

7. Disconnect the mixture control solenoid with the cooling fan **OFF** and check for an idle drop of at least 50 rpm. If not as specified, inspect the idle air bleed circuit for restrictions, leaks, etc.

8. Run the engine at 3,000 rpm for a few moments and note the dwell reading. The dwell reading should be varying with an average reading of 35°.

9. If not as specified, reset lean mixture screw and then readjust the idle mixture screw to obtain a dwell reading of 25°. If dwell reading is as specified, reconnect all hoses and lines previously removed and set the idle to specification following the information on the Emission Control Information Label.

IDLE SPEED SOLENOID ADJUSTMENT

Without Air Conditioning

1. Ensure ignition timing is set to specification.

2. Prepare the vehicle for adjustments per emission label on the vehicle.

3. Start the engine and allow the engine to thoroughly warm up.

4. Set the emergency brake and place automatic transmission in **D** or manual transmission in neutral.

5. With the idle speed solenoid energized, open the throttle slightly to allow the solenoid plunger to fully extend.

6. Turn the solenoid screw to adjust the curb idle speed.

7. Disconnect the electrical lead to the solenoid to de-energize and set the basic idle to specification.

8. Reconnect the solenoid lead after adjustment.

With Air Conditioning

1. Ensure ignition timing is set to specification.

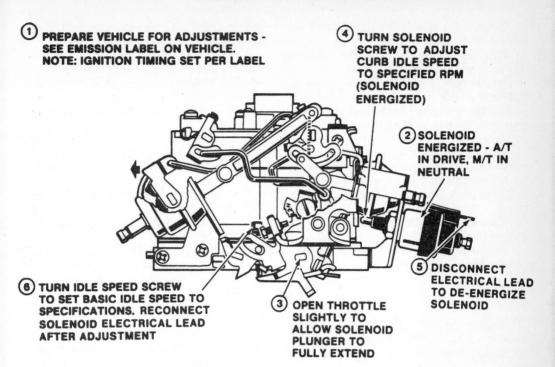

1. PREPARE VEHICLE FOR ADJUSTMENTS - SEE EMISSION LABEL ON VEHICLE. NOTE: IGNITION TIMING SET PER LABEL

4. TURN SOLENOID SCREW TO ADJUST CURB IDLE SPEED TO SPECIFIED RPM (SOLENOID ENERGIZED)

2. SOLENOID ENERGIZED - A/T IN DRIVE, M/T IN NEUTRAL

5. DISCONNECT ELECTRICAL LEAD TO DE-ENERGIZE SOLENOID

6. TURN IDLE SPEED SCREW TO SET BASIC IDLE SPEED TO SPECIFICATIONS. RECONNECT SOLENOID ELECTRICAL LEAD AFTER ADJUSTMENT

3. OPEN THROTTLE SLIGHTLY TO ALLOW SOLENOID PLUNGER TO FULLY EXTEND

Idle speed adjustment—without A/C—2.8L engine

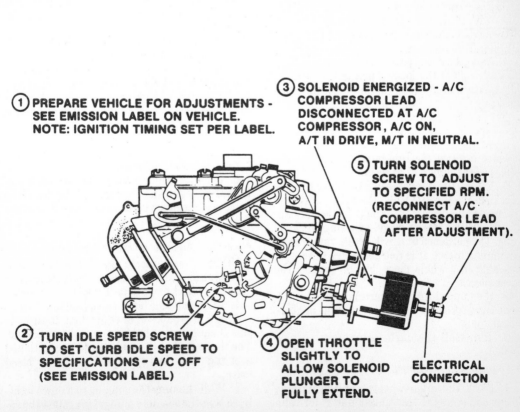

1. PREPARE VEHICLE FOR ADJUSTMENTS - SEE EMISSION LABEL ON VEHICLE. NOTE: IGNITION TIMING SET PER LABEL.

3. SOLENOID ENERGIZED - A/C COMPRESSOR LEAD DISCONNECTED AT A/C COMPRESSOR, A/C ON, A/T IN DRIVE, M/T IN NEUTRAL.

5. TURN SOLENOID SCREW TO ADJUST TO SPECIFIED RPM. (RECONNECT A/C COMPRESSOR LEAD AFTER ADJUSTMENT).

2. TURN IDLE SPEED SCREW TO SET CURB IDLE SPEED TO SPECIFICATIONS - A/C OFF (SEE EMISSION LABEL)

4. OPEN THROTTLE SLIGHTLY TO ALLOW SOLENOID PLUNGER TO FULLY EXTEND.

ELECTRICAL CONNECTION

Idle speed adjustment—with A/C—2.8L engine

2. Prepare the vehicle for adjustments per emission label on the vehicle.

3. Start the engine and allow the engine to thoroughly warm up. Set the idle speed screw to set the curb idle to specification with the air conditioning **OFF** per the emission label.

4. Set the emergency brake and place automatic transmission in **D** or manual transmission in neutral.

5. With the idle speed solenoid energized, the air conditioning compressor lead disconnected and air conditioning **ON**, open the throttle slightly to allow the solenoid plunger to fully extend.

6. Turn the solenoid screw to adjust the curb idle speed to specification.

7. Reconnect the electrical lead to the compressor after adjustment.

5.0L Engine

MIXTURE PLUG REMOVAL

1. Remove the carburetor from the engine, following normal service procedures to gain access to the plugs covering the idle mixture needles.

2. Invert carburetor and drain fuel into a suitable container.

CAUTION: *Take precautions to avoid the risk of fire.*

3. Place carburetor on a suitable holding fixture, with the intake manifold side up. Use care to avoid damaging linkage, tubes and parts protruding from air horn.

4. Make 2 parallel cuts in the throttle body, 1 on each side of the locator points beneath the idle mixture needle plug (manifold side), with a hacksaw.

NOTE: *The cuts should reach down to the steel plug, but should not extend more than ⅛ in. (3mm) beyond the locator points. The distance between the saw cuts depends on the size of the punch to be used.*

5. Place a flat punch near the ends of the saw marks in the throttle body. Hold the punch at a 45° angle and drive it into the throttle body until the casting breaks away, exposing the steel plug. The hardened plug will break, rather than remaining intact. It is not necessary to remove the plug in a whole piece, but do remove the loose pieces.

6. If equipped with a 4 barrel carburetor, repeat the procedure for the remaining mixture needle plug.

7. Reinstall the carburetor using a new gasket.

PRE-ADJUSTMENT PROCEDURE

1. Block the drive wheels, set the parking brake and place the transmission in **P** for vehicles equipped with an automatic transmission or neutral for manual transmissions.

2. Remove the idle mixture needle plugs and turn the idle mixture screw in until lightly seated, then back out approximately 3⅜ turns using tool J–29030 or equivalent.

3. Reinstall the carburetor, if previously removed.

4. Do not install the air cleaner.

5. Disconnect and plug the hoses as directed on the Emission Control Information Label under the hood.

6. Check the ignition timing as shown on the Emission Control Information Label.

7. Connect the positive lead of a dwell meter to the mixture control solenoid test lead (green connector generally located on right fenderwell) and connect the other lead to ground. Set the dwell meter to the 6-cylinder position.

MIXTURE ADJUSTMENT PROCEDURE

1. Start the engine and allow it run until thoroughly warm and dwell begins to vary.

2. Check idle speed and compare to the specifications on the underhood Emission Control Information Label. If necessary adjust the curb idle speed.

3. With the engine idling in **D** for automatic transmissions or neutral for manual transmissions, observe the dwell reading on the 6 cylinder scale.

4. If the reading is varying within the 10–50° range, the adjustment is correct.

5. If the reading is not as specified remove the idle air bleed valve cover. Refer to Fuel System, Chapter 5. With cover removed, look for presence (or absence) of a letter identification on top of idle air bleed valve.

NOTE: *A missing cover indicates that the idle air bleed valve setting has been changed from its original factory setting.*

6. If no identifying letter appears on top of the valve, begin with Procedure A, below. If the valve is identified with a letter, begin Procedure B.

Procedure A (No Letter On Idle Air Bleed Valve)

NOTE: *Presetting the idle air bleed valve to a gauge dimension is necessary only if the valve was serviced prior to on-vehicle adjustment.*

1. Install idle air bleed valve gauging Tool J–33815–2, BT–8253–B, or equivalent, in throttle side D-shaped vent hole in the air horn casting. The upper end of the tool should be positioned over the open cavity next to the idle air bleed valve.

2. While holding the gauging tool down lightly, so that the solenoid plunger is against the so-

**IDLE AIR BLEED VALVE — CHECK FOR
LETTER IDENTIFICATION THIS LOCATION**

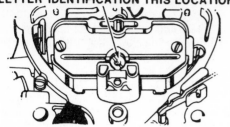

Idle air bleed valve identification letter location—5.0L engine

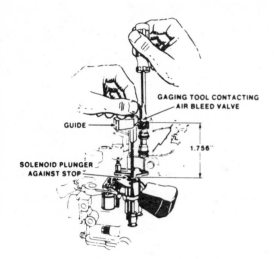

GAGING TOOL CONTACTING
AIR BLEED VALVE

GUIDE

1.756"

SOLENOID PLUNGER
AGAINST STOP

Adjusting idle air bleed—5.0L engine

lenoid stop, adjust the idle air bleed valve so that the gauging tool will pivot over and just contact the top of the valve. The valve is now preset for on-vehicle adjustment. Remove the gauging tool and proceed as follows:

a. Disconnect the vacuum hose from the canister purge valve and plug it.

b. Start engine and allow it to reach normal operating temperature.

c. While idling in **D** for automatic transmission or neutral for manual transmission, use a screwdriver to slowly turn the valve counterclockwise or clockwise, until the dwell reading varies within the 25–35° range, attempting to be as close to 30° as possible. NOTE: *Perform this step carefully. The air bleed valve is very sensitive and should be turned in ⅛ turn increments only.*

d. If the reading is not as specified, the idle mixture needles will have to be adjusted.

e. If the reading is within specifications, reconnect all hoses previously removed and install air cleaner.

3. If unable to set dwell to 25–35°, and the dwell is below 25°, turn both mixture needles counterclockwise an additional turn. If dwell is above 35°, turn both mixture needles clockwise an additional turn. Readjust idle air bleed valve to obtain dwell limits.

4. After adjustments are complete, seal the idle mixture needle openings in the throttle body, using silicone sealant, RTV rubber, or equivalent. The sealer is required to discourage unnecessary adjustment of the setting, and to prevent fuel vapor loss in that area.

5. On vehicles without a carburetor-mounted Idle Speed Control or Idle Load Compensator, adjust curb idle speed if necessary.

6. Check, and only if necessary adjust, fast idle speed as described on Vehicle Emission Control Information label.

Procedure B (Letter Appears On Idle Air Bleed Valve)

1. Install idle air bleed valve gauging Tool J–33815–2, BT–8253–B, or equivalent, in throttle side D-shaped vent hole in the air horn casting. The upper end of the tool should be positioned over the open cavity next to the idle air bleed valve.

2. While holding the gauging tool down lightly, so that the solenoid plunger is against the solenoid stop, adjust the idle air bleed valve so that the gauging tool will pivot over and just contact the top of the valve.

3. The valve is now set properly. No further adjustment of the valve is necessary. Remove gauging tool.

4. Disconnect vacuum hose to canister purge valve and plug it.

5. Start engine and allow it to reach normal operating temperature.

6. While idling in **D** for automatic transmissions or neutral for manual transmission, adjust both mixture needles equally, ⅛ turn increments, until dwell reading varies within the 25–35° range, attempting to be as close to 30° as possible.

7. If reading is too low, turn mixture needles counterclockwise. If reading is too high, turn mixture needles clockwise. Allow time for dwell reading to stabilize after each adjustment.

NOTE: *After adjustments are complete, seal the idle mixture needle openings in the throttle body, using silicone sealant, RTV rubber, or equivalent. The sealer is required to discourage unnecessary readjustment of the setting, and to prevent fuel vapor loss in that area.*

8. On vehicles without a carburetor-mounted Idle Speed Control or Idle Load Compensator, adjust curb idle speed if necessary.

9. Check, and if necessary, adjust fast idle

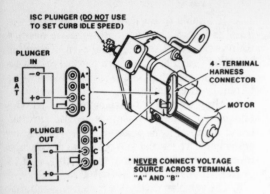

Idle Speed Control Assembly—5.0L engine

speed, as described on the Vehicle Emission Control Information label.

IDLE SPEED CONTROL (ISC) MOTOR ADJUSTMENT

The Idle Speed Control (ISC) is controlled by the Electronic Control Module (ECM), which has the desired idle speed programmed in its memory. The ECM compares the actual idle speed to the desired idle speed and the plunger is moved in or out. This automatically adjusts the throttle to hold an idle rpm independent of the engine loads.

An integral part of the ISC is the throttle contact switch. The position of the switch determines whether or not the ISC should control idle speed. When the throttle lever is resting against the ISC plunger, the switch contacts are closed, at which time the ECM moves the ISC to the programmed idle speed. When the throttle lever is not contacting the ISC plunger, the switch contacts are open; the ECM stops sending idle speed commands and the drive controls engine speed.

NOTE: *Before starting engine, place transmission selector lever in Park or Neutral position, set the parking brake and block the drive wheels.*

When a new ISC assembly is installed, a base (minimum authority) and high (maximum authority) rpm speed check must be performed and adjustments made as required. These adjustments limit the low and high rpm speeds to the ECM. When making a low and high speed adjustment, the low speed adjustment is always made first. DO NOT use the ISC plunger to adjust curb idle speed as the idle speed is controlled by the ECM.

NOTE: *Do not disconnect or connect the ISC connector with the ignition in the ON position, or damage to the ECM may occur.*

1. Connect a tachometer to the engine (distributor side of tach filter, if used).

2. Connect a dwell meter to the mixture control (M/C) solenoid dwell lead. Remember to set the dwell meter on the 6-cylinder scale, regardless of the engine being tested.

3. Turn the A/C off.

4. Start and run the engine until it is stabilized by entering closed loop (dwell meter needle starts to vary).

5. Turn the ignition off.

6. Unplug the connector from ISC motor.

7. Fully retract the ISC plunger by applying 12 volts DC (battery voltage) to terminal **C** of the ISC motor and ground terminal **D** of the ISC motor or use an approved ISC motor tool. It may be necessary to install jumper leads from the ISC motor in order to make proper connections.

NOTE: *Do not apply battery voltage to the motor longer than necessary to retract the ISC plunger. Prolonged contact will damage the motor. Also, never connect a voltage source across terminals **A** and **B** or damage to the internal throttle contact switch will result.*

8. Start the engine and wait until the dwell meter needle starts to vary, indicating closed loop operation.

9. With the parking brake applied and the drive wheels blocked, place the transmission in **D**.

10. With the ISC plunger fully retracted, adjust carburetor base (slow) idle stop screw to the minimum idle specified rpm (see specifications). The ISC plunger should not be left in the fully retracted position.

11. Place the transmission in the **P** or **N** position and fully extend the ISC plunger by applying 12 volts DC to terminal **D** of the ISC motor connection and ground lead to terminal **C** of the ISC motor connection.

WARNING: *Never connect voltage source across terminals A and B as damage to the internal throttle contact switch will result.*

12. Automatic Transmission — with transmission in **P** position, using Tool J–29607 or BT–8022 or equivalent, preset ISC plunger to obtain 1500 rpm.

13. With parking brake set and drive wheels blocked, place transmission in **D** position. Using tool J–29607 or BT–8022 or equivalent, turn ISC plunger to obtain ISC adjustment rpm (maximum authority).

14. Recheck ISC Maximum Authority Adjustment rpm with voltage applied to motor. Motor will ratchet at full extension with power applied.

15. Fully retract ISC plunger. Place transmission in **P** or **N** position and turn ignition in OFF position. Disconnect 12 volt power source, ground lead, tachometer and dwell meter. With ignition in OFF position, reconnect four terminal harness connector to ISC motor. To prevent

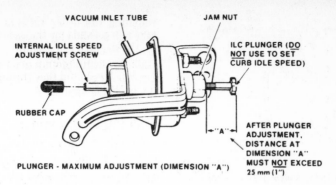

VACUUM INLET TUBE **JAM NUT**

INTERNAL IDLE SPEED ADJUSTMENT SCREW

ILC PLUNGER (DO NOT USE TO SET CURB IDLE SPEED)

RUBBER CAP

AFTER PLUNGER ADJUSTMENT, DISTANCE AT DIMENSION "A" MUST NOT EXCEED 25 mm (1")

PLUNGER - MAXIMUM ADJUSTMENT (DIMENSION "A")

Idle Load Compensator (ILC) adjustment—2.8L engine

internal damage to ISC, apply finger pressure to ISC plunger while retracting.

16. Remove block from drive wheels.

IDLE LOAD COMPENSATOR (ILC) ADJUSTMENT

1. Prepare the vehicle for adjustments, see emission label.

2. Connect a tachometer (distributor side of TACH filter, if used).

3. Remove the air cleaner and plug vacuum hose to thermal vacuum valve (TVV).

4. Disconnect and plug the vacuum hose to EGR.

5. Disconnect and plug the vacuum hose to canister purge port.

6. Disconnect and plug the vacuum hose to ILC.

7. Back out the idle stop screw on the carburetor 3 turns.

8. Turn the air conditioning **OFF**.

CAUTION: *Before starting engine, place transmission in P position, set parking brake and block drive wheels.*

9. With the engine running (engine warm, choke off), transmission in **D** position and ILC plunger fully extended (no vacuum applied), using tool J–29607, BT–8022, or equivalent, adjust plunger to obtain 725 rpm. Locknut on plunger must be held with wrench to prevent damage to guide tabs.

10. Remove plug from vacuum hose, reconnect hose to ILC and observe idle speed. Idle speed should be 500 rpm in **D** position.

11. If rpm in Step 10 is correct, proceed to Step 13. No further adjustment of the ILC is necessary.

12. If rpm in Step 10 is not correct:

a. Stop engine and remove the ILC. Plug vacuum hose to ILC.

b. With the ILC removed, remove the rubber cap from the center outlet tube and remove the metal plug (if used) from this same tube.

c. Install ILC on carburetor and re-attach throttle return spring and any other related

parts removed during disassembly. Remove plug from vacuum hose and reconnect hose to ILC.

d. Using a spare rubber cap with hole punched to accept a $3/32$ in. hex key wrench, install cap on center outlet tube (to seal against vacuum loss) and insert wrench through cap to engage adjusting screw inside tube. Start engine and turn adjusting screw with wrench to obtain 550 rpm in **D** position. Turning the adjusting screw will change the idle speed approximately 75–100 rpm for each complete turn. Turning the screw counterclockwise will increase the engine speed.

e. Remove wrench and cap (with hole) from center outlet tube and install new rubber cap.

f. Engine running, transmission in **D** position, observe idle speed. If a final adjustment is required, it will be necessary to repeat Steps 12a through 12e.

13. After adjustment of the ILC plunger, measure distance from the lock nut to tip of the plunger, dimension must not exceed 1 in. (25mm).

14. Disconnect and plug vacuum hose to ILC. Apply vacuum source such as hand vacuum pump J–23768, BT–7517 or equivalent to ILC vacuum inlet tube to fully retract the plunger.

15. Adjust the idle stop on the carburetor float bowl to obtain 500 rpm in **D** position.

16. Place transmission in **P** position and stop engine.

17. Remove plug from vacuum hose and install hose on ILC vacuum inlet tube.

18. Remove plugs and reconnect all vacuum hoses.

19. Install air cleaner and gasket.

20. Remove block from drive wheels.

Differential Vacuum Delay Valve (DVDV) Adjustment

The DVDV is located in the vacuum line between the Idle Load Compensator (ILC) and

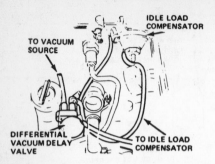

Differential Vacuum Delay Valve (DVDV) hose routing—5.0L engine

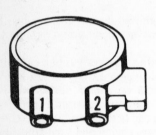

Differential Vacuum Delay Valve (DVDV) port identification-5.0L engine

the vacuum source. It is used on all 5.0L engines (engine code Y).

The DVDV acts as cushioning device by slightly delaying the operation of the ILC until a constant vacuum change has occurred. Without the DVDV the ILC would react too quickly to changes in engine vacuum, causing a stalling or run-on condition.

To check the operation of the DVDV, install a vacuum gauge with a tee between the hose from the DVDV to the ILC. Install a vacuum pump to port 1 of the DVDV and apply 17.8 in. Hg while watching the other vacuum gauge, it should take 6–9 seconds for the vacuum to rise to 16.9 in. Hg Remove the vacuum gauge with tee, install the vacuum pump to port 2 and leave port 1 open. Air should flow through the valve after 0.5 in. Hg is applied.

Fuel Injected Engines

NOTE: *The fuel/air mixture is controlled by the ECM and is non-adjustable.*

MINIMUM IDLE SPEED ADJUSTMENT

NOTE: *This adjustment should be performed only when throttle body parts have been replaced. Engine must be at normal operating temperature before making an adjustment.*

Throttle Body Injection

2.5L ENGINE

The throttle stop screw that is used to adjust the idle speed of the vehicle, is adjusted to specifications at the factory. The throttle stop screw is then covered with a steel plug to prevent the unnecessary readjustment in the field. However, if it is necessary to gain access to the throttle stop screw, the procedure given below eliminates removing the TBI unit from the engine.

1. Using a small punch or equivalent, mark over the center line of the throttle stop screw. Drill a $5/32$ in. (4mm) diameter hole through the casting to the hardened steel plug.
2. Using a $1/16$ in. (1.6mm) diameter punch or equivalent, punch out the steel plug.
3. Proceed with the idle speed adjustment as follows:

    a. With the vehicle in the **P** position, the parking brake applied and the drive wheels

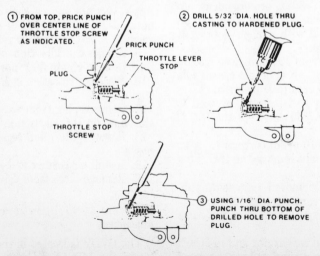

Throttle stop screw plug removal procedure—2.5L engine

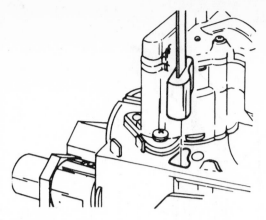

Install tool J-33047 in idle air passage—2.5L engine

blocked, remove the air cleaner and plug the thermactor vacuum port.

b. Remove the transmission T.V. cable from the throttle control bracket in order to gain access to the minimum air adjustment screw (automatic transmission only).

5. Connect a tachometer to the engine and disconnect the idle air control motor connector.

6. Start the engine. Let the engine reach normal operating temperature and the rpm to stabilize.

7. Install the special tool No. J-33047 or equivalent to the idle air passage of the throttle body. Ensure the tool is firmly seated in the passage and no air leaks exist.

8. Using a No. 20 Torx® head bit or equivalent, turn the throttle stop screw until the idle is set at 500 ± 25 rpm if equipped with automatic transmission or 775 ± 25 rpm with manual transmission.

9. Reinstall the transmission T.V. cable into the throttle control bracket (automatic transmission only).

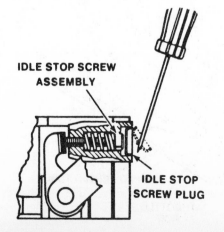

IDLE STOP SCREW ASSEMBLY

IDLE STOP SCREW PLUG

Throttle stop screw plug removal procedure—except 2.5L engine

10. Shut down the engine and remove the special tool or equivalent from the throttle body.

11. Reconnect the idle air control motor connector and seal the drilled hole through the throttle body housing with silicone sealant or equivalent.

12. Check the throttle position sensor voltage. Reinstall the air cleaner and thermac vacuum lines.

5.0L ENGINE

Without Cross-Fire Injection

1. Using a suitable tool, pierce the idle stop screw plug and remove it. Plug any necessary vacuum ports and connect a tachometer to the engine.

2. With the IAC valve connected, ground the diagnostic terminal (ALDL connector).

3. Turn ignition switch to the **ON** position, but do not start the engine. Wait for at least 45 seconds, allowing the IAC valve pintle to fully extend and seat.

4. With the ignition switch still **ON** and test terminal grounded, disconnect Idle Air Control (IAC) electrical connector.

5. Remove the ground from diagnostic lead and start the engine.

6. Adjust the idle speed screw to obtain 400–450 rpm with the transmission in **N**.

7. Turn the ignition OFF and reconnect connector at IAC motor.

8. Adjust the Throttle Position Sensor (TPS) to specifications.

9. Recheck the setting, start the engine and check for proper idle operation.

Cross-Fire Injection (CFI)

NOTE: *The throttle position of each throttle body must be balanced so the throttle plates are synchronized and open simultaneously. The adjustment should be performed only if there are signs of tampering or replacement of the throttle body assemblies, minimum air adjustment screw or idle balance screw.*

1. Remove the air cleaner and the gasket.

2. Disconnect and plug the thermactor vacuum port at the rear TBI unit.

3. If necessary, remove the plug covering the minimum air adjusting screw.

4. Block the wheels, set the parking brake, connect a tachometer to the engine.

5. Disconnect the IAC electrical connectors. Using tool J-33047, plug the idle air passages of each throttle body. Make sure that the tools are seated and no air leaks exist.

6. Start the engine and allow the engine speed to stabilize.

7. Place the automatic transmission in **D**.

NOTE: *When the plugs are installed, the rpm should drop below the curb idle speed. If the speed does not drop, check for an air leak.*

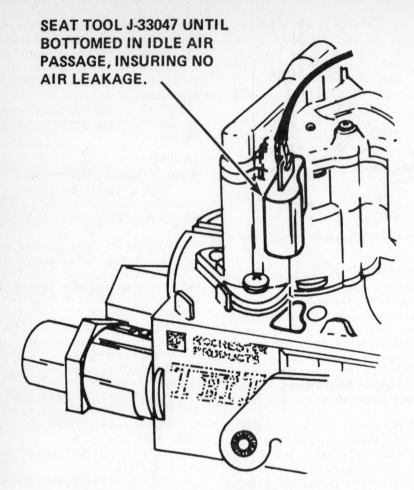

SEAT TOOL J-33047 UNTIL
BOTTOMED IN IDLE AIR
PASSAGE, INSURING NO
AIR LEAKAGE.

Install tool J-33047 in idle air passage—5.0L (VIN 7) engine

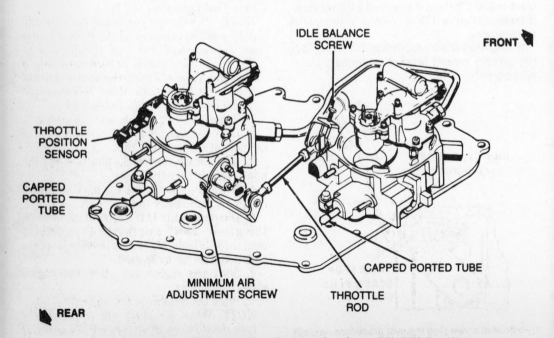

IDLE BALANCE
SCREW

FRONT

THROTTLE
POSITION
SENSOR

CAPPED
PORTED
TUBE

MINIMUM AIR
ADJUSTMENT SCREW

THROTTLE
ROD

CAPPED PORTED TUBE

REAR

Cross-Fire Injection (CFI) assembly adjustment locations—5.0L (VIN 7) engine

8. At the rear TBI unit, remove the cap from the ported tube and connect a water manometer J–23951 or equivalent.

9. Adjust the minimum air adjustment screw to obtain 6 in. (152mm) of water on the manometer. Remove the manometer and install the cap on the ported tube.

10. At the front TBI unit, remove the cap from the ported tube and connect the water manometer J–23951. The reading should be 6 in. (152mm) of water on the manometer.

11. If the manometer reading is not correct, locate the idle balance screw on the throttle linkage. If the screw is welded, break the weld and install a new screw with thread sealing compound. Adjust the screw to obtain 6 in. (152mm) of water on the manometer.

12. Remove the manometer and install the cap on the ported tube.

13. At the rear TBI unit, adjust the minimum air adjustment screw to obtain 475 rpm.

14. Stop the engine and remove the idle air passage plugs.

15. Place the transmission in **N** and start the engine.

NOTE: *The engine will run at a high rpm but will decrease when the IAC motors close the air passages. When the rpm drops, stop the engine.*

16. Check the Throttle Position Sensor (TPS) voltage and ad
just, if necessary. Install the air cleaner and connect vacuum lines.

NOTE: *To reset the IAC motors, drive the vehicle at 30 mph or if equipped with cruise control, disconnect the speedometer cable at the transducer, turn the key ON and rotate the cable to 30 mph.*

Tuned Port Injection (TPI)

NOTE: *The idle speed should only be adjusted if it is absolutely necessary.*

1. Using an awl or equivalent, pierce the idle stop plug and remove it.

2. Leave the Idle Air Control motor connected and ground the ALDL diagnostic terminal. Turn the ignition to the **ON** position, but do not start the engine.

3. Wait 30 seconds, and with the ignition switch still in the **ON** position, disconnect the idle air control connector.

4. Disconnect the distributor set-timing connector.

5. Start the engine, allowing it to go into Closed-Loop operation.

6. Remove the ground from the diagnostic terminal.

7. Adjust the idle stop screw to 400 rpm on the 5.0L engine or 450 rpm on the 5.7L engine.

Adjust the rpm with the transmission in the **N** position.

8. Turn the ignition **OFF** and reconnect the Idle Air Control motor connector.

9. Adjust the throttle position sensor, as necessary. Start the engine and check the engine for proper idle operation.

Multi-Port Injection

2.8L ENGINE

1. Using an awl or equivalent, pierce the idle stop plug and remove it.

2. Leave the Idle Air Control motor connected and ground the ALDL diagnostic terminal. Turn the ignition to the **ON** position, but do not start the engine.

3. Wait 30 seconds, and with the ignition switch still in the **ON** position, disconnect the idle air control connector.

4. Disconnect the distributor set-timing connector.

5. Start the engine, allowing it to go into Closed-Loop operation.

6. Remove the ground from the diagnostic terminal.

7. Adjust the idle stop screw to 550 rpm in **D** if equipped with automatic transmission or 650 rpm in neutral if equipped with a manual transmission.

8. Turn the ignition **OFF** and reconnect the Idle Air Control motor connector.

9. Adjust the throttle position sensor, as necessary. Start the engine and check the engine for proper idle operation.

3.1L ENGINE

1. Disconnect the negative battery cable. Using an awl or equivalent, pierce the idle stop plug and remove it.

2. Ensure the throttle or cruise control cables are not holding the throttle lever from returning fully. Back the throttle stop screw out until an air gap is visible between the screw and throttle lever.

3. Turn the screw in until it just contacts the throttle lever; then turn the screw in an additional 1½ turns.

4. Connect the negative battery cable and a suitable scanner to the ALDL connector to monitor the IAC valve counts.

5. Place the transmission in **P** if equipped with automatic transmission or neutral if equipped with a manual transmission.

6. Start the engine and allow it to reach normal operating temperature and enter Closed Loop operation.

7. Monitor the IAC valve counts with all accessories **OFF**, the IAC reading should be 10–20 counts. If not as specified, repeat the procedure.

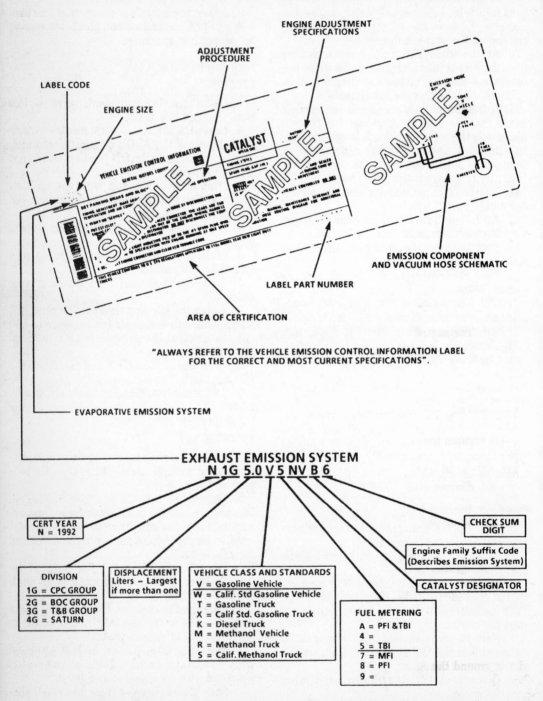

LABEL CODE

ENGINE SIZE

ADJUSTMENT PROCEDURE

ENGINE ADJUSTMENT SPECIFICATIONS

EMISSION COMPONENT AND VACUUM HOSE SCHEMATIC

LABEL PART NUMBER

AREA OF CERTIFICATION

"ALWAYS REFER TO THE VEHICLE EMISSION CONTROL INFORMATION LABEL FOR THE CORRECT AND MOST CURRENT SPECIFICATIONS".

EVAPORATIVE EMISSION SYSTEM

EXHAUST EMISSION SYSTEM
N 1G 5.0 V 5 NV B 6

CERT YEAR
N = 1992

CHECK SUM DIGIT

Engine Family Suffix Code
(Describes Emission System)

CATALYST DESIGNATOR

DIVISION

1G = CPC GROUP
2G = BOC GROUP
3G = T&B GROUP
4G = SATURN

DISPLACEMENT
Liters – Largest
if more than one

VEHICLE CLASS AND STANDARDS

V = Gasoline Vehicle
W = Calif. Std Gasoline Vehicle
T = Gasoline Truck
X = Calif Std. Gasoline Truck
K = Diesel Truck
M = Methanol Vehicle
R = Methanol Truck
S = Calif. Methanol Truck

FUEL METERING

A = PFI &TBI
4 =
5 = TBI
7 = MFI
8 = PFI
9 =

Sample of vehicle emission label located under the hood on the radiator support

Engine and Engine Overhaul

3

ENGINE ELECTRICAL

The engine electrical system can be broken down into three separate and distinct systems:
1. The starting system.
2. The charging system.
3. The ignition system.

Battery and Starting System

The battery is the first link in the chain of mechanisms which work together to provide cranking of the automobile engine. In most modern cars, the battery is a lead-acid electrochemical device consisting of six two-volt (2 V) subsections connected in series so the unit is capable of producing approximately 12 V of electrical pressure. Each subsection, or cell, consists of a series of positive and negative plates held a short distance apart in a solution of sulfuric acid and water. The two types of plates are of dissimilar metals. This causes a chemical reaction to be set up, and it is this reaction which produces current flow from the battery when its positive and negative terminals are connected to an electrical appliance such as a lamp or motor.

The continued transfer of electrons would eventually convert the sulfuric acid in the electrolyte to water and make the two plates identical in chemical composition. As electrical energy is removed from the battery, its voltage output tends to drop. Thus, measuring battery voltage and battery electrolyte composition are two ways of checking the ability of the unit to supply power. During the starting of the engine, electrical energy is removed from the battery. However, if the charging circuit is in good condition and the operating conditions are normal, the power removed from the battery will be replaced by the generator (or alternator) which will force electrons back through the battery, reversing the normal flow, and restoring the battery to its original chemical state.

The battery and starting motor are linked by very heavy electrical cables designed to minimize resistance to the flow of current. Generally, the major power supply cable that leaves the battery goes directly to the starter, while other electrical system needs are supplied by a smaller cable. During the starter operation, power flows from the battery to the starter and is grounded through the car's frame and the battery's negative ground strap.

The starting motor is a specially designed, direct current electric motor capable of producing a very great amount of power for its size. One thing that allows the motor to produce a great deal of power is its tremendous rotating speed. It drives the engine through a tiny pinion gear (attached to the starter's armature), which drives the very large flywheel ring gear at a greatly reduced speed. Another factor allowing it to produce so much power is that only intermittent operation is required of it. Thus, little allowance for air circulation is required, and the windings can be built into a very small space.

The starter solenoid is a magnetic device which employs the small current supplied by the starting switch circuit of the ignition switch. This magnetic action moves a plunger which mechanically engages the starter and electrically closes the heavy switch which connects it to the battery. The starting switch circuit consists of the starting switch contained within the ignition switch, a transmission neutral safety switch or clutch pedal switch, and the wiring necessary to connect these with the starter solenoid or relay.

A pinion, which is a small gear, is mounted to a one-way drive clutch. This clutch is splinted to the starter armature shaft. When the ignition switch is moved to the **START** position, the solenoid plunger slides the pinion toward the flywheel ring gear via a collar and spring. If the teeth on the pinion and flywheel match properly, the pinion will engage the flywheel immediately. If the gear teeth butt one another, the spring will be compressed and will force the gears to mesh as soon as the starter turns far enough to allow them to do so. As the solenoid plunger reaches the end of its travel, it closes the contacts that connect the battery and starter and then the engine is cranked.

As soon as the engine starts, the flywheel ring gear begins turning fast enough to drive the pinion at an extremely high rate of speed. At this point, the one-way clutch begins allowing the pinion to spin faster than the starter shaft so that the starter will not operate at excessive speed. When the ignition switch is released from the starter position, the solenoid is de-energized, and a spring contained within the solenoid assembly pulls the gear out of mesh and interrupts the current flow to the starter.

Some starters employ a separate relay, mounted away from the starter, to switch the motor and solenoid current on and off. The relay thus replaces the solenoid electrical switch, but does not eliminate the need for a solenoid mounted on the starter used to mechanically engage the starter drive gears. The relay is used to reduce the amount of current the starting switch must carry.

The Charging System

The automobile charging system provides electrical power for operation of the vehicle's ignition and starting systems and all the electrical accessories. The battery serves as an electrical surge or storage tank, storing (in chemical form) the energy originally produced by the engine driven generator. The system also provides a means of regulating alternator output to protect the battery from being overcharged and to avoid excessive voltage to the accessories.

The storage battery is a chemical device incorporating parallel lead plates in a tank containing a sulfuric acid-water solution. Adjacent plates are slightly dissimilar, and the chemical reaction of the two dissimilar plates produces electrical energy when the battery is connected to a load such as the starter motor. The chemical reaction is reversible, so that when the generator is producing a voltage (electrical pressure) greater than that produced by the battery, electricity is forced into the battery, and the battery is returned to its fully charged state.

Alternators are used on the modern automobiles for they are lighter, more efficient, can rotate at higher speeds and have fewer brush problems. In an alternator, the field rotates while all the current produced passes only through the stators windings. The brushes bear against continuous slip rings rather than a commutator. This causes the current produced to periodically reverse the direction of its flow. Diodes (electrical one-way switches) block the flow of current from traveling in the wrong direction. A series of diodes is wired together to permit the alternating flow of the stator to be converted to a pulsating, but unidirectional flow at the alternator output. The alternator's field is wired in series with the voltage regulator.

NOTE: *Please refer to Chapter 2 for all ignition system testing procedures.*

Ignition Coil
REMOVAL AND INSTALLATION
Coil In Cap

1. Disconnect wires from cap.
2. Remove distributor cap from distributor.
3. On the distributor cap, remove coil cover attaching screws and remove cover.
4. Remove ignition coil attaching screws and lift coil with leads from the cap.
5. To install, position the coil into position and secure with attaching screws.
6. Install coil cover and attaching screws.
7. Install distributor cap.
8. Connect the wires to the cap.

Externally Mounted Coil

1. Disconnect wires from coil.
2. Remove ignition coil mounting bolts and remove coil.
3. To install, position coil into place and secure with the mounting bolts.
4. Connect the wires to the coil.

Ignition Module
REMOVAL AND INSTALLATION

1. Disconnect wires from cap.
2. Remove distributor cap from distributor.
3. Remove the two module attaching screws and capacitor attaching screw. Lift module, capacitor and harness assembly from base.
4. Disconnect wiring harness and capacitor assembly.
5. To install, apply silicone lubricant on housing under module.
6. Connect wiring harness and capacitor assembly.
7. Install module and attaching screws.
8. Install distributor cap and wires.

HEI Distributor
REMOVAL AND INSTALLATION

NOTE: *The distributor will have to be removed from the engine and disassembled if the pickup coil or distributor shaft need to be replaced.*

1. Disconnect the negative battery cable.
2. Remove the air cleaner assembly.
3. Disconnect the electrical connectors from the side of the distributor.
4. Remove the distributor cover and wire retainer, if equipped. Turn the retaining screws counterclockwise and remove the cap.
5. Mark the relationship of the rotor to the distributor housing and the housing relationship to the engine.
6. Remove the distributor retaining bolt and hold-down clamp.
7. Pull the distributor up until the rotor just stops turning counterclockwise and again note the position of the rotor.
8. Remove the distributor from the engine.

To install:
9. Insert the distributor into the engine, with the rotor aligned to the last mark made, then slowly install the distributor the rest of the way until all marks previously made are aligned.
10. Install the distributor hold-down clamp and retaining bolt.
11. If removed, install the wiring harness retainer and secondary wires.
12. Install the distributor cap.
13. Reconnect the wire connectors to the side of the distributor. Make certain the connectors are fully seated and latched.
14. Reconnect the negative battery cable.

NOTE: *If the engine was accidentally cranked after the distributor was removed, the following procedure can be used during installation.*

15. Remove the No. 1 spark plug.
16. Place a finger over the spark plug hole and have a helper crank the engine slowly until compression is felt.
17. Align the timing mark on the pulley to 0 on the engine timing indicator.
18. Turn the rotor to point between No. 1 spark plug tower on the distributor cap.
19. Install the distributor assembly in the engine and ensure the rotor is pointing toward the No. 1 spark plug tower.
20. Install the cap and spark plug wires.
21. Check and adjust engine timing.

Alternator

DESCRIPTION

An alternator differs from a DC shunt generator in that the armature is stationary, and is called the stator, while the field rotates and is called the rotor. The higher current values in the alternator's stator are conducted to the external circuit through fixed leads and connections, rather than through a rotating commutator and brushes as in a DC generator. This eliminates a major point of maintenance.

The rotor assembly is supported in the drive end frame by a ball bearing and at the other end by a roller bearing. These bearings are lubricated during assembly and require no maintenance. There are six diodes in the end frame assembly. These diodes are electrical check valves that also change the alternating current developed within the stator windings to a direct (DC) current at the output (BAT) terminal. Three of these diodes are negative and are mounted flush with the end frame while the other three are positive and are mounted into a strip called a heat sink. The positive diodes are easily identified as the ones within small cavities or depressions.

The alternator charging system is a negative (–) ground system which consists of an alternator, a regulator, a charge indicator, a storage battery and wiring connecting the components, and fuse link wire.

The alternator is belt-driven from the engine. Energy is supplied from the alternator/regulator system to the rotating field through two brushes to two slip-rings. The slip-rings are mounted on the rotor shaft and are connected to the field coil. This energy supplied to the rotating field from the battery is called excitation current and is used to initially energize the field to begin the generation of electricity. Once the alternator starts to generate electricity, the excitation current comes from its own output rather than the battery.

The alternator produces power in the form of alternating current. The alternating current is rectified by 6 diodes into direct current. The direct current is used to charge the battery and power the rest of the electrical system.

When the ignition key is turned on, current flows from the battery, through the charging system indicator light on the instrument panel, to the voltage regulator, and to the alternator. Since the alternator is not producing any current, the alternator warning light comes on. When the engine is started, the alternator begins to produce current and turns the alternator light off. As the alternator turns and produces current, the current is divided in two ways: part to the battery to charge the battery and power the electrical components of the vehicle, and part is returned to the alternator to enable it to increase its output. In this situation, the alternator is receiving current from the battery and from itself. A voltage regulator is wired into the current supply to the alternator to prevent it from receiving too much current which would cause it to put out too much current. Conversely, if the voltage regulator does not allow the alternator to receive enough current, the battery will not be fully charged and will eventually go dead.

The battery is connected to the alternator at all times, whether the ignition key is turned on or not. If the battery were shorted to ground, the alternator would also be shorted. This would damage the alternator. To prevent this, a fuse link is installed in the wiring between the battery and the alternator. If the battery is shorted, the fuse link is melted, protecting the alternator.

An alternator is better that a conventional, DC shunt generator because it is lighter and more compact, because it is designed to supply the battery and accessory circuits through a wide range of engine speeds, and because it eliminates the necessary maintenance of replacing brushes and servicing commutators.

PRECAUTIONS

To prevent serious damage to the alternator and the rest of the charging system, the following precautions must be observed:

• Never reverse the battery connections.

• Booster batteries for starting must be connected properly: positive-to-positive and negative-to-ground.

• Disconnect the battery cables before using a fast charger; the charger has a tendency to force current through the diodes in the opposite direction for which they were designed. This burns out the diodes.

• Never use a fast charger as a booster for starting the vehicle.

• Never disconnect the voltage regulator while the engine is running.

• Avoid long soldering times when replacing diodes or transistors. Prolonged heat is damaging to AC generators.

• Do not use test lamps of more than 12 volts (V) for checking diode continuity.

• Do not short across or ground any of the terminals on the AC generator.

• The polarity of the battery, generator, and regulator must be matched and considered before making any electrical connections within the system.

• Never operate the alternator on an open circuit. make sure that all connections within the circuit are clean and tight.

• Disconnect the battery terminals when performing any service on the electrical system. This will eliminate the possibility of accidental reversal of polarity.

• Disconnect the battery ground cable if arc welding is to be done on any part of the car.

CHARGING SYSTEM TROUBLESHOOTING

There are many possible ways in which the charging system can malfunction. Often the source of a problem is difficult to diagnose, requiring special equipment and a good deal of experience. However, when the charging system fails completely and causes the dash board warning light to come on or the battery to become dead the following items may be checked:

1. The battery is known to be good and fully charged.

2. The alternator belt is in good condition and adjusted to the proper tension.

3. All connections in the system are clean and tight.

REMOVAL AND INSTALLATION

While internal alternator repairs are possible, they require specialized tools and training. Therefore, it is advisable to replace a defective alternator as an assembly, or have it repaired by a qualified shop.

1. Disconnect the battery ground cable.

2. Tag and disconnect the alternator wiring.

3. Remove the alternator brace bolt. If the car is equipped with power steering, loosen the pump brace and mount nuts. Detach the drive belt(s).

4. Support the alternator and remove the mount bolt(s). Remove the unit from the vehicle.

5. To install, position the alternator into place and install the mount bolt(s) loosely.

6. Install the drive belt(s). Tighten belt enough to allow approximately ½ in. (13mm) of play on the longest run between pulleys.

7. Connect the alternator wiring.

8. Connect the battery ground cable.

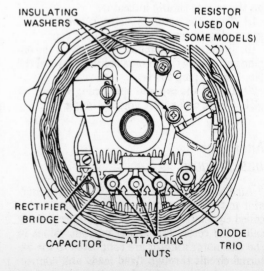

View of the alternator end frame

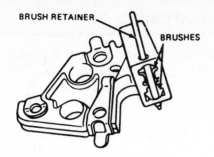

BRUSH RETAINER

BRUSHES

Voltage regulator with brushes depressed

Voltage Regulator

REMOVAL AND INSTALLATION

NOTE: *This procedure is to be performed with the alternator removed from the vehicle. The new style CS alternators on 1987–92 vehicles are non-serviceable and must be replaced as an assembly.*

1. Make scribe marks on the end frames to make reassembly easier.
2. Remove the 4 through-bolts and separate the drive end frame assembly from the rectifier end frame assembly.
3. Remove the 3 diode trio attaching nuts and the 3 regulator attaching screws.
4. Remove the diode trio and the regulator from the end frame.
5. To install, push the brushes into the brush holder and install a brush retainer or a tooth pick to hold the brushes in place.
6. Install the regulator into the alternator.
7. Install the diode trio.
8. Install the halves of the alternator and secure the halves with the 4 through-bolts. After the alternator is assembled, remove the brush retainer.

Battery

REMOVAL AND INSTALLATION

1. Remove the negative battery cable and then the positive battery cable.
2. Remove the battery retainer screw and the retainer. Remove the battery.
3. To install, position the battery into place.
4. Install the battery retainer and secure it with the retaining screw.

ALTERNATOR SPECIFICATIONS

Year	VIN	Engine Displacement Liters (cc)	Output (Amps)
1982	2	2.5L (2500)	42, 63, 70, 85
	1	2.8L (2800)	42, 63, 70, 85
	H	5.0L (5000)	55, 70, 70, 85
	7	5.0L (5000)	55, 70, 70, 85
1983	2	2.5L (2500)	42, 63, 78
	1	2.8L (2800)	42, 63, 78
	H	5.0L (5000)	42, 78, 78
	7	5.0L (5000)	70, 70, 85
1984	2	2.5L (2500)	42, 66
	1	2.8L (2800)	42, 66, 78
	H	5.0L (5000)	42, 78
	G	5.0L (5000)	94
1985	2	2.5L (2500)	42, 66, 78
	S	2.8L (2800)	66, 78, 97
	H	5.0L (5000)	108
	G	5.0L (5000)	42, 78
	F	5.0L (5000)	66, 78, 94
1986	2	2.5L (2500)	42, 66, 78
	S	2.8L (2800)	66, 78, 97
	H	5.0L (5000)	42, 78
	G	5.0L (5000)	66, 78, 94
	F	5.0L (5000)	108
	8	5.7L (5700)	108

ALTERNATOR SPECIFICATIONS

Year	VIN	Engine Displacement Liters (cc)	Output (Amps)
1987	S	2.8L (2800)	85, 100
	H	5.0L (5000)	85, 100
	F	5.0L (5000)	105
	8	5.7L (5700)	74, 85
1988	S	2.8L (2800)	85, 100
	E	5.0L (5000)	85, 100
	F	5.0L (5000)	105
	8	5.7L (5700)	105
1989	S	2.8L (2800)	85, 100
	E	5.0L (5000)	85, 100
	F	5.0L (5000)	105
	8	5.7L (5700)	105
1990	T	3.1L (3100)	100
	E	5.0L (5000)	100
	F	5.0L (5000)	105
	8	5.7L (5700)	105
1991	T	3.1L (3100)	100
	E	5.0L (5000)	100
	F	5.0L (5000)	105
	8	5.7L (5700)	105
1992	T	3.1L (3100)	100
	E	5.0L (5000)	100
	F	5.0L (5000)	105
	8	5.7L (5700)	105

1. Contact disc
2. Plunger
3. Solenoid
4. Return spring
5. Shift lever
6. Bushing
7. Pinion stop
8. Clutch and drive assembly
9. Field coil
10. Armature
11. Brush
12. Terminals

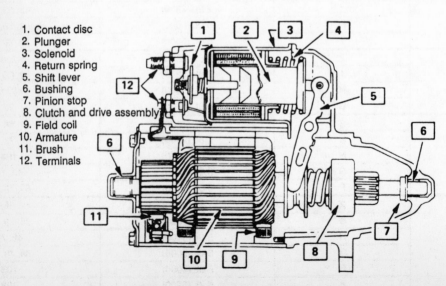

Cross section of starter assembly

5. Connect the positive battery cable then the negative battery cable. Torque the battery cables to 11 ft. lbs. (15) Nm).

Starter

REMOVAL AND INSTALLATION

1. Disconnect the negative battery cable.
2. Raise and safely support the vehicle.
3. Disconnect all wiring from the starter solenoid. Replace each nut as the connector is removed, as thread sizes differ from connector to connector. Note or tag the wiring positions for installation.
4. Remove the bracket from the starter and the two mounting bolts. On engines with a solenoid heat shield, remove the front bracket upper bolt and detach the bracket from the starter.
5. Remove the front bracket bolt or nut. Lower the starter front end first, and then remove the unit from the car.
6. To install, position the starter into place and secure it with the front bracket bolt and nut. Torque the two mounting bolts to 25–35 ft. lbs.
   CAUTION: *If shims were removed, they must be replaced to ensure proper pinion-to-flywheel engagement.*
7. On engines with a solenoid heat shield, attach the bracket to the starter. Install the bracket to the starter and the two mounting bolts. Install the front bracket upper bolt.

8. Connect all wiring to the starter solenoid and tighten wire lug nuts.
9. Lower the vehicle.
10. Connect the negative battery cable.

SOLENOID REPLACEMENT

1. Remove the screw and washer from the motor connector strap terminal.
2. Remove the two solenoid retaining screws.
3. Twist the solenoid housing clockwise to remove the flange key from the keyway in the housing. Then remove the housing.
4. To re-install the unit, place the return spring on the plunger and place the solenoid body on the drive housing. Turn counterclockwise to engage the flange key. Place the two retaining screws in position and install the screw and washer which secures the strap terminal. Install the unit on the starter.

Sending Units and Sensors

Refer to Chapter 4 for all sending unit and sensor testing.

REMOVAL AND INSTALLATION

Coolant Temperature

Replace the sensor by disconnecting the electrical connector, draining the coolant and then remove the sensor using the appropriate wrench or socket.

Oil Pressure

Replace the sensor by disconnecting the electrical connector and using a special oil pressure sensor socket, remove the sensor.

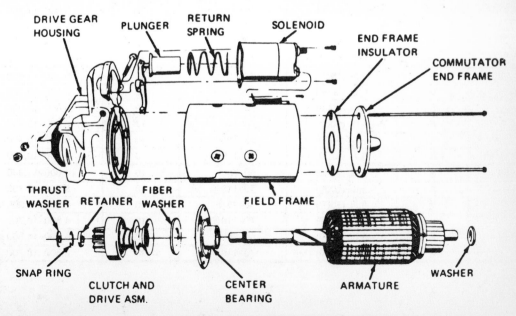

Exploded view of starter assembly

STARTER SPECIFICATIONS

Year	VIN	Engine Displacement Liters (cc)	No-Load Test		
			Amps Min.–Max.	Volts	Rpm Min.–Max.
1982	2	2.5L (2500)	45–70	10	7,000–11,900
	1	2.8L (2800)	45–70	10	7,000–11,900
	H	5.0L (5000)	45–70	10	7,000–11,900
	7	5.0L (5000)	45–70	10	7,000–11,900
1983	2	2.5L (2500)	55–85	10	6,000–12,000
	1	2.8L (2800)	45–70	10	7,000–11,900
	H	5.0L (5000)	45–70	10	7,000–11,900
	7	5.0L (5000)	45–70	10	7,000–11,900
1984	2	2.5L (2500)	50–75	10	6,000–11,900
	1	2.8L (2800)	45–70	10	7,000–11,900
	H	5.0L (5000)	50–75	10	6,000–11,900
	G	5.0L (5000)	52–76	10	6,000–12,000
1985	2	2.5L (2500)	52–76	10	6,000–11,500
	S	2.8L (2800)	52–76	10	6,000–11,500
	H	5.0L (5000)	70–120 ①	10	5,500–10,700
	H	5.0L (5000)	52–76 ②	10	6,000–11,500
	G	5.0L (5000)	52–76 ②	10	6,000–11,500
	F	5.0L (5000)	70–120 ①	10	5,500–10,700
1986	2	2.5L (2500)	52–76	10	6,000–11,500
	S	2.8L (2800)	52–76	10	6,000–11,500
	H	5.0L (5000)	70–120 ①	10	5,500–10,700
	H	5.0L (5000)	52–76 ②	10	6,000–11,500
	G	5.0L (5000)	52–76 ②	10	6,000–11,500
	F	5.0L (5000)	70–120 ①	10	5,500–10,700
	8	5.7L (5700)	70–120	10	5,500–10,700
1987	S	2.8L (2800)	50–75	10	6,000–11,500
	H	5.0L (5000)	70–120 ①	10	5,500–10,700
	H	5.0L (5000)	52–76 ②	10	6,000–11,500
	F	5.0L (5000)	70–110 ①	10	6,500–10,700
	F	5.0L (5000)	52–76 ②	10	6,500–10,700
	8	5.7L (5700)	70–110	10	6,500–10,700
1988	S	2.8L (2800)	50–75	10	6,000–11,500
	E	5.0L (5000)	70–110 ①	10	6,500–10,700
	E	5.0L (5000)	52–76 ②	10	6,000–12,000
	F	5.0L (5000)	70–110 ①	10	6,500–10,700
	F	5.0L (5000)	52–76 ②	10	6,500–10,700
	8	5.7L (5700)	70–110	10	6,500–10,700
1989	S	2.8L (2800)	50–75	10	6,000–11,900
	E	5.0L (5000)	70–110 ①	10	6,500–10,700
	E	5.0L (5000)	50–75 ②	10	6,000–11,900
	F	5.0L (5000)	70–110 ①	10	6,500–10,700
	F	5.0L (5000)	50–75 ②	10	6,000–11,900
	8	5.7L (5700)	70–110	10	6,500–10,700

STARTER SPECIFICATIONS

Year	VIN	Engine Displacement Liters (cc)	No-Load Test		
			Amps Min.–Max.	Volts	Rpm Min.–Max.
1990	T	3.1L (3100)	50–75	10	6,000–11,900
	E	5.0L (5000)	70–110①	10	6,500–10,700
	E	5.0L (5000)	50–75②	10	6,000–11,900
	F	5.0L (5000)	70–110①	10	6,500–10,700
	F	5.0L (5000)	50–75②	10	6,000–11,900
	8	5.7L (5700)	70–110	10	6,500–10,700
1991	T	3.1L (3100)	45–75	10	6,000–11,000
	E	5.0L (5000)	45–75	10	6,500–11,000
	F	5.0L (5000)	45–75	10	6,500–11,000
	8	5.7L (5700)	70–110	10	6,500–10,700
1992	T	3.1L (3100)	50–75	10	6,500–11,000
	E	5.0L (5000)	45–75	10	6,500–11,000
	F	5.0L (5000)	45–75	10	6,500–11,000
	8	5.7L (5700)	70–110	10	6,500–10,700

① Automatic Transmission
② Manual Transmission

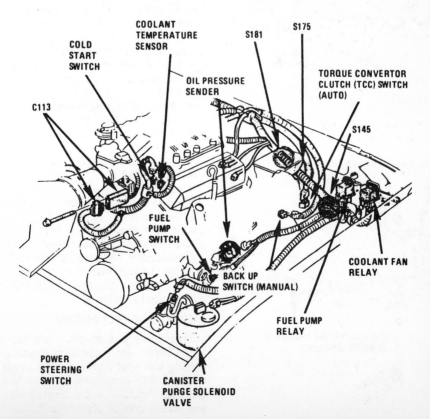

Engine coolant temperature and oil pressure sensor location—2.8L engine

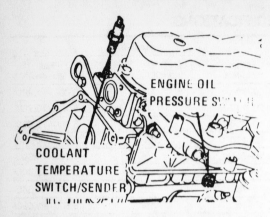

Engine coolant temperature and oil pressure sensor location—2.5L engine

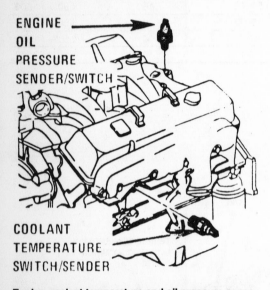

Engine coolant temperature and oil pressure sensor location—1982–86 V8 engine

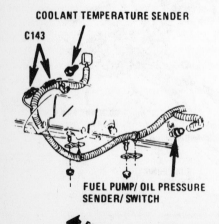

Engine coolant temperature and oil pressure sensor location—1986–92 V8 engine

ENGINE MECHANICAL

Engine Overhaul Tips

Most engine overhaul procedures are fairly standard. In addition to specific parts replacement procedures and complete specifications for your individual engine, this Chapter also is a guide to rebuilding procedures. Examples of standard rebuilding practice are shown and should be used along with specific details concerning your particular engine.

Competent and accurate machine shop services will ensure maximum performance, reliability and engine life.

In most instances it is more profitable for the do-it-yourself mechanic to remove, clean and inspect the component, buy the necessary parts and deliver these to a shop for actual machine work.

On the other hand, much of the rebuilding work (crankshaft, block, bearings, piston rods, and other components) is well within the scope of the do-it-yourself mechanic.

TOOLS

The tools required for an engine overhaul or parts replacement will depend on the depth of your involvement. With a few exceptions, they will be the tools found in a mechanic's tool kit (see Chapter 1). More in-depth work will require any or all of the following:
- a dial indicator (reading in thousandths) mounted on a universal base
- micrometers and telescope gauges
- jaw and screw-type pullers
- scraper
- valve spring compressor
- ring groove cleaner
- piston ring expander and compressor
- ridge reamer
- cylinder hone or glaze breaker
- Plastigage®
- engine stand

The use of most of these tools is illustrated in this Section. Many can be rented for a one-time use from a local parts jobber or tool supply house specializing in automotive work.

Occasionally, the use of special tools is called for. See the information on Special Tools and Safety Notice in the front of this book before substituting another tool.

INSPECTION TECHNIQUES

Procedures and specifications are given in this Chapter for inspecting, cleaning and assessing the wear limits of most major components. Other procedures such as Magnaflux® and Zyglo® can be used to locate material flaws and stress cracks. Magnaflux® is a magnetic process applicable only to ferrous materials. The Zyglo® process coats the material with a fluorescent dye penetrant and can be used on any material to check for suspected surface cracks. Other spray-type dyes are available through parts retailers and can also be used to check for cracks.

OVERHAUL TIPS

Aluminum has become extremely popular for use in engines, due to its low weight. Observe the following precautions when handling aluminum parts:

• Never hot tank aluminum parts (the caustic hot tank solution will eat the aluminum).

• Remove all aluminum parts (identification tag, etc.) from engine parts prior to the tanking.

• Always coat threads lightly with engine oil or anti-seize compounds before re-installation, to prevent seizure.

• Never overtorque bolts or spark plugs especially in aluminum threads.

Stripped threads in any component can be repaired using any of several commercial repair kits (Heli-Coil®, Microdot®, Keenserts®, etc.).

When assembling the engine, any parts that will be experiencing frictional contact must be prelubed to provide lubrication at initial start-up. Any product specifically formulated for this purpose can be used, but engine oil is not recommended as a prelube.

When semi-permanent (locked, but removable) installation of bolts or nuts is desired, threads should be cleaned and coated with Loctite® or other similar, commercial non-hardening sealant.

REPAIRING DAMAGED THREADS

Several methods of repairing damaged threads are available. Heli-Coil® (shown here), Keenserts® and Microdot® are among the most widely used. All involve basically the same principle, drilling out stripped threads, tapping the hole and installing a prewound insert, making

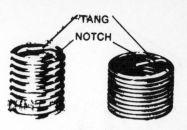

Standard thread repair insert (left) and a spark plug thread repair insert (right)

Using the specified drill to remove the damaged threads and prepare the hole for the specified tap. Drill completely through the hole or the bottom of a blind hole

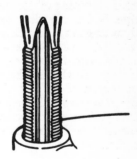

Using the tap supplied with the kit, tap the hole to receive the new thread insert. Keep the tap sufficiently oiled and back it out frequently to avoid clogging it

welding, plugging and oversize fasteners unnecessary.

Two types of thread repair inserts are usually supplied: a standard type for most Inch Coarse, Inch Fine, Metric Coarse and Metric Fine thread sizes and a spark lug type to fit most spark plug port sizes. Consult the individual manufacturer's catalog to determine exact applications. Typical thread repair kits will contain a selection of pre-wound threaded inserts, a tap (corresponding to the outside diameter threads of the insert) and an installation tool. Spark plug inserts usually differ because they require a tap equipped with pilot threads and a combined reamer/tap section. Most manufacturers also supply blister-packed thread repair

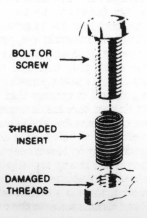

Using the thread repair kit to fix a damaged hole

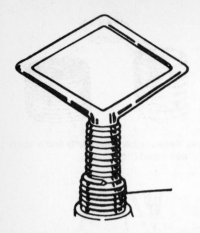

Screw the threaded insert onto the tool until the tang engages the slot. Screw the insert into the hole until it is ¼ to a ½ turn below the top of the hole. After installation break off the tang with a hammer and punch

inserts separately in addition to a master kit containing a variety of taps and inserts plus installation tools.

Prior to proceding with a repair to a threaded hole, remove any snapped, broken or damaged bolts or studs. Penetrating oil can be used to free frozen threads. The offending item can be removed with locking pliers or with a screw or stud extractor. Often when a bolt is overtightened and snaps it may be removed easily by the drilling 2 small holes right next to each other on the top of the bolt; then use a small screwdriver to remove the broken bolt or stud. After the hole is clear, the threads can be repaired if damaged, as shown in the series of accompanying illustrations.

Checking Engine Compression

A noticeable lack of engine power, excessive oil consumption and/or poor fuel mileage measured over an extended period are all indicators

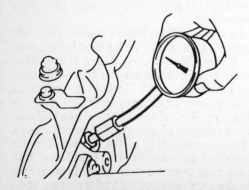

Screw-in type compression gauge is more accurate

of internal engine war. Worn piston rings, scored or worn cylinder bores, blown head gaskets, sticking or burnt valves and worn valve seats are all possible culprits here. A check of each cylinder's compression will help you locate the problems.

As mentioned in the Tools and Equipment section of Chapter 1, a screw-in type compression gauge is more accurate then the type you simply hold against the spark plug hole, although it takes slightly longer to use. It's worth it to obtain a more accurate reading. Follow the procedures below.

1. Warm up the engine to normal operating temperature.

2. Remove all the spark plugs.

3. Disconnect the high tension lead from the ignition coil.

4. Fully open the throttle, either by operating the carburetor throttle linkage by hand or by having an assistant hold the accelerator pedal to the floor.

5. Screw the compression gauge into the No. 1 spark plug hole until the fitting is snug.

WARNING: *Be careful not to crossthread the plug hole. On aluminum cylinder heads use extra care, as the threads in these heads are easily damaged.*

6. Ask an assistant to depress the accelerator pedal fully on both carbureted and fuel injected vehicles. Then, while you read the compression gauge, ask the assistant to crank the engine 4 to 6 revolutions using the ignition switch. Repeat the test two or three times until a consistent reading is obtained.

7. Read the compression gauge at the end of each series of cranks, and record the highest of these readings. Repeat this procedure for each of the engine's cylinders. The lowest reading recorded should not be less than 70% of the highest reading and no cylinder should be less than 100 psi.

For example, if the highest reading obtained was 150 psi. then the lowest acceptable cylinder reading would be 105 psi. (150 x 0.70 = 105). The difference between any two cylinders should be no more than 12–14 pounds.

8. If a cylinder is unusually low, pour a tablespoon of clean engine oil into the cylinder through the spark plug hole and repeat the compression test. If the compression comes up after adding the oil, it appears that the cylinder's piston rings or bore are damaged or worn. If the pressure remains low, the valves may not be seating properly (a valve job is needed), or the head gasket may be blown near that cylinder. If compression in any two adjacent cylinders is low, and if the addition of oil doesn't help the compression, there is leakage past the head gasket. Oil and coolant water in the combustion

GENERAL ENGINE SPECIFICATIONS

Year	VIN	No. Cylinders cu. in. (Liters)	Fuel System Type	Sae Net Horsepower @ rpm	Sae Net Torque @ rpm (ft. lbs.)	Bore × Stroke (in.)	Compression Ratio	Oil Pressure @ 2000 rpm
1982	2	4-151 (2.5L)	TBI	90 @ 4000	134 @ 2400	4.000 × 3.000	8.2:1	40
	1	6-173 (2.8L)	Carb	102 @ 4800	145 @ 2400	3.500 × 3.000	8.5:1	40
	H	8-305 (5.0L)	Carb	145 @ 4000	240 @ 2400	3.736 × 3.480	8.6:1	40
	7	8-305 (5.0L)	CFI	165 @ 4200	240 @ 2400	3.736 × 3.480	9.5:1	40
1983	2	4-151 (2.5L)	TBI	90 @ 4000	134 @ 2400	4.000 × 3.000	8.2:1	40
	1	6-173 (2.8L)	Carb	102 @ 4800	145 @ 2400	3.500 × 3.000	8.5:1	40
	H	8-305 (5.0L)	Carb	145 @ 4000	240 @ 2400	3.736 × 3.480	8.6:1	40
	7	8-305 (5.0L)	CFI	165 @ 4200	240 @ 2400	3.736 × 3.480	9.5:1	40
1984	2	4-151 (2.5L)	TBI	90 @ 4000	134 @ 2400	4.000 × 3.000	8.2:1	40
	1	6-173 (2.8L)	Carb	102 @ 4800	145 @ 2400	3.500 × 3.000	8.5:1	40
	H	8-305 (5.0L)	Carb	150 @ 4000	240 @ 2400	3.736 × 3.480	8.6:1	55
	G	8-305 (5.0L)	Carb	165 @ 4200	240 @ 2400	3.736 × 3.480	9.5:1	55
1985	2	4-151 (2.5L)	TBI	92 @ 4000	134 @ 2400	4.000 × 3.000	9.0:1	40
	S	6-173 (2.8L)	MPI	135 @ 5100	165 @ 3500	3.500 × 3.000	8.9:1	55
	H	8-305 (5.0L)	Carb	150 @ 4000	240 @ 2400	3.736 × 3.480	8.6:1	55
	G	8-305 (5.0L)	Carb	165 @ 4200	250 @ 2000	3.736 × 3.480	9.5:1	55
	F	8-305 (5.0L)	TPI	190 @ 4800	240 @ 3200	3.736 × 3.480	9.5:1	55
1986	2	4-151 (2.5L)	TBI	92 @ 4000	134 @ 2400	4.000 × 3.000	9.0:1	40
	S	6-173 (2.8L)	MPI	135 @ 5100	165 @ 3500	3.500 × 3.000	8.9:1	55
	H	8-305 (5.0L)	Carb	150 @ 4000	240 @ 2400	3.736 × 3.480	8.6:1	55
	G	8-305 (5.0L)	Carb	165 @ 4200	250 @ 2000	3.736 × 3.480	9.5:1	55
	F	8-305 (5.0L)	TPI	190 @ 4800	240 @ 3200	3.736 × 3.480	9.5:1	55
	8	8-350 (5.7L)	TPI	230 @ 4000	300 @ 3200	4.000 × 3.480	9.5:1	55
1987	S	6-173 (2.8L)	MPI	135 @ 5100	165 @ 3500	3.500 × 3.000	8.9:1	55
	H	8-305 (5.0L)	Carb	150 @ 4000	240 @ 2400	3.736 × 3.480	8.6:1	55
	F	8-305 (5.0L)	TPI	190 @ 4800	240 @ 3200	3.736 × 3.480	9.5:1	55
	8	8-350 (5.7L)	TPI	230 @ 4000	300 @ 3200	4.000 × 3.480	9.5:1	55
1988	S	6-173 (2.8L)	MPI	135 @ 5100	165 @ 3500	3.500 × 3.000	8.9:1	55
	E	8-305 (5.0L)	TBI	150 @ 4000	240 @ 2400	3.736 × 3.480	9.3:1	55
	F	8-305 (5.0L)	TPI	190 @ 4800	240 @ 3200	3.736 × 3.480	9.5:1	55
	8	8-350 (5.7L)	TPI	230 @ 4000	300 @ 3200	4.000 × 3.480	9.5:1	55
1989	S	6-173 (2.8L)	MPI	135 @ 5100	165 @ 3500	3.500 × 3.000	8.9:1	55
	E	8-305 (5.0L)	EFI	150 @ 4000	240 @ 2400	3.736 × 3.480	9.3:1	55
	F	8-305 (5.0L)	TPI	190 @ 4800	240 @ 3200	3.736 × 3.480	9.5:1	55
	8	8-350 (5.7L)	TPI	230 @ 4000	300 @ 3200	4.000 × 3.480	9.5:1	55
1990	T	6-191 (3.1L)	MPI	140 @ 4400	180 @ 3600	3.500 × 3.000	8.8:1	55
	E	8-305 (5.0L)	EFI	170 @ 4000	255 @ 2400	3.736 × 3.480	9.3:1	55
	F	8-305 (5.0L)	TPI	230 @ 4400	300 @ 3200	3.736 × 3.480	9.3:1	55
	8	8-350 (5.7L)	TPI	240 @ 4400	345 @ 3200	4.000 × 3.480	9.3:1	55
1991	T	6-191 (3.1L)	MPI	140 @ 4400	180 @ 3600	3.500 × 3.000	8.5:1	55
	E	8-305 (5.0L)	EFI	170 @ 4000	255 @ 2400	3.736 × 3.480	9.3:1	18
	F	8-305 (5.0L)	TPI	230 @ 4400	300 @ 3200	3.736 × 3.480	9.3:1	18
	8	8-350 (5.7L)	TPI	240 @ 4400	345 @ 3200	4.000 × 3.480	9.8:1	18

GENERAL ENGINE SPECIFICATIONS

Year	VIN	No. Cylinders cu. in. (Liters)	Fuel System Type	Sae Net Horsepower @ rpm	Sae Net Torque @ rpm (ft. lbs.)	Bore × Stroke (in.)	Compression Ratio	Oil Pressure @ 2000 rpm
1992	T	6-191 (3.1L)	MPI	140 @ 4400	180 @ 3600	3.500 × 3.000	8.5:1	55
	E	8-305 (5.0L)	EFI	170 @ 4000	255 @ 2400	3.736 × 3.480	9.3:1	18
	F	8-305 (5.0L)	TPI	205 @ 4200	285 @ 3200	3.736 × 3.480	9.3:1	18
	8	8-350 (5.7L)	TPI	245 @ 4400	345 @ 3200	4.000 × 3.480	9.8:1	18

NOTE: Horsepower and torque are SAE net figures. They are measured at the rear of the transmission with all accessories installed and operating. Since the figures vary when a given engine is installed in different models, some are representative rather than exact.

Carb—Carburetor
CFI—Cross Fire Injection
MPI—Multi-Point Injection
TBI—Throttle Body Injection
TPI—Tuned Port Injection

VALVE SPECIFICATIONS

Year	VIN	No. Cylinders/ cu. in. (Liters)	Seat Angle (deg.)	Face Angle (deg.)	Spring Test Pressure (lbs.)	Spring Installed Height (in.)	Stem-to-Guide Clearance (in.) Intake	Stem-to-Guide Clearance (in.) Exhaust	Stem Diameter (in.) Intake	Stem Diameter (in.) Exhaust
1982	2	4-151 (2.5L)	46	45	122–180 @ 1.25	1.69	0.0010–0.0027	0.0010–0.0027	0.3418–0.3425	0.3418–0.3425
	1	6-173 (2.8L)	46	45	195 @ 1.18	1.57	0.0010–0.0027	0.0010–0.0027	—	—
	H	8-305 (5.0L)	46	45	194–206 @ 1.25	1.72	0.0010–0.0027	0.0010–0.0027	—	—
	7	8-305 (5.0L)	46	45	194–206 @ 1.25	1.72	0.0010–0.0027	0.0010–0.0027	—	—
1983	2	4-151 (2.5L)	46	45	122–180 @ 1.25	1.69	0.0010–0.0027	0.0010–0.0027	—	—
	1	6-173 (2.8L)	46	45	195 @ 1.18	1.57	0.0010–0.0027	0.0010–0.0027	—	—
	H	8-305 (5.0L)	46	45	194–206 @ 1.25	1.72	0.0010–0.0027	0.0010–0.0027	—	—
	7	8-305 (5.0L)	46	45	194–206 @ 1.25	1.72	0.0010–0.0027	0.0010–0.0027	—	—
1984	2	4-151 (2.5L)	46	45	122–180 @ 1.25	1.69	0.0010–0.0027	0.0010–0.0027	—	—
	1	6-173 (2.8L)	46	45	195 @ 1.18	1.57	0.0010–0.0027	0.0010–0.0027	—	—
	H	8-305 (5.0L)	46	45	194–206 @ 1.25	1.72	0.0010–0.0027	0.0010–0.0027	—	—
	G	8-305 (5.0L)	46	45	194–206 @ 1.25	1.72	0.0010–0.0027	0.0010–0.0027	—	—
1985	2	4-151 (2.5L)	46	46	170–180 @ 1.26	1.69	0.0010–0.0027	0.0010–0.0027	—	—
	S	6-173 (2.8L)	46	45	195 @ 1.18	1.57	0.0010–0.0027	0.0010–0.0027	—	—
	H	8-305 (5.0L)	46	45	194–206 @ 1.25	1.72	0.0010–0.0027	0.0010–0.0027	—	—
	G	8-305 (5.0L)	46	45	194–206 @ 1.25	1.72	0.0010–0.0027	0.0010–0.0027	—	—
	F	8-305 (5.0L)	46	45	194–206 @ 1.25	1.72	0.0010–0.0027	0.0010–0.0027	—	—

VALVE SPECIFICATIONS

Year	VIN	No. Cylinders/ cu. in. (Liters)	Seat Angle (deg.)	Face Angle (deg.)	Spring Test Pressure (lbs.)	Spring Installed Height (in.)	Stem-to-Guide Clearance (in.)		Stem Diameter (in.)	
							Intake	Exhaust	Intake	Exhaust
1986	2	4-151 (2.5L)	46	45	170–180 @ 1.26	1.69	0.0010–0.0027	0.0010–0.0027	—	—
	S	6-173 (2.8L)	46	45	195 @ 1.18	1.57	0.0010–0.0027	0.0010–0.0027	—	—
	H	8-305 (5.0L)	46	45	194–206 @ ②	①	0.0010–0.0027	0.0010–0.0027	—	—
	G	8-305 (5.0L)	46	45	194–206 @ ②	①	0.0010–0.0027	0.0010–0.0027	—	—
	F	8-305 (5.0L)	46	45	194–206 @ ②	①	0.0010–0.0027	0.0010–0.0027	—	—
	8	8-350 (5.7L)	46	45	194–206 @ ②	①	0.0010–0.0027	0.0010–0.0027	—	—
1987	S	6-173 (2.8L)	46	45	195 @ 1.18	1.57	0.0010–0.0027	0.0010–0.0027	—	—
	H	8-305 (5.0L)	46	45	194–206 @ ②	①	0.0010–0.0027	0.0010–0.0027	—	—
	F	8-305 (5.0L)	46	45	194–206 @ ②	①	0.0010–0.0027	0.0010–0.0027	—	—
	8	8-350 (5.7L)	46	45	194–206 @ ②	①	0.0010–0.0027	0.0010–0.0027	—	—
1988	S	6-173 (2.8L)	46	45	195 @ 1.18	1.57	0.0010–0.0027	0.0010–0.0027	—	—
	E	8-305 (5.0L)	46	45	194–206 @ 1.25	①	0.0010–0.0027	0.0010–0.0027	—	—
	F	8-305 (5.0L)	46	45	194–206 @ 1.25	①	0.0010–0.0027	0.0010–0.0027	—	—
	8	8-350 (5.7L)	46	45	194–206 @ 1.25	①	0.0010–0.0027	0.0010–0.0027	—	—
1989	S	6-173 (2.8L)	46	45	195 @ 1.18	1.57	0.0010–0.0027	0.0010–0.0027	—	—
	E	8-305 (5.0L)	46	45	194–206 @ 1.25	①	0.0011–0.0027	0.0011–0.0027	—	—
	F	8-305 (5.0L)	46	45	194–206 @ 1.25	①	0.0011–0.0027	0.0011–0.0027	—	—
	8	8-350 (5.7L)	46	45	194–206 @ 1.25	①	0.0011–0.0027	0.0011–0.0027	—	—
1990	T	6-191 (3.1L)	46	45	195 @ 1.18	1.57	0.0010–0.0027	0.0010–0.0027	—	—
	E	8-305 (5.0L)	46	45	194–206 @ 1.25	①	0.0011–0.0027	0.0011–0.0027	—	—
	F	8-305 (5.0L)	46	45	194–206 @ 1.25	①	0.0011–0.0027	0.0011–0.0027	—	—
	8	8-350 (5.7L)	46	45	194–206 @ 1.25	①	0.0011–0.0027	0.0011–0.0027	—	—
1991	T	6-191 (3.1L)	46	45	189 @ 1.18	1.57	0.0014–0.0025	0.0016–0.0029	—	—
	E	8-305 (5.0L)	46	45	194–206 @ 1.25	①	0.0011–0.0027	0.0011–0.0027	—	—
	F	8-305 (5.0L)	46	45	194–206 @ 1.25	①	0.0011–0.0027	0.0011–0.0027	—	—
	8	8-350 (5.7L)	46	45	194–206 @ 1.25	①	0.0011–0.0027	0.0011–0.0027	—	—

VALVE SPECIFICATIONS (cont.)

Year	VIN	No. Cylinders/ cu. in. (Liters)	Seat Angle (deg.)	Face Angle (deg.)	Spring Test Pressure (lbs.)	Spring Installed Height (in.)	Stem-to-Guide Clearance (in.) Intake	Exhaust	Stem Diameter (in.) Intake	Exhaust
1992	T	6-191 (3.1L)	46	45	189 @ 1.18	1.57	0.0014– 0.0025	0.0016– 0.0029	—	—
	E	8-305 (5.0L)	46	45	194–206 @ 1.25	①	0.0011– 0.0027	0.0011– 0.0027	—	—
	F	8-305 (5.0L)	46	45	194–206 @ 1.25	①	0.0011– 0.0027	0.0011– 0.0027	—	—
	8	8-350 (5.7L)	46	45	194–206 @ 1.25	①	0.0011– 0.0027	0.0011– 0.0027	—	—

① Intake—1.72″
   Exhaust—1.59″
② Intake—1.25″
   Exhaust—1.16″

CAMSHAFT SPECIFICATIONS

Year	VIN	No. Cylinders cu. in. (Liters)	Journal Diameter (in.) 1	2	3	4	5	Lobe Lift Intake	Exhaust	Bearing Clearance (in.)	Camshaft End Play (in.)
1982	2	4-151 (2.5L)	1.8690	1.8690	1.8690	1.8690	1.8690	0.398	0.398	0.0007– 0.0027	0.0020– 0.0050
	1	6-173 (2.8L)	1.8678– 1.8697	1.8678– 1.8697	1.8678– 1.8697	1.8678– 1.8697	1.8678– 1.8697	0.231	0.263	0.0010– 0.0040	NA
	H	8-305 (5.0L)	1.8682– 1.8692	1.8682– 1.8692	1.8682– 1.8692	1.8682– 1.8692	1.8682– 1.8692	0.238	0.260	NA	0.0040– 0.0120
	7	8-305 (5.0L)	1.8682– 1.8692	1.8682– 1.8692	1.8682– 1.8692	1.8682– 1.8692	1.8682– 1.8692	0.260	0.273	NA	0.0040– 0.0120
1983	2	4-151 (2.5L)	1.8690	1.8690	1.8690	1.8690	1.8690	0.398	0.398	0.0007– 0.0027	0.0020– 0.0050
	1	6-173 (2.8L)	1.8678– 1.8697	1.8678– 1.8697	1.8678– 1.8697	1.8678– 1.8697	1.8678– 1.8697	0.231	0.263	0.0010– 0.0040	NA
	H	8-305 (5.0L)	1.8682– 1.8692	1.8682– 1.8692	1.8682– 1.8692	1.8682– 1.8692	1.8682– 1.8692	0.234	0.257	NA	0.0040– 0.0120
	7	8-305 (5.0L)	1.8682– 1.8692	1.8682– 1.8692	1.8682– 1.8692	1.8682– 1.8692	1.8682– 1.8692	0.269	0.276	NA	0.0040– 0.0120
1984	2	4-151 (2.5L)	1.8690	1.8690	1.8690	1.8690	1.8690	0.398	0.398	0.0007– 0.0027	0.0020– 0.0050
	1	6-173 (2.8L)	1.8678– 1.8697	1.8678– 1.8697	1.8678– 1.8697	1.8678– 1.8697	1.8678– 1.8697	0.231	0.263	0.0010– 0.0040	NA
	H	8-305 (5.0L)	1.8682– 1.8692	1.8682– 1.8692	1.8682– 1.8692	1.8682– 1.8692	1.8682– 1.8692	0.234	0.257	NA	0.0040– 0.0120
	G	8-305 (5.0L)	1.8682– 1.8692	1.8682– 1.8692	1.8682– 1.8692	1.8682– 1.8692	1.8682– 1.8692	0.269	0.276	NA	0.0040– 0.0120
1985	2	4-151 (2.5L)	1.8690	1.8690	1.8690	1.8690	1.8690	0.398	0.398	0.0007– 0.0027	0.0015– 0.0050
	S	6-173 (2.8L)	1.8678– 1.8697	1.8678– 1.8697	1.8678– 1.8697	1.8678– 1.8697	1.8678– 1.8697	0.263	0.273	0.0010– 0.0040	NA
	H	8-305 (5.0L)	1.8682– 1.8692	1.8682– 1.8692	1.8682– 1.8692	1.8682– 1.8692	1.8682– 1.8692	0.234	0.257	NA	0.0040– 0.0120
	G	8-305 (5.0L)	1.8682– 1.8692	1.8682– 1.8692	1.8682– 1.8692	1.8682– 1.8692	1.8682– 1.8692	0.269	0.276	NA	0.0040– 0.0120
	F	8-305 (5.0L)	1.8682– 1.8692	1.8682– 1.8692	1.8682– 1.8692	1.8682– 1.8692	1.8682– 1.8692	0.269	0.276	NA	0.0040– 0.0120

CAMSHAFT SPECIFICATIONS

Year	VIN	No. Cylinders cu. in. (Liters)	Journal Diameter (in.)					Lobe Lift		Bearing Clearance (in.)	Camshaft End Play (in.)
			1	2	3	4	5	Intake	Exhaust		
1986	2	4-151 (2.5L)	1.8690	1.8690	1.8690	1.8690	1.8690	0.398	0.398	0.0007–0.0027	0.0015–0.0050
	S	6-173 (2.8L)	1.8678–1.8697	1.8678–1.8697	1.8678–1.8697	1.8678–1.8697	1.8678–1.8697	0.263	0.273	0.0010–0.0040	NA
	H	8-305 (5.0L)	1.8682–1.8692	1.8682–1.8692	1.8682–1.8692	1.8682–1.8692	1.8682–1.8692	0.234	0.257	NA	0.0040–0.0120
	G	8-305 (5.0L)	1.8682–1.8692	1.8682–1.8692	1.8682–1.8692	1.8682–1.8692	1.8682–1.8692	0.269	0.276	NA	0.0040–0.0120
	F	8-305 (5.0L)	1.8682–1.8692	1.8682–1.8692	1.8682–1.8692	1.8682–1.8692	1.8682–1.8692	0.269	0.276	NA	0.0040–0.0120
	8	8-350 (5.7L)	1.8682–1.8692	1.8682–1.8692	1.8682–1.8692	1.8682–1.8692	1.8682–1.8692	0.273	0.282	NA	0.0040–0.0120
1987	S	6-173 (2.8L)	1.8678–1.8697	1.8678–1.8697	1.8678–1.8697	1.8678–1.8697	1.8678–1.8697	0.263	0.273	0.0010–0.0040	NA
	H	8-305 (5.0L)	1.8682–1.8692	1.8682–1.8692	1.8682–1.8692	1.8682–1.8692	1.8682–1.8692	0.234	0.257	NA	0.0040–0.0120
	F	8-305 (5.0L)	1.8682–1.8692	1.8682–1.8692	1.8682–1.8692	1.8682–1.8692	1.8682–1.8692	0.269	0.276	NA	0.0040–0.0120
	8	8-350 (5.7L)	1.8682–1.8692	1.8682–1.8692	1.8682–1.8692	1.8682–1.8692	1.8682–1.8692	0.273	0.282	NA	0.0040–0.0120
1988	S	6-173 (2.8L)	1.8678–1.8697	1.8678–1.8697	1.8678–1.8697	1.8678–1.8697	1.8678–1.8697	0.263	0.273	0.0010–0.0040	NA
	E	8-305 (5.0L)	1.8682–1.8692	1.8682–1.8692	1.8682–1.8692	1.8682–1.8692	1.8682–1.8692	0.234	0.257	NA	0.0040–0.0120
	F	8-305 (5.0L)	1.8682–1.8692	1.8682–1.8692	1.8682–1.8692	1.8682–1.8692	1.8682–1.8692	0.269	0.276	NA	0.0040–0.0120
	8	8-350 (5.7L)	1.8682–1.8692	1.8682–1.8692	1.8682–1.8692	1.8682–1.8692	1.8682–1.8692	0.273	0.282	NA	0.0040–0.0120
1989	S	6-173 (2.8L)	1.8678–1.8697	1.8678–1.8697	1.8678–1.8697	1.8678–1.8697	1.8678–1.8697	0.263	0.273	0.0010–0.0040	NA
	E	8-305 (5.0L)	1.8682–1.8692	1.8682–1.8692	1.8682–1.8692	1.8682–1.8692	1.8682–1.8692	0.234	0.257	NA	0.0040–0.0120
	F	8-305 (5.0L)	1.8682–1.8692	1.8682–1.8692	1.8682–1.8692	1.8682–1.8692	1.8682–1.8692	0.269	0.276	NA	0.0040–0.0120
	8	8-350 (5.7L)	1.8682–1.8692	1.8682–1.8692	1.8682–1.8692	1.8682–1.8692	1.8682–1.8692	0.273	0.282	NA	0.0040–0.0120
1990	T	6-191 (3.1L)	1.8677–1.8815	1.8677–1.8815	1.8677–1.8815	1.8677–1.8815	1.8677–1.8815	0.263	0.273	0.0010–0.0040	NA
	E	8-305 (5.0L)	1.8682–1.8692	1.8682–1.8692	1.8682–1.8692	1.8682–1.8692	1.8682–1.8692	0.234	0.257	NA	0.0040–0.0120
	F	8-305 (5.0L)	1.8682–1.8692	1.8682–1.8692	1.8682–1.8692	1.8682–1.8692	1.8682–1.8692	0.269	0.276	NA	0.0040–0.0120
	8	8-350 (5.7L)	1.8682–1.8692	1.8682–1.8692	1.8682–1.8692	1.8682–1.8692	1.8682–1.8692	0.273	0.282	NA	0.0040–0.0120
1991	T	6-191 (3.1L)	1.8677–1.8815	1.8677–1.8815	1.8677–1.8815	1.8677–1.8815	1.8677–1.8815	0.263	0.273	0.0010–0.0040	NA
	E	8-305 (5.0L)	1.8682–1.8692	1.8682–1.8692	1.8682–1.8692	1.8682–1.8692	1.8682–1.8692	0.234	0.257	NA	0.0040–0.0120
	F	8-305 (5.0L)	1.8682–1.8692	1.8682–1.8692	1.8682–1.8692	1.8682–1.8692	1.8682–1.8692	0.275	0.285	NA	0.0040–0.0120
	8	8-350 (5.7L)	1.8682–1.8692	1.8682–1.8692	1.8682–1.8692	1.8682–1.8692	1.8682–1.8692	0.275	0.285	NA	0.0040–0.0120

CAMSHAFT SPECIFICATIONS

Year	VIN	No. Cylinders cu. in. (Liters)	Journal Diameter (in.)					Lobe Lift		Bearing Clearance (in.)	Camshaft End Play (in.)
			1	2	3	4	5	Intake	Exhaust		
1992	T	6-191 (3.1L)	1.8677–1.8815	1.8677–1.8815	1.8677–1.8815	1.8677–1.8815	1.8677–1.8815	0.263	0.273	0.0010–0.0040	NA
	E	8-305 (5.0L)	1.8682–1.8692	1.8682–1.8692	1.8682–1.8692	1.8682–1.8692	1.8682–1.8692	0.234	0.257	NA	0.0040–0.0120
	F	8-305 (5.0L)	1.8682–1.8692	1.8682–1.8692	1.8682–1.8692	1.8682–1.8692	1.8682–1.8692	0.269	0.276	NA	0.0040–0.0120
	8	8-350 (5.7L)	1.8682–1.8692	1.8682–1.8692	1.8682–1.8692	1.8682–1.8692	1.8682–1.8692	0.273	0.282	NA	0.0040–0.0120

NA—Not available

CRANKSHAFT AND CONNECTING ROD SPECIFICATIONS

Year	VIN	No. Cylinders cu. in. (Liters)	Crankshaft				Connecting Rod		
			Main Brg. Journal Dia.	Main Brg. Oil Clearance	Shaft End-play	Thrust on No.	Journal Diameter	Oil Clearance	Side Clearance
1982	2	4-151 (2.5L)	2.3000	0.0005–0.0022	0.0035–0.0085	5	2.0000	0.0005–0.0026	0.0060–0.0220
	1	6-173 (2.8L)	2.4937–2.4946	0.0017–0.0029	0.0019–0.0066	3	1.9983–1.9994	0.0014–0.0037	0.0063–0.0173
	H	8-305 (5.0L)	①	②	0.0020–0.0060	5	2.0986–2.0998	0.0018–0.0039	0.0080–0.0140
	7	8-305 (5.0L)	①	②	0.0020–0.0060	5	2.0986–2.0998	0.0018–0.0039	0.0080–0.0140
1983	2	4-151 (2.5L)	2.3000	0.0005–0.0022	0.0035–0.0085	5	2.0000	0.0005–0.0026	0.0060–0.0220
	1	6-173 (2.8L)	⑥	③	0.0019–0.0066	3	1.9983–1.9994	0.0014–0.0037	0.0063–0.0173
	H	8-305 (5.0L)	①	②	0.0020–0.0060	5	2.0980–2.0990	0.0018–0.0039	0.0080–0.0140
	7	8-305 (5.0L)	①	②	0.0020–0.0060	5	2.0980–2.0990	0.0018–0.0039	0.0080–0.0140
1984	2	4-151 (2.5L)	2.3000	0.0005–0.0022	0.0035–0.0085	5	2.0000	0.0005–0.0026	0.0060–0.0220
	1	6-173 (2.8L)	⑥	③	0.0020–0.0060	3	1.9983–1.9994	0.0014–0.0037	0.0063–0.0173
	H	8-305 (5.0L)	①	②	0.0020–0.0060	5	2.0980–2.0990	0.0018–0.0039	0.0080–0.0140
	G	8-305 (5.0L)	①	②	0.0020–0.0060	5	2.0980–2.0990	0.0018–0.0039	0.0080–0.0140
1985	2	4-151 (2.5L)	2.3000	0.0005–0.0022	0.0035–0.0085	5	2.0000	0.0005–0.0026	0.0060–0.0220
	S	6-173 (2.8L)	2.6472–2.6482	③	0.0020–0.0060	3	1.9983–1.9994	0.0014–0.0037	0.0063–0.0173
	H	8-305 (5.0L)	①	②	0.0020–0.0060	5	2.0980–2.0990	0.0018–0.0039	0.0080–0.0140
	G	8-305 (5.0L)	①	②	0.0020–0.0060	5	2.0980–2.0990	0.0018–0.0039	0.0080–0.0140
	F	8-305 (5.0L)	①	②	0.0020–0.0060	5	2.0980–2.0990	0.0018–0.0039	0.0080–0.0140

CRANKSHAFT AND CONNECTING ROD SPECIFICATIONS

Year	VIN	No. Cylinders cu. in. (Liters)	Crankshaft				Connecting Rod		
			Main Brg. Journal Dia.	Main Brg. Oil Clearance	Shaft End-play	Thrust on No.	Journal Diameter	Oil Clearance	Side Clearance
1986	2	4-151 (2.5L)	2.3000	0.0005–0.0022	0.0035–0.0085	5	2.0000	0.0005–0.0026	0.0060–0.0220
	S	6-173 (2.8L)	2.6472–2.6482	③	0.0024–0.0083	3	1.9983–1.9994	0.0014–0.0037	0.0063–0.0173
	H	8-305 (5.0L)	①	②	0.0020–0.0060	5	2.0986–2.0998	0.0018–0.0039	0.0080–0.0140
	G	8-305 (5.0L)	①	②	0.0020–0.0060	5	2.0986–2.0998	0.0018–0.0039	0.0080–0.0140
	F	8-305 (5.0L)	①	②	0.0020–0.0060	5	2.0986–2.0998	0.0018–0.0039	0.0080–0.0140
	8	8-350 (5.7L)	①	②	0.0020–0.0060	5	2.0986–2.0998	0.0018–0.0039	0.0080–0.0140
1987	S	6-173 (2.8L)	2.6472–2.6482	③	0.0024–0.0083	3	1.9983–1.9994	0.0014–0.0037	0.0063–0.0173
	H	8-305 (5.0L)	①	②	0.0020–0.0060	5	2.0986–2.0998	0.0018–0.0039	0.0080–0.0140
	F	8-305 (5.0L)	①	②	0.0020–0.0060	5	2.0986–2.0998	0.0018–0.0039	0.0080–0.0140
	8	8-350 (5.7L)	①	②	0.0020–0.0060	5	2.0986–2.0998	0.0018–0.0039	0.0080–0.0140
1988	S	6-173 (2.8L)	2.6472–2.6482	③	0.0024–0.0083	3	1.9983–1.9994	0.0014–0.0037	0.0063–0.0173
	E	8-305 (5.0L)	①	②	0.0020–0.0060	5	2.0986–2.0998	0.0018–0.0039	0.0080–0.0140
	F	8-305 (5.0L)	①	②	0.0020–0.0060	5	2.0986–2.0998	0.0018–0.0039	0.0080–0.0140
	8	8-350 (5.7L)	①	②	0.0020–0.0060	5	2.0986–2.0998	0.0018–0.0039	0.0080–0.0140
1989	S	6-173 (2.8L)	2.6472–2.6482	③	0.0024–0.0083	3	1.9983–1.9994	0.0014–0.0037	0.0063–0.0173
	E	8-305 (5.0L)	①	②	0.0020–0.0060	5	2.0986–2.0998	0.0018–0.0039	0.0080–0.0140
	F	8-305 (5.0L)	①	②	0.0020–0.0060	5	2.0986–2.0998	0.0018–0.0039	0.0080–0.0140
	8	8-350 (5.7L)	①	②	0.0020–0.0060	5	2.0986–2.0998	0.0018–0.0039	0.0080–0.0140
1990	T	6-191 (3.1L)	2.6472–2.6482	④	0.0024–0.0083	3	1.9983–1.9994	0.0014–0.0037	0.0140–0.0270
	E	8-305 (5.0L)	①	②	0.0020–0.0060	5	2.0986–2.0998	0.0018–0.0039	0.0080–0.0140
	F	8-305 (5.0L)	①	②	0.0020–0.0060	5	2.0986–2.0998	0.0018–0.0039	0.0080–0.0140
	8	8-350 (5.7L)	①	②	0.0020–0.0060	5	2.0986–2.0998	0.0018–0.0039	0.0080–0.0140
1991	T	6-191 (3.1L)	2.6472–2.6482	⑤	0.0024–0.0083	3	1.9983–1.9994	0.0014–0.0037	0.0140–0.0290
	E	8-305 (5.0L)	①	②	0.0020–0.0060	5	2.0986–2.0998	0.0018–0.0039	0.0080–0.0140
	F	8-305 (5.0L)	①	②	0.0020–0.0060	5	2.0986–2.0998	0.0018–0.0039	0.0080–0.0140
	8	8-350 (5.7L)	①	②	0.0020–0.0060	5	2.0986–2.0998	0.0018–0.0039	0.0080–0.0140

CRANKSHAFT AND CONNECTING ROD SPECIFICATIONS (cont.)

Year	VIN	No. Cylinders cu. in. (Liters)	Crankshaft				Connecting Rod		
			Main Brg. Journal Dia.	Main Brg. Oil Clearance	Shaft End-play	Thrust on No.	Journal Diameter	Oil Clearance	Side Clearance
1992	T	6-191 (3.1L)	2.6472–2.6482	⑤	0.0024–0.0083	3	1.9983–1.9994	0.0014–0.0037	0.0140–0.0290
	E	8-305 (5.0L)	①	②	0.0020–0.0060	5	2.0986–2.0998	0.0018–0.0039	0.0080–0.0140
	F	8-305 (5.0L)	①	②	0.0020–0.0060	5	2.0986–2.0998	0.0018–0.0039	0.0080–0.0140
	8	8-350 (5.7L)	①	②	0.0020–0.0060	5	2.0986–2.0998	0.0018–0.0039	0.0080–0.0140

① No. 1—2.4484–2.4493
No. 2, 3, 4—2.4481–2.4490
No. 5—2.4479–2.4488
② No. 1—0.0008–0.0020
No. 2, 3, 4—0.0011–0.0023
No. 5—0.0017–0.0032
③ Main Thrust Bearing—0.0021–0.0033
All other main bearings—0.0016–0.0032
④ Main Thrust Bearing—0.0016–0.0027
All other main bearings—0.0012–0.0027
⑤ Main Thrust Bearing—0.0016–0.0030
All other main bearings—0.0012–0.0030
⑥ No. 1, 2, 4—2.4937–2.4946
No. 3—2.4931–2.4941

PISTON AND RING SPECIFICATIONS

Year	VIN	No. Cylinders cu. in. (Liters)	Piston Clearance	Ring Gap			Ring Side Clearance		
				Top Compression	Bottom Compression	Oil Control	Top Compression	Bottom Compression	Oil Control
1982	2	4-151 (2.5L)	0.0025–0.0033	0.010–0.022	0.010–0.027	0.015–0.055	0.0015–0.0030	0.0015–0.0030	0.0150–0.0550
	1	6-173 (2.8L)	0.0007–0.0017	0.010–0.020	0.010–0.020	0.020–0.055	0.0012–0.0028	0.0016–0.0037	0.0078 Max.
	H	8-305 (5.0L)	0.0007–0.0017	0.010–0.020	0.010–0.025	0.015–0.055	0.0012–0.0032	0.0012–0.0032	0.0020–0.0070
	7	8-305 (5.0L)	0.0007–0.0017	0.010–0.020	0.010–0.025	0.015–0.055	0.0012–0.0032	0.0012–0.0032	0.0020–0.0070
1983	2	4-151 (2.5L)	0.0025–0.0033	0.010–0.022	0.010–0.027	0.015–0.055	0.0015–0.0030	0.0015–0.0030	0.0150–0.0550
	1	6-173 (2.8L)	0.0007–0.0017	0.010–0.020	0.010–0.020	0.020–0.055	0.0012–0.0028	0.0016–0.0037	0.0078 Max.
	H	8-305 (5.0L)	0.0007–0.0017	0.010–0.020	0.010–0.025	0.015–0.055	0.0012–0.0032	0.0012–0.0032	0.0020–0.0070
	7	8-305 (5.0L)	0.0007–0.0017	0.010–0.020	0.010–0.025	0.015–0.055	0.0012–0.0032	0.0012–0.0032	0.0020–0.0070
1984	2	4-151 (2.5L)	0.0025–0.0033	0.010–0.022	0.010–0.027	0.015–0.055	0.0015–0.0030	0.0015–0.0030	0.0150–0.0550
	1	6-173 (2.8L)	0.0007–0.0017	0.010–0.020	0.010–0.020	0.020–0.055	0.0012–0.0028	0.0016–0.0037	0.0078 Max.
	H	8-305 (5.0L)	0.0007–0.0017	0.010–0.020	0.010–0.025	0.015–0.055	0.0012–0.0032	0.0012–0.0032	0.0020–0.0070
	G	8-305 (5.0L)	0.0007–0.0017	0.010–0.020	0.010–0.025	0.015–0.055	0.0012–0.0032	0.0012–0.0032	0.0020–0.0070

PISTON AND RING SPECIFICATIONS

| Year | VIN | No. Cylinders cu. in. (Liters) | Piston Clearance | Ring Gap | | | Ring Side Clearance | | |
				Top Compression	Bottom Compression	Oil Control	Top Compression	Bottom Compression	Oil Control
1985	2	4-151 (2.5L)	0.0014–0.0022	0.010–0.020	0.010–0.020	0.020–0.060	0.0020–0.0030	0.0010–0.0030	0.0150–0.0550
	S	6-173 (2.8L)	0.0007–0.0017	0.010–0.020	0.010–0.020	0.020–0.055	0.0012–0.0028	0.0016–0.0037	0.0078 Max.
	H	8-305 (5.0L)	0.0007–0.0017	0.010–0.020	0.010–0.025	0.015–0.055	0.0012–0.0032	0.0012–0.0032	0.0020–0.0070
	G	8-305 (5.0L)	0.0007–0.0017	0.010–0.020	0.010–0.025	0.015–0.055	0.0012–0.0032	0.0012–0.0032	0.0020–0.0070
	F	8-305 (5.0L)	0.0007–0.0017	0.010–0.020	0.010–0.025	0.015–0.055	0.0012–0.0032	0.0012–0.0032	0.0020–0.0070
1986	2	4-151 (2.5L)	0.0014–0.0022	0.010–0.020	0.010–0.020	0.020–0.060	0.0020–0.0030	0.0010–0.0030	0.0150–0.0550
	S	6-173 (2.8L)	0.0007–0.0017	0.010–0.020	0.010–0.020	0.020–0.055	0.0012–0.0028	0.0016–0.0037	0.0078 Max.
	H	8-305 (5.0L)	0.0007–0.0017	0.010–0.020	0.010–0.025	0.015–0.055	0.0012–0.0032	0.0012–0.0032	0.0020–0.0070
	G	8-305 (5.0L)	0.0007–0.0017	0.010–0.020	0.010–0.025	0.015–0.055	0.0012–0.0032	0.0012–0.0032	0.0020–0.0070
	F	8-305 (5.0L)	0.0007–0.0017	0.010–0.020	0.010–0.025	0.015–0.055	0.0012–0.0032	0.0012–0.0032	0.0020–0.0070
	8	8-305 (5.0L)	0.0025–0.0035	0.010–0.020	0.010–0.025	0.015–0.055	0.0012–0.0032	0.0012–0.0032	0.0020–0.0070
1987	S	6-173 (2.8L)	0.0007–0.0017	0.010–0.020	0.010–0.020	0.020–0.055	0.0012–0.0028	0.0016–0.0037	0.0078 Max.
	H	8-305 (5.0L)	0.0007–0.0017	0.010–0.020	0.010–0.025	0.015–0.055	0.0012–0.0032	0.0012–0.0032	0.0020–0.0070
	F	8-305 (5.0L)	0.0007–0.0017	0.010–0.020	0.010–0.025	0.015–0.055	0.0012–0.0032	0.0012–0.0032	0.0020–0.0070
	8	8-305 (5.0L)	0.0007–0.0017	0.010–0.020	0.010–0.025	0.015–0.055	0.0012–0.0032	0.0012–0.0032	0.0020–0.0070
1988	S	6-173 (2.8L)	0.0007–0.0017	0.010–0.020	0.010–0.020	0.020–0.055	0.0012–0.0028	0.0016–0.0037	0.0078 Max.
	E	8-305 (5.0L)	0.0007–0.0017	0.010–0.020	0.010–0.025	0.015–0.055	0.0012–0.0032	0.0012–0.0032	0.0020–0.0070
	F	8-305 (5.0L)	0.0007–0.0017	0.010–0.020	0.010–0.025	0.015–0.055	0.0012–0.0032	0.0012–0.0032	0.0020–0.0070
	8	8-350 (5.7L)	0.0007–0.0017	0.010–0.020	0.010–0.025	0.015–0.055	0.0012–0.0032	0.0012–0.0032	0.0020–0.0070
1989	S	6-173 (2.8L)	0.0007–0.0017	0.010–0.020	0.010–0.020	0.020–0.055	0.0012–0.0028	0.0016–0.0037	0.0078 Max.
	E	8-305 (5.0L)	0.0007–0.0017	0.010–0.020	0.010–0.025	0.015–0.055	0.0012–0.0032	0.0012–0.0032	0.0020–0.0070
	F	8-305 (5.0L)	0.0007–0.0017	0.010–0.020	0.010–0.025	0.015–0.055	0.0012–0.0032	0.0012–0.0032	0.0020–0.0070
	8	8-350 (5.7L)	0.0007–0.0017	0.010–0.020	0.010–0.025	0.015–0.055	0.0012–0.0032	0.0012–0.0032	0.0020–0.0070
1990	T	6-191 (3.1L)	0.0012–0.0029	0.010–0.020	0.010–0.020	0.010–0.030	0.0020–0.0035	0.0020–0.0035	0.0080 Max.
	E	8-305 (5.0L)	0.0007–0.0021	0.010–0.020	0.010–0.025	0.015–0.055	0.0012–0.0032	0.0012–0.0032	0.0020–0.0070
	F	8-305 (5.0L)	0.0007–0.0021	0.010–0.020	0.010–0.025	0.015–0.055	0.0012–0.0032	0.0012–0.0032	0.0020–0.0070
	8	8-350 (5.7L)	0.0007–0.0021	0.010–0.020	0.010–0.025	0.015–0.055	0.0012–0.0032	0.0012–0.0032	0.0020–0.0070

PISTON AND RING SPECIFICATIONS (cont.)

Year	VIN	No. Cylinders cu. in. (Liters)	Piston Clearance	Ring Gap			Ring Side Clearance		
				Top Compression	Bottom Compression	Oil Control	Top Compression	Bottom Compression	Oil Control
1991	T	6-191 (3.1L)	0.0012–0.0029	0.010–0.020	0.010–0.028	0.010–0.030	0.0020–0.0035	0.0020–0.0035	0.0071 Max.
	E	8-305 (5.0L)	0.0007–0.0021	0.010–0.020	0.010–0.025	0.015–0.055	0.0012–0.0032	0.0012–0.0032	0.0020–0.0070
	F	8-305 (5.0L)	0.0007–0.0021	0.010–0.020	0.010–0.025	0.015–0.055	0.0012–0.0032	0.0012–0.0032	0.0020–0.0070
	8	8-350 (5.7L)	0.0007–0.0021	0.010–0.020	0.018–0.026	0.010–0.030	0.0012–0.0032	0.0012–0.0032	0.0020–0.0070
1992	T	6-191 (3.1L)	0.0007–0.0017	0.010–0.020	0.010–0.020	0.020–0.055	0.0012–0.0028	0.0016–0.0037	0.0071 Max.
	E	8-305 (5.0L)	0.0007–0.0021	0.010–0.020	0.010–0.025	0.015–0.055	0.0012–0.0032	0.0012–0.0032	0.0020–0.0070
	F	8-305 (5.0L)	0.0007–0.0021	0.010–0.020	0.010–0.025	0.015–0.055	0.0012–0.0032	0.0012–0.0032	0.0020–0.0070
	8	8-350 (5.7L)	0.0007–0.0021	0.010–0.020	0.018–0.026	0.010–0.030	0.0012–0.0032	0.0012–0.0032	0.0020–0.0070

TORQUE SPECIFICATIONS
All readings in ft. lbs.

Year	VIN	No. Cylinders cu. in. (Liters)	Cylinder Head	Main Bearing	Rod Bearing	Crankshaft Damper	Flywheel	Manifold		Spark Plugs
								Intake	Exhaust	
1982	2	4-151 (2.5L)	85	70	32	160	44	29	44	12
	1	6-173 (2.8L)	70	68	37	75	50	23	25	12
	H	8-305 (5.0L)	65	70	45	60	60	30	20	22
	7	8-305 (5.0L)	65	70	45	60	60	30	20	22
1983	2	4-151 (2.5L)	85	70	32	160	44	29	44	12
	1	6-173 (2.8L)	70	68	37	75	50	23	25	12
	H	8-305 (5.0L)	65	70	45	60	60	30	20	22
	7	8-305 (5.0L)	65	70	45	60	60	30	20	22
1984	2	4-151 (2.5L)	85	70	32	160	44	29	44	12
	1	6-173 (2.8L)	70	68	37	75	50	23	25	12
	H	8-305 (5.0L)	65	70	45	60	60	30	20	22
	G	8-305 (5.0L)	65	70	45	60	60	30	20	22
1985	2	4-151 (2.5L)	92	70	32	200	44	④	44	12
	S	6-173 (2.8L)	77	73	40	71	50	19	25	12
	H	8-305 (5.0L)	68	①	45	60	60	35	②	22
	G	8-305 (5.0L)	68	①	45	60	60	35	②	22
	F	8-305 (5.0L)	68	①	45	60	60	35	②	22
1986	2	4-151 (2.5L)	92	70	32	200	44	④	44	12
	S	6-173 (2.8L)	77	73	40	71	50	19	25	12
	H	8-305 (5.0L)	68	①	45	60	75	35	②	22
	G	8-305 (5.0L)	68	①	45	60	75	35	②	22
	F	8-305 (5.0L)	68	①	45	60	75	35	②	22
	8	8-350 (5.7L)	68	①	45	60	75	35	②	22
1987	S	6-173 (2.8L)	77	73	40	71	50	19	25	12
	H	8-305 (5.0L)	68	①	45	60	75	35	②	22
	F	8-305 (5.0L)	68	①	45	60	75	35	②	22
	8	8-350 (5.7L)	68	①	45	60	75	35	②	22

TORQUE SPECIFICATIONS

All readings in ft. lbs.

Year	VIN	No. Cylinders cu. in. (Liters)	Cylinder Head	Main Bearing	Rod Bearing	Crankshaft Damper	Flywheel	Manifold Intake	Manifold Exhaust	Spark Plugs
1988	S	6-173 (2.8L)	③	73	40	71	50	19	25	12
	E	8-305 (5.0L)	68	①	45	60	75	35	②	22
	F	8-305 (5.0L)	68	①	45	60	75	35	②	22
	8	8-350 (5.7L)	68	①	45	60	75	35	②	22
1989	S	6-173 (2.8L)	③	73	40	75	52	19	25	12
	E	8-305 (5.0L)	68	77	44	70	75	35	②	22
	F	8-305 (5.0L)	68	77	44	70	75	35	②	22
	8	8-350 (5.7L)	68	77	44	70	75	35	②	22
1990	T	6-191 (3.1L)	③	73	40	75	52	19	25	12
	E	8-305 (5.0L)	68	77	44	70	75	35	②	22
	F	8-305 (5.0L)	68	77	44	70	75	35	②	22
	8	8-350 (5.7L)	68	77	44	70	75	35	②	22
1991	T	6-191 (3.1L)	③	73	40	70	52	19	25	12
	E	8-305 (5.0L)	68	77	44	70	75	35	②	22
	F	8-305 (5.0L)	68	77	44	70	75	35	②	22
	8	8-350 (5.7L)	68	77	44	70	75	35	②	22
1992	T	6-191 (3.1L)	③	73	40	70	52	19	25	12
	E	8-305 (5.0L)	68	77	44	70	75	35	②	22
	F	8-305 (5.0L)	68	77	44	70	75	35	②	22
	8	8-350 (5.7L)	68	77	44	70	75	35	②	22

① Inner 70–85 ft. lbs.
　Outer 60–75 ft. lbs.
② Inner 20–32 ft. lbs.
　Outer 14–26 ft. lbs.
③ 40 ft. lbs. + 90 degree additional turn
④ See text procedure.

chamber can result from this problem. There may be evidence of water droplets on the engine dipstick when a head gasket has blown.

Engine

REMOVAL AND INSTALLATION

In the process of removing the engine you will come across a number of steps which call for the removal of a separate component or system, i.e. Disconnect the exhaust system or Remove the radiator. In all of these instances, a detailed removal procedure can be found elsewhere in this section.

It is virtually impossible to list each individual wire and hose which must be disconnected, simply because so many different model and engine combinations have been manufactured. Careful observation and common sense are the best possible additions to any repair procedure. Be absolutely sure to tag any wire or hose before disconnecting it, so that it may be reconnected properly during installation.

CAUTION: *The EPA warns that prolonged contact with used engine oil may cause a number of skin disorders, including cancer! You should make every effort to minimize your exposure to used engine oil. Protective gloves should be worn when changing the oil. Wash your hands and any other exposed skin areas as soon as possible after exposure to used engine oil. Soap and water, or waterless hand cleaner should be used.*

When draining the coolant, keep in mind that cats and dogs are attracted by the ethylene glycol antifreeze, and are quite likely to drink any that is left in an uncovered container or in puddles on the ground. This will prove fatal in sufficient quantity. Always drain the coolant into a sealable container. Coolant should be reused unless it is contaminated or several years old.

2.5L ENGINE

1. Disconnect the negative battery cable.
2. Remove the air cleaner duct.

| 1 | P/S BRACE | 3 | ENGINE MOUNT (6Q-P2) | 5 | TRANS ASM. |
| 2 | STARTER MOTOR BRACKET | 4 | CROSSMEMBER (2B) | 6 | ENGINE MOUNT |

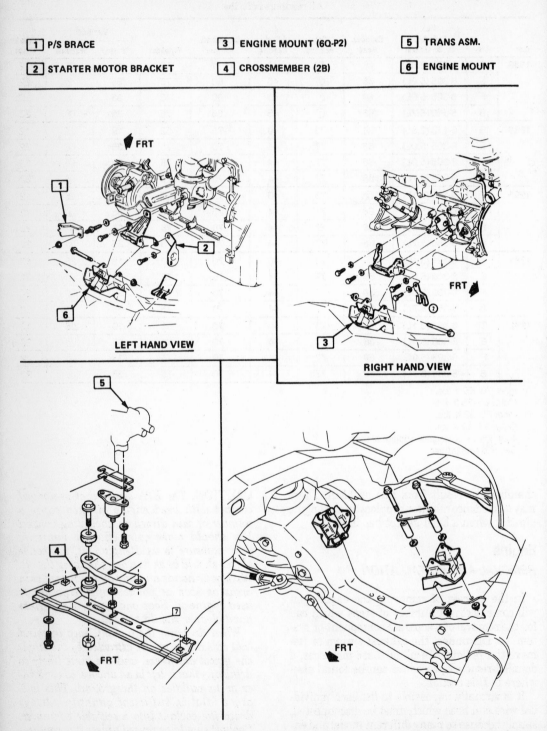

LEFT HAND VIEW

RIGHT HAND VIEW

Engine mount through bolt removal is necessary to raise or remove the engine from the vehicle—2.5L engine

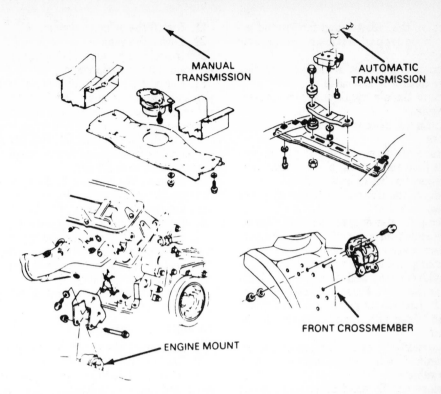

Transmission and engine mounts—2.8L and 3.1L engine. Only engine-to-mount through bolt removal is necessary for engine removal

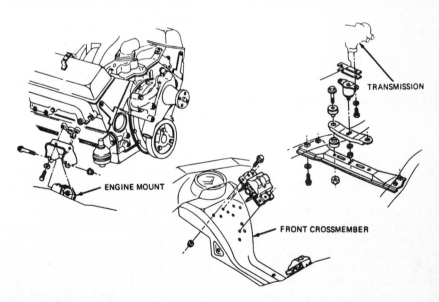

Transmission and engine mounts—5.0L and 5.7L engine. Only engine-to-mount through bolt removal is necessary for engine removal

3. Mark the hood location on the hood supports and remove the hood.

4. Remove the water pump drive belt.

5. Drain the radiator and remove the radia-tor hoses. Disconnect the heater hoses and the transmission cooler lines.

6. Remove the upper half of the radiator shroud, if equipped with a manual transmis-

sion. Remove the radiator and fan shroud assembly, if equipped with an automatic transmission.

7. Disconnect the throttle linkage, including the cruise control detent cable.

8. Remove the air conditioning compressor and lay aside.

NOTE: *Do not disconnect the air conditioning lines.*

9. Disconnect the power steering pump and drain the fluid into a suitable container. Remove the vacuum brake booster line.

10. Remove the distributor cap and spark plug wires.

11. Disconnect the engine electrical connection at the bulkhead connection and disconnect any necessary vacuum hoses.

12. Working inside the vehicle, remove the right-hand hush panel and disconnect the ECM harness at the ECM. Raise and safely support the vehicle. Remove the right fenderwell splash shield and feed the harness through the fenderwell.

13. Disconnect the exhaust pipes at the exhaust manifolds and remove exhaust system from the vehicle.

14. Remove the flywheel cover and remove the converter bolts, if equipped with automatic transmission.

15. Disconnect the transmission and starter wire connections.

16. Remove the bellhousing and the motor mount through bolts.

17. Disconnect the clutch fork return spring, if equipped with a manual transmission. Lower the vehicle.

18. Relieve the fuel system pressure. Disconnect the fuel lines.

19. Support the transmission with a suitable jack. Attach an engine lifting device.

20. Remove the engine assembly.

To install:

21. Position the engine assembly in the vehicle.

22. Attach the motor mount to engine brackets and lower the engine in place. Remove the engine lifting device and the transmission jack.

23. Raise and support the vehicle safely.

24. Install the motor mount through bolts and tighten the nuts to specification. Install the bellhousing bolts and tighten to 35 ft. lbs. (47 Nm).

25. On vehicles with automatic transmission, install the converter to flywheel attaching bolts to 46 ft. lbs. (63 Nm).

26. Install the flywheel splash shield and tighten to 89 inch lbs. (10 Nm). Install the clutch return spring, if equipped with manual transmission.

27. Connect the starter wires and the fuel lines.

28. Install the exhaust system.

29. Lower the vehicle.

30. Install the power steering pump and the air conditioning compressor.

31. Connect the bulkhead harness connector, wires and hoses. Reroute the ECM harness in its' original location. Install the hush panel and fenderwell splash panel.

32. Install the radiator, fan and fan shroud. Connect the radiator and heater hoses and the transmission cooler lines.

33. Connect the vacuum brake booster line, the throttle linkage and cruise control cable. Install the distributor cap.

34. Fill the cooling system with the proper type and amount of coolant and the crankcase with the proper type of oil to the correct level.

35. Install the water pump drive belt, the air cleaner duct and the hood.

36. Connect the negative battery cable, start the engine and check for leaks.

2.8L AND 3.1L ENGINES

1. Disconnect the negative battery cable.

2. Remove the air cleaner duct.

3. Mark the hood location on the hood supports and remove the hood.

4. Remove the water pump drive belt.

5. Drain the radiator and remove the radiator hoses. Disconnect the heater hoses and the transmission cooler lines.

6. Remove the fan shroud, fan and radiator.

7. Disconnect the throttle linkage, including the cruise control detent cable.

8. Remove the air conditioning compressor and lay aside. Remove the power steering pump and lay aside.

NOTE: *Do not disconnect the air conditioning or power steering lines.*

9. Remove the vacuum brake booster line.

10. Remove the distributor cap and spark plug wires.

11. Disconnect the necessary electrical connections and hoses.

12. Raise and safely support the vehicle.

13. Disconnect the exhaust pipes at the exhaust manifolds.

14. Remove the flywheel cover and remove the converter bolts.

15. Disconnect the starter wire connections.

16. Remove the bellhousing and the motor mount through bolts.

17. Lower the vehicle.

18. Relieve the fuel system pressure. Disconnect the fuel lines.

19. Support the transmission with a suitable jack. Attach an engine lifting device.

20. Remove the engine assembly.

To install:

21. Position the engine assembly in the vehicle.

22. Attach the motor mount to engine brackets and lower the engine in place. Remove the engine lifting device and the transmission jack.

23. Raise and support the vehicle safely.

24. Install the motor mount through bolts and tighten the nuts to 50 ft. lbs. (68 Nm). Install the bellhousing bolts and tighten to 35 ft. lbs. (47 Nm).

25. On vehicles with automatic transmission, install the converter to flywheel attaching bolts to 46 ft. lbs. (63 Nm).

26. Install the flywheel splash shield and tighten to 89 inch lbs. (10 Nm).

27. Connect the starter wires and the fuel lines.

28. Install the exhaust pipe on the exhaust manifold.

29. Lower the vehicle.

30. Install the power steering pump and the air conditioning compressor.

31. Connect the necessary wires and hoses.

32. Install the radiator, fan and fan shroud. Connect the radiator and heater hoses and the transmission cooler lines.

33. Connect the vacuum brake booster line, the throttle linkage and cruise control cable. Install the distributor cap.

34. Fill the cooling system with the proper type and amount of coolant and the crankcase with the proper type of oil to the correct level.

35. Install the water pump drive belt, the air cleaner duct and the hood.

36. Connect the negative battery cable, start the engine and check for leaks.

5.0L AND 5.7L ENGINES

1. Disconnect the negative battery cable.

2. Mark the location of the hood on the hood hinges and remove the hood.

3. Remove the air cleaner.

4. Drain the cooling system.

5. Remove the radiator hoses.

6. Disconnect the transmission cooler lines, the electrical connectors and retaining clips at the fan and remove the fan and shroud.

7. Remove the radiator.

8. Remove the accessory drive belt.

9. Disconnect the throttle cable.

10. Remove the plenum extension screws and the plenum extension, if equipped.

11. Disconnect the spark plug wires at the distributor and remove the distributor.

12. Disconnect the necessary vacuum hoses and wiring.

13. Disconnect the power steering and air conditioning compressors from their respective brackets and lay them aside.

14. Properly relieve the fuel system pressure. Disconnect the fuel lines.

15. Disconnect the negative battery cable at the engine block.

16. Raise and safely support the vehicle.

17. Remove the exhaust pipes at the exhaust manifolds.

18. Remove the flywheel cover and remove the converter to flywheel bolts.

19. Disconnect the starter wires.

20. Remove the bellhousing bolts and the motor mount through bolts.

21. Lower the vehicle.

22. Support the transmission with a suitable jack.

23. Remove the AIR/converter bracket and ground wires from the rear of the cylinder head.

24. Attach a suitable lifting device and remove the engine assembly.

To install:

25. Position the engine assembly in the vehicle.

26. Attach the motor mount to engine brackets and lower the engine into place.

27. Remove the engine lifting device and the transmission jack.

28. Raise and safely support the vehicle.

29. Install the motor mount through bolts and tighten to 50 ft. lbs. (68 (Nm).

30. Install the bellhousing bolts and tighten to 35 ft. lbs. (47 Nm).

31. On vehicles with automatic transmission, install the converter to flywheel bolts. Tighten the bolts to 46 ft. lbs. (63 Nm). Install the flywheel cover.

32. Connect the starter wires and the fuel lines.

33. Connect the exhaust pipe at the exhaust manifold.

34. Lower the vehicle.

35. Connect the necessary wires and hoses.

36. Install the power steering pump and air conditioning compressor in their respective brackets.

37. Install the radiator, fan and fan shroud, radiator hoses and heater hoses.

38. Connect the transmission cooler lines and cooling fan electrical connectors.

39. Install the distributor.

40. Install the plenum extension, if equipped.

41. Fill the cooling system with the proper type and quantity of coolant and the crankcase with the proper type of oil to the correct level.

42. Install the air cleaner and the hood.

43. Connect the negative battery cable, start the engine, check for leaks and check timing.

Rocker Arm Cover

REMOVAL AND INSTALLATION

2.5L Engine

1. Disconnect the negative battery cable.

2. Remove the air cleaner assembly.

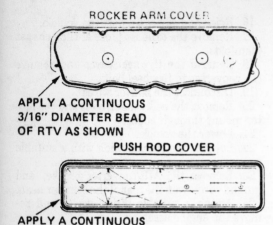

ROCKER ARM COVER

APPLY A CONTINUOUS
3/16" DIAMETER BEAD
OF RTV AS SHOWN

PUSH ROD COVER

APPLY A CONTINUOUS
3/16" DIAMETER BEAD
OF RTV AS SHOWN

Valve cover and pushrod cover RTV application—2.5L
engine

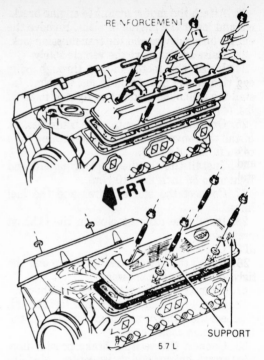

Valve cover removal—1982–86 5.0L and 5.7L engine

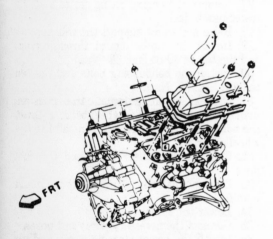

Valve cover removal—2.8L and 3.1L engine

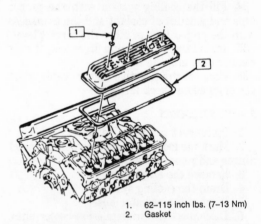

1. 62–115 inch lbs. (7–13 Nm)
2. Gasket

Valve cover removal—1987–92 5.0L and 5.7L engine

3. Disconnect the throttle cable at the throttle body.

4. Remove the PCV valve from the cover.

5. Remove the spark plug wires from the clips. Remove the clips from the valve cover.

6. Remove the EGR valve. Loosen the throttle body to gain clearance, as required.

7. Remove the valve cover retaining bolts and remove the cover. Tap on the valve cover with the palm of your hand or use a soft mallet to loosen.

8. To install, clean sealing surface on cylinder head and intake manifold of all old RTV or gasket. Make sure no oil or old gasket is present when applying new RTV or gasket.

9. Place a $\frac{3}{16}$ in. (5mm) bead of RTV sealant all around the rocker arm sealing surface or use a cork style gasket. (When going around the attaching bolt holes, always flow the RTV on the inboard side of the holes).

10. Install cover and torque bolts to 8 ft. lbs. (11 Nm) will RTV is still wet.

11. Finish installation by reversing removal procedure.

2.8L and 3.1L Engines

1. Disconnect the negative battery cable.

2. For left side valve cover removal proceed as follows:

  a. Remove the accessory drive belt.

  b. Remove the transmission dipstick, if required.

  c. Remove the air management hose and air conditioning bracket, if equipped.

d. Remove the intake plenum and throttle body assembly, if equipped with 3.1L engine.

e. Remove the valve cover reinforcements and nuts.

3. For right side valve cover removal proceed as follows:

a. Remove the EGR valve adapter with the EGR valve and shield from the exhaust manifold.

b. Remove the coil and coil mounting bracket from the cylinder head.

c. Disconnect the crankcase vent pipe.

d. Remove the intake plenum and throttle body assembly.

e. Remove the valve cover reinforcements and nuts.

4. Remove cover. If cover adheres to cylinder head, shear off by bumping end of rocker arm cover with palm of hand or rubber mallet. If cover still will not come loose, CAREFULLY pry until loose. DO NOT DISTORT SEALING FLANGE.

5. To install, clean sealing surface on cylinder head and intake manifold of all old RTV or gasket. Make sure no oil or old gasket is present when applying new RTV or gasket.

6. Place a ⅛ in. (3mm) bead of RTV sealant all around the rocker arm sealing surface or use a cork style gasket. (When going around the attaching bolt holes, always flow the RTV on the inboard side of the holes).

7. Install cover and torque bolts to 8 ft. lbs. (10 Nm) will RTV is still wet.

8. Finish installation by reversing removal procedure.

5.0L AND 5.7L ENGINES

1. Disconnect the negative battery cable.

2. Remove the air cleaner, if necessary.

3. To remove the right side valve cover, perform the following:

a. Pre-1988 vehicles: Disconnect the wire EGR solenoid transfer tube from the plenum. Remove the coil and mounting bracket from the cylinder head. Remove the plenum, runners and throttle body assembly. Remove the valve cover retainers and nuts. Remove the valve cover.

b. 1989–92 vehicles: Remove the EGR pipe assembly, if necessary. Disconnect the electrical connections and wiring harnesses as necessary. Disconnect the spark plug wires from the distributor. Remove the crankcase vent hoses and valves. Remove the coil and disconnect the heater hose from the throttle body on 1991–92 vehicles. Remove the AIR control valve, check valve, pipes and hoses. Remove the valve cover bolts and remove the cover.

4. To remove the left side valve cover, perform the following:

a. Pre-1988 vehicles: Remove the air management hose, if equipped. Remove the plenum and throttle body assembly. Remove the air conditioning bracket. Remove the valve cover reinforcements and nuts. Remove the valve cover.

b. 1989–92 vehicles: Disconnect the electrical connections and the wiring harnesses, as necessary. Remove the alternator and disconnect the crankcase hoses and the PCV valve. Remove the valve cover bolts and remove the valve cover.

5. If cover adheres to cylinder head, shear off by bumping end of rocker arm cover with palm of hand or rubber mallet. If cover still will not come loose, CAREFULLY pry until loose. DO NOT DISTORT SEALING FLANGE.

6. To install, clean sealing surface on cylinder head and intake manifold of all old RTV or gasket. Make sure no oil or old gasket is present when applying new RTV or gasket.

7. Place a ⅛ in. (3mm) bead of RTV sealant all around the rocker arm sealing surface or use a cork style gasket. (When going around the attaching bolt holes, always flow the RTV on the inboard side of the holes).

8. Install cover and torque bolts to 8 ft. lbs. (11 Nm) will RTV is still wet.

9. Finish installation by reversing removal procedure.

Pushrod Side Cover

REMOVAL AND INSTALLATION

2.5L Engine

1. Disconnect the negative battery cable.

2. Mark and remove the distributor assembly.

3. Remove the ignition coil and bracket.

4. Remove the side cover retaining nuts and remove the cover.

5. To install, clean the cover sealing surfaces of all RTV or gasket material.

6. Place a ³⁄₁₆ in. (5mm) bead of RTV sealant all around the rocker arm sealing surface or use a cork style gasket. (When going around the attaching bolt holes, always flow the RTV on the inboard side of the holes).

7. Install cover and torque bolts to 89 inch lbs. (10 Nm) will RTV is still wet.

8. Finish installation by reversing removal procedure.

Rocker Arms

REMOVAL AND INSTALLATION

Rocker arms are removed by removing the adjusting nut. Be sure to keep all the components in the exact order of removal so they may be installed in there original location; adjust the valve lash after replacing the rocker arms. Coat the replacement rocker arm and ball with engine oil before installation.

Rocker arms studs that have damaged threads or are loose in the cylinder heads may be replaced by reaming the bore and installing oversize studs. Oversizes available are 0.003 in. (0.076mm) and 0.013 in. (0.33mm). The bore may also be tapped and screw-in studs installed.

Several aftermarket companies produce complete rocker arm stud kits with installation tools.

NOTE: *2.5L engines use bolts instead of studs, 2.8L and 3.1L engines use threaded studs, the 5.0L and 5.7L engines use press fit studs.*

Thermostat

REMOVAL AND INSTALLATION

1. Drain the cooling system to below the thermostat level.

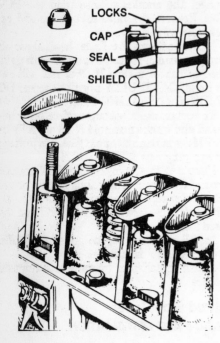

Rocker arm components

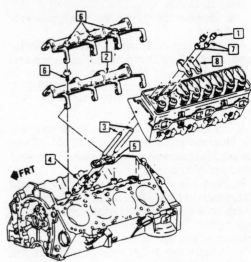

1. 6–14 N·m
   (55–125 IN. LB.)
2. Retainer
3. Push rod
4. Lifter
5. Restrictor
6. 13–19 N·m
   (10–14 ft. lbs.)
7. Ball
8. Rocker arm

Rocker arm and pushrod assembly—5.0L and 5.7L engines

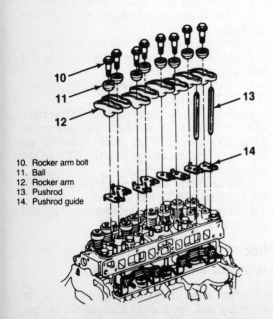

10. Rocker arm bolt
11. Ball
12. Rocker arm
13. Pushrod
14. Pushrod guide

Exploded view of the rocker arm assembly—2.5L engine

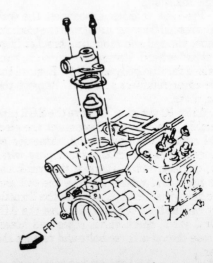

Thermostat servicing—3.1L engine

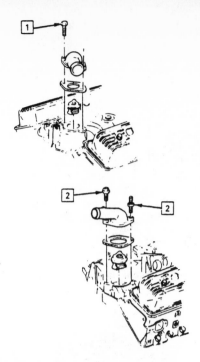

Thermostat servicing—5.0L and 5.7L engines

Coolant should be reused unless it is contaminated or several years old.

2. It is not necessary to remove the radiator hose from the thermostat housing.

3. Remove the two retaining bolts from the thermostat housing and remove the thermostat.

4. Use a new gasket when replacing the thermostat.

5. Fill and bleed the cooling system.

Intake Manifold

REMOVAL AND INSTALLATION

NOTE: *When servicing all vehicles, be absolutely sure to mark vacuum hoses and wiring so that these items may be properly reconnected during installation. Also, when disconnecting fitting lines (fuel lines, power brake vacuum lines, transmission and engine cooler lines, etc.), always use two flare nut (or line) wrenches. Hold the wrench on the large fitting with pressure on the wrench as if you were tightening the fitting (clockwise), THEN loosen and disconnect the smaller fitting from the larger fitting. If this is not done, damage to the line will result.*

CAUTION: *When draining the coolant, keep in mind that cats and dogs are attracted by the ethylene glycol antifreeze, and are quite likely to drink any that is left in an uncovered container or in puddles on the ground. This will prove fatal in sufficient quantity. Always drain the coolant into a sealable container.*

CAUTION: *When draining the coolant, keep in mind that cats and dogs are attracted by the ethylene glycol antifreeze, and are quite likely to drink any that is left in an uncovered container or in puddles on the ground. This will prove fatal in sufficient quantity. Always drain the coolant into a sealable container.*

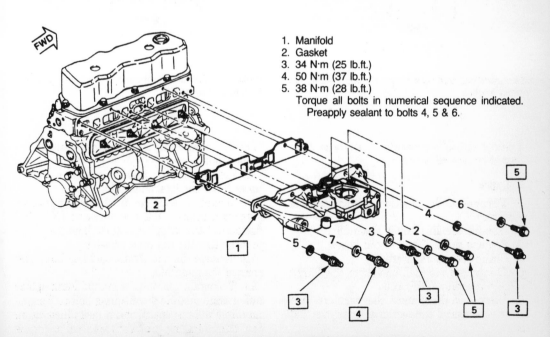

1. Manifold
2. Gasket
3. 34 N·m (25 lb.ft.)
4. 50 N·m (37 lb.ft.)
5. 38 N·m (28 lb.ft.)
   Torque all bolts in numerical sequence indicated.
   Preapply sealant to bolts 4, 5 & 6.

Intake bolt torque and sequence—1987–88 2.5L engine

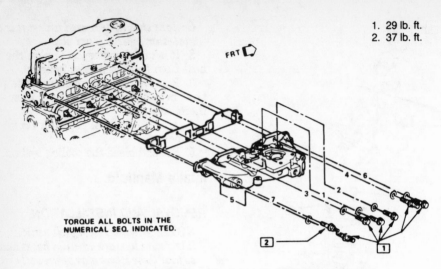

1. 29 lb. ft.
2. 37 lb. ft.

TORQUE ALL BOLTS IN THE
NUMERICAL SEQ. INDICATED.

Intake manifold bolt torque and sequence—1982–86 2.5L engine

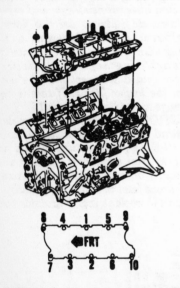

Intake manifold bolt tightening sequence—2.8L carbureted engine

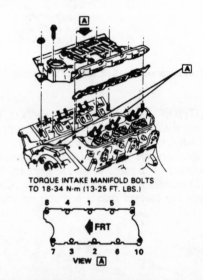

TORQUE INTAKE MANIFOLD BOLTS
TO 18-34 N·m (13-25 FT. LBS.)

Intake manifold bolt tightening sequence—2.8L and 3.1L engine with MPI

Coolant should be reused unless it is contaminated or several years old.

2.5L Engine

1. Disconnect the negative battery cable at the battery.
2. Remove the air cleaner assembly.
3. Remove the PCV valve and hose.
4. Drain the cooling system.
5. Disconnect the fuel lines from the Throttle Body Injection (TBI) unit.
6. Mark and disconnect the vacuum lines and the electrical connections from the TBI unit.
7. Disconnect the linkage from the TBI unit

(throttle, downshift, and/or cruise control, as applicable).
8. Disconnect the coolant inlet and outlet hoses from the intake manifold.
9. Remove the air conditioning compressor support brackets and the compressor. DO NOT disconnect the refrigerant lines from the compressor. Lay the compressor aside.
10. Remove the manifold attaching bolts and remove the manifold.
11. To install, position the manifold into place and install manifold attaching bolts. Torque manifold bolts to specification (see illustration for tightening sequence and torque specifications).

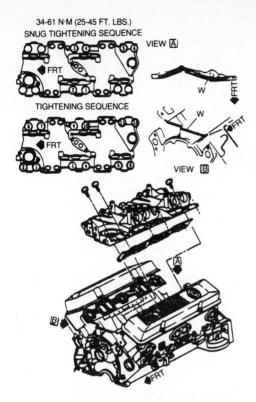

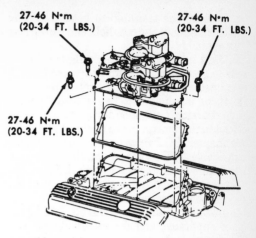

Cross-Fire Injection upper plenum and gasket

Intake manifold bolt tightening sequence—V8 engine with TPI

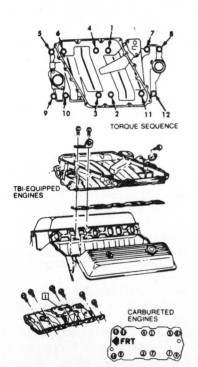

Intake manifold bolt tightening sequence of all V8 engines. Lower sequence is for all carbureted engines and upper sequence is for all TBI equipped engines

12. Install the air conditioning compressor and compressor support brackets, if so equipped.

13. Connect the coolant inlet and outlet hoses to the intake manifold.

14. Connect the linkage to the TBI unit (throttle, downshift, and/or cruise control, as applicable).

15. Connect the vacuum lines and the electrical connections to the TBI unit.

16. Connect the fuel lines to the Throttle Body Injection (TBI) unit.

17. Install the PCV valve and hose.

18. Install the air cleaner assembly.

19. Connect the negative battery cable at the battery.

20. Fill the cooling system.

2.8L and 5.0L Engines With Carburetor

1. Remove the air cleaner.
2. Drain the radiator.
3. Disconnect:
    a. Battery cables at the battery.
    b. Upper radiator and heater hoses at the manifold.
    c. Crankcase ventilation hoses as required.
    d. Fuel line at the carburetor.
    e. Accelerator linkage.
    f. Vacuum hose at the distributor, if equipped.
    g. Power brake hose at the carburetor base or manifold, if applicable.
    h. Temperature sending switch wires.
4. Remove the distributor cap and scribe the rotor position relative to the distributor body, and engine.
5. Remove the distributor.
6. If applicable, remove the alternator upper bracket. As required, remove the air cleaner bracket, and accelerator bellcrank.

7. Remove the manifold-to-head attaching bolts, then remove the manifold and carburetor as an assembly.

8. Mark and disconnect all emission related items (e.g.: wiring, vacuum hoses, etc.) which are connected to manifold mounted items.

9. If the manifold is to be replaced, transfer the carburetor (and mounting studs), water outlet and thermostat (use a new gasket) heater hose adapter, EGR valve (use new gasket) and, if applicable, TVS switch(s) and the choke coil.

10. Before installing the manifold, thoroughly clean the gasket and sealing surfaces of the cylinder heads and manifold.

11. Install the manifold end seals, folding the tabs if applicable, and the manifold/head gaskets, using a sealing compound around the water passages.

NOTE: *Make sure that the new manifold gaskets match the old ones EXACTLY.*

12. When installing the manifold, care should be taken not to dislocate the end seals. It is helpful to use a pilot in the distributor opening. Tighten the manifold bolts to 30 ft. lbs. (40 Nm) for 5.0L or 20–25 ft. lbs. (27–34 Nm) for 2.8L in the sequence illustrated.

13. Install the distributor with the rotor in its original location as indicated by the scribe line. If the engine has been disturbed, refer to the previous Distributor Removal and Installation procedure.

14. If applicable, install the alternator upper bracket and adjust the belt tension.

15. Connect all disconnected components at their original locations.

16. Fill the cooling system, start the engine, check for leaks and adjust the ignition timing and carburetor idle speed and mixture.

2.8L and 5.7L Engine With MPI

1. Disconnect the negative battery cable. Remove the air cleaner assembly. Drain the coolant system.

2. Remove the plenum, fuel rail and runners.

3. Remove the spark plug wires from the spark plugs and disconnect the wires at the coil.

4. Remove the distributor cap along with the spark plug wires, mark the position of the distributor, remove the distributor hold down bolt and lift the distributor out of the vehicle.

5. Disconnect the emission canister hoses. Remove the pipe bracket on the front left valve cover and remove the left valve cover.

6. Remove the right valve cover and the upper radiator hose. Disconnect the coolant switches.

7. Remove the manifold bolts along with the intake manifold. Discard the old gaskets and clean the sealing from the manifold and engine.

8. To install, apply a $^3/_{16}$ in. (5mm) bead of

RTV sealant on the front and rear ridge of the cylinder case.

9. Install the new gaskets on the cylinder heads. Hold the gaskets in place by extending the RTV bead up onto the gasket ends. Certain GM intake gaskets will have to be cut to be install behind the pushrods. Cut these gaskets as required and only where necessary.

10. Install the intake manifold along with the intake manifold bolts. Torque bolts in sequence to 13–25 ft. lbs. (18–34 Nm) on 2.8L engine and 25–45 ft. lbs. (34–61 Nm) on 5.7L engine.

11. Connect the coolant switches.

12. Install the upper radiator hose.

13. Install the right and left valve covers.

14. Install the pipe bracket on the front left valve cover and connect the emission canister hoses.

15. Install the distributor to the match marks, hold down bolt, spark plug wires and distributor cap.

16. Install the spark plug wires to the spark plugs and connect the wires at the coil.

17. Install the plenum, fuel rail and runner.

18. Install the air cleaner. Connect the negative battery cable. Fill the coolant system.

TBI Equipped 5.0L Engine

1. Disconnect the negative battery cable at the battery.

2. Remove the air cleaner assembly.

3. Drain the cooling system.

4. Disconnect the fuel inlet line at the front Throttle Body Injection (TBI) unit.

5. Remove the exhaust gas recirculation (EGR) solenoid.

6. Disconnect the wiring from the idle air motors, injectors, and the throttle position sensor (TPS).

7. Disconnect the fuel return line at the rear TBI unit.

8. Remove the power brake booster line.

9. Disconnect the accelerator and cruise control cables, unbolt the cable bracket from the manifold and tie the cable and bracket assembly out of the way.

10. Disconnect the air injection hose at the check valve and the air control valve.

11. Unbolt the air injection pump and move it out of the way.

12. Disconnect the positive crankcase ventilation valve hose at the manifold and move the hose aside.

13. Mark and disconnect any vacuum hoses which will interfere with removal of the manifold.

14. If you plan on removing the TBI units from the upper manifold plate, remove the fuel balance tube (connecting the units) at this time.

15. Remove the bolts which attach the upper

manifold plate (or TBI plate) to the intake manifold. Lift the TBI and plate assembly off of the intake manifold.

16. Remove the distributor as previously outlined.

17. Disconnect the upper radiator hose from the thermostat housing.

18. Disconnect the heater hose from the intake manifold.

19. Remove the intake manifold-to-cylinder head bolts and lift the intake manifold assembly off of the engine.

20. To install, position the intake manifold assembly onto the engine and install the intake manifold-to-cylinder head bolts. Torque bolt in sequence to 25–45 ft. lbs. (34–61 Nm).

21. Connect the heater hose to the intake manifold.

22. Connect the upper radiator hose to the thermostat housing.

23. Install the distributor.

24. Position the TBI and plate assembly on the intake manifold. Install the bolts which attach the upper manifold plate (or TBI plate) to the intake manifold.

25. If the TBI units on CFI engines were removed, install the fuel balance tube (connecting the units).

26. Connect vacuum hoses which were disconnected for removal of the manifold.

27. Connect the positive crankcase ventilation valve hose.

28. Install the air injection pump.

29. Connect the air injection hose at the check valve and the air control valve.

30. Install the cable bracket to the manifold and connect the accelerator and cruise control cables.

31. Install the power brake booster line.

32. Connect the fuel return line at the TBI unit.

33. Connect the wiring to the idle air motors, injectors, and the throttle position sensor (TPS).

34. Install the exhaust gas recirculation (EGR) solenoid.

35. Connect the fuel inlet line to the TBI unit.

36. Install the air cleaner assembly.

37. Connect the negative battery cable at the battery.

38. Fill the cooling system.

39. Start the engine and check for leaks.

Exhaust Manifold

REMOVAL AND INSTALLATION

2.5L Engine

1. Disconnect the negative battery cable at the battery.

2. Remove the air cleaner assembly, being

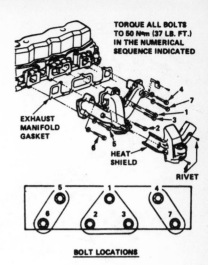

Exhaust manifold bolt torque sequence—2.5L engine

sure to mark any disconnected hoses for proper reinstallation.

3. Remove the E.F.I. preheat tube.

4. Remove the oxygen sensor and disconnect the exhaust pipe from the exhaust manifold.

5. Remove the engine oil level dipstick and tube.

6. Remove the exhaust manifold attaching bolts and remove the manifold.

7. To install, position the exhaust manifold onto the engine and torque the bolts, follow the sequence in the accompanying diagram and tighten each bolt to 44 ft. lbs.

8. Install the engine oil level dipstick tube and dipstick.

9. Connect the exhaust pipe to the exhaust manifold and install the oxygen sensor.

10. Install the E.F.I. preheat tube.

11. Install the air cleaner assembly and connecting hoses.

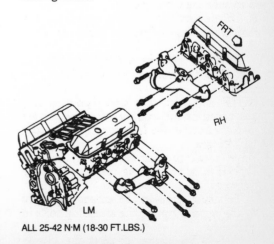

ALL 25-42 N·M (18-30 FT.LBS.)

Exhaust manifold bolt torque sequnce—3.1L engine

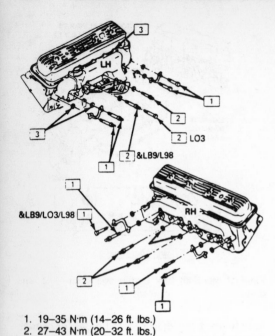

1. 19–35 N·m (14–26 ft. lbs.)
2. 27–43 N·m (20–32 ft. lbs.)
3. Heat stove (LO3)

Exhaust manifold bolt torque sequence—V8 engines

12. Connect the negative battery cable at the battery.

2.8L, 5.0L and 5.7L Engines

1. If equipped with AIR, remove the air injector manifold assembly. The ¼ in. pipe threads in the manifold are straight threads. Do not use a ¼ in. tapered pipe tap to clean the threads.
2. Disconnect the battery.
3. If applicable, remove the air cleaner preheater shroud.
4. Remove the spark plug wire heat shields.
5. On the left exhaust manifold, disconnect and remove the alternator.
6. Disconnect the exhaust pipe from the manifold and hang it from the frame out of the way.
7. Bend the locktabs and remove the end bolts, then the center bolts. Remove the manifold.
NOTE: *A ⁹⁄₁₆ in. thin wall 6-point socket, sharpened at the leading edge and tapped onto the head of the bolt, simplifies bending the locktabs.*
When installing a new manifold on the right side you must transfer the heat stove from the old manifold to the new one.
8. To install, position the exhaust manifold onto the engine. Torque the attaching bolts in sequence to:
  • 1982–84 V6 engine: 22–28 ft. lbs. (30–38 Nm)

  • 1985–92 V6 engine: 19–31 ft. lbs. (25–42 Nm)
  • 1982–84 V8 engine: 20 ft. lbs. (15 Nm)
  • 1985–92 V8 engine (4 outer bolts): 14–26 ft. lbs. (19–35 Nm)
  • 1985–92 V8 engine (2 inner bolts): 20–32 ft. lbs. (27–43 Nm)
9. Bend the locktabs over bolts.
10. Connect the exhaust pipe to the manifold.
11. Install the alternator and connect wiring.
12. Install the spark plug wire heat shields.
13. If equipped, install the air cleaner preheater shroud.
14. If equipped with AIR, install the air injector manifold assembly.
15. Connect the battery.

Radiator

REMOVAL AND INSTALLATION

1. Drain the cooling system.
CAUTION: *When draining the coolant, keep in mind that cats and dogs are attracted by the ethylene glycol antifreeze, and are quite likely to drink any that is left in an uncovered container or in puddles on the ground. This will prove fatal in sufficient quantity. Always drain the coolant into a sealable container. Coolant should be reused unless it is contaminated or several years old.*
2. Remove the fan.
NOTE: *On fan clutch equipped cars, store clutch in upright position to prevent seal leakage.*
3. Disconnect upper and lower radiator hoses.
4. On vehicles equipped with automatic transmission, disconnect and plug transmission cooler lines.
5. Remove fan shield assembly if applicable.
6. Remove radiator and shroud assembly by lifting straight up.
NOTE: *The radiator assembly is held at the bottom by two cradles secured to the radiator support.*
7. If installing a new radiator, transfer fittings from old radiator to new radiator.
8. Replace radiator assembly by reversing the above steps, checking to assure radiator lower cradles are located properly in radiator recess.
9. Refill radiator. Run engine for a short period of time and check for leaks. If the radiator was removed from a car with an automatic transmission, recheck the transmission fluid.

Engine Oil Cooler

The engine oil cooler consists of an adapter bolted to the engine block which the oil filter is

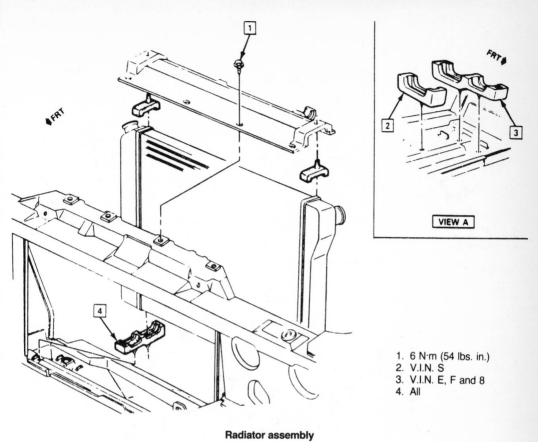

1. 6 N·m (54 lbs. in.)
2. V.I.N. S
3. V.I.N. E, F and 8
4. All

Radiator assembly

screwed onto. The adapter has 2 hoses which attach to the oil cooler and the radiator, these hoses are the inlet and return lines.

REMOVAL AND INSTALLATION

1. Disconnect the negative battery cable. Drain the cooling system into a suitable container.

CAUTION: *When draining the coolant, keep in mind that cats and dogs are attracted by the ethylene glycol antifreeze, and are quite likely to drink any that is left in an uncovered container or in puddles on the ground. This will prove fatal in sufficient quantity. Always drain the coolant into a sealable container. Coolant should be reused unless it is contaminated or several years old.*

2. Remove the radiator, if the oil cooler is to be repaired or replaced, otherwise remove the engine oil cooler from the radiator as necessary.

3. Remove the oil filter.

4. Remove the hoses from the oil cooler adapter.

5. Unscrew the oil cooler adapter retainer and remove the assembly. Discard the gasket.

6. Installation is the reverse of the removal procedure. Use new gaskets.

Electric Fan

REMOVAL AND INSTALLATION

1. Disconnect the battery ground cable.

2. Remove the air cleaner top, if equipped.

3. Remove the fan harness connector from the fan motor and frame.

4. Remove the fan frame to radiator support mounting bolts and remove the fan assembly.

5. Install the cooling fan frame to the radiator support bolt. Reconnect the wiring harness, the negative battery cable and check fan operation.

Clutch Fan

REMOVAL AND INSTALLATION

1. Disconnect the negative battery cable.

2. Remove the fan shroud, as required.

3. Remove the fan-to-water pump attaching bolts or nuts.

4. Remove the fan belts.

5. Remove the fan and clutch assembly. Separate the clutch assembly from the fan.

6. Installation is the reverse of the removal procedure.

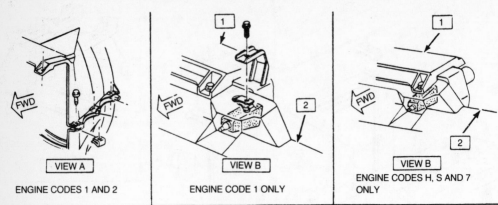

VIEW A

ENGINE CODES 1 AND 2

VIEW B

ENGINE CODE 1 ONLY

VIEW B

ENGINE CODES H, S AND 7 ONLY

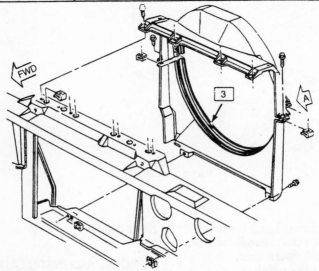

1. Fan shroud
2. Tie Bar—front end upper
3. Engine codes H and 7 fan shroud shown
4. Condenser
5. Radiator support

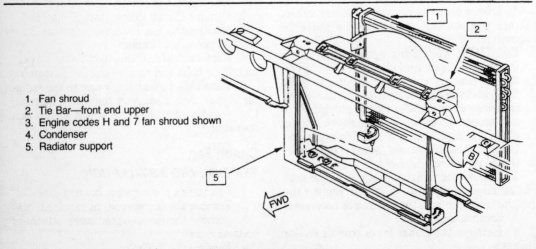

Radiator shroud assembly

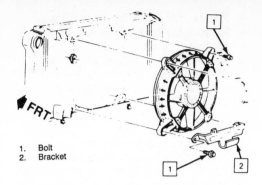

1. Bolt
2. Bracket

Electric cooling fan—without A/C

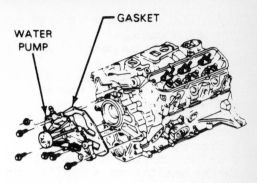

Water pump assembly—2.8L and 3.1L engines

Water Pump

REMOVAL AND INSTALLATION

CAUTION: *When draining the coolant, keep in mind that cats and dogs are attracted by the ethylene glycol antifreeze, and are quite likely to drink any that is left in an uncovered container or in puddles on the ground. This will prove fatal in sufficient quantity. Always drain the coolant into a sealable container. Coolant should be reused unless it is contaminated or several years old.*

Except 2.5L Engine

1. Disconnect the negative battery terminal.
2. Drain the cooling system.
3. If equipped with MPFI, remove the air intake tube and the mass air flow sensor.
4. Remove the fan shroud and/or radiator support, as applicable.

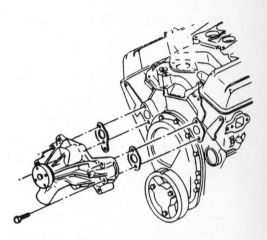

Water pump assembly—5.0L and 5.7L engines

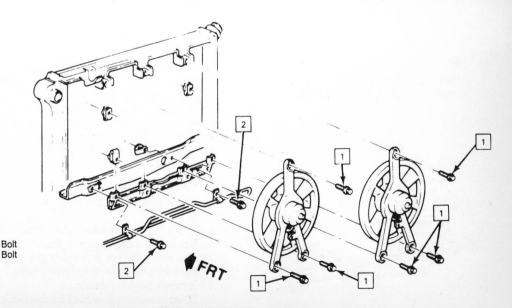

1. Bolt
2. Bolt

Electric cooling fan—with A/C

5. Remove all drive belts or remove the serpentine belt, as applicable.

6. Remove the fan and pulley from the water pump.

7. Remove the alternator upper and lower brackets. Remove the power steering pump lower bracket and swing aside.

8. Remove the bottom radiator hose and heater hose from the pump.

9. Remove the water pump.

10. To install, coat the new gasket with RTV Sealer and install the water pump. Torque the bolts to:

- 1982–84 V6 engine (M6 × 1.0 bolt): 6–9 ft. lbs. (8–12 Nm)
- 1982–84 V6 engine (M8 × 1.25 bolt): 13–18 ft. lbs. (18–24 Nm)
- 1982–84 V6 engine (M10 × 1.5 bolt): 20–30 ft. lbs. (27–41 Nm)
- 1985–92 V6 engine (M8 × 1.25 bolt): 13–22 ft. lbs. (18–30 Nm)
- 1985–92 V6 engine (M10 × 1.5 bolt): 20–35 ft. lbs. (27–48 Nm)
- V8 engine: 30 ft. lbs. (40 Nm)

11. Install the bottom radiator hose and heater hose to the pump.

12. Install the power steering pump bracket and pump. Install the alternator upper and lower brackets and alternator.

13. Install the pulley and fan to the water pump.

14. Install all drive belts. On V6 models, remove serpentine belt.

15. Install the fan shroud and/or radiator support.

16. If equipped with MFI, install the air intake tube and the mass air flow sensor.

17. Connect the negative battery terminal.

18. Fill the cooling system, start the engine and check for leaks.

2.5L Engine

1. Drain the cooling system.
2. Remove the accessory drive belts.

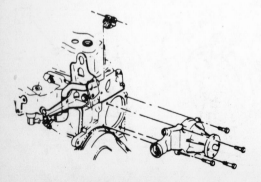

Water pump assembly—2.5L engine

3. Remove the fan and pump pulley.

4. Remove the heater hose and lower radiator hose from the water pump.

5. Remove the pump from the block.

6. To install, coat the new gasket with RTV Sealer. Install the pump and torque bolts to 25 ft. lbs. (34 Nm).

7. Install the hose and lower radiator hose to the water pump.

8. Install the pump pulley and fan.

9. Install the accessory drive belts.

10. Fill the cooling system, start the engine and check for leaks.

Cylinder Head
REMOVAL AND INSTALLATION

NOTE: *When servicing the engine, be absolutely sure to mark vacuum hoses and wiring so that these items may be properly reconnected during installation. Also, when disconnecting fittings of metal lines (fuel, power brake vacuum), always use two flare nut (or line) wrenches. Hold the wrench on the large fitting with pressure on the wrench as if you were tightening the fitting (clockwise), THEN loosen and disconnect the smaller fitting from the larger fitting. If this is not done, damage to the line will result.*

CAUTION: *When draining the coolant, keep in mind that cats and dogs are attracted by the ethylene glycol antifreeze, and are quite likely to drink any that is left in an uncovered container or in puddles on the ground. This will prove fatal in sufficient quantity. Always drain the coolant into a sealable container. Coolant should be reused unless it is contaminated or several years old.*

Properly relieve the fuel system pressure before disconnecting any lines.

The EPA warns that prolonged contact with used engine oil may cause a number of skin disorders, including cancer! You should make every effort to minimize your exposure to used engine oil. Protective gloves should be worn when changing the oil. Wash your hands and any other exposed skin areas as soon as possible after exposure to used engine oil. Soap and water, or waterless hand cleaner should be used.

2.5L Engine

1. Disconnect the battery cables at the battery.

2. Drain the engine block of coolant.

3. Raise and safely support the vehicle. Remove the exhaust pipe and lower the vehicle.

4. Remove the oil level indicator tube.

5. Remove the air cleaner.

6. Disconnect the electrical connections and linkage from the TBI unit.

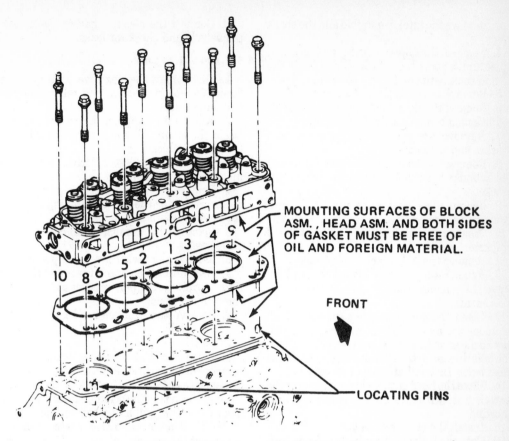

MOUNTING SURFACES OF BLOCK
ASM. , HEAD ASM. AND BOTH SIDES
OF GASKET MUST BE FREE OF
OIL AND FOREIGN MATERIAL.

FRONT

LOCATING PINS

Cylinder head tightening sequence—2.5L engine

7. Disconnect the heater hoses from the intake manifold.

8. Disconnect all electrical connections from the intake manifold and cylinder head.

9. If the vehicle has air conditioning, remove the compressor and position it out of the way. Do not disconnect the refrigerant lines.

10. Remove the alternator and lay the unit aside. If necessary, remove the alternator brackets.

11. Remove the power steering pump bracket-upper, if top mounted.

12. Remove the upper radiator hose.

13. Remove the rocker arm cover and back off the rocker arm nuts/bolts and pivot the rocker arms out of the way so that the pushrods can be removed. Identify the pushrods so that they can be reinstalled in their original locations.

14. Remove the cylinder head bolts and cylinder head. Remove the intake and exhaust manifolds, as required.

To install:

15. Thoroughly clean all mating surfaces of oil, grease and old gasket material. Clean the head bolts and cylinder block threads, otherwise an accurate torque specification will not be attained.

16. Install new gaskets and cylinder head.
   NOTE: *Clean the bolt threads, apply sealing compound and install the bolts finger tight.*

17. Tighten the head bolts a little at a time in the sequence illustrated and torque to 92 ft. lbs. (125 Nm).

18. Adjust the valves. Refill the cooling system and check for leaks. The remaining installation is the reverse of the removal procedure.

2.8L and 3.1L Engines

1. Disconnect the negative battery cable.

2. Relieve the fuel system pressure and drain the engine coolant from the radiator into a suitable container.

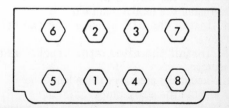

Cylinder head tightening sequence—2.8L and 3.1L
engines

3. Remove the intake manifold and the spark plugs.

4. Remove the dipstick tube and bracket. Raise and support the vehicle safely. Drain the oil and remove the oil filter. Lower the vehicle.

5. Remove the exhaust manifolds.

6. Remove the drive belt and remove the air conditioning compressor and lay aside.

7. Remove the power steering pump and bracket and lay aside.

8. Remove the ground cable from the rear of the cylinder head and remove the engine lift bracket.

9. Loosen the rocker arms until the push-rods can be removed.

10. Remove the belt tensioner, alternator and brackets.

11. Remove the AIR bracket, if equipped.

12. Remove the cylinder head bolts and remove the cylinder heads.

To install:

13. Clean the gasket mating surfaces of all components. Be careful not to nick or scratch any surfaces as this will allow leak paths. Clean the bolt threads in the cylinder block and on the head bolts. Dirt will affect bolt torque.

14. Place the head gaskets in position over the dowel pins, with the note "This Side Up" showing.

15. Install the cylinder heads.

16. Coat the cylinder head bolts threads with GM sealer 1052080 or equivalent, and install the bolts. Tighten the bolts in the proper sequence to:

- 1982–87 V6 engine: 70 ft. lbs. (95 Nm)
- 1988–92 V6 engine:
   1st step: 40 ft. lbs. (55 Nm)
        2nd step: an additional ¼ (90 degree) turn

17. Install the pushrods and loosely retain them with the rocker arms. Make sure the lower ends of the pushrods are in the lifter seats.

18. Install the power steering pump bracket and pump and the air conditioning compressor bracket and compressor.

19. Install the ground cable to the rear of the cylinder head.

20. Install the exhaust manifolds.

21. Install the dipstick tube and bracket.

22. Adjust the valve lash.

23. Install the intake manifold.

24. Install the AIR bracket and the belt tensioner.

25. Install the alternator bracket and alternator.

26. Install the accessory drive belt.

27. Install the spark plugs.

28. Fill the cooling system with the proper type and quantity of coolant. Install a new oil filter and fill the crankcase with the proper type and quantity of oil.

29. Connect the negative battery cable, start the vehicle and check for leaks.

5.0L and 5.7L Engines

1. Disconnect the negative battery cable. Drain the cooling system and relieve the fuel system pressure.

2. Raise and support the vehicle safely. Drain the engine oil and remove the oil filter. Lower the vehicle.

3. Remove the accessory drive belt and remove the intake manifold.

4. Remove the power steering pump, alternator bracket or the air conditioning compressor mounting bracket, as necessary.

5. Remove the exhaust manifolds and the valve covers.

6. Remove the rocker arms and pushrods.

7. Disconnect the ground wires and the catalytic converter AIR pipe bracket at the rear of the cylinder heads.

8. Remove the cylinder head bolts and the cylinder head.

To install:

9. Clean the gasket mating surfaces of all components. Be careful not to nick or scratch any surfaces as this will allow leak paths. Clean the bolt threads in the cylinder block and on the head bolts. Dirt will affect bolt torque.

NOTE: *When using a steel gasket, coat both sides of the new gasket with a thin even coat of sealer.*

If using a composition gasket, do not use any sealer.

10. Position the head gasket over the dowel pins with the bead up. Install the cylinder head over the dowel pins and gasket.

11. Coat the threads of the head bolts with GM 1052080 thread sealer or equivalent. Install the head bolts and tighten in sequence to 68 ft. lbs. (92 Nm).

12. Install the exhaust manifolds.

13. Install the pushrods and rocker arms and adjust the valve lash. Install the valve covers.

14. Install the power steering pump and alternator bracket or air conditioning compressor mounting bracket, as necessary.

15. Connect the ground wires and the catalytic converter AIR bracket to the rear of the cylinder head.

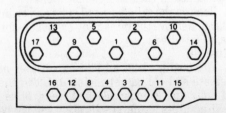

Cylinder head tightening sequence—5.0L and 5.7L engines

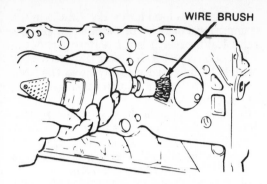

WIRE BRUSH

Removing carbon from the cylinder head chamber

16. Install the intake manifold.
17. Install the accessory drive belt.
18. Fill the cooling system with the proper type and amount of coolant. Connect the negative battery cable.
19. Raise and support the vehicle safely. Install a new oil filter, lower the vehicle. Fill the crankcase with the proper type and quantity of engine oil.
20. Start the engine, check for leaks and check the ignition timing.

CLEANING AND INSPECTION

Chip carbon away from the valve heads, combustion chambers, and ports, using a chisel made of hardwood. Remove the remaining deposits with a stiff wire brush.

NOTE: *Be sure that the deposits are actually removed, rather than burnished.*

Have the cast iron cylinder heads hot-tanked to remove grease, corrosion, and scale from the water passages. Aluminum cylinder heads must be cleaned by hand with a safe aluminum cleaning solvent. Clean the remaining cylinder head parts in an engine cleaning solvent. Do not remove the protective coating from the springs.

Place a straightedge across the gasket surface of the cylinder head. Using feeler gauges, determine the clearance at the center of the straightedge. If warpage exceeds 0.003 in. (0.037mm) in a 6 in. (152mm) span, or 0.006 in. (0.15mm) over the total length, the cylinder head must be resurfaced.

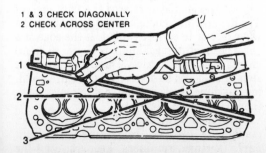

1 & 3 CHECK DIAGONALLY
2 CHECK ACROSS CENTER

Checking the cylinder head for warpage

NOTE: *If warpage exceeds the manufacturer's maximum tolerance for material removal, the cylinder head must be replaced.*

When milling the cylinder heads of V-type engines, the intake manifold mounting position is altered, and must be corrected by milling the manifold flange a proportionate amount.

RESURFACING

NOTE: *This procedure should only be performed by a machine shop.*

When the cylinder head is removed, check the flatness of the cylinder head gasket surfaces.

1. Place a straightedge across the gasket surface of the cylinder head. Using feeler gauges, determine the clearance at the center of the straightedge.
2. If warpage exceeds 0.003 in. (0.076mm) in a 6 in. (152mm) span, or 0.006 in. (0.152mm) over the total length, the cylinder head must be resurfaced.
3. If it is necessary to refinish the cylinder head gasket surface, do not plane or grind off more than 0.254mm (0.010 in.) from the original gasket surface.

NOTE: *When milling the cylinder heads of V6 and V8 engines, the intake manifold mounting position is altered, and must be corrected by milling the manifold flange a proportionate amount. Consult an experienced machinist about this.*

Valves and Springs

REMOVAL AND INSTALLATION

1. Block the head on its side, or install a pair of head-holding brackets made especially for valve removal.
2. Using a socket slightly larger than the

Valve spring compressor

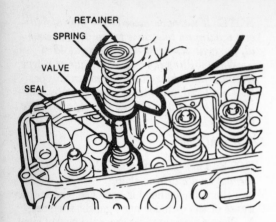

Valve spring and seal removal and installation

valve stem and keepers, place the socket over the valve stem and gently hit the socket with a plastic hammer to break loose any varnish buildup.

3. Remove the valve keepers, retainer, spring shield and valve spring using a valve spring compressor (the locking C-clamp type is the easiest kind to use).

4. Put the parts in a separate container numbered for the cylinder being worked on; do not mix them with other parts removed.

5. Remove and discard the valve stem oil seals. A new seal will be used at assembly time.

6. Remove the valves from the cylinder head and place them, in order, through numbered holes punched in a stiff piece of cardboard or wood valve holding stick.

NOTE: *The exhaust valve stems, on some engines, are equipped with small metal caps. Take care not to lose the caps. Make sure to reinstall them at assembly time. Replace any caps that are worn.*

7. Use an electric drill and rotary wire brush to clean the intake and exhaust valve ports, combustion chamber and valve seats. In some cases, the carbon will need to be chipped away. Use a blunt pointed drift for carbon chipping. Be careful around the valve seat areas.

8. Use a wire valve guide cleaning brush and safe solvent to clean the valve guides.

9. Clean the valves with a revolving wires brush. Heavy carbon deposits may be removed with the blunt drift.

NOTE: *When using a wire brush to clean carbon on the valve ports, valves etc., be sure that the deposits are actually removed, rather than burnished.*

10. Wash and clean all valve springs, keepers, retaining caps etc., in safe solvent.

11. Clean the head with a brush and some safe solvent and wipe dry.

12. Check the head for cracks. Cracks in the cylinder head usually start around an exhaust valve seat because it is the hottest part of the combustion chamber. If a crack is suspected but cannot be detected visually have the area checked with dye penetrant or other method by the machine shop.

13. After all cylinder head parts are reasonably clean, check the valve stem-to-guide clearance. If a dial indicator is not on hand, a visual inspection can give you a fairly good idea if the guide, valve stem or both are worn.

14. Insert the valve into the guide until slight away from the valve seat. Wiggle the valve sideways. A small amount of wobble is normal, excessive wobble means a worn guide or valve stem. If a dial indicator is on hand, mount the indicator so that the stem of the valve is at 90° to the valve stem, as close to the valve guide as possible. Move the valve off the seat, and measure the valve guide-to-stem clearance by rocking the stem back and forth to actuate the dial indicator. Measure the valve stem using a micrometer and compare to specifications to determine whether stem or guide wear is causing excessive clearance.

15. The valve guide, if worn, must be repaired before the valve seats can be resurfaced. Chevrolet supplies valves with oversize stems to fit valve guides that are reamed to oversize for repair. The machine shop will be able to handle the guide reaming for you. In some cases, if the guide is not too badly worn, knurling may be all that is required.

16. Reface, or have the valves and valve seats refaced. The valve seats should be a true 45° angle. Remove only enough material to clean up any pits or grooves. Be sure the valve seat is not too wide or narrow. Use a 60° grinding wheel to remove material from the bottom of the seat for raising and a 30° grinding wheel to remove material from the top of the seat to narrow.

17. After the valves are refaced by machine, hand lap them to the valve seat. Clean the grinding compound off and check the position of face-to-seat contact. Contact should be close to the center of the valve face. If contact is close to the top edge of the valve, narrow the seat; if too close to the bottom edge, raise the seat.

18. Valves should be refaced to a true angle of 44°. Remove only enough metal to clean up the valve face or to correct runout. If the edge of a valve head, after machining, is $\frac{1}{32}$ in. (0.8mm) or less replace the valve. The tip of the valve stem should also be dressed on the valve grinding machine, however, do not remove more than 0.010 in. (0.254mm).

19. After all valve and valve seats have been machined, check the remaining valve train parts (springs, retainers, keepers, etc.) for

Testing valve spring tension using tool J-8056 and torque wrench

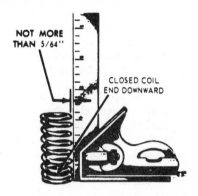

NOT MORE
THAN 5/64"

CLOSED COIL
END DOWNWARD

Checking valve spring free length and straightness

wear. Check the valve springs for straightness and tension.

20. Install the valves in the cylinder head and metal caps.

21. Install new valve stem oil seals.

22. Install the valve keepers, retainer, spring shield and valve spring using a valve spring compressor (the locking C-clamp type is the easiest kind to use).

23. Check the valve spring installed height, shim or replace as necessary.

CHECKING SPRINGS

Place the spring on a flat surface next to a square. Measure the height of the spring, and rotate it against the edge of the square to measure distortion. If spring height varies (by comparison) by more than $\frac{1}{16}$ in. (1.6mm) or if distortion exceeds $\frac{1}{16}$ in. (1.6mm), replace the spring.

In addition to evaluating the spring as above, test the spring pressure at the installed and compressed (installed height minus valve lift) height using a valve spring tester. Springs used on small displacement engines (up to 3 liters) should be ± 1 lb. of all other springs in either position. A tolerance of ± 5 lbs is permissible on larger engines.

VALVE SPRING INSTALLED HEIGHT

After installing the valve spring, measure the distance between the spring mounting pad and the lower edge of the spring retainer. Compare the measurement to specifications. If the installed height is incorrect, add shim washers between the spring mounting pad and the spring. Use only washers designed for valve springs, available at most parts houses.

VALVE STEM OIL SEALS

When installing valve stem oil seals, ensure that a small amount of oil is able to pass the seal to lubricate the valve stems and guide walls, otherwise, excessive wear will occur.

Valve Seats

NOTE: *The valve seats are not removable, they are an integral part of the cylinder head. Any cutting or grinding operation performed on the valve guides, should be done by a qualified machine shop.*

LAPPING THE VALVES

When valve faces and seats have been refaced and recut, or if they are determined to be in good condition, the valves must be lapped in to ensure efficient sealing when the valve closes against the seat.

1. Invert the cylinder head so that the combustion chambers are facing up.

2. Lightly lubricate the valve stems with clean oil, and coat the valve seats with valve grinding compound. Install the valves in the head as numbered.

3. Attach the suction cup of a valve lapping tool to a valve head. You'll probably have to moisten the cup to securely attach the tool to the valve.

HAND
DRILL

ROD

SUCTION
CUP

Homemade valve lapping tool

Lapping the valves using a hand valve lapping stick

4. Rotate the tool between the palms, changing position and lifting the tool often to prevent grooving. Lap the valve until a smooth, polished seat is evident (you may have to add a bit more compound after some lapping is done).

5. Remove the valve and tool, and remove ALL traces of grinding compound with solvent-soaked rag, or rinse the head with solvent.

NOTE: *Valve lapping can also be done by fastening a suction cup to a piece of drill rod in a hand eggbeater type drill. Proceed as above, using the drill as a lapping tool. Due to the higher speeds involved when using the hand drill, care must be exercised to avoid grooving the seat. Lift the tool and change direction of rotation often.*

Valve Guides

NOTE: *The valve guides are not removable, they are an integral part of the cylinder head. Any cutting or grinding operation performed on the valve guides, should be done by a qualified machine shop.*

REAMING VALVE GUIDES

If it becomes necessary to ream a valve guide to install with an oversize stem, a reaming kit is available which contains a oversize reamers and pilot tools.

When replacing a standard size valve with an oversize valve always use the reamer in sequence (smallest oversize first, then next smallest, etc.) so as not to overload the reamers. Always reface the valve seat after the valve guide has been reamed, and use a suitable scraper to brake the sharp corner at the top of the valve guide.

KNURLING

Valve guides which are not excessively worn or distorted may, in some cases, be knurled. Knurling is a process in which metal is displaced and raised, thereby reducing clearance. Knurling also provides excellent oil control.

NOTE: *This procedure should only be performed by a qualified machine shop.*

STEM-TO-GUIDE CLEARANCE

Valve stem-to-guide clearance should be checked upon assembling the cylinder head, and is especially necessary if the valve guides have been reamed or knurled, or if oversize valve have been installed. Excessive oil consumption often is a result of too much clearance between the valve guide and valve stem.

1. Clean the valve stem with lacquer thinner or a similar solvent to remove all gum and varnish. Clean the valve guides using solvent and an expanding wire-type valve guide cleaner (a rifle cleaning brush works well here).

2. Mount a dial indicator so that the stem is 90° to the valve stem and as close to the valve guide as possible.

3. Move the valve off its seat, and measure the valve guide-to-stem clearance by rocking the stem back and forth to actuate the dial indicator. Measure the valve stems using a micrometer and compare to specifications, to determine whether stem or guide wear is responsible for excessive clearance.

Valve Lifters

REMOVAL AND INSTALLATION

1. Remove the intake manifold, valve cover and push rod cover (4-cylinder). Disassemble the rocker arms and remove the push rods.

2. Remove the lifters. If they are coated with varnish, clean with carburetor cleaning solvent.

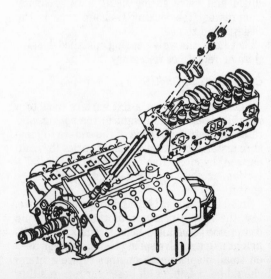

Exploded view of lifters, rockers and pushrods—V8 engine

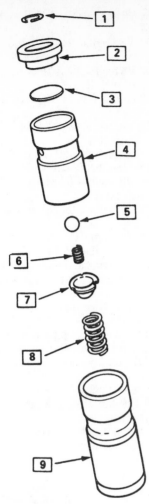

1. Retainer spring
2. Push rod seat
3. Rocker feed metering valve
4. Plunger
5. Ball check valve
6. Ball check valve spring (high ball lifter only)
7. Ball check valve retainer
8. Plunger spring
9. Lifter body

Exploded view of hydraulic lifter

3. If installing new lifters or you have disassembled the lifters, they must be primed before installation. Submerge the lifters in SAE 10 oil and carefully push down on the plunger with a ⅛ in. (3mm) drift. Hold the plunger down (DO NOT pump), then release the plunger slowly. The lifter is now primed.

4. Coat the bottoms of the lifters with Molykote® before installation. Install the lifters and pushrods into the engine in their original position.

5. Install the rocker arms and adjust the valves. Complete the installation by reversing the removal procedure.

Oil Pan

REMOVAL AND INSTALLATION

CAUTION: *The EPA warns that prolonged contact with used engine oil may cause a number of skin disorders, including cancer! You should make every effort to minimize your exposure to used engine oil. Protective gloves should be worn when changing the oil. Wash your hands and any other exposed skin*

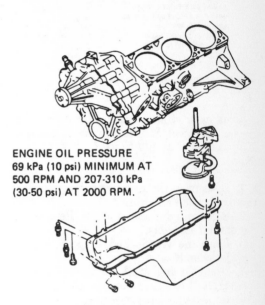

ENGINE OIL PRESSURE
69 kPa (10 psi) MINIMUM AT
500 RPM AND 207-310 kPa
(30-50 psi) AT 2000 RPM.

Oil pan assembly—1982–86 V6 engine

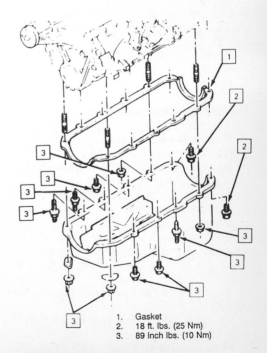

1. Gasket
2. 18 ft. lbs. (25 Nm)
3. 89 inch lbs. (10 Nm)

Oil pan assembly—1987–92 V6 engine

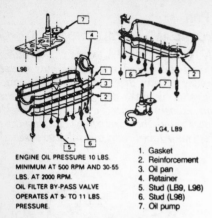

ENGINE OIL PRESSURE 10 LBS.
MINIMUM AT 500 RPM AND 30-55
LBS. AT 2000 RPM.
OIL FILTER BY-PASS VALVE
OPERATES AT 9- TO 11 LBS.
PRESSURE.

1. Gasket
2. Reinforcement
3. Oil pan
4. Retainer
5. Stud (LB9, L98)
6. Stud (L98)
7. Oil pump

Oil pan assembly—1987–92 V8 engine

areas as soon as possible after exposure to used engine oil. Soap and water, or waterless hand cleaner should be used.

Except 2.5L Engine

1. Disconnect the negative battery cable at the battery and air cleaner.
2. Remove the distributor cap. Remove the fan shroud assembly.
3. Raise the vehicle and support it safely with jackstands.
4. Drain the engine oil.
CAUTION: *Be sure that the catalytic converter is cool before proceeding.*
5. Remove the air injection pipe at the catalytic convertor.
6. Remove the catalytic converter hanger bolts. Disconnect the exhaust pipe at the manifold.
7. Remove the starter bolts, loosen the starter brace, then lay the starter aside.
8. Remove the front engine mount through-bolts.
9. Raise the engine enough to provide sufficient clearance for oil pan removal.
10. Remove the oil pan bolts.
NOTE: *If the front crankshaft throw prohibits removal of the pan, turn the crankshaft to position the throw horizontally.*
11. Remove the oil pan from the vehicle.
12. Remove all old RTV from the oil pan and engine block.
13. To install, run a ⅛ in. (3mm) bead of RTV around the oil pan sealing surface. Remember to keep the RTV on the INSIDE of the bolt holes.
14. Install the pan and pan bolts. Torque the pan bolts to:
- V6 engine (M6 × 1 X 16.0 bolts): 6–9 ft. lbs. (8–12 Nm)
- V6 engine (M8 × 1.25 × 14.0 bolts): 15–22 ft. lbs. (20–30 Nm)

- 1982–84 V8 engine ($^5/_{16}$–18 bolts): 165 inch lbs. (10 Nm)
- 1982–84 V8 engine (¼–20 bolts): 80 inch lbs. (8 Nm)
- 1985–92 V8 engine ($^5/_{16}$–18 × 1.44 studs): minimum of 10 inch lbs.
- 1985 V8 engine (stud nuts): 150–180 inch lbs. (17–20 Nm)
- 1985 V8 engine (¼–20 × 0.56 bolts): 72–90 inch lbs. (8–10 Nm)
- 1985 V8 engine (¼–20 × 0.50 × 0.56 studs): 72–90 inch lbs. (8–10 Nm)
- 1986–92 V8 engine (stud nuts): 150–250 inch lbs. (17–28 Nm)
- 1986–92 V8 engine (¼–20 × 0.56 bolts): 72–130 inch lbs. (8–14 Nm)
- 1986–92 V8 engine (¼–20 × 0.50 × 0.56 studs): 72–130 inch lbs. (8–14 Nm)
15. Lower the engine and install the front engine mount through-bolts. Torque bolts to 48 ft. lbs. (65 Nm).
16. Install the starter and starter brace, and secure with starter bolts.
17. Connect the exhaust pipe at the manifold. Install the catalytic converter hanger bolts.
18. Install the air injection pipe at the catalytic convertor.
19. Lower the vehicle.
20. Install the fan shroud assembly. Install the distributor cap.
21. Connect the negative battery cable at the battery and air cleaner.

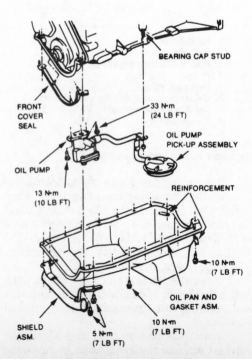

Oil pan and pump assembly—2.5L engine

22. Fill the engine with engine oil.

23. Start the engine and check for leaks.

2.5L Engine

1. Disconnect the negative battery cable at the battery.

2. Raise the vehicle and support it safely with jackstands.

3. Drain the engine oil.

4. Disconnect the exhaust pipe at the manifold.

5. Loosen the exhaust pipe hanger bracket.

6. Remove the starter assembly.

7. Remove the flywheel dust cover.

8. Remove the front engine mount through-bolts.

9. Carefully raise the engine enough to provide sufficient clearance to lower the oil pan.

10. Remove the oil pan retaining bolts and remove the oil pan.

11. Clean all old RTV from the mating surfaces.

12. Install the rear gasket into the rear main bearing cap and apply a small amount of RTV where the gasket engages into the engine block.

13. Install the front gasket.

14. Install the side gaskets, using grease as a retainer. Apply a small amount of RTV where the side gaskets meet the front gasket.

15. Install the oil pan.

NOTE: *Install the oil pan-to-timing cover bolts last, as these holes will not align until the other pan bolts are snug.*

16. Torque the pan bolts to 53 inch lbs. (6 Nm) for 1982–85 models and 90 inch lbs. (10 Nm) for 1986–88 models.

17. Lower the engine and install the front mount through-bolts. Torque bolts to 48 ft. lbs. (65 Nm).

18. Install the flywheel dust cover.

19. Install the starter assembly.

20. Connect the exhaust pipe at the manifold.

21. Tighten the exhaust pipe hanger bracket.

22. Lower the vehicle.

23. Connect the negative battery cable at the battery.

24. Fill the engine with engine oil and start engine. Check for leaks.

Oil Pump

REMOVAL

1. Drain and remove the oil pan.

CAUTION: *The EPA warns that prolonged contact with used engine oil may cause a number of skin disorders, including cancer! You should make every effort to minimize your exposure to used engine oil. Protective gloves should be worn when changing the oil. Wash your hands and any other exposed skin*

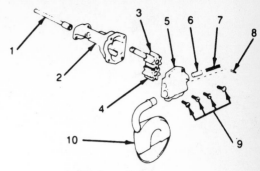

1. Shaft extension
2. Pump body
3. Drive gear and shaft
4. Idler gear
5. Pump cover
6. Pressure regulator valve
7. Pressure regulator spring
8. Retaining pin
9. Screws
10. Pickup screen and pipe

Exploded view of oil pump—V8 engine

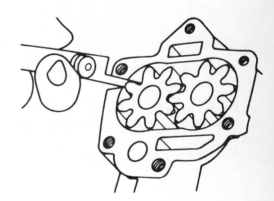

Measuring gear side clearance

Measuring oil pump end clearance

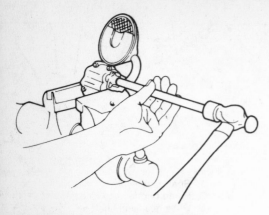

Installing the oil pump pickup and screen

areas as soon as possible after exposure to used engine oil. Soap and water, or waterless hand cleaner should be used.

2. Remove the oil pump-to-rear main bearing cap bolt. Remove the pump and the extension shaft.

3. Remove the cotter pin, spring and pressure regulator valve.

NOTE: *Place your thumb over the pressure regulators bore before removing the cotter pin, as the spring is under pressure.*

OVERHAUL

1. Remove the pump cover attaching screws and the pump cover.

2. Mark gear teeth so they may be reassembled with the same teeth indexing. Remove the idler gear, drive gear and shaft from the pump body.

3. Remove the pressure regulator valve retaining pin, pressure regulator valve and related parts.

4. If the pickup screen and pipe assembly need replacing, mount the pump in a soft-jawed vise and extract pipe from pump. Do not disturb the pickup screen on the pipe. This is serviced as an assembly.

5. Wash all parts in cleaning solvent and dry with compressed air.

6. Inspect the pump body and cover for cracks or excessive wear. Inspect pump gears for damage or excessive wear.

NOTE: *The pump gears and body are not serviced separately. If the pump gears or body are damaged or worn, replacement of the entire oil pump assembly is necessary.*

7. Check the drive gear shaft for looseness in the pump body. Inspect inside of pump cover for wear that would permit oil to leak past the ends of the gears.

8. Inspect the pickup screen and pipe assembly for damage to screen, pipe or relief grommet.

9. Check the pressure regulator valve for fit.

10. If the pickup screen and pipe assembly was removed, it should be replaced with a new part. Loss of press fit condition could result in an air leak and loss of oil pressure. Mount the pump in a soft-jawed vise, apply sealer to end of pipe, and use a suitable tool to tap the pipe in place.

NOTE: *Be careful of twisting, shearing or collapsing pipe while installing in pump. Do not use excessive force.*

11. Install the pressure regulator valve and related parts.

12. Install the drive gear and shaft in the pump body.

13. Install the idler gear in the pump body with the smooth side of gear towards pump cover opening.

NOTE: *Pack the inside of the pump completely with petroleum jelly. DO NOT use engine oil. The pump MUST be primed this way or it won't produce any oil pressure when the engine is started.*

14. Install the pump cover and torque attaching screws to specifications.

15. Turn drive shaft by hand to check for smooth operation.

INSTALLATION

1. Assemble pump and extension shaft to rear main bearing cap, aligning slot on top end of extension shaft with drive tang on lower end of distributor drive shaft.

NOTE: *When assembling the drive shaft extension to the drive shaft, the end of the extension nearest the washers must be inserted into the drive shaft.*

2. Insert the drive shaft extension through the opening in the main bearing cap and block until the shaft mates into the distributor drive gear.

3. Install the pump onto the rear main bearing cap and install the attaching bolts. Torque the bolts to specifications:

- All L4 engines: 22 ft. lbs. (30 Nm)
- All V6 engines: 25–35 ft. lbs. (35–47 Nm)
- All V8 engines: 60–70 ft. lbs. (81–95 Nm)

4. Install the oil pan and fill the crankcase with engine oil.

Crankshaft Damper

The damper may be replaced by removing the fan shroud, belts, crankshaft pulley bolts and then remove the damper center bolts. Install a suitable damper removing tool (J–23523 or equivalent), remove the damper from the crankshaft. Use the appropriate end of the removal tool for reinstalling the damper.

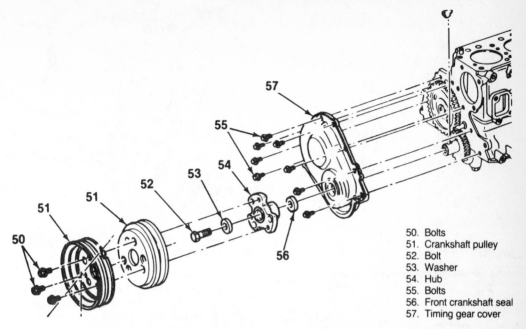

50. Bolts
51. Crankshaft pulley
52. Bolt
53. Washer
54. Hub
55. Bolts
56. Front crankshaft seal
57. Timing gear cover

Exploded view of pulley, damper, timing cover and gears—2.5L engine

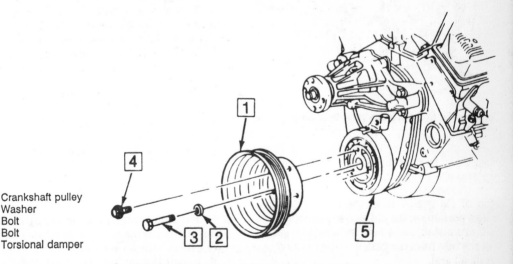

1. Crankshaft pulley
2. Washer
3. Bolt
4. Bolt
5. Torsional damper

Crankshaft pulley and damper assembly—V8 engine

Timing Cover

REMOVAL AND INSTALLATION

CAUTION: *When draining the coolant, keep in mind that cats and dogs are attracted by the ethylene glycol antifreeze, and are quite likely to drink any that is left in an uncovered container or in puddles on the ground. This will prove fatal in sufficient quantity. Always drain the coolant into a sealable container. Coolant should be reused unless it is contaminated or several years old.*

4-Cylinder Engine

1. Remove the drive belts. Remove the hub center bolt, then slide the hub and pulleys from the crankshaft.

NOTE: *If only removing the oil seal, simply pry the oil seal from the front cover using a large screwdriver. Be careful not to distort the sheet metal timing gear cover.*

2. Remove the oil pan-to-front cover screws and the front cover-to-block screws. Pull the cover forward enough to permit the cutting of

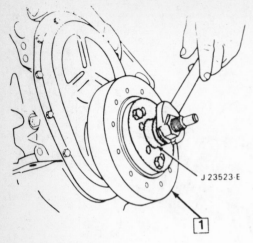

1. Torsional damper

Crankshaft damper remover and installer

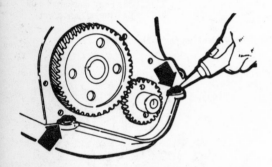

Apply sealer to these joints prior to assembly—2.5L engine

the oil pan front seal. Using a sharp knife, cut the seal close to the block at both corners.

3. Remove the front cover and clean any portion of old gasket from the sealing surfaces. Clean portions of the old gasket from the block.

4. To install, use a new front oil pan gasket, cut the tabs from the gasket. Replace the crankshaft oil seal.

5. Place RTV sealer in the corners of the new oil pan gasket and the new timing gear cover gasket.

6. Install the front cover and install the oil pan-to-front cover screws and the front cover-to-block screws. Torque screws to 90 inch lbs. (10 Nm).

7. Install the hub and pulleys onto the crankshaft. Install the hub center bolt and torque to 162 ft. lbs. (220 Nm).

8. Install the drive belts and adjust.

V6 and V8 Engine

1. Disconnect the battery ground cable. Drain the cooling system.

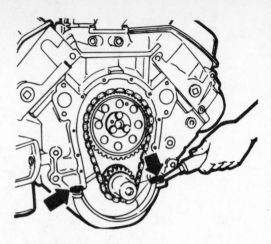

Apply sealer to these joints prior to assembly—except 2.5L engine

2. Remove the fan shroud or the upper radiator support and drive belts. Remove the fan and pulley from the water pump.

3. Remove the generator upper and lower brackets, air brace and brackets, and lower bracket of the power steering, move it aside.

4. Remove the radiator lower hose and the heater hose from the water pump. Remove the water pump bolts and the water pump.

5. If A/C equipped, remove the compressor and move aside. Remove the compressor mounting bracket.

6. Remove the damper pulley retaining bolt and the damper pulley.

7. Remove the timing gear cover bolts and the timing gear cover.

NOTE: *With the timing gear cover removed, use a large screwdriver to pry the oil seal from the cover. To install the new oil seal, lubricate it with engine oil and drive it into place.*

8. To install, prepare the mating surfaces for reinstallation of the timing gear cover. Coat the new gasket with RTV sealer.

9. Install the timing gear cover and timing gear cover bolts. Torque the cover bolts to specifications:
- V6 engines (M8 × 1.25 bolts): 13–22 ft. lbs. (18–30 Nm)
- V6 engines (M10 × 1.5 bolts): 20–35 ft. lbs. (27–48 Nm)
- V8 engines (all bolts): 69–130 inch lbs. (8–14 Nm)

10. Install the damper pulley by pulling the damper onto the crankshaft. Use tool J–23523 or equivalent. Install the damper pulley retaining bolt and torque bolts to 67–85 ft. lbs. (90–110 Nm).

11. If A/C equipped, install the compressor mounting bracket and compressor.

12. Install the water pump and the water pump bolts.

13. Install the radiator lower hose and the heater hose to the water pump.

14. Install the generator upper and lower brackets, air brace and brackets, and lower bracket of the power steering.

15. Install the fan and pulley to the water pump. Install the fan shroud or the upper radiator support and drive belts and adjust.

16. Connect the battery ground cable.

17. Fill the cooling system, start the engine and check for leaks.

TIMING GEAR COVER OIL SEAL REPLACEMENT

All Engines

1. After removing the gear cover, pry the oil seal out of the front of the cover with a small prybar or an oil seal removal tool.

2. Install a new lip seal with the lip (open side of seal) inside and drive or press the seal into place.

3. Lightly coat seal with engine oil before installing cover on block.

Installing oil seal with front cover on engine

Installing oil seal with front cover removed from engine

Timing Chain or Gear

REMOVAL AND INSTALLATION

4-Cylinder

The 4-cylinder engine uses a gear driven camshaft. To remove the timing gear, refer to the camshaft removal section. The camshaft must be removed from the engine so that the timing gear may be pressed from the shaft.

WARNING: *The thrust plate must be positioned so that the woodruff key in the shaft does not damage it when the shaft is pressed out of the gear. Properly support the hub of the gear or the gear will be seriously damaged. The crankshaft gear may be removed with a gear puller while in place in the block.*

V6 and V8 Engine

NOTE: *To remove the timing gear cover, refer to Timing Gear Cover – Removal and Installation.*

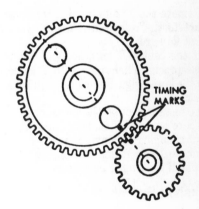

Timing gear alignment—2.5L engine

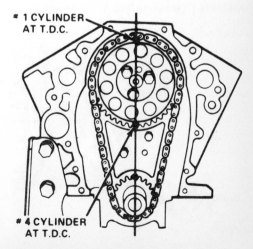

Timing gear and chain alignment—V6 engine

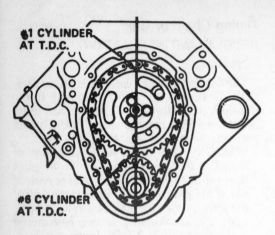

Timing gear and chain alignment—V8 engine

Crankshaft sprocket removal—2.5L engines

1. With the timing gear cover removed, rotate the engine so that the No. 6 cylinder T.D.C. mark (V8 engine) or the No. 4 cylinder T.D.C. mark (V6 engine) on the camshaft sprocket, aligns with the mark on the crankshaft sprocket.

2. Remove the 3 bolts holding the camshaft sprocket to the camshaft. Pull the camshaft sprocket forward.

3. If the camshaft sprocket will not move, give the sprocket a light blow with a plastic mallet, on the lower edge. Remove the sprocket and timing chain.

4. To install, position the sprocket into place and secure with the 3 camshaft sprocket bolts without changing the engines position. Torque the bolts to 15–25 ft. lbs. (20–35 Nm).

5. Install the timing gear cover.

Crankshaft Sprocket

REMOVAL AND INSTALLATION

1. Should it be necessary to remove the crankshaft sprocket, it may be necessary to re- move the radiator to gain sufficient clearance.

2. Using the proper puller, remove the crankshaft sprocket.

3. To install, pay attention to the position of the woodruff key. Slide the sprocket onto the crankshaft.

4. To complete the removal procedure, reverse the above.

Camshaft and Bearings

REMOVAL AND INSTALLATION

CAUTION: *When draining the coolant, keep in mind that cats and dogs are attracted by the ethylene glycol antifreeze, and are quite likely to drink any that is left in an uncovered container or in puddles on the ground. This will prove fatal in sufficient quantity. Always drain the coolant into a sealable container. Coolant should be reused unless it is contaminated or several years old.*

The EPA warns that prolonged contact with used engine oil may cause a number of skin disorders, including cancer! You should make every effort to minimize your exposure to used engine oil. Protective gloves should be worn when changing the oil. Wash your hands and any other exposed skin areas as soon as possible after exposure to used engine oil. Soap and water, or waterless hand cleaner should be used.

Crankshaft sprocket removal—V6 and V8 engines

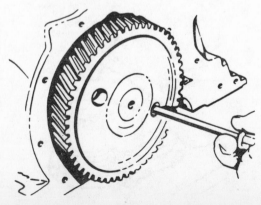

Removing the camshaft thrust plate retaining screws—2.5L engine

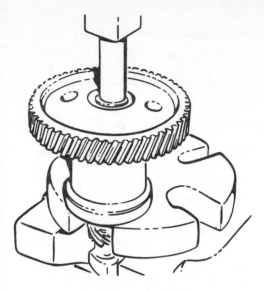

Using a press to remove the timing gear from the camshaft-2.5L engine

4-Cylinder Engine

There are two ways to go about this task: either remove the engine from the car, or remove the radiator, grill and any supports which are directly in front of the engine. If the second alternative is chosen, you may have to disconnect the motor mounts, and raise the front of the engine. This will give you the necessary clearance to remove the cam from the engine.

1. Drain the crankcase and the radiator. Refer to the radiator removal and installation procedure at the beginning of this Chapter and remove the radiator.

2. Remove the fan, drive belts and water pump pulley. Remove the valve cover. Loosen the rocker arms and pivot them, then remove the push rods.

3. Remove the oil pump drive shaft and gear assembly. Remove the spark plugs.

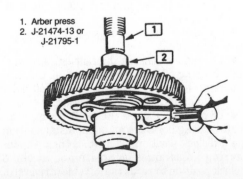

1. Arber press
2. J-21474-13 or J-21795-1

Installing the camshaft gear using a press and checking thrust plate clearance during the process—2.5L engine

4. Mark the position of the distributor rotor, housing, and engine block. Remove the distributor.

5. Remove the valve lifters. Refer to the timing gear cover removal and installation in this chapter and remove the timing gear cover.

6. Insert a screwdriver through the holes in the timing gear and remove the 2 camshaft thrust plate screws.

7. Pull the camshaft and gear assembly out through the front of the engine block.

NOTE: *When removing the camshaft, be careful not to damage the camshaft bearings.*

8. If the camshaft is to be removed from the timing gear, place the assembly in an arbor press and separate.

CAUTION: *When removing the timing gear from the camshaft, the thrust plate must be positioned so that the woodruff key does not damage it.*

9. To install the timing gear to the camshaft, press the assembly together and measure the end clearance. There should be 0.0015–0.0050 in. (0.038–0.127mm) between the thrust plate and the camshaft.

NOTE: *If the clearance is less than 0.0015 in. (0.038mm), replace the spacer ring; if more than 0.0050 in. (0.127mm), replace the thrust ring.*

10. To install, lubricate the camshaft, bearings, and lifters. Slide the camshaft assembly into the engine and align the timing marks of the camshaft gear and crankshaft gear.

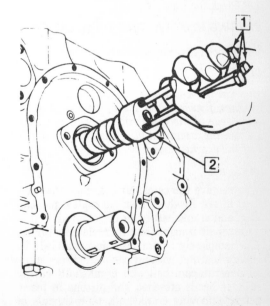

1. Bolts
2. Camshaft

Install 3 long bolts in camshaft to aid in removal and installation of camshaft

11. Complete the installation by reversing the removal procedure.

V6 and V8 Engine

1. Drain the cooling system and remove the radiator by referring to the radiator removal and installation in this chapter

2. Refer to the timing gear cover and timing chain removal and installation in this chapter, then remove the timing gear cover and chain.

3. Mark the distributor rotor, housing and engine block, then remove the distributor. Remove the fuel pump and fuel pump push rod.

4. Remove the intake manifold and valve covers. Loosen the rocker arms and pivot out of way. Remove the push rods and valve lifters.

5. Slide the camshaft toward the front of the engine (be careful not to damage the camshaft bearings).

6. To install, lubricate all parts. Slide the camshaft onto the camshaft bearings.

7. Install the fuel pump and fuel pump push rod.

8. Install the distributor and align all match marks.

9. Install the valve lifters, push rods and rocker arms.

10. Install the intake manifold and valve covers.

11. Install the timing and timing chain cover.

12. Install the radiator.

13. Fill the cooling system, start the engine and check for leaks.

BEARING REMOVAL AND INSTALLATION

NOTE: *It is recommended that the engine be removed from the vehicle before attempting this procedure.*

On the 4-Cylinder engine, the camshaft, lifters, flywheel and the expansion plug (at the rear of the camshaft) must be removed. Drive the expansion plug out from the inside of the engine block.

All Engines

To remove the camshaft bearings, the camshaft lifters, flywheel, rear camshaft expansion plug, and crankshaft must be removed.

Camshaft bearings can be replaced with engine completely or partially disassembled. To replace bearings without complete disassembly remove the camshaft and crankshaft leaving cylinder heads attached and pistons in place. Before removing crankshaft, tape threads of connecting rod bolts to prevent damage to crankshaft. Fasten connecting rods against sides of engine so they will not be in the way while replacing camshaft bearings.

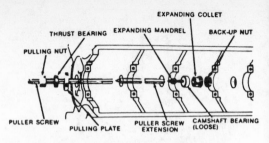

Camshaft bearing removal and installation tool

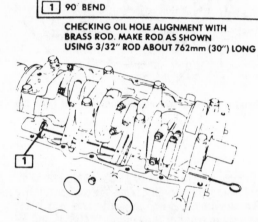

Checking camshaft bearing oil hole alignment

If excessive wear is indicated, or if the engine is being completely rebuilt, camshaft bearings should be replaced as follows: Drive the camshaft rear plug from the block. Assembly the removal puller with its shoulder on the bearing to be removed. Gradually tighten the puller nut until bearing is removed. Remove remaining bearings, leaving the front and rear for last. To remove front and rear bearings, reverse position of the tool, so as to pull the bearings in toward the center of the block. Leave the tool in this position, pilot the new front and rear bearings on the installer, and pull them into position as follows:

• 4 cylinder engines: Ensure oil holes are properly aligned.

• V6 engines: Ensure the rear and intermediate bearing oil holes are aligned at the 2:30 o'clock position and the front bearing oil holes are at 1:00 and 2:30 o'clock position.

• V8 engines: Ensure the No. 1 (front) camshaft bearing holes are an equal distance from the 6 o'clock position. The No. 2 thru 4 inner bearing holes must be positioned at the 5 o'clock position towards the left side (drivers) of the engine, even with the bottom of the cylinder bore. The No. 5 bearing oil holes must be positioned at 12 o'clock.

Return the tool to its original position and pull remaining bearings into position.

NOTE: *Ensure that oil holes are properly aligned. Replace camshaft rear plug, and stake it into position to aid retention.*

CHECKING CAMSHAFT

Camshaft Lobe Lift

Check the lift of each lobe in consecutive order and make a note of the reading.

1. Remove the fresh air inlet tube and the air cleaner. Remove the heater hose and crankcase ventilation hoses. Remove valve rocker arm cover(s).

2. Remove the rocker arm stud nut or fulcrum bolts, fulcrum seat and rocker arm.

3. Make sure the pushrod is in the valve tappet socket. Install a dial indicator so that the actuating point of the indicator is in the push rod socket (or the indicator ball socket adaptor tool is on the end of the push rod) and in the same plane as the push rod movement.

4. Disconnect the I terminal and the S terminal at the starter relay. Install an auxiliary

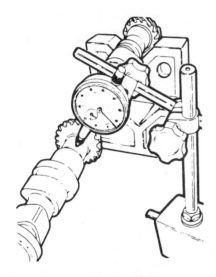

Checking the camshaft for straightness

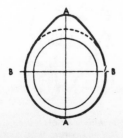

Camshaft lobe measurement

starter switch between the battery and S terminals of the start relay. Crank the engine with the ignition switch off. Turn the crankshaft over until the tappet is on the base circle of the camshaft lobe. At this position, the push rod will be in its lowest position.

5. Zero the dial indicator. Continue to rotate the crankshaft slowly until the push rod is in the fully raised position.

6. Compare the total lift recorded on the dial indicator with the specification shown on the Camshaft Specification chart.

To check the accuracy of the original indicator reading, continue to rotate the crankshaft until the indicator reads zero. If the left on any lobe is below specified wear limits listed, the camshaft and the valve tappet operating on the worn lobe(s) must be replaced.

7. Install the dial indicator and auxiliary starter switch.

8. Install the rocker arm, fulcrum seat and stud nut or fulcrum bolts. Check the valve clearance. Adjust if required (refer to procedure in this Section).

9. Install the valve rocker arm cover(s) and the air cleaner.

Camshaft End Play

NOTE: *On all gasoline V8 engines, prying against the aluminum-nylon camshaft sprocket, with the valve train load on the camshaft, can break or damage the sprocket. Therefore, the rocker arm adjusting nuts must be backed off, or the rocker arm and shaft assembly must be loosened sufficiently to free the camshaft. After checking the camshaft end play, check the valve clearance. Adjust if required (refer to procedure in this Section).*

1. Push the camshaft toward the rear of the engine. Install a dial indicator or equivalent so that the indicator point is on the camshaft sprocket attaching screw.

2. Zero the dial indicator. Position a prybar between the camshaft gear and the block. Pull the camshaft forward and release it. Compare the dial indicator reading with the specifications.

3. If the end play is excessive, check the spacer for correct installation before it is removed. If the spacer is correctly installed, replace the thrust plate.

4. Remove the dial indicator.

Pistons and Connecting Rods

REMOVAL

Before removal of piston(s), connecting rod(s) and cap(s), mark the piston assembly

RIDGE CAUSED BY CYLINDER WEAR

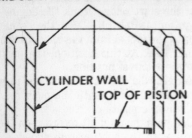

Cylinder bore ridge

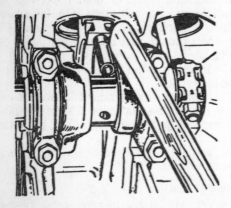

Pushing the piston assembly from the engine using a hammer handle

with their respective cylinder numbers. Place the mark on the side of the connecting rod and also on the top of the piston, nearest to the front of the engine. This will ensure a proper match during reinstallation.

NOTE: *This procedure is easily completed if the engine has been removed from the car.*

1. Remove the cylinder head(s), intake manifold, exhaust manifold, oil pan, and oil pump as outlined in this Section.

2. Mount the engine on a stand. In order to facilitate removal of the piston and connecting rod, the ridge at the top of the cylinder (unworn area; see illustration) must be removed. Place the piston at the bottom of the bore, and cover it with a rag. Cut the ridge away using a ridge reamer, exercising extreme care to avoid cutting too deeply. Remove the rag, and remove cuttings that remain on the piston.

CAUTION: *If the ridge is not removed, and new rings are installed, damage to rings will result.*

3. Remove the connecting rod bearing caps and bearings.

4. Install a section of rubber hose over the connecting rod bolts to prevent damage to the crankshaft.

5. Slide the piston/connecting rod assembly through the top of the cylinder block.

CAUTION: *Do not attempt to force the piston past the cylinder ridge (see above).*

POSITIONING

NOTE: *Most pistons are notched or marked to indicate which way they should be installed. If your pistons are not marked, mark them before removal. Then reinstall them in the proper position.*

CLEANING AND INSPECTING

A piston ring expander is necessary for removing piston rings without damaging them; any other method (screwdriver blades, pliers, etc.) usually results in the rings being bent, scratched or distorted, or the piston itself being damaged. When the rings are removed, clean the ring grooves using an appropriate ring groove cleaning tool, using care not to cut too deeply. Thoroughly clean all carbon and varnish from the piston with solvent.

CAUTION: *Do not use a wire brush or caustic solvent (acids, etc.) on piston.*

Install the pistons with the notch facing the front of the engine and the oil bearing tang slots facing the opposite side of the camshaft

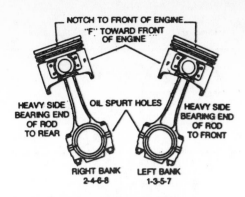

Piston-to-rod relationship-V8 engines

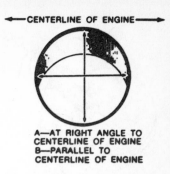

Cylinder bore measuring points

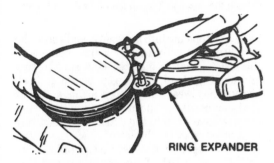

Piston ring remover

Measuring the cylinder bore with a dial gauge

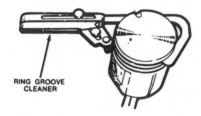

Ring groove cleaner removes carbon deposits

Correct cylinder bore honing pattern

Inspect the pistons for scuffing, scoring, cracks, pitting, or excessive ring groove wear. If these are evident, the piston must be replaced.

The piston should also be checked in relation to the cylinder diameter. Using a telescoping gauge and micrometer, or a dial gauge, measure the cylinder bore diameter perpendicular (90%) to the piston pin, 2½ in. (63.5mm) below the cylinder block deck (surface where the block mates with the heads). Then, with the micrometer, measure the piston perpendicular to its wrist pin on the skirt. The difference between the two measurements is the piston clearance.

If the clearance is within specifications or slightly below (after the cylinders have been bored or honed), finish honing is all that is necessary. If the clearance is excessive, try to obtain a slightly larger piston to bring clearance to within specifications. If this is not possible ob-

tain the first oversize piston and hone (or if necessary, bore) the cylinder to size. Generally, if the cylinder bore is tapered 0.005 in. (0.127mm) or more or is out-of-round 0.003 in. (0.076mm) or more, it is advisable to re-bore for the smallest possible oversize piston and rings. After measuring, mark pistons with a felt-tip pen for reference and for assembly.

NOTE: *Cylinder block boring should be performed by a reputable machine shop with the*

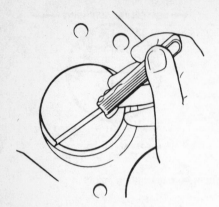

Checking the piston ring end gap

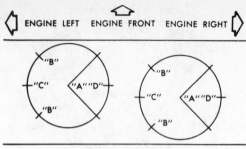

"A" OIL RING SPACER GAP
(Tang in Hole or Slot within Arc)
"B" OIL RING RAIL GAPS
"C" 2ND COMPRESSION RING GAP
"D" TOP COMPRESSION RING GAP

Placing the ring end gaps in their correct locations

proper equipment. In some cases, cleanup honing can be done with the cylinder block in the car, but most excessive honing and all cylinder boring must be done with the block stripped and removed from the car.

CHECKING RING END GAP

Piston ring end gap should be checked while the rings are removed from the pistons. Incorrect end gap indicates that the wrong size rings are being used; ring breakage could occur.

Compress the piston rings to be used in a cylinder, one at a time, into that cylinder. Squirt clean oil into the cylinder, so that the rings and the top 2 in. (51mm) of cylinder wall are coated. Using an inverted piston, press the rings approximately 1 in. (25mm) below the deck of the block. Measure the ring end gap with a feeler gauge, and compare to the Ring Gap chart in this Section. Carefully pull the ring out of the cylinder and file the ends squarely with a fine file to obtain the proper clearance.

INSTALLATION AND SIDE CLEARANCE MEASUREMENT

Check the pistons to see that the ring grooves and oil return holes have been properly cleaned.

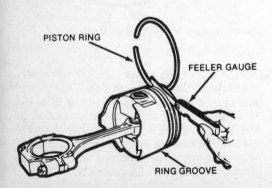

PISTON RING

FEELER GAUGE

RING GROOVE

Checking the piston ring side clearance

Slide a piston ring into its groove, and check the side clearance with a feeler gauge. Make sure the feeler gauge is inserted between the ring and its lower land (lower edge of the groove), because any wear that occurs forms a step at the inner portion of the lower land. If the piston grooves have worn to the extent that relatively high steps exist on the lower land, the piston should be replaced, because these will interfere with the operation of the new rings and ring clearances will be excessive. Piston rings are not furnished in oversize widths to compensate for ring groove wear.

Install the rings on the piston, lowest ring first, using a piston ring expander. There is a high risk of breaking or distorting the rings, or scratching the piston, if the rings are installed by hand or other means.

Position the rings on the piston as illustrated; spacing of the various piston ring gaps is crucial to proper oil retention and even cylinder wear. When installing new rings, refer to the installation diagram furnished with the new parts.

PISTON PIN REPLACEMENT

The piston pins are made of chromium steel. The fit within the piston is floating and in the connecting rod is pressed.

NOTE: *Pin replacement should only be attempted by a qualified machine shop.*

Connecting Rod Bearings

Connecting rod bearings for the engines covered in this guide consist of two halves or shells which are interchangeable in the rod and cap. When the shells are placed in position, the ends extend slightly beyond the rod and cap surfaces so that when the rod bolts are torqued the shells will be clamped tightly in place to insure positive seating and to prevent turning. A tang holds the shells in place.

NOTE: *The ends of the bearing shells must never be filed flush with the mating surface of the rod and cap.*

If a rod bearing becomes noisy or is worn so that its clearance on the crank journal is excessive, a new bearing of the correct undersize must be selected and installed since there is no provision for adjustment.

CAUTION: *Under no circumstances should the rod end or cap be filed to adjust the bearing clearance, nor should shims of any kind be used.*

Inspect the rod bearings while the rod assemblies are out of the engine. If the shells are scored or show flaking, they should be replaced. If they are in good shape check for proper clearance on the crank journal (see below). Any scoring or ridges on the crank journal means the crankshaft must be replaced, or re-ground and fitted with undersized bearings.

NOTE: *If journals are deeply scored or ridged the crankshaft must be replaced, as regrinding will reduce the durability of the crankshaft.*

ROD BEARING INSPECTION AND REPLACEMENT

NOTE: *Make sure connecting rods and their caps are kept together, and that the caps are installed in the proper direction.*

Replacement bearings are available in standard size, and in undersizes for reground crankshafts. Connecting rod-to-crankshaft bearing clearance is checked using Plastigage® at either the top or bottom of each crank journal. The Plastigage® has a range of 0.001–0.003 in. (0.0254–0.0762mm).

1. Remove the rod cap with the bearing shell, Completely clean the bearing shell and the crank journal, and blow any oil from the oil hole in the crankshaft; Plastigage® lengthwise along the bottom center of the lower bearing shell, then install the cap with shell and torque the

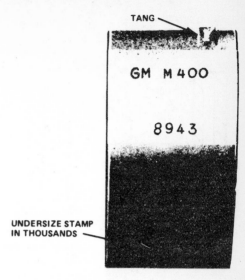

TANG

GM M400

8943

UNDERSIZE STAMP IN THOUSANDS

Undersize marks are stamped on the bearing shells. The tang fits in the notch on the rod and cap

bolt or nuts to specification. DO NOT turn the crankshaft with Plastigage® in the bearing.

2. Remove the bearing cap with the shell. The flattened Plastigage® will be found sticking to either the bearing shell or crank journal. Do not remove it yet.

3. Use the scale printed on the Plastigage® envelope to measure the flattened material at its widest point. The number within the scale which most closely corresponds to the width of the Plastigage® indicates bearing clearance in thousandths of an inch and hundreths of a milimeter.

4. Check the specifications chart in this Chapter for the desired clearance. It is advisable to install a new bearing if clearance exceeds 0.003 in. (0.076mm); however, if the bearing is in good condition and is not being checked because of bearing noise, bearing replacement is not necessary.

5. If you are installing new bearings, try a standard size, then each undersize in order until one is found that is within the specified limits when checked for clearance with Plastigage. Each undersize shell has its size stamped on it.

6. When the proper size shell is found, clean off the Plastigage, oil the bearing thoroughly, reinstall the cap with its shell and torque the rod bolt nuts to specification.

NOTE: *With the proper bearing selected and the nuts torqued, it should be possible to move the connecting rod back and forth freely on the crank journal as allowed by the specified connecting rod end clearance. If the rod cannot be moved, either the rod bearing is too far undersize or the rod is misaligned.*

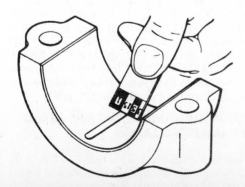

Use Plastigage® to determine bearing clearances

1. Gaging point
2. Sizing point

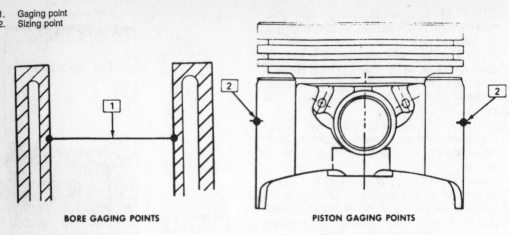

BORE GAGING POINTS   PISTON GAGING POINTS

Cylinder bore and piston gauging points

MEASURING THE OLD PISTONS

Check used piston-to-cylinder bore clearance as follows:

1. Measure the cylinder bore diameter with a telescope gauge.

2. Measure the piston diameter. When measuring the pistons for size or taper, measurements must be made with the piston pin removed.

3. Subtract the piston diameter from the cylinder bore diameter to determine piston-to-bore clearance.

4. Compare the piston-to-bore clearances obtained with those clearances recommended. Determine if the piston-to-bore clearance is in the acceptable range.

5. When measuring taper, the largest reading must be at the bottom of the skirt.

SELECTING NEW PISTONS

1. If the used piston is not acceptable, check the service piston size and determine if a new piston can be selected. (Service pistons are available in standard, high limit and standard oversize.

2. If the cylinder bore must be reconditioned, measure the new piston diameter, then hone the cylinder bore to obtain the preferred clearance.

3. Select a new piston and mark the piston to identify the cylinder for which it was fitted. On some vehicles, oversize pistons may be found. These pistons will be 0.254mm (0.010 in.) oversize.

CYLINDER HONING

1. When cylinders are being honed, follow the manufacturer's recommendations for the use of the hone.

2. Occasionally, during the honing operation, the cylinder bore should be thoroughly cleaned and the selected piston checked for correct fit.

3. When finish-honing a cylinder bore, the hone should be moved up and down at a sufficient speed to obtain a very fine uniform surface finish in a cross-hatch pattern of approximately 45–65° included angle. The finish marks should be clean but not sharp, free from embedded particles and torn or folded metal.

4. Permanently mark the piston for the cylinder to which it has been fitted and proceed to hone the remaining cylinders.

WARNING: *Handle the pistons with care. Do not attempt to force the pistons through the cylinders until the cylinders have been honed to the correct size. Pistons can be distorted through careless handling.*

5. Thoroughly clean the bores with hot water and detergent. Scrub well with a stiff bristle brush and rinse thoroughly with hot water. It is extremely essential that a good cleaning operation be performed. If any of the abrasive material is allowed to remain in the cylinder bores, it will rapidly wear the new rings and cylinder bores. The bores should be swabbed several times with light engine oil and a clean cloth and then wiped with a clean dry cloth. CYLINDERS SHOULD NOT BE CLEANED WITH KEROSENE OR GASOLINE! Clean the remainder of the cylinder block to remove the excess material spread during the honing operation.

PISTON AND CONNECTING ROD ASSEMBLY AND INSTALLATION

Install the connecting rod to the piston, making sure piston installation notches and marks on the rod are in proper relation to one another. Lubricate the wrist pin with clean engine oil,

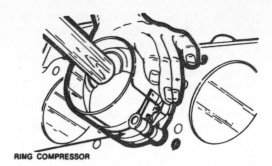

RING COMPRESSOR

Install the piston ring compressor, then tap the piston into the cylinder bore. Make sure that the piston marks are correctly positioned

Check the connecting rod side clearance with a feeler gauge. Use a small pry bar to carefully spread the rods to specified clearance

and install the pin into the rod and piston assembly, by using a wrist pin press. Install snaprings if equipped, and rotate them in their grooves to make sure they are seated. To install the piston and connecting rod assembly:

1. Make sure connecting rod bearings are of the correct size and properly installed.

2. Fit rubber hoses over the connecting rod bolts to protect the crankshaft journals, as in the Piston Removal procedure. Coat the rod bearings with clean oil.

3. Using the proper ring compressor, insert the piston assembly into the cylinder so that the notch in the top of the piston faces the front of the engine and the connecting rod bearing tang slots on the side opposite the camshaft (this assumes that the dimple(s) or other mark-

ings on the connecting rods are in correct relation to the piston notch).

4. From beneath the engine, coat each crank journal with clean oil. Pull the connecting rod, with the bearing shell in place, into position against the crank journal.

5. Remove the rubber hoses. Install the bearing cap and cap nuts and torque to specification.

NOTE: *When more than one rod and piston assembly is being installed, the connecting rod cap attaching nuts should only be tightened enough to keep each rod in position until all have been installed. This will ease the installation of the remaining piston assembles.*

6. Check the clearance between the sides of the connecting rods and the crankshaft using a feeler gauge. Spread the rods slightly with a small prybar to insert the gauge. If clearance is below the minimum tolerance, the rod may be machined to provide adequate clearance. If clearance is excessive, substitute an unworn rod, and recheck. If clearance is still outside specifications, the crankshaft must be welded and reground, or replaced.

7. Replace the oil pump, if removed, and the oil pan.

8. Install the cylinder head(s) and intake manifold, as previously described.

Freeze Plugs

REMOVAL AND INSTALLATION

CAUTION: *When draining the coolant, keep in mind that cats and dogs are attracted by the ethylene glycol antifreeze, and are quite likely to drink any that is left in an uncovered container or in puddles on the ground. This will prove fatal in sufficient quantity. Always drain the coolant into a sealable container. Coolant should be reused unless it is contaminated or several years old.*

1. Disconnect the negative battery cable.

2. Drain the cooling system.

3. Raise and support the vehicle safely.

4. Remove the coolant drain plug on the side of the block, if equipped. Or you can use a punch to put a small hole in the center of the freeze plug.

5. Remove all components in order to gain access to the freeze plug(s).

6. Using a punch, tap the bottom corner of the freeze plug to cock it in the bore. Remove the plug using pliers.

7. Clean the freeze plug hole and coat the new plug with sealer.

8. Using a suitable tool, install the freeze plug into the block.

9. Connect the negative battery cable, fill the

cooling system, start the engine and check for leaks.

Crankshaft Servicing

CAUTION: *The EPA warns that prolonged contact with used engine oil may cause a number of skin disorders, including cancer! You should make every effort to minimize your exposure to used engine oil. Protective gloves should be worn when changing the oil. Wash your hands and any other exposed skin areas as soon as possible after exposure to used engine oil. Soap and water, or waterless hand cleaner should be used.*

Crankshaft servicing literally makes or breaks any engine; especially a high performance one. The most critical maintenance operation is the replacement of the crankshaft main bearings. These bearings are of the precision insert design and do not require adjustment through shims. They are offered in undersizes of 0.001 in. (0.0254mm), 0.002 in. (0.0508mm), 0.009 in. (0.228mm), 0.010 in. (0.254mm), 0.020 in. (0.508mm) in. 0.030 in. (0.762mm).

Despite the advent of these inserts and accompanying precision machine work, it does happen that sizing mistakes are made and no crankshaft should be installed in a block without checking clearances. One of the simplest means of doing so is to use Plastigage®. This is a wax-like plastic material that is formed into

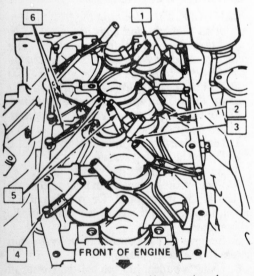

1. Rubber hose
2. #4 rod
3. #3 rod
4. Oil pan bolt
5. Note overlap of adjacent rods
6. Rubber bands

Support the connecting rods with rubber bands and install rubber hose over the cap bolts during crankshaft removal and installation

precision threads. It will compress evenly between two surfaces, without damage, and when measured, will indicate the actual clearance.

It is easiest to check bearing clearance with the engine removed from the car and the block inverted. This ensures that the crank is resting against the upper bearing shells. If Plastigage® is to be used on an engine still in the vehicle, it will be necessary to support the crankshaft at both ends so that clearance between the crankshaft and the upper bearing shells is eliminated.

REMOVAL

1. Drain the engine oil and remove the engine from the car. Mount the engine on a work stand in a suitable working area. Invert the engine, so the oil pan is facing up.
2. Remove the engine water pump and front (timing) cover.
3. Remove the timing chain (if equipped) and gears.
4. Remove the oil pan.
5. Remove the oil pump.
6. Stamp or mark the cylinder number on the machined surfaces of the bolt bosses of the connecting rods and caps for identification when reinstalling. If the pistons are to be removed from the connecting rod, mark the cylinder number on the pistons with silver paint or felt-tip pen for proper cylinder identification and cap-to-rod location.
7. Remove the connecting rod caps. Install lengths of rubber hose on each of the connecting rod bolts, to protect the crank journals when the crank is removed.
8. Mark the main bearing caps with a number punch or punch so that they can be reinstalled in their original positions.
9. Remove all main bearing caps.
10. Note the position of the keyway in the crankshaft so it can be installed in the same position.
11. Install rubber bands between a bolt on each connecting rod and oil pan bolts that have been reinstalled in the block (see illustration). This will keep the rods from banging on the block when the crank is removed.
12. Carefully lift the crankshaft out of the block. The rods will pivot to the center of the engine when the crank is removed.

MAIN BEARING INSPECTION

Like connecting rod big-end bearings, the crankshaft main bearings are shell-type inserts that do not utilize shims and cannot be adjusted. The bearings are available in various standard and undersizes; if main bearing clearance

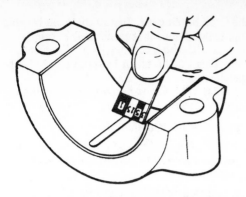

Measure the main bearing clearance by comparing the flattened strip of Plastigage® with the scale

is found to be excessive, a new bearing (both upper and lower halves) is required.

NOTE: *Factory-undersized crankshafts are marked, sometimes with a "9" and/or a large spot of light green paint; the bearing caps also will have the paint on each side of the undersized journal.*

Generally, the lower half of the bearing shell (except No. 1 bearing) shows greater wear and fatigue. If the lower half only shows the effects of normal wear (no heavy scoring or discoloration), it can usually be assumed that the upper half is also in good shape; conversely, if the lower half is heavily worn or damaged, both halves should be replaced. Never replace one bearing half without replacing the other.

MEASURING MAIN BEARING CLEARANCE

Main bearing clearance can be checked both with the crankshaft in the car and with the engine out of the car. If the engine block is still in the car, the crankshaft should be supported both front and rear (by the damper and the transmission) to remove clearance from the upper bearing. Total clearance can then be measured between the lower bearing and journal. If the block has been removed from the car, and is inverted, the crank will rest on the upper bearings and the total clearance can be measured between the lower bearing and journal. Clearance is checked in the same manner as the connecting rod bearings, with Plastigage®.

NOTE: *Crankshaft bearing caps and bearing shells should NEVER be filed flush with the cap-to-block mating surface to adjust for wear in the old bearings. Always install new bearings.*

1. If the crankshaft has been removed, install it (block removed from car). If the block is still in the car, remove the oil pan and oil pump. Starting with the rear bearing cap, remove the cap and wipe all oil from the crank journal and bearing cap.

2. Place a strip of Plastigage® the full width of the bearing, (parallel to the crankshaft), on the journal.

NOTE: *Plastigage® is soluble in oil; therefore, oil on the journal or bearing could result in erroneous readings.*

CAUTION: *Do not rotate the crankshaft while the gaging material is between the bearing and the journal.*

3. Install the bearing cap and evenly torque the cap bolts to specification.

4. Remove the bearing cap. The flattened Plastigage® will be sticking to either the bearing shell or the crank journal.

5. Use the graduated scale on the Plastigage® envelope to measure the material at its widest point. If the flattened Plastigage® tapers toward the middle or ends, there is a difference in clearance indicating the bearing or journal has a taper, low spot or other irregularity. If this is indicated, measure the crank journal with a micrometer.

6. If bearing clearance is within specifications, the bearing insert is in good shape. Replace the insert if the clearance is not within specifications. Always replace both upper and lower inserts as a unit.

7. Standard, 0.001 in. (0.0254mm) or 0.002 in. (0.508mm) undersize bearings should produce the proper clearance. If these sizes still produce too sloppy a fit, the crankshaft must be reground for use with the next undersize bearing. Recheck all clearances after installing new bearings.

8. Replace the rest of the bearings in the same manner. After all bearings have been checked, rotate the crankshaft to make sure there is no excessive drag. When checking the No. 1 main bearing, loosen the accessory drive belts (engine in car) to prevent a tapered reading with the Plastigage®.

MAIN BEARING REPLACEMENT

Engine Out of Car

1. Remove and inspect the crankshaft.
2. Remove the main bearings from the bear-

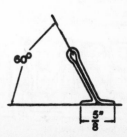

Fabricated cotter pin for removal of main bearings

ing saddles in the cylinder block and main bearing caps.

3. Coat the bearing surfaces of the new, correct size main bearings with clean engine oil and install them in the bearing saddles in the block and in the main bearing caps.

4. Install the crankshaft. See Crankshaft Installation.

Engine In Car

1. With the oil pan, oil pump and spark plugs removed, remove the cap from the main bearing needing replacement and remove the bearing from the cap.

2. Make a bearing roll-out pin, using a bent cotter pin as shown in the illustration. Install the end of the pin in the oil hole in the crankshaft journal.

3. Rotate the crankshaft clockwise as viewed from the front of the engine. This will roll the upper bearing out of the block.

4. Lube the new upper bearing with clean engine oil and insert the plain (un-notched) end between the crankshaft and the indented or notched side of the block. Roll the bearing into place, making sure that the oil holes are aligned. Remove the roll pin from the oil hole.

5. Lube the new lower bearing and install

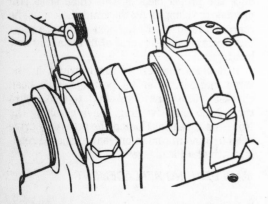

Use a feeler gauge to check the crankshaft end play during assembly

the main bearing cap. Install the main bearing cap, making sure it is positioned in proper direction with the matchmarks in alignment.

6. Torque the main bearing cap bolts to specification.

NOTE: *The thrust bearing must be aligned before torquing cap bolts.*

REGRINDING JOURNALS

NOTE: *Regrinding rod and/or main bearing journals should be performed by a qualified machine shop.*

CRANKSHAFT INSTALLATION

When main bearing clearance has been checked, bearings examined and/or replaced, the crankshaft can be installed. Thoroughly clean the upper and lower bearing surfaces, and lube them with clean engine oil. Install the crankshaft and main bearing caps.

Dip all main bearing cap bolts in clean oil, and torque all main bearing caps, excluding the thrust bearing cap, to specifications (see the Crankshaft and Connecting Rod chart in this Chapter to determine which bearing is the thrust bearing). Tighten the thrust bearing bolts finger tight. To align the thrust bearing, pry the crankshaft the extent of its axial travel several times, holding the last movement toward the front of the engine. Add thrust washers if required for proper alignment. Torque the thrust bearing cap to specifications.

To check crankshaft end-play, pry the crankshaft to the extreme rear of its axial travel, then to the extreme front of its travel. Using a feeler gauge, measure the end-play at the front of the rear main bearing. End play may also be measured at the thrust bearing. Install a new rear main bearing oil seal in the cylinder block and main bearing cap. Continue to reassemble the engine in reverse of disassembly procedures.

Rear Main Oil Seal

REMOVAL AND INSTALLATION

CAUTION: *The EPA warns that prolonged contact with used engine oil may cause a*

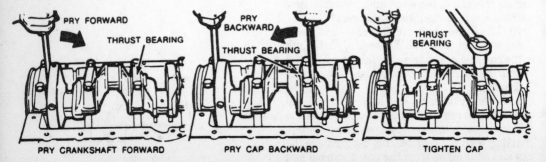

PRY FORWARD   THRUST BEARING   PRY BACKWARD   THRUST BEARING   THRUST BEARING

PRY CRANKSHAFT FORWARD   PRY CAP BACKWARD   TIGHTEN CAP

Align the thrust bearing as illustrated. Torque the main caps to specification

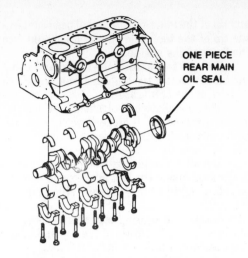

The 1-piece type oil seal and crankshaft assembly—
2.5L engine

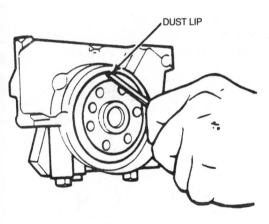

Rear main 1-piece oil seal removal

number of skin disorders, including cancer! You should make every effort to minimize your exposure to used engine oil. Protective gloves should be worn when changing the oil. Wash your hands and any other exposed skin areas as soon as possible after exposure to used engine oil. Soap and water, or waterless hand cleaner should be used.

1-Piece Neoprene Seal

NOTE: *The rear main seal is a one piece unit. It can be removed or installed without removing the oil pan or crankshaft.*

1. Jack up your vehicle and support it with jackstands.

2. Remove the transmission and flywheel assembly.

3. If equipped with a manual transmission, remove the clutch and pressure plate.

4. Using a suitable tool, pry the old seal out.

5. Inspect the crankshaft for nicks or burrs, correct as required.

6. To install, clean the area and coat the seal with engine oil. Install the seal onto tool J–34686 or equivalent. Install the seal into the engine.

7. Install the flywheel and torque to specification.

8. Install the transmission. (If equipped with a manual transmission, install the clutch and pressure plate.)

9. Check the fluid levels, start the engine and check for leaks.

2-Piece Neoprene Seal

Both halves of the rear main oil seal can be replaced without removing the crankshaft. Always replace the upper and lower seal together. The lip should face the front of the engine. Be very careful that you do not break the sealing

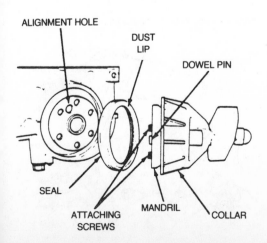

Rear main 1-piece oil seal tool and installation

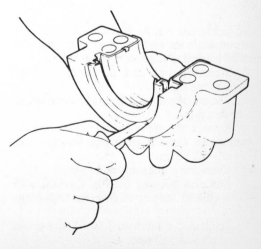

Rear main 2-piece oil seal lower half removal

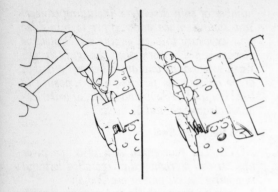

Rear main 2-piece oil seal upper half removal

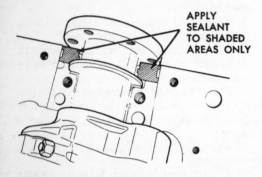

APPLY SEALANT TO SHADED AREAS ONLY

Applying sealer to main bearing cap

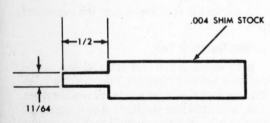

.004 SHIM STOCK

1/2

11/64

Fabricated oil seal installation tool

bead in the channel on the outside portion of the seal while installing it. An installation tool can be fabricated to protect the seal bead.

1. Remove the oil pan, oil pump and rear main bearing cap.

2. Remove the oil seal from the bearing cap by prying it out.

3. Remove the upper half of the seal with a small punch. Drive it around far enough to be gripped with pliers.

4. Clean the crankshaft and bearing cap.

5. Coat the lips and bead of the seal with light engine oil, keeping oil from the ends of the seal.

6. Position the fabricated tool between the crankshaft and seal seat.

7. Position the seal between the crankshaft

and tip of the tool so that the seal bead contacts the tip of the tool. The oil seal lip should face the front of the engine.

8. Roll the seal around the crankshaft using the tool to protect the seal bead from the sharp corners of the crankcase.

9. The installation tool should be left installed until the seal is properly positioned with both ends flush with the block.

10. Remove the tool.

11. Install the other half of the seal in the bearing cap using the tool in the same manner as before. Light thumb pressure should install the seal.

12. Install the bearing cap with sealant applied to the mating areas of the cap and block. Keep sealant from the ends of the seal.

13. Torque the rear main bearing cap to specifications.

14. Install the oil pump and oil pan.

15. Fill the engine with engine oil, start the engine and check for leaks.

Rope Seal

NOTE: *The following procedure is only to be used as an oil seal repair while the engine is*

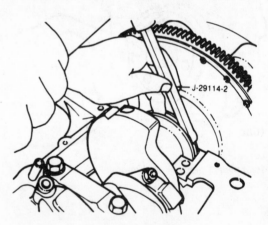

J-29114-2

Using the rope seal packing tool

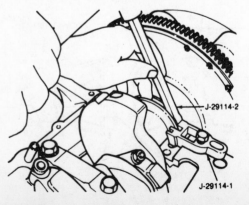

J-29114-2

J-29114-1

Using the rope seal guide tool

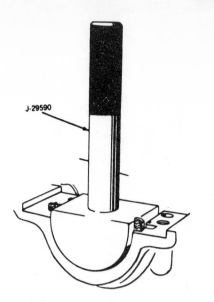

J-29590

Install the rope seal in the cap using tool J-29590 and cut the seal ends flush with the main cap

in the vehicle. Whenever possible the crankshaft should be removed and a new complete rope seal installed.

1. Disconnect the negative battery cable.
2. Drain the engine oil and remove the oil pan.
3. Remove the rear main bearing cap.
4. Insert packing tool J–29114–2 or equivalent, against 1 end of the seal in the cylinder block. Drive the old seal gently into the groove until it is packed tight. This will vary from ¼ in. (6mm) to ¾ in. (19mm) depending on the amount of pack required.
5. Repeat the procedure on the other end of the seal.
6. Measure the amount the seal was driven up on one side and add ¹⁄₁₆ in. (1.6mm). Using a suitable cutting tool, cut that length from the old seal removed from the rear main bearing cap. Repeat the procedure for the other side. Use the rear main bearing cap as a holding fixture when cutting the seal.
7. Install guide tool J–29114–1 or equivalent, onto the cylinder block.
8. Using the packing tool, work the short pieces cut in Step 6 into the guide tool and then pack into the cylinder block. The guide tool and packing tool are machined to provide a built in stop. Use this procedure for both sides. It may help to use oil on the short pieces of the rope seal when packing them into the cylinder block.
9. Remove the guide tool.
10. Apply Loctite 414 or equivalent, to the seal groove in the rear main bearing cap. Within 1 minute, insert a new seal into the groove and push into place with tool J-29590 until the seal

is flush with the block. Cut the excess seal material with a sharp cutting tool at the bearing cap parting line.
11. Apply a thin film of chassis grease to the rope seal. Apply a thin film of RTV sealant on the bearing cap mating surface around the seal groove. Use the sealer sparingly.
12. Plastigage the rear main bearing cap as outlined in MEASURING REAR MAIN CLEARANCE in this Chapter and check with specification. If out of specification, check for frying of the rope seal which may be causing the cap to not seat properly.
13. Install all remaining components and inspect for leaks.

Flywheel and Ring Gear

REMOVAL AND INSTALLATION

The ring gear is an integral part of the flywheel and is not replaceable.
1. Remove the transmission.
2. Remove the six bolts attaching the flywheel to the crankshaft flange. Remove the flywheel.
3. Inspect the flywheel for cracks, and inspect the ring gear for burrs or worn teeth. Replace the flywheel if any damage is apparent. Remove burrs with a mill file.
4. Install the flywheel. The flywheel will only attach to the crankshaft in one position, as the bolt holes are unevenly spaced. Install the bolts and torque to specification. Tighten bolts in crisscross pattern.

EXHAUST SYSTEM

Safety Precautions

For a number of reasons, exhaust system work can be the most dangerous type of work you can do on your car. Always observe the following precautions:

• Support the car safely. Not only will you often be working directly under it, but you'll frequently be using a lot of force, say, heavy hammer blows, to dislodge rusted parts. This can cause a car that's improperly supported to shift and possibly fall.

• Wear goggles. Exhaust system parts are always rusty. Metal chips can be dislodged, even when you're only turning rusted bolts. Attempting to pry pipes apart with a chisel makes the chips fly even more frequently.

• If you're using a cutting torch, keep it a safe distance from either the fuel tank or lines. Stop what you're doing and feel the temperature of the fuel bearing pipes on the tank frequently. Even slight heat can expand and/or vaporize fuel, resulting in accumulated vapor, or even a liquid leak, near your torch.

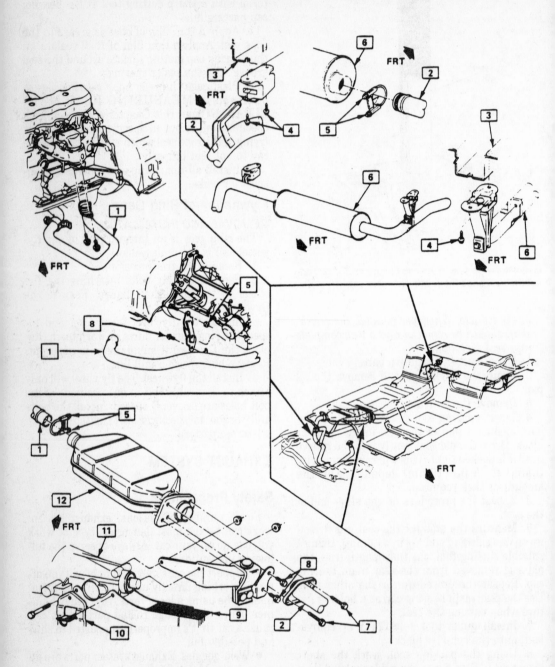

1. Front exhaust pipe
2. Intermediate exhaust pipe asm.
3. Underbody
4. 10 N·m (8 lb. ft.)
5. 30 N·m (22 lb. ft.)
6. Resonator & tailpipe asm.
7. 16 N·m (12 lb. ft.)
8. 34 N·m (25 lb. ft.)
9. Damper asm.
10. Inner brkt. asm.
11. Transmission
12. Converter asm.

Exhaust system—2.5L engine

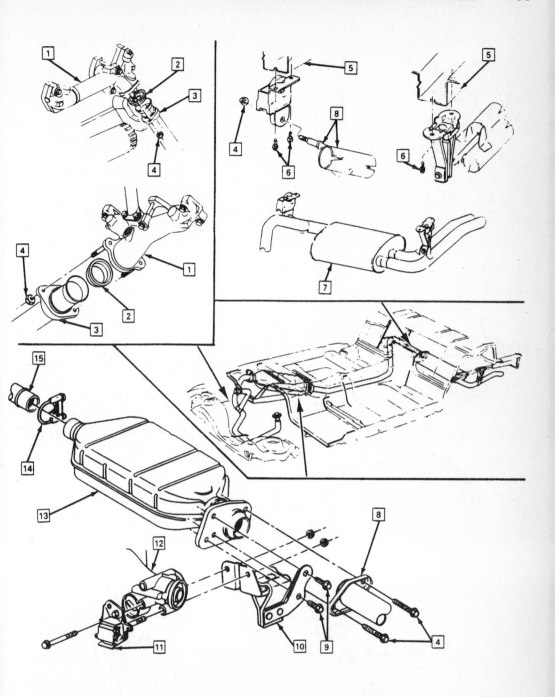

1. Manifold
2. Seal
3. Crossover pipe
4. 20 N·m (15 lbs. ft.)
5. Underbody
6. 10 N·m (8 lbs. ft.)
7. Muffler
8. Intermediate exhaust pipe assembly

9. 50 N·m (37 lbs. ft.)
10. Hanger
11. Inner bracket assembly
12. Transmission
13. Converter assembly
14. 60 N·m (44 lbs. ft.)
15. Front exhaust pipe

Exhaust system—V6 engine

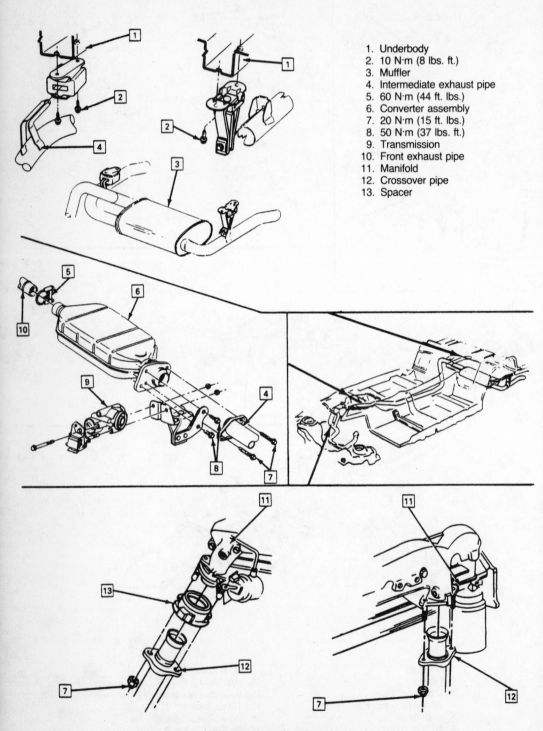

1. Underbody
2. 10 N·m (8 lbs. ft.)
3. Muffler
4. Intermediate exhaust pipe
5. 60 N·m (44 ft. lbs.)
6. Converter assembly
7. 20 N·m (15 ft. lbs.)
8. 50 N·m (37 lbs. ft.)
9. Transmission
10. Front exhaust pipe
11. Manifold
12. Crossover pipe
13. Spacer

Exhaust system—V8 engine

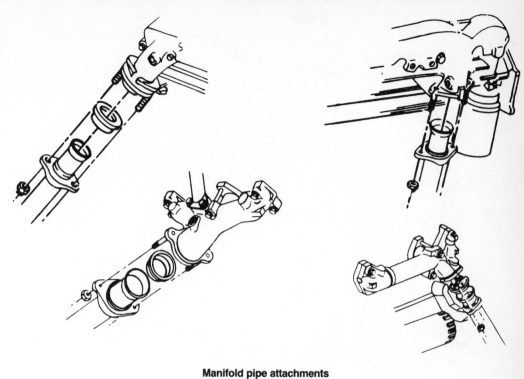

Manifold pipe attachments

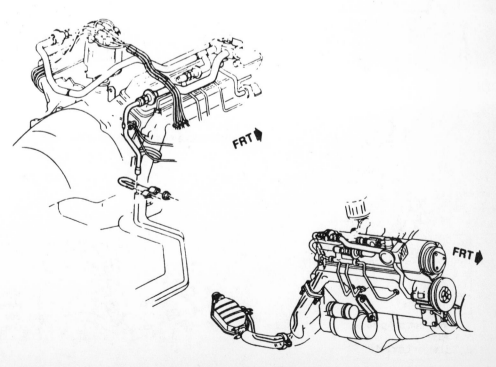

Air injection system attachments

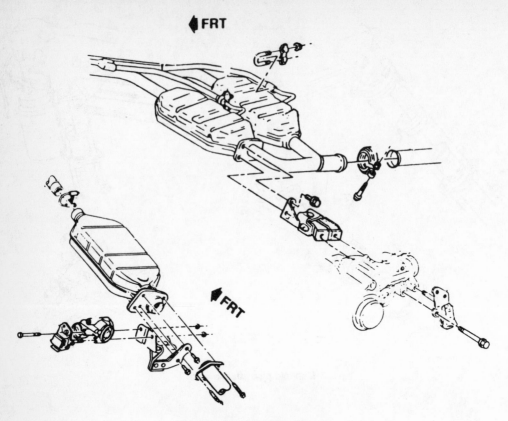

Catalytic converter attachments

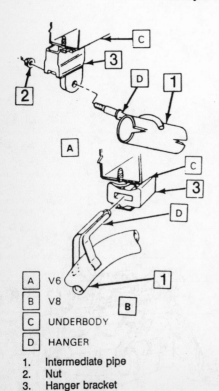

A	V6
B	V8
C	UNDERBODY
D	HANGER

1. Intermediate pipe
2. Nut
3. Hanger bracket

Intermediate pipe hanger

1. Intermediate pipe
2. Clamp
3. Muffler

Intermediate pipe attachment at muffler

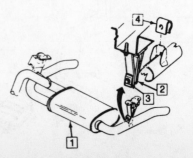

1. Muffler
2. Hanger
3. Bolt
4. Clip

Muffler hanger attachment

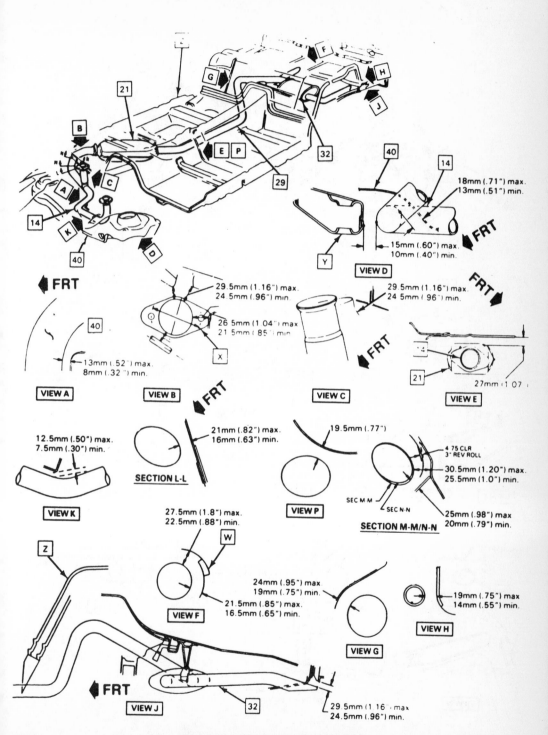

Exhaust to body clearances—V8 engine

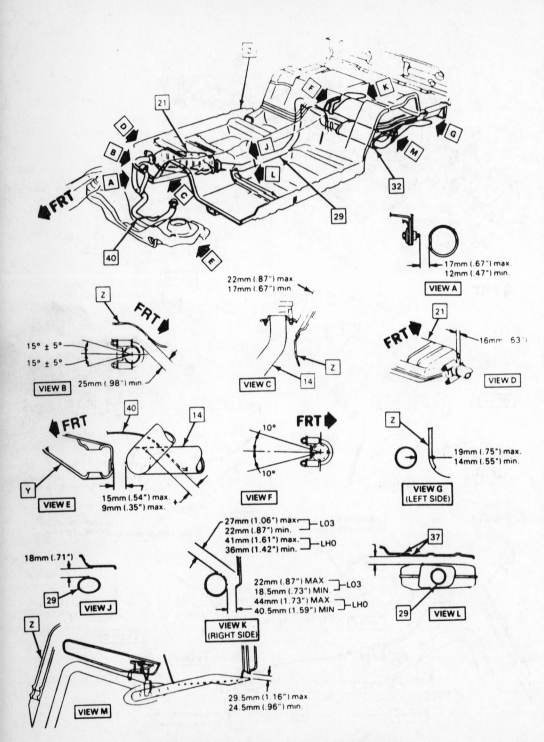

Exhaust to body clearances—V6 and V8 engines

• Watch where you're hammering and make sure you hit squarely. You could easily tap a brake or fuel line when you hit an exhaust system part with a glancing blow. Inspect all lines and hoses in the area where you've been working.

Special Tools

A number of special exhaust system tools can be rented from auto supply houses or local stores that rent special equipment. A common one is a tail pipe expander, designed to enable you to join pipes of identical diameter.

It may also be quite helpful to use solvents designed to loosen rusted bolts or flanges. Soaking rusted parts the night before you do the job can speed the work of freeing rusted parts considerably. Remember that these solvents are often flammable. Apply only to parts after they are cool!

Checking

Check complete exhaust system and nearby body areas and trunk lid for broken, damaged, missing or mispositioned parts, open seams, holes, loose connections or other deterioration which could permit exhaust fumes to seep into the trunk or passenger compartment. Dust or water in the trunk may be an indication of a problem in one of these areas. Any defects should be corrected immediately. To help insure continued integrity, the exhaust system pipe rearward of the muffler must be replaced whenever a new muffler is installed. Also perform the following checks:

• After completing any repairs to the exhaust system check for possible leaks by performing the following: start the vehicle, ensure the emergency brake is on and the transmission is in **P** for automatic transmission or neutral for manual transmission, then have an assistant hold a rag up the tailpipe(s), listen for exhaust leaks, if possible carefully listen under the vehicle and if the exhaust system is still cool place hands around the pipes and feel for leaks. The engine may begin to stall because of excessive backpressure, which is normal and so the test should be performed quickly.

• After completing any repairs to the exhaust system, lower the vehicle so the suspension is fully compressed and with the aid of an assistant rock the back end of the vehicle up and down while you listen and carefully look for any system components which might be rubbing on fuel, brake or other items such as: shock absorbers, the rear axle, driveshaft and the body or floor of the vehicle.

Exhaust Pipe
REMOVAL AND INSTALLATION

The exhaust manifold-to-crossover pipe connections are of the ball type, which eliminates the need for gaskets. Remove the front pipe retaining nuts, space and heat riser, if equipped. Separate the front pipe from the converter using a torch (to heat the pipe to aid in removal), or if the pipe is be replaced you can cut the outside pipe carefully and remove it. Remove the air injection pipes, as required. Installation is the reverse of the removal, pay special attention to the fit and alignment of the system. Secure with new clamps.

Muffler
REMOVAL AND INSTALLATION

The mufflers are a tri-flow design. Some muffler installations have a slot in the inlet and/or outlet pipe which indexes to a key (tab) welded on the exhaust and/or tail pipe to help maintain alignment. Remove any necessary clamps and carefully separate the pipe from the muffler using a suitable tool. Installation is the reverse of the removal procedure, pay special attention to the fit and alignment of the system. Secure with new clamps.

Resonator
REMOVAL AND INSTALLATION

A resonator is used on some series exhaust systems. It allows the use of mufflers with less back pressure and provides for optimum tuning characteristics of the exhaust system. Removal is the same as a muffler assembly.

Catalytic Converter
REMOVAL AND INSTALLATION

The catalytic converter is an emission control device added to the exhaust system to reduce pollutants from the exhaust gas stream. Remove the front crossover pipe assembly and front pipe to converter. Remove any AIR injection tubes, as necessary. Remove the converter hanger and intermediate pipe-to-flange retaining bolts. Installation is the reverse of the removal procedure, pay special attention to the fit and alignment of the system. Secure with new clamps.

Periodic maintenance of the exhaust system is not required, however, if the car is raised for other service, it is advisable to check the general condition of the catalytic converter, pipes and mufflers.

Emission Controls

AIR POLLUTION

The earth's atmosphere, at or near sea level, consists of 78% nitrogen, 21% oxygen and 1% other gases, approximately. If it were possible to remain in this state, 100% clean air would result. However, many varied causes allow other gases and particulates to mix with the clean air, causing the air to become unclean or polluted.

Certain of these pollutants are visible while others are invisible, with each having the capability of causing distress to the eyes, ears, throat, skin and respiratory system. Should these pollutants be concentrated in a specific area and under the right conditions, death could result due to the displacement or chemical change of the oxygen content in the air. These pollutants can cause much damage to the environment and to the many man made objects that are exposed to the elements.

To better understand the causes of air pollution, the pollutants can be categorized into 3 separate types, natural, industrial and automotive.

Natural Pollutants

Natural pollution has been present on earth before man appeared and is still a factor to be considered when discussing air pollution, although it causes only a small percentage of the present overall pollution problem existing in our country. It is the direct result of decaying organic matter, wind born smoke and particulates from such natural events as plains and forest fires (ignited by heat or lightning), volcanic ash, sand and dust which can spread over a large area of the countryside.

Such a phenomenon of natural pollution has been recent volcanic eruptions, with the resulting plume of smoke, steam and volcanic ash blotting out the sun's rays as it spreads and rises higher into the atmosphere, where the upper air currents catch and carry the smoke and ash, while condensing the steam back into water vapor. As the water vapor, smoke and ash traveled on their journey, the smoke dissipates into the atmosphere while the ash and moisture settle back to earth in a trail hundred of miles long. In many cases, lives are lost and millions of dollars of property damage result, and ironically, man can only stand by and watch it happen.

Industrial Pollution

Industrial pollution is caused primarily by industrial processes, the burning of coal, oil and natural gas, which in turn produces smoke and fumes. Because the burning fuels contain much sulfur, the principal ingredients of smoke and fumes are sulfur dioxide (SO_2) and particulate matter. This type of pollutant occurs most severely during still, damp and cool weather, such as at night. Even in its less severe form, this pollutant is not confined to just cities. Because of air movements, the pollutants move for miles over the surrounding countryside, leaving in its path a barren and unhealthy environment for all living things.

Working with Federal, State and Local mandated rules, regulations and by carefully monitoring the emissions, industries have greatly reduced the amount of pollutant emitted from their industrial sources, striving to obtain an acceptable level. Because of the mandated industrial emission clean up, many land areas and streams in and around the cities that were formerly barren of vegetation and life, have now begun to move back in the direction of nature's intended balance.

Automotive Pollutants

The third major source of air pollution is the automotive emissions. The emissions from the internal combustion engine were not an appreciable problem years ago because of the small number of registered vehicles and the nation's small highway system. However, during the early 1950's, the trend of the American people was to move from the cities to the surrounding suburbs. This caused an immediate problem in the transportation areas because the majority of the suburbs were not afforded mass transit conveniences. This lack of transportation created an attractive market for the automobile manufacturers, which resulted in a dramatic increase in the number of vehicles produced and sold, along with a marked increase in highway construction between cities and the suburbs. Multi-vehicle families emerged with much emphasis placed on the individual vehicle per family member. As the increase in vehicle ownership and usage occurred, so did the pollutant levels in and around the cities, as the suburbanites drove daily to their businesses and employment in the city and its fringe area, returning at the end of the day to their homes in the suburbs.

It was noted that a fog and smoke type haze was being formed and at times, remained in suspension over the cities and did not quickly dissipate. At first this "smog", derived from the words "smoke" and "fog", was thought to result from industrial pollution but it was determined that the automobile emissions were largely to blame. It was discovered that as normal automobile emissions were exposed to sunlight for a period of time, complex chemical reactions would take place.

It was found the smog was a photo chemical layer and was developed when certain oxides of nitrogen (NOx) and unburned hydrocarbons (HC) from the automobile emissions were exposed to sunlight and was more severe when the smog would remain stagnant over an area in which a warm layer of air would settle over the top of a cooler air mass at ground level, trapping and holding the automobile emissions, instead of the emissions being dispersed and diluted through normal air flows. This type of air stagnation was given the name "Temperature Inversion".

Temperature Inversion

In normal weather situations, the surface air is warmed by the heat radiating from the earth's surface and the sun's rays and will rise upward, into the atmosphere, to be cooled through a convection type heat expands with the cooler upper air. As the warm air rises, the surface pollutants are carried upward and dissipated into the atmosphere.

When a temperature inversion occurs, we find the higher air is no longer cooler but warmer than the surface air, causing the cooler surface air to become trapped and unable to move. This warm air blanket can extend from above ground level to a few hundred or even a few thousand feet into the air. As the surface air is trapped, so are the pollutants, causing a severe smog condition. Should this stagnant air mass extend to a few thousand feet high, enough air movement with the inversion takes place to allow the smog layer to rise above ground level but the pollutants still cannot dissipate. This inversion can remain for days over an area, with only the smog level rising or lowering from ground level to a few hundred feet high. Meanwhile, the pollutant levels increases, causing eye irritation, respirator problems, reduced visibility, plant damage and in some cases, cancer type diseases.

This inversion phenomenon was first noted in the Los Angeles, California area. The city lies in a basin type of terrain and during certain weather conditions, a cold air mass is held in the basin while a warmer air mass covers it like a lid.

Because this type of condition was first documented as prevalent in the Los Angeles area, this type of smog was named Los Angeles Smog, although it occurs in other areas where a large concentration of automobiles are used and the air remains stagnant for any length of time.

Internal Combustion Engine Pollutants

Consider the internal combustion engine as a machine in which raw materials must be placed so a finished product comes out. As in any machine operation, a certain amount of wasted material is formed. When we relate this to the internal combustion engine, we find that by putting in air and fuel, we obtain power from this mixture during the combustion process to drive the vehicle. The by-product or waste of this power is, in part, heat and exhaust gases with which we must concern ourselves.

HEAT TRANSFER

The heat from the combustion process can rise to over 4000°F (2204°C). The dissipation of this heat is controlled by a ram air effect, the use of cooling fans to cause air flow and having a liquid coolant solution surrounding the combustion area and transferring the heat of combustion through the cylinder walls and into the coolant. The coolant is then directed to a thin-finned, multi-tubed radiator, from which the excess heat is transferred to the outside air by 1 or all of the 3 heat transfer methods, conduction, convection or radiation.

The cooling of the combustion area is an important part in the control of exhaust emissions. To understand the behavior of the combustion and transfer of its heat, consider the air/fuel charge. It is ignited and the flame front burns progressively across the combustion chamber until the burning charge reaches the cylinder walls. Some of the fuel in contact with the walls is not hot enough to burn, thereby snuffing out or Quenching the combustion process. This leaves unburned fuel in the combustion chamber. This unburned fuel is then forced out of the cylinder along with the exhaust gases and into the exhaust system.

Many attempts have been made to minimize the amount of unburned fuel in the combustion chambers due to the snuffing out or "Quenching", by increasing the coolant temperature and lessening the contact area of the coolant around the combustion area. Design limitations within the combustion chambers prevent the complete burning of the air/fuel charge, so a certain amount of the unburned fuel is still expelled into the exhaust system, regardless of modifications to the engine.

EXHAUST EMISSIONS

Composition Of The Exhaust Gases

The exhaust gases emitted into the atmosphere are a combination of burned and unburned fuel. To understand the exhaust emission and its composition review some basic chemistry.

When the air/fuel mixture is introduced into the engine, we are mixing air, composed of nitrogen (78%), oxygen (21%) and other gases (1%) with the fuel, which is 100% hydrocarbons (HC), in a semi-controlled ratio. As the combustion process is accomplished, power is produced to move the vehicle while the heat of combustion is transferred to the cooling system. The exhaust gases are then composed of nitrogen, a diatomic gas (N_2), the same as was introduced in the engine, carbon dioxide ($CO2$), the same gas that is used in beverage carbonation and water vapor (H_2O). The nitrogen (N_2), for the most part passes through the engine unchanged, while the oxygen (O_2) reacts (burns) with the hydrocarbons (HC) and produces the carbon dioxide (CO_2) and the water vapors (H_2O). If this chemical process would be the only process to take place, the exhaust emissions would be harmless. However, during the combustion process, other pollutants are formed and are considered dangerous. These pollutants are carbon monoxide (CO), hydrocarbons (HC), oxides of nitrogen (NOx) oxides of sulfur (SOx) and engine particulates.

Lead (Pb), is considered 1 of the particulates and is present in the exhaust gases whenever leaded fuels are used. Lead (Pb) does not dissipate easily. Levels can be high along roadways when it is emitted from vehicles and can pose a health threat. Since the increased usage of unleaded gasoline and the phasing out of leaded gasoline for fuel, this pollutant is gradually diminishing. While not considered a major threat lead is still considered a dangerous pollutant.

HYDROCARBONS

Hydrocarbons (HC) are essentially unburned fuel that have not been successfully burned during the combustion process or have escaped into the atmosphere through fuel evaporation. The main sources of incomplete combustion are rich air/fuel mixtures, low engine temperatures and improper spark timing. The main sources of hydrocarbon emission through fuel evaporation come from the vehicle's fuel tank and carburetor bowl.

To reduce combustion hydrocarbon emission, engine modifications were made to minimize dead space and surface area in the combustion chamber. In addition the air/fuel mixture was made more lean through improved carburetion, fuel injection and by the addition of external controls to aid in further combustion of the hydrocarbons outside the engine. Two such methods were the addition of an air injection system, to inject fresh air into the exhaust manifolds and the installation of a catalytic converter, a unit that is able to burn traces of hydrocarbons without affecting the internal combustion process or fuel economy.

To control hydrocarbon emissions through fuel evaporation, modifications were made to the fuel tank and carburetor bowl to allow storage of the fuel vapors during periods of engine shut-down, and at specific times during engine operation, to purge and burn these same vapors by blending them with the air/fuel mixture.

CARBON MONOXIDE

Carbon monoxide is formed when not enough oxygen is present during the combustion process to convert carbon (C) to carbon dioxide (CO_2). An increase in the carbon monoxide (CO) emission is normally accompanied by an increase in the hydrocarbon (HC) emission because of the lack of oxygen to completely burn all of the fuel mixture.

Carbon monoxide (CO) also increases the rate at which the photo chemical smog is formed by speeding up the conversion of nitric oxide (NO) to nitrogen dioxide (NO_2). To accomplish this, carbon monoxide (CO) combines with oxygen (O_2) and nitrogen dioxide (NO_2) to produce carbon dioxide (CO_2)

and nitrogen dioxide (NO_2). ($CO + O_2 + NO = CO_2 + NO_2$).

The dangers of carbon monoxide, which is an odorless, colorless toxic gas are many. When carbon monoxide is inhaled into the lungs and passed into the blood stream, oxygen is replaced by the carbon monoxide in the red blood cells, causing a reduction in the amount of oxygen being supplied to the many parts of the body. This lack of oxygen causes headaches, lack of coordination, reduced mental alertness and should the carbon monoxide concentration be high enough, death could result.

NITROGEN

Normally, nitrogen is an inert gas. When heated to approximately 2500°F (1371°C) through the combustion process, this gas becomes active and causes an increase in the nitric oxide (NOx) emission.

Oxides of nitrogen (NOx) are composed of approximately 97–98% nitric oxide (NO2). Nitric oxide is a colorless gas but when it is passed into the atmosphere, it combines with oxygen and forms nitrogen dioxide (NO2). The nitrogen dioxide then combines with chemically active hydrocarbons (HC) and when in the presence of sunlight, causes the formation of photo chemical smog.

OZONE

To further complicate matters, some of the nitrogen dioxide (NO_2) is broken apart by the sunlight to form nitric oxide and oxygen. (NO_2 + sunlight = NO + O). This single atom of oxygen then combines with diatomic (meaning 2 atoms) oxygen (O_2) to form ozone (O_3). Ozone is 1 of the smells associated with smog. It has a pungent and offensive odor, irritates the eyes and lung tissues, affects the growth of plant life and causes rapid deterioration of rubber products. Ozone can be formed by sunlight as well as electrical discharge into the air.

The most common discharge area on the automobile engine is the secondary ignition electrical system, especially when inferior quality spark plug cables are used. As the surge of high voltage is routed through the secondary cable, the circuit builds up an electrical field around the wire, acting upon the oxygen in the surrounding air to form the ozone. The faint glow along the cable with the engine running that may be visible on a dark night, is called the "corona discharge." It is the result of the electrical field passing from a high along the cable, to a low in the surrounding air, which forms the ozone gas. The combination of corona and ozone has been a major cause of cable deterioration. Recently, different types and better quality insulating materials have lengthened the life of the electrical cables.

Although ozone at ground level can be harmful, ozone is beneficial to the earth's inhabitants. By having a concentrated ozone layer called the 'ozonosphere', between 10 and 20 miles (16–32km) up in the atmosphere much of the ultra violet radiation from the sun's rays are absorbed and screened. If this ozone layer were not present, much of the earth's surface would be burned, dried and unfit for human life.

There is much discussion concerning the ozone layer and its density. A feeling exists that this protective layer of ozone is slowly diminishing and corrective action must be directed to this problem. Much experimenting is presently being conducted to determine if a problem exists and if so, the short and long term effects of the problem and how it can be remedied.

OXIDES OF SULFUR

Oxides of sulfur (SOx) were initially ignored in the exhaust system emissions, since the sulfur content of gasoline as a fuel is less than $\frac{1}{10}$ of 1%. Because of this small amount, it was felt that it contributed very little to the overall pollution problem. However, because of the difficulty in solving the sulfur emissions in industrial pollutions and the introduction of catalytic converter to the automobile exhaust systems, a change was mandated. The automobile exhaust system, when equipped with a catalytic converter, changes the sulfur dioxide (SO_2) into the sulfur trioxide (SO_3).

When this combines with water vapors (H_2O), a sulfuric acid mist (H_2SO_4) is formed and is a very difficult pollutant to handle and is extremely corrosive. This sulfuric acid mist that is formed, is the same mist that rises from the vents of an automobile storage battery when an active chemical reaction takes place within the battery cells.

When a large concentration of vehicles equipped with catalytic converters are operating in an area, this acid mist will rise and be distributed over a large ground area causing land, plant, crop, paints and building damage.

PARTICULATE MATTER

A certain amount of particulate matter is present in the burning of any fuel, with carbon constituting the largest percentage of the particulates. In gasoline, the remaining percentage of particulates is the burned remains of the various other compounds used in its manufacture. When a gasoline engine is in good internal condition, the particulate emissions are low but as the engine wears internally, the particulate emissions increase. By visually inspecting the tail pipe emissions, a determination can be made as to where an engine defect may exist. An engine with light gray smoke emitting from the tail pipe normally indicates an increase in the oil consumption through burning due to internal engine wear. Black smoke would indicate a defective fuel delivery system, causing the engine to operate in a rich mode. Regardless of the color of the smoke, the internal part of the engine or the fuel delivery system should be repaired to a "like new" condition to prevent excess particulate emissions.

Diesel and turbine engines emit a darkened plume of smoke from the exhaust system because of the type of fuel used. Emission control regulations are mandated for this type of emission and more stringent measures are being used to prevent excess emission of the particulate matter. Electronic components are being introduced to control the injection of the fuel at precisely the proper time of piston travel, to achieve the optimum in fuel ignition and fuel usage. Other particulate after-burning components are being tested to achieve a cleaner particular emission.

Good grades of engine lubricating oils should be used, meeting the manufacturers specification. "Cut-rate" oils can contribute to the particulate emission problem because of their low "flash" or ignition temperature point. Such oils burn prematurely during the combustion process causing emissions of particulate matter.

The cooling system is an important factor in the reduction of particulate matter. With the cooling system operating at a temperature specified by the manufacturer, the optimum of combustion will occur. The cooling system must be maintained in the same manner as the engine oiling system, as each system is required to perform properly in order for the engine to operate efficiently for a long time.

Other Automobile Emission Sources

Before emission controls were mandated on the internal combustion engines, other sources of engine pollutants were discovered, along with the exhaust emission. It was determined the engine combustion exhaust produced 60% of the total emission pollutants, fuel evaporation from the fuel tank and carburetor vents produced 20%, with the another 20% being produced through the crankcase as a by-product of the combustion process.

CRANKCASE EMISSIONS

Crankcase emissions are made up of water, acids, unburned fuel, oil fumes and particulates. The emissions are classified as hydrocarbons (HC) and are formed by the small amount of unburned, compressed air/fuel mixture entering the crankcase from the combustion area during the compression and power strokes, between the cylinder walls and piston rings. The head of the compression and combustion help to form the remaining crankcase emissions.

Since the first engines, crankcase emissions were allowed to go into the air through a road draft tube, mounted on the lower side of the engine block. Fresh air came in through an open oil filler cap or breather. The air passed through the crankcase mixing with blow-by gases. The motion of the vehicle and the air blowing past the open end of the road draft tube caused a low pressure area at the end of the tube. Crankcase emissions were simply drawn out of the road draft tube into the air.

To control the crankcase emission, the road draft tube was deleted. A hose and/or tubing was routed from the crankcase to the intake manifold so the blow-by emission could be burned with the air/fuel mixture. However, it was found that intake manifold vacuum, used to draw the crankcase emissions into the manifold, would vary in strength at the wrong time and not allow the proper emission flow. A regulating type valve was needed to control the flow of air through the crankcase.

Testing, showed the removal of the blow-by gases from the crankcase as quickly as possible, was most important to the longevity of the engine. Should large accumulations of blow-by gases remain and condense, dilution of the engine oil would occur to form water, soots, resins, acids and lead salts, resulting in the formation of sludge and varnishes. This condensation of the blow-by gases occur more frequently on vehicles used in numerous starting and stopping conditions, excessive idling and when the engine is not allowed to attain normal operating temperature through short runs. The crankcase purge control or PCV system will be described in detail later in this Chapter.

FUEL EVAPORATIVE EMISSIONS

Gasoline fuel is a major source of pollution, before and after it is burned in the automobile engine. From the time the fuel is refined, stored, pumped and transported, again stored until it is pumped into the fuel tank of the vehicle, the gasoline gives off unburned hydrocarbons (HC) into the atmosphere. Through redesigning of the storage areas and venting systems, the pollution factor has been diminished but not eliminated, from the refinery standpoint. However, the automobile still remained the primary source of vaporized, unburned hydrocarbon (HC) emissions.

Fuel pumped form an underground storage

tank is cool but when exposed to a warner ambient temperature, will expand. Before controls were mandated, an owner would fill the fuel tank with fuel from an underground storage tank and park the vehicle for some time in warm area, such as a parking lot. As the fuel would warm, it would expand and should no provisions or area be provided for the expansion, the fuel would spill out the filler neck and onto the ground, causing hydrocarbon (HC) pollution and creating a severe fire hazard. To correct this condition, the vehicle manufacturers added overflow plumbing and/or gasoline tanks with built in expansion areas or domes.

However, this did not control the fuel vapor emission from the fuel tank and the carburetor bowl. It was determined that most of the fuel evaporation occurred when the vehicle was stationary and the engine not operating. Most vehicles carry 5–25 gallons (19–95 liters) of gasoline. Should a large concentration of vehicles be parked in one area, such as a large parking lot, excessive fuel vapor emissions would take place, increasing as the temperature increases.

To prevent the vapor emission from escaping into the atmosphere, the fuel system is designed to trap the fuel vapors while the vehicle is stationary, by sealing the fuel system from the atmosphere. A storage system is used to collect and hold the fuel vapors from the carburetor and the fuel tank when the engine is not operating. When the engine is started, the storage system is then purged of the fuel vapors, which are drawn into the engine and burned with the air/fuel mixture.

EMISSION CONTROLS

Crankcase Ventilation System

OPERATION

The positive crankcase ventilation (PCV) system is used to control crankcase blow-by vapors. The system functions as follows:

The crankcase (blow-by) gases are recycled in the following way:

As the engine is running, clean, filtered air is drawn through the air filter and into the crankcase. As the air passes through the crankcase, it picks up the combustion gases and carries them out of the crankcase, through the PCV valve, and into the induction system. As they enter the intake manifold, they are drawn into the combustion chamber where they are reburned.

The most critical component in the system is the PCV valve. This valve controls the amount of gases which are recycled into the combustion chamber. At low engine speeds, the valve is partially closed, limiting the flow of gases into the intake manifold. As engine speed increases, the

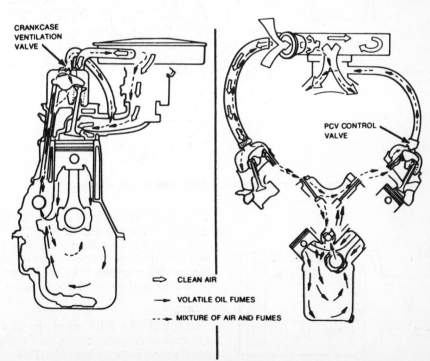

CRANKCASE VENTILATION VALVE

PCV CONTROL VALVE

⇨ CLEAN AIR

➤ VOLATILE OIL FUMES

--➤ MIXTURE OF AIR AND FUMES

PCV system operation—4 cyl. to the left; V6 & V8 to the right

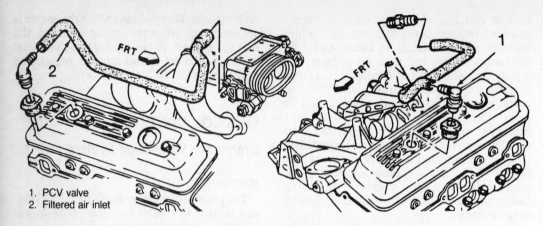

1. PCV valve
2. Filtered air inlet

Positive Crankcase Ventilation (PCV) system—5.7L (TPI) engine

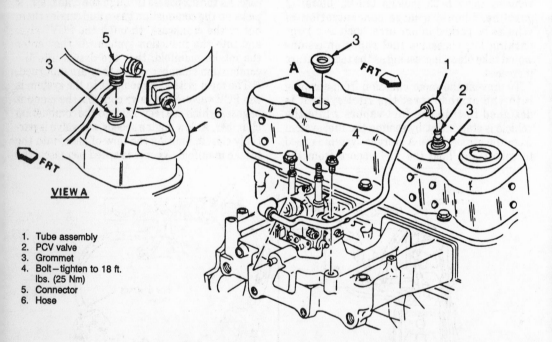

1. Tube assembly
2. PCV valve
3. Grommet
4. Bolt—tighten to 18 ft.
   lbs. (25 Nm)
5. Connector
6. Hose

Positive Crankcase Ventilation (PCV) system—2.5L engine

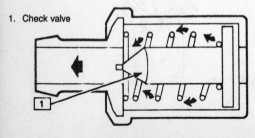

1. Check valve

Cross-section of standard PCV valve

valve opens to admit greater quantities of gases into the intake manifold. If the PCV valve becomes clogged, the system is designed to allow excessive amounts of blow-by gases to back flow through the crankcase tube into the air cleaner to be consumed by normal combustion.

SERVICE

Inspect the PCV system hose and connections at each tune-up and replace any deteriorated hoses. Check the PCV valve at every tune-up and replace it at 30,000 mile intervals.

TESTING

1. Remove the PCV valve from the intake manifold or valve cover.
2. Run the engine at idle.
3. Place your thumb over the end of the valve. Check for vacuum. If there is no vacuum at the valve, check for plugged valve or vacuum lines.
4. Shut off the engine. Shake the valve and listen for the rattle. If valve doesn't rattle, replace it.

Evaporative Emission Controls

OPERATION

This system reduces the amount of gasoline vapors escaping into the atmosphere. Some models employ a purge control solenoid which is controlled by the ECM, to open and close the EEC system. Other models use a canister mounted vacuum purge valve; when the engine vacuum reaches a certain pressure, the valve opens allowing the gas vapors to be drawn off to the carburetor for burning.

Carburetor models use an exhaust tube from the float bowl to the charcoal canister; fuel injected models eliminate the fuel bowl tube. Fuel vapors from the gas tank travel from the tank to the vapor canister, where they are collected. Although the system may varies from vehicle to vehicle, the operations are basically the same.

Canister

REMOVAL AND INSTALLATION

1. Loosen the screw holding the canister retaining bracket.
2. Rotate the canister retaining bracket and remove the canister.
3. Tag and disconnect the hoses leading from the canister.
4. To install, connect the hoses to the canister according to the tags.
5. Install the canister into the retaining bracket.
6. Tighten the screw holding the canister retaining bracket.

FILTER REPLACEMENT

1. Remove the vapor canister.
2. Pull the filter out from the bottom of the canister.
3. Install a new filter and then replace the canister.

CANISTER PURGE SOLENOID REPLACEMENT

1. Disconnect the negative battery cable.
2. Remove the bolt, cover and solenoid.
3. Disconnect the electrical connector and hoses from the solenoid.
4. Remove the solenoid.

To install:

5. Install the solenoid, cover and bolt.

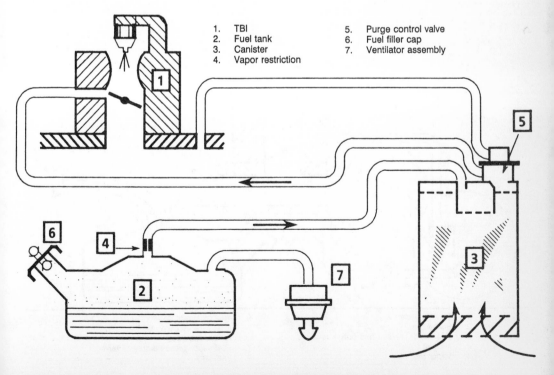

1.	TBI	5.	Purge control valve
2.	Fuel tank	6.	Fuel filler cap
3.	Canister	7.	Ventilator assembly
4.	Vapor restriction		

Evaporative Emission Control system—2.5L engine

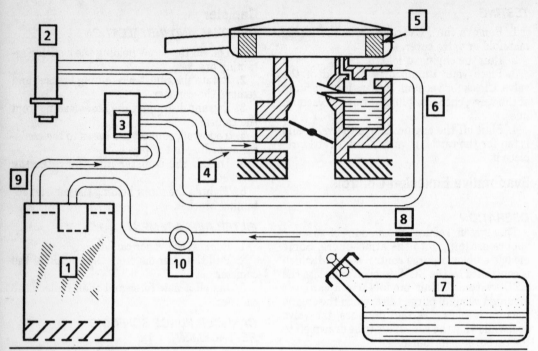

1. Canister
2. Thermal vacuum switch
3. Fuel vapor canister control valve
4. To manifold vacuum
5. Air cleaner carbon element

6. Bowl vent
7. Fuel tank
8. Vapor restriction
9. Purge hose
10. Tank pressure control valve

Evaporative Emission Control system—5.0L (VIN G & H) engines

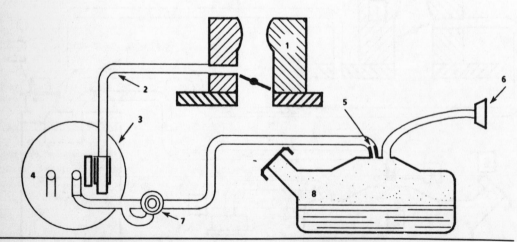

1. Throttle body
2. Purge line
3. Fuel vapor canister and purge solenoid
4. Air inlet
5. Vapor restriction

6. Fuel tank vent valve
   (pressure/vacuum relief)
   remote mounted
7. Fuel vapor pressure control valve
8. Fuel tank

Evaporative Emission Control system with fuel injection—3.1L, 5.0L & 5.7L engines

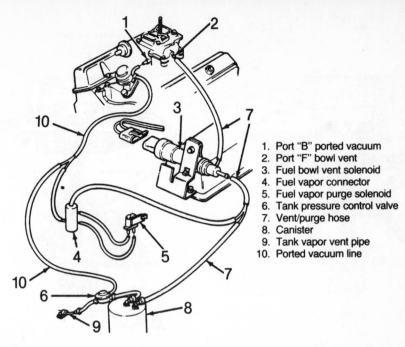

1. Port "B" ported vacuum
2. Port "F" bowl vent
3. Fuel bowl vent solenoid
4. Fuel vapor connector
5. Fuel vapor purge solenoid
6. Tank pressure control valve
7. Vent/purge hose
8. Canister
9. Tank vapor vent pipe
10. Ported vacuum line

Evaporative Emission Control system with carburetor bowl vent solenoid—2.8L engine

6. Connect the hoses and electrical connector to the solenoid.

7. Connect the negative battery cable.

Tank Pressure Control Valve

TESTING

1. Using a hand-held vacuum pump, apply a vacuum of 15 in. Hg. (51kPa) through the control vacuum signal tube to the purge valve diaphragm. If the diaphragm does not hold 5 in Hg. at least for 10 seconds, the diaphragm is leaking. Replace the control valve.

2. With the vacuum still applied to the control vacuum tube, attach a short piece of hose to the valve's tank tube side and blow into the hose. Air should pass through the valve. If it does not, replace the control valve.

REMOVAL AND INSTALLATION

1. Disconnect the hoses from the control valve.

2. Remove the mounting hardware.

3. Remove the control valve from the vehicle.

4. Installation is the reverse of the removal procedure. Refer to the Vehicle Emission Control Information label, located in the engine compartment, for proper routing of the vacuum hoses.

Exhaust Gas Recirculation (EGR) System

OPERATIONS

All models are equipped with this system, which consists of a metering valve, a vacuum line to the carburetor or intake manifold, and cast-in exhaust passages in the intake manifold. The EGR valve is controlled by vacuum, and opens and closes in response to the vacuum signals to admit exhaust gases into the air/fuel mixture. The exhaust gases lower peak combustion temperatures, reducing the formation of NOx. The valve is closed at idle and wide open throttle, but is open between the two extreme positions.

There are actually three types of EGR systems: Ported, Positive Back-Pressure and Negative Backpressure. The principle of all the systems are the same; the only difference is in the method used to control how the EGR valve opens.

Ported Valve

In the Ported system, the amount of exhaust gas admitted into the intake manifold depends on a ported vacuum signal. A ported vacuum signal is one taken from the carburetor above the throttle plates; thus, the vacuum signal (amount of vacuum) is dependent on how far

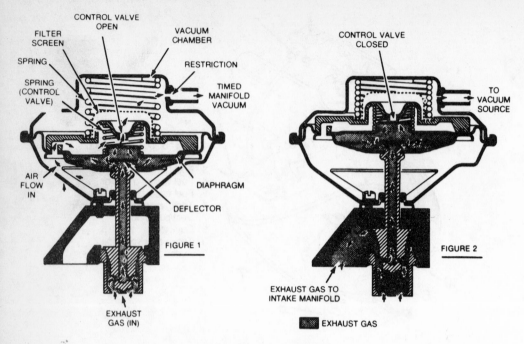

Positive backpressure EGR valve

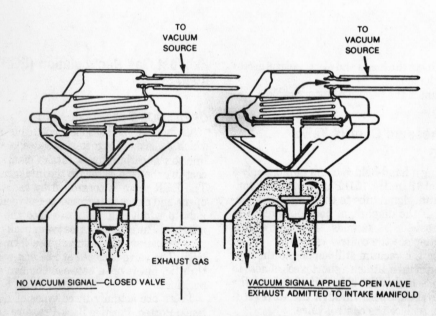

Vacuum operated EGR valve

the throttle plates are opened. When the throttle is closed (idle or deceleration) there is no vacuum signal. Thus, the EGR valve is closed, and no exhaust gas enters the intake manifold. As the throttle is opened, a vacuum is produced, which opens the EGR valve, admitting exhaust gas into the intake manifold.

Positive Backpressure Valve

This valve operates the same as the ported, except, it has an internal air bleed that acts as a vacuum regulator. The bleed valve controls the

amount of vacuum inside the vacuum chamber during operation. When the valve receives sufficient exhaust back-pressure through the hollow shaft, it closes the bleed; at this point the EGR valve opens.

NOTE: *This valve will not open, with vacuum applied to it, while the engine is idling or stopped.*

Negative Backpressure Valve

This valve is similar to the Positive Type, except, the bleed valve spring is moved from

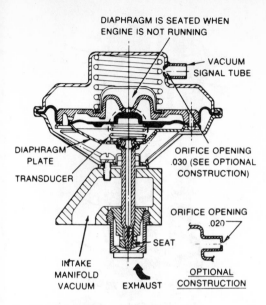

DIAPHRAGM IS SEATED WHEN
ENGINE IS NOT RUNNING

VACUUM
SIGNAL TUBE

DIAPHRAGM
PLATE

TRANSDUCER

ORIFICE OPENING
.030 (SEE OPTIONAL
CONSTRUCTION)

ORIFICE OPENING
.020

SEAT

INTAKE
MANIFOLD
VACUUM

EXHAUST

OPTIONAL
CONSTRUCTION

Negative backpressure EGR valve

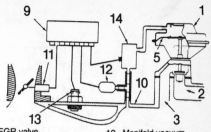

1. EGR valve
2. Exhaust gas
3. Intake air
5. Diaphragm
9. Electronic control module

10. Manifold vacuum
11. Throttle position sensor
12. Manifold pressure sensor
13. Coolant temperature sensor
14. EGR control solenoid

Electronic controlled EGR system

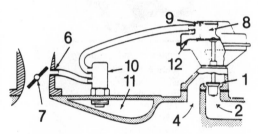

1. EGR valve
2. Exhaust gas
4. Intake flow
6. Vacuum port
7. Throttle valve

8. Vacuum chamber
9. Valve return spring
10. Thermal vacuum switch
11. Coolant
12. Diaphragm

Thermostatic vacuum switch controlled EGR valve

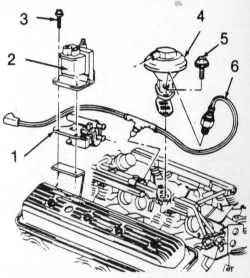

1. EGR solenoid
2. Coil
3. Bolt (2) 21 N·m
   (16 ft. lbs.)

4. EGR valve
5. Bolts (2)
6. EGR diag temp switch
   12 N·m (105 in. lbs.)

EGR and solenoid servicing—V8 engine

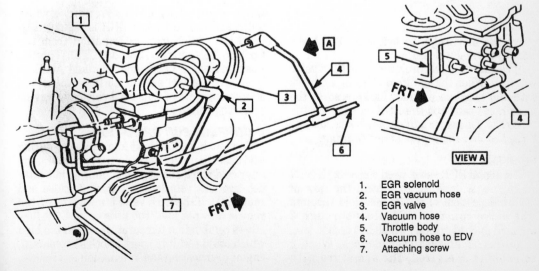

1. EGR solenoid
2. EGR vacuum hose
3. EGR valve
4. Vacuum hose
5. Throttle body
6. Vacuum hose to EDV
7. Attaching screw

EGR control solenoid

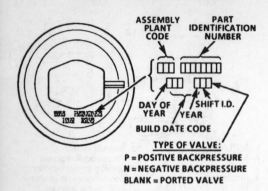

ASSEMBLY PLANT CODE

PART IDENTIFICATION NUMBER

DAY OF YEAR

SHIFT I.D. YEAR

BUILD DATE CODE

TYPE OF VALVE:
P = POSITIVE BACKPRESSURE
N = NEGATIVE BACKPRESSURE
BLANK = PORTED VALVE

EGR identification

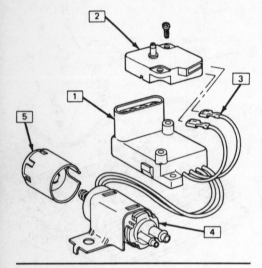

1. EGR vacuum control assembly base
2. EGR vacuum diagnostic switch
3. Diagnostic switch connectors
4. EGR solenoid
5. Filter

EGR vacuum control assembly—2.8L engine

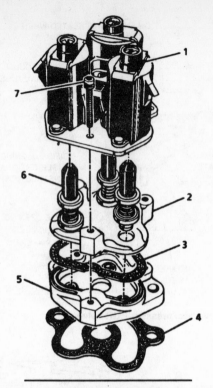

1. Solenoid and mounting plate assembly
2. EGR base plate
3. EGR base gasket
4. Insulator gasket
5. EGR base
6. Armature assembly
7. Screw assembly

Digital EGR valve—3.1L engine

above the diaphragm to below it. The bleed valve is normally closed.

At certain manifold pressures, the EGR valve will open. When the manifold vacuum combines with the negative exhaust backpressure, the bleed hole opens and the EGR valve closes.

NOTE: *This valve will open when vacuum is applied and the engine is not running.*

Digital EGR Valve

The digital EGR valve, used on the 3.1L (VIN T) engine, is designed to control the flow of EGR independent of intake manifold vacuum. The valve controls EGR flow through 3 solenoid-opened orifices, which increase in size, to produce 7 possible combinations. When a solenoid is energized, the armature with attached shaft and swivel pintle, is lifted, opening the orifice.

The digital EGR valve is opened by the ECM QDR, grounding each solenoid circuit individually. The flow of EGR is regulated by the ECM which uses information from the Coolant Temperature Sensor (CTS), Throttle Position Sensor (TPS) and Manifold Absolute Pressure (MAP) sensor to determine the appropriate rate of flow for a particular engine operating condition.

INCORRECT EGR OPERATION

Too much EGR flow at idle, cruise or during cold operation may result in the engine stalling after cold start, the engine stalling at idle after deceleration, vehicle surge during cruise and rough idle. If the EGR valve is always open, the vehicle may not idle. Too little or no EGR flow allows combustion temperatures to get too high which could result in spark knock (detonation), engine overheating and/or emission test failure.

EGR VALVE IDENTIFICATION

• Positive backpressure EGR valves will have a "P" stamped on the top side of the valve below the date built.

• Negative backpressure EGR valves will have a "N" stamped on the top side of the valve below the date built.

• Port EGR valves have no identification stamped below the date built.

Optional Controls

THERMOSTATIC VACUUM SWITCH (TVS)

The switch is sometimes used in combination with the EGR valve to close off vacuum during cold operation.

VACUUM/SOLENOID CONTROL

Some systems use a coolant temperature switch, throttle position switch and pressure sensor with the EGR valve. The vacuum control solenoid uses a Pulse Width Modulation system which turns the solenoid **ON** and **OFF** numerous times a second and varies the amount of **ON** time (pulse width) to vary the amount of ported vacuum supplied the EGR valve.

SERVICE

1. Check to see if the EGR valve diaphragm moves freely. Use your finger to reach up under the valve and push on the diaphragm. If it doesn't move freely, the valve should be replaced. The use of a mirror will aid the inspection process.

CAUTION: *If the engine is hot, wear a glove to protect your hand.*

2. Install a vacuum gauge into the vacuum line between the EGR valve and the carburetor. Start the engine and allow it to reach operating temperature.

3. With the car in either **P** or **N**, increase the engine speed until at least 5 in.Hg is showing on the gauge.

4. Remove the vacuum hose from the EGR valve. The diaphragm should move downward (valve closed). The engine speed should increase.

5. Install the vacuum hose and watch for the EGR valve to open (diaphragm moving upward). The engine speed should decrease to its former level, indicating exhaust recirculation.

6. If the diaphragm doesn't move, check engine vacuum; it should be at least 5 in.Hg with the throttle open and engine running.

7. Check to see that the engine is at normal operating temperature.

8. Check for vacuum at the EGR hose. If no vacuum is present, check the hose for leaks, breaks, kinks, improper connections, etc., and replace as necessary.

9. If the diaphragm moves, but the engine speed doesn't change, check the EGR passages in the intake manifold for blockage.

REMOVAL AND INSTALLATION

EGR VALVE

Except 3.1L Engine

1. Disconnect the negative battery cable.
2. Remove the air cleaner assembly.

NOTE: *If equipped with the 5.0L (VIN F) and 5.7L (VIN 8) engines with Tuned Port Injection, it will be necessary to remove the intake plenum to gain access to the EGR valve.*

3. Tag and disconnect the necessary hoses and wiring to gain access to the EGR valve.
4. Remove the EGR valve retaining bolts.
5. Remove the EGR valve. Discard the gasket.
6. Buff the exhaust deposits from the mounting surface and around the valve using a wire wheel.
7. Remove deposits from the valve outlet.
8. Clean the mounting surfaces of the intake manifold and valve assembly.

To install:

9. Install a new EGR gasket.
10. Install the EGR valve to the manifold.
11. Install the retaining bolts.
12. Connect the wiring and hoses.
13. Install the air cleaner assembly.
14. Connect the negative battery cable.

3.1L Engine

1. Disconnect the negative battery cable.
2. Disconnect the electrical connector at the solenoid.
3. Remove the 2 base-to-flange bolts.
4. Remove the digital EGR valve.

To install:

5. Install the digital EGR valve.
6. Install the 2 base-to-flange bolts. Tighten to 22 ft. lbs. (30 Nm).
7. Connect the negative battery cable.

EGR Solenoid

NOTE: *If equipped with the 5.0L (VIN F) and 5.7L (VIN 8) engines with Tuned Port Injection, it will be necessary to remove the intake plenum to gain access to the EGR solenoid.*

1. Disconnect the negative battery cable.
2. Remove the air cleaner, as required.
3. Disconnect the electrical connector at the solenoid.
4. Disconnect the vacuum hoses.
5. Remove the retaining bolts and the solenoid.
6. Remove the filter, as required.

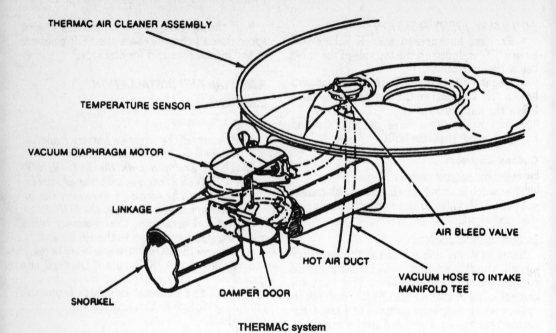

THERMAC AIR CLEANER ASSEMBLY

TEMPERATURE SENSOR

VACUUM DIAPHRAGM MOTOR

LINKAGE

AIR BLEED VALVE

HOT AIR DUCT

VACUUM HOSE TO INTAKE MANIFOLD TEE

SNORKEL

DAMPER DOOR

THERMAC system

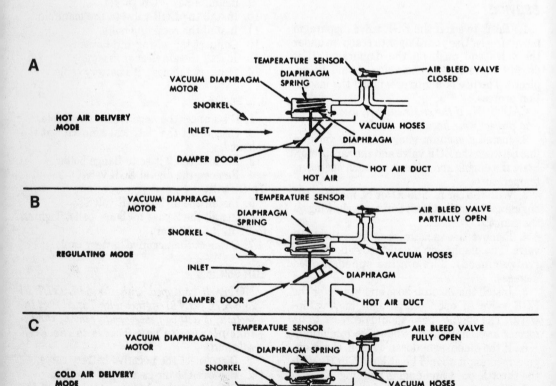

A

HOT AIR DELIVERY MODE

TEMPERATURE SENSOR
DIAPHRAGM SPRING
AIR BLEED VALVE CLOSED
VACUUM DIAPHRAGM MOTOR
SNORKEL
VACUUM HOSES
INLET
DIAPHRAGM
DAMPER DOOR
HOT AIR DUCT
HOT AIR

B

REGULATING MODE

VACUUM DIAPHRAGM MOTOR
TEMPERATURE SENSOR
DIAPHRAGM SPRING
AIR BLEED VALVE PARTIALLY OPEN
SNORKEL
VACUUM HOSES
INLET
DIAPHRAGM
DAMPER DOOR
HOT AIR DUCT

C

COLD AIR DELIVERY MODE

TEMPERATURE SENSOR
AIR BLEED VALVE FULLY OPEN
VACUUM DIAPHRAGM MOTOR
DIAPHRAGM SPRING
SNORKEL
VACUUM HOSES
INLET
DIAPHRAGM
DAMPER DOOR
HOT AIR DUCT

Schematic of the vacuum motor operation

To install:

7. If removed, install the filter.
8. Install the solenoid and retaining bolts.
9. Connect the vacuum hoses.
10. Connect the electrical connector.
11. If removed, install the air cleaner.
12. Connect the negative battery cable.

Thermostatic Air Cleaner (THERMAC)

OPERATION

All engines use the THERMAC system. This system is designed to warm the air entering the carburetor when underhood temperatures are low, and to maintain a controlled air temperature into the carburetor at all times. By allowing preheated air to enter the carburetor, the amount of time the choke is on is reduced, resulting in better fuel economy and lower emissions. Engine warm-up time is also reduced.

The THERMAC system is composed of the air cleaner body, a filter, sensor unit, vacuum diaphragm, damper door, and associated hoses and connections. Heat radiating from the exhaust manifold is trapped by a heat stove and is ducted to the air cleaner to supply heated air to the carburetor. A movable door in the air cleaner case snorkel allows air to be drawn in from the heat stove (cold operation). The door position is controlled by the vacuum motor, which receives intake manifold vacuum as modulated by the temperature sensor.

NOTE: *A vacuum door which remains open will cause carburetor icing and poor cold driveability and a door which remains closed during normal engine operating temperatures can cause sluggishness, engine knocking and overheating.*

SYSTEM CHECK

1. Check the vacuum hoses for leaks, kinks, breaks, or improper connections and correct any defects.
2. With the engine off, check the position of the damper door within the snorkel. A mirror can be used to make this job easier. The damper door should be open to admit outside air.
3. Apply at least 7 in.Hg of vacuum to the damper diaphragm unit. The door should close. If it doesn't, check the diaphragm linkage for binding and correct hookup.
4. With the vacuum still applied and the door closed, clamp the tube to trap the vacuum. If the door doesn't remain closed, there is a leak in the diaphragm assembly.

REMOVAL AND INSTALLATION

Vacuum Motor

1. Remove the air cleaner.
2. Disconnect the vacuum hose from the motor.
3. Drill out the spot welds with a ⅛ in. (3mm) hole, then enlarge as necessary to remove the retaining strap.
4. Remove the retaining strap.
5. Lift up the motor and cock it to one side to

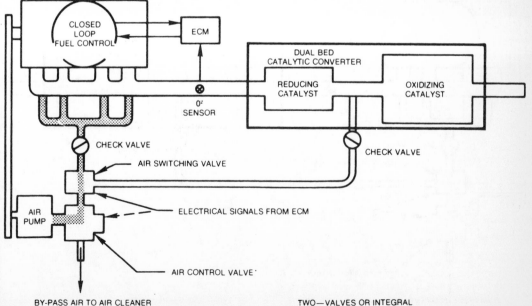

Air Injection Reaction system—cold engine

unhook the motor linkage at the control damper assembly.

6. To install the new vacuum motor, drill a $\frac{7}{64}$ in. (2.8mm) hole in the snorkel tube as the center of the vacuum motor retaining strap.

7. Insert the vacuum motor linkage into the control damper assembly.

8. Use the motor retaining strap and a sheet metal screw to secure the retaining strap and motor to the snorkel tube.

NOTE: *Make sure the screw does not interfere with the operation of the damper assembly. Shorten the screw if necessary.*

Temperature Sensor

1. Remove the air cleaner.
2. Disconnect the hoses at the air cleaner.
3. Pry up the tabs on the sensor retaining clip and remove the clip and sensor from the air cleaner.
4. To install, position sensor into air cleaner.
5. Install retaining clip.
6. Connect the hoses to the air cleaner.
7. Install the air cleaner.

Air Injection Reaction (A.I.R.) System

OPERATION

The AIR management system, is used to provide additional oxygen to continue the combustion process after the exhaust gases leave the combustion chamber. Air is injected into either the exhaust port(s), the exhaust manifold(s) or the catalytic converter by an engine driven air pump. The system is in operation at all times and will bypass air only momentarily during deceleration and at high speeds. The bypass function is performed by the Air Control Valve, while the check valve protects the air pump by preventing any backflow of exhaust gases.

The AIR system helps reduce HC and CO content in the exhaust gases by injecting air into the exhaust ports during cold engine operation. This air injection also helps the catalytic

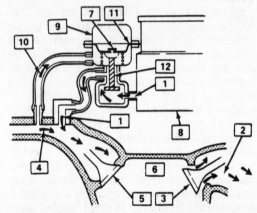

1. Air flow	7. Vacuum bleed valve
2. Exhaust gas	8. Air cleaner
3. Exhaust valve	9. Deceleration valve
4. Intake flow	10. Manifold vacuum
5. Intake valve	11. Diaphragm
6. Combustion chamber	12. Valve

Anti-Backfire control valve—2.8L carbureted engine

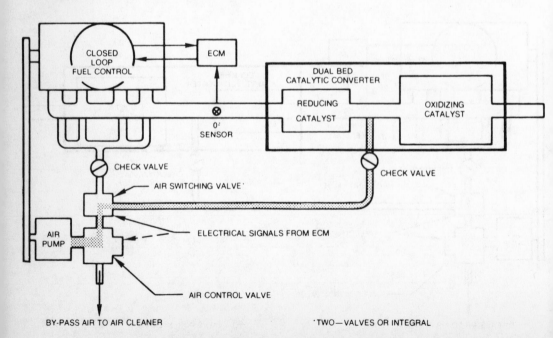

Air Injection Reaction system—warm engine

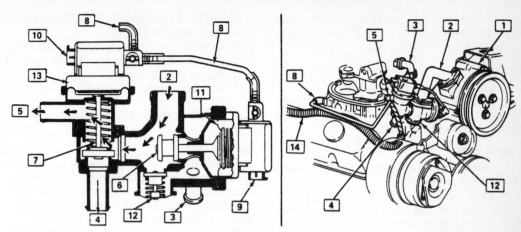

1. Air pump
2. Air from pump
3. Diverted air to air cleaner
4. Air to exhaust ports
5. Air to catalytic converter
6. Air control valve
7. Air switching valve
8. Manifold vacuum
9. ECM (term. 16 blk) control
10. ECM (term. 14 blk) control
11. Diaphragm
12. Pressure relief valve
13. Vacuum chamber
14. Wiring harness

AIR system control valve

converter to reach the proper temperature quicker during warmup. When the engine is warm (Closed Loop), the AIR system injects air into the beds of a three-way converter to lower the HC and the CO content in the exhaust.

The Air Injection Reduction system utilizes the following components:

1. An engine driven AIR pump.
2. AIR Control valves (Air Control, Air Switching).
3. Air flow and control hoses.
4. Check valves.
5. A dual-bed, three-way catalytic converter.
6. A deceleration back-fire control valve-2.8L only.

The belt driven, vane-type air pump is located at the front of the engine and supplies clean air to the AIR system for purposes already stated. When the engine is cold, the Electronic Control Module (ECM) energizes an AIR control solenoid. This allows air to flow to the AIR switching valve. The AIR switching valve is then energized to direct air to the exhaust ports.

When the engine is warm, the ECM de-energizes the AIR switching valve, thus directing the air between the beds of the catalytic converter. This provides additional oxygen for the oxidizing catalyst in the second bed to decrease HC and CO, while at the same time keeping oxygen levels low in the first bed, enabling the reducing catalyst to effectively decrease the levels of NOx.

If the AIR control valve detects a rapid increase in manifold vacuum (deceleration), certain operating modes (wide open throttle, etc.)

or if the ECM self-diagnostic system detects any problem in the system, air is diverted to the air cleaner or directly into the atmosphere.

The primary purpose of the ECM's divert mode is to prevent backfiring. Throttle closure at the beginning of deceleration will temporarily create air/fuel mixtures which are too rich to burn completely. These mixtures become burnable when they reach the exhaust if combined with the injection air. The next firing of the engine will ignite this mixture causing an exhaust backfire. Momentary diverting of the injection air from the exhaust prevents this.

The AIR system check valves and hoses should be checked periodically for any leaks, cracks or deterioration.

To help prevent backfire during high vacuum deceleration conditions, on 2.8L only, a anti-backfire (gulp) valve is used to allow air to flow into the intake manifold. The extra air enters the intake system to lean the rich air/fuel mixture. The valve is operated by the intake manifold vacuum to allow air from the air filter to flow into the intake manifold.

COMPONENT CHECK

Anti-Backfire Valve

1. Remove the air cleaner and plug the air cleaner vacuum source. Connect a tachometer to the engine.
2. With the engine idling, remove the vacuum signal hose from the intake manifold.
3. Reconnect the signal hose and listen for air flow through the ventilation tube into the anti-backfire valve. A speed drop should be noticed when the hose is reconnected.

4. If these conditions are not found, check hoses for restrictions or leaks. If hoses are OK, replace the anti-backfire valve.

Air Pump

1. Check the drive belt tension.
2. Increase the engine speed and observe an increase in air flow. If air flow does not increase, replace the air pump.

Control Valve

1. Remove the hoses. Blow through the valve (toward the cylinder head).
2. Then, suck through the valve. If air flows in one direction, the valve is operative. If not, replace the control valve.

REMOVAL AND INSTALLATION
Air Pump

1. Remove the AIR control valves and/or adapter at the pump.
2. Loosen the air pump adjustment bolt and remove the drive belt.
3. Unscrew the pump mounting bolts and then remove the pump pulley.
4. Unscrew the pump mounting bolts and then remove the pump.
5. To install, position the pump into place and secure it with the mounting bolts.
6. Install the pump pulley.
7. Install the air pump drive belt and adjust pump belt with the pump adjustment bolt.
8. Install the AIR control valves and/or adapter.

Check Valve

1. Release the clamp and disconnect the air hoses from the valve.
2. Unscrew the check valve from the air injection pipe.
3. Installation is in the reverse order of removal.

Air Control Valve

1. Disconnect the negative battery cable.
2. Remove the air cleaner.
3. Tag and disconnect the vacuum hose from the valve.
4. Tag and disconnect the air outlet hoses from the valve.
5. Bend back the lock tabs and then remove the bolts holding the elbow to the valve.
6. Tag and disconnect any electrical connections at the valve and then remove the valve from the elbow.
7. To install, position the valve into the elbow.
8. Connect any electrical connections at the valve.

9. Install the bolts holding the elbow to the valve and bend the lock tabs.
10. Connect the air outlet hoses to the valve.
11. Connect the vacuum hose to the valve.
12. Install the air cleaner.
13. Connect the negative battery cable.

Early Fuel Evaporation (EFE)

OPERATION

The EFE system is used on some of the engines to provide a source of rapid engine heat up during cold operations. It helps reduce the time that carburetor choking is required and helps reduce exhaust emissions.

Of the 2 types of EFE systems, the Vacuum Servo type, consisting of a valve, an actuator and a Thermal Vacuum Switch (TVS), the valve is located in the exhaust manifold and the TVS switch is on the engine coolant housing.

The electrical type, consisting of a ceramic grid is located under the base of the carburetor, it supplies heat to the incoming air/fuel mixture. The system uses a relay which is mounted on the left side of the firewall in the engine compartment.

A check of the operation should be made at regular maintenance intervals.

SYSTEM CHECK
Vacuum Servo Type

1. With the engine cold, observe the position of the actuator arm. Start the engine. The arm

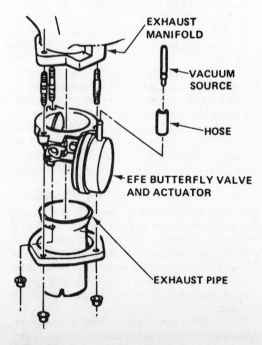

EFE system—vacuum servo type

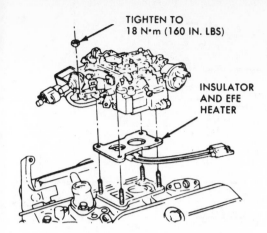

TIGHTEN TO
18 N•m (160 IN. LBS)

INSULATOR
AND EFE
HEATER

Early Fuel Evaporation (EFE)—2.8L carbureted engine

should move toward the diaphragm (closing the valve).

2. If the arm does not move, remove the hose and check for vacuum. If still no vacuum, remove the top hose from the TVS switch and check for vacuum.

3. If vacuum is present in the top hose, replace the TVS switch.

4. If vacuum is present at the actuator and it does not move, try to free the valve or replace the valve.

Electrical Type

1. Turn the ignition **ON** with the engine cold and probe both terminals of the heater switch connector with a test light.

2. If 1 wire has power, replace the heater switch; if neither wire has power, repair the ignition circuit. If both wires have power, probe the pink wire at the heater connector; if no power, repair the connector of the heater switch.

3. If power exists, disconnect the heater connector and connect a tester across the harness terminal. If no power, repair the ground wire; if power exists, check the resistance of the heater.

4. If heater is over 3Ω, replace the heater. If under 3Ω, replace the connector, start the engine (operate to normal temperature) and probe the pink wire. If no power, the system is OK; if power exists, replace the heater switch.

REMOVAL AND INSTALLATION

Vacuum Servo Type

1. Disconnect the vacuum hose at the EFE.
2. Remove exhaust pipe to manifold nuts.
3. Remove the crossover pipe. Complete removal is not always necessary.
4. Remove the EFE valve.

5. To install, position the EFE valve into place.
6. Install the crossover pipe.
7. Install the exhaust pipe to manifold nuts.
8. Connect the vacuum hose at the EFE.

Electrically Heated Type

1. Remove the air cleaner and disconnect the negative battery cable.
2. Disconnect all electrical, vacuum and fuel connections from the carburetor.
3. Disconnect the EFE heater electrical lead.
4. Remove the carburetor as detailed later in this Chapter.
5. Lift off the EFE heater grid.
6. To install, position the EFE heater grid onto the manifold.
7. Install the carburetor.
8. Connect the EFE heater electrical lead.
9. Connect all electrical, vacuum and fuel connection to the carburetor.
10. Install the air cleaner and connect the negative battery cable.

EFE HEATER RELAY REPLACEMENT

1. Disconnect the negative battery cable.
2. Remove the retaining bracket.
3. Tag and disconnect all electrical connections.
4. Unscrew the retaining bolts and remove the relay.
5. To install, position the relay into place and secure the relay with the retaining bolt.
6. Connect all electrical connections.
7. Install the retaining bracket.
8. Connect the negative battery cable.

ELECTRONIC ENGINE CONTROLS

Computer Command Control (CCC) System

The Computer Command Control System (CCC) is an electronically controlled exhaust emission system that can monitor and control a large number of interrelated emission control systems. It can monitor up to 15 various engine/vehicle operating conditions and then use this information to control as many as 9 engine related systems. The system is thereby making constant adjustments to maintain good vehicle performance under all normal driving conditions while at the same time allowing the catalytic converter to effectively control the emissions of HC, CO and NOx.

Electronic Control Module

The Electronic Control Module (ECM) is required to maintain the exhaust emissions at ac-

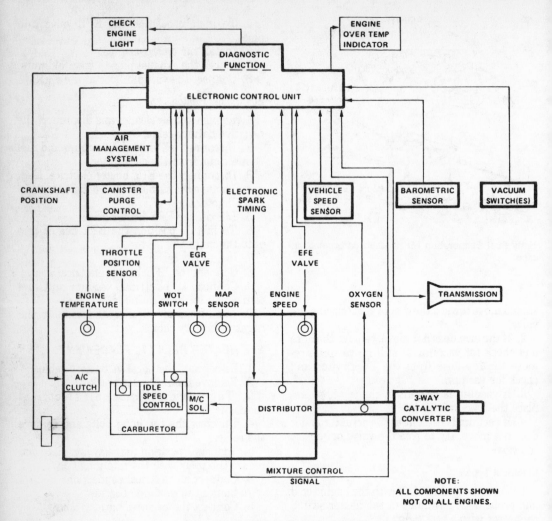

CHECK
ENGINE
LIGHT

ENGINE
OVER TEMP
INDICATOR

DIAGNOSTIC
FUNCTION

ELECTRONIC CONTROL UNIT

AIR
MANAGEMENT
SYSTEM

CRANKSHAFT
POSITION

CANISTER
PURGE
CONTROL

ELECTRONIC
SPARK
TIMING

VEHICLE
SPEED
SENSOR

BAROMETRIC
SENSOR

VACUUM
SWITCH(ES)

THROTTLE
POSITION
SENSOR

EGR
VALVE

EFE
VALVE

ENGINE
TEMPERATURE

WOT
SWITCH

MAP
SENSOR

ENGINE
SPEED

OXYGEN
SENSOR

TRANSMISSION

A/C
CLUTCH

IDLE
SPEED
CONTROL

M/C
SOL.

DISTRIBUTOR

3-WAY
CATALYTIC
CONVERTER

CARBURETOR

MIXTURE CONTROL
SIGNAL

NOTE:
ALL COMPONENTS SHOWN
NOT ON ALL ENGINES.

Computer Command Control schematic

ceptable levels. The module is a small, solid state computer which receives signals from many sources and sensors; it uses these data to make judgements about operating conditions and then control output signals to the fuel and emission systems to match the current requirements.

Inputs are received from many sources to form a complete picture of engine operating conditions. Some inputs are simply Yes or No messages, such as that from the Park/Neutral switch; the vehicle is either in gear or in Park/Neutral; there are no other choices. Other data is sent in quantitative input, such as engine RPM or coolant temperature. The ECM is pre-programmed to recognize acceptable ranges or combinations of signals and control the outputs to control emissions while providing good driveability and economy. The ECM also monitors some output circuits, making sure that the components function as commanded. For prop-

er engine operation, it is essential that all input and output components function properly and communicate properly with the ECM.

Since the control module is programmed to recognize the presence and value of electrical inputs, it will also note the lack of a signal or a radical change in values. It will, for example, react to the loss of signal from the vehicle speed sensor or note that engine coolant temperature has risen beyond acceptable (programmed) limits. Once a fault is recognized, a numeric code is assigned and held in memory. The dashboard warning lamp — CHECK ENGINE or SERVICE ENGINE SOON — will illuminate to advise the operator that the system has detected a fault.

More than one code may be stored. Although not every engine uses every code, possible codes range from 12 to 999. Additionally, the same code may carry different meanings relative to each engine or engine family. For example, a

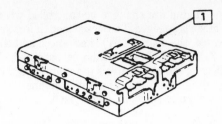

1. Electronic control module (ECM)

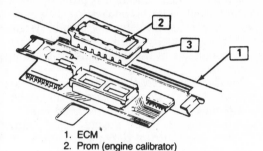

1. ECM *
2. Prom (engine calibrator)
3. Prom carrier

PROM and ECM assembly

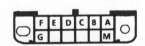

TERMINAL IDENTIFICATION
A. Ground
B. Diagnostic terminal
C. A.I.R. (if used)
D. Service engine soon light
E. Serial data
F. TCC (if used)
G. Fuel pump (if used)
M. Serial data (if used)

ALDL connector—connect terminals A & B to retrieve any stored ECM codes

3.3L (VIN N), code 46 indicates a fault found in the power steering pressure switch circuit. The same code on the 5.7L (VIN F) engine indicates a fault in the VATS anti-theft system.

In the event of an ECM failure, the system will default to a pre-programmed set of values. These are compromise values which allow the engine to operate, although possibly at reduced efficiency. This is variously known as the default, limp-in or back-up mode. Driveability is almost always affected when the ECM enters this mode.

LEARNING ABILITY

The ECM can compensate for minor variations within the fuel system through the block learn and fuel integrator systems. The fuel integrator monitors the oxygen sensor output voltage, adding or subtracting fuel to drive the mixture rich or lean as needed to reach the ideal air fuel ratio of 14.7:1. The integrator values may be read with a scan tool; the display will range from 0–255 and should center on 128 if the oxygen sensor is seeing a 14.7:1 mixture.

The temporary nature of the integrator's control is expanded by the block learn function. The name is derived from the fact that the entire engine operating range (load vs. rpm) is divided into 16 Chapters or blocks. Within each memory block is stored the correct fuel delivery value for that combination of load and engine speed. Once the operating range enters a certain block, that stored value controls the fuel delivery unless the integrator steps in to change it. If changes are made by the integrator, the new value is memorized and stored within the block. As the block learn makes the correction, the integrator correction will be reduced until the integrator returns to 128; the block learn then controls the fuel delivery with the new value.

The next time the engine operates within the block's range, the new value will be used. The block learn data can also be read by a scan tool; the range is the same as the integrator and should also center on 128. In this way, the systems can compensate for engine wear, small air or vacuum leaks or reduced combustion.

Any time the battery is disconnected, the block learn values are lost and must be relearned by the ECM. This loss of corrected values may be noticed as a significant change in driveability. To reteach the system, make certain the engine is fully warmed up. Drive the vehicle at part throttle using moderate acceleration and idle until normal performance is felt.

DASHBOARD WARNING LAMP

The primary function of the dash warning lamp is to advise the operator and the technician that a fault has been detected, and, in most cases, a code stored. Under normal conditions, the dash warning lamp will illuminate when the ignition is turned **ON**. Once the engine is started and running, the ECM will perform a system check and extinguish the warning lamp if no fault is found.

Additionally, the dash warning lamp can be used to retrieve stored codes after the system is placed in the Diagnostic Mode. Codes are transmitted as a series of flashes with short or long pauses. When the system is placed in the Field Service Mode, the dash lamp will indicate open loop or closed loop function to the technician.

Intermittents

If a fault occurs intermittently, such as a loose connector pin breaking contact as the vehicle hits a bump, the ECM will note the fault as it occurs and energize the dash warning lamp. If the problem self-corrects, as with the terminal pin again making contact, the dash lamp will extinguish after 10 seconds but a code will remain stored in the ECM memory.

When an unexpected code appears during diagnostics, it may have been set during an intermittent failure that self-corrected; the codes are still useful in diagnosis and should not be discounted.

TOOLS AND EQUIPMENT

Scan Tools

Although stored codes may be read with only the use of a small jumper wire, the use of a hand-held scan tool such as GM's TECH 1 or equivalent is recommended. There are many manufacturers of these tools; a purchaser must be certain that the tool is proper for the intended use.

The scan tool allows any stored codes to be read from the ECM memory. The tool also allows the operator to view the data being sent to the ECM while the engine is running. This ability has obvious diagnostic advantages; the use of the scan tool is frequently required by the diagnostic charts. Use of the scan tool provides additional data but does not eliminate the need for use of the charts. The scan tool makes collecting information easier; the data must be correctly interpreted by an operator familiar with the system.

An example of the usefulness of the scan tool may be seen in the case of a temperature sensor which has changed its electrical characteristics. The ECM is reacting to an apparently warmer engine (causing a driveability problem), but the sensor's voltage has not changed enough to set a fault code. Connecting the scan tool, the voltage signal being sent to the ECM may be viewed; comparison to either a chart of normal values or a known good vehicle reveals the problem quickly.

The ECM is capable of communicating with a scan tool in 3 modes:

Normal or Open Mode

This mode is not applicable to all engines. When engaged, certain engine data can be observed on the scanner without affecting engine operating characteristics. The number of items readable in this mode varies with engine family. Most scan tools are designed to change automatically to the ALDL mode if this mode is not available.

ALDL MODE

Also referred to as the 10K or SPECIAL mode, the scanner will present all readable data as available. Certain operating characteristics

of the engine are changed or controlled when this mode is engaged. The closed loop timers are bypassed, the spark (EST) is advanced and the PARK/NEUTRAL restriction is bypassed. If applicable, the IAC controls the engine speed to 1000 rpm ± 50, and, on some engines, the canister purge solenoid is energized.

FACTORY TEST

Sometimes referred to as BACK-UP mode, this level of communication is primarily used during vehicle assembly and testing. This mode will confirm that the default or limp-in system is working properly within the ECM. Other data obtainable in this mode has little use in diagnosis.

NOTE: *A scan tool that is known to display faulty data should not be used for diagnosis. Although the fault may be believed to be in only one area, it can possibly affect many other areas during diagnosis, leading to errors and incorrect repair.*

To properly read system values with a scan tool, the following conditions must be met. All normal values given in the charts will be based on these conditions:

- Engine running at idle, throttle closed
- Engine warm, upper radiator hose hot
- Vehicle in park or neutral
- System operating in closed loop
- All accessories **OFF**

Electrical Tools

The most commonly required electrical diagnostic tool is the Digital Multimeter, allowing voltage, ohmage (resistance) and amperage to be read by one instrument. The multimeter must be a high-impedance unit, with $10m\Omega$ of impedance in the voltmeter. This type of meter will not place an additional load on the circuit it is testing; this is extremely important in low voltage circuits. The multimeter must be of high quality in all respects. It should be handled carefully and protected from impact or damage. Replace batteries frequently in the unit.

Other necessary tools include an unpowered test light, a quality tachometer with inductive (clip-on) pick upand the proper tools for releasing GM's Metri-Pack, Weather Pack and Micro-Pack terminals as necessary. The Micro-Pack connectors are used at the ECM connector. A vacuum pump/gauge may also be required for checking sensors, solenoids and valves.

Diagnosis and Testing

TROUBLESHOOTING

Diagnosis of a driveablility and/or emissions problems requires attention to detail and following the diagnostic procedures in the correct order. Resist the temptation to perform any repairs before performing the preliminary diagnostic steps. In many cases this will shorten diagnostic time and often cure the problem without electronic testing.

The proper troubleshooting procedure for these vehicles is as follows:

Visual/Physical Underhood Inspection

This is possibly the most critical step of diagnosis. A detailed examination of connectors, wiring and vacuum hoses can often lead to a repair without further diagnosis. Performance of this step relies on the skill of the technician performing it; a careful inspector will check the undersides of hoses as well as the integrity of hard-to-reach hoses blocked by the air cleaner or other component. Wiring should be checked carefully for any sign of strain, burning, crimping, or terminal pull-out from a connector. Checking connectors at components or in harnesses is required; usually, pushing them together will reveal a loose fit.

Diagnostic Circuit Check

This step is used to check that the on-board diagnostic system is working correctly. A system which is faulty or shorted may not yield correct codes when placed in the Diagnostic Mode. Performing this test confirms that the diagnostic system is not failed and is able to communicate through the dash warning lamp.

If the diagnostic system is not operating correctly, or if a problem exists without the dash warning lamp being lit, refer to the specific vehicle's A-Charts. These charts cover such conditions as Engine Cranks but Will Not Run or No Service Engine Soon Light.

Reading Codes and Use of Scan Tool

Once the integrity of the system is confirmed, enter the Diagnostic Mode and read any stored codes. To enter the diagnostic mode:

1. Turn the ignition switch **OFF**. Locate the Assembly Line Diagnostic Link (ALDL), usually under the instrument panel. It may be within a plastic cover or housing labeled DIAGNOSTIC CONNECTOR. This link is used to communicate with the ECM.

2. The code(s) stored in memory may be read either through the flashing of the dashboard warning lamp or through the use of a hand-held scan tool. If using the scan tool, connect it correctly to the ALDL.

3. If reading codes via the dash warning lamp, use a small jumper wire to connect Terminal B of the ALDL to Terminal A. As the ALDL connector is viewed from the front, Terminal A is on the extreme right of the upper row; Terminal B is second from the right on the upper row.

4. After the terminals are connected, turn the ignition switch to the **ON** position but do not start the engine. The dash warning lamp should begin to flash Code 12. The code will display as one flash, a pause and two flashes. Code 12 is not a fault code. It is used as a system acknowledgement or handshake code; its presence indicates that the ECM can communicate as requested. Code 12 is used to begin every diagnostic sequence. Some vehicles also use Code 12 after all diagnostic codes have been sent.

5. After Code 12 has been transmitted 3 times, the fault codes, if any, will each be transmitted 3 times. The codes are stored and transmitted in numeric order from lowest to highest.

NOTE: *The order of codes in the memory does not indicate the order of occurrence.*

6. If there are no codes stored, but a driveability or emissions problem is evident, refer to the Symptoms and Intermittents Chart for the specific fuel system.

7. If one or more codes are stored, record them. At the end of the procedure, refer to the applicable Diagnostic Code chart.

8. If no fault codes are transmitted, connect the scan tool (if not already connected). Use the scan functions to view the values being sent to the ECM. Compare the actual values to the typical or normal values for the engine.

9. Switch the ignition **OFF** when finished with code retrieval or scan tool readings.

Circuit/Component Diagnosis and Repair

Using the appropriate chart(s) based on the Diagnostic Circuit Check, the fault codes and the scan tool data will lead to diagnosis and checking of a particular circuit or component. It is important to note that the fault code indicates a fault or loss of signal in an ECM-controlled system, not necessarily in the specific component. Detailed procedures to isolate the problem are included in each code chart; these procedures must be followed accurately to insure timely and correct repair. Following the procedure will also insure that only truly faulty components are replaced.

DIAGNOSTIC MODE

The ECM may be placed into the diagnostic mode by turning the ignition switch from **OFF** to **ON**, then grounding ALDL Terminal B to Terminal A. When in the Diagnostic Mode, the ECM will:

• Display Code 12, indicating the system is operating correctly.

• Display any stored fault codes 3 times in succession.

• Energize all the relays controlled by the ECM except the fuel pump relay. This will allow the relays and circuits to be checked in the shop without recreating certain driving conditions.

• Move the IAC valve to its fully extended position, closing the idle air passage.

NOTE: *Due to increased battery draw, do not allow the vehicle to remain in the Diagnostic Mode for more than 30 minutes. If longer periods are necessary, connect a battery charger.*

FIELD SERVICE MODE

If ALDL terminal B is grounded to terminal A with the engine running, the system enters the Field Service Mode. In this mode, the dash warning lamp will indicate whether the system is operating in open loop or closed loop.

If working in open loop, the dash warning lamp will flash rapidly 2½ times per second. In closed loop, the flash rate slows to once per second. Additionally, if the system is running lean in closed loop, the lamp will be off most of the cycle. A rich condition in closed loop will cause the lamp to remain lit for most of the 1 second cycle.

When operating in the Field Service Mode, additional codes cannot be stored by the ECM. The closed loop timer is bypassed in this mode.

CLEARING THE TROUBLE CODES

Stored fault codes may be erased from memory at any time by removing power from the ECM for at least 30 seconds. It may be necessary to clear stored codes during diagnosis to check for any recurrence during a test drive, but the stored codes must be written down when retrieved. The codes may still be required for subsequent troubleshooting. Whenever a repair is complete, the stored codes must be erased and the vehicle test driven to confirm correct operation and repair.

NOTE: *The ignition switch must be OFF any time power is disconnected or restored to the ECM. Severe damage may result if this precaution is not observed.*

Depending on the electric distribution of the particular vehicle, power to the ECM may be disconnected by removing the ECM fuse in the fusebox, disconnecting the inline fuse holder near the positive battery terminal or disconnecting the ECM power lead at the battery terminal. Disconnecting the negative battery cable to clear codes is not recommended as this will also clear other memory data in the vehicle such as radio presets or seat memory.

NOTE: *Have a professional certified technician perform all testing and repairs of the components and sensors.*

Oxygen Sensor

OPERATION

An oxygen sensor is used on all models. The sensor protrudes into the exhaust stream and

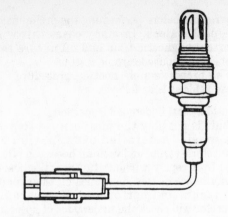

Oxygen sensor

monitors the oxygen content of the exhaust gases. The difference between the oxygen content of the exhaust gases and that of the outside air generates a voltage signal to the ECM. The ECM monitors this voltage and, depending upon the value of the signal received, issues a command to adjust for a rich or a lean condition.

No attempt should ever be made to measure the voltage output of the sensor. The current drain of any conventional voltmeter would be such that it would permanently damage the sensor. No jumpers, test leads or any other electrical connections should ever be made to the sensor. Use these tools ONLY on the ECM side of the wiring harness connector AFTER disconnecting it from the sensor.

REMOVAL AND INSTALLATION

The oxygen sensor must be replaced every 30,000 miles (48,000 km.). The sensor may be difficult to remove when the engine temperature is below 120°F (48°C). Excessive removal force may damage the threads in the exhaust manifold or pipe; follow the removal procedure carefully.

1. Locate the oxygen sensor. It protrudes from the center of the exhaust manifold at the front of the engine compartment (it looks somewhat like a spark plug).

2. Disconnect the electrical connector from the oxygen sensor.

3. Spray a commercial solvent onto the sensor threads and allow it to soak in for at least five minutes.

4. Carefully unscrew and remove the sensor.

5. To install, first coat the new sensor's threads with G.M. anti-seize compound No. 5613695 or the equivalent. This is not a conventional anti-seize paste. The use of a regular compound may electrically insulate the sensor, rendering it inoperative. You must coat the

threads with an electrically conductive anti-seize compound.

6. Installation torque is 30 ft. lbs. (42 Nm). Do not overtighten.

7. Reconnect the electrical connector. Be careful not to damage the electrical pigtail. Check the sensor boot for proper fit and installation.

Coolant Temperature Sensor (CTS)

OPERATION

Most engine functions are effected by the coolant temperature. Determining whether the engine is hot or cold is largely dependent on the temperature of the coolant. An accurate temperature signal to the ECM is supplied by the coolant temperature sensor. The coolant temperature sensor is a thermistor mounted in the engine coolant stream. A thermistor is an electrical device that varies its resistance in relation to changes in temperature. Low coolant temperature produces a high resistance (100,000Ω at −40°F/−40°C) and high coolant temperature produces low resistance (70Ω at 266°F/130°C). The ECM supplies a signal of 5 volts to the coolant temperature sensor through a resistor in the ECM and measures the voltage. The voltage will be high when the engine is cold and low when the engine is hot.

TESTING

1. Disconnect the negative battery cable.
2. Disconnect the coolant temperature sensor wire connector.
3. Connect a volt/ohmmeter to the terminals of the coolant temperature sensor and verify the reading is within range on the appropriate CODE chart.

REMOVAL AND INSTALLATION

1. Disconnect the negative battery cable.
2. Drain the cooling system into a clean container for reuse.
3. Disconnect the electrical connector from the coolant temperature sensor.

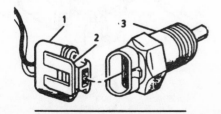

1. Harness connector to ECM
2. Locking tab
3. Temperature sensor

Coolant temperature sensor (CTS)

A. Distance of pintle extension
B. Diameter and shape of pintle
C. IAC valve gasket

Idle Air Control (IAC) valve

4. Remove the coolant temperature sensor.
To install:
5. Install the coolant temperature sensor.
6. Connect the electrical connector.
7. Fill the cooling system.
8. Connect the negative battery cable.
9. Start the engine and check for leaks.

Idle Air Control (IAC) Valve

OPERATION

Engine idle speeds are controlled by the ECM through the IAC valve mounted on the throttle body. The ECM sends voltage pulses to the IAC motor windings causing the IAC motor shaft and pintle to move **IN** or **OUT** a given distance (number of steps) for each pulse (called counts). The movement of the pintle controls the airflow around the throttle plate, which in turn, controls engine idle speed. IAC valve pintle position counts can be observed using a Scan tool. Zero counts correspond to a fully closed passage, while 140 counts or more corresponds to full flow.

Idle speed can be categorized in 2 ways: actual (controlled) idle speed and minimum idle speed. Controlled idle speed is obtained by the ECM positioning the IAC valve pintle. Resulting idle speed is determined by total air flow (IAC/passage + PCV + throttle valve + calibrated vacuum leaks). Controlled idle speed is specified at normal operating conditions, which consists of engine coolant at normal operating temperature, air conditioning compressor **OFF**, manual transmission in neutral or automatic transmission in **D**.

Minimum idle air speed is set at the factory with a stop screw. This setting allows enough air flow by the throttle valves to cause the IAC valve pintle to be positioned a calibrated number of steps (counts) from the seat during normal controlled idle operation.

The idle speed is controlled by the ECM through the IAC valve. No adjustment is required during routine maintenance. Tampering with the minimum idle speed adjustment may result in premature failure of the IAC valve.

REMOVAL AND INSTALLATION

1. Disconnect the negative battery cable. Disconnect the IAC valve electrical connector.
2. Remove the IAC valve by performing the following:

   a. On thread-mounted units, use a 1¼ in. (32mm) wrench.

   b. On flange-mounted units, remove the mounting screw assemblies.
3. Remove the IAC valve gasket or O-ring and discard.

To install:
4. Clean the mounting surfaces by performing the following:

   a. If servicing a thread-mounted valve, remove the old gasket material from the surface of the throttle body to ensure proper sealing of the new gasket.

   b. If servicing a flange-mounted valve, clean the IAC valve surfaces on the throttle body to assure proper seal of the new O-ring and contact of the IAC valve flange.
5. If installing a new IAC valve, measure the distance between the tip of the IAC valve pintle and the mounting flange. If the distance is greater than 1.102 in. (28mm), use finger pressure to slowly retract the pintle. The force required to retract the pintle of a new valve will not cause damage to the valve. If reinstalling the original IAC valve, do not attempt to adjust the pintle in this manner.
6. Install the IAC valve into the throttle body by performing the following:

   a. If installing a thread-mounted valve, install with a new gasket. Using a 1¼ in. (32mm) wrench, tighten to 13 ft. lbs. (18 Nm).

   b. If installing a flange-mounted valve, lubricate a new O-ring with transmission fluid and install on the IAC valve. Install the IAC valve to the throttle body. Install the mounting screws using a suitable thread locking compound. Tighten to 28 inch lbs. (3.2 Nm).
7. Connect the IAC valve electrical connector.
8. Connect the negative battery cable.
9. No physical adjustment of the IAC valve assembly is required after installation. Reset the IAC valve pintle position by performing the following:

   a. Depress the accelerator pedal slightly.

   b. Start the engine and run for 5 seconds.

   c. Turn the ignition switch to the **OFF** position for 10 seconds.

   d. Restart the engine and check for proper idle operation.

Manifold Absolute Pressure (MAP) Sensor

OPERATION

The MAP sensor measures the changes in intake manifold pressure, which result from engine load and speed changes and converts this information to a voltage output. The MAP sensor reading is the opposite of a vacuum gauge reading: when manifold pressure is high, MAP sensor value is high and vacuum is low. A MAP sensor will produce a low output on engine coastdown with a closed throttle while a wide open throttle will produce a high output. The high output is produced because the pressure inside the manifold is the same as outside the manifold, so 100 percent of the outside air pressure is measured.

The MAP sensor is also used to measure barometric pressure under certain conditions, which allows the ECM to automatically adjust for different altitudes.

The MAP sensor changes the 5 volt signal supplied by the ECM, which reads the change and uses the information to control fuel delivery and ignition timing.

REMOVAL AND INSTALLATION

1. Disconnect the negative battery cable.
2. Disconnect the vacuum harness assembly.
3. Release the electrical connector locking tab.
4. Remove the bolts or release the MAP sensor locking tabs and remove the sensor.

To install:
5. Install the bolts or snap sensor onto the bracket.

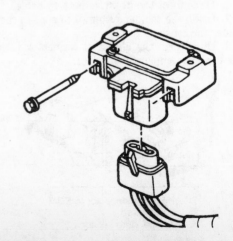

Manifold Absolute Pressure (MAP) sensor

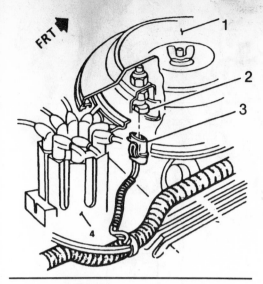

1.   Air cleaner
2.   Intake Air TGemperature (IAT) sensor
3.   Harness connector to ECM
4.   Distributor

Intake Air Temperature (IAT) sensor—5.0L (VIN E) engine

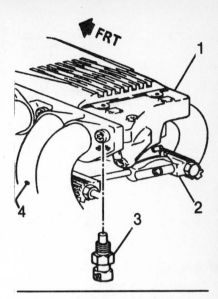

1.   Intake manifold
2.   Fuel rail
3.   Intake Air TGemperature (IAT) sensor
4.   Left intake runners

Intake Air Temperature (IAT) sensor—5.0L (VIN F) engine and 5.7L (VIN 8) engines

6. Connect the MAP sensor electrical connector.

7. Connect the MAP sensor vacuum harness connector.

8. Connect the negative battery cable.

Manifold or Intake Air Temperature (MAT or IAT) Sensor

OPERATION

The MAT or IAT sensor is a thermistor which supplies manifold air temperature information to the ECM. The MAT sensor produces high resistance (100,000Ω at −40°F/−40°C) at low temperatures and low resistance (180Ω at 210°F/100°C) at high temperatures. The ECM supplies a 5 volt signal to the MAT sensor and measures MAT sensor output voltage. The voltage signal will be low when the air is cold and high when the air is hot.

REMOVAL AND INSTALLATION

1. Disconnect the negative battery cable.

2. Disconnect the sensor electrical connector locking tab.

3. Remove the sensor.

To install:

4. Install the sensor.

5. Connect the electrical connector.

6. Connect the negative battery cable.

Throttle Position Sensor (TPS)

OPERATION

The TPS is mounted to the throttle body, opposite the throttle lever and is connected to the throttle shaft. Its function is to sense the current throttle valve position and relay that information to the ECM. Throttle position information allows the ECM to generate the required injector control signals. The TPS consists of a potentiometer which alters the flow of voltage according to the position of a wiper on the variable resistor windings, in proportion to the movement of the throttle shaft.

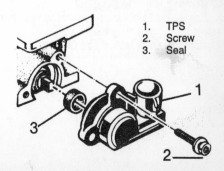

1.   TPS
2.   Screw
3.   Seal

Throttle Position Sensor (TPS)—5.0L (VIN E) engine

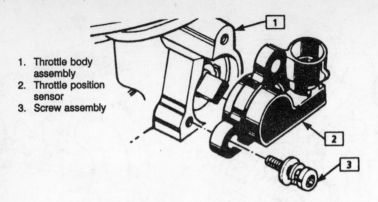

1. Throttle body assembly
2. Throttle position sensor
3. Screw assembly

Throttle Position Sensor (TPS)—2.5L engine

REMOVAL AND INSTALLATION

1. Disconnect the negative battery cable.
2. Disconnect the TPS electrical connector.
3. Remove the 2 mounting screws.
4. Remove the TPS and, if equipped, TPS seal from the throttle body.

To install:

5. Place the TPS in position. Align the TPS lever with the TPS drive lever on the throttle body.
6. Install the 2 TPS mounting screws.
7. Connect the electrical connector.
8. Connect the negative battery cable.

Vehicle Speed Sensor

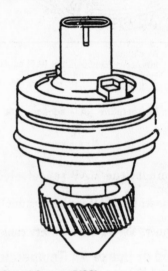

Vehicle Speed Sensor (VSS)

OPERATION

The VSS is located on the transmission and sends a pulsing voltage signal to the ECM which is converted to miles per hour. This sensor mainly controls the operation of the TCC system, shift light, cruise control and activation of the EGR system.

REMOVAL AND INSTALLATION

1. Disconnect the negative battery cable.
2. Raise and safely support the vehicle.
3. Disconnect the VSS electrical connector.
4. Remove the retaining bolt.
5. Have a clean container to catch the transmission fluid and remove the VSS.
6. Remove and discard the O-ring.

To install:

7. Lubricate a new O-ring with a thin film of transmission fluid. Install the O-ring and VSS.
8. Install the retaining bolt.
9. Connect the electrical connector.
10. Lower the vehicle.
11. Connect the negative battery cable.
12. Refill transmission to proper level.

NOTE: *Due to the intricacy of the system and the special testing equipment required, it is recommended to have a qualified technician perform any testing, adjusting, or replacement of the system components.*

CARBURETED FUEL SYSTEM

Mechanical Fuel Pump

The fuel pump is a single action AC diaphragm type. All fuel pumps used on V6 and V8 engines are of the diaphragm type and because of the design are serviced by replacement only. No adjustments or repairs are possible. The fuel pump is mounted on the left front (V6) and right front (V8) of the engine.

The fuel pumps are also equipped with vapor return lines for purposes of emission control and to reduce vapor lock. All pumps are operated by an eccentric on the camshaft. On V6 and V8 engines, a pushrod between the camshaft eccentric and the fuel pump operates the pump.

REMOVAL AND INSTALLATION

NOTE: When disconnecting the fuel pump outlet fitting, always use 2 wrenches to avoid twisting the line.

1. Disconnect the fuel intake and outlet lines at the pump and plug the pump intake line.

2. Remove the two pump mounting bolts and lockwashers; remove the pump and its gasket.

3. If the pump pushrod is to be removed from the V8, remove the two adapter bolts and lockwashers and remove the adapter and its gasket.

4. Install the fuel pump with a new gasket reversing the removal procedure. Coat the mating surfaces with sealer.

5. Connect the fuel lines and check for leaks.

TESTING

To determine if the pump is in good condition, tests for both volume and pressure should be performed. The tests are made with the pump installed, and the engine at normal operating temperature and idle speed. Never replace a fuel pump without first performing these simple tests.

Ensure the fuel filter has been changed at the specified interval. If in doubt, install a new filter first. Always check for broken or deteriorated

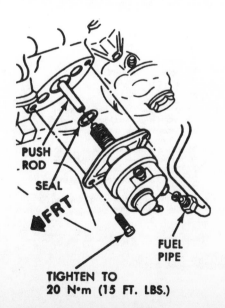

PUSH ROD
SEAL
FRT
FUEL PIPE
TIGHTEN TO 20 N•m (15 FT. LBS.)

V6 carbureted engine fuel pump

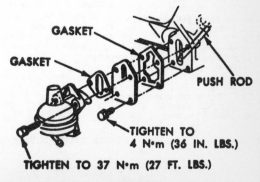

GASKET
GASKET
PUSH ROD
TIGHTEN TO 4 N•m (36 IN. LBS.)
TIGHTEN TO 37 N•m (27 FT. LBS.)

V8 carbureted engine fuel pump

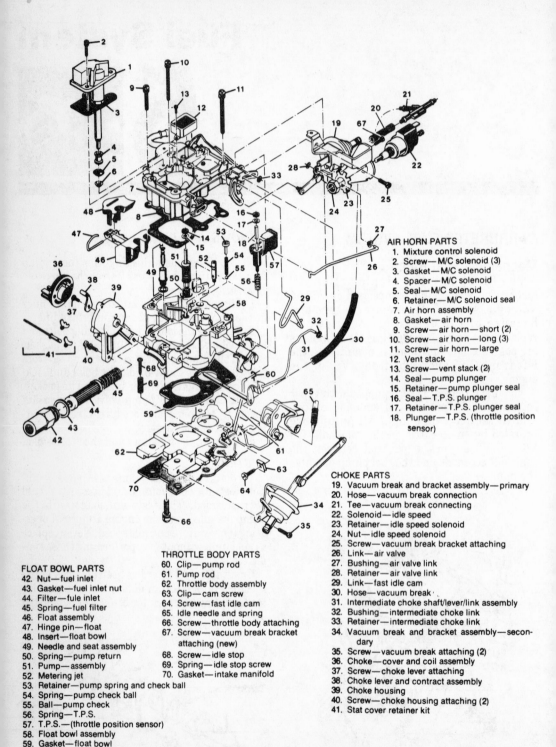

AIR HORN PARTS
1. Mixture control solenoid
2. Screw—M/C solenoid (3)
3. Gasket—M/C solenoid
4. Spacer—M/C solenoid
5. Seal—M/C solenoid
6. Retainer—M/C solenoid seal
7. Air horn assembly
8. Gasket—air horn
9. Screw—air horn—short (2)
10. Screw—air horn—long (3)
11. Screw—air horn—large
12. Vent stack
13. Screw—vent stack (2)
14. Seal—pump plunger
15. Retainer—pump plunger seal
16. Seal—T.P.S. plunger
17. Retainer—T.P.S. plunger seal
18. Plunger—T.P.S. (throttle position sensor)

CHOKE PARTS
19. Vacuum break and bracket assembly—primary
20. Hose—vacuum break connection
21. Tee—vacuum break connecting
22. Solenoid—idle speed
23. Retainer—idle speed solenoid
24. Nut—idle speed solenoid
25. Screw—vacuum break bracket attaching
26. Link—air valve
27. Bushing—air valve link
28. Retainer—air valve link
29. Link—fast idle cam
30. Hose—vacuum break
31. Intermediate choke shaft/lever/link assembly
32. Bushing—intermediate choke link
33. Retainer—intermediate choke link
34. Vacuum break and bracket assembly—secondary
35. Screw—vacuum break attaching (2)
36. Choke—cover and coil assembly
37. Screw—choke lever attaching
38. Choke lever and contract assembly
39. Choke housing
40. Screw—choke housing attaching (2)
41. Stat cover retainer kit

FLOAT BOWL PARTS
42. Nut—fuel inlet
43. Gasket—fuel inlet nut
44. Filter—fule inlet
45. Spring—fuel filter
46. Float assembly
47. Hinge pin—float
48. Insert—float bowl
49. Needle and seat assembly
50. Spring—pump return
51. Pump—assembly
52. Metering jet
53. Retainer—pump spring and check ball
54. Spring—pump check ball
55. Ball—pump check
56. Spring—T.P.S.
57. T.P.S.—(throttle position sensor)
58. Float bowl assembly
59. Gasket—float bowl

THROTTLE BODY PARTS
60. Clip—pump rod
61. Pump rod
62. Throttle body assembly
63. Clip—cam screw
64. Screw—fast idle cam
65. Idle needle and spring
66. Screw—throttle body attaching
67. Screw—vacuum break bracket attaching (new)
68. Screw—idle stop
69. Spring—idle stop screw
70. Gasket—intake manifold

Exploded view of the E2SE carburetor—2.8L engine

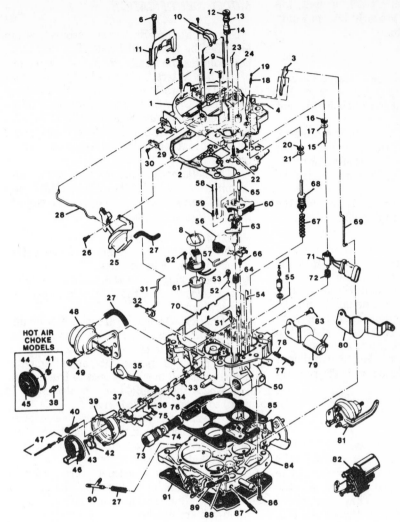

49. Screw—vacuum break attaching (2)
50. Float Bowl Assembly
51. Jet—primary metering (2)
52. Ball—pump discharge
53. Retainer—pump discharge ball
54. Baffle—pump well
55. Needle & seat assembly
56. Float assembly
57. Hinge pin—float assembly
58. Rod—primary metering (2)
59. Spring—primary metering rod (2)
60. Insert—float bowl
61. Insert—bowl cavity
62. Screw—connector attaching
63. Mixture control (M/C) solenoid & plunger assembly
64. Spring—solenoid tension
65. Screw—solenoid adjusting (lean mixture)
66. Spring—solenoid adjusting screw
67. Spring—pump return
68. Pump assembly
69. Link—pump
70. Baffle—secondary bores
71. Throttle position sensor (TPS)
72. Spring—TPS Tension
73. Filter nut—fuel inlet
74. Gasket—filter nut
75. Filter—fuel inlet
76. Spring—fuel filter
77. Screw—idle stop
78. Spring—idle stop screw
79. Idle speed solenoid & bracket assembly
80. Bracket—throttle return spring
81. Idle load compensator & bracket assembly
82. Idle speed control & bracket assembly
83. Screw—bracket attaching
84. Throttle body assembly
85. Gasket—throttle body
86. Screw—throttle body
87. Idle needle & spring assembly (2)
88. Screw—fast idle adjusting
89. Spring fast idle screw
90. Tee—vacuum hose
91. Gasket—flange

HOT AIR CHOKE MODELS

1. Air horn assembly
2. Gasket—air horn
3. Lever—pump actuating
4. Roll pin—pump lever hinge
5. Screw—air horn, long (2)
6. Screw—air horn, short
7. Screw—air horn, countersunk (2)
8. Gasket—solenoid connector to air horn
9. Metering rod—secondary (2)
10. Holder & screw—secondary metering rod
11. Baffle—secondary air
12. Valve—idle air bleed
13. "O" ring (thick)—idle air bleed valve
14. "O" ring (thin)—idle air bleed valve
15. Plunger—TPS actuator
16. Seal—TPS plunger
17. Retainer—TPS seal
18. Screw—TPS adjusting
19. Plug—TPS screw
20. Seal—pump plunger
21. Retainer—pump seal
22. Screw—solenoid plunger stop (rich mixture stop)
23. Plug—plunger stop screw (rich mixture stop)
24. Plug—solenoid adjusting screw (lean mixture)
25. Vacuum break & bracket—front
26. Screw—vacuum break attaching (2)
27. Hose—vacuum
28. Rod—air valve
29. Lever—choke rod (upper)
30. Screw—choke lever
31. Rod—choke
32. Lever—choke rod (lower)
33. Seal—intermediate choke shaft
34. Lever—secondary lockout
35. Link—rear vacuum break
36. Intermediate choke shaft & lever
37. Cam—fast idle
38. Seal—choke housing to bowl (hot air choke)
39. Choke housing
40. Screw—choke housing to bowl
41. Seal—intermediate choke shaft (hot air choke)
42. Lever—choke coil
43. Screw—choke coil lever
44. Gasket—Stat cover (hot air choke)
45. Stat cover & coil assembly (hot air choke)
46. Stat cover & coil assembly (electric choke)
47. Kit—stat cover attaching
48. Vacuum break assembly—rear

Exploded view of the E4MC/E4ME carburetor—5.0L (VIN G & H) engine

fuel hoses. If a line has a crack or split, the pump may be operating properly, but the pump will only draw air, not fuel.

Pressure Test

1. Disconnect the fuel line at the carburetor and connect a fuel pump pressure gauge. Ensure the carburetor float bowl has a sufficient amount of gasoline.
2. Start the engine and check the pressure with the engine at idle. If the pump has a vapor return hose, squeeze it off so that an accurate reading can be obtained. Pressure should be 5½–6½ psi.
3. If the pressure is incorrect, replace the pump. If it is ok, go on to the volume test.

Volume Test

1. Disconnect the pressure gauge. Run the fuel line into a graduated container.
2. Run the engine at idle until one pint of gasoline has been pumped. One pint should be delivered in 30 seconds or less. There is normally enough fuel in the carburetor float bowl to perform this test, but refill it if necessary.
3. If the delivery rate is below the minimum, check the lines for restrictions or leaks, then replace the pump.

Carburetors

The V6 engine is equipped with the Rochester E2SE carburetor, V8 engines use the E4ME and E4MC. These carburetors are of the downdraft design used in conjunction with the CCC system of fuel control. They have special design features for optimum air/fuel mixture control during all ranges of engine operation.

An electrical solenoid in the carburetor controls the air/fuel ratio. The solenoid is connected to an electronic module (ECM) which is an on board computer. The ECM provides a controlling signal to the solenoid. The solenoid controls the metering rod(s) and an idle air bleed valve to closely control the air/fuel ratio throughout the operating range of the engine.

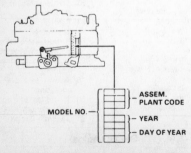

MODEL NO. —

– ASSEM.
  PLANT CODE

– YEAR

– DAY OF YEAR

Location of the carburetor identification number

MODEL IDENTIFICATION

General Motors Rochester carburetors are identified by their model code. The first number indicates the number of barrels, while one of the last letters indicates the type of choke used. These are V for the manifold mounted choke coil, C for the choke coil mounted in the carburetor body, and E for electric choke, also mounted on the carburetor. Model codes ending in A indicate an altitude-compensating carburetor.

NOTE: *Because of the intricate nature and computer controls, the E2SE, E4ME and E4MC carburetors should only be serviced by a qualified technician.*

PRELIMINARY CHECK

The following should be observed before attempting any adjustments.

1. Thoroughly warm the engine. If the engine is cold, be sure that it reaches operating temperature.
2. Check the torque of all carburetor mounting nuts and assembly screws. Also check the intake manifold-to-cylinder head bolts. If air is leaking at any of these points, any attempts at adjustment will inevitably lead to frustration.
3. Check the manifold heat control valve (if used) to be sure that it is free.
4. Check and adjust the choke as necessary.
5. Adjust the idle speed and mixture. If the mixture screws are capped, don't adjust them unless all other causes of rough idle have been eliminated. If any adjustments are performed that might possibly change the idle speed or mixture, adjust the idle and mixture again when you are finished.

NOTE: *Before you make any carburetor adjustments make sure that the engine is in tune. Many problems which are thought to be carburetor related can be traced to an engine which is simply out-of-tune. Any trouble in these areas will have symptoms like those of carburetor problems.*

ADJUSTMENTS

Fast Idle

ROCHESTER E2SE

1. Refer to the emission label and prepare the vehicle for adjustment.
2. Place the transmission in **P** or **D**.
3. Place the fast idle screw on the highest step of the fast idle cam.
4. Turn the fast idle screw to obtain the fast idle speed.

ROCHESTER E4ME AND E4MC

NOTE: *The fast idle adjustment must be performed according to the directions of the emissions label.*

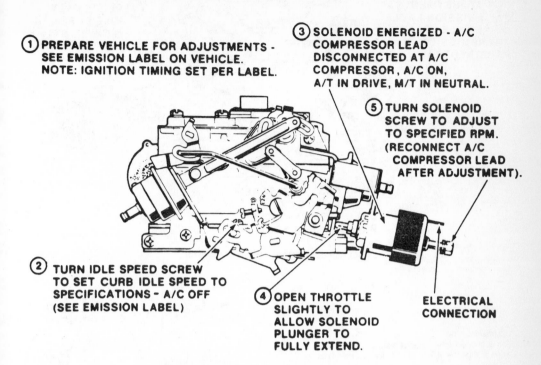

① PREPARE VEHICLE FOR ADJUSTMENTS -
SEE EMISSION LABEL ON VEHICLE.
NOTE: IGNITION TIMING SET PER LABEL.

③ SOLENOID ENERGIZED - A/C
COMPRESSOR LEAD
DISCONNECTED AT A/C
COMPRESSOR, A/C ON,
A/T IN DRIVE, M/T IN NEUTRAL.

⑤ TURN SOLENOID
SCREW TO ADJUST
TO SPECIFIED RPM.
(RECONNECT A/C
COMPRESSOR LEAD
AFTER ADJUSTMENT).

② TURN IDLE SPEED SCREW
TO SET CURB IDLE SPEED TO
SPECIFICATIONS - A/C OFF
(SEE EMISSION LABEL)

④ OPEN THROTTLE
SLIGHTLY TO
ALLOW SOLENOID
PLUNGER TO
FULLY EXTEND.

ELECTRICAL
CONNECTION

Idle speed adjustment without A/C—E2SE carburetor

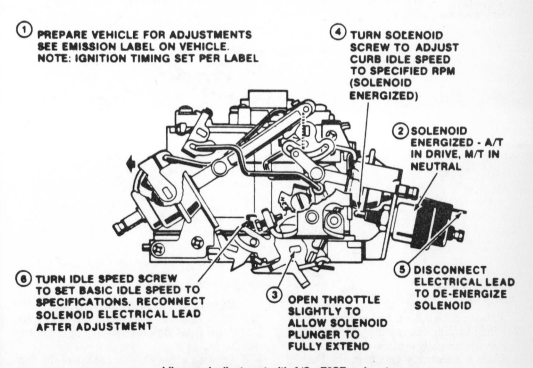

① PREPARE VEHICLE FOR ADJUSTMENTS
SEE EMISSION LABEL ON VEHICLE.
NOTE: IGNITION TIMING SET PER LABEL

④ TURN SOLENOID
SCREW TO ADJUST
CURB IDLE SPEED
TO SPECIFIED RPM
(SOLENOID
ENERGIZED)

② SOLENOID
ENERGIZED - A/T
IN DRIVE, M/T IN
NEUTRAL

⑥ TURN IDLE SPEED SCREW
TO SET BASIC IDLE SPEED TO
SPECIFICATIONS. RECONNECT
SOLENOID ELECTRICAL LEAD
AFTER ADJUSTMENT

③ OPEN THROTTLE
SLIGHTLY TO
ALLOW SOLENOID
PLUNGER TO
FULLY EXTEND

⑤ DISCONNECT
ELECTRICAL LEAD
TO DE-ENERGIZE
SOLENOID

Idle speed adjustment with A/C—E2SE carburetor

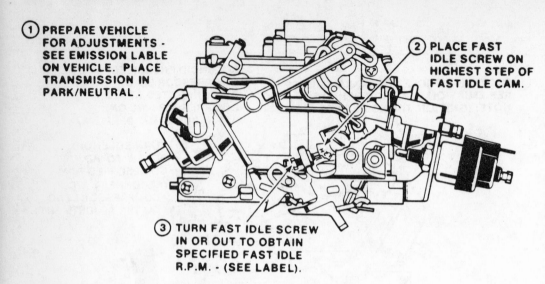

① PREPARE VEHICLE FOR ADJUSTMENTS - SEE EMISSION LABLE ON VEHICLE. PLACE TRANSMISSION IN PARK/NEUTRAL.

② PLACE FAST IDLE SCREW ON HIGHEST STEP OF FAST IDLE CAM.

③ TURN FAST IDLE SCREW IN OR OUT TO OBTAIN SPECIFIED FAST IDLE R.P.M. - (SEE LABEL).

Fast idle adjustment—E2SE carburetor

1. Hold retainer in place
2. Push float down lightly against needle
3. Gauge at large toe of float, at point farthest from float hinge
4. Remove float and bend float arm up or down to adust. (Some models have float stabilizer spring. Use care in removing.)
5. Visually check float alignment

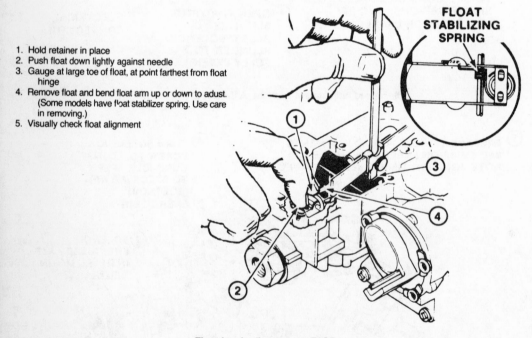

Float level adjustment—E2SE

Float and Fuel Level
ROCHESTER E2SE

1. Remove the air horn and gasket.

2. While holding the retainer in place, push the float down lightly against the needle.

3. Place a measuring gauge on the float at the farthest point from the float hinge.

4. To adjust, remove the float and bend the arm up or down. Also check the float alignment.

5. Install the air horn and gasket.

ROCHESTER E4ME AND E4MC

1. Remove the air horn and gasket from the float bowl. Hold the float retainer down firmly. Push the float down (lightly) against the needle.

2. Position a T-scale over the toe of the float $\frac{1}{16}$ in. (1.6mm) from the end of the float toe.

3. If the float level varies more than $\frac{1}{16}$ in. (1.6mm) from the specified setting, it must be reset.

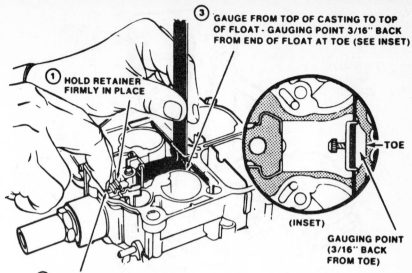

③ GAUGE FROM TOP OF CASTING TO TOP
OF FLOAT - GAUGING POINT 3/16" BACK
FROM END OF FLOAT AT TOE (SEE INSET)

① HOLD RETAINER
FIRMLY IN PLACE

◄—TOE

(INSET)

GAUGING POINT
(3/16" BACK
FROM TOE)

② PUSH FLOAT DOWN LIGHTLY
AGAINST NEEDLE

IF FLOAT LEVEL VARIES OVER ± 1/16" FROM SPECIFICATIONS,
FOR LEVEL TOO HIGH, HOLD RETAINER IN PLACE AND PUSH DOWN ON
CENTER OF FLOAT PONTOON TO OBTAIN CORRECT SETTING.
FOR LEVEL TOO LOW,
IF E4M REMOVE METERING RODS, SOLENOID CONNECTOR
SCREW. COUNT, AND RECORD FOR REASSEMBLY, THE NUMBER OF
TURNS NEEDED TO LIGHTLY BOTTOM LEAN MIXTURE SCREW. BACK
OUT AND REMOVE SCREW, SOLENOID, CONNECTOR. REMOVE FLOAT
AND FLOAT ARM UPWARD TO ADJUST. REINSTALL PARTS, RESET
LEAN MIXTURE SCREW. VISUALLY CHECK FLOAT ALIGNMENT.

Float level adjustment—E4ME/E4MC

FLOAT LEVEL TOO HIGH

1. Hold the float retainer in place.
2. Push down on the center of the float until
the correct level is obtained.

FLOAT LEVEL TOO LOW

1. Lift out the metering rods and remove the
solenoid connector screws.
2. Turn the lean mixture solenoid screw
clockwise, counting and recording the number
of turns required to seat the screw in the float
bowl.
3. Turn the screw counterclockwise and remove it. Lift the solenoid and the connector
from the float bowl.
4. Remove the float and bend the arm up to
adjust. The float must be correctly aligned after
adjustment.
5. To install the components, reverse the order of removal. Back out the solenoid mixture
screw the number of turns that were recorded
in step 2.

Throttle Linkage

ROCHESTER E2SE

No adjustment of the throttle linkage is
possible.

ROCHESTER E4ME AND E4MC

Due to the design of the throttle cable for the
carburetor systems, no adjustments of the
throttle linkage are possible.

Choke Unloader (Primary)

ROCHESTER E2SE

1. Connect a rubber band to the intermediate choke lever and open the throttle to allow
the choke valve to close.
2. Set up the angle gauge and set the gauge
to specifications.
3. Using a vacuum source, retract the vacuum break plunger. Make sure that the air valve
rod does not interfere with the retraction of the
vacuum break plunger.
4. Support the vacuum break rod and make
the adjustment by bending the rod.

ROCHESTER E4ME AND E4MC

1. Connect a rubber band to the green tang
of the intermediate choke shaft.
2. Open the throttle to allow the choke valve
to close.
3. Set up the angle gauge and set to
specifications.

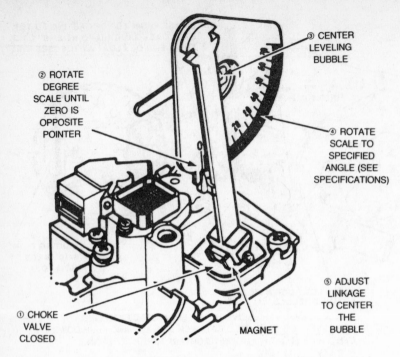

② ROTATE DEGREE SCALE UNTIL ZERO IS OPPOSITE POINTER

③ CENTER LEVELING BUBBLE

④ ROTATE SCALE TO SPECIFIED ANGLE (SEE SPECIFICATIONS)

⑤ ADJUST LINKAGE TO CENTER THE BUBBLE

① CHOKE VALVE CLOSED

MAGNET

Choke angle gauge installation

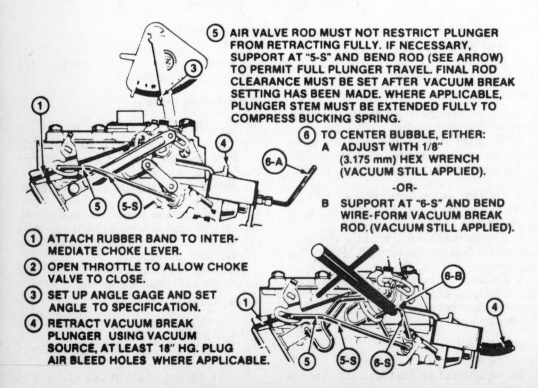

⑤ AIR VALVE ROD MUST NOT RESTRICT PLUNGER FROM RETRACTING FULLY. IF NECESSARY, SUPPORT AT "5-S" AND BEND ROD (SEE ARROW) TO PERMIT FULL PLUNGER TRAVEL. FINAL ROD CLEARANCE MUST BE SET AFTER VACUUM BREAK SETTING HAS BEEN MADE. WHERE APPLICABLE, PLUNGER STEM MUST BE EXTENDED FULLY TO COMPRESS BUCKING SPRING.

⑥ TO CENTER BUBBLE, EITHER:
A ADJUST WITH 1/8" (3.175 mm) HEX WRENCH (VACUUM STILL APPLIED).

-OR-

B SUPPORT AT "6-S" AND BEND WIRE-FORM VACUUM BREAK ROD. (VACUUM STILL APPLIED).

① ATTACH RUBBER BAND TO INTER-MEDIATE CHOKE LEVER.

② OPEN THROTTLE TO ALLOW CHOKE VALVE TO CLOSE.

③ SET UP ANGLE GAGE AND SET ANGLE TO SPECIFICATION.

④ RETRACT VACUUM BREAK PLUNGER USING VACUUM SOURCE, AT LEAST 18" HG. PLUG AIR BLEED HOLES WHERE APPLICABLE.

Primary vacuum break adjustment—E2SE

4. Using a vacuum source, retract the vacuum break plunger. The air valve rod must not restrict the breaker plunger from fully retracting.

5. With the vacuum applied, turn the adjusting screw until the centering bubble of the angle gauge is level.

Choke Unloader (Secondary)

ROCHESTER E2SE

1. Connect a rubber band to the intermediate choke lever and open the throttle to allow the choke to close.

2. Set up the angle gauge and set the angle to specifications.

3. Using a vacuum source, retract the vacuum break plunger and retain the vacuum pressure.

4. Refer to the accompanying illustration to perform this procedure. Center the angle gauge bubble by turning an ⅛ in. (3mm) allen wrench or bending vacuum break rod.

ROCHESTER E4ME AND E4MC

1. Connect a rubber band to the green tang of the intermediate choke shaft.

2. Open the throttle to allow the choke valve to close.

3. Set up the angle gauge and set the angle to specification.

4. Using a vacuum source, retract the vacuum break plunger.

NOTE: *The air valve rod must not restrict the vacuum break plunger from fully retracting.*

5. With the vacuum applied, turn the adjusting screw or bend the vacuum break rod until the bubble of the angle gauge is centered.

Air Valve Spring Adjustment

ROCHESTER E2SE

1. If necessary, remove the intermediate choke rod to gain access to the lock screw.

2. Loosen the lock screw and turn the tension adjusting screw clockwise until the air valve opens slightly.

3. Turn the adjusting screw counterclockwise until the air valve just closes; continue turning the screw counterclockwise according to specifications.

4. Tighten the lock screw. Apply lithium grease to the spring and pin.

ROCHESTER E4ME AND E4MC

1. Loosen the lock screw and turn the tension adjusting screw counterclockwise until the air valve partly opens.

2. Turn the tension adjusting screw clockwise until the air valve just closes, then turn

① ATTACH RUBBER BAND TO GREEN TANG OF INTERMEDIATE CHOKE SHAFT

② OPEN THROTTLE TO ALLOW CHOKE VALVE TO CLOSE

③ SET UP ANGLE GAGE AND SET TO SPECIFICATION

④ RETRACT VACUUM BREAK PLUNGER USING VACUUM SOURCE, AT LEAST 18" HG. PLUG AIR BLEED HOLES WHERE APPLICABLE

ON QUADRAJETS, AIR VALVE ROD MUST NOT RESTRICT PLUNGER FROM RETRACTING FULLY. IF NECESSARY, BEND ROD (SEE ARROW) TO PERMIT FULL PLUNGER TRAVEL. FINAL ROD CLEARANCE MUST BE SET AFTER VACUUM BREAK SETTING HAS BEEN MADE.

⑤ WITH AT LEAST 18" HG STILL APPLIED, ADJUST SCREW TO CENTER BUBBLE

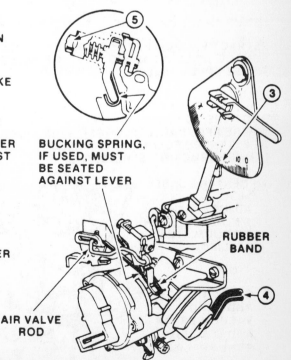

BUCKING SPRING, IF USED, MUST BE SEATED AGAINST LEVER

RUBBER BAND

AIR VALVE ROD

Front vacuum break adjustment—E4ME/E4MC

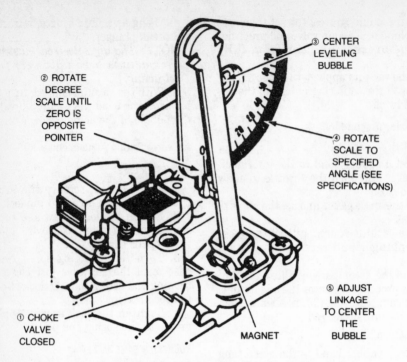

② ROTATE
DEGREE
SCALE UNTIL
ZERO IS
OPPOSITE
POINTER

③ CENTER
LEVELING
BUBBLE

④ ROTATE
SCALE TO
SPECIFIED
ANGLE (SEE
SPECIFICATIONS)

⑤ ADJUST
LINKAGE
TO CENTER
THE
BUBBLE

① CHOKE
VALVE
CLOSED

MAGNET

Secondary vacuum break adjustment—E2SE

① ATTACH RUBBER BAND TO GREEN TANG OF INTERMEDIATE CHOKE SHAFT.

② OPEN THROTTLE TO ALLOW CHOKE VALVE TO CLOSE.

③ SET UP ANGLE GAGE AND SET ANGLE TO SPECIFICATION.

④ RETRACT VACUUM BREAK PLUNGER. USING VACUUM
SOURCE. AT LEAST 18" HG. PLUG AIR BLEED HOLES
WHERE APPLICABLE.

④A ON QUADRAJETS, AIR VALVE ROD MUST NOT RESTRICT
PLUNGER FROM RETRACTING FULLY. IF NECESSARY BEND
ROD HERE TO PERMIT FULL PLUNGER TRAVEL.
WHERE APPLICABLE, PLUNGER STEM MUST
BE EXTENDED FULLY TO COMPRESS
PLUNGER BUCKING SPRING.

⑤ TO CENTER BUBBLE,
EITHER:
A. ADJUST WITH
1/8" HEX WRENCH
(VACUUM STILL
APPLIED)

-OR-

B. SUPPORT AT "S"
AND BEND
VACUUM BREAK
ROD (VACUUM
STILL APPLIED)

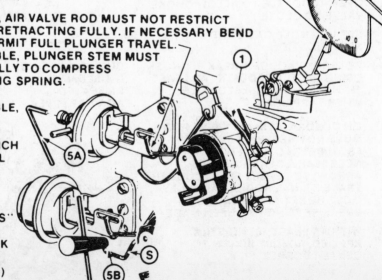

Rear vacuum break adjustment—E4ME/E4MC

the screw clockwise a specified number of turns.

3. Tighten the lock screw and apply lithium grease to the spring contact area.

Air Valve Rod Adjustment

ROCHESTER E2SE

1. Set up the angle gauge on the air valve and set the angle to specification.

2. Use a vacuum source to seat the vacuum break plunger.

3. By applying light pressure to the air valve lever, rotate it in the opening direction.

4. Support the air valve rod and bend it to make the adjustment.

ROCHESTER E4ME AND E4MC

1. Using a vacuum source, seat the vacuum break plunger. The air valve must be closed.

2. Insert a 0.025 in. plug gauge between the rod and the end of the slot.

3. To adjust, bend the air valve rod.

Choke Lever Adjustment

ROCHESTER E2SE

1. If the choke cover is riveted, drill out the rivets and remove the choke cover with the spring assembly.

2. Place the fast idle screw on the high step

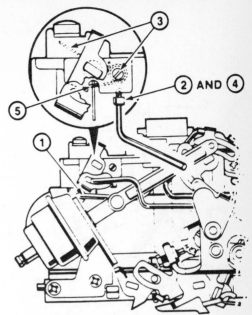

1. If necessary, remove intermediate choke rod, to gain access to lock screw
2. Loosen lock screw using 3/32″ (2.381mm) hex wrench
3. Turn tension-adjusting screw clockwise until air valve opens slightly
   Turn adjusting screw counterclockwise until air valve just closes. Continue counterclockwise specified number of turns
4. Tighten lock screw
5. Apply lithium base grease to lubricate pin and spring contact area

Air valve spring adjustment—E2SE

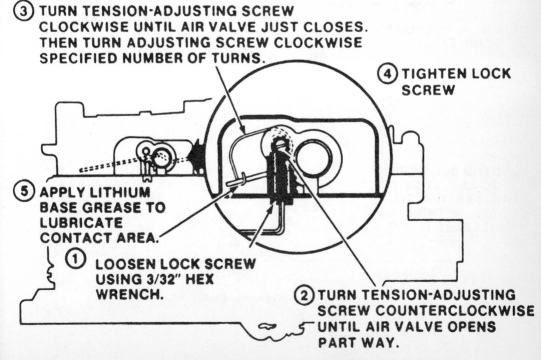

③ TURN TENSION-ADJUSTING SCREW CLOCKWISE UNTIL AIR VALVE JUST CLOSES. THEN TURN ADJUSTING SCREW CLOCKWISE SPECIFIED NUMBER OF TURNS.

④ TIGHTEN LOCK SCREW

⑤ APPLY LITHIUM BASE GREASE TO LUBRICATE CONTACT AREA.

① LOOSEN LOCK SCREW USING 3/32″ HEX WRENCH.

② TURN TENSION-ADJUSTING SCREW COUNTERCLOCKWISE UNTIL AIR VALVE OPENS PART WAY.

Air valve spring adjustment—E4ME/E4MC

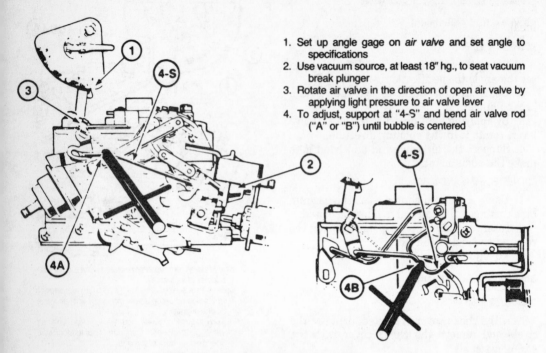

1. Set up angle gage on *air valve* and set angle to specifications
2. Use vacuum source, at least 18" hg., to seat vacuum break plunger
3. Rotate air valve in the direction of open air valve by applying light pressure to air valve lever
4. To adjust, support at "4-S" and bend air valve rod ("A" or "B") until bubble is centered

Air valve spring adjustment—E2SE

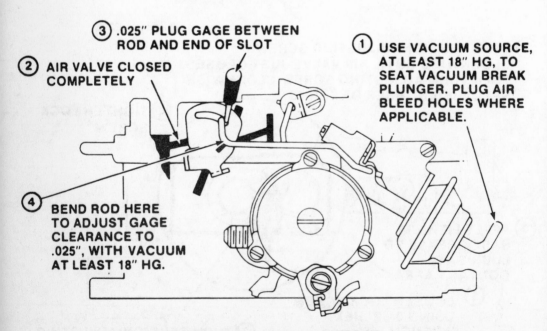

③ .025" PLUG GAGE BETWEEN ROD AND END OF SLOT

② AIR VALVE CLOSED COMPLETELY

① USE VACUUM SOURCE, AT LEAST 18" HG, TO SEAT VACUUM BREAK PLUNGER. PLUG AIR BLEED HOLES WHERE APPLICABLE.

④ BEND ROD HERE TO ADJUST GAGE CLEARANCE TO .025", WITH VACUUM AT LEAST 18" HG.

Front air valve rod adjustment—E4ME/E4MC

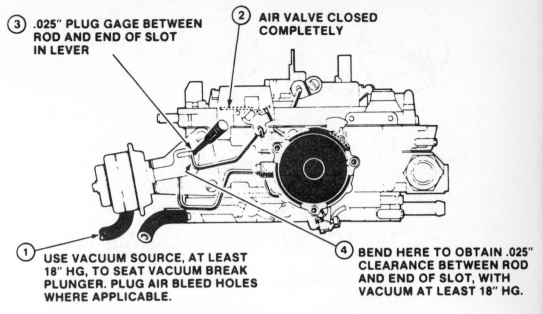

③ .025" PLUG GAGE BETWEEN ROD AND END OF SLOT IN LEVER

② AIR VALVE CLOSED COMPLETELY

① USE VACUUM SOURCE, AT LEAST 18" HG, TO SEAT VACUUM BREAK PLUNGER. PLUG AIR BLEED HOLES WHERE APPLICABLE.

④ BEND HERE TO OBTAIN .025" CLEARANCE BETWEEN ROD AND END OF SLOT, WITH VACUUM AT LEAST 18" HG.

Rear air valve rod adjustment—E4ME/E4MC

1. If riveted, drill out and remove rivets. Remove choke cover and coil assembly
2. Place fast idle screw on high step of fast idle cam
3. Push on intermediate choke lever until choke valve is closed
4. Insert .085" (2.18mm) plug gage in hole
5. Edge of lever should just contact side of gage
6. Support at "S" and bend intermediate choke rod to adjust

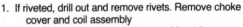

Choke lever adjustment—E2SE

of the fast idle cam. Push the intermediate choke lever until the choke valve is closed.

3. Place a 0.085 in. plug gauge in the choke housing hole and move the choke lever to touch the plug gauge.

4. Support the intermediate choke rod and bend it to make adjustment.

5. To install choke cover, use pop rivets.

ROCHESTER E4ME AND E4MC

1. If the choke cover plate is riveted, drill out the rivets and remove the plate assembly.

2. Place the fast idle cam follower on the high step of the fast idle cam.

3. Lift up on the choke lever to close the choke valve and insert a 0.120 in. (3mm) plug gauge into the choke housing hole. The choke lever should just touch the gauge.

4. To adjust, bend the choke rod.

5. To replace the cover plate, rivet in place.

Choke Rod Fast Idle Cam Adjustment

ROCHESTER E2SE

1. Attach a rubber band to the intermediate choke lever and open the throttle to allow the choke plate to close.

2. Set up the angle gauge and set the angle to specifications.

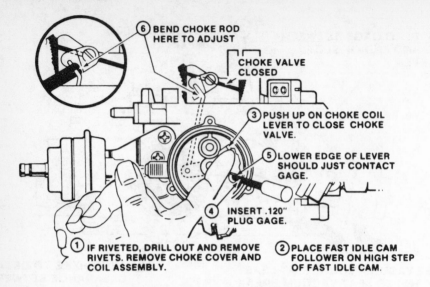

Choke lever adjustment—E4ME/E4MC

3. Place the fast idle screw on the second step of the cam, against the high step.

4. Move the choke shaft lever, to open the choke valve, make contact with the black closing tang.

5. Support the fast idle cam rod and bend the rod to make the adjustment. Adjustment is when the bubble of the angle gauge is level.

ROCHESTER E4ME AND E4MC

1. Connect a rubber band to the green tang of the intermediate choke shaft.

2. Open the throttle to allow the choke valve to close.

3. Set up the angle gauge and set the angle to specifications.

4. Place the cam follower on the second step of the fast idle cam, against the rise of the first step. If the cam follower does not contact the cam, turn the fast idle screw additional turns.

5. To adjust, bend the tang of the fast idle cam until the gauge bubble is centered.

NOTE: *The final fast idle speed adjustment must be performed according to the emission control label.*

Unloader Adjustment

ROCHESTER E2SE

1. Connect a rubber band to the intermediate choke lever and open throttle to allow the choke to close.

2. Set up the angle gauge and set the angle to specifications.

3. Hold the throttle lever in wide-open position and push on the choke lever to open the choke, making contact with the black closing tang.

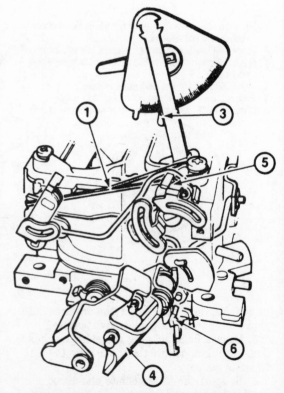

1. Attach rubber band to intermediate choke lever
2. Open throttle to allow choke valve to close
3. Set up angle gage and set angle to specifications
4. Hold throttle lever in wide open position
5. Push on choke shaft lever to open choke valve and to make contact with black closing tang
6. Adjust by bending tang until bubble is centered

Choke unloader adjustment—E2SE

1. Attach rubber band to intermediate choke lever
2. Open throttle to allow choke valve to close
3. Set up angle gage and set angle to specifications
4. Place fast idle screw on second step of cam against rise of high step
5. Push on choke shaft lever to open choke valve and to make contact with black closing tang
6. Support at "S" and adjust by bending fast idle cam rod until bubble is centered

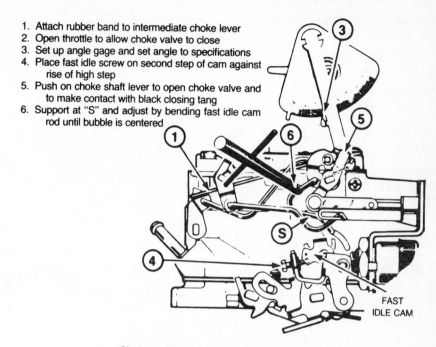

Choke rod fast idle cam adjustment—E2SE

① ATTACH RUBBER BAND TO GREEN TANG OF INTERMEDIATE CHOKE SHAFT

② OPEN THROTTLE TO ALLOW CHOKE VALVE TO CLOSE

③ SET UP ANGLE GAGE AND SET ANGLE TO SPECIFICATIONS

④ PLACE CAM FOLLOWER ON SECOND STEP OF CAM, AGAINST RISE OF HIGH STEP. IF CAM FOLLOWER DOES NOT CONTACT CAM, TURN IN FAST IDLE SPEED SCREW ADDITIONAL TURN(S).

NOTICE: FINAL FAST IDLE SPEED ADJUSTMENT MUST BE PERFORMED ACCORDING TO UNDER-HOOD EMISSION CONTROL INFORMATION LABEL.

⑤ ADJUST BY BENDING TANG OF FAST IDLE CAM UNTIL BUBBLE IS CENTERED.

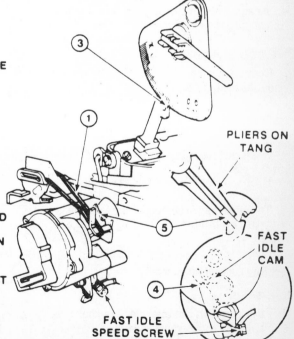

Choke rod fast idle cam adjustment—E4ME/E4MC

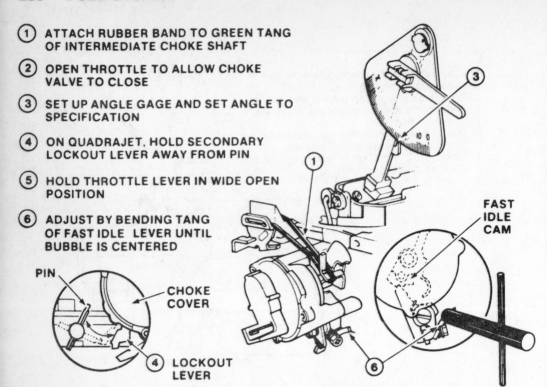

① ATTACH RUBBER BAND TO GREEN TANG OF INTERMEDIATE CHOKE SHAFT

② OPEN THROTTLE TO ALLOW CHOKE VALVE TO CLOSE

③ SET UP ANGLE GAGE AND SET ANGLE TO SPECIFICATION

④ ON QUADRAJET, HOLD SECONDARY LOCKOUT LEVER AWAY FROM PIN

⑤ HOLD THROTTLE LEVER IN WIDE OPEN POSITION

⑥ ADJUST BY BENDING TANG OF FAST IDLE LEVER UNTIL BUBBLE IS CENTERED

PIN

CHOKE COVER

④ LOCKOUT LEVER

FAST IDLE CAM

Choke unloader adjustment—E4ME/E4MC

4. To adjust, bend the tang until the bubble of the angle gauge is centered.

ROCHESTER E4ME AND E4MC

1. Connect a rubber band to the green tang of the intermediate shaft.

2. Open the throttle to allow the choke valve to close.

3. Set up the angle gauge and set the angle to specification.

4. Hold the secondary lockout lever away from the pin.

5. Hold the throttle lever in the wide-open position.

6. To adjust, bend the tang of the fast idle lever until the bubble of the angle gauge is centered.

Secondary Lockout Adjustment

ROCHESTER E2SE

1. Push down on the intermediate choke lever to hold the choke valve wide-open.

2. Open the throttle lever until the end of the secondary actuating lever is opposite the toe of the lockout lever.

3. Insert a 0.025 in. plug gauge.

4. To adjust, bend the lockout lever tang into contact with the fast idle cam.

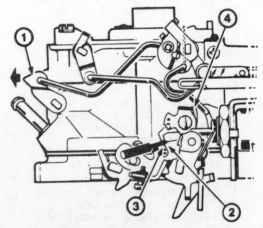

1. Hold choke valve wide open by pushing down on intermediate choke lever
2. Open throttle lever until end of secondary actuating lever is opposite toe of lockout lever
3. Gage clearance—dimension should be .025"
4. If necessary to adjust, bend lockout lever gang contacting fast idle cam

Secondary lockout adjustment—E2SE

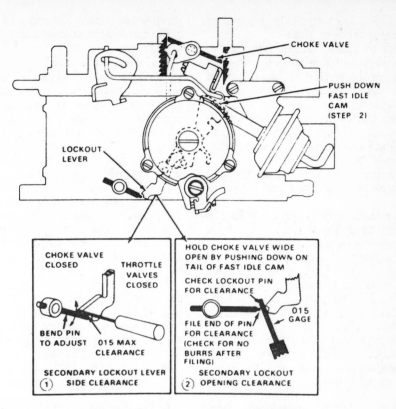

Secondary lockout adjustment—E4ME/E4MC

ROCHESTER E4ME AND E4MC

1. With the choke and the throttle valves closed, insert a 0.015 in. (0.38mm) plug gauge between the lockout lever and the pin. To establish clearance, bend the pin.

2. Push down on the fast idle cam and hold the choke valve wide open.

3. Insert a 0.015 in. (0.38mm) plug gauge sideways between the lockout lever and the pin. To adjust, file the end of the pin.

Mixture Control Solenoid

ROCHESTER E4ME AND E4MC

Travel Test

Before checking the mixture control solenoid travel, it may be necessary to modify the float

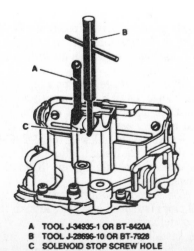

A TOOL J-34935-1 OR BT-8420A
B TOOL J-28696-10 OR BT-7928
C SOLENOID STOP SCREW HOLE

Adjusting the solenoid stop screw—E4MC/E4ME carburetor

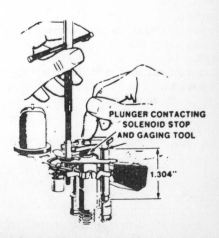

PLUNGER CONTACTING SOLENOID STOP AND GAGING TOOL

1.304"

Adjusting the lean mixture solenoid screw—E4MC/E4ME carburetor

gauge J–9789–130 or equivalent (used to externally check the float level).

This should be done by filing or grinding the sufficient material off the gauge to allow for insertion down the vertical D-shaped hole in the air horn casting (located next to the idle air bleed valve cover).

Check that the gauge freely enters the D-shaped vent hole and does not bind. The gauge will also be used to determine the total mixture control solenoid travel.

With the engine off and the air cleaner removed, measure the control solenoid travel as follows:

1. Insert a modified float gauge J–9789–130 or equivalent down the D-shaped vent hole. Press down on the gauge and release it.

2. Observe that the gauge moves freely and does not bind. With the gauge released (solenoid in the up position), be sure to read it at eye level and record the mark on the gauge (in inches/millimeters) that lines up with the top of the air horn casting (upper edge).

3. Lightly press down on the gauge until bottomed (solenoid in the down position). Record (in inches/millimeters) the mark on the gauge that lines up with the top of the air horn casting.

4. Subtract the gauge up dimension from gauge dimension. Record the difference (in inches/millimeters). This difference is total solenoid travel.

5. If total solenoid travel is not within $\frac{3}{32}$–$\frac{5}{32}$ in. (2.4–3.9mm), perform the mixture control solenoid adjustments. If the difference is within $\frac{3}{32}$–$\frac{5}{32}$ in. (2.4–3.9mm), proceed to the idle air bleed valve adjustment.

NOTE: *If adjustment is required, it will be necessary to remove the air horn and drive out the mixture control solenoid screw plug from the under side of the air horn.*

Adjustments

Before making adjustment to mixture control solenoid, verify that the plunger travel is not correct.

1. Remove air horn, mixture control solenoid plunger, air horn gasket and plastic filler block, using normal service procedures.

2. Check carburetor for cause of incorrect mixture:

   a. M/C solenoid bore or plunger worn or sticking

   b. Metering rods for incorrect part number, sticking or rods or springs not installed properly

   c. Foreign material in jets

3. Remove throttle side metering rod. Install mixture control solenoid gauging tool, J–33815–1, BT–8253–A, or equivalent, over the

throttle side metering jet rod guide and temporarily reinstall the solenoid plunger into the solenoid body.

4. Holding the solenoid plunger in the down position, use tool J–28696–10, BT–7928, or equivalent, to turn lean mixture solenoid screw counterclockwise until the plunger breaks contact with the gauging tool. Turn slowly clockwise until the plunger makes contact with the gauging tool. The adjustment is correct when the solenoid plunger is contacting both the solenoid stop and the gauging tool.

NOTE: *If the total difference in adjustment required less than ¾ turn of the lean mixture solenoid screw, the original setting was within the manufacturer's specifications.*

5. Remove solenoid plunger and gauging tool and reinstall metering rod and plastic filler block.

6. Invert air horn and remove rich mixture stop screw from bottom side of air horn, using tool J–28696–4, BT–7967–A, or equivalent.

7. Remove lean mixture screw plug and the rich mixture stop screw plug from air horn, using a suitable sized punch.

8. Reinstall rich mixture stop screw in air horn and bottom lightly, then back screw out ¼ turn.

9. Reinstall air horn gasket, mixture control solenoid plunger and air horn to carburetor.

10. Adjust M/C Solenoid Plunger travel as follows:

   a. Insert float gauge down D-shaped vent hole. Press down on gauge and release, observing that the gauge moves freely and does not bind. With gauge released, (plunger UP position), read at eye level and record the reading of the gauge mark (in inches/millimeters) that lines up with the top of air horn casting, (upper edge).

   b. Lightly press down on gauge until bottomed, (plunger DOWN position). Read and record (in inches/millimeters) the reading of the gauge mark that lines up with top of air horn casting.

   c. Subtract gauge **UP** position (Step 1) from gauge **DOWN** position (Step 2) and record the difference. This difference is the total plunger travel. Insert external float gauge in vent hole and, with tool J–28696–10, BT–7928, or equivalent, adjust rich mixture stop screw to obtain $\frac{5}{32}$ in. (3.9mm) total plunger travel.

11. With solenoid plunger travel correctly set, install plugs (supplied in service kits) in the air horn, as follows:

   a. Install plug, hollow end down, into the access hole to lean mixture (solenoid) screw. Use suitably sized punch to drive plug into the air horn until the top of plug is even with the lower. Plug must be installed to retain the screw setting and to prevent fuel vapor loss.

b. Install plug, with hollow end down, over the rich mixture stop screw access hole and drive plug into place so that the top of the plug is $\frac{3}{16}$ in. (4.7mm) below the surface of the air horn casting.

NOTE: *Plug must be installed to retain screw setting.*

12. To check the M/C solenoid dwell, first disconnect vacuum line to the canister purge valve and plug it. Ground diagnostic TEST terminal and run engine until it is at normal operation temperature (upper radiator hose hot) and in closed loop.

13. Check M/C dwell at 3000 rpm. If within 10–50 degrees, calibration is complete. If higher than 50 degrees, check carburetor for cause of rich condition. If below 10 degrees, look for cause of lean engine condition such as vacuum leaks. If none found, check for cause of lean carburetor.

Idle Air Valve

A cover is in place over the idle air bleed valve and the access holes to the idle mixture needles are sealed with hardened plugs, to seal the factory settings, during original equipment production. These items are NOT to be removed unless required for cleaning, part replacement, improper dwell readings or if the System Performance Check indicates the carburetor is the cause of the trouble.

ROCHESTER E4ME AND E4MC

1. With engine **OFF**, cover the internal bowl vents and inlet to bleed valve and the carburetor air intakes with masking tape, to prevent metal chips from entering.

2. Carefully drill rivet head of idle air bleed cover, with 0.110 in. (2.8mm) drill bit.

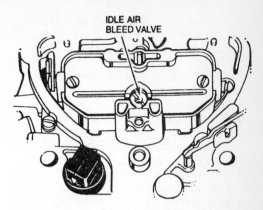

Idle air bleed adjustment—E4MC/E4ME carburetor

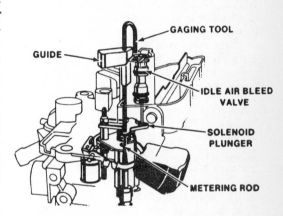

Installing the air bleed valve gauging tool—E4MC/E4ME carburetor

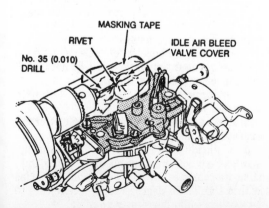

Idle air bleed cover removal—E4MC/E4ME carburetor

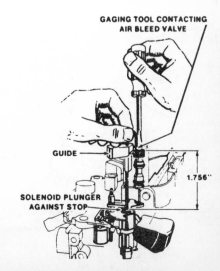

Setting the idle air bleed valve until it just contacts the gauging tool—E4MC/E4ME carburetor

3. Remove rivet head and all pieces of rivet.

4. Lift cover off air bleed valve and blow out any metal shavings, or use a magnet to remove excess metal.

CAUTION: *Always wear eye protection when using compressed air.*

5. Remove masking tape.

6. Start engine allow to reach normal operating temperature.

7. Disconnect the vacuum hose from the canister purge valve and plug it.

8. While idling in **D** for automatic transmission or **N** for manual transmission, slowly turn the valve counterclockwise or clockwise, until the dwell reading varies within the 25–35 degree range, attempting to be as close to 30 degrees as possible.

NOTE: *Perform this step carefully. The air bleed valve is very sensitive and should be turned in ⅛ turn increments only.*

9. If the dwell reading does not vary and is not within the 25–35 degree range, it will be necessary to remove the plugs and to adjust the idle mixture needles.

Idle Mixture

E4ME CARBURETORS
(ELECTRIC CHOKE)

1. Using tool J–29030, BT–7610–B, or equivalent, turn both idle mixture needles clockwise until they are lightly seated, then turn each mixture needle counterclockwise 3 turns.

2. Reinstall carburetor on engine using a new flange mounting gasket, but do not install air cleaner and gasket at this time.

3. Disconnect the vacuum hose to canister purge valve and plug it. Readjust the idle air bleed valve to finalize correct dwell reading.

4. Start engine and run until fully warm and repeat the idle air bleed valve adjustment.

5. If unable to set dwell to 25–35 degrees and the dwell is below 25 degrees, turn both mix-

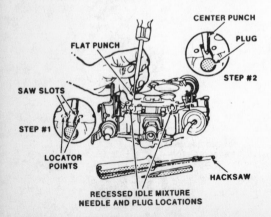

Removing the idle mixture needle plugs—E4MC/E4ME carburetor

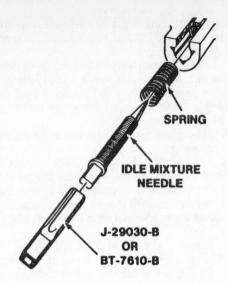

Idle mixture needle assembly—E4MC-E4ME carburetor

ture needles counterclockwise an additional turn. If dwell is above 35 degrees, turn both mixture needles clockwise an additional turn. Readjust idle air bleed valve to obtain dwell limits. Repeat as needed.

6. After adjustments are complete, seal the idle mixture needle openings in the throttle body, using silicone sealant, RTV rubber, or equivalent. The sealer is required to discourage unnecessary adjustment of the setting and to prevent fuel vapor loss in that area. Reconnect canister vacuum hose.

7. On vehicles without an Idle Load Compensator (ILC), adjust curb idle speed if necessary.

8. Check, and if necessary, adjust fast idle speed as described on Vehicle Emission Control Information label.

E4MC CARBURETOR
(HOT AIR CHOKE)

1. Using tool J–29030–B, BT–7610–B, or equivalent, turn each idle mixture needle clockwise until lightly seated, then turn each mixture needle counterclockwise 3 turns.

2. Reinstall carburetor on engine, using a new flange mounting gasket, but do not install air cleaner or gasket at this time.

3. Disconnect vacuum hose to canister purge valve and plug it.

4. Start engine and allow it to reach normal operating temperature.

5. While idling in **D** (**N** for manual transmission), adjust both mixture needles equally, in ⅛ turn increments, until dwell reading varies within the 25–35 degree range, attempting to be as close to 30 degrees as possible.

6. If reading is too low, turn mixture needles counterclockwise. If reading is too high, turn

mixture needles clockwise. Allow time for dwell reading to stabilize after each adjustment.

NOTE: *After adjustments are complete, seal the idle mixture needle openings in the throttle body, using silicone sealant, RTV rubber, or equivalent. The sealer is required to discourage unnecessary readjustment of the setting and prevent fuel vapor loss in that area.*

7. On vehicles without a carburetor-mounted Idle Load Compensator, adjust curb idle speed if necessary.

8. Check, and if necessary, adjust fast idle speed, as described on the Vehicle Emission Control Information label.

Idle Load Compensator

The idle load compensator is adjusted at the factory. Do not make any adjustments unless diagnosis or curb idle speed is not to specification.

1. Make certain ignition timing, mixture adjustment, vacuum hoses, fuel pressure and CCC system meets specifications.

2. Remove air cleaner and plug hose to thermal vacuum valve.

3. Connect a tachometer.

4. Disconnect and plug hose to EGR valve.

5. Disconnect and plug hose to canister purge port.

6. Disconnect and plug hose to idle load compensator.

7. Back out idle stop screw on carburetor 3 turns.

8. Turn air conditioning **OFF**.

9. Block drive wheels, set parking brake, place transmission in **P**, start and warm engine to normal operating temperature. Make certain choke is open.

10. With engine running, place transmission in **D** and idle load compensator fully extended (no vacuum applied). Using tool J–29607, or

equivalent, adjust plunger to obtain 650–750 rpm. Locknut on plunger must be held with a wrench to prevent damage to guide tabs.

11. Measure distance from the locknut to tip of the plunger. This distance must not exceed 1 in. (25mm). If it does check for low idle condition.

12. Reconnect vacuum hose to idle load compensator and observe idle speed.

13. Idle speed should be 425–475 rpm in **D**.

14. If idle speed is correct no further adjustment is necessary, proceed with Step 18. If idle speed is still incorrect continue with Step 15.

NOTE: *It may be necessary to remove the idle load compensator from the engine unless a hex key wrench is modified to clear obstructions.*

15. Stop engine, remove rubber cap from the center outlet tube.

16. Using a 0.90 in. (23mm) hex wrench, insert through open center tube to engage idle speed adjusting screw.

17. If idle speed in Step 13, was low turn the adjusting screw counterclockwise 1 turn for every 85 rpm low. If idle speed was high turn screw 1 turn for every 85 rpm high.

18. Disconnect and plug vacuum hose to the idle load compensator.

19. Using a hand pump, apply vacuum to the idle load compensator until fully retracted.

20. Adjust the idle stop screw on carburetor float bowl to obtain 450 rpm in **D**.

21. Place transmission in **P** and stop engine.

22. Reconnect the idle load compensator.

23. Reconnect all vacuum hoses.

24. Install air cleaner and gasket. Remove wheel blocks.

Throttle Position Sensor (TPS)

Before the throttle position sensor voltage output setting can be accurately checked or adjusted the idle rpm must be within specifications. The plug covering the TPS adjustment screw is used to provide a tamper-resistant de-

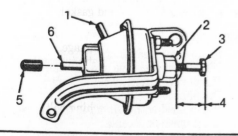

1. Vacuum inlet tube
2. Jam nut
3. ILC plunger (do not use to set curb idle speed)
4. Dimension "A" distance must not exceed 1 in. (25mm) after plunger adj.
5. Rubber cap
6. Idle speed adj. screw

Idle Load Compensator (ILC)—E4MC/E4ME carburetor

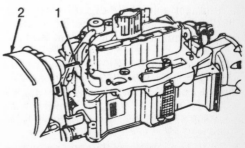

1. Plug (TPS adjusting screw)
2. Drill

Removing the Throttle Positioning Sensor (TPS) plug—E4MC/E4ME carburetor

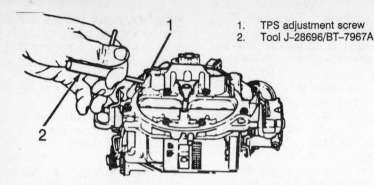

1.   TPS adjustment screw
2.   Tool J–28696/BT–7967A

Adjusting the TPS using the proper tool—E4MC/E4ME carburetor

sign and retain the factory setting during vehicle operation. Do not remove the plug unless diagnosis indicates the TPS is not adjusted correctly, or it is necessary to replace the air horn assembly, float bowl, TPS, or TPS adjustment screw. This is a critical adjustment that must be performed accurately to ensure proper vehicle performance and control of exhaust emissions. Remove TPS plug if not already removed.

NOTE: *Adjustment is required only if voltage is above the following readings, as the ECM automatically zeros below 0.70 Volts.*

1. Using a $^5/_{64}$ in. (2mm) drill bit, carefully drill a hole in the steel or aluminum plug. Be sure to drill only far enough to start a self tapping screw, the approximate drilling depth is $^1/_{16}$–$^1/_8$ in. (1.6–3mm).

NOTE: *Use care in drilling so as not to damage the TPS adjustment screw head.*

2. Start a long self tapping screw (No. 8 × ½ in.) into the drilled pilot hole in the plug. Turn the screw in only enough to ensure a good thread engagement in the drilled hole.

3. Place a suitable tool between the screw head and the air horn casting. Then pry against the screw head to remove the plug. A small slide hammer may also be used in this procedure. Be sure to discard the plug when it has been removed.

4. Connect a suitable digital voltmeter (J–29125 or equivalent) from the TPS connector center terminal (B) to the bottom terminal (C).

NOTE: *Jumper wires for access can be made using terminals 12014836 and 12014837 or equivalent. Make jumper wires up with 16 gauge (1.0mm), 18 gauge (0.8mm) or 20 gauge (0.5mm) wire approximately 6 in. (152mm) long.*

5. With the ignition **ON** and the engine stopped, install the TPS adjustment screw and turn the screw with a suitable tool to obtain the specified voltage at the specified throttle position with the A/C controls in the **OFF** position.

6. After the adjustment has been made, install a new plug kit (supplied in the service kits), into the air horn. Drive the plug into place until it is flush with the raised pump lever boss on the casting. Clear trouble code memory after adjustment.

NOTE: *The plug must be installed to retain the TPS adjustment screw setting. If a plug kit is not available, remove the TPS adjusting screw and apply thread sealer adhesive X–10 or equivalent to the screw threads. Now repeat the TPS adjustment procedure to obtain the correct TPS voltage.*

REMOVAL AND INSTALLATION

Always replace all internal gaskets that are removed. Base gasket should be inspected and replaced only if damaged. Flooding, stumble on acceleration and other performance complaints are in many instances, caused by presence of dirt, water, or other foreign matter in carburetor. To aid in diagnosis, carburetor should be carefully removed from engine without draining fuel from bowl. Contents of fuel bowl may then be examined for contamination as carburetor is disassembled. Check fuel filter.

Rochester E2SE

1. Remove air cleaner and gasket.
2. Disconnect fuel pipe and vacuum lines.
3. Disconnect electrical connectors.
4. Disconnect accelerator linkage.
5. If equipped with automatic transmission, disconnect downshift cable.
6. If equipped with cruise control, disconnect linkage.
7. Remove carburetor attaching bolts.
8. Remove carburetor and EFE heater/insulator (if used).
9. Fill carburetor bowl before installing carburetor. A small supply of no-lead fuel will enable the carburetor to be filled and the operation of the float and inlet needle and seat to be

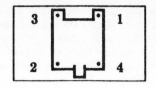

1. Left rear
2. Right front
3. Right rear
4. Left front

Correct carburetor-to-manifold torquing procedure—E4MC/E4ME carburetor

checked. Operate throttle lever several times and check discharge from pump jets before installing carburetor.

10. Inspect EFE heater/insulator for damage. Be certain throttle body and EFE heater/insulator surfaces are clean.

11. Install EFE heater; insulator.

12. Install carburetor and tighten nuts alternately to the correct torque.

13. Connect downshift cable as required.

14. Connect cruise control cable as required.

15. Connect accelerator linkage.

16. Connect electrical connections.

17. Connect fuel pipe sand vacuum hoses.

18. Check base (slow) and fast idle.

19. Install air cleaner.

Rochester E4ME and E4MC

1. Disconnect the battery and remove the air cleaner.

2. Disconnect the accelerator linkage.

3. Disconnect the transmission detent cable.

4. If equipped, remove the cruise control.

5. Disconnect all of the necessary vacuum lines.

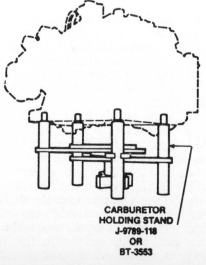

CARBURETOR
HOLDING STAND
J-9789-118
OR
BT-3553

Carburetor holding fixture

6. Disconnect the fuel line at the carburetor inlet.

7. Remove the attaching bolts and remove the carburetor.

8. To install, position the carburetor onto the manifold and install the attaching bolts.

9. Connect the fuel line at the carburetor inlet.

10. Connect all of the vacuum lines.

11. If equipped, install the cruise control.

12. Connect the transmission detent cable.

13. Connect the accelerator linkage.

14. Install the air cleaner and connect the battery.

OVERHAUL

Efficient carburetion depends greatly on careful cleaning and inspection during overhaul, since dirt, gum, water, or varnish in or on the carburetor parts are often responsible for poor performance.

Overhaul your carburetor in a clean, dust-free area. Carefully disassemble the carburetor, referring often to the exploded views and directions packaged with the rebuilding kit. Keep all similar and look-alike parts separated during disassembly and cleaning to avoid accidental interchange during assembly. Make a note of all jet sizes.

When the carburetor is disassembled, wash all parts (except diaphragms, electric components, pump plunger, and any other plastic, leather, fiber, or rubber parts) in clean carburetor solvent. Do not leave parts in the solvent any longer than is necessary to sufficiently loosen the deposits. Excessive cleaning may remove the special finish from the float bowl and choke valve bodies, leaving these parts unfit for service. Rinse all parts in clean solvent and blow them dry with compressed air or allow them to air dry. Wipe clean all cork, plastic, leather, and fiber parts with a clean, lint-free cloth.

Blow out all passages and jets with compressed air and be sure that there are no restrictions or blockages. Never use wire or similar tools to clean jets, fuel passages, or air bleeds. Clean all jets and valves separately to avoid accidental interchange.

Check all parts for wear or damage. If wear or damage is found, replace the defective parts. Especially check the following:

1. Check the float needle and seat for wear. If wear is found, replace the complete assembly.

2. Check the float hinge pin for wear and the float(s) for dents or distortion. Replace the float if fuel has leaked into it.

3. Check the throttle and choke shaft bores for wear or an out-of-round condition. Damage or wear to the throttle arm, shaft, or shaft bore

will often require replacement of the throttle body. These parts require a close tolerance of fit; wear may allow air leakage, which could affect starting and idling.

NOTE: *Throttle shafts and bushings are not included in overhaul kits. They can be purchased separately or repaired by a qualified carburetor overhaul shop.*

4. Inspect the idle mixture adjusting needles for burrs or grooves. Any such condition requires replacement of the needle, since you will not be able to obtain a satisfactory idle.

5. Test the accelerator pump check valves. They should pass air one way but not the other. Test for proper seating by blowing and sucking on the valve. Replace the valve check ball and spring as necessary. If the valve is satisfactory, wash the valve parts again to remove breath moisture.

6. Check the bowl cover for warped surfaces with a straightedge.

7. Closely inspect the accelerator pump plunger for wear and damage, replacing as necessary.

8. After the carburetor is assembled, check the choke valve for freedom of operation.

Carburetor overhaul kits are recommended for each overhaul. These kits contain all gaskets and new parts to replace those which deteriorate most rapidly. Failure to replace all parts supplied with the kit (especially gaskets) can result in poor performance later.

Some carburetor manufacturers supply overhaul kits for three basic types: minor repair; major repair; and gasket kits. Basically, they contain the following:

Minor Repair Kits:
- All gaskets
- Float needle valve
- All diagrams
- Spring for the pump diaphragm

Major Repair Kits:
- All jets and gaskets
- All diaphragms
- Float needle valve
- Pump ball valve
- Float
- Complete intermediate rod
- Intermediate pump lever
- Some cover holddown screws and washers

Gasket kits:
- All gaskets

After cleaning and checking all components, reassemble the carburetor, using new parts and referring to the exploded view. When reassembling, make sure that all screws and jets are tight in their seats, but do not overtighten as the tips will be distorted. Tighten all screws gradually, in rotation. Do not tighten needle valves into their seats; uneven jetting will result. Always use new gaskets. Be sure to follow all assembly and adjustment procedures.

NOTE: *Before performing any service on the carburetor, it is essential that it be placed on a suitable holding fixture, such as tool J–9789–118, BY–30–15 or equivalent. Without the use of the holding fixture, it is possible to damage throttle valves or other parts of the carburetor.*

E2SE Carburetor Disassembly

SECONDARY VACUUM BREAK REMOVAL

Remove the secondary vacuum break/bracket assembly-to-throttle body screw. Then, rotate the assembly to disengage the vacuum break link ("T" pin) from the choke lever slot.

Do not immerse the idle speed solenoid or the vacuum break units in any type of carburetor cleaner. These items must always be removed before complete cleaning or damage to the components will result.

AIR HORN REMOVAL

1. Remove the clip from the hole in the pump rod.

NOTE: *Do not remove the pump lever retaining screw or the pump lever from the air horn assembly.*

2. Reomve and discard the retaining clip from the intermediate choke link at the choke lever. A new retaining clip is required for reassembly. Remove the choke link and the plastic busing from the choke lever, then save the bushing for laster reuse.

3. Remove the mixture control solenoid-to-air horn screws; then, using a slight twisting motion, carefully lift the solenoid out of the air horn. Remove and discard the solenoid gasket.

4. Remove the seal retainer and the rubber seal from the end of the solenoid stem, being careful not to damage or nick end of the solenoid stem. Discard the seal and retainer. Retain the spacer for use at time of reassembly.

5. Remove the air horn-to-fuel bowl screws and lockwashers.

6. Rotate the fast idle cam to the full UP position and remove the air horn assembly by tilting to disengage the fast idle cam rod from the slot in the fast idle cam and the pump rod from the pump lever hole. If the pump plunger comes out of the float bowl with the air horn removal, remove the pump plunger from the air horn. The air horn gasket should remain on the float bowl for removal later. Do not remove the fast idle cam screw and the cam from the float bowl. These parts are not serviced separately and are to remain permanently in place as installed by

the factory. The new service replacement float bowl will include the secondary lockout lever, the fast idle cam and screw installed as required.

7. Remove the fast idle cam link from the choke lever by rotating the rod to align the upset on the link with the small slot in the lever.

AIR HORN DISASSEMBLY

1. Remove the Throttle Position Sensor (TPS) plunger by pushing it downward through the air horn seal.

NOTE: *Use your fingers only to remove the plunger to prevent damage to the sealing surface of the plunger.*

2. Remove the TPS seal by inverting the air horn and use a small screwdriver to remove the staking, holding the seal retaining the ideal retainer in place. Remove and discard the retainer and seal.

3. Remove the pump plunger stem seal by inverting the air horn and using a small screwdriver to remove the staking, holding the seal retainer in place. Remove and discard the retainer and seal.

NOTE: *Use care in removing the TPS plunger seal retainer and the pump plunger stem seal retainer to prevent damage to the air horn casting. New seals and retainers are required for reassembly.*

4. Remove the vent/screen assembly by removing the 2 small attaching screws.

5. Further disassembly of the air horn is not require for cleaning purposes or air horn replacement. A new service air horn assembly includes the secondary metering rod-air valve assembly with adjustments pre-set to factory specifications. No attempt should be made to change the air valve settings. The air valve and the choke valve attaching screws are staked in place and are not removable. A new service air horn assembly will also include a TPS adjustment screw. The new service air horn assembly will have the thermostatic pump bypass assembly installed, this temperature sensitive device is pressed permanently into place and is not serviceable, separately.

FLOAT BOWL DISASSEMBLY

1. Remove the air horn gasket.

2. Remove the pump plunger from the pump well, if not removed with the air horn.

3. Remove the pump return spring from the pump well.

4. Push up from the bottom on the electrical connector and remove the "Throttle Position Sensor (TPS) and the connector assembly from the float bowl. Remove the spring from the bottom of the TPS well in the bowl.

NOTE: *Use care in removing the sensor and connector assembly to prevent damage to this critical electrical part.*

5. Remove the plastic filler block over the float valve.

6. Remove the float assembly and the float valve by pulling up the hinge pin (hold the float valve clip in place with your finger while tilting the float to clear the bowl vapor purge tube).

7. Using a removal tool or a wide-blade screwdriver, remove the float valve seat (with gasket) and the extended metering jet from the float bowl.

NOTE: *Do not remove or change the adjustment of the small calibration screw located deep inside the metering jet during routine servicing. The adjustment screw is pre-set at the factory and no attempt should be made to change this adjustment in the field except as the result of a Computer Command Control system performance check.*

8. Using a small slidehammer or equivalent, remove the plastic retainer holding the pump discharge spring and check ball in place. Discard the plastic retainer, a new retainer is required for reassembly.

NOTE: *Do not attempt to remove the plastic retainer by prying it out with a tool such as a punch or screwdriver as this will damage the sealing beads on the bowl casting surface and require complete float bowl replacement.*

Turn the fuel bowl upside down catching the pump discharge spring and the check ball in palm of your hand.

Return the bowl to the upright position.

9. Remove the fuel inlet nut, the gasket, the check valve filter assembly and the spring.

CHOKE DISASSEMBLY

A tamper resistant choke cover design is used to discourage readjustment of the choke thermostatic coil thermostatic coil assembly in the field.However, it is necessary to remove the cover and coil assembly during normal carburetor disassembly for cleaning and overhaul using the following procedures:

1. Support the float bowl and the throttle body as an assembly on a suitable holding fixture.

2. Carefully align a No. 21 drill (0.159 in./ 4mm) on the rivet head and drill only enough to remove the rivet head. After removing the rivet heads and retainers, use a drift and a small hammer to drive the remainder of the rivets out of the choke housing.

NOTE: *Use care in drilling to prevent damage to the choke cover or housing.*

3. Remove the screw from the end of the intermediate choke shaft inside the choke housing.

4. Remove the choke coil lever from the end of the shaft.

5. Remove the intermediate choke shaft assembly from the float bowl by sliding the shaft rearward and out of the throttle lever side.

6. Remove the choke housing by removing the 2 attaching screws.

THROTTLE BODY REMOVAL

1. Remove the throttle body-to-bowl screws and the throttle body assembly from the float bowl.

2. Remove the throttle body gasket.

THROTTLE BODY DISASSEMBLY

1. Place the throttle body assembly on the carburetor holding fixture to avoid damaging the throttle valves.

2. Hold the primary throttle lever wide-open and disengage the pump rod from the throttle lever by rotating the rod until the ridge on the rod aligns with slot in the lever.

Further disassembly of the throttle body is not required for cleaning purpose.

NOTE: *The primary and secondary throttle valve screws are permanently staked in place and should not be removed. The throttle body is serviced as a complete assembly.*

3. Do not remove the plugs covering the idle mixture needle unless it is necessary to replace the mixture needle or normal soakings and air pressure fails to clean the idle mixture passages. If necessary, remove the idle mixture plug and needle as follows:

   a. Invert the throttle body and place it on a suitable holding fixture-manifold side up.

   b. Make 2 parallel cuts into the throttle body on either side of the locator point beneath the idle mixture needle plug (manifold side) with a hacksaw. The cuts should reach down to the steel plug but should not extend more than 1.8 in. (46mm) beyond the locator point. The distance between the saw marks depends on the size of the punch to be used.

   c. Place a flat punch at a point near the end of the saw marks in the throttle body. Holding the punch at a 45 degree angle, drive it into the throttle body until the casting breaks away, exposing the steel plug.

   d. Holding a center punch vertical, drive it into the steel plug. Then holding the punch at a 45 degree angle, drive the plug out of the casting.

NOTE: *The hardened plug will break rather than remaining intact. It is not necessary to remove the plug whole; instead, remove loose pieces to allow use of Idle Mixture Adjusting tool J-29030, BT-7610B or equivalent.*

4. Using the tool J-29030, BT-7610B or equivalent, remove the idle mixture needle and spring from the throttle body.

CLEANING AND INSPECTION

The carburetor parts should be cleaned in a cold immersion-type cleaner such as Carbon X (X-55) or equivalent.

NOTE: *The idle speed solenoid, the mixture control solenoid, the throttle position sensor, the electric choke, the rubber parts, the plastic parts, the diaphragms, the pump plunger, the plastic filler block, should not be immersed in carburetor cleaner as they will hardened, swell or distort.*

The plastic busing in the throttle lever will withstand normal cleaning in the carburetor cleaner.

1. Thoroughly clean all of the metal parts and blow dry with shop air. Make sure all the fuel passages and metering parts are free of burrs and dirt. Do not pass the drills or wires through the jets and passages.

2. Inspect the upper and lower surface of the carburetor castings for damage.

3. Inspect the holes in the levers for excessive wear or out of round conditions. If worn, the levers should be replaced. Inspect the plasticbushings in the levers for damage and excessive wear, replace as required.

4. Check, repair or replace parts, if the following problems are encountered:

A. Flooding

1. Inspect the float valve and seat for dirt, deep wear grooves, scores and improper sealing.

2. Inspect the float vale pull clip for proper installation; be careful not to bend the pull clip.

3. Inspect the float, the float arms and the hinge pin for distortion, binds, and burrs. Check the density of the material in the float; if heavier than normal, replace the float.

4. Clean or replace the fuel inlet filter and check the valve assembly.

B. Hesitation

1. Inspect the pump plunger for cracks, scores or cup excessive wear. A used pump cup will shrink when dry. If dried out, soak in fuel for 8 hours before testing.

2. Inspect the pump duration and return springs for weakness or distortion.

3. Check the pump passages and the jet(s) for dirt, improper seating of the discharge checkball or the temperature bypass disc and/or scores in the pumpwell. Check the condition of the pump discharge check ball spring, replace as necessary.

4. Check the pump linkage for excessive wear; repair or replace as necessary.

C. Hard Starting — Poor Cold Operation

1. Check the choke valve and linkage for excessive wear, binds or distortion.

2. Test the vacuum break diaphragm(s) for leaks.

3. Clean or replace the fuel filter.

4. Inspect the float valve for sticking, dirt, etc.

5. Also check the items under "Flooding".

D. Poor Performance – Poor Gas Mileage

1. Clean all fuel and vacuum passages in the castings.

2. Check the choke valve for freedom of movement.

3. Check the Mixture Control solenoid for sticking, binding or leaking as follows:

a. Connect 1 end of a jumper wire to either terminal of the solenoid connector and the other end to the positive (+) terminal of a 12-volt battery source.

b. Connect a jumper wire to the other terminal of the solenoid connector and the other end of a known good ground.

c. With the rubber seal, retainer and spacer removed from the end of the solenoid stem, attach a hose from a hand vacuum pump.

d. With the solenoid fully energized (lean position), apply 25 in. Hg vacuum and time the leak-down rate from 20–15 in. Hg vacuum in 5 seconds. If the leakage exceeds that amount, replace the solenoid.

e. To check the solenoid for sticking in the down position, remove the jumper lead to a 12V source and observe the hand vacuum pump reading; the reading should go to 0 in less than 1 second.

4. Inspect the metering jet for dirt, loose parts or damage.

NOTE: *Do not attempt to readjust the mixture screw located inside the metering jet. The screw if factory adjusted and a change can upset the fuel system calibration. No attempt should be made to change this adjustment in the field except as the result of a Computer Command Control system performance check.*

5. Check the air valve and secondary metering rod for binding conditions. If the air valve or metering rod is damaged or the metering rod adjustment is changed from the factory setting, the air horn assembly must be replaced. Also check the air valve lever spring for proper installation (tension against the air valve shaft pin.

E. Rough Idle

1. Inspect the gasket and gasket mating surfaces on the casting for nicks, burrs or damage to the sealing beads.

2. Check the operation and sealing of the mixture control solenoid.

3. Clean all of the idle field passages.

4. If removed, inspect the idle mixture needle for ridges, burrs or being bent.

5. Check the throttle lever and valves for binds, nicks. or other damage.

6. Check all of the diaphragms for possible ruptures or leaks.

E2SE Carburetor Reassembly

THROTTLE BODY ASSEMBLY

1. Holding the primary throttle lever wide-open, install the lower end of the pump rod in the throttle lever by aligning the squirt on the rod with the slot in the lever.

2. If removed, install the idle mixture needle and spring using tool J–029030 or equivalent. Lightly seat the needle and then back out 3 turns as a preliminary idle mixture adjustment. Final idle mixture adjustment must be made on-vehicle. Refer to the "On-Vehicle Service" Chapter for the idle mixture adjustment procedures.

FLOAT BOWL ASSEMBLY

1. Install a new throttle-to-bowl gasket over the 2 locating dowels on the bowl.

NOTE: *If a new float bowl assembly is used, stamp or engrave the model number on the new float bowl.*

2. Rotate the fast idle cam so the steps face fast the idle screw on the throttle lever when properly installed, install the throttle body making certain the throttle body is properly located over the dowels on the float bowl; then install the throttle body-to-bowl screws and lockwashers, then tighten evenly and securely.

Inspect the linkage to insure the lockout tang is located properly to engage the slot in the secondary lockout lever and that the linkage moves freely and does not bind.

3. Place the carburetor on suitable holding fixture.

4. Install the fuel inlet filter spring, the filter assembly, a new gasket and inlet nut, then tighten the nut to 18 ft. lbs.

When installing a service replacement filter,

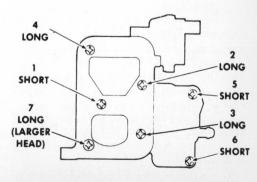

Air horn tightening sequence—E2SE carburetor

make sure the filter is the type that includes the check valve to meet Federal Motor Vehicle Safety Standards (FMVSS). When properly installed, the hole (check valve end) in the filter faces toward the inlet nut.

NOTE: *Tightening beyond the specified torque can damage the nylon gasket to cause a fuel leak.*

5. Install the choke housing on the throttle body, making sure the raised boss and locating lug on the rear of the housing fit into the recesses in the float bowl casting. Install the choke housing attaching screws and lockwashers, then tighten the screw evenly and securely.

6. Install the immediate choke shaft assembly in the float bowl by pushing the shaft through from the throttle lever side.

7. With the intermediate choke lever in the UP (12 o'clock) position, install the choke coil lever inside the choke housing onto flats on the intermediate choke shaft. The choke coil lever is properly aligned when the coil pick-up tang is in the UP position. Install the choke coil lever retaining screws into the end of the intermediate choke shaft and tighten securely.

8. Install the pump discharge check ball, the spring and a new plastic retainer in the float bowl. Tap lightly into place until the top of retainer is flush with the bowl casting surface.

9. Using a wide-blade screwdriver, install the float valve seat (with gasket) and the metering jet; tighten securely.

10. To make the adjustment easier, carefully bend the float arm upward at the notch in the arm before assembly.

11. Install the float valve onto the float arm by sliding the float lever under the pull clip. The correct installation of the pull clip is to hook the clip over the edge of the float on the float arm facing the float pontoon.

12. Install the float hinge pin into the float arm with the end of loop of pin facing the pump well. Then, install the float assembly by aligning the valve in the seat and the float pin into locating channels in the float bowl.

13. To adjust the float level, perform the following procedures:

   a. Hold the float pin firmly in place and push down lightly on the arm at the outer end against the top of the float valve.

   b. Using adjustment "T" scale, measure from the top of the float bowl casting surface (air horn gasket removed) to the top of the float at the toe.

   c. Bend the float arm, as necessary, for proper adjustment by pushing on the pontoon (see Adjustment Chart for specifications).

   d. Visually check the float alignment after adjustment.

14. Install the plastic filler block over the float valve by pressing downward until properly seated (flush with the bowl casting surface).

15. Install the Throttle Position Sensor (TPS) return spring in the bottom of the well in the float bowl.

16. Install the Throttle position Sensor (TPS) and the connector assembly in the float bowl by aligning the groove in the electrical connector with the "V" in the float bowl casting, push down on the connector and sensor assembly so the connector wires and sensor are located below the bowl casting surface.

NOTE: *Care must be taken when installing the throttle position sensor to assure that the electrical integrity is maintained. Make sure the wires between the connector and sensor assembly are not pinched or the insulation broken upon final assembly. Accidental electrical grounding of the TPS must be avoided.*

17. Install the air horn gasket on the float bowl, locating the gasket over the 2 dowel locating pins on the bowl.

18. Install the pump return spring and plunger in the pump well.

Air Horn Assembly

1. Install the new pump plunger stem seal and retainer in the air horn casting. Lightly stake the seal retainer in 3 places, choosing locations different from the original .

2. Install new Throttle Position Sensor (TPS) actuator plunger seal and retainer in the air horn casting. Lightly stake the seal retainer in 3 places, choosing locations different from the original .

3. Install the vent/screen assembly by install the 2 small attaching screws; tighten securely.

4. Inspect the air valve shaft pin for lubrication, apply a liberal quantity of lithuim base grease to the air valve shaft pin. Make sure to lubricate the pin surface contacted by the wind-up spring.

5. Install the fast idle cam rod in lower hole of the choke lever, aligning the squirt on the rod with small slot in the lever.

6. Install the TPS plunger through seal in the air horn until about ½ of the plunger extends above the surface of the air horn casting. Seal pressure should hold the plunger in place during the air horn installation on the float bowl.

Air Horn to Bowl Installation

1. Rotate the fast idle cam to the full UP position and tilt the air horn assembly to engage the lower end of the fast idle cam rod in the slot in the fast idle cam and install the pump rod end into hole in the pump lever; check the intermediate choke rod for position, then, holding

down on the pump plunger assembly, carefully lower the air horn assembly onto the float bowl, guiding the pump plunger stem through the seal in the air horn casting.

Do not force the air horn assembly onto the bowl but rather lightly lower it into place. Make sure the TPS actuator plunger engages the sensor plunger in the bowl by checking the plunger movement.

2. Install the air horn-to-bowl screws and lockwashers, tighten evenly and securely.

3. Install the new retainer clip through the hole in the end of the pump rod extending through the pump lever, making sure the clip securely locked in place.

4. If not tested previously, test the mixture control solenoid for sticking, binding or leaking, following the steps in the cleaning and inspection procedure. Then, install the spacer and new rubber seal on the mixture control solenoid stem making sure the seal is up against the spacer. Then, using a $3/16$ in. socket and light hammer, carefully drive a new retainer on the stem. Drive the retainer onto the stem only far enough to retain the rubber seal on the stem leaving a flight clearance between the retainer and seal to allow for seal expansion.

5. Prior to installing the mixture control solenoid, lightly coat the rubber seal on the end of the solenoid stem with a silicone grease or light engine oil. Using a new mounting gasket, install the mixture control solenoid on the air horn, carefully aligning the solenoid stem with recess in bottom of the bowl. Use a slight twisting motion of the solenoid during installation to ensure the rubber seal on stem is guided into the recess in the bottom of the bowl, to prevent distortion or damage to the rubber seal. Install the solenoid attaching screw sand tighten securely.

6. Install the plastic bushing in the hole in the choke lever, making sure the small end of the busing faces the retaining clip, when installed, With the inner coil lever and intermediate choke lever is at the 12 o'clock position, install the intermediate choke rod in the bushing. Retain the rod with new clip, pressing the clip securely in place with needle nose plier. Make sure the clip has full contact on the rod is not seated tightly against the bushing. The rod-to-bushing clearance should be 0.030 in. (0.762mm).

7. Install the secondary vacuum break assembly. Rotate the assembly and insert the end ("T" pin) of the vacuum break link into the upper slot of the choke lever. Attach the bracket-to-throttle body with countersunk screws and tighten the screws securely.

8. If the air valve rod has been removed from the primary side vacuum break plunger, install a plastic bushing in the hole in the primary side vacuum break plunger, making sure the small end of the bushing faces the retaining clip when install. Then insert the end of the air valve rod through the bushing. Retain with a new clip, pressing the clip into place using needlenose pliers. make sure the clip has full contact on the rod but is not seated tightly against the bushing. The rod-to-bushing clearance should be 0.030 in. (0.762mm).

9. Rotate the primary side vacuum break assembly(with the idle speed solenoid and bracket), then insert the end of the air valve rod into the slot of the air valve lever and end ("T" pin) of the vacuum break link into the lower slot of the choke lever. Connect the primary vacuum break hose-to-tube on the throttle body and tube on the vacuum break unit. Position the bracket over the locating lug on the air horn and install the 2 counter sunk screws on the air horn and screw with lockwasher in the throttle body; tighten the screws securely.

10. Perform the choke coil lever adjustment procedure as specified in carburetor adjustment section.

11. Install the choke cover and coil assembly in the choke housing, aligning the notch in the cover with the raised casting projection on the housing cover flange. Make sure the coil pickup tank engages the inside choke coil lever.

The tang on the thermostatic coil is the "trapped stat" design. This means that the coil tank is formed so it will completely encircle the coil pick-up lever. Make sure the coil pick-up lever is located inside the coil tang when installing the choke cover and coil assembly.

NOTE: *The ground contact for the electric choke is provided by a metal plate located at the rear of the choke cover assembly. Do not install a choke cover gasket between the electrical choke assembly and the choke housing. A choke cover retainer kit is required to attach the choke cover-to-choke housing. Install the proper retainers and rivets contained in kit, using a blind rivet installation tool.*

E4ME/E4MC Carburetor Disassembly

IDLE SPEED CONTROL (ISC) SOLENOID REMOVAL

Remove the attaching screws, then remove the Idle Speed Control solenoid (ISC). The ISC should not be immersed in any carburetor cleaner. They must always be removed before complete carburetor overhaul, as carburetor cleaner will damage the internal components.

IDLE MIXTURE NEEDLE PLUG REMOVAL

1. Use a hacksaw to make 2 parallel cuts in the throttle body, 1 on each side of the locator points near an idle mixture needle plug. The distance between the cuts will depend on the

size of the punch to be used. Cuts should reach down to the steel plug, but should but extend more than ⅛ in. (3mm) beyond the locator points.

2. Place a flat punch at a point near the ends of the saw marks in the throttle body. Hold the punch at a 45 degree angle and drive it into the throttle body until the casting breaks away, exposing the hardened steel plug. The plug will break, rather than remaining intact. Remove all the loose pieces.

3. Repeat the procedure for the other idle mixture needle plug.

IDLE AIR BLEED VALVE REMOVAL

1. Cover internal bowl vents and air inlets to the bleed valve with masking tape.

2. Carefully align a $^{7}/_{64}$ in. drill bit on rivet head. Drill only enough to remove head of each rivet holding the idle air bleed valve cover.

3. Use a suitably sized punch to drive out the remainder of the rivet from the castings. Repeat procedure with other rivet.

CAUTION: *For the next operation, safety glasses must be worn to protect eyes from possible metal shaving damage.*

4. Lift off cover and remove any pieces of rivet still inside tower. Use shop air to blow out any remaining chips.

5. Remove idle air bleed valve from the air horn.

6. Remove and discard O-ring seals from valve. New O-ring seals are required for reassembly. The idle air bleed valve is serviced as a complete assembly only.

AIR HORN REMOVAL

1. Remove upper choke lever from the end of choke shaft by removing retaining screw. Rotate upper choke lever to remove choke rod from slot in lever.

2. Remove choke rod from lower lever inside the float bowl casting. Remove rod by holding

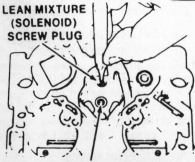

LEAN MIXTURE (SOLENOID) SCREW PLUG

RICH MIXTURE STOP SCREW PLUG LOCATION

Removing the lean and rich mixture screw plugs from the top of the air horn—E4MC/E4ME carburetor

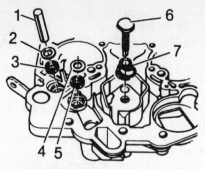

1. Senor actuator plunger
2. TPS seal retainer
3. TPS plunger seal
4. Pump stem seal retainer
5. Pump stem seal
6. Rich mixture solenoid stop screw (some models)
7. Rich authority adjusting spring (some models)

Bottom view of the air horn assembly—E4MC/E4ME carburetor

lower lever outward with small suitable tool and twisting rod counterclockwise.

3. Remove secondary metering rods by removing the small screw in the top of the metering rod hanger. Lift upward on the metering rod hanger until the secondary metering rods are completely out of the air horn. Metering rods may be disassembled from the hanger by rotating the ends out of the holes in the end of the hanger.

4. Remove pump link retainer and remove link from pump lever.

NOTE: *Do not attempt to remove the lever, as damage to the air horn could result.*

5. Remove front vacuum break hose from tube on float bowl.

6. Remove 11 air horn-to-bowl screws; then remove the 2 countersunk attaching screws located next to the venturi. If used, remove secondary air baffle deflector from beneath the 2 center air horn screws.

7. Remove air horn from float bowl by lifting it straight up. The air horn gasket should remain on the float bowl for removal later.

NOTE: *When removing air horn from float bowl, use care to prevent damaging the mixture control solenoid connector, Throttle Position Sensor (TPS) adjustment lever and the small tubes protruding from the air horn. These tubes are permanently pressed into the air horn casting. Do not remove them. Do not place vacuum break assembly in carburetor cleaner, as damage to vacuum break will occur.*

8. Remove front vacuum break bracket attaching screws. The vacuum break assembly may now be removed from the air valve dashpot

CHILTON'S
FUEL ECONOMY
& TUNE-UP TIPS

55 WAYS TO IMPROVE FUEL ECONOMY

Tune-up • Spark Plug Diagnosis • Emission Controls

Fuel System • Cooling System • Tires and Wheels

General Maintenance

CHILTON'S FUEL ECONOMY & TUNE-UP TIPS

Fuel economy is important to everyone, no matter what kind of vehicle you drive. The maintenance-minded motorist can save both money and fuel using these tips and the periodic maintenance and tune-up procedures in this Repair and Tune-Up Guide.

There are more than 130,000,000 cars and trucks registered for private use in the United States. Each travels an average of 10-12,000 miles per year, and, and in total they consume close to 70 billion gallons of fuel each year. This represents nearly ⅔ of the oil imported by the United States each year. The Federal government's goal is to reduce consumption 10% by 1985. A variety of methods are either already in use or under serious consideration, and they all affect you driving and the cars you will drive. In addition to "down-sizing", the auto industry is using or investigating the use of electronic fuel delivery, electronic engine controls and alternative engines for use in smaller and lighter vehicles, among other alternatives to meet the federally mandated Corporate Average Fuel Economy (CAFE) of 27.5 mpg by 1985. The government, for its part, is considering rationing, mandatory driving curtailments and tax increases on motor vehicle fuel in an effort to reduce consumption. The government's goal of a 10% reduction could be realized — and further government regulation avoided — if every private vehicle could use just 1 less gallon of fuel per week.

How Much Can You Save?

Tests have proven that almost anyone can make at least a 10% reduction in fuel consumption through regular maintenance and tune-ups. When a major manufacturer of spark plugs sur-

TUNE-UP

1. Check the cylinder compression to be sure the engine will really benefit from a tune-up and that it is capable of producing good fuel economy. A tune-up will be wasted on an engine in poor mechanical condition.

2. Replace spark plugs regularly. New spark plugs alone can increase fuel economy 3%.

3. Be sure the spark plugs are the correct type (heat range) for your vehicle. See the Tune-Up Specifications.

Heat range refers to the spark plug's ability to conduct heat away from the firing end. It must conduct the heat away in an even pattern to avoid becoming a source of pre-ignition, yet it must also operate hot enough to burn off conductive deposits that could cause misfiring.

The heat range is usually indicated by a number on the spark plug, part of the manufacturer's designation for each individual spark plug. The numbers in bold-face indicate the heat range in each manufacturer's identification system.

Manufacturer	Typical Designation
AC	R **45** TS
Bosch (old)	WA **145** T30
Bosch (new)	HR **8** Y
Champion	RBL **15** Y
Fram/Autolite	**415**
Mopar	P-**62** PR
Motorcraft	BRF-**42**
NGK	BP **5** ES-15
Nippondenso	W **16** EP
Prestolite	14GR **5** 2A

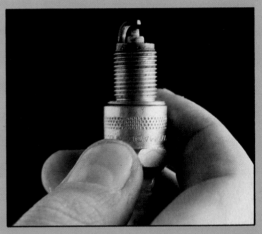

Periodically, check the spark plugs to be sure they are firing efficiently. They are excellent indicators of the internal condition of your engine.

On AC, Bosch (new), Champion, Fram/Autolite, Mopar, Motorcraft and Prestolite, a higher number indicates a hotter plug. On Bosch (old), NGK and Nippondenso, a higher number indicates a colder plug.

4. Make sure the spark plugs are properly gapped. See the Tune-Up Specifications in this book.

5. Be sure the spark plugs are firing efficiently. The illustrations on the next 2 pages show you how to "read" the firing end of the spark plug.

6. Check the ignition timing and set it to specifications. Tests show that almost all cars have incorrect ignition timing by more than 2°.

veyed over 6,000 cars nationwide, they found that a tune-up, on cars that needed one, increased fuel economy over 11%. Replacing worn plugs alone, accounted for a 3% increase. The same test also revealed that 8 out of every 10 vehicles will have some maintenance deficiency that will directly affect fuel economy, emissions or performance. Most of this mileage-robbing neglect could be prevented with regular maintenance.

Modern engines require that all of the functioning systems operate properly for maximum efficiency. A malfunction anywhere wastes fuel. You can keep your vehicle running as efficiently and economically as possible, by being aware of your vehicle's operating and performance characteristics. If your vehicle suddenly develops performance or fuel economy problems it could be due to one or more of the following:

PROBLEM	POSSIBLE CAUSE
Engine Idles Rough	Ignition timing, idle mixture, vacuum leak or something amiss in the emission control system.
Hesitates on Acceleration	Dirty carburetor or fuel filter, improper accelerator pump setting, ignition timing or fouled spark plugs.
Starts Hard or Fails to Start	Worn spark plugs, improperly set automatic choke, ice (or water) in fuel system.
Stalls Frequently	Automatic choke improperly adjusted and possible dirty air filter or fuel filter.
Performs Sluggishly	Worn spark plugs, dirty fuel or air filter, ignition timing or automatic choke out of adjustment.

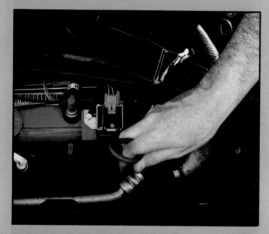

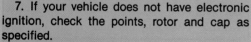

Check spark plug wires on conventional point type ignition for cracks by bending them in a loop around your finger.

Be sure that spark plug wires leading to adjacent cylinders do not run too close together. (Photo courtesy Champion Spark Plug Co.)

7. If your vehicle does not have electronic ignition, check the points, rotor and cap as specified.

8. Check the spark plug wires (used with conventional point-type ignitions) for cracks and burned or broken insulation by bending them in a loop around your finger. Cracked wires decrease fuel efficiency by failing to deliver full voltage to the spark plugs. One misfiring spark plug can cost you as much as 2 mpg.

9. Check the routing of the plug wires. Misfiring can be the result of spark plug leads to adjacent cylinders running parallel to each other and too close together. One wire tends to

pick up voltage from the other causing it to fire "out of time".

10. Check all electrical and ignition circuits for voltage drop and resistance.

11. Check the distributor mechanical and/or vacuum advance mechanisms for proper functioning. The vacuum advance can be checked by twisting the distributor plate in the opposite direction of rotation. It should spring back when released.

12. Check and adjust the valve clearance on engines with mechanical lifters. The clearance should be slightly loose rather than too tight.

SPARK PLUG DIAGNOSIS

Normal

APPEARANCE: This plug is typical of one operating normally. The insulator nose varies from a light tan to grayish color with slight electrode wear. The presence of slight deposits is normal on used plugs and will have no adverse effect on engine performance. The spark plug heat range is correct for the engine and the engine is running normally.

CAUSE: Properly running engine.

RECOMMENDATION: Before reinstalling this plug, the electrodes should be cleaned and filed square. Set the gap to specifications. If the plug has been in service for more than 10-12,000 miles, the entire set should probably be replaced with a fresh set of the same heat range.

Oil Deposits

APPEARANCE: The firing end of the plug is covered with a wet, oily coating.

CAUSE: The problem is poor oil control. On high mileage engines, oil is leaking past the rings or valve guides into the combustion chamber. A common cause is also a plugged PCV valve, and a ruptured fuel pump diaphragm can also cause this condition. Oil fouled plugs such as these are often found in new or recently overhauled engines, before normal oil control is achieved, and can be cleaned and reinstalled.

RECOMMENDATION: A hotter spark plug may temporarily relieve the problem, but the engine is probably in need of work.

Incorrect Heat Range

APPEARANCE: The effects of high temperature on a spark plug are indicated by clean white, often blistered insulator. This can also be accompanied by excessive wear of the electrode, and the absence of deposits.

CAUSE: Check for the correct spark plug heat range. A plug which is too hot for the engine can result in overheating. A car operated mostly at high speeds can require a colder plug. Also check ignition timing, cooling system level, fuel mixture and leaking intake manifold.

RECOMMENDATION: If all ignition and engine adjustments are known to be correct, and no other malfunction exists, install spark plugs one heat range colder.

Carbon Deposits

APPEARANCE: Carbon fouling is easily identified by the presence of dry, soft, black, sooty deposits.

CAUSE: Changing the heat range can often lead to carbon fouling, as can prolonged slow, stop-and-start driving. If the heat range is correct, carbon fouling can be attributed to a rich fuel mixture, sticking choke, clogged air cleaner, worn breaker points, retarded timing or low compression. If only one or two plugs are carbon fouled, check for corroded or cracked wires on the affected plugs. Also look for cracks in the distributor cap between the towers of affected cylinders.

RECOMMENDATION: After the problem is corrected, these plugs can be cleaned and reinstalled if not worn severely.

Photos Courtesy Fram Corporation

MMT Fouled

APPEARANCE: Spark plugs fouled by MMT (Methycyclopentadienyl Maganese Tricarbonyl) have reddish, rusty appearance on the insulator and side electrode.

CAUSE: MMT is an anti-knock additive in gasoline used to replace lead. During the combustion process, the MMT leaves a reddish deposit on the insulator and side electrode.

RECOMMENDATION: No engine malfunction is indicated and the deposits will not affect plug performance any more than lead deposits (see Ash Deposits). MMT fouled plugs can be cleaned, regapped and reinstalled.

High Speed Glazing

APPEARANCE: Glazing appears as shiny coating on the plug, either yellow or tan in color.

CAUSE: During hard, fast acceleration, plug temperatures rise suddenly. Deposits from normal combustion have no chance to fluff-off; instead, they melt on the insulator forming an electrically conductive coating which causes misfiring.

RECOMMENDATION: Glazed plugs are not easily cleaned. They should be replaced with a fresh set of plugs of the correct heat range. If the condition recurs, using plugs with a heat range one step colder may cure the problem.

Ash (Lead) Deposits

APPEARANCE: Ash deposits are characterized by light brown or white colored deposits crusted on the side or center electrodes. In some cases it may give the plug a rusty appearance.

CAUSE: Ash deposits are normally derived from oil or fuel additives burned during normal combustion. Normally they are harmless, though excessive amounts can cause misfiring. If deposits are excessive in short mileage, the valve guides may be worn.

RECOMMENDATION: Ash-fouled plugs can be cleaned, gapped and reinstalled.

Detonation

APPEARANCE: Detonation is usually characterized by a broken plug insulator.

CAUSE: A portion of the fuel charge will begin to burn spontaneously, from the increased heat following ignition. The explosion that results applies extreme pressure to engine components, frequently damaging spark plugs and pistons.

Detonation can result by over-advanced ignition timing, inferior gasoline (low octane) lean air/fuel mixture, poor carburetion, engine lugging or an increase in compression ratio due to combustion chamber deposits or engine modification.

RECOMMENDATION: Replace the plugs after correcting the problem.

Photos Courtesy Champion Spark Plug Co.

EMISSION CONTROLS

13. Be aware of the general condition of the emission control system. It contributes to reduced pollution and should be serviced regularly to maintain efficient engine operation.

14. Check all vacuum lines for dried, cracked or brittle conditions. Something as simple as a leaking vacuum hose can cause poor performance and loss of economy.

15. Avoid tampering with the emission control system. Attempting to improve fuel econ-

FUEL SYSTEM

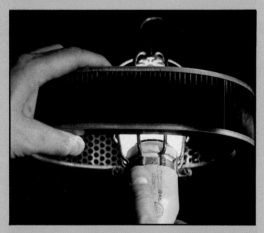

Check the air filter with a light behind it. If you can see light through the filter it can be reused.

Extremely clogged filters should be discarded and replaced with a new one.

18. Replace the air filter regularly. A dirty air filter richens the air/fuel mixture and can increase fuel consumption as much as 10%. Tests show that ⅓ of all vehicles have air filters in need of replacement.

19. Replace the fuel filter at least as often as recommended.

20. Set the idle speed and carburetor mixture to specifications.

21. Check the automatic choke. A sticking or malfunctioning choke wastes gas.

22. During the summer months, adjust the automatic choke for a leaner mixture which will produce faster engine warm-ups.

COOLING SYSTEM

29. Be sure all accessory drive belts are in good condition. Check for cracks or wear.

30. Adjust all accessory drive belts to proper tension.

31. Check all hoses for swollen areas, worn spots, or loose clamps.

32. Check coolant level in the radiator or expansion tank.

33. Be sure the thermostat is operating properly. A stuck thermostat delays engine warm-up and a cold engine uses nearly twice as much fuel as a warm engine.

34. Drain and replace the engine coolant at least as often as recommended. Rust and scale

TIRES & WHEELS

38. Check the tire pressure often with a pencil type gauge. Tests by a major tire manufacturer show that 90% of all vehicles have at least 1 tire improperly inflated. Better mileage can be achieved by over-inflating tires, but never exceed the maximum inflation pressure on the side of the tire.

39. If possible, install radial tires. Radial tires deliver as much as ½ mpg more than bias belted tires.

40. Avoid installing super-wide tires. They only create extra rolling resistance and decrease fuel mileage. Stick to the manufacturer's recommendations.

41. Have the wheels properly balanced.

omy by tampering with emission controls is more likely to worsen fuel economy than improve it. Emission control changes on modern engines are not readily reversible.

16. Clean (or replace) the EGR valve and lines as recommended.

17. Be sure that all vacuum lines and hoses are reconnected properly after working under the hood. An unconnected or misrouted vacuum line can wreak havoc with engine performance.

23. Check for fuel leaks at the carburetor, fuel pump, fuel lines and fuel tank. Be sure all lines and connections are tight.

24. Periodically check the tightness of the carburetor and intake manifold attaching nuts and bolts. These are a common place for vacuum leaks to occur.

25. Clean the carburetor periodically and lubricate the linkage.

26. The condition of the tailpipe can be an excellent indicator of proper engine combustion. After a long drive at highway speeds, the inside of the tailpipe should be a light grey in color. Black or soot on the insides indicates an overly rich mixture.

27. Check the fuel pump pressure. The fuel pump may be supplying more fuel than the engine needs.

28. Use the proper grade of gasoline for your engine. Don't try to compensate for knocking or "pinging" by advancing the ignition timing. This practice will only increase plug temperature and the chances of detonation or pre-ignition with relatively little performance gain.

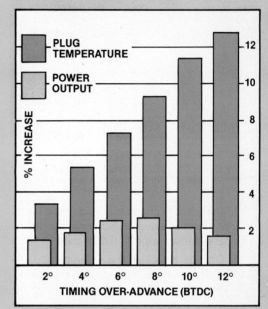

Increasing ignition timing past the specified setting results in a drastic increase in spark plug temperature with increased chance of detonation or preignition. Performance increase is considerably less. (Photo courtesy Champion Spark Plug Co.)

that form in the engine should be flushed out to allow the engine to operate at peak efficiency.

35. Clean the radiator of debris that can decrease cooling efficiency.

36. Install a flex-type or electric cooling fan, if you don't have a clutch type fan. Flex fans use curved plastic blades to push more air at low speeds when more cooling is needed; at high speeds the blades flatten out for less resistance. Electric fans only run when the engine temperature reaches a predetermined level.

37. Check the radiator cap for a worn or cracked gasket. If the cap does not seal properly, the cooling system will not function properly.

42. Be sure the front end is correctly aligned. A misaligned front end actually has wheels going in differed directions. The increased drag can reduce fuel economy by .3 mpg.

43. Correctly adjust the wheel bearings. Wheel bearings that are adjusted too tight increase rolling resistance.

Check tire pressures regularly with a reliable pocket type gauge. Be sure to check the pressure on a cold tire.

GENERAL MAINTENANCE

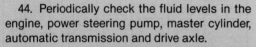

Check the fluid levels (particularly engine oil) on a regular basis. Be sure to check the oil for grit, water or other contamination.

A vacuum gauge is another excellent indicator of internal engine condition and can also be installed in the dash as a mileage indicator.

44. Periodically check the fluid levels in the engine, power steering pump, master cylinder, automatic transmission and drive axle.

45. Change the oil at the recommended interval and change the filter at every oil change. Dirty oil is thick and causes extra friction between moving parts, cutting efficiency and increasing wear. A worn engine requires more frequent tune-ups and gets progressively worse fuel economy. In general, use the lightest viscosity oil for the driving conditions you will encounter.

46. Use the recommended viscosity fluids in the transmission and axle.

47. Be sure the battery is fully charged for fast starts. A slow starting engine wastes fuel.

48. Be sure battery terminals are clean and tight.

49. Check the battery electrolyte level and add distilled water if necessary.

50. Check the exhaust system for crushed pipes, blockages and leaks.

51. Adjust the brakes. Dragging brakes or brakes that are not releasing create increased drag on the engine.

52. Install a vacuum gauge or miles-per-gallon gauge. These gauges visually indicate engine vacuum in the intake manifold. High vacuum = good mileage and low vacuum = poorer mileage. The gauge can also be an excellent indicator of internal engine conditions.

53. Be sure the clutch is properly adjusted. A slipping clutch wastes fuel.

54. Check and periodically lubricate the heat control valve in the exhaust manifold. A sticking or inoperative valve prevents engine warm-up and wastes gas.

55. Keep accurate records to check fuel economy over a period of time. A sudden drop in fuel economy may signal a need for tune-up or other maintenance.

© 1980 Chilton Book Company, Radnor, PA 19089

rod and the dashpot rod from the air valve lever.

9. Remove TPS plunger by pushing plunger down through seal in air horn.

10. Remove TPS seal and pump plunger stem seal by inverting air horn and using a small suitable tool to remove staking holding seal retainers in place. Remove and discard retainers and seals.

NOTE: *Use care in removing the TPS plunger seal retainer and pump plunger stem seal retainer to prevent damage to air horn casting. New seals and retainers are required for reassembly.*

11. Invert air horn and use tool J-28696-4, BT-7967A, or equivalent, to remove rich mixture stop screw and spring.

12. Use a suitable punch to drive the lean mixture screw plug and rich mixture stop screw plug out of the air horn. Discard the plugs.

13. Further disassembly of the air horn is not required for cleaning purposes.

NOTE: *The choke valve and choke valve screws, the air valves and air valve shaft should not be removed. However, if it is necessary to replace the air valve closing springs or center plastic eccentric cam, a repair kit is available. Instructions for assembly are included in the repair kit.*

FLOAT BOWL DISASSEMBLY

1. Remove solenoid metering rod plunger by lifting straight up.

2. Remove air horn gasket by lifting it from the dowel locating pins on float bowl. Discard gasket.

3. Remove pump plunger from pump well.

4. Remove staking holding Throttle Position Sensor (TPS) in bowl as follows:

   a. Lay a flat tool or metal piece across bowl casting to protect gasket sealing surface.

   b. Use a small suitable tool to depress TPS sensor lightly and hold against spring tension.

   c. Observing safety precautions, pry upward with a small prybar, or other suitable tool, to remove bowl staking, making sure prying force is exerted against the metal piece and not against the bowl casting. Use care not to damage the TPS sensor.

   d. Push up from bottom on electrical connector and remove TPS and connector assembly from bowl. Use care in removing sensor and connector assembly to prevent damage to this critical electrical part.

   e. Remove spring from bottom of TPS well in float bowl.

5. Remove plastic bowl insert from float bowl.

6. Carefully lift each metering rod out of the guided metering jet, checking to be sure the return spring is removed with each metering rod.

NOTE: *Use extreme care when handling these critical parts to avoid damage to the metering rod and spring.*

7. Remove the mixture control solenoid from the float bowl as follows:

   a. Remove screw attaching solenoid connector to float bowl. Do not remove solenoid connector from float bowl until called for in text.

   b. Use tool J-28696-10, BT-7928, or equivalent, to remove lean mixture (solenoid) screw. Do not remove plunger return spring or connector and wires from the solenoid body. The mixture control solenoid, with plunger and connector, is only serviced as a complete assembly.

   c. Remove rubber gasket from top of solenoid connector and discard.

   d. Remove solenoid screw tension spring (next to float hanger pin).

8. Remove float assembly and float needle by pulling up on retaining pin. Remove needle and seat and gasket using set remover tool J-22769, BT-3006M, or equivalent.

9. Remove large mixture control solenoid tension spring from boss on bottom of float bowl located between guided metering jets.

10. If necessary, remove the primary main metering jets using special tool J-28696-4, BT-7928, or equivalent.

NOTE: *Use care installing tool on jet, to prevent damage to the metering rod guide (upper area), and locating tool over vertical float sections on lower area of jet. Also, no attempt should be made to remove the secondary metering jets (metering orifice plates). These jets are fixed and, if damaged, entire bowl replacement is required.*

11. Remove pump discharge check ball retainer and turn bowl upside down, catching discharge ball as it falls.

12. Remove secondary air baffle, if replacement is required.

13. Remove pump well fill slot baffle only if necessary.

CHOKE DISASSEMBLY

The tamper-resistant choke cover is used to discourage unnecessary readjustment of the choke thermostatic cover and coil assembly. However, if it is necessary to remove the cover and coil assembly during normal carburetor disassembly for cleaning and normal carburetor disassembly for cleaning and overhaul, the procedures below should be followed.

1. Support float bowl and throttle body, as an assembly, on a suitable holding fixture such as tool J-9789-118, BT-30-15, or equivalent.

2. Carefully align a $5/32$ in. drill (0.159 in.) on rivet head and drill only enough to remove rivet head. Drill the 2 remaining rivet heads, then use a drift and small hammer to drive the remainder of the rivets out of the choke housing.

NOTE: *Use care in drilling to prevent damage to the choke cover or housing.*

3. Remove the 2 conventional retainers, retainer with tab and choke cover assembly from choke housing.

4. Remove choke housing assembly from float bowl by removing retaining screw and washer inside the choke housing. The complete choke assembly can be removed from the float bowl by sliding outward.

5. Remove secondary throttle valve lock-out lever from float bowl.

6. Remove lower choke lever from inside float bowl cavity by inverting bowl.

7. To disassemble intermediate choke shaft from choke housing, remove coil lever retaining screw at end of shaft inside the choke housing. Remove thermostatic coil lever from flats on intermediate choke shaft.

8. Remove intermediate choke shaft from the choke housing by sliding it outward. The fast idle cam can now be removed from the intermediate choke shaft. Remove the cup seal from the float bowl cleaning purposes. Do not attempt to remove the insert.

9. Remove fuel inlet nut, gasket, check valve, filter assembly and spring. Discard check valve filter assembly and gasket.

10. Remove 3 throttle body-to-bowl attaching screws and lockwashers and remove throttle body assembly.

11. Remove throttle body-to-bowl insulator gasket.

THROTTLE BODY DISASSEMBLY

Place throttle body assembly on carburetor holding fixture to avoid damage to throttle valves.

1. Remove pump rod from the throttle lever by rotating the rod until the tang on the rod aligns with the slot in the lever.

2. Use tool J–29030–B, BT–7610B, or equivalent, to remove idle mixture needles for thorough throttle body cleaning.

3. Further disassembly of the throttle body is not required for cleaning purposes. The throttle valve screws are permanently staked in place and should not be removed. The throttle body is serviced as a complete assembly.

E4MC/E4ME Carburetor Reassembly

1. Install the lower end of the pump rod in the throttle lever by aligning the tang on the rod with the slot in the lever. The end of the rod should point outward toward the throttle lever.

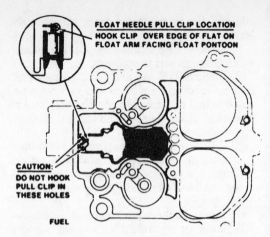

Float needle pull clip installation—E4MC/E4ME carburetor

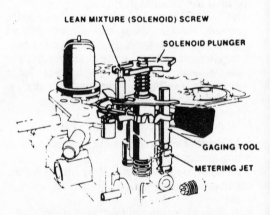

Installing the mixture control solenoid gauging tool—E4MC/E4ME carburetor

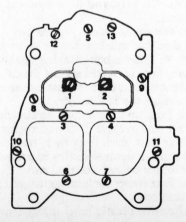

Air horn screw location and tightening sequence—E4MC/E4ME carburetor

2. Install idle mixture needles and springs using tool J–29030–B, BT–07610B, or equivalent. Lightly seat each needle and then turn counterclockwise the number of specified turns, the final idle mixture adjustment is made on the vehicle.

3. If a new float bowl assembly is used, stamp or engrave the model number on the new float bowl. Install new throttle body-to-bowl insulator gasket over 2 locating dowels on bowl.

4. Install throttle body making certain throttle body is properly located over dowels on float bowl. Install 3 throttle body-to-bowl screws and lockwashers and tighten evenly and securely.

5. Place carburetor on proper holding fixture such as J–9789–118, BT–30–15 or equivalent.

6. Install fuel inlet filter spring, a new check valve filter assembly, new gasket and inlet nut. Tighten nut to 18 ft. lbs. (24 Nm).

NOTE: *When installing a service replacement filter, make sure the filter is the type that includes the check valve to meet government safety standard. New service replacement filters with check valve meet this requirement. When properly installed, the hole in the filter faces toward the inlet nut. Ribs on the closed end of the filter element prevent it from being installed incorrectly, unless forced. Tightening beyond the specified torque can damage the nylon gasket.*

7. Install a new cup seal into the insert on the side of the float bowl for the intermediate choke shaft. The lip on the cup seal faces outward.

8. Install the secondary throttle valve lockout lever on the boss of the float bowl, with the recess hole in the lever facing inward.

9. Install the fast idle cam on the intermediate choke shaft (steps on cam face downward).

10. Carefully install fast idle cam and intermediate choke shaft assembly in the choke housing. Install the thermostatic coil lever on the flats on the intermediate choke shaft. Inside thermostatic choke coil lever is properly aligned when both inside and outside levers face toward the fuel inlet. Install inside lever retaining screw into the end of the intermediate choke shaft.

11. Install lower choke rod (inner) lever into cavity in float bowl.

12. Install choke housing to bowl, sliding intermediate choke shaft into lower (inner) lever. tool J–23417, BT–6911 or equivalent, can be used to hold the lower choke lever in correct position while installing the choke housing. The intermediate choke shaft lever and fast idle cam are in correct position when the tang on lever is beneath the fast idle cam.

13. Install choke housing retaining screws and washers. Check linkage for freedom of movement. Do not install choke cover and coil assembly until inside coil lever is adjusted.

14. If removed, install air baffle in secondary side of float bowl with notches toward the top. Top edge of baffle must be flush with bowl casting.

15. If removed, install baffle inside of the pump well with slot toward the bottom.

16. Install pump discharge check ball and retainer screw in the passage next to the pump well.

17. If removed, carefully install primary main metering jets in bottom of float bowl using tool J–28696–4, BT–7928, or equivalent.

NOTE: *Use care in installing jets to prevent damage to metering rod guide.*

18. Install large mixture control solenoid tension spring over boss on bottom of float bowl.

19. Install needle seat assembly, with gasket, using seat installer J–22769, BT–3006M, or equivalent.

20. To make adjustment easier, carefully bend float arm before assembly.

21. Install float needle onto float arm by sliding float lever under needle pull clip. Proper installation of the needle pull clip is to hook the clip over the edge of the float on the float arm facing the float pontoon.

22. Install float hinge pin into float arm with end of loop of pin facing pump well. Install float assembly by aligning needle in the seat and float hinge pin into locating channels in float bowl. Do not install float needle pull clip into holes in float arm.

23. Perform a float level adjustment, as necessary.

24. Install mixture control solenoid screw tension spring between raised bosses next to float hanger pin.

25. Install mixture control solenoid and connector assembly as follows:

   a. Install new rubber gasket on top of solenoid connector.

   b. Install solenoid carefully in the float chamber, aligning pin on end of solenoid with hole in raised boss at bottom of bowl. Align solenoid connector wires to fit in slot in bowl.

   c. Install lean mixture (solenoid) screw through hole in solenoid bracket and tension spring in bowl, engaging first 6 screw threads to assure proper thread engagement.

   d. Install mixture control solenoid gauging tool J–33815–1, BT–8253–A, or equivalent over the throttle side metering jet rod guide and temporarily install solenoid plunger.

   e. Holding the solenoid plunger against the solenoid stop, use tool J–28696–10, BT–7928, or equivalent, to turn the lean mixture (solenoid) screw slowly clockwise, until the solenoid plunger just contacts the gauging tool. The adjustment is correct when the solenoid plunger is contacting both the solenoid stop and the gauging tool.

f. Remove solenoid plunger and gauging tool.

26. Install connector attaching screw, but do not overtighten, as that could cause damage to the connector.

27. Install Throttle Position Sensor (TPS) return spring in bottom of well in float bowl.

28. Install the TPS and connector assembly in float bowl by aligning groove in electrical connector with slot in float bowl casting. Push down on connector and sensor assembly so that connector and wires are located below bowl casting surface.

29. Install plastic bowl insert over float valve, pressing downward until properly seated (flush with bowl casting surface).

30. Slide metering rod return spring over metering rod tip until small end of spring stops against shoulder on rod. Carefully install metering rod and spring assembly through holding in plastic bowl insert and gently lower the metering rod into the guided metering jet, until large end of spring seats on the recess on end of jet guide.

NOTE: *Do not force metering rod down in jet. Use extreme care when handling these critical parts to avoid damage to rod and spring. If service replacement metering rods, springs and jets are installed, they must be installed in matched sets.*

31. Install pump return spring in pump well.

32. Install pump plunger assembly in pump well.

33. Holding down on pump plunger assembly against return spring tension, install air horn gasket by aligning pump plunger stem with hole in gasket and aligning holes in gasket over TPS plunger, solenoid plunger return spring metering rods, solenoid attaching screw and electrical connector. Position gasket over the 2 dowel locating pins on the float bowl.

34. Holding down on air horn gasket and pump plunger assembly, install the solenoid-metering rod plunger in the solenoid, aligning slot in end of plunger with solenoid attaching screw. Be sure plunger arms engage top of each metering.

35. If a service replacement mixture control solenoid package is installed, the solenoid and plunger MUST be installed as a matched set.

Air Horn Assembly

1. If removed, install Throttle Position Sensor (TPS) adjustment screw in air horn using tool J–28696–10, BT–7967A, or equivalent. Final adjustment of the TPS is made on the vehicle.

2. Inspect the air valve shaft pin for lubrication. Apply a liberal quantity of lithium base grease to the air valve shaft pin, especially in the area contacted by the air valve spring.

3. Install new pump plunger and TPS plunger seals and retainers in air horn casting. The lip on the seal faces outward, away from the air horn mounting surface. Lightly stake seal retainer in 3 places, choosing locations different from the original stakings.

4. Install rich mixture stop screw and rich authority adjusting spring from bottom side of the air horn. Use tool J–2869–4, BT–7967A, or equivalent, to bottom the stop screw lightly, then back out ¼ turn. Final adjustment procedure will be covered later in this Chapter.

5. Install TPS actuator plunger in the seal.

6. Carefully lower the air horn assembly onto the float bowl while positioning the TPS adjustment lever over the TPS sensor and guiding pump plunger stem through the seal in the air horn casting. To ease installation, insert a thin suitable tool between the air horn gasket and float bowl to raise the TPS Adjustment Lever, positioning it over the TPS sensor.

7. Make sure that the bleed tubes and accelerating well tubes are positioned properly through the holes in the air horn gasket. Do not force the air horn assembly onto the bowl, but lower it lightly into place over the 2 dowel locating pins.

8. Install 2 long air horn screws and lockwashers, 9 short screws and lockwashers and 2 countersunk screws located next to the carburetor venturi area. Install secondary air baffle beneath the No. 3 and 4 screws. Tighten all screws evenly and securely.

9. Install air valve rod into slot in the lever on the end of the air valve shaft. Install the other end of the rod in hole in front vacuum break plunger. Install front vacuum break and bracket assembly on the air horn, using 2 attaching screws. Tighten screw securely. Connect pump link to pump lever and install retainer.

NOTE: *Use care installing the roll pin to prevent damage to the pump lever bearing surface and casting bosses.*

10. Install 2 secondary metering rods into the secondary metering rod hanger (upper end of rods point toward each other). Install secondary metering rod holder, with rods, onto air valve cam follower. Install retaining screw and tighten securely. Work air valves up and down several times to make sure they remove freely in both directions.

11. Connect choke rod into lower choke lever inside bowl cavity. Install choke rod in slot in upper choke lever. Position the lever on end of choke shaft, making sure flats on end of shaft align with flats in lever. Install attaching screw

and tighten securely. When properly installed, the number on the lever will face outward.

12. Adjust the rich mixture stop screw:

a. Insert external float gauging tool J–34935–1, BT–8420A, or equivalent, in the vertical D-shaped vent hole in the air horn casting (next to the idle air bleed valve) and allow it to float freely.

b. Read (at eye level) the mark on the gauge, in inches, that lines up with the tip of the air horn casting.

c. Lightly press down on gauge, reading and recording the mark on the gauge that lines up with the top of the air horn casting.

d. Subtract gauge **UP** dimension, found in Step b, from gauge **DOWN** dimension, found in Step c and record the difference in inches. This difference in dimension is the total solenoid plunger travel.

e. Insert tool J–28696–10, BT–7928, or equivalent, in the access hole in the air horn and adjust the rich mixture stop screw to obtain ⅛ in. (3mm) total solenoid plunger travel.

13. With the solenoid plunger travel correctly set, install the plugs supplied in the service kit into the air horn to retain the setting and prevent fuel vapor loss:

a. Install the plug, hollow end down, into the access hole to the lean mixture (solenoid) screw and use a suitably sized punch to drive the plug into the air horn until top of plug is even with the lower edge of the hole chamber.

b. In a similar manner, install the plug over the rich mixture screw access hole and drive the plug into place so that the tip of the plug is $\frac{3}{16}$ in. (5mm) below the surface of the air horn casting.

14. Install the idle air bleed valve as follows:

a. Lightly coat 2 new O-ring seals with automatic transmission fluid, to aid in their installation on the idle air bleed valve body. The thick seal goes in the upper groove and the thin seal goes in the lower groove.

b. Install the idle air bleed valve in the air horn, making sure that there is proper thread engagement.

c. Insert idle air bleed valve gauging tool J–33815–2, BT–8353B, or equivalent, in throttle side D-shaped vent hole of the air horn casting. The upper end of the tool should be positioned over the open cavity next to the idle air bleed valve.

d. Hold the gauging tool down lightly so that the solenoid plunger is against the solenoid stop, then adjust the idle air bleed valve so that the gauging tool will pivot over and just contact the top of the valve.

e. Remove the gauging tool.

f. The final adjustment of the idle air bleed valve is made on the vehicle to obtain idle mixture control.

15. Perform the air valve spring adjustment and choke coil Lever Adjustment.

16. Install the cover and coil assembly in the choke housing, as follows:

a. Place the cam follower on the highest step of the fast idle cam.

b. Install the thermostatic cover and coil assembly in the choke housing, making sure the coil tang engages the inside coil pickup lever. Ground contact for the electric choke is provided by a metal plate located at the rear of the choke cover assembly. Do not install a choke cover gasket between the electric choke assembly and the choke housing.

c. A choke cover retainer kit is required to attach the choke cover to the choke housing. Follow the instructions found in the kit and install the proper retainer and rivets using a suitable blind rivet tool.

d. It may be necessary to use an adapter (tube) if the installing tool interferes with the electrical connector tower on the choke cover.

17. Install the hose on the front vacuum brake and on the tube on the float bowl.

18. Position the idle speed solenoid and bracket assembly on the float bowl, retaining it with 2 large countersunk screws.

19. Perform the choke rod-fast idle cam adjustment, primary (front) vacuum break adjustment, air valve rod adjustment-front, unloader adjustment and the secondary lockout adjustment.

20. Reinstall the carburetor on the vehicle with a new flange gasket.

THROTTLE BODY INJECTION (TBI) SYSTEM

NOTE: *This book contain simple testing and service procedures for your fuel injection system.*

Releiving Fuel System Presure

1. Remove the fuel pump fuse from the fuse block.

2. Start the engine. Allow it to run out of fuel.

3. Engage starter to make sure it is out of fuel.

4. Turn the car off. Replace the fuse.

Electric Fuel Pump
REMOVAL AND INSTALLATION

NOTE: *To reduce the risk of fire and personal injury the fuel pressure must be relieved.*

E2SE CARBURETOR SPECIFICATIONS

Year	Carburetor Identification	Float Level (in.)	Pump Rod (in.)	Air Valve Spring (Turns)	Choke Coil Level (in.)	Fast Idle Cam (deg.)	Air Valve Rod (deg.)	Primary Vacuum Break (deg.)	Choke Setting (notches)	Secondary Vacuum Break (deg.)	Choke Unloader (deg.)
1982	17082390	13/32	Fixed	1	.085	17°	1°	26°	Fixed	34°	35°
	17082391	13/32	Fixed	1	.085	25°	1°	29°	Fixed	35°	35°
	17082490	13/32	Fixed	1	.085	17°	1°	26°	Fixed	34°	35°
	17082491	13/32	Fixed	1	.085	25°	1°	29°	Fixed	35°	35°
1983	17083356	13/32	Fixed	1	.085	22°	1°	25°	Fixed	35°	30°
	17083357	13/32	Fixed	1	.085	22°	1°	25°	Fixed	35°	30°
	17083358	13/32	Fixed	1	.085	22°	1°	25°	Fixed	35°	30°
	17083359	13/32	Fixed	1	.085	22°	1°	25°	Fixed	35°	30°
	17083368	1/8	Fixed	1	.085	22°	1°	25°	Fixed	35°	30°
	17083370	1/8	Fixed	1	.085	22°	1°	25°	Fixed	35°	30°
	17083450	1/8	Fixed	1	.085	28°	1°	27°	Fixed	35°	45°
	17083451	1/8	Fixed	1	.085	28°	1°	27°	Fixed	35°	45°
	17083452	1/8	Fixed	1	.085	28°	1°	27°	Fixed	35°	45°
	17083453	1/8	Fixed	1	.085	28°	1°	27°	Fixed	35°	45°
	17083454	1/8	Fixed	1	.085	28°	1°	27°	Fixed	35°	45°
	17083455	1/8	Fixed	1	.085	28°	1°	27°	Fixed	35°	45°
	17083456	1/8	Fixed	1	.085	28°	1°	27°	Fixed	35°	45°
	17083630	1/4	Fixed	1	.085	28°	1°	27°	Fixed	35°	45°
	17083631	1/4	Fixed	1	.085	28°	1°	27°	Fixed	35°	45°
	17083632	1/4	Fixed	1	.085	28°	1°	27°	Fixed	35°	45°
	17083633	1/4	Fixed	1	.085	28°	1°	27°	Fixed	35°	45°
	17083634	1/4	Fixed	1	.085	28°	1°	27°	Fixed	35°	45°
	17083635	1/4	Fixed	1	.085	28°	1°	27°	Fixed	35°	45°
	17083636	1/4	Fixed	1	.085	28°	1°	27°	Fixed	35°	45°
	17083650	1/8	Fixed	1/2	.085	28°	1°	27°	Fixed	35°	45°
1984 & Later	17072683	9/32	Fixed	1/2	.085	28°	1°	25°	Fixed	35°	45°
	17074812	9/32	Fixed	1/2	.085	28°	1°	25°	Fixed	35°	45°
	17084356	9/32	Fixed	3/4	.085	22°	1°	25°	Fixed	30°	30°
	17084357	9/32	Fixed	3/4	.085	22°	1°	25°	Fixed	30°	30°
	17084358	9/32	Fixed	3/4	.085	22°	1°	25°	Fixed	30°	30°
	17084359	9/32	Fixed	3/4	.085	22°	1°	25°	Fixed	30°	30°
	17084368	1/8	Fixed	3/4	.085	22°	1°	25°	Fixed	30°	30°
	17084370	1/8	Fixed	3/4	.085	22°	1°	25°	Fixed	30°	30°
	17084430	11/32	Fixed	1	.085	15°	1°	26°	Fixed	38°	42°
	17084431	11/32	Fixed	1	.085	15°	1°	26°	Fixed	38°	42°
	17084434	11/32	Fixed	1	.085	15°	1°	26°	Fixed	38°	42°
	17084435	11/32	Fixed	1	.085	15°	1°	26°	Fixed	38°	42°
	17084452	5/32	Fixed	1/2	.085	28°	1°	25°	Fixed	35°	45°
	17084453	5/32	Fixed	1/2	.085	28°	1°	25°	Fixed	35°	45°
	17084455	5/32	Fixed	1/2	.085	28°	1°	25°	Fixed	35°	45°
	17084456	5/32	Fixed	1/2	.085	28°	1°	25°	Fixed	35°	45°
	17084458	5/32	Fixed	1/2	.085	28°	1°	25°	Fixed	35°	45°
	17084532	5/32	Fixed	1/2	.085	28°	1°	25°	Fixed	35°	45°
	17084534	5/32	Fixed	1/2	.085	28°	1°	25°	Fixed	35°	45°
	17084535	5/32	Fixed	1/2	.085	28°	1°	25°	Fixed	35°	45°
	17084537	5/32	Fixed	1/2	.085	28°	1°	25°	Fixed	35°	45°
	17084538	5/32	Fixed	1/2	.085	28°	1°	25°	Fixed	35°	45°

E2SE CARBURETOR SPECIFICATIONS

Year	Carburetor Identification	Float Level (in.)	Pump Rod (in.)	Air Valve Spring (Turns)	Choke Coil Level (in.)	Fast Idle Cam (deg.)	Air Valve Rod (deg.)	Primary Vacuum Break (deg.)	Choke Setting (notches)	Secondary Vacuum Break (deg.)	Choke Unloader (deg.)
	17084540	5/32	Fixed	1/2	.085	28°	1°	25°	Fixed	35°	45°
	17084542	1/8	Fixed	1/2	.085	28°	1°	25°	Fixed	35°	45°
	17084632	9/32	Fixed	1/2	.085	28°	1°	25°	Fixed	35°	45°
	17084633	9/32	Fixed	1/2	.085	28°	1°	25°	Fixed	35°	45°
	17084635	9/32	Fixed	1/2	.085	28°	1°	25°	Fixed	35°	45°
	17084636	9/32	Fixed	1/2	.085	28°	1°	25°	Fixed	35°	45°

E4ME AND E4MC CARBURETOR SPECIFICATIONS

Year	Carburetor Identification	Float Level (in.)	Air Valve Spring (turn)	Pump Rod (in.)	Primary Vacuum Break (deg.)	Secondary Vacuum Break (deg.)	Air Valve Rod (in.)	Choke Rod (deg.)	Choke Unloader (deg.)	Fast Idle Speed (rpm)
1982	17082202	11/32	7/8	Fixed	27°	—	.025	20°	38°	①
	17082204	11/32	7/8	Fixed	27°	—	.025	20°	38°	①
	17082203	11/32	7/8	Fixed	27°	—	.025	38°	38°	①
	17082207	11/32	7/8	Fixed	27°	—	.025	38°	38°	①
1983	17083204	11/32	7/8	Fixed	—	27°	.025	20°	38°	②
	17083206	11/32	7/8	Fixed	—	27°	.025	20°	38°	②
	17083207	11/32	7/8	Fixed	—	27°	.025	38°	38°	②
	17083218	11/32	7/8	Fixed	—	27°	.025	20°	38°	②
	17083236	11/32	7/8	Fixed	—	27°	.025	20°	38°	②
	17083506	7/16	7/8	Fixed	27°	36°	.025	20°	36°	②
	17083508	7/16	7/8	Fixed	27°	36°	.025	20°	36°	②
	17083524	7/16	7/8	Fixed	25°	36°	.025	20°	36°	②
	17083526	7/16	7/8	Fixed	25°	36°	.025	20°	36°	②
1984 & Later	17084201	11/32	7/8	Fixed	27°	—	.025	20°	38°	②
	17084205	11/32	7/8	Fixed	27°	—	.025	38°	38°	②
	17084208	11/32	7/8	Fixed	27°	—	.025	20°	38°	②
	17084209	11/32	7/8	Fixed	27°	—	.025	38°	38°	②
	17084210	11/32	7/8	Fixed	27°	—	.025	20°	38°	②
	17084507	7/16	1	Fixed	27°	36°	.025	20°	36°	②
	17084509	7/16	1	Fixed	27°	36°	.025	20°	36°	②
	17084525	7/16	1	Fixed	25°	36°	.025	20°	36°	②
	17084527	7/16	1	Fixed	25°	36°	.025	20°	36°	②

① 3 turns after contacting lever for preliminary setting
② Refer to Emission Label

Perform the following steps:

1. Remove the fuel pump fuse from the fuse block.

2. Start the engine. Allow it to run out of fuel.

3. Engage starter to make sure it is out of fuel.

4. Turn the car off. Replace the fuse.

5. Drain the fuel tank into a suitable container.

6. Jack up your vehicle and support it with jack stands.

7. Disconnect the exhaust system allowing it to hang over the axle assembly.

8. Remove the heat shield.

9. Remove the filler neck shield.

10. Remove the rear suspension track bar and its brace.

11. Disconnect the fuel pump/gauge connector.

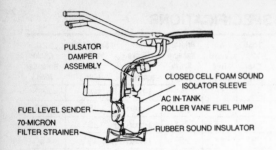

PULSATOR DAMPER ASSEMBLY

CLOSED CELL FOAM SOUND ISOLATOR SLEEVE

FUEL LEVEL SENDER

AC IN-TANK ROLLER VANE FUEL PUMP

70-MICRON FILTER STRAINER

RUBBER SOUND INSULATOR

Electric in-tank fuel pump with sending unit

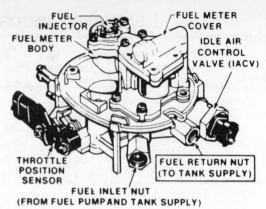

FUEL INJECTOR

FUEL METER COVER

FUEL METER BODY

IDLE AIR CONTROL VALVE (IACV)

THROTTLE POSITION SENSOR

FUEL RETURN NUT (TO TANK SUPPLY)

FUEL INLET NUT (FROM FUEL PUMP AND TANK SUPPLY)

TBI assembly

NOTE: *The wiring harness on the fuel pump/gauge assembly is a permanent part of the assembly. Do not pry on the cover connector. Disconnect at body harness connector.*

12. Disconnect all fuel lines.

13. Remove the fuel pipe retaining bracket on the left side. Also remove the brake line clip from the bracket.

14. Position a jack under the axle assembly.

15. Disconnect the lower end of the shock absorbers.

16. Lower the axle and remove the coil springs.

17. Remove the tank strap bolts.

18. Remove the tank. The rear suspension must be lowered as far as possible without damaging the brake lines.

19. Remove fuel pump/gauge from the tank.

20. Installation is the reverse of removal.

TESTING

1. Turn the engine off and relieve the fuel pressure.

2. Remove the air cleaner and plug the thermac vacuum port on TBI.

3. On 2.5L engine, install fuel pressure gage between the throttle body unit and fuel filter by removing the steel fuel line. Use a back-up wrench to hold fuel nut on the TBI when removing the fuel line.

4. Start the car and observe the fuel pressure reading. It should be 9–13 psi (62–90 kPa).

5. Relieve the fuel pressure.

6. Remove the fuel pressure gauge.

7. Reinstall the fuel line.

8. Start the car and check for fuel leaks.

9. Remove plug covering thermac vacuum port on the TBI and install the air cleaner.

Throttle Body Assembly

The throttle body injection used on 2.5L and 5.0L (VIN 7 & E) engines is centrally located on the intake manifold. Its function is to supply an air/fuel mixture to the intake manifold, which is controlled by the ECM.

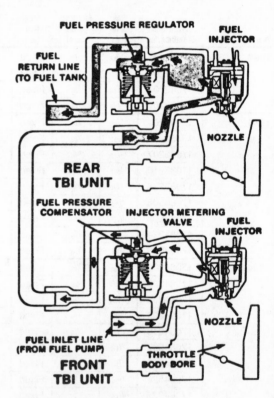

FUEL PRESSURE REGULATOR

FUEL INJECTOR

FUEL RETURN LINE (TO FUEL TANK)

NOZZLE

REAR TBI UNIT

FUEL PRESSURE COMPENSATOR

INJECTOR METERING VALVE

FUEL INJECTOR

NOZZLE

FUEL INLET LINE (FROM FUEL PUMP)

THROTTLE BODY BORE

FRONT TBI UNIT

CFI fuel and air mixture schematic

The assembly is simple. It consists of two casting assemblies: a throttle body and a fuel metering assembly. The assembly contains a pressure regulator, idle air control valve, electrical solenoid that activates the fuel injector, throttle position sensor, fuel inlet and a fuel return fitting.

The Throttle Body Injection identification number is stamped on the lower mounting flange located near the TPS. The number is in alphabetical code and should be noted before servicing the unit.

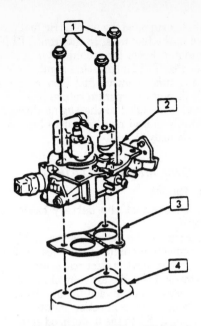

1. Bolt—tighten to 16 N·m (12 ft. lbs.)
2. TBI unit
3. Gasket (must be installed with stripe facing up)
5. Engine intake manifold

Throttle Body assembly removal—5.0L (VIN E) engine

An oxygen sensor in the main exhaust system functions to provide feedback information to the ECM as to oxygen content, lean or rich in the exhaust. The ECM then uses this information to modify fuel delivery to achieve as near as possible an ideal air/fuel ratio of 14.7:1. This ratio permits the catalytic converter to become more effective in reducing emissions while providing acceptable driveability.

Trouble diagnosis of the injection system is nearly impossible for the novice mechanic to perform, because of the interaction between the injection, emissions, and ignition systems; all of which are controlled by the ECM. Should you encounter any type of engine performance problem, have a complete CCC system test performed by a qualified, professional technician. If the fault lies in the injection system, you can use the following procedures to remove the TBI unit(s) and replace the defective component(s).

REMOVAL AND INSTALLATION

1. Disconnect the THERMAC hose from the engine fitting and remove the air cleaner.

2. Disconnect the electrical connectors at the idle air control, throttle position sensor, and the injector.

3. Disconnect the throttle linkage, return spring, and cruise control (if equipped).

4. Disconnect the throttle body vacuum hoses, fuel supply and fuel return lines.

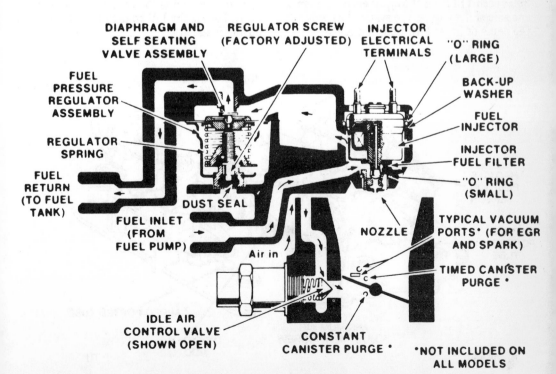

TBI fuel and air mixture schematic

5. Disconnect the 3 bolts securing the throttle body and remove the throttle body.

6. To install, reverse the removal procedures. Replace the manifold gasket and O-rings.

Idle Air Control Assembly (IAC)

REMOVAL AND INSTALLATION

1. Remove the air cleaner.

2. Disconnect the electrical connection from the idle air control assembly.

3. Using a 1¼ in. wrench, remove the IAC from the throttle body.

NOTE: *Before installing a new IAC measure the distance that the conical valve is extended. Measurement should be made from motor housing to end of cone. Distance should be no greater than 1.259 in. (32mm). If the cone is extended too far damage may result when the motor is installed. If necessary push on the end of cone, until it is retracted.*

4. Installation is the reverse of removal. Torque the motor bolts to 13 ft. lbs. (17 Nm).

Cross-Fire Injection (CFI)

The Model 400 Electronic Fuel Injection (EFI) system is a computer controlled system that uses a pair of Throttle Body Injection (TBI) units, which are mounted on a single manifold cover on the 5.0L (VIN 7) engine. Since each TBI feeds the cylinders on the opposite side of the engine, the system has acquired the name of Cross-Fire Injection (CFI).

Fuel is supplied, by an electric fuel pump located in the fuel tank, to the front TBI fuel accumulator. From the accumulator, it is carried to the rear TBI fuel pressure regulator by a connecting tube. Unused fuel is sent to the fuel tank through a separate return line.

Fuel is supplied to the engine through electronically pulsed injector valves located in the throttle body.

REMOVAL AND INSTALLATION

Front TBI Unit

1. Disconnect the battery cables at the battery.

2. Remove the air cleaner assembly, noting the connection points of the vacuum lines.

3. Disconnect the electrical connectors at the injector and the idle air control motor.

4. Disconnect the vacuum lines from the TBI unit, noting the connection points. During installation, refer to the underhood emission control information decal for vacuum line routing information.

5. Disconnect the transmission detent cable from the TBI unit.

6. Disconnect the fuel inlet (feed) and fuel balance line connections at the front TBI unit.

7. Disconnect the throttle control rod between the two TBI units.

8. Unbolt and remove the TBI unit.

9. Installation is the reverse of the previous steps. Torque the TBI bolts to 120–168 inch lbs. during installation.

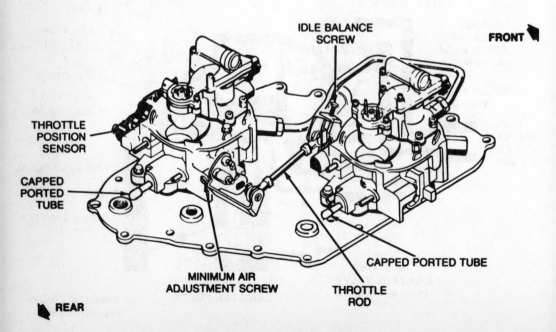

Cross-Fire Injection (CFI) system

Rear TBI Unit

1. Disconnect the battery cables at the battery.

2. Remove the air cleaner assembly, noting the connection points of the vacuum lines.

3. Disconnect the electrical connectors at the injector, idle air control motor, and throttle position sensor.

4. Disconnect the vacuum lines from the TBI unit, noting the connection points. During installation, refer to the underhood emission control information decal for vacuum line routing information.

5. Disconnect the throttle and cruise control (if so equipped) cables at the TBI unit.

6. Disconnect the fuel return and balance line connections from the rear TBI unit.

7. Disconnect the throttle control rod between the two units.

8. Unbolt and remove the TBI unit.

9. Installation is the reverse of the previous steps. Torque the TBI bolts to 120–168 inch lbs. during installation.

TBI Disassembly

CAUTION: *Use extreme care when handling the TBI unit to avoid damage to the swirl plates located beneath the throttle valve.*

NOTE: *If both TBI units are to be disassembled, DO NOT mix parts between either unit.*

1. Remove the fuel meter cover assembly (five screws). Remove the gaskets after the cover has been removed. The fuel meter cover assembly is serviced only as a unit. If necessary, the entire unit must be replaced.

CAUTION: *DO NOT remove the four screws which retain the pressure regulator (rear unit) or pressure compensator (front unit). There is a spring beneath the cover which is under great pressure. If the cover is accidentally released, personal injury could result.*

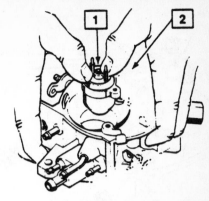

1. Fuel injector assembly
2. Fuel meter body assembly

Fuel Injector Installation—5.0L (VIN E) engine

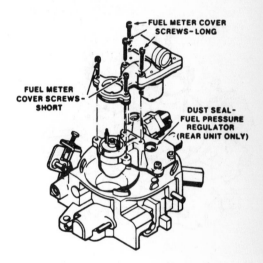

Fuel meter cover removal—2.5L & 5.0L (CFI) engines

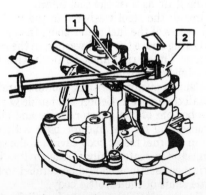

1. Fuel meter cover gasket
2. Fuel injector assembly

Fuel Injector removal—5.0L (VIN E) engine

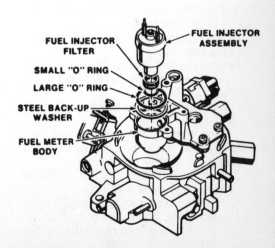

Fuel Injector Installation—2.5L & 5.0L (CFI) engines

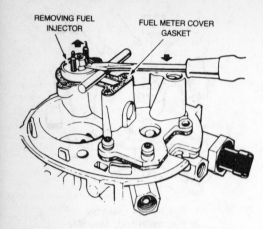

Removing the Injector—2.5L & 5.0L (CFI) engines

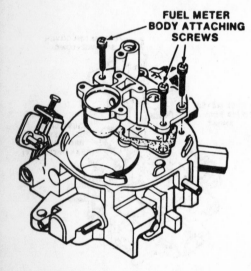

Fuel meter body attaching screws—2.5L & 5.0L engines

Do not immerse the fuel meter cover in any type of cleaning solvent.

2. Remove the foam dust seal from the meter body of the rear unit.

3. Remove the fuel injector by:

    a. Using a screwdriver and rod, lift the fuel injector from the TBI.

    b. Use a twisting motion when removing the fuel injector.

    c. If the injectors are to be removed from both TBI units, mark them so that they may be reinstalled in their original units.

4. Remove the filter from the base of the injector by rotating it back and forth.

5. Remove the O-ring and the steel washer from the top of the fuel meter body, then remove the small O-ring from the bottom of the injector cavity.

6. Remove the fuel inlet and outlet nuts (and gaskets) from the fuel meter body.

7. Remove the fuel meter body assembly and the gasket from the throttle body assembly (three screws).

8. For the rear TBI unit only: Remove the throttle position sensor (TPS) from the throttle body (two screws). If necessary, remove the screw which holds the TPS actuator lever to the end of the throttle shaft.

9. Remove the idle air control motor from the throttle body.

CAUTION: *Because the TPS and idle air control motors are electrical units, they must not be immersed in any type of cleaning solvent.*

Assembly

NOTE: *During assembly, replace the gaskets, injector washer, O-rings, and pressure regulator dust seal with new equivalents.*

1. Install the idle air control motor in the throttle body, using a new gasket. Torque the retaining screws to 13 ft. lbs.

NOTE: *DO NOT overtighten the screws.*

2. For the rear TBI unit only: If removed, install the TPS actuator lever by aligning the flats of the lever and the shaft. Install and tighten the retaining screw.

3. Install the fuel meter body on the throttle body, using a new gasket. Also, apply thread locking compound to the three fuel meter body screws according to the chemical manufacturers instructions. Torque the screws to 35 inch lbs.

4. Install the fuel inlet and outlet nuts, using new gaskets. Torque the nuts to 260 inch lbs.

5. Carefully twist the fuel filter onto the injector base.

6. Lubricate the new O-rings with lithium grease.

7. Install the small O-ring onto the injector, pressing it up against the fuel filter.

8. Install the steel washer into the injector cavity recess of the fuel meter body. Install the large O-ring above the steel washer, in the cavity recess. The O-ring must be flush with the fuel meter body surface.

9. Using a pushing/twisting motion, carefully install the injector. Center the nozzle O-ring in the bottom of the injector cavity and align the raised lug on the injector base with the notch in the fuel meter body cavity. Make sure the injector is seated fully in the cavity. The electrical connections should be parallel to the throttle shaft of the throttle body.

10. For the rear TBI unit only: Install the new pressure regulator dust seal into the fuel meter body recess.

11. Install the new fuel meter cover and fuel outlet passage gaskets on the fuel meter cover.

12. Install the fuel meter cover assembly, using thread locking compound on the five retaining screws. Torque the screws to 28 inch lbs. Note that the two short screws must be installed alongside the fuel injector (one screw each side).

13. For the rear TBI unit only: With the throttle valve in the closed (idle) position, install the TPS but do not tighten the attaching screws. The TPS lever must be located ABOVE the tang on the throttle actuator lever.

14. Install the TBI unit(s) as previously outlined and adjust the throttle position sensor.

Adjustments

No internal adjustments of the TBI units are possible. Any time the TPS is removed, it must be readjusted according to the following procedure.

THROTTLE POSITION SENSOR (TPS) ADJUSTMENT

NOTE: *An accurate digital voltmeter is needed to perform this adjustment.*

1. Remove the TPS attaching screws and apply thread locking compound to the screws. Reinstall the screws loosely.

2. Install three jumper wires between the TPS and the TPS wiring terminal connections.

3. Turn the ignition ON and measure the voltage between the GROUND and TPS SIGNAL terminals.

NOTE: With the ignition switch ON, the GROUND terminal will have a 0 volt reading, the TPS SIGNAL terminal should be below 0.960 volts with the throttle closed and the 5 VOLT REFERENCE terminal will have a minimum of 4.0 volts.

4. Rotate the TPS to obtain a voltmeter reading of 0.450–0.960 volts. Tighten TPS and turn the ignition OFF, remove the jumpers, and reconnect the TPS wiring to the TPS.

MINIMUM IDLE AND THROTTLE VALVE SYNCHRONIZING

The throttle position of each throttle body must be balanced so that the throttle plates are synchronized and open simultaneously. Adjustment should be performed only when a manifold cover, TBI unit or throttle body has been replaced. See Chapter 2 for more complete detail of adjustment.

1. Remove the air cleaner and plug the vacuum port on the rear TBI unit for the thermostatic air cleaner.

2. Remove the tamper resistant plugs covering both unit throttle stop screws. Make sure both throttle valves are slightly open to allow fuel to bypass them.

3. Block the drive wheels and apply the parking brake.

4. Connect a tachometer to measure rpm.

5. Disconnect the idle air control (IAC) valve electrical connectors.

6. Plug the idle air passages of each throttle body with plugs (J–33047 or equivalent). Make sure the plugs are seated fully in the passage so that no air leaks exist.

CAUTION: *To prevent the engine from running at high rpm, be sure the ignition switch is OFF and transmission is in N before connecting IAC valves or removing or installing idle air passage plugs. Failure to do this may result in vehicle movement and possible personal injury.*

7. Start the engine and allow the engine rpm to stabilize at normal operating temperature.

8. Place the transmission in **D** while holding the brake pedal to prevent vehicle movement. The engine rpm should decrease below curb idle speed. If the engine rpm does not decrease, check for a vacuum leak.

9. Remove the cap from the ported tube on the rear TBI unit and connect a vacuum gauge or water manometer.

10. Adjust the rear unit throttle stop screw to obtain approximately ½ in.Hg as read on the vacuum gauge, or 6 in.H$_2$O as read on the manometer. If not able to adjust to this level, check that the front unit throttle stop is not limiting throttle travel.

11. Remove the vacuum gauge or manometer from the rear unit and install the cap on the ported vacuum tube.

12. Remove the cap from the ported vacuum tube on the front TBI unit and install the gauge or manometer as before. If the reading is not the same as the rear unit, proceed as follows:

a. Locate the throttle synchronizing screw and collar on the front TBI unit. The screw retaining collar is welded to the throttle lever to discourage tampering with this adjustment.

b. If the collar is in place, grind off the weld from the screw collar and throttle lever.

c. Block possible movement of the throttle lever as illustrated, relieving the force of the heavy spring against the throttle synchronizing screw, to prevent the levers from coming into contact.

NOTE: *If the lever is not blocked before the throttle synchronizing screw is removed, the screw may be damaged and reinstallation will be done only with great difficulty.*

d. Remove the screw and collar and discard the collar.

e. Reinstall the throttle synchronizing screw, using thread locking compound.

f. Adjust the screw to obtain ½ in.Hg on the vacuum gauge, or 6 in.H$_2$O on the manometer.

13. Remove the gauge or manometer from the ported tube and reinstall the cap.

14. Adjust the rear throttle stop screw to obtain 475 rpm, with the transmission in **D** and the parking brake applied. On manual transmission models, leave the gear selector in **N**.

15. Turn the ignition OFF and place automatic transmission in **N**.

16. Adjust the front throttle stop screw to obtain 0.005 in. (0.127mm) clearance between the front throttle stop screw and the throttle lever tang.

17. Remove idle air passage plugs and reconnect IAC valves.

18. Start the engine. It may run at a high rpm but the engine speed should decrease when the idle air control valves close the air passages. Stop the engine when the rpm decreases.

19. The throttle position sensor (TPS) voltage should be checked and adjusted, if necessary. See TPS Adjustment for procedures.

20. Install the air cleaner gasket, connect the vacuum line to the TBI unit and install the air cleaner.

21. Reset the idle speed control motors by driving the vehicle to 30 mph.

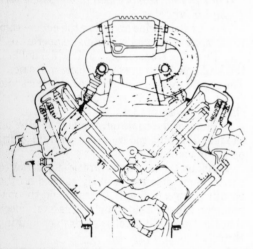

Cross-section view of TPI system—5.0L (VIN F) & 5.7L engines

MULTI-PORT FUEL INJECTION (MPFI)
TUNED PORT INJECTION (TPI)

NOTE: *This book contain simple testing and service procedures for your fuel injection system.*

On 1985 models, two new fuel injection systems were introduced: Multi-Port Fuel Injection (MFI) for use with the 2.8L engine and Tuned Port Injection (TPI) for use with the 5.0L engine. Although both systems are basically identical, the Tuned Port Injection (TPI) offers a significant increase in engine torque and power.

The systems are controlled by an Electronic Control Module (ECM) which monitors the engine operations and generates output signals to

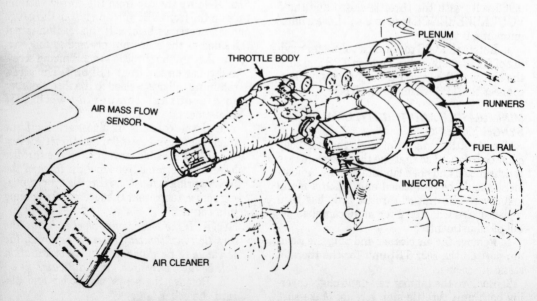

Tuned Port Injection (TPI) system—5.0L (VIN F) & 5.7L engines

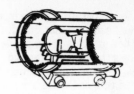

Sectional view of Mass Air Flow (MAF) sensor—TPI & MPI systems

25 N·m (18 FT. LBS.)

21 N·m (15 FT. LBS.)

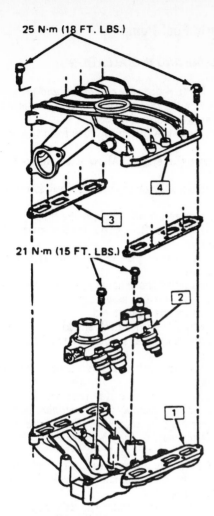

1. Intake manifold
2. Fuel rail assembly
3. Gasket
4. Plenum

Multi-Port Injection components—2.8L (VIN S) & 3.1L engines

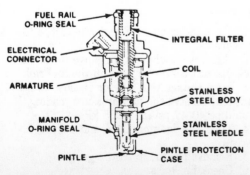

FUEL RAIL O-RING SEAL
ELECTRICAL CONNECTOR
ARMATURE
MANIFOLD O-RING SEAL
PINTLE
INTEGRAL FILTER
COIL
STAINLESS STEEL BODY
STAINLESS STEEL NEEDLE
PINTLE PROTECTION CASE

Sectional view of fuel injector—TPI & MPI systems

provide the correct air/fuel mixture, ignition timing and idle speed. Input information to the ECM is provided by the oxygen sensor, temperature sensor, detonation sensor, mass air flow sensor and throttle position sensor. The ECM also receives information concerning engine rpm, road speed, transmission gear position, power steering and air conditioning.

The systems consist of a large front mounted air cleaner, a mass air flow sensor (TPI uses a burn off filament), a cast throttle body assembly (TPI has dual throttle blades), a large cast plenum (TPI uses individual tuned runners) and dual (TPI) or single (MFI) fuel rail assemblies with computer controlled injectors.

The tuned runners (TPI) are designed to provide excellent throttle responses throughout the driving range. Their configuration enables large volumes of high pressure air to be present at each intake valve, resulting in improved cylinder charging and operation efficiency.

Both systems use Bosch injectors, one at each intake port, rather than the single injector found on the earlier throttle body system. The injectors are mounted on a fuel rail and are activated by a signal from the electronic control module. The injector is a solenoid-operated valve which remains open depending on the width of the electronic pulses (length of the signal) from the ECM; the longer the open time, the more fuel is injected. In this manner, the air/fuel mixture can be precisely controlled for maximum performance with minimum emissions.

Fuel is pumped from the tank by a high pressure fuel pump, located inside the fuel tank. It is a positive displacement roller vane pump. The impeller serves as a vapor separator and pre-charges the high pressure assembly. A pressure regulator maintains 44 psi in the fuel line to the injectors and the excess fuel is fed back to the tank. A fuel accumulator is used to dampen the hydraulic line hammer in the system created when all injectors open simultaneously.

The Mass Air Flow Sensor is used to measure the mass of air that is drawn into the engine cylinders. It is located just ahead of the air throttle in the intake system and consists of a heated film which measures the mass of air, rather than just the volume. A resistor is used to measure the temperature of the incoming air and the air mass sensor maintains the temperature of the film at 75 degrees above ambient temperature. As the ambient (outside) air temperature rises, more energy is required to maintain the heated film at the higher temperature and the control unit uses this difference in required energy to calculate the mass of the incoming air. The control unit uses this information to determine the duration of fuel injection pulse, timing and EGR.

The throttle body incorporates an idle air control (IAC) that provides for a bypass channel through which air can flow. It consists of an orifice and pintle which is controlled by the ECM through a stepper motor. The IAC provides air flow for idle and allows additional air during cold start until the engine reaches operating temperature. As the engine temperature rises, the opening through which air passes is slowly closed.

The throttle position sensor (TPS) provides the control unit with information on throttle position, in order to determine injector pulse width and hence correct mixture. The TPS is connected to the throttle shaft on the throttle body and consists of a potentiometer with one end connected to a 5 volt source from the ECM and the other to ground. A third wire is connected to the ECM to measure the voltage output from the TPS which changes as the throttle valve angle is changed (accelerator pedal moves). At the closed throttle position, the output is low (approximately 0.4 volts); as the throttle valve opens, the output increases to a maximum 5 volts at wide open throttle (WOT). The TPS can be misadjusted open, shorted, or loose and if it is out of adjustment, the idle quality or WOT performance may be poor. A loose TPS can cause intermittent bursts of fuel from the injectors and an unstable idle because the ECM thinks the throttle is moving. This should cause a trouble code to be set. Once a trouble code is set, the ECM will use a preset value for TPS and some vehicle performance may return. A small amount of engine coolant is routed through the throttle assembly to prevent freezing inside the throttle bore during cold operation.

Releiving Fuel System Presure

1. Remove the fuel pump fuse from the fuse block.
2. Start the engine. Allow it to run out of fuel.
3. Engage starter to make sure it is out of fuel.
4. Turn the car off. Replace the fuse.

Electric Fuel Pump

REMOVAL AND INSTALLATION

NOTE: *To reduce the risk of fire and personal injury the fuel pressure must be relieved. Perform the following steps:*
1. Remove the fuel pump fuse from the fuse block.
2. Start the engine. Allow it to run out of fuel.
3. Engage starter to make sure it is out of fuel.
4. Turn the car off. Replace the fuse.
5. Drain the fuel tank into a suitable container.
6. Jack up your vehicle and support it with jack stands.
7. Disconnect the exhaust system allowing it to hang over the axle assembly.
8. Remove the heat shield.
9. Remove the filler neck shield.
10. Remove the rear suspension track bar and its brace.
11. Disconnect the fuel pump/gauge connector.
NOTE: *The wiring harness on the fuel pump/gauge assembly is a permanent part of the assembly. Do not pry on the cover connector. Disconnect at body harness connector.*
12. Disconnect all fuel lines.
13. Remove the fuel pipe retaining bracket on the left side. Also remove the brake line clip from the bracket.
14. Position a jack under the axle assembly.
15. Disconnect the lower end of the shock absorbers.
16. Lower the axle and remove the coil springs.
17. Remove the tank strap bolts.
18. Remove the tank. The rear suspension must be lowered as far as possible without damaging the brake lines.
19. Remove fuel pump/gauge from the tank.
20. Installation is the reverse of removal.

TESTING

1. Turn the engine off and relieve the fuel pressure.
2. Connect a fuel pressure gauge to the fuel pressure test connector port on the fuel rail.
3. Turn the ignition ON for at least 10 seconds and observe the fuel pressure reading. It should be 40–47 psi (280–325 kPa).
4. Turn the ignition OFF and relieve fuel pressure.
5. Remove the fuel pressure gauge.
6. Check for leaks.

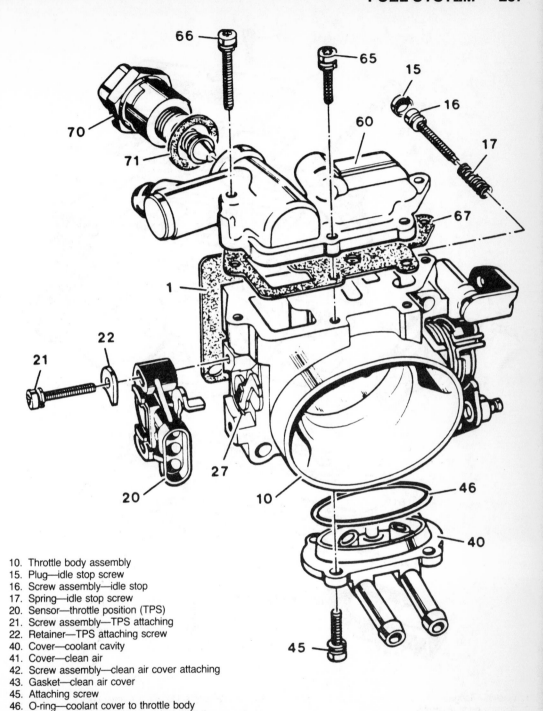

10. Throttle body assembly
15. Plug—idle stop screw
16. Screw assembly—idle stop
17. Spring—idle stop screw
20. Sensor—throttle position (TPS)
21. Screw assembly—TPS attaching
22. Retainer—TPS attaching screw
40. Cover—coolant cavity
41. Cover—clean air
42. Screw assembly—clean air cover attaching
43. Gasket—clean air cover
45. Attaching screw
46. O-ring—coolant cover to throttle body
60. Idle air/vacuum signal housing assembly
61. IACV/coolant cover assembly
62. Screw assembly—IACV cover assembly to throttle
    body
63. Gasket—IACV/coolant cover to throttle body
65. Screw assembly—idle air/vacuum signal assembly
66. Screw assembly—idle air/vacuum signal assembly
67. Gasket—idle air/vacuum signal assembly
70. Valve assembly—idle air control (IAC)
71. Gasket—IACV valve assembly

Exploded view of MPI throttle body assembly—2.8L (VIN F) & 3.1L engines

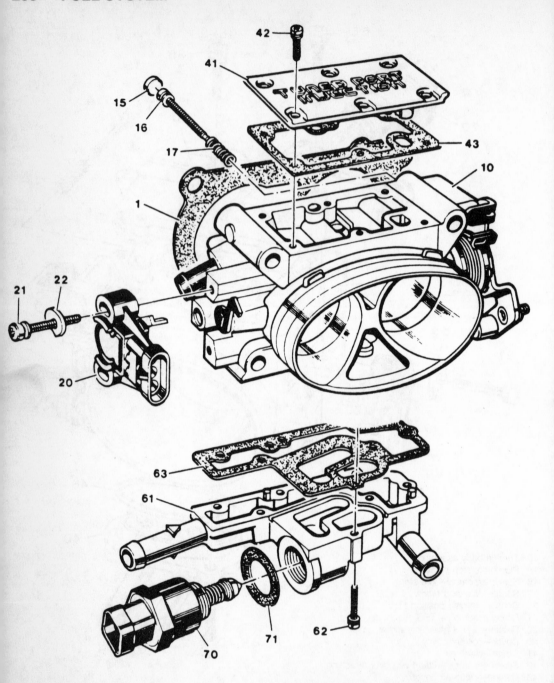

1. Gasket—flange
10. Throttle body assembly
15. Plug—idle stop screw
16. Screw assembly—idle stop
17. Spring—idle stop screw
20. Sensor—throttle position (TPS)
21. Screw assembly—TPS attaching
22. Retainer—TPS attaching screw
41. Cover—clean air
42. Screw assembly—clean air cover attaching
43. Gasket—clean air cover
45. Attaching screw

46. O-ring—coolant cover to throttle body
60. Idle air/vacuum signal housing assembly
61. IACV/coolant cover assembly
62. Screw assembly—IACV cover assembly to throttle body
63. Gasket—IACV/coolant cover to throttle body
65. Screw assembly—idle air/vacuum signal assembly
66. Screw assembly—idle air/vacuum signal assembly
67. Gasket—idle air/vacuum signal assembly
70. Valve assembly—idle air control (IAC)
71. Gasket—IAC valve assembly

Exploded view of TPI throttle body assembly—5.0L (VIN F) & 5.7L engines

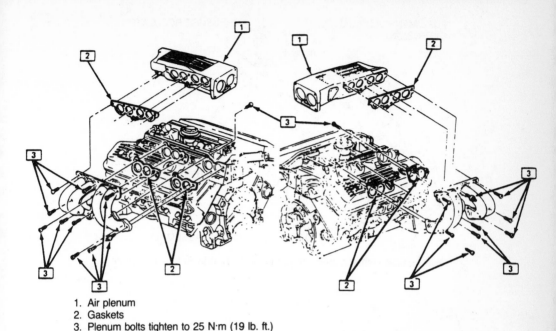

1. Air plenum
2. Gaskets
3. Plenum bolts tighten to 25 N·m (19 lb. ft.)

Plenum removal—5.0L (VIN F) & 5.7L engines

Throttle Body

REMOVAL AND INSTALLATION

1. Remove the air inlet duct, Idle Air Control (IAC) and Throttle Position Sensor (TPS) connectors.

2. Remove the vacuum lines and coolant hoses.

3. Remove the throttle cable and the cruise control cables, if equipped.

4. Remove the throttle body retaining screws and the throttle body.

5. To install, reverse the removal procedures.

Plenum

2.8L ENGINE

1. Remove the negative battery cable.

2. Remove the air inlet duct at the throttle body.

3. Remove the throttle body retaining bolts and the throttle body.

4. Remove the EGR pipe bolts and the EGR valve.

5. Remove the throttle cable bracket.

6. Remove the plenum bolts and the plenum. Clean the gasket material from the sealing surfaces.

7. To install, use new gaskets and reverse the removal procedures.

5.0L AND 5.7L ENGINE

1. Remove the negative battery cable.

2. Remove the throttle cable, thermal vacuum connector, and the cruise control cable, if equipped.

3. Remove the cable retaining bracket.

4. Remove the Throttle Position Sensor (TPS) and the Idle Air Control (IAC) connectors.

5. Remove the throttle body bolts and the throttle body.

6. Remove the brake booster pipe, vacuum hose and the canister control valve fresh air pipe.

7. Remove the right runners, the plenum retaining bolts and the plenum. Clean the gasket material from the sealing surfaces.

8. To install, use new gaskets and reverse the removal procedures.

Fuel Rail and Pressure Regulator Assembly

NOTE: *When servicing the fuel system, be sure to relieve the pressure of the system and drain the fuel into an approved container. DO NOT allow dirt or other contaminants to enter the system.*

1. Refer to the Plenum Removal and Installation procedures in this Chapter and remove the plenum.

2. Remove the fuel lines and the cold start valve. Remove the injector harness connectors.

3. On the 2.8L engine, remove the vacuum line at the pressure regulator.

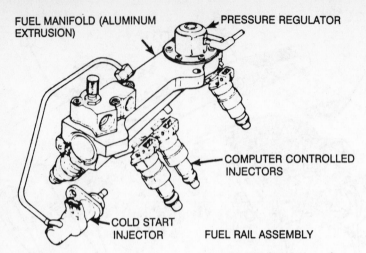

Fuel injection rail and pressure regulator—2.8L (VIN S) & 3.1L engines

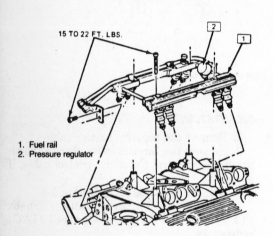

1. Fuel rail
2. Pressure regulator

Fuel injection rail and pressure regulator—5.0L (VIN F) & 5.7 L engines

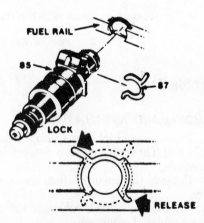

85. Injector—port
87. Clip—injector retainer

Removing the fuel injector and lock clip—TPI & MPI systems

4. Remove the fuel rail retaining bolts, the fuel rail and injectors.

5. To install, replace the O-rings of the fuel injectors, coat the O-rings with engine oil and reverse the removal procedure.

6. Turn the ignition **ON** and **OFF** several times and inspect for leaks.

Fuel Injectors

1. Refer to the Fuel Rail and Pressure Regulator Removal and Installation procedures in this Chapter and remove the fuel rail.

2. Rotate the injector retaining clips to the **UNLOCKED** position and remove the injectors.

3. To install, replace the O-rings, coat them with engine oil and reverse the removal procedures.

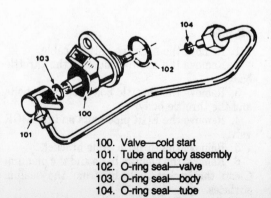

100. Valve—cold start
101. Tube and body assembly
102. O-ring seal—valve
103. O-ring seal—body
104. O-ring seal—tube

Cold start valve assembly

Cold Start Valve

NOTE: *On the 2.8L engine, refer to the Plenum Removal and Installation procedures in this Chapter and remove the plenum. Also remove the distributor cap.*

1. Remove the negative battery cable and brake booster line.
2. Disconnect the fuel line at the fuel rail.
3. Disconnect the wiring harness.
4. Remove the pollution control valve pipe retaining screw.
5. Remove the valve retaining bolt and valve.
6. To install, use new O-rings and reverse the removal procedures.

Idle Air Control Valve

1. Remove electrical connector from idle air control valve.
2. Remove the idle air control valve.
3. Installation is the reverse of removal. Before installing the idle air control valve, measure the distance that the valve is extended. Measurement should be made from the motor housing to the end of the cone. The distance should not exceed 1⅛ in. (28.6mm), or damage to the valve may occur when installed. Use a new gasket and turn the ignition on then off again to allow the ECM to reset the idle air control valve.

NOTE: *Identify replacement IAC valve as being either Type 1 (with collar at electric terminal end) or Type 2 (without collar). If measuring distance is greater than specified above, proceed as follows:*
Type 1: Press on valve firmly to retract it.
Type 2: Compress retaining spring from valve while turning valve in with a clockwise motion. Return spring to original position with straight portion of spring end aligned with flat surface of valve.

Throttle Position Sensor (TPS)

1. Disconnect the electrical connector from the sensor.
2. Remove the attaching screws, lockwashers and retainers.
3. Remove the throttle position sensor. If necessary, remove the screw holding the actuator to the end of the throttle shaft.
4. With the throttle valve in the normal closed idle position, install the throttle position sensor on the throttle body assembly, making sure the sensor pickup lever is located above the tang on the throttle actuator lever.
5. Install the retainers, screws and lockwashers using a thread locking compound. DO NOT tighten the screws until the throttle position switch is adjusted.
6. Install three jumper wires between the throttle position switch and the harness connector.
7. With the ignition switch ON, use a digital voltmeter connected to terminals B and C and adjust the switch to obtain 0.35–0.45 volts.
8. Tighten the mounting screws, then recheck the reading to insure that the adjustment hasn't changed.
9. Turn ignition OFF, remove jumper wires, then reconnect harness to throttle position switch.

ADJUSTMENTS

NOTE: *Due to the complexity of the system, any adjustments should be performed by a qualified mechanic.*

Idle Speed Adjustment

1. Remove the idle stop screw plug by piercing it with an awl.
2. With idle air control motor connected, ground the diagnostic connector.

DIM. "A"
28mm

60
71
70

60. Idle air/vacuum signal housing
70. Idle air control valve (IAC)
71. IAC gasket

Idle Air Control (IAC) valve pintle length

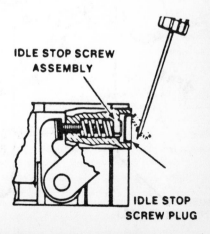

IDLE STOP SCREW
ASSEMBLY

IDLE STOP
SCREW PLUG

Removing the idle stop screw plug

3. Turn the ignition **ON** and wait 30 seconds, DO NOT start the engine.

4. Disconnect the idle air control connector with the ignition **ON**.

5. Remove the ground from the diagnostic connector and start the engine.

6. On 2.8L engines, adjust the idle stop screw to 450–550 rpm, in **D** for automatic transmissions or 550–650 rpm for manual transmissions.

7. On 5.0L engines, adjust the idle stop screw to 450–550 rpm, in **D**.

8. Turn the ignition **OFF** and reconnect the idle air control motor connector.

9. Remove the throttle position sensor connector and install three jumper wires between the connector and the sensor. Connect a digital voltmeter to terminals **A** and **B**.

10. Turn the ignition **ON** and adjust the sensor to 0.50–0.60 volt for the 2.8L engine or 0.475–0.615 volt for the 5.0L engine.

11. Tighten the screws, remove the jumper wires with the ignition **OFF** and reconnect the harness connector.

12. Start the engine and check for proper idle operation.

Cold Start Valve Adjustment

1. With the valve removed from the engine, turn the valve completely into the body.

2. Turn the valve back one complete turn until the electrical connector is at the top position.

3. Bend the body tang forward so the valve cannot turn more than one full turn.

4. Reinstall the valve to the engine.

FUEL TANK

REMOVAL AND INSTALLATION

NOTE: *To reduce the risk of fire and personal injury the fuel pressure must be relieved. Perform the following steps:*

1. Remove the fuel pump fuse from the fuse block.

2. Start the engine. Allow it to run out of fuel.

3. Engage starter to make sure it is out of fuel.

4. Turn the car off. Replace the fuse.

5. Drain the fuel tank.

6. Jack up your vehicle and support it with jack stands.

7. Disconnect the exhaust system allowing it to hang over the axle assembly.

8. Remove the heat shield.

9. Remove the filler neck shield.

10. Remove the rear suspension track bar and its brace.

11. Disconnect the fuel pump/gauge connector.

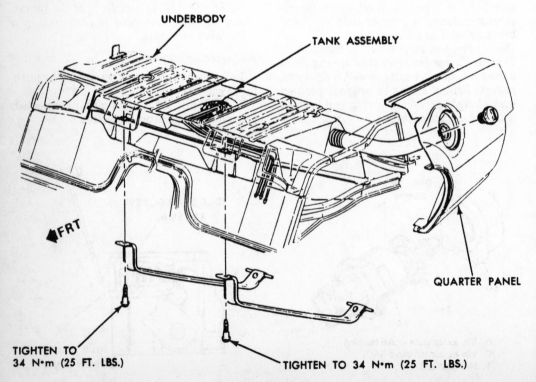

UNDERBODY

TANK ASSEMBLY

FRT

QUARTER PANEL

TIGHTEN TO
34 N•m (25 FT. LBS.)

TIGHTEN TO 34 N•m (25 FT. LBS.)

Fuel tank removal

NOTE: *The wiring harness on the fuel pump/gauge assembly is a permanent part of the assembly. Do not pry on the cover connector. Disconnect at body harness connector.*

12. Disconnect all fuel lines.

13. Remove the fuel pipe retaining bracket on the left side. Also remove the brake line clip from the bracket.

14. Position a jack under the axle assembly.

15. Disconnect the lower end of the shock absorbers.

16. Lower the axle and remove the coil springs.

17. Remove the tank strap bolts.

18. Remove the tank. The rear suspension must be lowered as far as possible without damaging the brake lines.

20. To install, use new O-ring in the fuel tank. Install the fuel tank.

21. Install the tank strap bolts.

22. Lower the axle and install the coil springs.

23. Connect the lower end of the shock absorbers.

24. Install the brake line clip to the bracket. Install the fuel pipe retaining bracket on the left side.

25. Connect all fuel lines.

26. Connect the fuel pump/gauge connector.

27. Install the rear suspension track bar and its brace.

28. Install the filler neck shield.

29. Install the heat shield.

30. Connect the exhaust system.

31. Lower the vehicle.

32. Fill the fuel tank and check for leaks.

SENDING UNIT AND FUEL PUMP ASSEMBLY REPLACEMENT

The electric fuel pump and sensing unit are an assembly, which is located inside the fuel tank.

1. Release the fuel pressure and disconnect the negative battery cable. Drain the fuel from the tank into a safe container.

2. Raise and support the vehicle safely. Disconnect the exhaust pipe at the catalytic converter and the rear hanger. Allow the exhaust system to hang over the rear axle assembly.

3. Remove the tail pipe and muffler heat shields. Remove the fuel filler neck shield from behind the left rear tire.

4. Remove the rear track bar and brace.

5. Disconnect the fuel pump/sending unit electrical connector, at the body harness connector. Do not pry up on the cover connector, as the pump/sending unit wiring harness is an integral part of the sending unit.

6. Disconnect the fuel pipes. Remove the fuel pipe retaining bracket on the left side and the brake line clip from the retaiing bracket.

7. Position a jack under the rear axle assembly in order to support the rear axle.

8. Disconnect the lower ends of the shock ab-

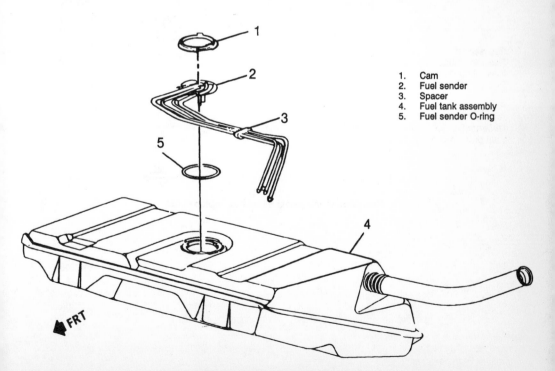

1. Cam
2. Fuel sender
3. Spacer
4. Fuel tank assembly
5. Fuel sender O-ring

Fuel sender assembly replacement

sorbers, lower the axle assembly enough to release the tension on the coil springs. Remove the coil springs.

9. Lower the rear axle assembly as far as possible without causing damage to the brake lines and cables.

10. Remove the fuel tank strap bolts. Remove the tank by rotating the front of the tank downward and sliding it to the right side.

11. Remove the fuel pump/sending unit from the tank, by loosening the cam nut. When removing the cam nut, use brass tool or equivalent to tap the nut loose.

12. Remove the O-ring from under the unit. Replace the O-ring if defective.

13. Separate the fuel pump from the sending unit.

To install:

14. Install the fuel pump to the sending unit.

15. Install the O-ring in the groove around the tank opening and install the fuel pump/sending unit. Install the cam nut and tighten until is it against the stop.

16. Raise the fuel tank into position and install the tank strap bolts.

17. Install the coil springs and raise the rear axle into position. Connect the shcok absorbers.

18. Connect the fuel lines and the electrical connector.

19. Install the rear suspension track bar and the track bar brace.

20. Install the fuel filler neck shield and the tail pipe and muffler heat shields.

21. Connect the exhaust system and lower the vehicle.

22. Fill the fuel tank.

23. Connect the negative battery cable, start the engine and check for fuel leaks.

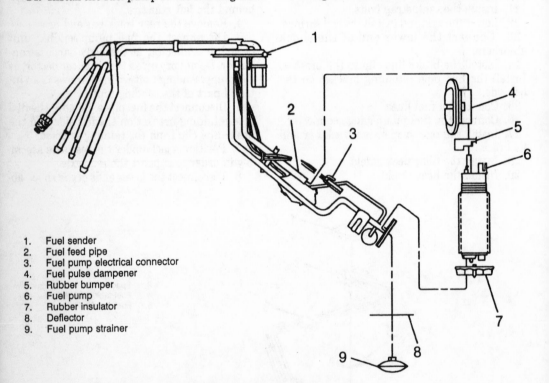

1. Fuel sender
2. Fuel feed pipe
3. Fuel pump electrical connector
4. Fuel pulse dampener
5. Rubber bumper
6. Fuel pump
7. Rubber insulator
8. Deflector
9. Fuel pump strainer

Fuel sender and pump assembly replacement

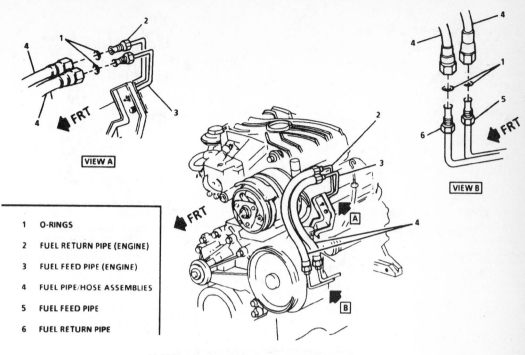

Fuel line connections—2.8L engine with MPFI

1	O-RINGS
2	FUEL RETURN PIPE (ENGINE)
3	FUEL FEED PIPE (ENGINE)
4	FUEL PIPE/HOSE ASSEMBLIES
5	FUEL FEED PIPE
6	FUEL RETURN PIPE

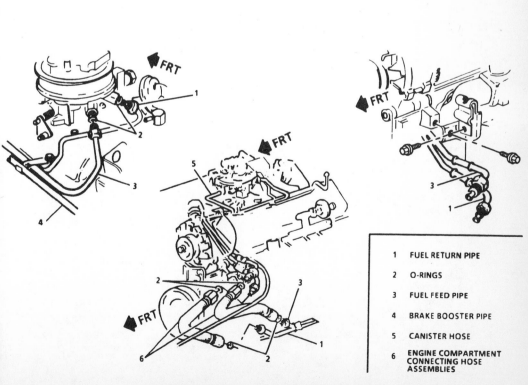

1	FUEL RETURN PIPE
2	O-RINGS
3	FUEL FEED PIPE
4	BRAKE BOOSTER PIPE
5	CANISTER HOSE
6	ENGINE COMPARTMENT CONNECTING HOSE ASSEMBLIES

Fuel line connections—V8 engine with carburetor

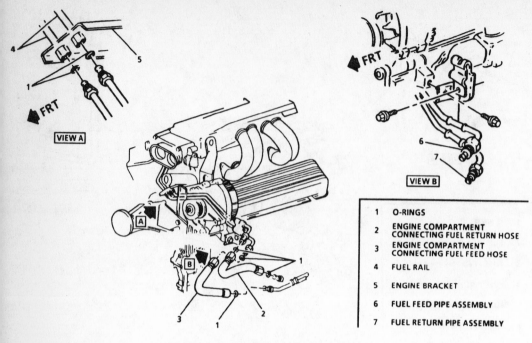

1   O-RINGS

2   ENGINE COMPARTMENT
    CONNECTING FUEL RETURN HOSE

3   ENGINE COMPARTMENT
    CONNECTING FUEL FEED HOSE

4   FUEL RAIL

5   ENGINE BRACKET

6   FUEL FEED PIPE ASSEMBLY

7   FUEL RETURN PIPE ASSEMBLY

Fuel line connections—V8 engine with TPI

Chassis Electrical

6

UNDERSTANDING AND TROUBLE SHOOTING ELECTRICAL SYSTEMS

At the rate which both import and domestic manufacturers are incorporating electronic control systems into their production lines, it won't be long before every new vehicle is equipped with one or more on-board computer. These electronic components (with no moving parts) should theoretically last the life of the vehicle, provided nothing external happens to damage the circuits or memory chips.

While it is true that electronic components should never wear out, in the real world malfunctions do occur. It is also true that any computer-based system is extremely sensitive to electrical voltages and cannot tolerate careless or haphazard testing or service procedures. An inexperienced individual can literally do major damage looking for a minor problem by using the wrong kind of test equipment or connecting test leads or connectors with the ignition switch **ON**. When selecting test equipment, make sure the manufacturers instructions state that the tester is compatible with whatever type of electronic control system is being serviced. Read all instructions carefully and double check all test points before installing probes or making any test connections.

The following Chapter outlines basic diagnosis techniques for dealing with computerized automotive control systems. Along with a general explanation of the various types of test equipment available to aid in servicing modern electronic automotive systems, basic repair techniques for wiring harnesses and connectors is given. Read the basic information before attempting any repairs or testing on any computerized system, to provide the background of information necessary to avoid the most common and obvious mistakes that can cost both time and money. Although the replacement and testing procedures are simple in themselves, the systems are not, and unless one has a thorough understanding of all components and their function within a particular computerized control system, the logical test sequence these systems demand cannot be followed. Minor malfunctions can make a big difference, so it is important to know how each component affects the operation of the overall electronic system to find the ultimate cause of a problem without replacing good components unnecessarily. It is not enough to use the correct test equipment; the test equipment must be used correctly.

Safety Precautions

CAUTION: *Whenever working on or around any computer based microprocessor control system, always observe these general precautions to prevent the possibility of personal injury or damage to electronic components.*

• Never install or remove battery cables with the key ON or the engine running. Jumper cables should be connected with the key OFF to avoid power surges that can damage electronic control units. Engines equipped with computer controlled systems should avoid both giving and getting jump starts due to the possibility of serious damage to components from arcing in the engine compartment when connections are made with the ignition ON.

• Always remove the battery cables before charging the battery. Never use a high output charger on an installed battery or attempt to use any type of "hot shot" (24 volt) starting aid.

• Exercise care when inserting test probes into connectors to insure good connections without damaging the connector or spreading the pins. Always probe connectors from the rear (wire) side, NOT the pin side, to avoid accidental shorting of terminals during test procedures.

• Never remove or attach wiring harness

connectors with the ignition switch ON, especially to an electronic control unit.

• Do not drop any components during service procedures and never apply 12 volts directly to any component (like a solenoid or relay) unless instructed specifically to do so. Some component electrical windings are designed to safely handle only 4 or 5 volts and can be destroyed in seconds if 12 volts are applied directly to the connector.

• Remove the electronic control unit if the vehicle is to be placed in an environment where temperatures exceed approximately 176°F (80°C), such as a paint spray booth or when arc or gas welding near the control unit location in the car.

ORGANIZED TROUBLESHOOTING

When diagnosing a specific problem, organized troubleshooting is a must. The complexity of a modern automobile demands that you approach any problem in a logical, organized manner. There are certain troubleshooting techniques that are standard:

1. Establish when the problem occurs. Does the problem appear only under certain conditions? Were there any noises, odors, or other unusual symptoms?

2. Isolate the problem area. To do this, make some simple tests and observations; then eliminate the systems that are working properly. Check for obvious problems such as broken wires, dirty connections or split or disconnected vacuum hoses. Always check the obvious before assuming something complicated is the cause.

3. Test for problems systematically to determine the cause once the problem area is isolated. Are all the components functioning properly? Is there power going to electrical switches and motors? Is there vacuum at vacuum switches and/or actuators? Is there a mechanical problem such as bent linkage or loose mounting screws? Doing careful, systematic checks will often turn up most causes on the first inspection without wasting time checking components that have little or no relationship to the problem.

4. Test all repairs after the work is done to make sure that the problem is fixed. Some causes can be traced to more than one component, so a careful verification of repair work is important to pick up additional malfunctions that may cause a problem to reappear or a different problem to arise. A blown fuse, for example, is a simple problem that may require more than another fuse to repair. If you don't look for a problem that caused a fuse to blow, for example, a shorted wire may go undetected.

Experience has shown that most problems tend to be the result of a fairly simple and obvious cause, such as loose or corroded connectors or air leaks in the intake system; making careful inspection of components during testing essential to quick and accurate troubleshooting. Special, hand held computerized testers designed specifically for diagnosing the system are available from a variety of aftermarket sources, as well as from the vehicle manufacturer, but care should be taken that any test equipment being used is designed to diagnose that particular computer controlled system accurately without damaging the control unit (ECM) or components being tested.

NOTE: *Pinpointing the exact cause of trouble in an electrical system can sometimes only be accomplished by the use of special test equipment. The following describes commonly used test equipment and explains how to put it to best use in diagnosis. In addition to the information covered below, the manufacturer's instructions booklet provided with the tester should be read and clearly understood before attempting any test procedures.*

TEST EQUIPMENT

Jumper Wires

Jumper wires are simple, yet extremely valuable, pieces of test equipment. Jumper wires are merely wires that are used to bypass sections of a circuit. The simplest type of jumper wire is merely a length of multi-strand wire with an alligator clip at each end. Jumper wires are usually fabricated from lengths of standard automotive wire and whatever type of connector (alligator clip, spade connector or pin connector) that is required for the particular vehicle being tested. The well equipped tool box will have several different styles of jumper wires in several different lengths. Some jumper wires are made with three or more terminals coming from a common splice for special purpose testing. In cramped, hard-to-reach areas it is advisable to have insulated boots over the jumper wire terminals in order to prevent accidental grounding, sparks, and possible fire, especially when testing fuel system components.

Jumper wires are used primarily to locate open electrical circuits, on either the ground (–) side of the circuit or on the hot (+) side. If an electrical component fails to operate, connect the jumper wire between the component and a good ground. If the component operates only with the jumper installed, the ground circuit is open. If the ground circuit is good, but the component does not operate, the circuit between the power feed and component is open. You can sometimes connect the jumper wire directly from the battery to the hot terminal of the component, but first make sure the component uses 12 volts in operation. Some electrical components, such as fuel injectors, are designed to operate on about 4 volts and running 12 volts directly to the injector terminals can burn out the wiring. By inserting an in-line fuseholder between a set of test leads, a fused jumper wire can be used for bypassing open circuits. Use a 5 amp fuse to provide protection against voltage spikes. When in doubt, use a voltmeter to check the voltage input to the component and measure how much voltage is being applied normally. By moving the jumper wire successively back from the lamp toward the power source, you can isolate the area of the circuit where the open is located. When the component stops functioning, or the power is cut off, the open is in the segment of wire between the jumper and the point previously tested.

CAUTION: *Never use jumpers made from wire that is of lighter gauge than used in the circuit under test. If the jumper wire is of too small gauge, it may overheat and possibly melt. Never use jumpers to bypass high resistance loads in a circuit. Bypassing resistances, in effect, creates a short circuit which may, in turn, cause damage and fire. Never use a jumper for anything other than temporary bypassing of components in a circuit.*

12 Volt Test Light

The 12 volt test light is used to check circuits and components while electrical current is flowing through them. It is used for voltage and ground tests. Twelve volt test lights come in different styles but all have three main parts; a ground clip, a probe, and a light. The most commonly used 12 volt test lights have pick-type probes. To use a 12 volt test light, connect the ground clip to a good ground and probe wherever necessary with the pick. The pick should be sharp so that it can penetrate wire insulation to make contact with the wire, without making a large hole in the insulation. The wrap-around light is handy in hard to reach areas or where it is difficult to support a wire to push a probe pick into it. To use the wrap around light, hook the wire to probed with the hook and pull the trigger. A small pick will be forced through the wire insulation into the wire core.

CAUTION: *Do not use a test light to probe electronic ignition spark plug or coil wires. Never use a pick-type test light to probe wiring on computer controlled systems unless specifically instructed to do so. Any wire insulation that is pierced by the test light probe should be taped and sealed with silicone after testing.*

Like the jumper wire, the 12 volt test light is used to isolate opens in circuits. But, whereas the jumper wire is used to bypass the open to operate the load, the 12 volt test light is used to locate the presence of voltage in a circuit. If the test light glows, you know that there is power up to that point; if the 12 volt test light does not glow when its probe is inserted into the wire or connector, you know that there is an open circuit (no power). Move the test light in successive steps back toward the power source until the light in the handle does glow. When it does glow, the open is between the probe and point previously probed.

NOTE: *The test light does not detect that 12 volts (or any particular amount of voltage) is present; it only detects that some voltage is present. It is advisable before using the test light to touch its terminals across the battery posts to make sure the light is operating properly.*

Self-Powered Test Light

The self-powered test light usually contains a 1.5 volt penlight battery. One type of self-powered test light is similar in design to the 12 volt test light. This type has both the battery and the light in the handle and pick-type probe tip. The second type has the light toward the open tip, so that the light illuminates the contact point. The self-powered test light is dual purpose piece of test equipment. It can be used to test for either open or short circuits when power is isolated from the circuit (continuity test). A powered test light should not be used on any computer controlled system or component unless specifically instructed to do so. Many engine sensors can be destroyed by even this small amount of voltage applied directly to the terminals.

Open Circuit Testing

To use the self-powered test light to check for open circuits, first isolate the circuit from the vehicle's 12 volt power source by disconnecting the battery or wiring harness connector. Connect the test light ground clip to a good ground and probe sections of the circuit sequentially with the test light. (start from either end of the circuit). If the light is out, the open is between the probe and the circuit ground. If the light is on, the open is between the probe and end of the circuit toward the power source.

Short Circuit Testing

By isolating the circuit both from power and from ground, and using a self-powered test light, you can check for shorts to ground in the circuit. Isolate the circuit from power and ground. Connect the test light ground clip to a good ground and probe any easy-to-reach test point in the circuit. If the light comes on, there is a short somewhere in the circuit. To isolate the short, probe a test point at either end of the isolated circuit (the light should be on). Leave the test light probe connected and open connectors, switches, remove parts, etc., sequentially, until the light goes out. When the light goes out, the short is between the last circuit component opened and the previous circuit opened.

NOTE: *The 1.5 volt battery in the test light does not provide much current. A weak battery may not provide enough power to illuminate the test light even when a complete circuit is made (especially if there are high resistances in the circuit). Always make sure that the test battery is strong. To check the battery, briefly touch the ground clip to the probe; if the light glows brightly the battery is strong enough for testing. Never use a self-powered test light to perform checks for opens or shorts when power is applied to the electrical system under test. The 12 volt vehicle power will quickly burn out the 1.5 volt light bulb in the test light.*

Voltmeter

A voltmeter is used to measure voltage at any point in a circuit, or to measure the voltage drop across any part of a circuit. It can also be used to check continuity in a wire or circuit by indicating current flow from one end to the other. Voltmeters usually have various scales on the meter dial and a selector switch to allow the selection of different voltages. The voltmeter has a positive and a negative lead. To avoid damage to the meter, always connect the negative lead to the negative (–) side of circuit (to ground or nearest the ground side of the circuit) and connect the positive lead to the positive (+) side of the circuit (to the power source or the nearest power source). Note that the negative voltmeter lead will always be black and that the positive voltmeter will always be some color other than black (usually red). Depending on how the voltmeter is connected into the circuit, it has several uses.

A voltmeter can be connected either in parallel or in series with a circuit and it has a very high resistance to current flow. When connected in parallel, only a small amount of current will flow through the voltmeter current path; the rest will flow through the normal circuit current path and the circuit will work normally. When the voltmeter is connected in series with a circuit, only a small amount of current can flow through the circuit. The circuit will not work properly, but the voltmeter reading will show if the circuit is complete or not.

Available Voltage Measurement

Set the voltmeter selector switch to the 20V position and connect the meter negative lead to the negative post of the battery. Connect the positive meter lead to the positive post of the battery and turn the ignition switch ON to provide a load. Read the voltage on the meter or digital display. A well charged battery should register over 12 volts. If the meter reads below 11.5 volts, the battery power may be insufficient to operate the electrical system properly. This test determines voltage available from the battery and should be the first step in any electrical trouble diagnosis procedure. Many electrical problems, especially on computer controlled systems, can be caused by a low state of charge in the battery. Excessive corrosion at the battery cable terminals can cause a poor contact that will prevent proper charging and full battery current flow.

Normal battery voltage is 12 volts when fully charged. When the battery is supplying current to one or more circuits it is said to be "under load". When everything is off the electrical system is under a "no-load" condition. A fully charged battery may show about 12.5 volts at no load; will drop to 12 volts under medium load; and will drop even lower under heavy load. If the battery is partially discharged the voltage decrease under heavy load may be excessive, even though the battery shows 12 volts or more at no load. When allowed to discharge further, the battery's available voltage under load will decrease more severely. For this reason, it is important that the battery be fully charged during all testing procedures to avoid errors in diagnosis and incorrect test results.

Voltage Drop

When current flows through a resistance, the voltage beyond the resistance is reduced (the larger the current, the greater the reduction in voltage). When no current is flowing, there is no voltage drop because there is no current flow. All points in the circuit which are connected to the power source are at the same voltage as the power source. The total voltage drop always equals the total source voltage. In a long circuit with many connectors, a series of small, unwanted voltage drops due to corrosion at the connectors can add up to a total loss of voltage which impairs the operation of the normal loads in the circuit.

INDIRECT COMPUTATION OF VOLTAGE DROPS

1. Set the voltmeter selector switch to the 20 volt position.
2. Connect the meter negative lead to a good ground.
3. Probe all resistances in the circuit with the positive meter lead.

4. Operate the circuit in all modes and observe the voltage readings.

DIRECT MEASUREMENT OF VOLTAGE DROPS

1. Set the voltmeter switch to the 20 volt position.

2. Connect the voltmeter negative lead to the ground side of the resistance load to be measured.

3. Connect the positive lead to the positive side of the resistance or load to be measured.

4. Read the voltage drop directly on the 20 volt scale.

Too high a voltage indicates too high a resistance. If, for example, a blower motor runs too slowly, you can determine if there is too high a resistance in the resistor pack. By taking voltage drop readings in all parts of the circuit, you can isolate the problem. Too low a voltage drop indicates too low a resistance. If, for example, a blower motor runs too fast in the MED and/or LOW position, the problem can be isolated in the resistor pack by taking voltage drop readings in all parts of the circuit to locate a possibly shorted resistor. The maximum allowable voltage drop under load is critical, especially if there is more than one high resistance problem in a circuit because all voltage drops are cumulative. A small drop is normal due to the resistance of the conductors.

HIGH RESISTANCE TESTING

1. Set the voltmeter selector switch to the 4 volt position.

2. Connect the voltmeter positive lead to the positive post of the battery.

3. Turn on the headlights and heater blower to provide a load.

4. Probe various points in the circuit with the negative voltmeter lead.

5. Read the voltage drop on the 4 volt scale. Some average maximum allowable voltage drops are:

FUSE PANEL: 7 volts
IGNITION SWITCH: 5 volts
HEADLIGHT SWITCH: 7 volts
IGNITION COIL (+): 5 volts
ANY OTHER LOAD: 1.3 volts
NOTE: *Voltage drops are all measured while a load is operating; without current flow, there will be no voltage drop.*

Ohmmeter

The ohmmeter is designed to read resistance (ohms) in a circuit or component. Although there are several different styles of ohmmeters, all will usually have a selector switch which permits the measurement of different ranges of resistance (usually the selector switch allows the multiplication of the meter reading by 10, 100, 1,000, and 10,000). A calibration knob allows the meter to be set at zero for accurate measurement. Since all ohmmeters are powered by an internal battery (usually 9 volts), the ohmmeter can be used as a self-powered test light. When the ohmmeter is connected, current from the ohmmeter flows through the circuit or component being tested. Since the ohmmeter's internal resistance and voltage are known values, the amount of current flow through the meter depends on the resistance of the circuit or component being tested.

The ohmmeter can be used to perform continuity test for opens or shorts (either by observation of the meter needle or as a self-powered test light), and to read actual resistance in a circuit. It should be noted that the ohmmeter is used to check the resistance of a component or wire while there is no voltage applied to the circuit. Current flow from an outside voltage source (such as the vehicle battery) can damage the ohmmeter, so the circuit or component should be isolated from the vehicle electrical system before any testing is done. Since the ohmmeter uses its own voltage source, either lead can be connected to any test point.

NOTE: *When checking diodes or other solid state components, the ohmmeter leads can only be connected one way in order to measure current flow in a single direction. Make sure the positive (+) and negative (–) terminal connections are as described in the test procedures to verify the one-way diode operation.*

In using the meter for making continuity checks, do not be concerned with the actual resistance readings. Zero resistance, or any resistance readings, indicate continuity in the circuit. Infinite resistance indicates an open in the circuit. A high resistance reading where there should be none indicates a problem in the circuit. Checks for short circuits are made in the same manner as checks for open circuits except that the circuit must be isolated from both power and normal ground. Infinite resistance indicates no continuity to ground, while zero resistance indicates a dead short to ground.

RESISTANCE MEASUREMENT

The batteries in an ohmmeter will weaken with age and temperature, so the ohmmeter must be calibrated or "zeroed" before taking measurements. To zero the meter, place the selector switch in its lowest range and touch the two ohmmeter leads together. Turn the calibration knob until the meter needle is exactly on zero.

NOTE: *All analog (needle) type ohmmeters must be zeroed before use, but some digital ohmmeter models are automatically calibrated when the switch is turned on. Self-calibrating digital ohmmeters do not have an adjusting knob, but its a good idea to check for a zero readout before use by touching the leads together. All computer controlled systems require the use of a digital ohmmeter with at least 10 megohms impedance for testing. Before any test procedures are attempted, make sure the ohmmeter used is compatible with the electrical system or damage to the on-board computer could result.*

To measure resistance, first isolate the circuit from the vehicle power source by disconnecting the battery cables or the harness connector. Make sure the key is OFF when disconnecting any components or the battery. Where necessary, also isolate at least one side of the circuit to be checked to avoid reading parallel resistances. Parallel circuit resistances will always give a lower reading than the actual resistance of either of the branches. When measuring the resistance of parallel circuits, the total resistance will always be lower than the smallest resistance in the circuit. Connect the meter leads to both sides of the circuit (wire or component) and read the actual measured ohms on the meter scale. Make sure the selector switch is set to the proper ohm scale for the circuit being tested to avoid misreading the ohmmeter test value.

WARNING: *Never use an ohmmeter with power applied to the circuit. Like the self-powered test light, the ohmmeter is designed to operate on its own power supply. The normal 12 volt automotive electrical system current could damage the meter!*

Ammeters

An ammeter measures the amount of current flowing through a circuit in units called amperes or amps. Amperes are units of electron flow which indicate how fast the electrons are flowing through the circuit. Since Ohms Law dictates that current flow in a circuit is equal to the circuit voltage divided by the total circuit resistance, increasing voltage also increases the current level (amps). Likewise, any decrease in resistance will increase the amount of amps in a circuit. At normal operating voltage, most circuits have a characteristic amount of amperes, called "current draw" which can be measured using an ammeter. By referring to a specified current draw rating, measuring the amperes, and comparing the two values, one can determine what is happening within the circuit to aid in diagnosis. An open circuit, for example, will not allow any current to flow so the ammeter reading will be zero. More current flows through a heavily loaded circuit or when the charging system is operating.

An ammeter is always connected in series with the circuit being tested. All of the current that normally flows through the circuit must also flow through the ammeter; if there is any other path for the current to follow, the ammeter reading will not be accurate. The ammeter itself has very little resistance to current flow and therefore will not affect the circuit, but it will measure current draw only when the circuit is closed and electricity is flowing. Excessive current draw can blow fuses and drain the battery, while a reduced current draw can cause motors to run slowly, lights to dim and other components to not operate properly. The ammeter can help diagnose these conditions by locating the cause of the high or low reading.

Multimeters

Different combinations of test meters can be built into a single unit designed for specific tests. Some of the more common combination test devices are known as Volt/Amp testers, Tach/Dwell meters, or Digital Multimeters. The Volt/Amp tester is used for charging system, starting system or battery tests and consists of a voltmeter, an ammeter and a variable resistance carbon pile. The voltmeter will usually have at least two ranges for use with 6, 12 and 24 volt systems. The ammeter also has more than one range for testing various levels of battery loads and starter current draw and the carbon pile can be adjusted to offer different amounts of resistance. The Volt/Amp tester has heavy leads to carry large amounts of current and many later models have an inductive ammeter pickup that clamps around the wire to simplify test connections. On some models, the ammeter also has a zero-center scale to allow testing of charging and starting systems without switching leads or polarity. A digital multimeter is a voltmeter, ammeter and ohmmeter combined in an instrument which gives a digital readout. These are often used when testing solid state circuits because of their high input impedance (usually 10 megohms or more).

The tach/dwell meter combines a tachometer and a dwell (cam angle) meter and is a specialized kind of voltmeter. The tachometer scale is marked to show engine speed in rpm and the dwell scale is marked to show degrees of distributor shaft rotation. In most electronic ignition systems, dwell is determined by the control unit, but the dwell meter can also be used to check the duty cycle (operation) of some electronic engine control systems. Some tach/dwell meters are powered by an internal battery, while others take their power from the car battery in use. The battery powered testers usually require calibration much like an ohmmeter before testing.

Special Test Equipment

A variety of diagnostic tools are available to help troubleshoot and repair computerized engine control systems. The most sophisticated of these devices are the console type engine analyzers that usually occupy a garage service bay, but there are several types of aftermarket electronic testers available that will allow quick circuit tests of the engine control system by plugging directly into a special connector located in the engine compartment or under the dashboard. Several tool and equipment manufacturers offer simple, hand held testers that measure various circuit voltage levels on command to check all system components for proper operation. Although these testers usually cost about $300-500, consider that the average computer control unit (or ECM) can cost just as much and the money saved by not replacing perfectly good sensors or components in an attempt to correct a problem could justify the purchase price of a special diagnostic tester the first time it's used.

These computerized testers can allow quick and easy test measurements while the engine is operating or while the car is being driven. In addition, the on-board computer memory can be read to access any stored trouble codes; in effect allowing the computer to tell you where it hurts and aid trouble diagnosis by pinpointing exactly which circuit or component is malfunctioning. In the same manner, repairs can be tested to make sure the problem has been corrected. The biggest advantage these special testers have is their relatively easy hookups that minimize or eliminate the chances of making the wrong connections and getting false voltage readings or damaging the computer accidentally.

NOTE: *It should be remembered that these testers check voltage levels in circuits; they don't detect mechanical problems or failed components if the circuit voltage falls within the preprogrammed limits stored in the tester PROM unit. Also, most of the hand held testers are designed to work only on one or two systems made by a specific manufacturer.*

A variety of aftermarket testers are available to help diagnose different computerized control systems. Owatonna Tool Company (OTC), for example, markets a device called the OTC Monitor which plugs directly into the assembly line diagnostic link (ALDL). The OTC tester makes diagnosis a simple matter of pressing the correct buttons and, by changing the internal PROM or inserting a different diagnosis cartridge, it will work on any model from full size to subcompact, over a wide range of years. An adapter is supplied with the tester to allow connection to all types of ALDL links, regardless of the number of pin terminals used. By inserting an updated PROM into the OTC tester, it can be easily updated to diagnose any new modifications of computerized control systems.

Wiring Harnesses

The average automobile contains about ½ mile of wiring, with hundreds of individual connections. To protect the many wires from damage and to keep them from becoming a confusing tangle, they are organized into bundles, enclosed in plastic or taped together and called wire harnesses. Different wiring harnesses serve different parts of the vehicle. Individual wires are color coded to help trace them through a harness where sections are hidden from view.

A loose or corroded connection or a replacement wire that is too small for the circuit will add extra resistance and an additional voltage drop to the circuit. A ten percent voltage drop can result in slow or erratic motor operation, for example, even though the circuit is complete. Automotive wiring or circuit conductors can be in any one of three forms:

1. Single strand wire
2. Multi-strand wire
3. Printed circuitry

Single strand wire has a solid metal core and is usually used inside such components as alternators, motors, relays and other devices. Multi-strand wire has a core made of many small strands of wire twisted together into a single conductor. Most of the wiring in an automotive electrical system is made up of multi-strand wire, either as a single conductor or grouped together in a harness. All wiring is color coded on the insulator, either as a solid color or as a colored wire with an identification stripe. A printed circuit is a thin film of copper or other conductor that is printed on an insulator backing. Occasionally, a printed circuit is sandwiched between two sheets of plastic for more protection and flexibility. A complete printed circuit, consisting of conductors, insulating material and connectors for lamps or other components is called a printed circuit board. Printed circuitry is used in place of individual wires or harnesses in places where space is limited, such as behind instrument panels.

Wire Gauge

Since computer controlled automotive electrical systems are very sensitive to changes in resistance, the selection of properly sized wires is critical when systems are repaired. The wire gauge number is an expression of the cross section area of the conductor. The most common system for expressing wire size is the American Wire Gauge (AWG) system.

Wire cross section area is measured in circular mils. A mil is $\frac{1}{1000}$ in. (0.001 in. or 0.0254mm); a circular mil is the area of a circle one mil in diameter. For example, a conductor ¼ in. (6mm) in diameter is 0.250 in. or 250 mils. The circular mil cross section area of the wire is 250 squared (250^2)or 62,500 circular mils. Imported car models usually use metric wire gauge designations, which is simply the cross section area of the conductor in square millimeters (mm^2).

Gauge numbers are assigned to conductors of various cross section areas. As gauge number increases, area decreases and the conductor becomes smaller. A 5 gauge conductor is smaller than a 1 gauge conductor and a 10 gauge is smaller than a 5 gauge. As the cross section area of a conductor decreases, resistance increases and so does the gauge number. A conductor with a higher gauge number will carry less current than a conductor with a lower gauge number.

NOTE: *Gauge wire size refers to the size of the conductor, not the size of the complete wire. It is possible to have two wires of the same gauge with different diameters because one may have thicker insulation than the other.*

12 volt automotive electrical systems generally use 10, 12, 14, 16 and 18 gauge wire. Main power distribution circuits and larger accessories usually use 10 and 12 gauge wire. Battery cables are usually 4 or 6 gauge, although 1 and 2 gauge wires are occasionally used. Wire length must also be considered when making repairs to a circuit. As conductor length increases, so does resistance. *An 18 gauge wire, for example, can carry a 10 amp load for 10 feet without excessive voltage drop; however if a 15 foot wire is required for the same 10 amp load, it must be a 16 gauge wire.*

An electrical schematic shows the electrical current paths when a circuit is operating properly. It is essential to understand how a circuit works before trying to figure out why it doesn't. Schematics break the entire electrical system down into individual circuits and show only one particular circuit. In a schematic, no attempt is made to represent wiring and components as they physically appear on the vehicle; switches and other components are shown as simply as possible. Face views of harness connectors show the cavity or terminal locations in all multi-pin connectors to help locate test points.

If you need to backprobe a connector while it is on the component, the order of the terminals must be mentally reversed. The wire color code can help in this situation, as well as a keyway, lock tab or other reference mark.

NOTE: *Wiring diagrams are not included in this book. As trucks have become more complex and available with longer option lists, wiring diagrams have grown in size and complexity. It has become almost impossible to provide a readable reproduction of a wiring diagram in a book this size. Information on ordering wiring diagrams from the vehicle manufacturer can be found in the owner's manual.*

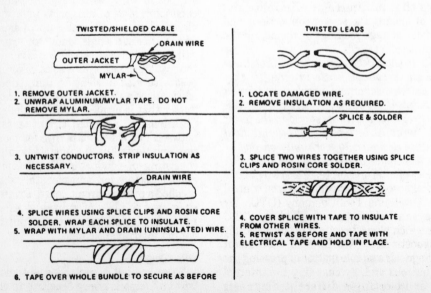

TWISTED/SHIELDED CABLE

ORAIN WIRE
OUTER JACKET
MYLAR

1. REMOVE OUTER JACKET.
2. UNWRAP ALUMINUM/MYLAR TAPE. DO NOT REMOVE MYLAR.

3. UNTWIST CONDUCTORS. STRIP INSULATION AS NECESSARY.

DRAIN WIRE

4. SPLICE WIRES USING SPLICE CLIPS AND ROSIN CORE SOLDER. WRAP EACH SPLICE TO INSULATE.
5. WRAP WITH MYLAR AND DRAIN (UNINSULATED) WIRE.

6. TAPE OVER WHOLE BUNDLE TO SECURE AS BEFORE

TWISTED LEADS

1. LOCATE DAMAGED WIRE.
2. REMOVE INSULATION AS REQUIRED.

SPLICE & SOLDER

3. SPLICE TWO WIRES TOGETHER USING SPLICE CLIPS AND ROSIN CORE SOLDER.

4. COVER SPLICE WITH TAPE TO INSULATE FROM OTHER WIRES.
5. RETWIST AS BEFORE AND TAPE WITH ELECTRICAL TAPE AND HOLD IN PLACE.

Wiring repairs

WIRING REPAIR

Soldering is a quick, efficient method of joining metals permanently. Everyone who has the occasion to make wiring repairs should know how to solder. Electrical connections that are soldered are far less likely to come apart and will conduct electricity much better than connections that are only "pig-tailed" together. The most popular (and preferred) method of soldering is with an electrical soldering gun. Soldering irons are available in many sizes and wattage ratings. Irons with higher wattage ratings deliver higher temperatures and recover lost heat faster. A small soldering iron rated for no more than 50 watts is recommended, especially on electrical systems where excess heat can damage the components being soldered.

There are three ingredients necessary for successful soldering; proper flux, good solder and sufficient heat. A soldering flux is necessary to clean the metal of tarnish, prepare it for soldering and to enable the solder to spread into tiny crevices. When soldering, always use a resin flux or resin core solder which is non-corrosive and will not attract moisture once the job is finished. Other types of flux (acid core) will leave a residue that will attract moisture and cause the wires to corrode. Tin is a unique metal with a low melting point. In a molten state, it dissolves and alloys easily with many metals. Solder is made by mixing tin with lead. The most common proportions are 40/60, 50/50 and 60/40, with the percentage of tin listed first. Low priced solders usually contain less tin, making them very difficult for a beginner to use because more heat is required to melt the solder. A common solder is 40/60 which is well suited for all-around general use, but 60/40 melts easier, has more tin for a better joint and is preferred for electrical work.

Soldering Techniques

Successful soldering requires that the metals to be joined be heated to a temperature that will melt the solder, usually 360-460°F (182-238°C). Contrary to popular belief, the purpose of the soldering iron is not to melt the solder itself, but to heat the parts being soldered to a temperature high enough to melt the solder when it is touched to the work. Melting flux-cored solder on the soldering iron will usually destroy the effectiveness of the flux.

NOTE: *Soldering tips are made of copper for good heat conductivity, but must be "tinned" regularly for quick transference of heat to the project and to prevent the solder from sticking to the iron. To "tin" the iron, simply heat it and touch the flux-cored solder to the tip; the solder will flow over the hot tip. Wipe the*
excess off with a clean rag, but be careful as the iron will be hot.

After some use, the tip may become pitted. If so, simply dress the tip smooth with a smooth file and "tin" the tip again. An old saying holds that "metals well cleaned are half soldered." Flux-cored solder will remove oxides but rust, bits of insulation and oil or grease must be removed with a wire brush or emery cloth. For maximum strength in soldered parts, the joint must start off clean and tight. Weak joints will result in gaps too wide for the solder to bridge.

If a separate soldering flux is used, it should be brushed or swabbed on only those areas that are to be soldered. Most solders contain a core of flux and separate fluxing is unnecessary. Hold the work to be soldered firmly. It is best to solder on a wooden board, because a metal vise will only rob the piece to be soldered of heat and make it difficult to melt the solder. Hold the soldering tip with the broadest face against the work to be soldered. Apply solder under the tip close to the work, using enough solder to give a heavy film between the iron and the piece being soldered, while moving slowly and making sure the solder melts properly. Keep the work level or the solder will run to the lowest part and favor the thicker parts, because these require more heat to melt the solder. If the soldering tip overheats (the solder coating on the face of the tip burns up), it should be retinned. Once the soldering is completed, let the soldered joint stand until cool. Tape and seal all soldered wire splices after the repair has cooled.

Wire Harness and Connectors

The on-board computer (ECM) wire harness electrically connects the control unit to the various solenoids, switches and sensors used by the control system. Most connectors in the engine compartment or otherwise exposed to the elements are protected against moisture and dirt which could create oxidation and deposits on the terminals. This protection is important because of the very low voltage and current levels used by the computer and sensors. All connectors have a lock which secures the male and female terminals together, with a secondary lock holding the seal and terminal into the connector. Both terminal locks must be released when disconnecting ECM connectors.

These special connectors are weather-proof and all repairs require the use of a special terminal and the tool required to service it. This tool is used to remove the pin and sleeve terminals. If removal is attempted with an ordinary pick, there is a good chance that the terminal will be bent or deformed. Unlike standard blade type terminals, these terminals cannot be straightened once they are bent. Make certain that the connectors are properly seated and all of the sealing rings in place when connecting leads. On some models, a hinge-type flap provides a backup or secondary locking feature for the terminals. Most secondary locks are used to improve the connector reliability by retaining the terminals if the small terminal lock tangs are not positioned properly.

Molded-on connectors require complete replacement of the connection. This means splicing a new connector assembly into the harness. All splices in on-board computer systems should be soldered to insure proper contact. Use care when probing the connections or replacing terminals in them as it is possible to short between opposite terminals. If this happens to the wrong terminal pair, it is possible to damage certain components. Always use jumper wires between connectors for circuit checking and never probe through weatherproof seals.

Open circuits are often difficult to locate by sight because corrosion or terminal misalignment are hidden by the connectors. Merely wiggling a connector on a sensor or in the wiring harness may correct the open circuit condition. This should always be considered when an open circuit or a failed sensor is indicated. Intermittent problems may also be caused by oxidized or loose connections. When using a circuit tester for diagnosis, always probe connections from the wire side. Be careful not to damage sealed connectors with test probes.

All wiring harnesses should be replaced with identical parts, using the same gauge wire and connectors. When signal wires are spliced into a harness, use wire with high temperature insulation only. With the low voltage and current levels found in the system, it is important that the best possible connection at all wire splices be made by soldering the splices together. It is seldom necessary to replace a complete harness. If replacement is necessary, pay close attention to insure proper harness routing. Secure the harness with suitable plastic wire clamps to prevent vibrations from causing the harness to wear in spots or contact any hot components.

NOTE: *Weatherproof connectors cannot be replaced with standard connectors. Instructions are provided with replacement connector and terminal packages. Some wire harnesses have mounting indicators (usually pieces of colored tape) to mark where the harness is to be secured.*

In making wiring repairs, it's important that you always replace damaged wires with wires that are the same gauge as the wire being replaced. The heavier the wire, the smaller the gauge number. Wires are color-coded to aid in identification and whenever possible the same color coded wire should be used for replacement. A wire stripping and crimping tool is necessary to install solderless terminal connectors. Test all crimps by pulling on the wires; it should not be possible to pull the wires out of a good crimp.

Wires which are open, exposed or otherwise damaged are repaired by simple splicing. Where possible, if the wiring harness is accessible and the damaged place in the wire can be located, it is best to open the harness and check for all possible damage. In an inaccessible harness, the wire must be bypassed with a new insert, usually taped to the outside of the old harness.

When replacing fusible links, be sure to use fusible link wire, NOT ordinary automotive wire. Make sure the fusible segment is of the same gauge and construction as the one being replaced and double the stripped end when crimping the terminal connector for a good contact. The melted (open) fusible link segment of the wiring harness should be cut off as close to the harness as possible, then a new segment spliced in as described. In the case of a damaged fusible link that feeds two harness wires, the harness connections should be replaced with two fusible link wires so that each circuit will have its own separate protection.

NOTE: *Most of the problems caused in the wiring harness are due to bad ground connections. Always check all vehicle ground connections for corrosion or looseness before performing any power feed checks to eliminate the chance of a bad ground affecting the circuit.*

Repairing Hard Shell Connectors

Unlike molded connectors, the terminal contacts in hard shell connectors can be replaced. Weatherproof hard-shell connectors with the leads molded into the shell have non-replaceable terminal ends. Replacement usually involves the use of a special terminal removal tool that depress the locking tangs (barbs) on the connector terminal and allow the connector to be removed from the rear of the shell. The connector shell should be replaced if it shows any evidence of burning, melting, cracks, or breaks. Replace individual terminals that are burnt, corroded, distorted or loose.

NOTE: *The insulation crimp must be tight to prevent the insulation from sliding back on the wire when the wire is pulled. The insulation must be visibly compressed under the crimp tabs, and the ends of the crimp should be turned in for a firm grip on the insulation.*

The wire crimp must be made with all wire strands inside the crimp. The terminal must be fully compressed on the wire strands with the ends of the crimp tabs turned in to make a firm grip on the wire. Check all connections with an ohmmeter to insure a good contact. There should be no measurable resistance between the wire and the terminal when connected.

Mechanical Test Equipment

Vacuum Gauge

Most gauges are graduated in inches of mercury (in. Hg.), although a device called a manometer reads vacuum in inches of water (in. Hg.). The normal vacuum reading usually varies between 18 and 22 in.Hg at sea level. To test engine vacuum, the vacuum gauge must be connected to a source of manifold vacuum. Many engines have a plug in the intake manifold which can be removed and replaced with an adapter fitting. Connect the vacuum gauge to the fitting with a suitable rubber hose or, if no manifold plug is available, connect the vacuum gauge to any device using manifold vacuum, such as EGR valves, etc. The vacuum gauge can be used to determine if enough vacuum is reaching a component to allow its actuation.

Hand Vacuum Pump

Small, hand-held vacuum pumps come in a variety of designs. Most have a built-in vacuum gauge and allow the component to be tested without removing it from the vehicle. Operate the pump lever or plunger to apply the correct amount of vacuum required for the test specified in the diagnosis routines. The level of vacuum in inches of Mercury (in.Hg) is indicated on the pump gauge. For some testing, an additional vacuum gauge may be necessary.

Intake manifold vacuum is used to operate various systems and devices on late model vehicles. To correctly diagnose and solve problems in vacuum control systems, a vacuum source is necessary for testing. In some cases, vacuum can be taken from the intake manifold when the engine is running, but vacuum is normally provided by a hand vacuum pump. These hand vacuum pumps have a built-in vacuum gauge that allow testing while the device is still attached to the component. For some tests, an additional vacuum gauge may be necessary.

Fuse Link

The fuse link is a short length of special, Hypalon (high temperature) insulated wire, integral with the engine compartment wiring harness and should not be confused with standard wire. It is several wire gauges smaller than the circuit which it protects. Under no circumstances should a fuse link replacement repair be made using a length of standard wire

cut from bulk stock or from another wiring harness.

To repair any blown fuse link use the following procedure:

1. Determine which circuit is damaged, its location and the cause of the open fuse link. If the damaged fuse link is one of three fed by a common No. 10 or 12 gauge feed wire, determine the specific affected circuit.

2. Disconnect the negative battery cable.

3. Cut the damaged fuse link from the wiring harness and discard it. If the fuse link is one of three circuits fed by a single feed wire, cut it out of the harness at each splice end and discard it.

4. Identify and procure the proper fuse link and butt connectors for attaching the fuse link to the harness.

5. To repair any fuse link in a 3-link group with one feed:

   a. After cutting the open link out of the harness, cut each of the remaining undamaged fuse links close to the feed wire weld.

   b. Strip approximately ½ in. (13mm) of insulation from the detached ends of the two good fuse links, Then insert two wire ends into one end of a butt connector and carefully push one stripped end of the replacement fuse link into the same end of the butt connector and crimp all three firmly together. NOTE: *Care must be taken when fitting the three fuse links into the butt connector as the internal diameter is a snug fit for three wires. Make sure to use a proper crimping tool. Pliers, side cutter, etc. will not apply the proper crimp to retain the wires and withstand a pull test.*

   c. After crimping the butt connector to the three fuse links, cut the weld portion from the feed wire and strip approximately ½ in. (13mm) of insulation from the cut end. Insert the stripped end into the open end of the butt connector and crimp very firmly.

   d. To attach the remaining end of the replacement fuse link, strip approximately ½ in. (13mm) of insulation from the wire end of the circuit from which the blown fuse link was removed, and firmly crimp a butt connector or equivalent to the stripped wire. Then, insert the end of the replacement link into the other end of the butt connector and crimp firmly.

   e. Using rosin core solder with a consistency of 60 percent tin and 40 percent lead, solder the connectors and the wires at the repairs and insulate with electrical tape.

6. To replace any fuse link on a single circuit in a harness, cut out the damaged portion, strip approximately ½ in. (13mm) of insulation from the two wire ends and attach the appropriate replacement fuse link to the stripped wire ends

with two proper size butt connectors. Solder the connectors and wires and insulate with tape.

7. To repair any fuse link which has an eyelet terminal on one end such as the charging circuit, cut off the open fuse link behind the weld, strip approximately ½ in. (13mm) of insulation from the cut end and attach the appropriate new eyelet fuse link to the cut stripped wire with an appropriate size butt connector. Solder the connectors and wires at the repair and insulate with tape.

8. Connect the negative battery cable to the battery and test the system for proper operation.

NOTE: *Do not mistake a resistor wire for a fuse link. The resistor wire is generally longer and has print stating, "Resistor-don't cut or splice".*

When attaching a single No. 16, 17, 18 or 20 gauge fuse link to a heavy gauge wire, always double the stripped wire end of the fuse link before inserting and crimping it into the butt connector for positive wire retention.

HEATER

Blower Motor
REMOVAL AND INSTALLATION

1. Disconnect the negative battery cable. If necessary, remove the diagonal fender brace at the right rear corner of the engine compartment to gain access to the blower motor.

2. Disconnect the electrical wiring from the blower motor. If equipped with air conditioning, remove the blower relay and bracket as an assembly and swing them aside.

3. Remove the blower motor cooling tube.

4. Remove the blower motor retaining screws.

5. Remove the blower motor and fan as an assembly from the case.

6. To install, position the blower motor into place and install the retaining screws.

7. Install the blower motor cooling tube.

8. Connect all the electrical connections.

9. Connect the negative battery cable.

Heater Core

REMOVAL AND INSTALLATION

CAUTION: *When draining the coolant, keep in mind that cats and dogs are attracted by the ethylene glycol antifreeze, and are quite likely to drink any that is left in an uncovered container or in puddles on the ground. This will prove fatal in sufficient quantity. Always drain the coolant into a sealable container. Coolant should be reused unless it is contaminated or several years old.*

1982–86

1. Drain the cooling system.

2. Remove both heater hoses.

3. Remove the lower right hush panel.

4. Remove the lower right instrument panel and the ESC module if necessary.

5. Remove the lower right instrument panel to cowl screw.

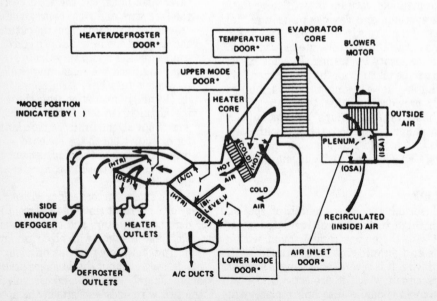

Heater and A/C airflow

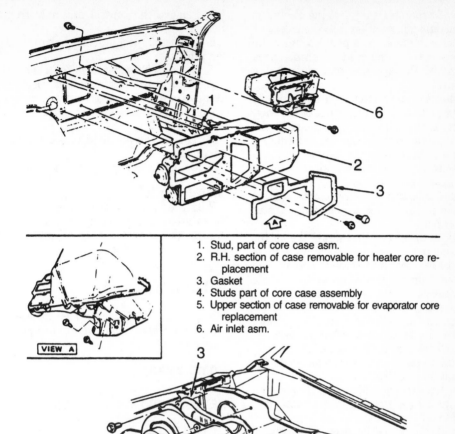

1. Stud, part of core case asm.
2. R.H. section of case removable for heater core replacement
3. Gasket
4. Studs part of core case assembly
5. Upper section of case removable for evaporator core replacement
6. Air inlet asm.

A/C module and heater core servicing

6. Remove the heater case screws.

NOTE: *The upper left screw may be reached with a long socket extension. Carefully lift the lower right corner of the instrument panel to align the extension.*

7. Remove the case cover.

8. Remove the support plate and baffle screws.

9. Remove the heater core and baffle plate from the housing.

10. To install, position the heater core and baffle plate into the housing.

11. Install the support plate and baffle screws.

12. Install the case cover.

13. Install the heater case screws.

14. Install the lower right instrument panel to cowl screw.

15. Install the lower right instrument panel and the ESC module if necessary.

16. Install the lower right hush panel.

17. Install both heater hoses.

18. Fill the cooling system and check for leaks.

1987–92

1. Disconnect the negative battery cable. Drain the cooling system. Disconnect the heater hoses.

2. Remove the right and left lower hush panel. Remove the upper dash pad.

3. Remove both front speaker retaining nuts. Remove the side window defrost duct retaining nuts, front carrier braces and carrier shelf. Remove both side window defrost ducts.

4. Remove the 2 screws securing the right

speaker and bracket. Disconnect the electronic control module and position it to the side.

5. Remove the radio trim plate. Remove the upper console trim. Remove the console glove box assembly. Remove the emergency brake handle grip.

6. Remove the screws that secure the console body and position the assembly out of the way.

7. Remove the trim plate from under the steering column. Remove the steering column retaining nuts and lower the column.

8. Remove the nuts and screws that retain the instrument panel carrier.

9. Move the instrument panel carrier back to gain access to the heater core and the heater core upper bolt.

10. Remove the screws that secure the heater core housing cover. Remove the screws that secure the heater core and shroud. Remove the heater core from the shroud assembly.

11. To install, install the heater core to the shroud assembly. Install the screws that secure the heater core and shroud. Install the screws that secure the heater core housing cover.

12. Install the instrument panel carrier.

13. Install the nuts and screws that retain the instrument panel carrier.

14. Install the trim plate to under the steering column. Install the steering column retaining nuts and lower the column.

15. Install the screws that secure the console body and position the assembly out of the way.

16. Install the emergency brake handle grip. Install the console glove box assembly. Install the upper console trim. Install the radio trim plate.

17. Connect the electronic control module and position it to the side. Install the 2 screws securing the right speaker and bracket.

18. Install both side window defrost ducts. Install the side window defrost duct retaining nuts, front carrier braces and carrier shelf. Install both front speaker retaining nuts.

19. Install the upper dash pad. Install the right and left lower hush panel.

20. Connect the heater hoses. Connect the negative battery cable. Fill the cooling system and check for leaks.

Control Head

REMOVAL AND INSTALLATION

1. Disconnect the negative battery cable.

2. Remove the air condition/radio console trim plate.

3. Remove the air condition control retaining screws.

4. Pull the assembly forward, disconnect the electrical and vacuum connections. Remove the temperature control cable.

5. Remove the control assembly from the vehicle.

6. To install, position the control head into the vehicle.

7. Install the temperature control cable.

8. Connect the electrical and vacuum connections and push the assembly rearward.

9. Install the air condition control retaining screws.

10. Install the air condition/radio console trim plate.

11. Connect the negative battery cable.

Blower Switch

With the control head removed from the vehicle the blower switch may be removed by pulling the blower switch knob off and removing the retaining clip from the switch.

AIR CONDITIONER

NOTE: *Refer to Chapter 1 for all air conditioning system evacuating and charging procedures.*

Compressor

REMOVAL AND INSTALLATION

1. Refer to Chapter 1 for discharging the A/C system.

2. Remove fitting block (coupled hose assembly) bolt at rear of compressor.

3. Remove mounting bracket bolt(s).

4. Remove drive belt (Route lower loop behind crankshaft pulley to gain additional slack if required).

5. Remove compressor.

6. To install, use new O-rings lubricated with refrigerant oil.

7. Install the compressor.

8. Install the drive belt.

9. Install the mounting bracket and bolts.

10. Install the fitting block bolt at the rear of the compressor.

11. Refer to Chapter 1 for charging the A/C system.

ENTERTAINMENT SYSTEMS

Radio

REMOVAL AND INSTALLATION

Except Berlinetta

1. Disconnect the negative battery cable.

2. Remove the console bezel screws.

3. Remove the radio to console attaching screws.

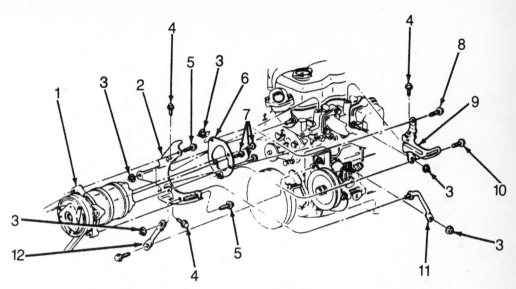

1. Compressor asm
2. Bracket
3. Nut 40–60 N·m (30–44 ft. lbs.)
4. Bolt/screw 40–60 N·m (30–44 ft. lbs.)
5. Bolt screw 40–60 N·m (30–44 ft. lbs.)
6. Bracket
7. Bolt/screw 20–34 N·m (15–25 ft. lbs.)
8. Bolt/screw
9. Bracket
10. Bolt/screw 40–60 N·m (30–44 ft. lbs.)
11. Brace
12. Brace

A/C compressor removal—4 cylinder engine

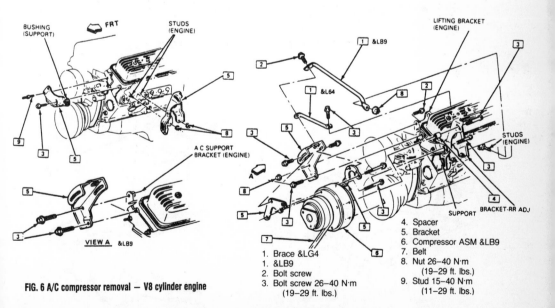

1. Brace &LG4
1. &LB9
2. Bolt screw
3. Bolt screw 26–40 N·m
   (19–29 ft. lbs.)
4. Spacer
5. Bracket
6. Compressor ASM &LB9
7. Belt
8. Nut 26–40 N·m
   (19–29 ft. lbs.)
9. Stud 15–40 N·m
   (11–29 ft. lbs.)

VIEW A &LB9

FIG. 6 A/C compressor removal – V8 cylinder engine

A/C compressor removal—V8 cylinder engine

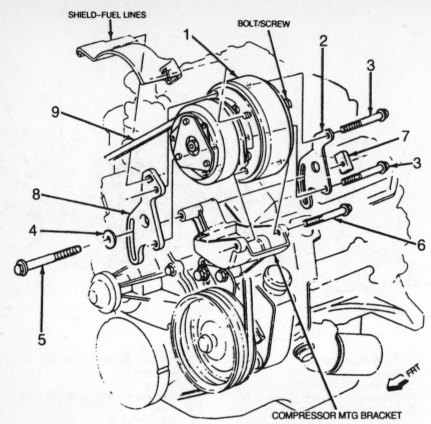

SHIELD–FUEL LINES

BOLT/SCREW

COMPRESSOR MTG BRACKET

FRT

1. Compressor asm
2. Bracket—rr adj
3. Bolt/screw 40–54 N·m (30–40 ft. lbs.)
4. Washer
5. Bolt/screw 40–50 N·m (30–40 ft. lbs.)
6. Bolt/screw 40–50 N·m (30–40 ft. lbs.)
7. Nut
8. Bracket—frt adj
9. Belt

A/C compressor removal—V6 cylinder engine

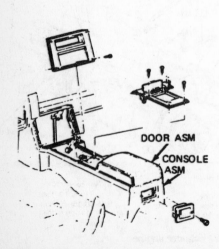

DOOR ASM

CONSOLE ASM

Console removal

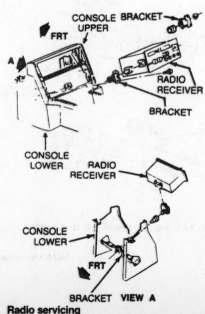

CONSOLE BRACKET UPPER

FRT

A

RADIO RECEIVER

BRACKET

CONSOLE LOWER

RADIO RECEIVER

CONSOLE LOWER

FRT

BRACKET **VIEW A**

Radio servicing

Radio removal

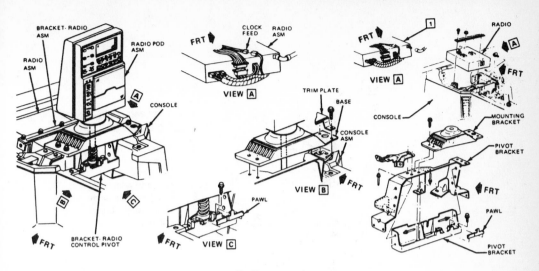

Radio removal

4. Remove the radio and disconnect the electrical connector.

5. To install, connect the electrical connector.

6. Install the radio to console attaching screws.

7. Install the console bezel screws.

8. Connect the negative battery cable.

NOTE: *Always connect the speakers before applying power to the radio as radio damage may result.*

Berlinetta

1. Disconnect the negative battery cable. Remove the 4 screws at the console trim plate.

2. Lift the receiver, with the connector attached, and turn to one side.

3. Remove the 4 control head mounting bracket screws. Remove the control head by pulling back on the pawl spring and pulling up on the control head.

4. Disconnect the electrical connectors from the control head.

5. Remove 4 screws at the receiver bracket and a slotted screw at the receiver.

6. Disconnect the electrical connector and remove the receiver.

7. To install, position the receiver into place and connect the electrical connector.

8. Install the 4 screws at the receiver bracket and a slotted screw at the receiver.

9. Connect the electrical connectors to the control head.

10. Install the control head. Install the 4 control head mounting bracket screws.

11. Install the 4 screws at the console trim plate.

12. Connect the negative battery cable.

Antenna

NOTE: *Placement of tape on the right inner door edge will help prevent scratches during the antenna removal and installation procedure.*

1. Disconnect the negative battery terminal.

2. Remove the right side lower instrument panel sound insulator and disconnect the antenna connection from the radio.

3. Raise and safely support the vehicle.

4. Disconnect the instrument panel harness from the radio.

5. Disconnect the power antenna lead, if equipped.

6. Disconnect the power antenna wire from the relay, if equipped.

7. Remove the right fender wheelhouse.

8. Loosen the fender-to-body attaching bolts and block the fender out.

9. Remove the antenna bezel and nut.

10. Remove the antenna assembly mounting screws.

11. Remove the grommet from the bulkhead and pull the harness from the vehicle interior.

12. Remove the antenna assembly from the vehicle.

NOTE: *In some cases, if the vehicle is equipped with a power antenna, it may be repaired. Seek a professional radio shop for proper repair of the antenna assembly.*

To install:

13. Install the antenna assembly into the vehicle.

14. Install the grommet and the harness into the vehicle interior.

15. Install the antenna assembly mounting screws.

16. Install the antenna bezel and nut.

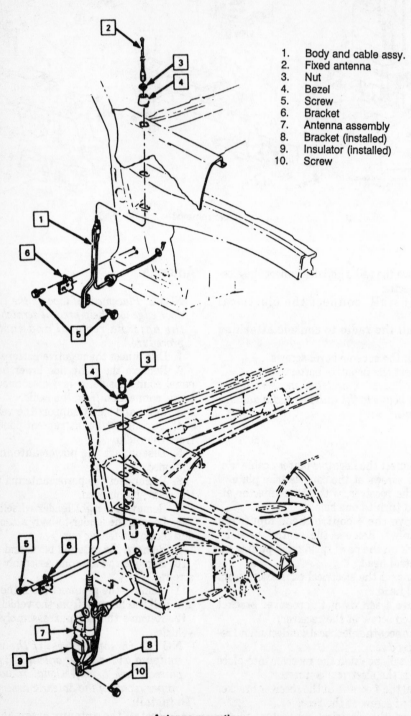

1. Body and cable assy.
2. Fixed antenna
3. Nut
4. Bezel
5. Screw
6. Bracket
7. Antenna assembly
8. Bracket (installed)
9. Insulator (installed)
10. Screw

Antenna mounting

1. Antenna lead-in
2. power antenna relay

Power antenna wiring

17. Remove the fender block, tighten the fender-to-body attaching bolts. Ensure any shims for the fender are reinstalled.
18. Install the right fender wheelhouse.
19. Lower the vehicle.
20. Connect the power antenna wire to the relay, if equipped.
21. Connect the power antenna lead, if equipped.
22. Connect the instrument panel harness to the radio.
23. Connect the antenna connection to the radio. Install the right side lower instrument panel sound insulator
24. Connect the negative battery cable.

1. Wiper arm
2. Transmission shaft
3. Wiper arm retaining latch
4. Wiper blade removal
5. Wiper insert removal
6. Wiper blade assembly
7. Wiper insert
8. Screwdriver
9. Blade retainer
10. Insert retainer

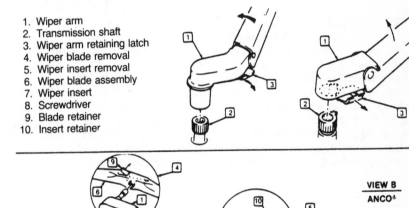

VIEW B
ANCO

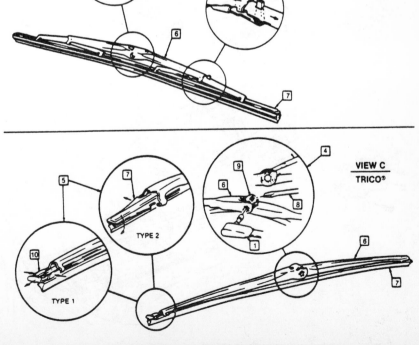

VIEW C
TRICO®

TYPE 2

TYPE 1

Wiper arm, blade and insert

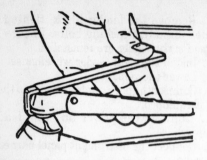

Windshield wiper removal tool

WINDSHIELD WIPERS AND WASHERS

Blade and Arm

REMOVAL AND INSTALLATION

If the wiper assembly has a press type release tab at the center, simply depress the tab and remove the blade. If the blade has no release tab, use a screwdriver to depress the spring at the center. This will release the assembly. To install the assembly, position the blade over the pin at the tip of the arm and press until the spring retainer engages the groove in the pin.

To remove the element, either depress the release button or squeeze the spring type retainer clip at the outer end together, and slide the blade element out. Just slide the new element in until it latches.

Removal of the wiper arms requires the use of a special tool, G.M. J–8966 or its equivalent. Versions of this tool are generally available in auto parts stores.

1. Insert the tool under the wiper arm and lever the arm off the shaft.

NOTE: *Raising the hood on most later models will facilitate easier wiper arm removal.*

2. Disconnect the washer hose from the arm (if so equipped). Remove the arm.

3. Installation is in the reverse order of removal. Be sure that the motor is in the park position before installing the arms.

Windshield Wiper Motor

REMOVAL AND INSTALLATION

1. Disconnect the negative battery cable at the battery.

2. Remove the screen or grille that covers the cowl area.

3. Working under the hood, disconnect the motor wiring. Then, reach through the cowl opening and loosen, but do not remove, the nuts which attach the transmission drive link to the motor crank arm. Then, disconnect the drive link from the crank arm.

4. Remove the three motor attaching screws,

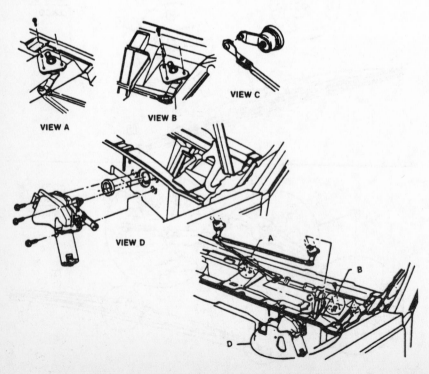

VIEW C

VIEW B

VIEW A

VIEW D

A

B

D

Wiper motor and transmission removal and installation

and remove the motor, guiding the crank arm through the hole.

5. To install, position the motor, guiding the crank arm through the hole, and install the 3 motor attaching screws.

6. Connect the drive link to the crank arm and connect the motor wiring.

NOTE: *The motor must be in the park position before assembling the crank arm to the transmission drive link(s).*

7. Install the screen or grille that covers the cowl area.

8. Connect the negative battery cable at the battery.

Park Switch

REMOVAL AND INSTALLATION

1. Disconnect the negative battery cable.

2. Remove the windshield wiper cover retaining screws and remove the cover.

3. If the wiper motor is in the **PARK** position, operate the motor as required to take it out of this position.

4. Remove the park switch assembly.

5. Installation is the reverse of the removal procedure. Ensure the motor is in the **PARK** before installing the cover assembly.

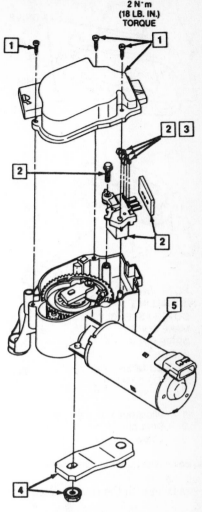

2 N·m
(18 LB. IN.)
TORQUE

SERVICE PACKAGES

1. Cover assembly
2. Park switch & contacts
3. Contacts
4. Crank arm
5. Wiper motor

Park switch assembly

1. Screwdriver (rotate)
2. Retaining clip
3. Align cam arm with this hole
4. Wiper in park position

Washer pump/cover removal and installation

Wiper Linkage

REMOVAL AND INSTALLATION

1. Remove the wiper arms and blades. Remove the cowl screen or grille.

2. Disconnect the wiring from the wiper motor. Loosen, but do not remove the nuts which attach the transmission drive link to the motor crank arm. Then, disconnect the drive link from the arm.

3. Remove the transmission-to-body attach-

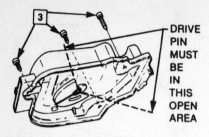

DRIVE PIN MUST BE IN THIS OPEN AREA

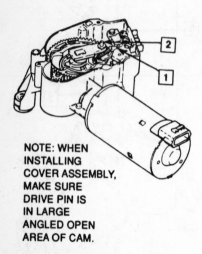

NOTE: WHEN INSTALLING COVER ASSEMBLY, MAKE SURE DRIVE PIN IS IN LARGE ANGLED OPEN AREA OF CAM.

1. Wiper motor in park position
2. Drive pin
3. Screw

Aligning cover with motor in park position

ing screws from both the right and left sides of the car.

4. Guide the transmissions and linkage out through the cowl opening.

5. To install, guide the transmissions and linkage in through the cowl opening.

6. Install the transmission-to-body attaching screws to both the right and left sides of the car.

7. Connect the drive link to the arm. Tighten the nuts which attach the transmission drive link to the motor crank arm. Connect the wiring to the wiper motor.

8. Install the cowl screen or grille.

9. Install the wiper arms and blades.

Washer Pump

REMOVAL AND INSTALLATION

In Wiper Motor

1. Using a screwdriver, lift the washer pump retainer clip on the wiper motor cover.

2. Pull the washer pump from the cover.

3. To install, position the washer pump to the cover. Be sure to push the washer pump all the way into the female socket.

4. Install the washer pump retainer clip on the wiper motor cover.

In Washer Tank

1. Drain the washer tank and disconnect the wire connectors.

2. Disconnect and remove the reservoir

3. Remove the washer pump from the reservoir.

4. Installation is the reverse of the removal procedure. Ensure pump is pushed fully into the reservoir.

Rear Window Wiper Motor

REMOVAL AND INSTALLATION

1. Remove the wiper arm blade using tool J–8966 or equivalent.

2. Remove the nut and spacer on the wiper motor shaft.

3. Raise the lid and remove the lift window trim panel.

4. Disconnect the electrical connectors to the wiper motor.

5. Remove the rivets holding the motor support to the lift window panel and remove the assembly from the car.

6. To remove the motor, remove the screws retaining wiper motor to motor support.

7. To install, position the motor onto the motor support and install the screws.

8. Install the motor support with the motor onto the lift window panel and secure it with rivets or nuts/bolts.

9. Connect the electrical connectors to the wiper motor.

10. Install the lift window trim panel and lower the lid.

11. Install the nut and spacer on the wiper motor shaft.

12. Install the wiper arm blade.

INSTRUMENTS AND SWITCHES

Instrument Cluster

REMOVAL AND INSTALLATION

Sport Coupe Model

1. Disconnect the negative battery cable.

2. Remove the instrument cluster bezel.

3. Remove the cluster attachment screws.

4. Pull the cluster out. Disconnect the speedometer cable and electrical connections.

5. Remove the cluster lens.

6. Install the cluster lens.

7. Connect the speedometer and electrical connections.

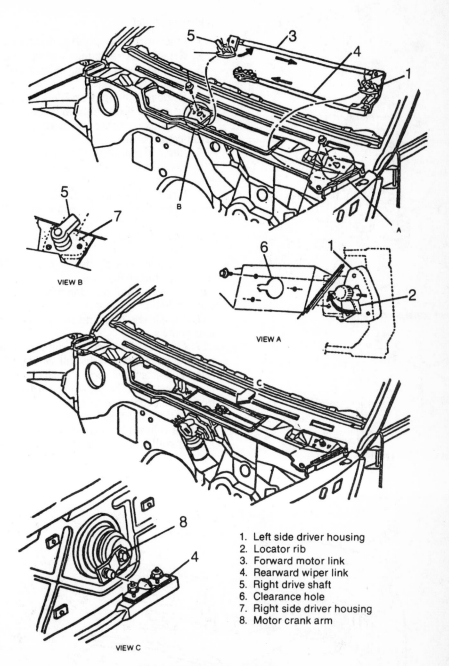

1. Left side driver housing
2. Locator rib
3. Forward motor link
4. Rearward wiper link
5. Right drive shaft
6. Clearance hole
7. Right side driver housing
8. Motor crank arm

VIEW B

VIEW A

VIEW C

Windshield wiper transmission

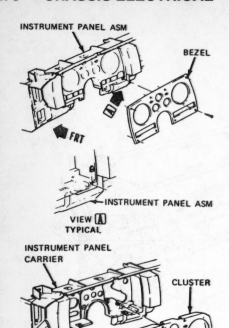

Instrument panel cluster and bezel

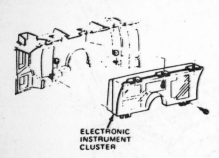

Instrument panel cluster and bezel

8. Push the cluster in.

9. Install the cluster attachment screws.

10. Install the instrument cluster bezel.

11. Connect the negative battery cable.

Berlinetta Model

1. Disconnect the negative battery cable.

2. Remove the instrument cluster bezel.

3. Remove the 8 steering column trim cover screws and trim cover.

4. Remove the right and left hand pod attaching screws at the bottom front of each pod. Pull the pods rearward and disconnect the electrical connection.

5. Remove the 5 cluster lens screws and lens.

6. Remove the 2 steering column bolts and lower the column.

7. Pull the instrument cluster rearward and disconnect the electrical connection. Remove the instrument cluster.

8. To install, position the instrument cluster into place.

9. Connect the electrical connection and push the cluster forward.

10. Lift the column and install the 2 steering column bolts.

11. Install the lens and install the 5 cluster lens screws.

12. Connect the electrical connection to each pod and push forward. Install the right and left hand pod attaching screws at the bottom front of each pod. Pull the pods rearward and disconnect the electrical connection.

13. Install the trim cover and install the 8 steering column trim cover screws.

14. Install the instrument cluster bezel.

15. Connect the negative battery cable.

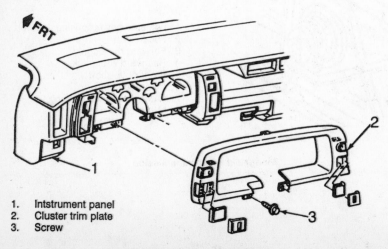

1. Intstrument panel
2. Cluster trim plate
3. Screw

Instrument panel bezel—1990–92

Wiper Switch

REMOVAL AND INSTALLATION

NOTE: *The wiper switch is part of the multi-function lever, located on the steering wheel column.*

1. Disconnect the electrical connector of the multi-function lever, located under the steering wheel.

2. Remove the protective cover from the wire.

3. Grasp the lever firmly, twist and pull (the tang on the lever must align with the socket) the lever straight out.

4. Pull the wire through the steering column.

5. To install, slide a music wire tool through the steering column and connect the lever wire to the tool wire; pull the wire through the steering column.

6. Push the control lever into the spring loaded socket (be sure to align the tang).

7. Install the protective cover to the wire.

8. Connect the electrical connector of the multi-function lever.

Headlight Switch

REMOVAL AND INSTALLATION

1. Disconnect the negative battery cable at the battery.

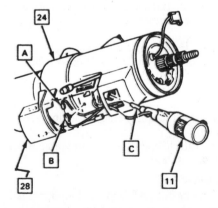

1. Multi-Function lever
2. Steering column
3. Housing cover end cap
A. Cruise control connector from column
B. Cruise control connector from switch
C. Tang

Multi-Function lever removal and installation

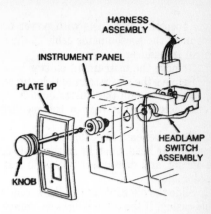

Headlight switch

2. Remove the four screws from inside the defroster duct (instrument panel pad securing screws).

3. Remove the screws which are under the lip of the instrument panel pad.

4. Remove the instrument panel pad.

5. On models equipped with air conditioning, remove the instrument panel cluster bezel and the cluster.

6. Remove the radio speaker bracket.

7. Pull the headlamp switch knob to the **ON** position, depress the locking button for the knob and shaft (located on the switch), and remove the knob and shaft.

8. Remove the switch bezel (retainer).

9. Disconnect the wiring from the switch and remove the switch.

10. To install, position the switch into place and connect the wiring to the switch.

11. Install the switch bezel (retainer).

12. Push the headlamp switch knob into the switch. (It may be necessary to depress the knob release button.

13. Install the radio speaker bracket.

14. On models equipped with air conditioning, install the instrument panel cluster bezel and the cluster.

15. Install the instrument panel pad.

16. Install the screws which are under the lip of the instrument panel pad.

17. Install the four screws from inside the defroster duct (instrument panel pad securing screws).

18. Connect the negative battery cable at the battery.

SPEEDOMETER CABLE

REMOVAL AND INSTALLATION

1. Disconnect the negative battery cable at the battery.

2. On models without cruise control, disconnect the speedometer cable strap at the power

brake booster. On models with power brakes, disconnect the speedometer cable at the cruise control transducer.

3. Remove the instrument cluster bezel.

4. Remove the six instrument cluster attaching screws and pull the cluster out far enough to gain access to the rear of the speedometer head.

5. Reach beneath the cable connection at the speedometer head, push in on the cable retaining spring, and disconnect the cable from the speedometer.

6. Slide the old cable out of the speedometer cable casing. If the cable is broken, remove the cable from both ends of the casing. Using a short piece of the old cable to fit the speedometer connection, turn the speedometer to increase the speed indicated on the dial and check for any binding during rotation. If binding is noted, the speedometer must be removed for repair or replacement. Check the entire cable casing for extreme bends, chafing, breaks, etc., and replace if necessary.

7. To install, wipe the cable clean using a lint-free cloth.

8. If the old casing is to be reused, flush the casing with petroleum spirits and blow dry with compressed air.

9. Lubricate the speedometer cable with an appropriate lubricant, being sure to cover the lower two-thirds of the cable.

10. Insert the cable into the casing, then connect the cable and casing assembly to the speedometer.

11. Install the cluster and install the 6 instrument cluster attaching screws.

12. Install the instrument cluster bezel.

13. On models without cruise control, connect the speedometer cable strap at the power brake booster. On models with power brakes, connect the speedometer cable at the cruise control transducer.

14. Connect the negative battery cable at the battery.

LIGHTING

Headlights

REMOVAL AND INSTALLATION

1. Remove headlamp bezel retaining screws and remove bezel.

2. Disengage spring from the retaining ring with a cotter pin removal tool and remove two attaching screws.

3. Remove retaining ring, disconnect sealed beam unit at wiring connector and remove the unit.

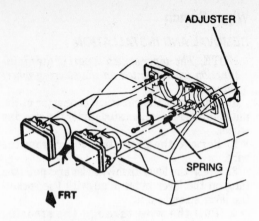

Headlamp and bezel assembly

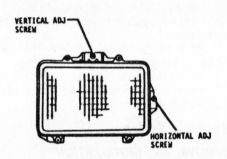

Headlamp aim adjusting screws

4. To install, attach the connector to replacement unit and position the unit in place making sure the number molded into the lens face is at the top.

NOTE: *In the dual headlamp installation the inboard unit (No. 1) takes a double connector plug, the outboard unit (No. 2) takes a triple connector plug.*

5. Position retaining ring into place and install the retaining ring attaching screws and spring.

6. Check operation of unit and install the headlamp bezel.

AIMING

The use of SAE approved equipment is preferred to achieve exact adjustment of the headlamps, although a farely accurate method of adjustment is as follows:

1. Position the vehicle approximately 25 ft. from a screen or wall, ensure the vehicle is facing the wall straight.

2. Measure the height from the ground to the center of the each headlamp.

3. Next measure from the ground up the same distance as previously measured and mark the appropriate spot on the screen or wall with chalk, ensuring the marks are straight ahead of each headlamp.

4. Turn the headlamps on and note the marks previously made.

5. The vertical aim, if properly adjusted, should be 2 in. (51mm) up to 2.5 in. (63.5mm) down from your center mark previously made.

6. Turn the vertical (top) adjusting screw if needed to correct the adjustment. The best overall setting is ½–1 in. (13–25mm) down for low beams and 0–½ in. (0–13mm), straight ahead, for high beams.

7. Next check the horizontal aim, if properly adjusted, should be 4 in. (102mm) to the right or 4 in. (102mm) to the left of the center mark previously made.

8. Turn the horizontal (side) adjuster screw if needed to obtain the correct setting. The best overall setting is 2 in. (51mm) to the right as not to blind oncoming traffic and better illumination of the sidewalk and curb.

9. After adjustment is complete, recheck previous adjustment, the headlamps will change slightly (up or down) when turning the opposite adjuster.

Signal and Marker Lights

REMOVAL AND INSTALLATION

Front Park/Turn and All Side Marker Lights

1. Reach around to the back side of the light assembly and unlock the bulb holder/wiring harness by grasping the bulb holder/wiring harness and turning it counterclockwise approximately ¼ turn.

2. Remove the bulb holder/wiring harness assembly.

3. To install, insert the bulb holder/wiring harness assembly into the light assembly and locking the holder by turning it ¼ turn clockwise.

Rear Brake, Park & Turn Lights

The tail light bulbs can be replaced by removing the plastic wing nuts which retain the light assemblies to the rear end panel and then removing the light assembly.

CIRCUIT PROTECTION

Fusible Links

In addition to circuit breakers and fuses, the wiring harness incorporates fusible links to protect the wiring. Links are used rather than a fuse, in wiring circuits that are not normally fused, such as the ignition circuit. Camaro fusible links are color coded red in the charging and load circuits to match the color coding of the circuits they protect. Each link is four gauges smaller than the cable it protects, and is

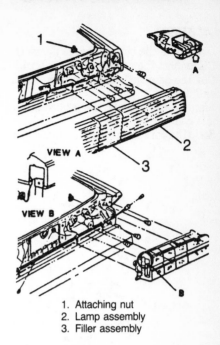

1. Attaching nut
2. Lamp assembly
3. Filler assembly

Rear tail lamp servicing

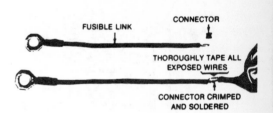

Repairing fusible links

marked on the insulation with the gauge size because the insulation makes it appear heavier than it really is.

The engine compartment wiring harness has several fusible links. The same size wire with a special hypalon insulation must be used when replacing a fusible link.

The links are located in the following areas:

1. A molded splice at the starter solenoid **Bat** terminal, a 14 gauge red wire.

2. A 16 gauge red fusible link at the junction block to protect the unfused wiring of 12 gauge or larger wire. This link stops at the bulkhead connector.

3. The alternator warning light and field circuitry is protected by a 20 gauge red wire fusible link used in the battery feed-to-voltage regulator #3 terminal. The link is installed as a molded splice in the circuit at the junction block.

4. The ammeter circuit is protected by two 20 gauge fusible links installed as molded splices in the circuit at the junction block and battery to starter circuit.

REPLACEMENT

1. Determine the circuit that is damaged.
2. Disconnect the negative battery terminal.
3. Cut the damaged fuse link from the harness and discard it.
4. Identify and procure the proper fuse link and butt connectors.
5. Strip the wire about ½ in. (13mm) on each end.

6. Connect the fusible link and crimp the butt connectors making sure that the wires are secure.
7. Solder each connection with resin core solder, and wrap the connections with plastic electrical tape.
8. Reinstall the wire in the harness.
9. Connect the negative battery terminal and test the system for proper operation.

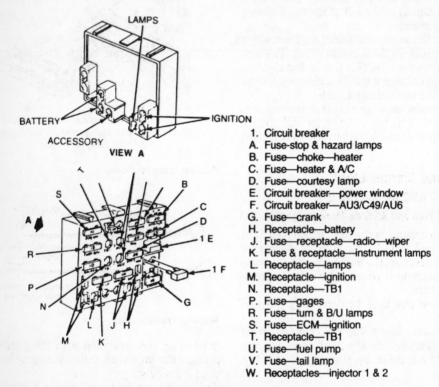

1. Circuit breaker
A. Fuse-stop & hazard lamps
B. Fuse—choke—heater
C. Fuse—heater & A/C
D. Fuse—courtesy lamp
E. Circuit breaker—power window
F. Circuit breaker—AU3/C49/AU6
G. Fuse—crank
H. Receptacle—battery
J. Fuse—receptacle—radio—wiper
K. Fuse & receptacle—instrument lamps
L. Receptacle—lamps
M. Receptacle—ignition
N. Receptacle—TB1
P. Fuse—gages
R. Fuse—turn & B/U lamps
S. Fuse—ECM—ignition
T. Receptacle—TB1
U. Fuse—fuel pump
V. Fuse—tail lamp
W. Receptacles—injector 1 & 2

Fuse blocks and designations—example

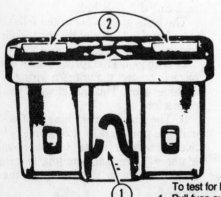

MINI FUSE COLOR CODES	
RATING	COLOR
5 AMP	TAN
10 AMP	RED
20 AMP	YELLOW
25 AMP	WHITE

To test for blown mini-fuse:
1. Pull fuse out and check visually
2. With the circuit activated use a test light across the points shown

Blown fuse

Circuit Breakers

Various circuit breakers are located under the instrument panel. In order to gain access to these components, it may be necessary to first remove the under dash padding. Most of the circuit breakers are located in the convenience center or the fuse panel.

Fuse Block

The fuse block on some models is located under the instrument panel next to the steering wheel and is a swing down unit. Other models have the fuse block located on the right side of the dash and access is gained through the glove box.

Each fuse block uses miniature fuses which are designed for increased circuit protection and greater reliability. The compact fuse is a blade terminal design which allows fingertip removal and replacement.

Although the fuses are interchangeable, the amperage values are molded in bold, color coded, easy to read numbers on the fuse body. Use only fuses of equal replacement valve.

A blown fuse can easily be checked by visual inspection or by continuity checking.

Buzzers, Relays, and Flashers

The electrical protection devices are located in the convenience center, which is a swing

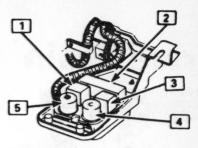

1. Horn relay
2. Seat belt—ignition key—headlight buzzer
3. Choke relay (vacant w/EFI)
4. Hazard flasher
5. Signal flasher

Convenience center—example

down unit located under the instrument panel. All units are serviced by plug-in replacements.

TURN SIGNAL FLASHER

The turn signal flasher is located inside the convenience center. In order to gain access to the turn signal flasher, it may be necessary to first remove the under dash padding.

HAZARD FLASHER

The hazard flasher is located inside the convenience center. In order to gain access to the turn signal flasher, it may be necessary to first remove the under dash padding.

Drive Train

7

MANUAL TRANSMISSION

Understanding the Manual Transmission

Because of the way the gasoline engine breathes, it can produce torque, or twisting force, only within a narrow speed range. Most modern engines must turn at about 2,500 rpm to produce their peak torque. By 4,500 rpm they are producing so little torque that continued increases in engine speed produce no power increases.

The transmission and clutch are employed to vary the relationship between engine speed and the speed of the wheels so that adequate engine power can be produced under all circumstances. The clutch allows engine torque to be applied to the transmission input shaft gradually, due to mechanical slippage. The car can, consequently, be started smoothly from a full stop.

The transmission changes the ratio between the rotating speeds of the engine and the wheels by the use of gears. 4-speed or 5-speed transmissions are most common. The lower gears allow full engine power to be applied to the rear wheels during acceleration at low speeds.

The clutch driven plate is a thin disc, the center of which is splined to the transmission input shaft. Both sides of the disc are covered with a layer of material which is similar to brake lining and which is capable of allowing slippage without roughness or excessive noise.

The clutch cover is bolted to the engine flywheel and incorporates a diaphragm spring which provides the pressure to engage the clutch. The cover also houses the pressure plate. The driven disc is sandwiched between the pressure plate and the smooth surface of the flywheel when the clutch pedal is released, thus forcing it to turn at the same speed as the engine crankshaft.

The transmission contains a mainshaft which passes all the way through the transmission, from the clutch to the driveshaft. This shaft is separated at one point, so that front and rear portions can turn at different speeds.

Power is transmitted by a countershaft in the lower gears and reverse. The gears of the countershaft mesh with gears on the mainshaft, allowing power to be carried from one to the other. All the countershaft gears are integral with that shaft, while several of the mainshaft gears can either rotate independently of the shaft or be locked to it. Shifting from one gear to the next causes one of the gears to be freed from rotating with the shaft, and locks another to it. Gears are locked and unlocked by internal dog clutches which slide between the center of the gear and the shaft. The forward gears usually employ synchronizers: friction members which smoothly bring gear and shaft to the same speed before the toothed dog clutches are engaged.

The clutch is operating properly if:

1. It will stall the engine when released with the vehicle held stationary.

2. The shift lever can be moved freely between first and reverse gears when the vehicle is stationary and the clutch disengaged.

A clutch pedal free-play adjustment is incorporated in the linkage. If there is about 1–2 in. (25–51mm) of motion before the pedal begins to release the clutch, it is adjusted properly. Inadequate free-play wears all parts of the clutch releasing mechanisms and may cause slippage. Excessive free-play may cause inadequate release and hard shifting of gears.

All 1984 and later clutches use a hydraulic system in place of a mechanical linkage. If the clutch fails to release, fill the clutch master cylinder with fluid to the proper level and pump the clutch pedal to fill the system with fluid.

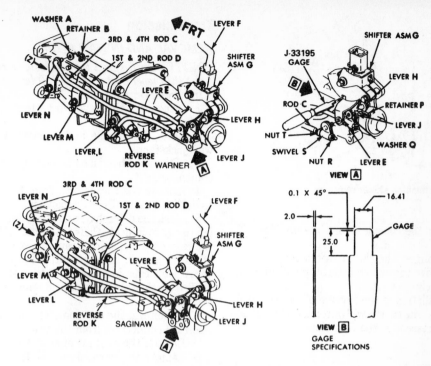

Transmission shift linkage adjustment

Bleed the system in the same way as a brake system. If leaks are located, tighten the loose connections or overhaul the master or slave cylinder as necessary.

Adjustments

LINKAGE

NOTE: *All terms used in the following procedure match those which are used in the accompanying illustration. No linkage adjustment is possible on the 5-speed transmission.*

1. Disconnect the negative battery cable at the battery.
2. Place the shift control lever (F) in Neutral.
3. Raise the vehicle and support it safely with jackstands.
4. Remove the swivel retainers (P) from the levers (E, H, and J).
5. Remove the swivels (S) from the shifter assembly (G), and loosen the swivel locknuts (R and T).
6. Make sure that levers L, M, and N are in their Neutral positions (center detents).
7. Align the holes of levers E, H, and J with the notch in the shifter assembly (G). Insert an alignment gauge (J–33195) to hold the levers in this position.
8. Insert swivel S into lever E and install washer Q. Secure with retainer P.
9. Apply rearward pressure (Z) to lever N.

Tighten locknuts R and T (at the same time) against swivel S to 25 ft. lbs.
10. Repeat steps 8 and 9 for rod D and levers J and M.
11. Repeat steps 8 and 9 for rod K and levers H and L.
12. Remove the alignment gauge, lower the vehicle, and check the operation of the shifting mechanism.
13. Reconnect the negative battery cable.

Clutch Switch

REMOVAL AND INSTALLATION

1. Disconnect the negative battery cable.
2. Remove the sound insulator on 1988–89

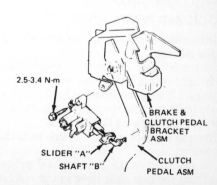

On some models the clutch safety switch is adjustable

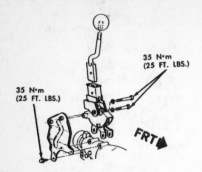

35 N·m
(25 FT. LBS.)

35 N·m
(25 FT. LBS.)

FRT

76mm transmission shifter removal

vehicles or the console trim plate on 1990–92 vehicles.

3. Disconnect the clutch switch connector.

4. Remove the switch attaching bolt and remove the clutch switch.

5. Installation is the reverse of the removal procedure. The switch will automatically adjust when depressed for the first time.

Shift Handle

REMOVAL AND INSTALLATION

1. Disconnect the negative battery cable.

2. Raise and safely support the vehicle.

3. Disconnect the shift rods from the control lever.

4. Lower the vehicle. Remove the shifter knob.

5. Remove the parking lever grip.

6. Remove the console cover.

7. Remove the shifter boot.

8. Remove the shifter mounting bolts and remove the shifter assembly.

9. Installation is the reverse of the removal procedure. Adjust the linkage per previous instructions.

Back-up Light Switch

REMOVAL AND INSTALLATION

1. Disconnect the negative battery terminal from the battery.

2. At the left-rear of the transmission, the back-up light switch is threaded into the transmission case. The speed sensor is held in with a separate bracket. Disconnect the electrical connector from the back-up light switch.

3. Remove the back-up light switch from the transmission.

4. To install, reverse the removal procedures. Place the gear shift lever in the reverse position and check that the back-up lights work.

Transmission

REMOVAL AND INSTALLATION

NOTE: *On 5-speed transmissions remove the shift lever boot and the shift lever prior to transmission removal.*

1. Disconnect the negative battery cable at the battery.

2. Raise the vehicle and support it safely with jackstands.

3. Drain the lubricant from the transmission.

4. Remove the torque arm from the vehicle as outlined under Rear Suspension.

5. Mark the driveshaft and the rear axle pinion flange to indicate their relationship. Unbolt the rear universal joint straps. Lower the rear of the driveshaft, being careful to keep the universal joint caps in place. Withdraw the driveshaft from the transmission and remove it from the vehicle.

6. Disconnect the speedometer cable and the electrical connectors from the transmission.

7. Remove the exhaust pipe brace.

8. Remove the transmission shifter support attaching bolts from the transmission.

9. On 4-speed transmissions only, disconnect the shift linkage at the shifter.

10. Raise the transmission slightly with a jack, then remove the crossmember attaching bolts.

11. Remove the transmission mount attaching bolts and remove the mount and crossmember from the vehicle.

12. Remove the transmission attaching bolts, and with the aid of an assistant, move the transmission rearward and downward out of the vehicle.

13. To install, apply a light coating of high temperature grease to the main drive gear bearing retainer and to the splined portion of the main drive gear. This will assure free movement of the clutch and transmission components during assembly.

14. Install the transmission and secure with transmission mounting bolts Torque transmission-to-clutch housing bolts to 55 ft. lbs. (74 Nm).

15. Install the mount and crossmember into the vehicle and install the transmission mount attaching bolts. Torque mount-to-crossmember bolts to 35 ft. lbs. and mount-to-transmission bolts to 35 ft. lbs. (47 Nm).

16. Install the crossmember attaching bolts. Torque crossmember-to-body bolts to 35 ft. lbs.

17. On 4-speed transmissions only, connect the shift linkage at the shifter and adjust the shift linkage.

18. Install the transmission shifter support attaching bolts to the transmission. Torque

shifter bracket-to-extension housing to 25 ft. lbs. (35 Nm).

19. Install the exhaust pipe brace.

20. Connect the speedometer cable and the electrical connectors to the transmission.

21. Install the driveshaft into the transmission. Then, align the marks on the driveshaft and the rear axle pinion flange. Bolt the rear universal joint straps.

22. Install the torque arm into the vehicle.

23. Fill the transmission with lubricant. Then install the filler plug and torque to 15 ft. lbs. (20 Nm).

24. Lower the vehicle.

25. Connect the negative battery cable at the battery.

CLUTCH

Understanding the Clutch

The purpose of the clutch is to disconnect and connect engine power from the transmission. A car at rest requires a lot of engine torque to get all that weight moving. An internal combustion engine does not develop a high starting torque (unlike steam engines), so it must be allowed to operate without any load until it builds up enough torque to move the car. Torque increases with engine rpm. The clutch allows the engine to build up torque by physically disconnecting the engine from the transmission, relieving the engine of any load or resistance. The transfer of engine power to the transmission (the load) must be smooth and gradual; if it weren't, drive line components would wear out or break quickly. This gradual power transfer is made possible by gradually releasing the clutch pedal. The clutch disc and pressure plate are the connecting link between the engine and transmission. When the clutch pedal is released, the disc and plate contact each other (clutch engagement), physically joining the engine and transmission. When the pedal is pushed in, the disc and plate separate (the clutch is disengaged), disconnecting the engine from the transmission.

The clutch assembly consists of the flywheel, the clutch disc, the clutch pressure plate, the throwout bearing and fork, the actuating linkage and the pedal. The flywheel and clutch pressure plate (driving members) are connected to the engine crankshaft and rotate with it. The clutch disc is located between the flywheel and pressure plate, and splined to the transmission shaft. A driving member is one that is attached to the engine and transfers engine power to a driven member (clutch disc) on the transmission shaft. A driving member (pressure plate) rotates (drives) a driven member (clutch disc) on contact and, in so doing, turns the transmission shaft. There is a circular diaphragm spring within the pressure plate cover (transmission side). In a relaxed state (when the clutch pedal is fully released), this spring is convex; that is, it is dished outward toward the transmission. Pushing in the clutch pedal actuates an attached linkage rod. Connected to the other end of this rod is the throwout bearing fork. The throwout bearing is attached to the fork. When the clutch pedal is depressed, the clutch linkage pushes the fork and bearing forward to contact the diaphragm spring of the pressure plate. The outer edges of the spring are secured to the pressure plate and are pivoted on rings so that when the center of the spring is compressed by the throwout bearing, the outer edges bow outward and, by so doing, pull the pressure plate in the same direction — away from the clutch disc. This action separates the disc from the plate, disengaging the clutch and allowing the transmission to be shifted into another gear. A coil type clutch return spring attached to the clutch pedal arm permits full release of the pedal. Releasing the pedal pulls the throwout bearing away from the diaphragm spring resulting in a reversal of spring position. As bearing pressure is gradually released from the spring center, the outer edges of the spring bow outward, pushing the pressure plate into closer contact with the clutch disc. As the disc and plate move closer together, friction between the two increases and slippage is reduced until, when full spring pressure is applied (by fully releasing the pedal), The speed of the disc and plate are the same. This stops all slipping, creating a direct connection between the plate and disc which results in the transfer of power from the engine to the transmission. The clutch disc is now rotating with the pressure plate at engine speed and, because it is splined to the transmission shaft, the shaft now turns at the same engine speed. Understanding clutch operation can be rather difficult at first; if you're still confused after reading this, consider the following analogy. The action of the diaphragm spring can be compared to that of an oil can bottom. The bottom of an oil can is shaped very much like the clutch diaphragm spring and pushing in on the can bottom and then releasing it produces a similar effect. As mentioned earlier, the clutch pedal return spring permits full release of the pedal and reduces linkage slack due to wear. As the linkage wears, clutch pedal free-travel will increase and free-travel will decrease as the clutch wears. Free-travel is actually throwout bearing lash.

The diaphragm spring type clutches used are

available in two different designs: flat diaphragm springs or bent spring. The bent fingers are bent back to create a centrifugal boost ensuring quick re-engagement at higher engine speeds. This design enables pressure plate load to increase as the clutch disc wears and makes low pedal effort possible even with a heavy duty clutch. The throwout bearing used with the bent finger design is 1¼ in. (31.75mm) long and is shorter than the bearing used with the flat finger design. These bearings are not interchangeable. If the longer bearing is used with the bent finger clutch, free-pedal travel will not exist. This results in clutch slippage and rapid wear.

The transmission varies the gear ratio between the engine and rear wheels. It can be shifted to change engine speed as driving conditions and loads change. The transmission allows disengaging and reversing power from the engine to the wheels.

Application

All 1982–83 vehicles use a mechanical (non-hydraulic) clutch; 1984 and later models use a hydraulic clutch. With the hydraulic clutch, no adjustment of the clutch pedal or the linkage is required. On the mechanical type, the only required adjustment is to maintain the proper clutch pedal freeplay. The freeplay adjustment is very important, for it determines the engaging and disengaging characteristics of the clutch assembly.

The clutch assembly consists of: a flywheel, a pressure plate, a throwout bearing and fork, a clutch pedal, and an actuating lever (non-hydraulic) or a master cylinder/slave cylinder (hydraulic).

The hydraulic system utilizes a remote reservoir which is mounted to the power brake booster, a master cylinder mounted to the cowl panel and a slave cylinder that is mounted to the bell housing. The system is operated directly by the clutch pedal. When adding fluid to the reservoir, always use a type which meets DOT 3 specifications.

CAUTION: *The clutch driven disc contains asbestos, which has been determined to be a cancer causing agent. Never clean clutch surfaces with compressed air! Avoid inhaling any dust from any clutch surface! When cleaning clutch surfaces, use a commercially available brake cleaning fluid.*

Adjustments
FREE-PLAY ADJUSTMENT

Non-Hydraulic

1. Disconnect the return spring at the clutch fork.

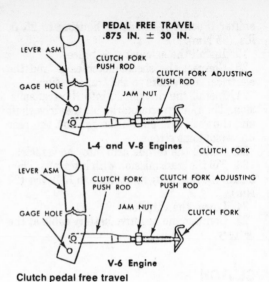

Clutch pedal free travel

Clutch pedal free-play adjustment—mechanical clutch linkage

2. Hold the pedal against the rubber bumper on the dash brace.
3. Push the clutch fork so that the throwout bearing lightly contacts the pressure plate fingers.
4. Loosen the locknut and adjust the length of the rod so that the swivel or rod can slip freely into the gauge hole in the lever. Increase the length of the rod until all free-play is removed.
5. Remove the rod or swivel from the gauge hole and insert it in the other (original) hole on the lever. Install the retainer and tighten the locknut.
6. Install the return spring and check freeplay measurement at the pedal pad.

Clutch Pedal

REMOVAL AND INSTALLATION

1. Disconnect the negative battery cable.
2. Disconnect the clutch return spring.
3. Remove the hush panel under the dash.
4. If equipped, remove the cruise control switch at the pedal.
5. Disconnect and remove the neutral start switch at the pedal.
6. Remove the turn signal and hazard warning flasher mounting bracket.
7. Disconnect the clutch pedal rod from the pedal.
8. Remove the clutch pedal pivot bolt far enough to permit removal of pedal assembly.
9. Clean all parts and relubricate. Install in reverse of removal.

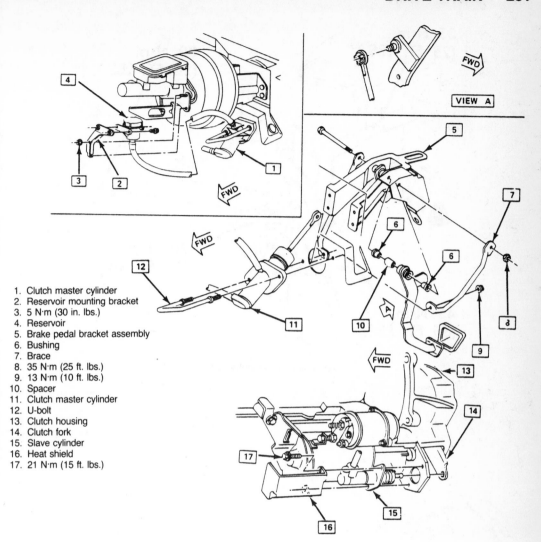

1. Clutch master cylinder
2. Reservoir mounting bracket
3. 5 N·m (30 in. lbs.)
4. Reservoir
5. Brake pedal bracket assembly
6. Bushing
7. Brace
8. 35 N·m (25 ft. lbs.)
9. 13 N·m (10 ft. lbs.)
10. Spacer
11. Clutch master cylinder
12. U-bolt
13. Clutch housing
14. Clutch fork
15. Slave cylinder
16. Heat shield
17. 21 N·m (15 ft. lbs.)

Hydraulic clutch and pedal assembly

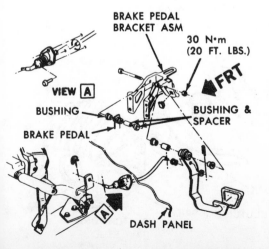

Clutch pedal assembly—mechanical clutch linkage

Clutch Linkage

REMOVAL AND INSTALLATION

1. Disconnect the negative battery cable.
2. Disconnect the return spring and rods from the pedal and fork assembly.
3. Loosen the outboard ball stud nut and slide stud out of bracket slot.
4. Move the cross shaft outboard, and as required to clear inboard ball stud, then lift out from the vehicle.
5. Inspect the nylon bushing and anti-rattle O-ring for wear and replace as required.
6. Installation is the reverse of the removal procedure. Adjust linkage as previously outlined.

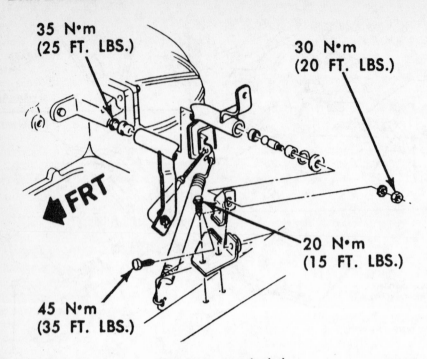

35 N•m
(25 FT. LBS.)

30 N•m
(20 FT. LBS.)

20 N•m
(15 FT. LBS.)

45 N•m
(35 FT. LBS.)

FRT

Clutch linkage—mechanical

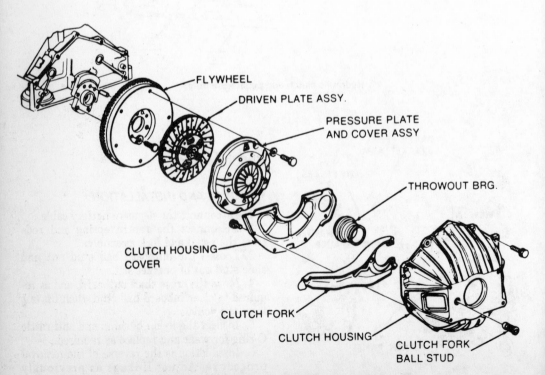

FLYWHEEL

DRIVEN PLATE ASSY.

PRESSURE PLATE
AND COVER ASSY

THROWOUT BRG.

CLUTCH HOUSING
COVER

CLUTCH FORK

CLUTCH HOUSING

CLUTCH FORK
BALL STUD

Exploded view of clutch and flywheel assembly

Driven Disc and Pressure Plate

REMOVAL AND INSTALLATION

1. Support engine and remove the transmission (as outlined in this chapter).

2. Disconnect the clutch fork push rod and spring.

3. Remove the flywheel housing.

4. Slide the clutch fork from the ball stud and remove the fork from the dust boot. The ball stud is threaded into the clutch housing and may be replaced, if necessary.

5. Install an alignment tool to support the clutch assembly during removal. Mark the flywheel and clutch cover for reinstallation, if they do not already have **X** marks.

6. Loosen the clutch-to-flywheel attaching bolts evenly, one turn at a time, until spring pressure is released. Remove the bolts and clutch assembly.

7. Clean the pressure plate and flywheel face.

8. Support the clutch disc and pressure plate with an alignment tool. The driven disc is installed with the damper springs on the transmission side.

9. Turn the clutch assembly until the mark on the cover lines up with the mark on the flywheel, then install the bolts. Tighten down evenly and gradually to avoid distortion.

10. Remove the alignment tool.

11. Lubricate the ball socket and fork fingers at the release bearing end with high melting point grease. Lubricate the recess on the inside of the throwout bearing and throwout fork groove with a light coat of graphite grease.

12. Install the clutch fork and dust boot into the housing. Install the throwout bearing to the throwout fork. Install the flywheel housing. Install the transmission.

13. Connect the fork push rod and spring. Lubricate the spring and pushrod ends.

14. Adjust the shift linkage and clutch pedal free-play.

Master Cylinder

NOTE: *Before removing the hydraulic components for repair, remove the clutch housing dust cover to verify the malfunction. Measure the movement of the slave cylinder push rod by pushing the clutch pedal to the floor; the minimum movement should be 14mm. Do not replace the cylinder if its movement exceeds the minimum.*

REMOVAL AND INSTALLATION

The clutch master cylinder is located in the engine compartment, on the left side of the firewall, above the steering column.

1. Disconnect negative battery terminal from the battery.

2. Remove hush panel from under the dash.

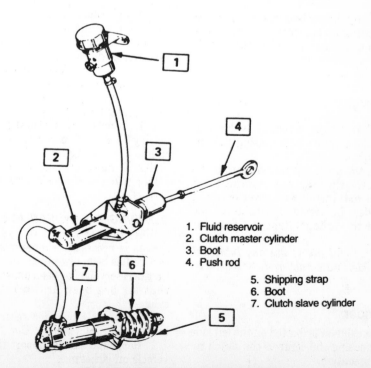

1. Fluid reservoir
2. Clutch master cylinder
3. Boot
4. Push rod

5. Shipping strap
6. Boot
7. Clutch slave cylinder

Hydraulic clutch slave and master cylinders

3. Disconnect push rod from clutch pedal.

4. Disconnect hydraulic line from the clutch master cylinder.

5. Remove the master cylinder-to-cowl brace nuts. Remove master cylinder and overhaul (if necessary).

6. Using a putty knife, clean the master cylinder and cowl mounting surfaces.

7. To install, reverse the removal procedures. Torque the master cylinder-to-cowl brace nuts to 10–15 ft. lbs. (14–20 Nm). Fill master cylinder with new hydraulic fluid conforming to Do 3 specifications. Bleed and check the hydraulic clutch sysemt for leaks.

OVERHAUL

1. Remove the filler cap and drain fluid from the master cylinder.

2. Remove the reservoir and seal from the master cylinder. Pull back the dust cover and remove the snapring.

3. Remove the push rod assembly. Using a block of wood, tap the master cylinder on it to eject the plunger aseembly from the cylinder bore.

4. Remove the seal (carefully) from the front of the plunger assembly, ensuring no damage oocurs to the plunger surfaces.

5. From the rear of the plunger assembly, remove the spring, the support, the seal and the shim.

6. Using clean brake fluid, clean all of the parts.

7. Inspect the cylinder bore and the plunger for ridges, pitting and/or scratches, the dust cover for wear and cracking; replace the parts if any of the conditions exist.

8. To install, use new seals, lubricate al of the parts in clean brake fluid, fit the plunger seal to the plunger and reverse the remove procedures.

9. Insert the plunger assembly, valve end leading into the cylinder bore (easing the entrance ofthe plunger seal).

10. Position the push rod aseembly into the cylinder bore, then install a new snapring to retain the push rod. Install dust cover onto the master cylinder. Lubricate the inside of the dust cover with Girling® Rubber Grease or equivalent.

NOTE: *Be careful not to use any lubricant that will deteriorate rubber dust covers or seals.*

Slave Cylinder

The slave cylinder is located on the left side of the bellhousing and controls the clutch release fork operation.

REMOVAL AND INSTALLATION

1. Disconnect the negative battery cable.

2. Raise and safely support the front of the vehicle on jackstands.

3. Disconnect the hydraulic line from clutch master cylinder. Remove the line-to-chassis screw and the clip from the chassis.

NOTE: *Be sure to plug the line opening to keep dirt and moisture out of the system.*

4. Remove the slave cylinder-to-bellhousing nuts.

5. Remove the push rod and the slave cylinder from the vehicle, then overhaul it (if necessary).

6. To install, reverse the removal procedures. Lubricat leading end of the slave cylinder with Girling® Rubber Lube or equivalent. Torque the slave cylinder-to-bellhousing nuts to 10–15 ft. lbs. (14–20 Nm). Fill the master cylinder with new brake fluid conformign to Dot 3 specifications. Bleed the hydraulic system.

OVERHAUL

1. Remove the shield, the pushrod and the dust cover from the slave cylinder, then inspect the cover for damage or deterioration.

2. Remove the snapring form the end of the cylinder bore.

3. Using a block of wood, tap the slave cylinder on it to eject the plunger, then remove the seal and the spring.

4. Using clean brake fluid, clean all of the parts.

5. Inspect the cylinder bore and the plunger for ridges, pitting and/or scratches, the dust cover for wear and cracking; replace the parts if anyoftheconditionsexist.

6. To install, use new seals and lubricate all of the parts in clean brake fluid. Install the spring, the plunger seal and the plunger into the cylinder bore, then install anew snapring.

7. Lubricate the inside of the dust cover with Girling® Rubber Grease or equivalent, then install it into the slave cylinder.

NOTE: *Be careful not to use any lubricant that will deteriorate rubber dust covers or seals.*

BLEEDING THE HYDRAULIC CLUTCH

Bleeding air from the hydraulic clutch system is necessary whenever any part of the system has been disconnected or teh fluid level (in the reservoir) has been allowed to fall so low that air has been drawn into the master cylinder.

1. Fill master cylinder reservoir with new brake fluid conforming to Dot 3 specifications.

2. Raise and safely support the front of the vehicle on jackstands.

3. Remove the slave cylinder attachign bolts.

4. Hold slave cylinder at approximately 45° with the bleeder at highest point. Fully depress clutch pedal and open the bleeder screw.

5. Close the bleeder screw and release clutch pedal.

6. Repeat the procedure until all of the air is evacuated from the system. Check and refill master cylinder reservoir as required to prevent air from being drawn through the master cylinder.

NOTE: *Never release a depressed clutch pedal with the bleeder screw open or air will be drawn into the system.*

AUTOMATIC TRANSMISSION

Understanding Automatic Transmissions

The automatic transmission allows engine torque and power to be transmitted to the rear wheels within a narrow range of engine operating speeds. The transmission will allow the engine to turn fast enough to produce plenty of power and torque at very low speeds, while keeping it at a sensible rpm at high vehicle speeds. The transmission performs this job entirely without driver assistance. The transmission uses a light fluid as the medium for the transmission of power. This fluid also works in the operation of various hydraulic control circuits and as a lubricant. Because the transmission fluid performs all of these three functions, trouble within the unit can easily travel from one part to another. For this reason, and because of the complexity and unusual operating principles of the transmission, a very sound understanding of the basic principles of operation will simplify troubleshooting.

THE TORQUE CONVERTER

The torque converter replaces the conventional clutch. It has three functions:

1. It allows the engine to idle with the vehicle at a standstill, even with the transmission in gear.

2. It allows the transmission to shift from range to range smoothly, without requiring that the driver close the throttle during the shift.

3. It multiplies engine torque to an increasing extent as vehicle speed drops and throttle opening is increased. This has the effect of making the transmission more responsive and reduces the amount of shifting required.

The torque converter is a metal case which is shaped like a sphere that has been flattened on opposite sides. It is bolted to the rear end of the engine's crankshaft. Generally, the entire metal case rotates at engine speed and serves as the engine's flywheel.

The case contains three sets of blades. One set is attached directly to the case. This set forms the torus or pump. Another set is directly connected to the output shaft, and forms the turbine. The third set is mounted on a hub which, in turn, is mounted on a stationary shaft through a one-way clutch. This third set is known as the stator.

A pump, which is driven by the converter hub at engine speed, keeps the torque converter full of transmission fluid at all times. Fluid flows continuously through the unit to provide cooling.

Under low speed acceleration, the torque converter functions as follows:

The torus is turning faster than the turbine. It picks up fluid at the center of the converter and, through centrifugal force, slings it outward. Since the outer edge of the converter moves faster than the portions at the center, the fluid picks up speed.

The fluid then enters the outer edge of the turbine blades. It then travels back toward the center of the converter case along the turbine blades. In impinging upon the turbine blades, the fluid loses the energy picked up in the torus.

If the fluid were now to immediately be returned directly into the torus, both halves of the converter would have to turn at approximately the same speed at all times, and torque input and output would both be the same.

In flowing through the torus and turbine, the fluid picks up two types of flow, or flow in two separate directions. It flows through the turbine blades, and it spins with the engine. The stator, whose blades are stationary when the vehicle is being accelerated at low speeds, converts one type of flow into another. Instead of allowing the fluid to flow straight back into the torus, the stator's curved blades turn the fluid almost 90° toward the direction of rotation of the engine. Thus the fluid does not flow as fast toward the torus, but is already spinning when the torus picks it up. This has the effect of allowing the torus to turn much faster than the turbine. This difference in speed may be compared to the difference in speed between the smaller and larger gears in any gear train. The result is that engine power output is higher, and engine torque is multiplied.

As the speed of the turbine increases, the fluid spins faster and faster in the direction of engine rotation. As a result, the ability of the stator to redirect the fluid flow is reduced. Under cruising conditions, the stator is eventually forced to rotate on its one-way clutch in the direction of engine rotation. Under these conditions, the torque converter begins to behave almost like a solid shaft, with the torus and turbine speeds being almost equal.

THE PLANETARY GEARBOX

The ability of the torque converter to multiply engine torque is limited. Also, the unit tends to be more efficient when the turbine is rotating at relatively high speeds. Therefore, a planetary gearbox is used to carry the power output of the turbine to the driveshaft.

Planetary gears function very similarly to conventional transmission gears. However, their construction is different in that three elements make up one gear system, and, in that all three elements are different from one another. The three elements are: an outer gear that is shaped like a hoop, with teeth cut into the inner surface; a sun gear, mounted on a shaft and located at the very center of the outer gear; and a set of three planet gears, held by pins in a ring-like planet carrier, meshing with both the sun gear and the outer gear. Either the outer gear or the sun gear may be held stationary, providing more than one possible torque multiplication factor for each set of gears. Also, if all three gears are forced to rotate at the same speed, the gearset forms, in effect, a solid shaft.

Most modern automatics use the planetary gears to provide either a single reduction ratio of about 1.8:1, or two reduction gears: a low of about 2.5:1, and an intermediate of about 1.5:1. Bands and clutches are used to hold various portions of the gearsets to the transmission case or to the shaft on which they are mounted. Shifting is accomplished, then, by changing the portion of each planetary gearset which is held to the transmission case or to the shaft.

THE SERVOS AND ACCUMULATORS

The servos are hydraulic pistons and cylinders. They resemble the hydraulic actuators used on many familiar machines, such as bulldozers. Hydraulic fluid enters the cylinder, under pressure, and forces the piston to move to engage the band or clutches.

The accumulators are used to cushion the engagement of the servos. The transmission fluid must pass through the accumulator on the way to the servo. The accumulator housing contains a thin piston which is sprung away from the discharge passage of the accumulator. When fluid passes through the accumulator on the way to the servo, it must move the piston against spring pressure, and this action smooths out the action of the servo.

THE HYDRAULIC CONTROL SYSTEM

The hydraulic pressure used to operate the servos comes from the main transmission oil pump. This fluid is channeled to the various servos through the shift valves. There is generally a manual shift valve which is operated by the transmission selector lever and an automatic shift valve for each automatic upshift the transmission provides: i.e., 2-speed automatics have a low/high shift valve, while 3-speeds have a 1–2 valve, and a 2–3 valve.

There are two pressures which effect the operation of these valves. One is the governor pressure which is affected by vehicle speed. The other is the modulator pressure which is affected by intake manifold vacuum or throttle position. Governor pressure rises with an increase in vehicle speed, and modulator pressure rises as the throttle is opened wider. By responding to these two pressures, the shift valves cause the upshift points to be delayed with increased throttle opening to make the best use of the engine's power output.

Most transmissions also make use of an auxiliary circuit for downshifting. This circuit may be actuated by the throttle linkage or the vacuum line which actuates the modulator, or by a cable or solenoid. It applies pressure to a special downshift surface on the shift valve or valves.

The transmission modulator also governs the line pressure, used to actuate the servos. In this way, the clutches and bands will be actuated with a force matching the torque output of the engine.

Identification

Two types of transmissions are used on the vehicles; Turbo Hydra-Matic 200C (3-Speed + reverse) and Turbo Hydra-Matic 700-R4/4L60 (4-Speed + reverse).

Fluid Pan

REMOVAL AND INSTALLATION
FLUID AND FILTER CHANGE

NOTE: *To remove an oil pan which has been installed with sealant refer to the oil pan removal section of Chapter 1. The fluid should be changed with the transmission warm. The vehicle should be driven at least 20 minutes at highway speeds to warm the fluid.*

1. Raise and support the vehicle.
2. Place a large pan under the transmission pan. Remove all the front and side pan bolts. Loosen the rear bolts about four turns.

CAUTION: *The fluid will be HOT. Protect hands, arms, etc.*

3. Pry the pan loose and let it drain.
4. Remove the pan and gasket. Clean the pan thoroughly with solvent and air dry it. Be very careful not to get any lint from rags in the pan.
5. Remove the filter and gasket.

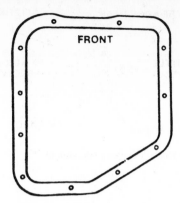

Turbo Hydra-Matic 200C transmission pan

Turbo Hydra-Matic 700R4 & 4L60 transmission pan

6. Install a new filter and gasket.

7. Reinstall the pan with a new gasket.

8. Lower the car. Add Dexron® II automatic transmission fluid through the fill tube.

9. Start the engine in Park and let it idle. Do not race the engine. Shift into each shift lever position, shift back into Park, and check the fluid level on the dipstick. The level should be ¼ in. (6mm) below ADD. Be very careful not to overfill. Recheck the level after the car has been driven long enough to thoroughly warm up the transmission. Add fluid as necessary. The level should then be at FULL.

Adjustments

BANDS

There are no band adjustments possible or required for the Turbo Hydra-Matic 200C, 700-R4 or 4L60 transmissions.

SHIFT CONTROL CABLE

1. Place the control lever in **N**.

2. Raise the car and support it with jackstands.

3. Loosen the cable attachment a the shift lever.

4. Rotate the shift lever clockwise to the park detent and then back to neutral.

5. Tighten cable attachment to 11 ft. lbs. (15 Nm).

NOTE: *The lever must be held out of P when torquing the nut.*

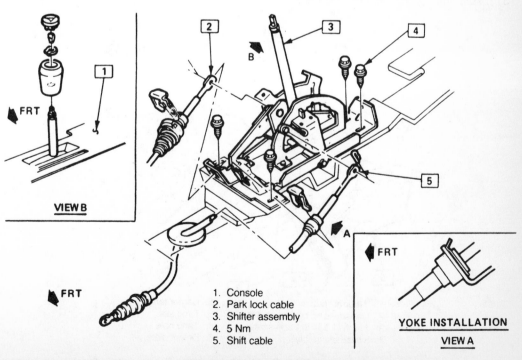

1. Console
2. Park lock cable
3. Shifter assembly
4. 5 Nm
5. Shift cable

Shift cable assembly at console

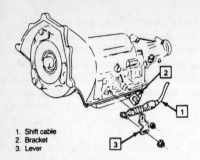

1. Shift cable
2. Bracket
3. Lever

Shift cable assembly at transmission

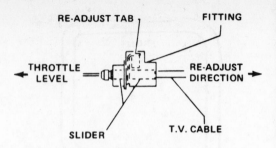

Throttle Value (TV) cable adjustment

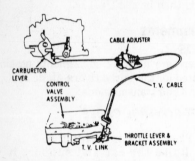

Throttle Valve (TV) cable and linkage assembly

SHIFT LINKAGE

1. Place the manual shaft of the transmission in **N**. Place the console shift lever in **N**.

2. Install the cable in the slot of the shift lever. Adjust the cable so that the pin has free movement.

3. Install and tighten the nut to the pin.

THROTTLE VALVE CABLE

1. After installation of the cable to the transmission, engine bracket, and the cable actuating lever, check to assure that the cable slider is in the zero or fully re-adjusted position.

2. If cable slider is not in the zero or fully re-adjusted, depress and hold the metal re-adjust tab. Move the slider back through the fitting in the direction away from the cable actuating lever until the slider stops against the fitting. Release the metal re-adjust tab.

3. Rotate the cable actuating lever to its full travel position.

4. The slider must move (ratchet) forward when the lever is rotated to the full travel position.

5. Release the lever.

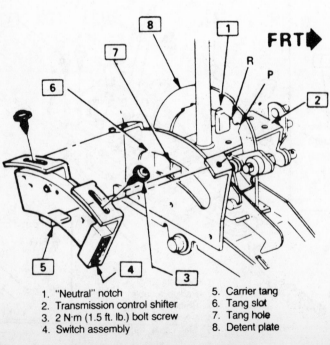

1. "Neutral" notch
2. Transmission control shifter
3. 2 N·m (1.5 ft. lb.) bolt screw
4. Switch assembly
5. Carrier tang
6. Tang slot
7. Tang hole
8. Detent plate

Neutral Safety/Back-Up Lamp switch

Neutral Start/Back-Up Light Switch

REPLACEMENT AND ADJUSTMENT

1. Remove the console trim from the console.
2. Disconnect the electrical connector from the switch.
3. Remove the 2 attaching screws from the switch and remove the switch.
4. To install a new switch:

a. Place the switch onto the transmission control shifter and loosely install the attaching screws. Position the transmission control shifter assembly in the N notch in the detent plate.

b. Assemble switch assembly to the transmission control shifter assembly by inserting the carrier tang into the hole in the shifter lever assembly.

c. Install the attaching screws and tighten.

d. Move the transmission control shifter assembly out of N position. This will shear the switch internal plastic pin.

5. To install the original switch:

a. Place the switch onto the transmission control shifter and loosely install the attaching screws. Position the transmission control shifter assembly in the N notch in the detent plate.

b. Rotate the switch on the shifter assembly to align the service adjustment hole with the carrier tang hole. Insert a $^3/_{32}$ in. (2.34mm) diameter gauge pin to a depth of $^{19}/_{32}$ in. (15mm) and tighten attaching screws.

c. Remove the gauge pin.

6. Connect the electrical connector to the switch.

7. Install the console trim to the console.

Park Lock Cable

REMOVAL AND INSTALLATION

1982–83

1. Remove the console and steering column covers. Remove cable retaining screw from the steering column slider and disconnect the cable.

2. At the shifter bracket, pull out the lock button on the cable housing and remove the yoke.

3. Disconnect the cable from the shifter.

4. To install, place the shifter lever in **P**. Rotate the steering column shift bowl to the **P** position and lock the column.

5. Connect the cable to the shifter.

6. Install the yoke and push in the lock button on the cable bracket.

7. Connect the cable and install cable retaining screw to the steering column slider.

8. Install the console and steering column covers.

1984–88

1. Place the shifter lever in the **P** position. Remove the negative battery cable.

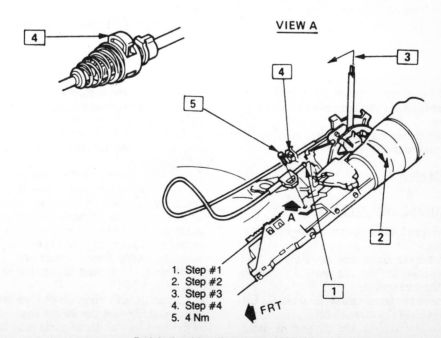

VIEW A

1. Step #1
2. Step #2
3. Step #3
4. Step #4
5. 4 Nm

FRT

Park lock cable adjustment—1982–83

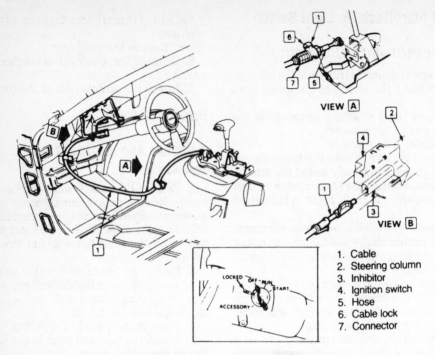

1. Cable
2. Steering column
3. Inhibitor
4. Ignition switch
5. Hose
6. Cable lock
7. Connector

Park lock cable assembly—1984–92

2. Turn the key to **RUN**. Release the cable from the inhibitor switch by inserting a screwdriver into the switch slot.

3. Push the cable lock button to the **UP** position and remove the cable from the park lever lock pin.

4. Depress the 2 cable connector latches at the shifter base and remove the cable. Remove the cable clips.

5. To install, place the shifter lever into the **P** position and the ignition key to the **RUN** position.

6. After installing the cable ends, push the cable connector nose toward the connector as far as possible and push the connector lock button down.

7. Complete the installation by reversing the removal procedure.

Transmission

REMOVAL AND INSTALLATION

1. Disconnect the negative battery cable at the battery.

2. Remove the air cleaner assembly.

3. Disconnect the throttle valve (TV) control cable at the carburetor.

4. Remove the transmission oil dipstick. Unbolt and remove the dipstick tube.

5. Raise the vehicle and support it safely with jackstands.

NOTE: *In order to provide adequate clearance for transmission removal, it may be necessary to raise both the front and the rear of the vehicle.*

6. Mark the relationship between the driveshaft and the rear pinion flange so that the driveshaft may be reinstalled in its original position.

7. Unbolt the universal joint straps from the pinion flange (use care to keep the universal joint caps in place), lower and remove the driveshaft from the vehicle. Place a transmission tailshaft plug or rag in place of the driveshaft to keep the transmission fluid from draining out.

8. Disconnect the catalytic converter support bracket at the transmission.

9. Disconnect the speedometer cable, electrical connectors and the shift control cable from the transmission.

CAUTION: *During the next step, rear spring force will cause the torque arm to move toward the floor pan. When disconnecting the arm from the transmission, carefully place a piece of wood between the floor pan and the torque arm. This will prevent possible personal injury and/or floor pan damage.*

10. Remove the torque arm-to-transmission bolts.

11. Remove the flywheel cover, then mark the relationship between the torque converter and the flywheel so that these parts may be reassembled in the same relationship.

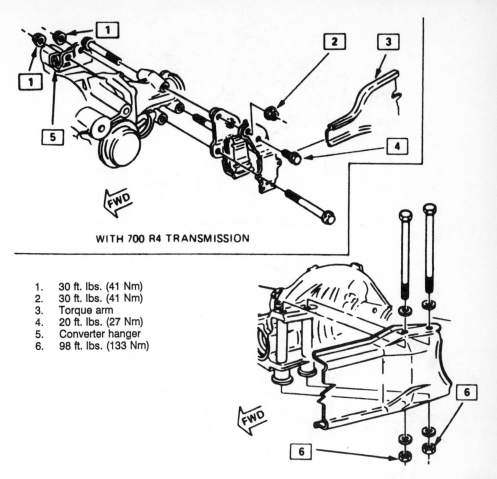

WITH 700 R4 TRANSMISSION

1. 30 ft. lbs. (41 Nm)
2. 30 ft. lbs. (41 Nm)
3. Torque arm
4. 20 ft. lbs. (27 Nm)
5. Converter hanger
6. 98 ft. lbs. (133 Nm)

Torque arm removal

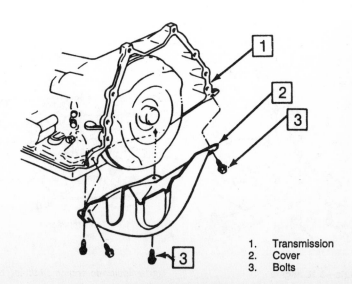

1. Transmission
2. Cover
3. Bolts

Flywheel cover removal

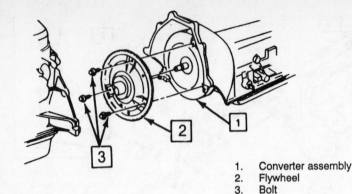

1. Converter assembly
2. Flywheel
3. Bolt

Converter-to-flywheel bolts

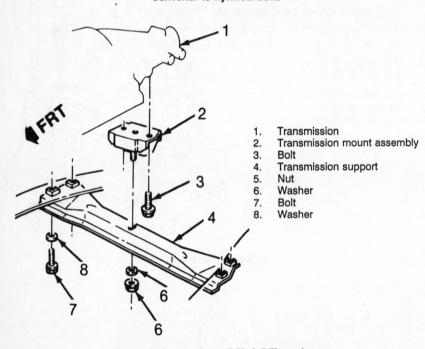

1. Transmission
2. Transmission mount assembly
3. Bolt
4. Transmission support
5. Nut
6. Washer
7. Bolt
8. Washer

Transmission mounts—5.0L & 5.7L engines

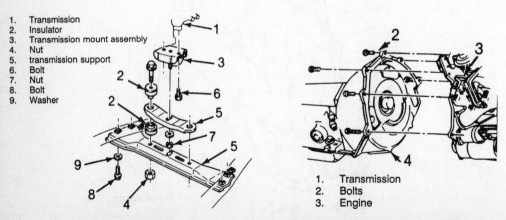

1. Transmission
2. Insulator
3. Transmission mount assembly
4. Nut
5. transmission support
6. Bolt
7. Nut
8. Bolt
9. Washer

1. Transmission
2. Bolts
3. Engine

Transmission mounts—3.1L engine   **Transmission-to-engine attaching bolts**

12. Remove the torque converter-to-flywheel attaching bolts.

13. Support the transmission with a jack, then remove the transmission mount bolt.

14. Unbolt and remove the transmission crossmember.

15. Lower the transmission slightly. Disconnect the throttle valve cable and oil cooler lines from the transmission.

16. Support the engine using Chevrolet special tool BT–6424 or its equivalent. Remove the transmission-to-engine mounting bolts.

CAUTION: *The transmission must be secured to the transmission jack.*

17. Remove the transmission from the vehicle. Be careful not to damage the oil cooler lines, throttle valve cable, or the shift control cable. Also, keep the rear of the transmission lower than the front to avoid the possibility of the torque converter disengaging from the transmission.

18. To install, position the transmission and converter into place.

19. Install the transmission-to-engine mounting bolts.

20. Connect the throttle valve cable and oil cooler lines to the transmission.

21. Install the transmission crossmember and secure with bolts.

22. Install the transmission mount bolt.

23. Match mark the torque converter to flywheel. Install the torque converter-to-flywheel attaching bolts.

NOTE: *Before installing the converter-to-flywheel bolts, be sure that the weld nuts on the converter are flush with the flywheel, and that the converter rotates freely by hand in this position.*

24. Install the flywheel cover.

25. Install the torque arm-to-transmission bolts.

26. Connect the speedometer cable, electrical connectors and the shift control cable from the transmission.

27. Connect the catalytic converter support bracket at the transmission.

28. Install the driveshaft to the match mark made earlier to the driveshaft and axle pinion. Bolt the universal joint straps to the pinion flange.

29. Lower the vehicle.

30. Install the dipstick tube using a new dipstick tube O-ring and secure with the bolt. Install the transmission oil dipstick.

31. Connect the throttle valve (TV) control cable at the carburetor.

32. Install the air cleaner assembly.

33. Connect the negative battery cable at the battery.

DRIVELINE

Driveshaft and U-Joints

The driveshaft (propeller shaft) is a long steel tube that transmits engine power from the transmission to the rear axle assembly. It is connected to, and revolves with, the transmission output shaft (remember, the transmission shaft is connected to and revolves with the engine crankshaft) whenever the transmission is put into gear. With the transmission in neutral, the driveshaft does not move. Located at each end of the driveshaft is a flexible joint that rotates with the shaft. These flexible joints, known as U-joints (universal joints) perform an important function. The rear axle assembly moves with the car. It moves up and down with every bump or dip in the road. The driveshaft by itself is a rigid tube incapable of bending. When combined with the flexing capabilities of the U-joints, however, it can do so.

A slip joint is coupled to the front of the driveshaft by a universal joint. This U-joint allows the yoke (slip joint) to move up and down with the car. The yoke is a cylinder containing splines that slide over the meshes with the splines on the transmission output shaft. When the rear axle moves up and down, the yoke slides back and forth a small amount on the transmission shaft. Therefore, it combines with the U-joints in allowing the driveshaft to move with the movements of the car. The rear universal joint is secured to a companion flange which is attached to, and revolves with, the rear axle drive pinion.

A U-joint consists of a cross piece (trunnion) and, on each of the four ends, a dust seal and a series of needle bearings that fit into a bearing cup. Each U-joint connects one yoke with another and the bearings allow the joints to revolve within each yoke.

A Camaro U-joint is secured to the yoke in one of two ways. Dana and Cleveland shafts use a conventional snapring to hold each bearing cup in the yoke. The snapring fits into a groove located in each yoke end just on top of each bearing cup. The Saginaw design shaft secures its U-joints in another way. Nylon material is injected through a small hole in the yoke and flows along a circular groove between the U-joint and the yoke, creating a synthetic snapring. Disassembly of the Saginaw U-joint requires the joint to be pressed from the yoke. This results in damage to the bearing cups and destruction of the nylon rings.

Replacement kits include new bearing cups and conventional snaprings to replace the

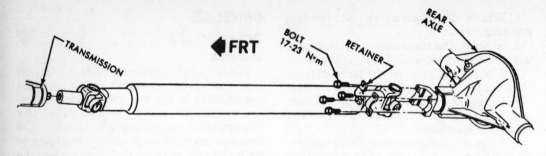

Rear driveshaft assembly

original nylon rings. These replacement rings must go inboard of the yoke in contrast to outboard mounting of the Dana and Cleveland designs. Previous service to the Saginaw U-joints can be recognized by the presence of snaprings inboard of the yoke.

Bad U-joints, requiring replacement, will produce a clunking sound when the car is put into gear. This is due to worn needle bearings or a scored trunnion end possibly caused by improper lubrication during assembly. Camaro U-joints require no periodic maintenance and therefore have no lubrication fittings.

Driveshaft

REMOVAL AND INSTALLATION

1. Raise the vehicle and safely support it on jackstands. Paint a reference line from the rear end of the driveshaft to the companion flange so that they can be reassembled in the same position.

2. Disconnect the rear universal joint by removing the U-bolts, retaining straps, or the flange bolts.

3. To prevent loss of the needle bearings, tape the bearing caps to the trunnion.

4. Remove the driveshaft from the transmission by sliding it rearward.

NOTE: *Do not be alarmed by oil leakage at the transmission output shaft. This oil is there to lubricate the splines of the front yoke.*

5. To install, check the yoke seal in the transmission case extension and replace it if necessary. See the transmission section for replacement procedures.

6. Position the driveshaft and insert the front yoke into the transmission so that the splines mesh with the splines of the transmission shaft.

7. Using reference marks made during removal, align the driveshaft with the companion flange and secure it with U-bolts or, retaining straps.

U-JOINT REPLACEMENT

1. Support the driveshaft horizontally in line with the base plate of a press.

2. Place the U-joint so the lower ear of the shaft yoke is supported on a 1⅛ in. (29mm) socket.

3. Remove the lower bearing cap out of the yoke ear by placing tool J–9522–3 or equivalent, on the open horizontal bearing caps and pressing the lower bearing cap out of the yoke ear.

NOTE: *This will shear the nylon injector ring, if the original U-joint is being removed. There are no bearing retaining grooves in the production bearing caps, therefore they cannot be reused. If a replacement U-joint is be-*

Internal snapring U-joint assembly

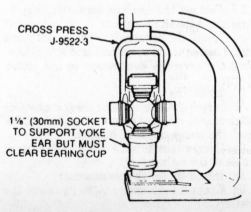

CROSS PRESS
J-9522-3

1⅛" (30mm) SOCKET
TO SUPPORT YOKE
EAR BUT MUST
CLEAR BEARING CUP

Pressing out the U-joint

Pressing out the old U-joint

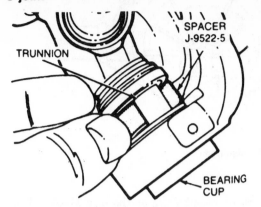

SPACER
J-9522-5

TRUNNION

BEARING
CUP

Insert spacer tool to push cup out of joint all the way

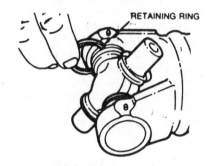

RETAINING RING

Installing snapring

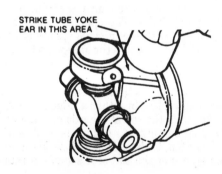

STRIKE TUBE YOKE
EAR IN THIS AREA

Seating the snapring

ing removed, ensure to remove the retaining clips from the U-joint.

4. If the bearing cap is not completely removed, lift tool J-9522-3 and insert tool J-9522-5 or equivalent between the bearing cap and seal and continue pressing the U-joint out of the yoke.

5. Repeat the procedure for the opposite side.

6. Remove the spider from the yoke.

To install:

7. Install 1 bearing cap part way into 1 side of the yoke. Turn this yoke ear to the bottom.

8. Using tool J-9522-3 or equivalent, seat the trunnion into the bearing cap.

9. Install the opposite bearing cap partially onto the trunnion.

10. Ensure both trunnions are straight and true in the bearing caps.

11. Press the spider against the opposite bearing cap, while working the spider back and forth to ensure free movement of the trunnions in the bearing caps.

12. If trunnion is binding, the needle bearings have tipped over under the end of the cap.

13. Stop pressing when 1 bearing cap clears the retainer groove inside the yoke.

14. Install a retaining ring.

15. Repeat the procedure for the remaining bearing caps and U-joints.

16. Installation of the driveshaft is the reverse of the removal procedure. Tighten the strap bolts to 16 ft. lbs. (22 Nm).

NOTE: *The Saginaw shaft uses two different sizes of bearing cups at the differential end. The larger cups (the ones with the groove) fit into the driveshaft yoke.*

REAR AXLE

Identification

The rear axle code and the manufacturers code, plus the date built, is stamped on the right axle tube on the forward side. Any reports made on the rear axle assemblies must include the full code letters and the date built numbers. The Limited-slip differentials are identified by a tag attached to the lower right section of the axle.

Understanding Drive Axles

The drive axle is a special type of transmission that reduces the speed of the drive from the engine and transmission and divides the power to the wheels. Power enters the axle from the driveshaft via the companion flange. The flange is mounted on the drive pinion shaft. The drive pinion shaft and gear which carry the power into the differential turn at engine speed. The gear on the end of the pinion shaft drives a large ring gear the axis of rotation of which is 90 degrees away from the of the pinion. The pinion and gear reduce the gear ratio of the axle, and change the direction of rotation to turn the axle shafts which drive both wheels. The axle gear ratio is found by dividing the number of pinion gear teeth into the number of ring gear teeth.

The ring gear drives the differential case. The

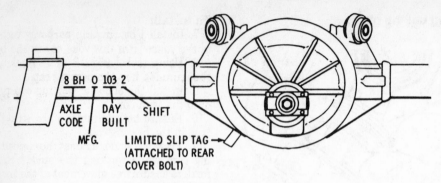

AXLE CODE
MFG.
DAY BUILT
SHIFT
LIMITED SLIP TAG → (ATTACHED TO REAR COVER BOLT)

8 BH O 103 2

Rear axle identification code

case provides the two mounting points for the ends of a pinion shaft on which are mounted two pinion gears. The pinion gears drive the two side gears, one of which is located on the inner end of each axle shaft.

By driving the axle shafts through the arrangement, the differential allows the outer drive wheel to turn faster than the inner drive wheel in a turn.

The main drive pinion and the side bearings, which bear the weight of the differential case, are shimmed to provide proper bearing preload, and to position the pinion and ring gears properly.

WARNING: *The proper adjustment of the relationship of the ring and pinion gears is critical. It should be attempted only by those with extensive equipment and/or experience.*

Limited-slip differentials include clutches which tend to link each axle shaft to the differential case. Clutches may be engaged either by spring action or by pressure produced by the torque on the axles during a turn. During turning on a dry pavement, the effects of the clutches are overcome, and each wheel turns at the required speed. When slippage occurs at either wheel, however, the clutches will transmit some of the power to the wheel which has the greater amount of traction. Because of the presence of clutches, limited-slip units require a special lubricant.

Determining Axle Ratio

An axle ratio is obtained by dividing the number of teeth on the drive pinion gear into the number of teeth on the ring gear. For instance, on a 4.11 ratio, the driveshaft will turn 4.11 times for every turn of the rear wheel.

The most accurate way to determine the axle ratio is to drain the differential, remove the cover, and count the number of teeth on the ring and pinion.

An easier method is to jack and support the car so that both rear wheels are off the ground.

Make a chalk mark on the rear wheel and the driveshaft. Block the front wheels and put the transmission in Neutral. Turn the rear wheel one complete revolution and count the number of turns made by the driveshaft. The number of driveshaft rotations is the axle ratio. More accuracy can be obtained by going more than one tire revolution and dividing the result by the number of tire rotations.

The axle ratio is also identified by the axle serial number prefix on the axle; the axle ratios are listed in dealer's parts books according to prefix number. Some axles have a tag on the cover.

Axle Shaft, Bearing and Seal

Axle shafts are the last link in the chain of components working to transmit engine power to the rear wheels. The splined end of each shaft meshes with the internal splines of each differential side gear. As the side gears turn, so do the axle shafts, and, since they are also connected, so do the wheels.

Each shaft passes through the side gear and is locked into place by either a C-lock or flange plate bolted to the end of the axle housing with pressed on bearings. As the name implies, the C-lock is a flat, C-shaped piece of metal that fits into a groove at the end of the shaft. A round

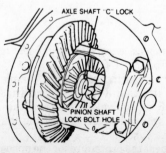

AXLE SHAFT "C" LOCK

PINION SHAFT LOCK BOLT HOLE

Removing the pinion shaft lock bolt, pin and C-Locks

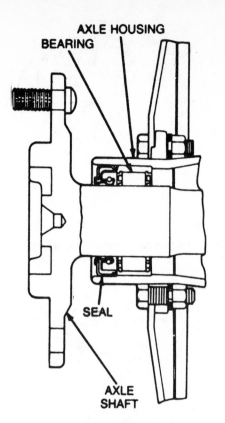

Axle, bearing and seal—side view

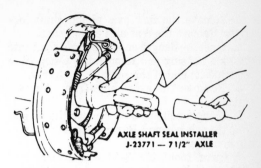

Installing the rear axle seal

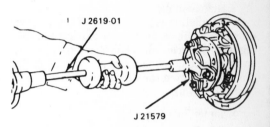

Axle shaft removal—Borg-Warner

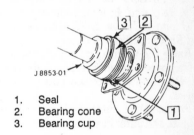

1. Seal
2. Bearing cone
3. Bearing cup

Bearing and seal pressed on axle—Borg-Warner

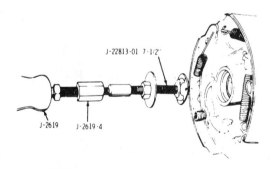

Removing the rear axle bearing

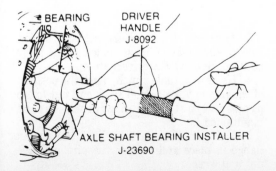

Installing the rear axle bearing

pinion shaft is wedged in between the end of the shafts. This pinion shaft prevents the shafts from sliding inward and makes the C-locks functional by pushing them tightly against each side gear. Removing this pinion shaft allows the shafts to slide inward making the C-locks accessible for removal. Once the C-locks are removed, the axle shafts can be pulled from the car.

The wheel end of each shaft is flanged and pressed into it are five wheel lug bolts serving to hold on the wheel. Each axle shaft is supported by an axle bearing (wheel bearing) and oil seal located within the axle shaft housing just to the outside of the brake backing plate.

REMOVAL AND INSTALLATION

Except Borg-Warner Rear Assembly

1. Raise and support the vehicle safely. Remove the rear wheels and drums or rotors.

2. Remove the carrier cover and drain the gear oil into a suitable container.

3. Remove the rear axle pinion shaft lock screw. Remove the rear axle pinion shaft.

4. Push the flanged end of the axle shaft into the axle housing and remove the C-clip from the opposite end of the shaft.

5. Remove the axle shaft from the axle housing.

6. Using a suitable tool, remove the oil seal from the axle housing. Be careful not to damage the housing.

7. Install tool J–22813–01 or equivalent, into the bore of the axle housing and position it behind the bearing, ensure the tangs of the tool engage the outer race. Remove the bearing using a slide hammer.

8. Installation is the reverse of the removal procedure. Lubricate the new bearing and sealing lips with gear lube before installing. Tighten the pinion gear shaft lock screw to 27 ft. lbs. (36 Nm). Tighten the carrier cover bolts to 22 ft. lbs. (30 Nm).

Borg-Warner Rear Assembly

NOTE: *The Borg Warner axle assembly can be quickly identified by checking the axle code. The Borg Warner axle numbers are 4EW, 4EU and 4ET on 1988 vehicles, BET, BEU and BEW on 1989 vehicles and 9EQ and 9ER on 1990 vehicles.*

1. Raise the vehicle and support is safely.

2. Remove the rear wheels and drums or rotors. Remove the brake components as required.

3. Remove the 4 nuts attaching the brake anchor plate and outer bearing retainer to the axle housing.

4. Remove the axle shaft and wheel bearing assembly using axle shaft removal tool J–21595 and slide hammer J–2619 or equivalent.

5. To remove the inner bearing retainer and the bearing from the axle shaft, split the retainer with a chisel and remove it from the shaft. Using tool J–22912–01, press the bearing off the shaft.

6. Installation is the reverse of the removal procedure. Ensure the axle seal is installed with the spring side facing the center of the axle. Tighten the backing plate bolts to 36 ft. lbs. (49 Nm).

NOTE: *There are right (black banded) and left (gold banded) axle seals; they cannot be interchanged.*

Pinion Seal

REMOVAL AND INSTALLATION

Except Borg-Warner Rear Axle Assembly

1. Raise and safely support the vehicle.

2. Remove both rear wheel and tire assemblies.

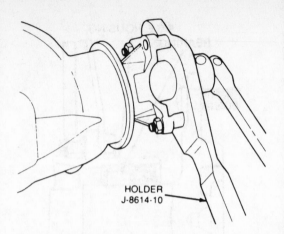

Rear axle pinion nut removal using special tool

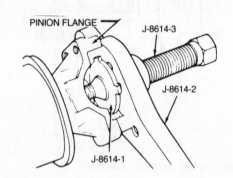

Rear axle flange removal

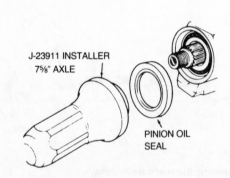

Rear axle pinion seal installation

3. Matchmark the driveshaft and pinion yoke so they may be reassembled in the same position. Remove the driveshaft.

4. Using a suitable punch, mark the position of the pinion yoke, pinion shaft and nut for so proper reinstallation preload can be maintained.

5. Using a suitable tool, hold the pinion flange in place and remove the pinion flange nut and washer.

6. Place a container under the differential to

catch any fluid that may drain from the rear axle. Using a suitable tool, remove the pinion yoke.

7. Use a suitable tool to remove the pinion seal.

To install:

8. Inspect the sealing surfaces of the pinion yoke for nicks or damage and replace, as necessary. Examine the carrier bore and remove any burrs that may cause leaks around the outside of the seal.

9. Install the seal using a suitable installer.

10. Apply a seal lubricant to the outer diameter of the pinion flange and the sealing lip of the new seal.

11. Install the pinion yoke on the drive pinion by taping with a soft-face hammer until a few pinion threads project through the pinion yoke.

12. Install the washer and pinion flange nut. While holding the pinion yoke, tighten the nut to the same position as marked earlier, then tighten an additional $\frac{1}{16}$ in. (1.6mm) turn beyond the marks.

13. Install the drive shaft.

14. Install the rear wheels and tires. Check and add the correct lubricant, as necessary.

Borg-Warner Rear Axle Assembly

1. Raise and safely support the vehicle.

2. Remove both rear wheel and tire assemblies.

3. Matchmark the driveshaft and pinion yoke so they may be reassembled in the same position. Remove the driveshaft.

4. Using a suitable inch pound torque wrench on the pinion yoke nut, mearsure and record the pinion bearing, axle bearings and seal preload.

5. Using a suitable tool to hold the pinion yoke in place, remove the pinion yoke nut and washer.

6. Place a suitable container under the differential to catch any fluid that may drain from the rear axle. Using a suitable tool, remove the pinion flange.

7. Use a suitable tool to remove the pinion seal.

To install:

8. Inspect the seal surface of the pinion flange for tool marks, nicks or damage and replace, as necessary. Examine the carrier bore and remove any burrs that might cause leaks around the outside of the seal.

9. Install the seal 0.010 in. (0.25mm) below the flange surface using a suitable seal installer.

10. Apply suitable seal lubricant to the outer diameter of the pinion flange and the sealing lip of the new seal.

11. Install the pinion flange on the drive pin-

ion by taping with a soft hammer until a few pinion threads project through the pinion flange.

12. Install the washer and pinion flange nut. While holding the pinion flange, tighten the nut a little at a time and turn the drive pinion several revolutions after each tightening, to set the bearing rollers. Check the preload each time with a suitable inch pound torque wrench until the preload is 5 inch lbs. (0.6 Nm) more then the reading obtained during disassembly.

13. Install the driveshaft.

14. Install the rear wheels and tires. Check and add the correct lubricant, as necessary.

Axle Housing

REMOVAL AND INSTALLATION

1. Raise the vehicle and support it safely. Be sure that the rear axle assembly is supported safely.

2. Disconnect shock absorbers from axle. Remove the wheel assemblies.

3. Mark drive shaft and pinion flange, then disconnect drive shaft and support out of the way.

4. Remove brake line junction block bolt at axle housing. If necessary, disconnect the brake lines at the junction block.

5. Disconnect the upper control arms from the axle housing.

6. Lower the rear axle assembly. Remove the springs.

7. Continue lowering the rear axle assembly and remove it from the vehicle.

8. To install, position the rear axle assembly into place and install the springs.

9. Connect the upper control arms to the axle housing.

10. Install the brake line junction block bolt at the axle housing. Connect any brake lines that were disconnected.

11. Install the driveshaft to the match marks made earlier and secure the driveshaft.

12. Connect the shock absorbers to the axle and install the wheel assemblies.

13. Lower the vehicle and replace any lost rear axle fluid.

Differential Assembly

REMOVAL AND INSTALLATION

1. Raise and safely support the vehicle.

2. Place a suitable container under the differential. Remove the carrier cover and drain the gear oil.

3. Remove the drive axles.

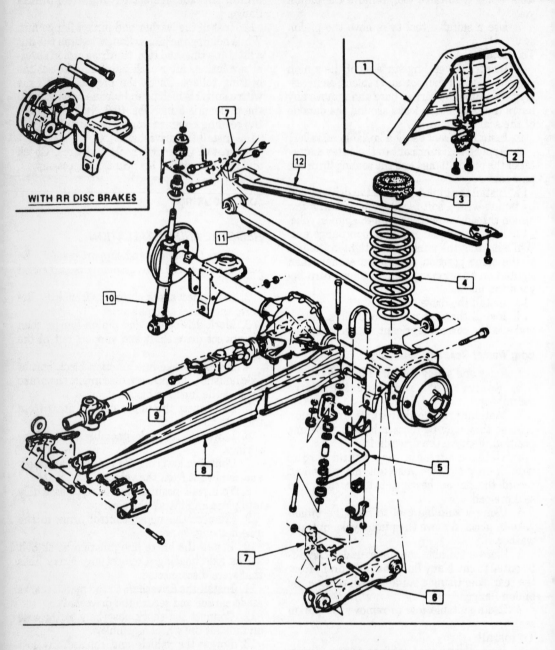

WITH RR DISC BRAKES

1. RAIL
2. JOUNCE BUMPER
3. SPRING INSULATOR ASSEMBLY
4. COIL SPRING
5. OPTIONAL STABILIZER BAR
6. LOWER CONTROL ARM
7. UNDERBODY
8. TORQUE ARM
9. PROP SHAFT
10. SHOCK ABSORBER
11. TRACK BAR
12. TRACK BAR BRACE

Exploded view of rear axle housing assembly

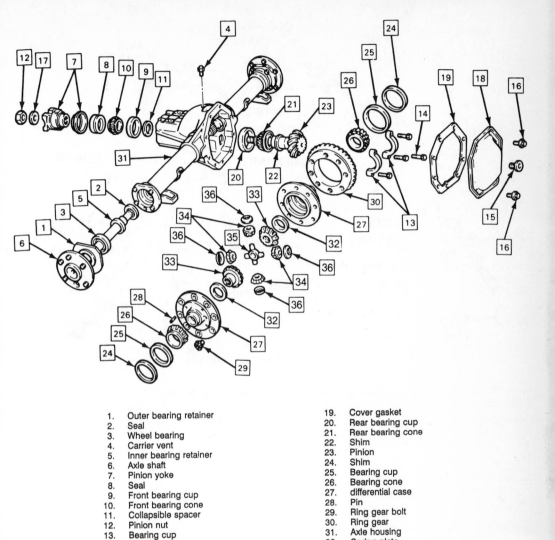

1.	Outer bearing retainer	19.	Cover gasket
2.	Seal	20.	Rear bearing cup
3.	Wheel bearing	21.	Rear bearing cone
4.	Carrier vent	22.	Shim
5.	Inner bearing retainer	23.	Pinion
6.	Axle shaft	24.	Shim
7.	Pinion yoke	25.	Bearing cup
8.	Seal	26.	Bearing cone
9.	Front bearing cup	27.	differential case
10.	Front bearing cone	28.	Pin
11.	Collapsible spacer	29.	Ring gear bolt
12.	Pinion nut	30.	Ring gear
13.	Bearing cup	31.	Axle housing
14.	Bolt	32.	Spring plate
15.	Axle drain plug	33.	Side gear
16.	Cover bolt	34.	Pinion gear
17.	Washer	35.	Pinion shaft
18.	Cover	36.	Thrust washer

Exploded view of Borg-Warner Rear axle assembly

4. Mark the differential bearing caps **L** and **R** to make sure they will be reassembled in their original location.

5. Using a suitable tool, remove the differential carrier. Be careful not to damage the gasket sealing surface when removing the unit. Place the right and left bearing outer races of the side bearing assemblies and shims in sets with the marked differential bearings caps so they can be reinstalled in their original positions.

To install:

6. Inspect the differential carrier housing for foreign material. Check the ring and pinion for chipped teeth, excessive wear and scoring.

Check the carrier bearings visually and by feel. Clean the differential housing and replace components, as necessary.

7. Install the differential carrier. Check the carrier bearing preload and ring and pinion backlash and adjust, as necessary. Tighten the differential bearing cap bolts to 55 ft. lbs. (75 Nm) except on Borg-Warner rear axles which are tighten to 40 ft. lbs. (54 Nm).

8. Install the axles.

9. Install the carrier cover using a new gasket. Tighten the carrier cover bolts to 20 ft. lbs. (27 Nm). Add the proper type and quantity of gear oil to axle assembly.

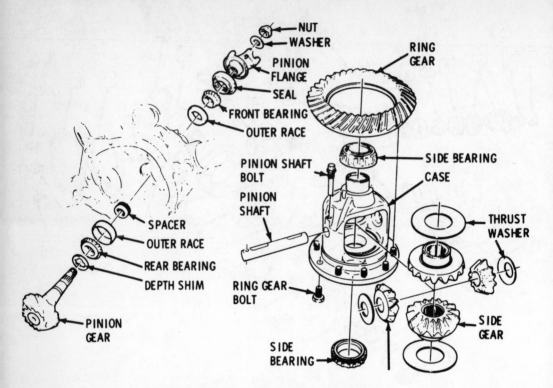

Exploded view of standard rear axle assembly

Suspension and Steering

8

FRONT SUSPENSION

The front suspension is designed to allow each wheel to compensate for changes in the road surface level without appreciably affecting the opposite wheel. Each wheel is independently connected to the frame by a steering knuckle, strut assembly, ball joint, and lower control arm. The steering knuckles move in a prescribed three dimensional arc. The front wheels are held in proper relationship to each other by two tie rods which are connected to the steering knuckles and to a relay rod assembly.

Coil chassis springs are mounted between the spring housings on the front crossmember and the lower control arms. Ride control is provided by double, direct acting strut assemblies. The upper portion of each strut assembly extends through the fender well and attaches to the upper mount assembly with a nut.

Side roll of the front suspension is controlled by a spring steel stabilizer shaft. It is mounted in rubber bushings which are held to the frame side rails by brackets. The ends of the stabilizer are connected to the lower control arms by link bolts isolated by rubber grommets.

The inner ends of the lower control arm have pressed-in bushings. Bolts, passing through the bushings, attach the arm to the suspension crossmember. The lower ball joint assembly is a press fit in the arm and attaches to the steering knuckle with a torque prevailing nut.

Rubber grease seals are provided at ball socket assemblies to keep dirt and moisture from entering the joint and damaging bearing surfaces.

Coil Springs

REMOVAL AND INSTALLATION

1. Raise the front of the vehicle and support it on jackstands.
2. Remove the road wheel(s).

3. Disconnect the stabilizer link from the lower control arm.
4. If the steering gear hinders removal procedures, detach the unit and move it out of the way.
5. Disconnect the tie rod from the steering knuckle using a ball joint remover.
6. Using an internal fit coil spring compressor, compress the coil spring so that it is loose in its seat.
CAUTION: *Be sure to follow manufacturer's instructions when using spring compressor. Coil springs in a compressed state contain enormous energy which, if released accidentally, could cause serious injury.*
7. To remove the coil spring, disconnect the lower control arm from the crossmember at the pivot bolts. If additional clearance is necessary, disconnect the lower control arm from the steering knuckle at the ball joint.
8. To install, compress the coil spring until spring height is the same as when removed, then position the spring on the control arm. Make sure the lower end of the coil spring is properly positioned in the lower control arm and that the upper end fits correctly in its pad.
9. Connect the lower control arm from the steering knuckle at the ball joint. Connect the lower control arm from the crossmember at the pivot bolts and install the coil spring.
10. Connect the tie rod to the steering knuckle.
11. Attach the steering gear unit.
12. Connect the stabilizer link to the lower control arm.
13. Install the wheel(s).
14. Lower the vehicle.

Struts

REMOVAL AND INSTALLATION

1. Place the ignition key in the unlocked position so that the front wheels can be moved.

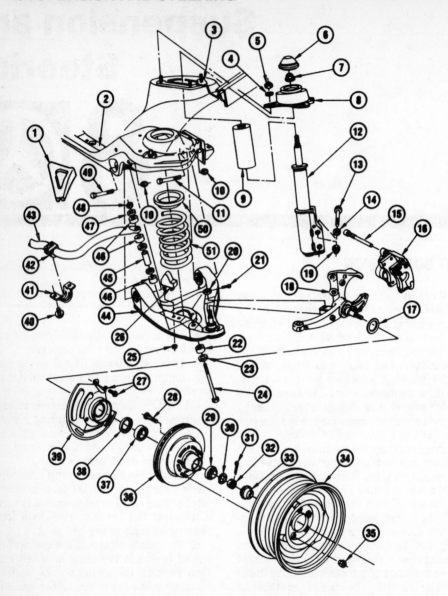

1. Crossmember brace	18. Knuckle	35. Nut
2. Crossmember	19. Nut (M16 × 2)	36. Hub
3. Retainer	20. Nut ($^9/_{16}$-18)	37. Inner front wheel bearing
4. Washer	21. Cotter pin (⅛ × 1)	38. Seal
5. Nut (M8 × 1.25)	22. Grommet	39. Shield
6. Washer	23. Retainer	40. Bolt (M10 × 1.5 × 30)
7. Nut (M14 × 2)	24. Bolt ($^5/_{16}$-18 × 7)	41. Bracket
8. Mount	25. Nut ($^7/_{16}$-14)	42. Insulator
9. Shield	26. Bumper	43. Front stabilizer shaft
10. Nut (M12 × 1.75)	27. Bolt	44. Lower control arm
11. Bolt (M12 × 1.75 × 95)	28. Bolt	45. Spacer
12. Absorber w/strut	29. Outer front wheel bearing	46. Grommet
13. Bolt	30. Washer	47. Retainer
14. Washer	31. Cotter pin (M3.2 × 25)	48. Nut
15. Bolt	32. Nut	49. Bolt (M12 × 1.75 × 115)
16. Caliper	33. Cap	50. Insulator
17. Gasket	34. Wheel	

Front suspension

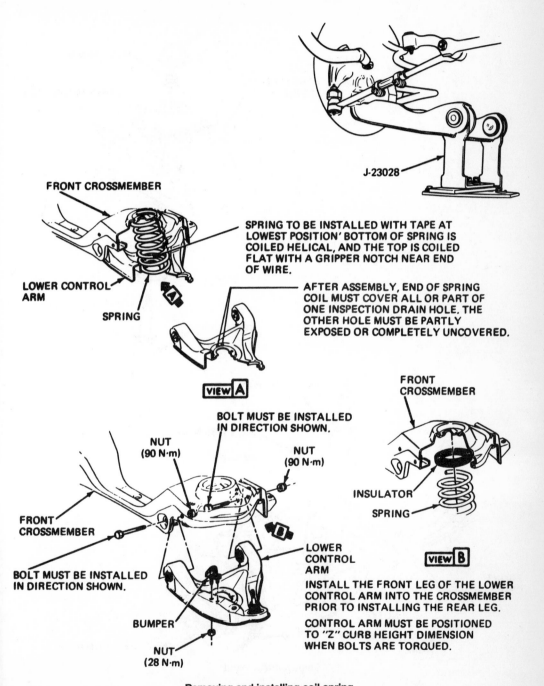

J-23028

FRONT CROSSMEMBER

SPRING TO BE INSTALLED WITH TAPE AT LOWEST POSITION' BOTTOM OF SPRING IS COILED HELICAL, AND THE TOP IS COILED FLAT WITH A GRIPPER NOTCH NEAR END OF WIRE.

LOWER CONTROL ARM

SPRING

AFTER ASSEMBLY, END OF SPRING COIL MUST COVER ALL OR PART OF ONE INSPECTION DRAIN HOLE. THE OTHER HOLE MUST BE PARTLY EXPOSED OR COMPLETELY UNCOVERED.

VIEW A

FRONT CROSSMEMBER

BOLT MUST BE INSTALLED IN DIRECTION SHOWN.

NUT (90 N·m)

NUT (90 N·m)

FRONT CROSSMEMBER

INSULATOR

SPRING

BOLT MUST BE INSTALLED IN DIRECTION SHOWN.

LOWER CONTROL ARM

VIEW B

INSTALL THE FRONT LEG OF THE LOWER CONTROL ARM INTO THE CROSSMEMBER PRIOR TO INSTALLING THE REAR LEG.

CONTROL ARM MUST BE POSITIONED TO "Z" CURB HEIGHT DIMENSION WHEN BOLTS ARE TORQUED.

BUMPER

NUT (28 N·m)

Removing and installing coil spring

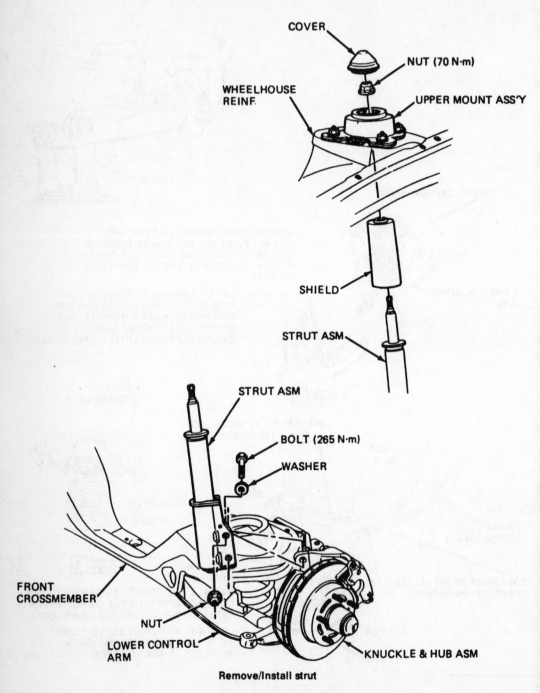

COVER

NUT (70 N·m)

WHEELHOUSE REINF.

UPPER MOUNT ASS'Y

SHIELD

STRUT ASM

STRUT ASM

BOLT (265 N·m)

WASHER

FRONT CROSSMEMBER

NUT

LOWER CONTROL ARM

KNUCKLE & HUB ASM

Remove/Install strut

Strut removal and installation

2. From inside the engine compartment, remove the upper strut to upper mount nut.

CAUTION: *Do not attempt to move the vehicle with the upper strut fastener disconnected.*

3. Raise the front of the vehicle and position safety stands under the vehicle.

4. Remove the wheel and tire assembly.

5. Remove the brake caliper without disconnecting the fluid hose, and hang out of the way on a wire. Do not allow the caliper to hang by its fluid hose.

6. Remove the two lower bolts attaching the strut to the steering knuckle.

7. Lift the strut up from the steering knuckle to compress the rod, then pull down and remove the strut.

8. To install, half extend the rod through the upper mount, then hand start the upper fastener, engaging as many threads as possible.

9. Extend the strut and position it onto the steering knuckle.

10. Install the lower mount bolts hand tight.

11. Tighten the upper fastener fully.

12. Fully tighten the lower bolts only when the front suspension is on the ground. Torque the steering knuckle-to-strut nuts to 125 ft. lbs. (170 Nm) followed by a 120 degree turn. Do not exceed a final torque of 148 Ft. lbs. (200 Nm).

13. Install the brake caliper

14. Install the wheel and tire assembly.

15. Lower the front of the vehicle.

16. From inside the engine compartment, tighten the upper strut to upper mount nut to 44 ft. lbs. (60 Nm).

17. Have the front end aligned.

OVERHAUL

The original equipment struts are serviced by replacement of the entire unit. There is no strut cartridge to replace.

Lower Ball Joint

INSPECTION

NOTE: *Before performing this inspection, make sure the wheel bearings are adjusted correctly and that the control arm bushings are in good condition.*

1. Jack the car up under the front lower control arm at the spring seat.

2. Raise the car until there is 1–2 in. (25–51mm) of clearance under the wheel.

3. Insert a bar under the wheel and pry upward. If the wheel raises more than 1/8 in. (3mm), the ball joints are worn. Determine if the lower ball joint is worn by visual inspection while prying on the wheel.

REMOVAL AND INSTALLATION

NOTE: *To prevent component damage, an on-car ball joint press, such as Kent-Moore tool J–9519–23 should be used.*

1. Raise the vehicle on a hoist and remove the wheel.

2. Support the lower control arm spring seat with a jack.

REMOVING BALL JOINT

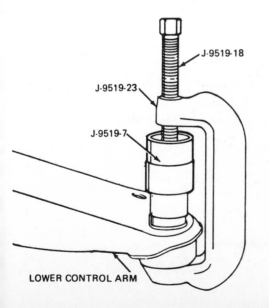

INSTALLING BALL JOINT

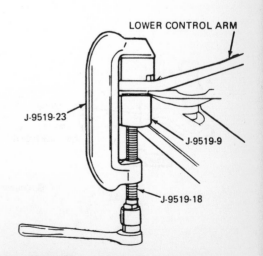

Removing and installing lower ball joint

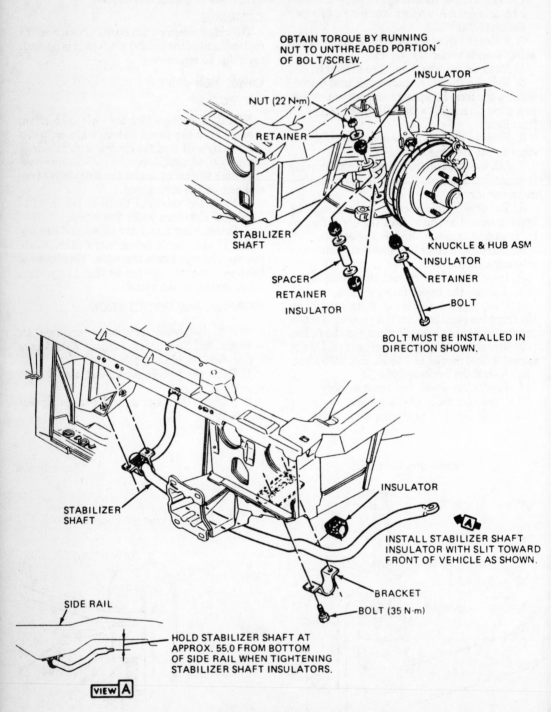

OBTAIN TORQUE BY RUNNING
NUT TO UNTHREADED PORTION
OF BOLT/SCREW.

INSULATOR

NUT (22 N·m)

RETAINER

STABILIZER
SHAFT

KNUCKLE & HUB ASM

SPACER

INSULATOR

RETAINER

RETAINER

INSULATOR

BOLT

BOLT MUST BE INSTALLED IN
DIRECTION SHOWN.

INSULATOR

STABILIZER
SHAFT

INSTALL STABILIZER SHAFT
INSULATOR WITH SLIT TOWARD
FRONT OF VEHICLE AS SHOWN.

BRACKET

BOLT (35 N·m)

SIDE RAIL

HOLD STABILIZER SHAFT AT
APPROX. 55.0 FROM BOTTOM
OF SIDE RAIL WHEN TIGHTENING
STABILIZER SHAFT INSULATORS.

VIEW A

Stabilizer shaft assembly

3. Loosen the lower ball stud nut. Break the ball stud loose. Remove the ball stud nut.

4. Remove the ball stud from the steering knuckle. Support the steering knuckle aside using a hanger or wire.

5. Using a ball joint press, remove the ball joint from the lower control arm.

6. Install the new ball joint, using the press.

7. Install the ball stud in the steering knuckle boss.

8. Install the nut on the ball stud, tightening to 77 ft. lbs. (105 Nm) on all models. Continue to tighten the nut until the cotter pin holes align and install the pin. Do not back off the nut to align the holes.

9. Install the lube fitting and grease the new joint.

Stabilizer Shaft

REMOVAL AND INSTALLATION

1. Raise the car and support the car on jackstands.

2. Remove the link bolt, nut, grommet, spacer and retainers.

3. Remove the insulators and brackets.

4. Remove the stabilizer shaft.

5. To install, position the stabilizer shaft into place and install the insulators and brackets.

6. Hold the stabilizer shaft approximately 55mm from the bottom of the side rail and torque the bracket bolts to 37 ft. lbs. (50 Nm).

7. Install the bolt, nut, grommets, spacer and retainers.

8. Lower the car.

Lower Control Arm

REMOVAL AND INSTALLATION

1. Raise the car and support the car on jackstands.

2. Remove the wheel and tire.

3. Remove the stabilizer link and bushings at the lower control arm.

4. Remove the pivot bolt nuts. DO NOT remove the pivot bolts at this time.

5. Install tool J–23028 or equivalent adapter to the jack and place into position with tool J–23028 or equivalent adapter supporting bushings.

6. Install the jackstand under the outside frame rail on the opposite side of the vehicle.

7. Raise tool J–23028 or equivalent adapter enough to remove both pivot bolts.

8. Lower tool J–23028 or equivalent adapter.

9. Remove the spring and insulator tape insulator to the spring.

10. Remove the ball joint from the knuckle.

11. To install, reverse the removal procedure.

Steering Knuckle and Spindle

REMOVAL AND INSTALLATION

1. Siphon some brake fluid from the master cylinder. Raise and support the vehicle.

2. Remove the wheel and tire. Remove the brake hose from the strut.

3. Remove the caliper and support on a wire. Refer to Chapter 9 for removal and installation procedures of the hub-and-disc, then remove the hub-and-disc.

4. Remove the splash shield. Disconnect the tie rod from the steering knuckle.

5. Support the lower control arm and disconnect the ball joint from the steering knuckle using tool J–24292A.

6. Remove the 2 bolts securing the strut to the steering knuckle and remove the steering knuckle.

7. To install, place the steering knuckle into position and install the 2 bolts securing the strut to the steering knuckle.

8. Support the lower control arm and connect the ball joint to the steering knuckle.

9. Connect the tie rod to the steering knuckle. Install the splash shield.

10. Install the caliper.

11. Install the brake hose from the strut. Install the wheel and tire.

12. Lower the vehicle and refill the master cylinder with brake fluid.

Front Wheel Bearings

ADJUSTMENT

1. Raise the car and support it at the lower arm.

2. Remove the hub dust cover and spindle cotter pin. Loosen the nut.

3. While spinning the wheel, snug the nut down to seat the bearings. Do not exert over 12 ft. lbs. of force on the nut.

4. Back the nut off ¼ turn or until it is just lose. Line up the cotter pin hole in the spindle with the hole in the nut.

5. Insert a new cotter pin. Endplay should be between 0.03–0.13mm. If play exceeds this tolerance, the wheel bearings should be replaced.

REMOVAL AND INSTALLATION

1. Raise the car and support it at the lower arm. Remove the wheel. Remove the brake caliper and support it on a wire.

2. Remove the dust cap, cotter pin, castle nut, thrust washer and outside wheel bearing. Pull the disc/hub assembly from the steering knuckle.

3. Pry out the inner seal and remove the inner bearing. If necessary to remove the inner

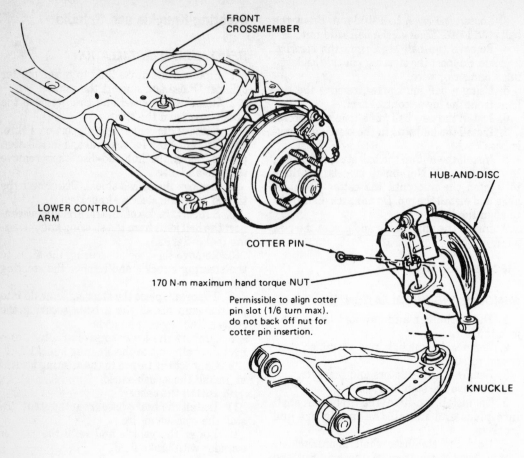

FRONT CROSSMEMBER

HUB-AND-DISC

LOWER CONTROL ARM

COTTER PIN

170 N·m maximum hand torque NUT

Permissible to align cotter pin slot (1/6 turn max). do not back off nut for cotter pin insertion.

KNUCKLE

Steering knuckle assembly

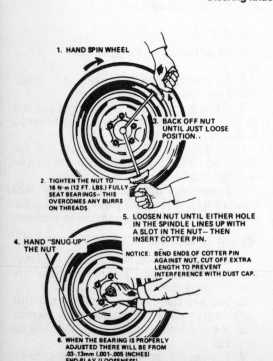

1. HAND SPIN WHEEL

3. BACK OFF NUT UNTIL JUST LOOSE POSITION..

2. TIGHTEN THE NUT TO 16 N·m (12 FT. LBS.) FULLY SEAT BEARINGS— THIS OVERCOMES ANY BURRS ON THREADS

5. LOOSEN NUT UNTIL EITHER HOLE IN THE SPINDLE LINES UP WITH A SLOT IN THE NUT-- THEN INSERT COTTER PIN.

4. HAND "SNUG-UP" THE NUT

NOTICE: BEND ENDS OF COTTER PIN AGAINST NUT, CUT OFF EXTRA LENGTH TO PREVENT INTERFERENCE WITH DUST CAP.

6. WHEN THE BEARING IS PROPERLY ADJUSTED THERE WILL BE FROM .03-.13mm (.001-.005 INCHES) END-PLAY (LOOSENESS).

Wheel bearing adjustment

bearing races, use a hammer and a brass drift to drive the bearing races from the hub.

4. Clean all parts in cleaning solvent; DO NOT use gasoline. After cleaning, check parts for excessive wear and replace damaged parts.

5. Smear grease inside of hub. Install the bearing races into hub, using a hammer and a brass drift. Drive the races in until they seat against the shoulder of the hub.

6. Pack the bearings with grease and install the inner bearing in the hub. Install a new grease seal, be careful not to damage the seal.

7. Install the disc/hub assembly onto the steering knuckle. Install the outer bearing, thrust washer and castle nut. Tighten the nut until the wheel does not turn freely.

8. Back off the nut until the wheel turns freely and install the cotter pin. Install the dust cap, caliper and wheel. Lower the car.

PACKING

Clean the wheel bearings thoroughly with solvent and check their condition before installation.

CAUTION: *Do not blow the bearing dry with compressed air as this would allow the bearing to turn without lubrication.*

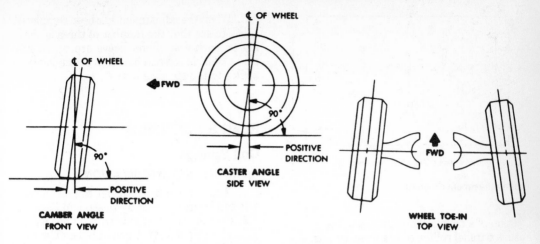

Caster, Camber and Toe-In diagrams

Apply a sizable amount of lubricant to the palm of one hand. Using your other hand, work the bearing into the lubricant so that the grease is pushed through the rollers and out the other side. Keep rotating the bearing while continuing to push the lubricant through it.

Front End Alignment

CAMBER

Camber is the inward or outward tilting of the front wheels from the vertical. When the wheels tilt outward at the top, the camber is said to be positive (+). When the wheels tilt in-

ward at the top, the camber is said to be negative (-). The amount of tilt is measured in degrees from the vertical and this measurement is called the camber angle.

CASTER

Caster is the tilting of the front steering axis either forward or backward from the vertical. A backward tilt is said to be positive (+) and a forward tilt is said to be negative (-).

TOE-IN

Toe-in is the turning in of the front wheels. The actual amount of toe-in is normally only a

An alignment verification label on the upper mount-to-wheelhouse tower verifies the accuracy of camber and caster adjustment. If a steering problem exists, it is important to check other possible causes before adjusting camber or caster.

(2) Using reliable alignment equipment, follow the manufacturer's instructions to obtain camber and caster readings. Adjust the camber by rotating the turnbuckle on J-29724 to allow the mount assembly to move inboard or outboard.

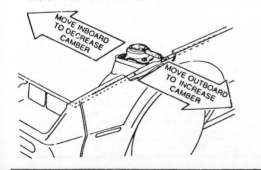

(1) Remove dust cap and fender bolt. Attach J-29724, using original fender bolt. Tighten the turnbuckle. Loosen (3) nuts attaching mount assembly.

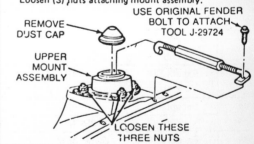

(3) After obtaining the correct camber reading, caster can be adjusted by lightly tapping the mount assembly forward or rearward.

(4) When the correct camber and caster readings are obtained, tighten the (3) nuts attaching the mount assembly to 28 N·m. Remove J-29724. Install the fender bolt and dust cap.

Caster and Camber adjustment

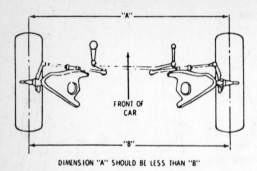

DIMENSION "A" SHOULD BE LESS THAN "B"

Toe-In adjustment diagram

fraction of a degree. The purpose of toe-in is to ensure parallel rolling of the front wheels. (Excessive toe-in or toe-out will cause tire wear.)

CASTER/CAMBER ADJUSTMENT

Caster and camber can be adjusted by moving the position of the upper strut mount assembly. Moving the mount forward/rearward adjusts caster. Movement inboard/outboard adjusts camber.

TOE-IN ADJUSTMENT

1. Loosen the clamp bolts at each end of the steering tie rod adjustable sleeves.
2. With the steering wheel set straight ahead, turn the adjusting sleeves to obtain the proper adjustment.

3. When the adjustment has been completed, check to see that the number of threads showing on each end of the sleeve are equal. Also check that tie rod end housings are at the right angles to the steering arm.

REAR SUSPENSION

Coil Springs

REMOVAL AND INSTALLATION

1. Raise the car by the frame so that the rear axle can be independently raised and lowered.
2. Support the rear axle with a floor jack.
3. If equipped with brake hose attaching brackets, disconnect the brackets allowing the hoses to hang free. Do not disconnect the hoses. Perform this step only if the hoses will be unduly stretched when the axle is lowered.
4. Disconnect the track bar from the axle.
5. Remove the lower shock absorber bolts and lower the axle. Make sure the axle is supported securely on the floor jack and that there is no chance of the axle slipping after the shock absorbers are disconnected.
NOTE: *On vehicles equipped with a 4-cylinder engine, remove the drive shaft.*
6. Lower the axle and remove the coil spring. Do not lower the axle past the limits of the brake lines or the lines will be damaged.

WHEEL ALIGNMENT

Year	Model	Caster (deg.) Range	Preferred Setting	Camber (deg.) Range	Preferred Setting	Toe-in (in.)
1982	Except Z28	2½P–3½P	3P	½P–1½P	1P	7/32
	Z28	2½P–3½P	3P	½P–1½P	1P	5/32
1983	Except Z28	2P–4P	3P	½P–1½P	1P	7/32
	Z28	2P–4P	3P	3/16P–1 13/16P	1P	5/32
1984	Except Z28	2P–4P	3P	½P–1½P	1P	7/32
	Z28	2P–4P	3P	3/16P–1 13/16P	1P	5/32
1985	Except Z28	2½P–3½P	3P	½P–1½P	1P	5/32
	Z28	3P–4P	3½P	½P–1½P	1P	5/32
1986	Except Z28	2½P–3½P	3P	½P–1½P	1P	5/32
	Z28	3P–4P	3½P	½P–1½P	1P	5/32
1987	All	4½P–5½P	5P	½P–1½P	1P	3/64
1988	All	4½P–5½P	5P	½N–½P	0	3/64
1989	All	4½P–5½P	5P	½N–½P	0	3/64
1990	All	4½P–5½P	5P	½N–½P	0	3/64
1991	All	4½P–5½P	5P	½N–½P	0	3/64
1992	All	4½P–5½P	5P	½N–½P	0	3/64

N—Negative
P—Positive

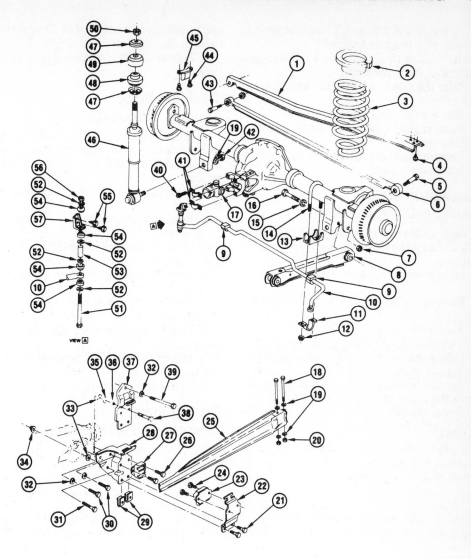

VIEW Ⓐ

1. Tie rod bracket brace
2. Upper spring insulator
3. Coil spring
4. Screw (M10 × 1.5 × 32)
5. Bolt
6. Tie rod
7. Nut (M12 × 1.75)
8. Lower control arm
9. Insulator
10. Rear stabilizer shaft
11. Clamp
12. Nut (M8 × 1.25)
13. Bracket
14. Bolt
15. Washer
16. Bolt (M12 × 1.75 × 95)
17. Driveshaft w/universal
    joint
18. Bolt (M14 × 2 × 185)
19. Washer

20. Nut (M14 × 2)
21. Bolt (M8 × 1.25 × 25)
22. Bracket
23. Insulator
24. Bolt (M5 × 0.8 × 10)
25. Torque arm
26. Bolt (M5 × 0.8 × 10)
27. Torque arm insulator
28. Torque arm bracket
29. Nut, "U" (M8 × 1.25)
30. Bolt (M10 × 1.5 × 20)
31. Bolt (M10 × 1.5 × 70)
32. Washer (M10 × 18.3)
33. Spacer
34. Bolt (M4 × 0.7 × 20)
35. Psh-nut
36. Spacer
37. Bracket
38. Bolt
39. Bolt (M10 × 1.5 × 110)

40. Bolt
41. Strap
42. Nut (M14.0 × 2)
43. Bolt w/screw
44. Bolt (M8 × 1.25 × 16)
45. Bumper
46. Rear shock absorber
47. Retainer
48. Grommet
49. Grommet
50. Nut (M10 × 1.5)
51. Bolt (M8 × 1.25 × 180)
52. Washer
53. Spacer
54. Grommet
55. Screw (M10 × 1.5 × 32)
56. Nut (M8 × 1.25)(*2)
57. Bracket

Rear suspension assembly

7. To install the coil spring, position spring into place with the axle lowered.

8. On vehicles equipped with 4-cylinder engines, install the drive shaft.

9. Raise the axle and install the lower shock absorber bolts.

10. Connect the track bar to the axle.

11. Connect the brake hose attaching brackets, if removed.

12. Remove the support from the rear axle.

13. Lower the vehicle.

Shock Absorbers
REMOVAL AND INSTALLATION

1. Jack up the car to a convenient working height. Support the axle assembly with jackstands.

2. Disconnect the upper shock attaching nuts.

3. Remove the lower shock to axle mounting bolt.

4. Remove the shock absorber.

5. To install, position the shock into place.

6. Install the lower shock to axle mounting bolt. Torque to 70 ft. lbs. (95 Nm).

7. Connect the upper shock attaching nuts. Torque the upper nuts to 13 ft. lbs. (17 Nm).

8. Lower the car.

TESTING

Visually inspect the shock absorber. If there is evidence of leakage and the shock absorber is covered with oil, the shock is defective and should be replaced.

If there is no sign of excessive leakage (a small amount of weeping is normal) bounce the car at one corner by pressing down on the fender or bumper and releasing. When you have the car bouncing as much as you can, release the fender or bumper. The car should stop bouncing after the first rebound. If the bouncing continues past the center point of the bounce more than once, the shock absorbers are worn and should be replaced.

Track Bar

REMOVAL AND INSTALLATION

1. Raise the rear of the vehicle, place jackstands under the rear axle, then lower the jack so that the stands are supporting all of the weight.

2. Remove the track bar mounting fasteners. Remove the track bar.

3. To install, clean all of the track bar fasteners.

4. Position the track bar in the body bracket and loosely install the bolt and the nut.

5. Position the track bar to the axle assembly and install the bolt and the nut. Torque the bolt to 59 ft. lbs. (80 Nm).

6. Torque the body bracket nut to 78 ft. lbs. (105 Nm).

Track Bar Brace
REMOVAL AND INSTALLATION

1. Raise the rear of the vehicle, place jackstands under the rear axle, then lower the jack so that the stands are supporting all of the weight.

2. Remove the heat shield screws from the track bar brace.

3. Remove the three track bar brace-to-body brace screws.

4. Remove the track bar-to-body bracket fasteners and remove the track bar brace.

5. To install, place the track bar brace into position.

6. Install the track bar-to-body bracket fasteners.

7. Install the three track bar brace-to-body brace screws.

8. Install the heat shield screws to the track bar brace.

9. Lower the vehicle.

Control Arms
REMOVAL AND INSTALLATION

NOTE: *Remove/reinstall only one lower control arm at a time. If both arms are removed at the same time, the axle could roll or slip sideways, making reinstallation of the arms very difficult.*

1. Raise the rear of the vehicle, place jackstands under the rear axle, then lower the jack so that the stands are supporting all of the weight.

2. Remove the control arm attaching fasteners, then remove the control arm.

3. Installation is a simple matter of bolting the arm into place. Torque the 3 bolts at the body brace bracket to 35 ft. lbs. (47 Nm) and the nut at the body bracket to 61 ft. lbs. (83 Nm).

Torque Arm
REMOVAL AND INSTALLATION

NOTE: *The coil springs must be removed BEFORE the torque arm. If the torque arm is removed first, vehicle damage will result.*

In order to proceed, the vehicle must be supported in a manner which will allow the rear axle height to be adjusted independently of the body height.

1. Remove the track bar mounting bolt at the axle assembly, then loosen the track bar bolt at the body brace.

2. Disconnect the rear brake hose clip at the

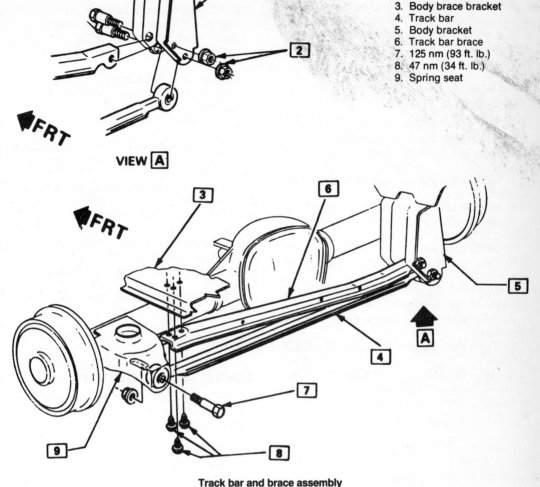

1. Body bracket
2. 78 nm (58 ft. lb.)
3. Body brace bracket
4. Track bar
5. Body bracket
6. Track bar brace
7. 125 nm (93 ft. lb.)
8. 47 nm (34 ft. lb.)
9. Spring seat

Track bar and brace assembly

axle assembly, which will allow additional drop of the axle.

3. Remove the lower attaching nuts from both rear shock absorbers.

4. Disconnect the shock absorbers from their lower attaching points.

5. On models with four cylinder engines, remove the driveshaft.

6. Carefully lower the rear axle assembly and remove the rear coil springs.

CAUTION: *DO NOT overstretch the brake hose when lowering the axle-damage to the hose will result.*

7. Remove the torque arm rear attaching bolts.

8. Remove the front torque arm outer bracket.

9. Remove the torque arm from the vehicle.

10. To install, place the torque arm in position and loosely install the rear torque arm bolts.

11. Install the front torque arm bracket and torque the nuts to 31 ft. lbs. (42 Nm).

12. Torque the rear torque arm nuts to 100 ft. lbs. (135 Nm).

13. Place the rear springs and insulators in position, then raise the rear axle assembly until all of the weight is supported by the spring.

14. Attach the shock absorbers to the rear axle and torque the fasteners to 70 ft. lbs. (95 Nm).

15. Clean and reinstall the track bar mounting bolt at the axle. Torque the bolt to 59 ft. lbs. (80 Nm).

16. Clean and reinstall the track bar-to-body brace nut. Torque the nut to 78 ft. lbs. (105 Nm).

17. Install the brake line clip to the underbody.

18. On four cylinder models, reinstall the driveshaft.

19. Lower the vehicle.

STEERING

WARNING: *Before attempting any repairs involving the steering wheel or disassembly of it, ensure the Supplemental Inflatable Restraint (Air Bag) system is properly disarmed.*

Air Bag

DISARMING

1. Turn the steering wheel to align the wheels in the straight-ahead position.
2. Turn the ignition switch to the **LOCK** position.
3. Remove the SIR air bag fuse from the fuse block.
4. Remove the left side trim panel and disconnect the yellow 2-way SIR harness wire connector at the base of the steering column.

To enable system:

5. Turn the ignition switch to the **LOCK** position.
6. Reconnect the yellow 2-way connector at the base of the steering column.
7. Reinstall the SIR fuse and the left side trim panel.
8. Turn the ignition switch to the **RUN** position.
9. Verify the SIR indicator light flashes 7–9 times. If it does not, inspect system for malfunction or contact a service facility.

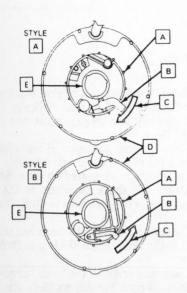

A. Locking tab
B. Spring
C. Hub direction
D. Coil housing
E. Coil hub

SIR (Air Bag) system coil centering

SUPPLEMENTAL INFLATABLE RESTRAINT (SIR) COIL ASSEMBLY

NOTE: *After performing repairs on the internals of the steering column the coil assembly must be centered in order to avoid damaging the coil or accidental deployment of the air bag.*

There are 2 different styles of coils, 1 rotates clockwise and the other rotates counterclockwise.

ADJUSTMENT

1. With the system properly disarmed, hold the coil assembly with the clear bottom up to see the coil ribbon.
2. While holding the coil assembly, depress the lock spring and rotate the hub in the direction of the arrow until it stops. The coil should now be wound up snug against the center hub.
3. Rotate the coil assembly in the opposite direction approximately 2½ turns and release the lock spring between the locking tabs in front of the arrow.
4. Install the coil assembly onto the steering shaft.

Steering Wheel

REMOVAL AND INSTALLATION

NOTE: *If the vehicle is equipped with S.I.R. (AIR BAG) system, ensure that the proper disarming procedure is followed.*

1982–89 VEHICLES

1. Disconnect the negative battery cable.
2. Remove the horn pad.
3. Disconnect the horn contact lead.
4. Remove the retainer and steering wheel nut.
5. Using a suitable steering wheel puller, remove the steering wheel.
6. Installation is the reverse of the removal procedure. Tighten the steering wheel nut to 31 ft. lbs. (42 Nm).

1990–92 VEHICLES

CAUTION: *The vehicle is equipped with a Supplemental Inflatable Restraint (SIR) system, follow the recommended disarming procedures before performing any work on or around the system. Failure to do so may result in possible deployment of the air bag and/or personal injury.*

1. Disconnect the negative battery cable.
2. Disable the Supplemental Inflatable Restraint (SIR) system as follows:
   a. Turn the steering wheel so the vehicle's wheels are pointing straight-ahead.
   b. Remove the left sound insulator by re-

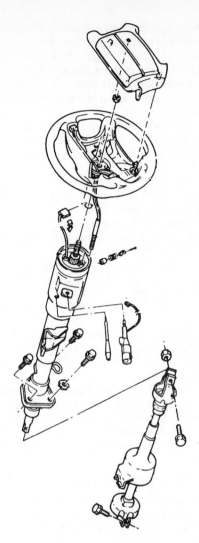

Steering column assembly—with SIR (Air Bag) system

moving the nut from the stud and gently prying the insulator from the knee bolster.

c. Disconnect the Connector Position Assurance (CPA) clip and yellow 2-way SIR harness connector at the base of the steering column.

d. Remove the SIR fuse from the fuse block.

3. Loosen the screws and locknuts from the back of the steering wheel using a suitable Torx® driver or equivalent, until the inflator module can be released from the steering wheel. Remove the inflator module from the steering wheel.

CAUTION: *When carrying a live inflator module, ensure the bag and trim cover are pointed away from the body. In case of an accidental deployment, the bag will then deploy with minimal chance of injury. When placing*

a live inflator module on a bench or other surface, always place the bag and trim cover up, away from the surface. This is necessary so a free space is provided to allow the air bag to expand in the unlikely event of accidental deployment. Otherwise, personal injury may result. Also, never carry the inflator module by the wires or connector on the underside of the module.

4. Disconnect the coil assembly connector and CPA clip from the inflator module terminal.

5. Remove the steering wheel locking nut.

6. Using a suitable puller, remove the steering wheel and disconnect the horn contact. When attaching the steering wheel puller, use care to prevent threading the side screws into the coil assembly and damaging the coil assembly.

To install:

7. Route the coil assembly connector through the steering wheel.

8. Connect the horn contact and install the steering wheel. When installing the steering wheel, align the block tooth on the steering wheel with the block tooth on the steering shaft within 1 female serration.

9. Install the steering wheel locking nut. Tighten the nut to 31 ft. lbs. (42 Nm).

10. Connect the coil assembly connector and CPA clip to the inflator module terminal.

11. Install the inflator module. Ensure the wiring is not exposed or trapped between the inflator module and the steering wheel. Tighten the inflator module screws to 25 inch lbs. (2.8 Nm).

12. Connect the negative battery cable.

13. Enable the SIR system as follows:

a. Connect the yellow 2-way SIR harness connector to base of the steering column and CPA.

b. Install the left sound insulator.

c. Install the SIR fuse in the fuse block.

d. Turn the ignition switch to the **RUN** position and verify that the inflatable restraint indicator flashes 7–9 times and then turns **OFF**. If the indicator does not respond as stated, a problem within the SIR system is indicated.

Turn Signal Switch

REMOVAL AND INSTALLATION

Standard Columns Without Air Bag

1. Remove the steering wheel as previously outlined. Remove the trim cover.

2. Pry the cover off, and lift the cover off the shaft.

3. Position the U-shaped lockplate compressing tool on the end of the steering shaft and

1. REMOVE AND INSTALL SHAFT LOCK AND/OR CANCELLING CAM

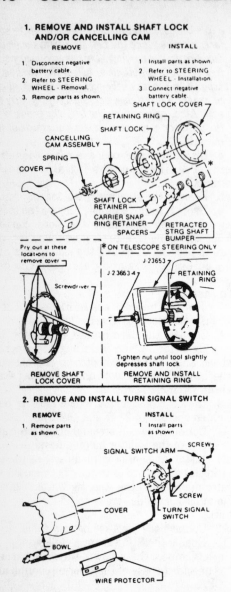

REMOVE

1. Disconnect negative battery cable.
2. Refer to STEERING WHEEL - Removal.
3. Remove parts as shown.

INSTALL

1. Install parts as shown.
2. Refer to STEERING WHEEL - Installation.
3. Connect negative battery cable.

SHAFT LOCK COVER
RETAINING RING
SHAFT LOCK
CANCELLING CAM ASSEMBLY
SPRING
COVER
SHAFT LOCK RETAINER
CARRIER SNAP RING RETAINER
SPACERS
RETRACTED STRG SHAFT BUMPER
*

Pry out at these locations to remove cover
Screwdriver
REMOVE SHAFT LOCK COVER

* ON TELESCOPE STEERING ONLY
J 23653
J 23663-4
RETAINING RING
Tighten nut until tool slightly depresses shaft lock
REMOVE AND INSTALL RETAINING RING

2. REMOVE AND INSTALL TURN SIGNAL SWITCH

REMOVE

1. Remove parts as shown.

INSTALL

1. Install parts as shown

SIGNAL SWITCH ARM
SCREW
SCREW
COVER
TURN SIGNAL SWITCH
BOWL
WIRE PROTECTOR

Turn signal switch assembly—without Air Bag system

compress the lock plate by turning the shaft nut clockwise. Pry the wire snapring out of the shaft groove.

4. Remove the tool and lift the lockplate off the shaft.

5. Remove the canceling cam assembly and upper bearing preload spring from the shaft.

6. Remove the turn signal lever. Push the flasher knob in and unscrew it. On models equipped with a button and a knob, remove the button retaining screw, then remove the button, spring, and knob.

7. Pull the switch connector out the mast jacket and tape the upper part to facilitate switch removal. Attach a long piece of wire to

the turn signal switch connector. When installing the turn signal switch, feed this wire through the column first, and then use this wire to pull the switch connector into position. On tilt wheels, place the turn signal and shifter housing in low position and remove the harness cover.

8. Remove the three switch mounting screws. Remove the switch by pulling it straight up while guiding the wiring harness cover through the column.

9. Install the replacement switch by working the connector and cover down through the housing and under the bracket. On tilt models, the connector is worked down through the housing, under the bracket, and then the cover is installed on the harness.

10. Install the switch mounting screws and the connector on the mast jacket bracket. Install the column-to-dash trim plate.

11. Install the flasher knob and the turn signal lever.

12. With the turn signal lever in neutral and the flasher knob out, slide the upper bearing preload spring, and canceling cam assembly onto the shaft.

13. Position the lock plate on the shaft and press it down until a new snapring can be inserted in the shaft groove. Always use a new snapring when assembling.

14. Install the cover and the steering wheel.

Tilt Columns Without Air Bag

CAUTION: *All elements of energy-absorbing (telescopic) steering columns are very sensitive to damage. Do not strike any part of the column (nuts, bolts, etc.) as this could ruin the entire assembly.*

1. Disconnect the battery cable.

2. Remove the steering wheel as outlined earlier.

3. Remove the cover from the steering column shaft.

4. Press down on the lockplate and pry the snapring from the shaft.

5. Remove the lockplate and the canceling cam.

6. Remove the upper bearing preload spring.

7. Remove the turn signal lever and the hazard flasher knob.

8. Lift up on the tilt lever and position the housing in its central position.

9. Remove the switch attaching screws.

10. Remove the lower trim cap from the instrument panel and disconnect the turn signal connector from the wiring harness.

11. Remove the four bolts which secure the bracket assembly to the jacket.

12. Loosen the screw that holds the shift indi-

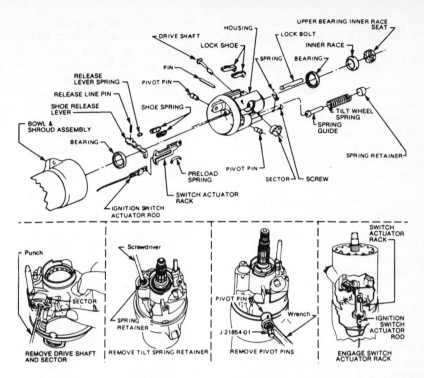

Tilt steering column assembly

cator needle and disconnect the clip from the link.

13. Remove the two nuts from the column support bracket while holding the column in position. Remove the bracket assembly and wire protector from the wiring, then loosely install the support column bracket.

14. Tape the turn signal wires at the connector to keep them fit and parallel.

15. Carefully remove the turn signal switch and wiring from the column.

16. To install, carefully install the turn signal switch and wiring into the column.

17. Remove the tape from the turn signal wires.

18. Install the wire protector and, while holding the column in position, install the two nuts to the column support bracket.

19. Connect the clip to the link and tighten the screw that holds the shift indicator needle.

20. Install the four bolts which secure the bracket assembly to the jacket.

21. Connect the turn signal connector to the wiring harness and install the lower trim cap to the instrument panel.

22. Install the switch attaching screws.

23. Install the turn signal lever and the hazard flasher knob.

24. Install the upper bearing preload spring.

25. Install the lockplate and the canceling cam.

26. Press down on the lockplate and install the snapring to the shaft using a new snapring.

27. Install the cover to the steering column shaft.

28. Install the steering wheel.

29. Connect the battery cable.

Steering Column With Air Bag

1. Properly disable the SIR air bag system, if equipped.

2. Disconnect the negative battery cable.

3. Remove the inflator module, if equipped with an air bag.

4. Remove the steering wheel.

5. Ensure the steering wheel is locked in the

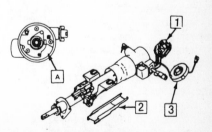

A. 6 o'clock position: harness through here
1. Coil assembly
2. Turn signal and hazard switch
3. Wiring protector

Turn signal switch removal—with Air Bag system

straight-ahead position and remove the coil assembly retaining ring on air bag equipped vehicles.

6. Pull the coil assembly out and allow it to hang.

7. Using a suitable tool, depress the lock plate to gain access to the snapring. Remove the snapring and remove the lockplate.

8. Remove the turn signal canceling cam, upper bearing spring and signal switch arm.

9. Remove the hazard warning knob, turn signal lever and steering column wiring protector.

10. Disconnect the turn signal switch connector from the harness connector.

11. Remove the switch retaining screws and remove the turn signal switch.

12. Installation is the reverse of the removal procedure. Make certain to follow the SIR coil recentering procedure previously described.

Ignition Switch

REPLACEMENT

The switch is located inside the channel section of the brake pedal support and is completely inaccessible without first lowering the steering column. The switch is actuated by a rod and rack assembly. A gear on the end of the lock cylinder engages the toothed upper end of the rod.

1. Lower the steering column; be sure to properly support it.

2. Put the switch in the **Off-Unlocked** position. **Off-Unlocked** position is two detents from the top.

3. Remove the two switch screws and remove the switch assembly.

4. Before installing, place the new switch in the **Off-Unlocked** position. Make sure the lock cylinder and actuating rod are in the **Off-Unlocked** (second detent from the top) position.

5. Install the activating rod into the switch and assemble the switch on the column. Tighten the mounting screws. Use only the specified screws since overlength screws could impair the collapsibility of the column.

6. Reinstall the steering column.

Ignition Lock Cylinder

REMOVAL AND INSTALLATION

1. Properly disable the SIR air bag system, if equipped.

2. Place the lock in the **RUN** position.

3. Remove the lock plate, turn signal switch and buzzer switch.

4. Remove the screw and lock cylinder. CAUTION: *If the screw is dropped on removal, it could fall into the column, requiring complete disassembly to retrieve the screw.*

5. Rotate the cylinder clockwise to align cylinder key with the keyway in the housing.

6. Push the lock all the way in.

7. Install the screw. Tighten the screw to 14 inch lbs. for adjustable columns and 25 inch lbs. for standard columns. Re-center the SIR coil assembly as previously directed.

Steering Column

REMOVAL AND INSTALLATION

NOTE: *The front of dash mounting plates must be loosened whenever the steering column is to be lowered from the instrument panel.*

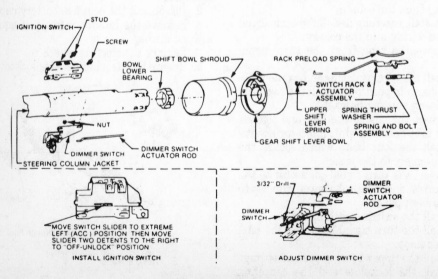

Ignition switch assembly

1. Disconnect the negative battery cable.

2. On 1990–92 vehicles, disable the Supplemental Inflatable Restraint (SIR) system as follows:

a. Turn the steering wheel so the vehicle's wheels are pointing straight-ahead.

NOTE: *The wheels of the vehicle must be in the straight-ahead position and the steering column in the locked position before proceeding with steering column removal. Failure to follow this procedure will cause the SIR coil to become uncentered, resulting in damage to the coil assembly.*

b. Remove the SIR fuse from the fuse block.

c. Remove the left sound insulator by removing the nut from the stud and gently prying the insulator from the knee bolster.

d. Disconnect the Connector Position Assurance (CPA) and yellow 2-way SIR harness connector at the base of the steering column.

3. Remove the nut and bolt from the upper intermediate shaft coupling. Separate the coupling from the lower end of the steering column.

4. Remove the steering wheel, if the column is to be replaced or repaired on the bench.

5. Remove the knee bolster and bracket, if equipped.

6. Remove the bolts attaching the toe plate to the cowl.

7. Disconnect the electrical connectors.

8. Remove the capsule nuts attaching the steering column support bracket to the instrument panel.

9. Disconnect the park lock cable from the ig-

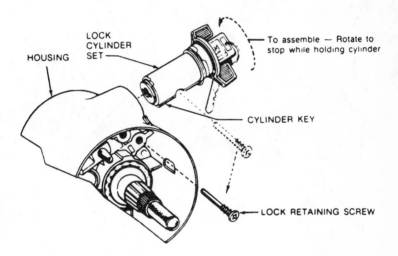

Ignition lock cylinder replacement

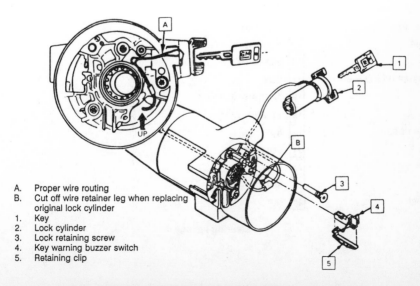

A. Proper wire routing
B. Cut off wire retainer leg when replacing original lock cylinder
1. Key
2. Lock cylinder
3. Lock retaining screw
4. Key warning buzzer switch
5. Retaining clip

Ignition lock cylinder replacement—with VATS security system

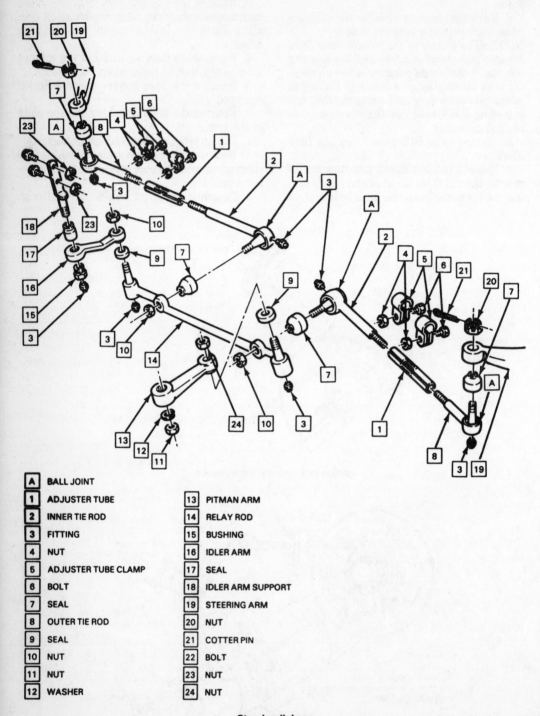

A	BALL JOINT		
1	ADJUSTER TUBE	13	PITMAN ARM
2	INNER TIE ROD	14	RELAY ROD
3	FITTING	15	BUSHING
4	NUT	16	IDLER ARM
5	ADJUSTER TUBE CLAMP	17	SEAL
6	BOLT	18	IDLER ARM SUPPORT
7	SEAL	19	STEERING ARM
8	OUTER TIE ROD	20	NUT
9	SEAL	21	COTTER PIN
10	NUT	22	BOLT
11	NUT	23	NUT
12	WASHER	24	NUT

Steering linkage

nition switch inhibitor, if equipped with automatic transmission.

10. Remove the steering column from the vehicle.

To install:

NOTE: *If a replacement steering column is being installed, do not remove the anti-rotation pin until after the steering column has been connected to the steering gear. Removing the anti-rotation pin before the steering column is connected to the steering gear may damage the SIR coil assembly.*

11. Position the steering column in the vehicle.

12. Connect the park lock cable to the ignition switch inhibitor on vehicles with automatic transmission.

13. Install the capsule nuts attaching the steering column support bracket to the instrument panel and tighten to 20 ft. lbs. (27 Nm).

14. Install the nut and bolt to the upper intermediate shaft coupling attaching the upper intermediate shaft to the steering column. Tighten the nut to 44 ft. lbs. (60 Nm).

15. Install the bolts attaching the toe plate to the cowl and tighten to 58 inch lbs. (6.5 Nm).

16. Connect the electrical connectors.

17. Remove the anti-rotation pin if a service replacement steering column is being installed.

18. Install the knee bolster and bracket, if equipped.

19. Install the sound insulator panel.

NOTE: *If SIR coil has become uncentered by turning of the steering wheel without the column connected to the steering gear, follow the proper adjustment procedure for the SIR coil assembly before proceeding.*

20. Install the steering wheel.

21. Connect the negative battery cable.

22. Enable the SIR system as follows:

a. Connect the yellow 2-way SIR harness connector to the base of the steering column and CPA clip and install the SIR fuse.

b. Install the left sound insulator.

c. Turn the ignition switch to the **RUN** position and verify that the inflatable restraint indicator flashes 7–9 times and then turns **OFF**. If the indicator does not respond as stated, a problem within the SIR system is indicated.

Steering Linkage

REMOVAL AND INSTALLATION

Pitman Arm

1. Raise the vehicle and support securely.

2. Remove the nut from the pitman arm ball stud.

3. Remove the relay rod from the pitman

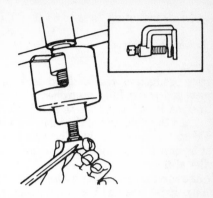

Using pitman arm puller—tie rod tool pictured in upper right

arm by using a tool such as J–24319–01 or equivalent. Pull down on the relay rod to remove it from the stud.

4. Remove the pitman arm nut from the pitman shaft and mark the relation of the arm position to the shaft.

5. Remove the pitman arm with tool J–5504 or tool J–6632 or equivalent. DO NOT HAMMER ON THE PULLER.

6. To install, position the pitman arm on the pitman shaft, lining up the marks made upon removal.

7. Position the relay rod on the pitman arm. Use J–29193 or J–29194 or equivalent to seat the tapers. A torque of 15 ft. lbs. (20 Nm) is required. With the tapers seated, remove the tool, then install a prevailing torque nut, and tighten to 35 ft. lbs. (48 Nm).

8. Set the relay rod height. Torque the idler arm-to-frame mounting bolts to 61 ft. lbs. (83 Nm).

9. Lower the vehicle.

Idler Arm

1. Raise the vehicle and support securely.

2. Remove the idler arm to frame nuts, washers, and bolts.

3. Remove the nut from the idler arm to relay rod ball stud.

4. Remove the relay rod from the idler arm by using J–24319–01 or equivalent.

5. Remove the idler arm.

6. To install, position the idler arm on the frame and LOOSELY install the mounting bolts, washers and nuts.

7. Install the relay rod to the idler arm, making certain seal is on the stud. Use J–29193 or J–29194 or equivalent to seat the tapers. A torque of 15 ft. lbs. (20 Nm) is required. With the tapers seated, remove the tool, then install a prevailing torque nut, and tighten to 35 ft. lbs. (48 Nm).

8. Set the relay rod height. Torque the idler

arm-to-frame mounting bolts to 61 ft. lbs. (83 Nm).

9. Lower the vehicle.

Relay Rod

During production, the installed position of the relay rod is carefully controlled to assure that the rod is at the proper height. Both the left end and the right end of the relay rod must be held at the same height. The side-to-side height is controlled by adjusting the position of the idler arm

Whenever disconnecting the relay rod assembly, it is important to first scribe the position of the idler arm-to-frame, and to reinstall the idler arm in the same position. Be sure to prevent the idler support from turning in the bushing, since that motion could result in improper relay rod height.

Whenever replacing the relay rod, or the idler arm, or the pitman arm, it is mandatory to establish the correct height.

1. Raise the vehicle and support on jackstands.

2. Remove the inner ends of the tie rods from the relay rod.

3. Remove the nut from the relay rod ball stud attachment at pitman arm.

4. Detach the relay rod from the pitman arm by using tool such as J–24319–01 or equivalent.

Shift the steering linkage as required to free the pitman arm from the relay rod.

5. Remove the nut from the idler arm and remove the relay rod from the idler arm.

6. Install the relay rod to idler arm, making certain idler stud seal is in place. Use J–29193 or J–29194 or equivalent to seat the tapers. A torque of 15 ft. lbs. (20 Nm) is required. With the tapers seated, remove the tool, then install a prevailing torque nut, and tighten to 35 ft. lbs. (48 Nm).

7. Raise the end of the rod and install on the pitman arm. Use J–29193 or J–29194 or equiv-

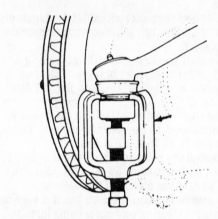

Using tie rod removing tool

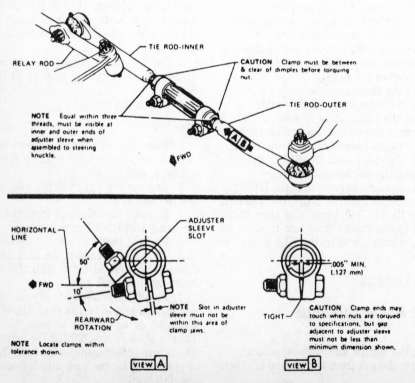

RELAY ROD

TIE ROD-INNER

CAUTION Clamp must be between & clear of dimples before torquing nut.

TIE ROD-OUTER

NOTE Equal within three threads, must be visible at inner and outer ends of adjuster sleeve when assembled to steering knuckle.

FWD

HORIZONTAL LINE

ADJUSTER SLEEVE SLOT

50°

FWD

10°

REARWARD ROTATION

NOTE Slot in adjuster sleeve must not be within this area of clamp jaws.

NOTE Locate clamps within tolerance shown.

TIGHT

.005" MIN. (.127 mm)

CAUTION Clamp ends may touch when nuts are torqued to specifications, but gap adjacent to adjuster sleeve must not be less than minimum dimension shown.

VIEW A

VIEW B

Proper tie rod and clamp positioning

alent to seat the tapers. A torque of 15 ft. lbs. (20 Nm) is required. With the tapers seated, remove the tool, then install a prevailing torque nut, and tighten to 35 ft. lbs. (48 Nm).

8. Install the tie rod ends to the relay rod. Lubricate the tie rod ends.

9. Install the damper, if equipped.

10. Set the relay rod height. Torque the idler arm-to-frame mounting bolts to 61 ft. lbs. (83 Nm).

11. Lower the vehicle.

12. Check and, if necessary, adjust front end alignment.

Tie Rod Ends

1. Raise the vehicle and support securely.

2. Remove the cotter pins from the ball studs and remove the castellated nuts.

3. Remove the outer ball stud by using the ball stud puller. If necessary, pull downward on the tie rod to disconnect it from the steering arm.

4. Remove the inner ball stud from the relay rod using a similar procedure.

5. Remove the tie rod end or ends to be replaced by loosening the clamp bolt and unscrewing them.

6. Lubricate tie rod threads with chassis grease and install new tie rod(s). Make sure both ends are an equal distance from the tie rod and tighten clamp bolts.

7. Make sure ball studs, tapered surfaces, and all threaded surfaces are clean and smooth, and free of grease. Install seals on ball studs. Install ball stud in steering arm and relay rod.

8. Rotate both inner and outer tie rod housings rearward to the limit of ball joint travel before tightening clamps. Make sure clamp slots and sleeve slots are aligned before tightening clamps. Make sure tightened bolts will be in horizontal position to 45 degrees upward (in the forward direction) when the tie rod is in its normal position. Make sure the tie rod end stays in position relative to the rod during the tightening operation. Tighten the clamps, and then return the assembly to the center of its travel.

9. Install ball stud nuts and torque to 35 ft. lbs. (47 Nm) Then tighten (do not loosen) further as required to align cotter pin holes in studs and nuts. Install new cotter pins.

10. Lubricate new tie rod ends and lower the vehicle.

Power Steering Gear

ADJUSTMENTS

NOTE: *Adjust the worm bearing preload first, then proceed with the pitman shaft over-center adjustment.*

WORM BEARING PRELOAD

1. Disconnect the negative battery cable.

2. Remove the steering gear.

3. Rotate the stub shaft and drain the power steering fluid into a suitable container.

4. Remove the adjuster plug nut.

5. Turn the adjuster plug in (clockwise) using a suitable spanner wrench until the adjuster plug and thrust bearing are firmly bottomed in the housing. Tighten the adjuster plug to 20 ft. lbs. (27 Nm).

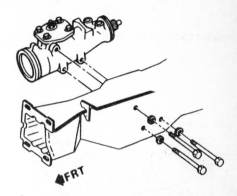

Power steering gear removal

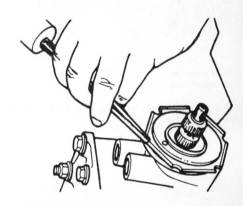

Loosening the power steering gear adjuster plug locknut

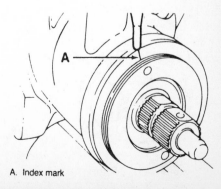

A. Index mark

Marking the housing even with the adjuster plug hole

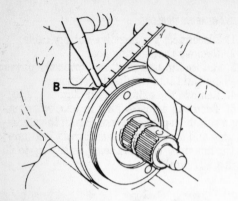

Making the second index mark

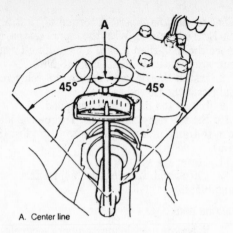

A. Center line

Checking the over-center rotational torque

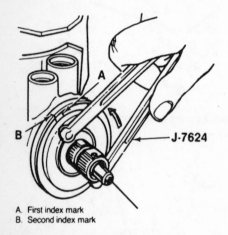

A. First index mark
B. Second index mark

Using a spanner wrench to align the adjuster plug with the second mark

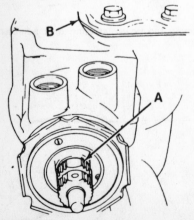

A. Stub shaft flat
B. Side cover

Aligning the stub shaft parallel with the top cover

6. Place an index mark on the housing even with 1 of the holes in the adjuster plug.

7. Measure back counterclockwise ½ in. (13mm) and place a second mark on the housing.

8. Turn the adjuster plug counterclockwise until the hole in the adjuster plug is aligned with the second mark on the housing.

9. Install the adjuster plug nut and using a suitable punch in a notch, tighten securely. Hold the adjuster plug to maintain alignment of the marks.

10. Install the steering gear and connect the negative battery cable.

PITMAN SHAFT OVER-CENTER

1. Disconnect the negative battery cable.

2. Remove the steering gear.

3. Rotate the stub shaft and drain the power steering fluid into a suitable container.

4. Turn the pitman shaft adjuster screw counterclockwise until fully extended, then turn back 1 full turn.

5. Rotate the stub shaft from stop to stop and count the number of turns.

6. Starting at either stop, turn the stub shaft back half the total number of turns. This is the "Center" position of the gear. When the gear is centered, the flat on the stub shaft should face upward and be parallel with the side cover and the master spline on the pitman shaft should be in line with the adjuster screw.

7. Rotate the stub shaft 45 degrees each side of the center using a suitable torque wrench with the handle in the vertical position. Record the worm bearing preload measured on or near the center gear position.

8. Adjust the over-center drag torque by loosening the adjuster locknut and turning the pitman shaft adjuster screw clockwise until the correct drag torque is obtained: Add 6–10 inch

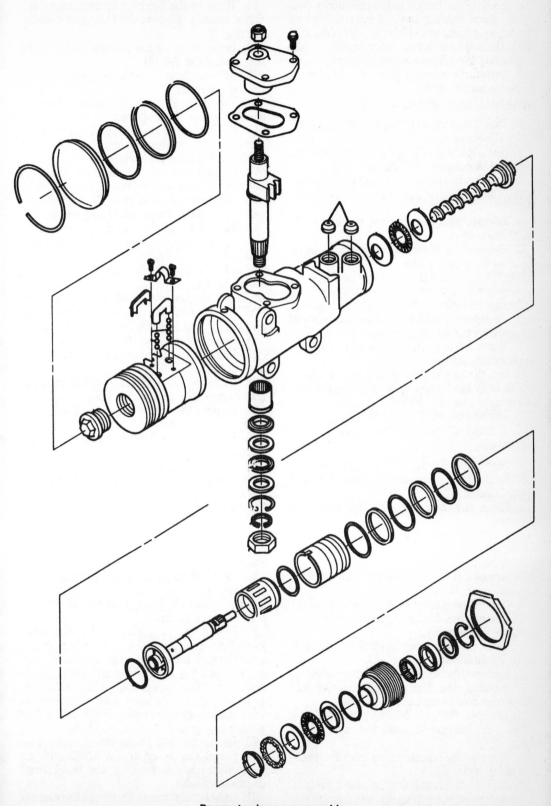

Power steering gear assembly

lbs. (0.7–1.1 Nm) torque to the previously measured worm bearing preload torque. Tighten the adjuster locknut to 20 ft. lbs. (27 Nm). Prevent the adjuster screw from turning while tightening the adjuster screw locknut.

9. Install the steering gear and connect the negative battery cable.

REMOVAL AND INSTALLATION

1. Disconnect the negative battery cable. Remove the coupling shield.

2. Remove the retaining bolts at the steering coupling to steering shaft flange.

3. Remove the pitman arm nut and washer. Mark the relation of the arm position to the shaft.

4. Remove pitman arm using special tool J–6632 or its equal.

5. Remove the steering box to frame bolts. Remove the steering box.

NOTE: *On vehicles with power steering, remove the fluid hoses and cap them to prevent foreign material from entering the system.*

6. To install, position the steering box and secure with the steering box-to-frame bolts.

7. Install the pitman arm to the match marks made earlier.

8. Install the pitman arm nut and washer.

9. Install the retaining bolts at the steering coupling to steering shaft flange.

10. Install the coupling shield.

11. Connect the negative battery cable.

OVERHAUL

1. Disconnect the negative battery cable.

2. Remove the power steering gear as previously directed.

3. Clean any external grease and dirt from the unit.

4. Rotate the stub shaft back and forth over a drain pan and remove any fluid remaining inside the unit.

5. Remove the pitman shaft adjuster lock nut and cover bolts.

6. Center the gear by turning the stub shaft.

7. Remove the side cover, gasket and pitman shaft as an assembly.

8. Remove the pitman shaft from the side cover by unscrewing it.

9. Remove the housing end plug by removing the retaining ring. Use a punch inserted into the access hole to unseat the ring.

10. Remove the adjuster plug nut using a punch and hammer against the edge of the slots.

11. Remove the adjuster plug from the housing using tool J–7624.

12. Remove the thrust washer bearing retainer from the adjuster plug by using a suitable tool and prying at raised area of bearing retainer.

13. Remove the bearing spacer, races and thrust bearing. Remove the O-ring and retaining ring.

14. Remove the needle bearing, dust and lip seals using tool J–6221.

15. Remove the stub shaft and valve assembly from the housing.

16. Tap the stub shaft lightly on a block of wood to loosen the shaft cap.

17. Pull the cap and valve spool out from the valve body ¼ in. (6mm) and disengage stub shaft pin from hole in valve spool.

18. Remove the valve spool from the valve body by pulling and rotating from the valve body. Remove the valve spool O-ring seal, the valve body teflon rings and O-ring seals.

19. Turn the stub shaft counterclockwise until the rack piston extends out of the housing.

20. Remove the rack piston end plug. Insert tool J–21552 into the bore of the rack piston. Hold the tool tight against the worm shaft while turning the stub shaft counterclockwise. This tool will force the rack piston onto the tool and hold the rack piston balls in place.

21. Remove the assembly from the housing.

22. Remove the worm shaft, thrust bearing and races.

23. Remove tool J–21552 from the rack piston. Remove the rack piston balls.

24. Remove the screws, clamp and ball guide from the rack piston.

25. Remove the teflon ring and O-ring seal from the rack piston.

26. Remove the steering gear check valve from the inlet and return lines of housing, as required.

To install:

27. Clean all parts in a suitable cleaner and lubricate with power steering fluid during assembly. Replace any worn bushings, bearings, races or seals.

28. Install the steering gear check valve from the inlet and return lines of housing, as required. Install the teflon ring and O-ring seal onto the rack piston.

29. Install the rack piston onto the worm shaft fully and align the worm shaft groove with the rack piston and align the worm shaft groove with the rack piston ball return guide hole. Install the black and silver balls alternately while turning the wormshaft counterclockwise. Install the remaining balls to the ball guide using grease to retain the balls.

30. Install the ball guide, clamp and screws onto the piston. Insert tool J–21552 onto the rack piston while turning the wormshaft counterclockwise.

31. Install the worm shaft, thrust bearing and races.

32. Install the assembly into the housing. In-

sert the worm shaft into the rack piston by holding tool J–21552 tightly against wormshaft and turning the stub shaft clockwise until rack piston is fully seated on worm shaft. Ensure the rack piston balls are installed properly.

33. Install the rack piston end plug and torque to 111 ft. lbs. (150 Nm).

34. Install the valve spool O-ring seal, the valve body teflon rings and O-ring seals.

35. Install the valve spool onto the valve body by pushing and rotating until hole in valve spool for stub shaft pin is accessible from the opposite end of the valve body.

36. The notch in the stub shaft cap must fully engage valve body pin and seat against valve body shoulder.

37. Install the stub shaft and valve assembly into the housing.

38. Install the needle bearing, dust and lip seals using tool J–6221.

39. The needle bearing must be installed with the identification on bearing facing the tool to prevent damaging the bearing.

40. Install the lip seal and dust seal onto the adjuster plug using tool J–6221. bearing spacer, races and thrust bearing. Install the O-ring and retaining ring.

41. Install the thrust washer bearing retainer onto the adjuster plug.

42. Install the adjuster plug onto the housing using tool J–7624. Use care not to damage the seals.

43. Install the adjuster plug nut.

44. Install the housing end plug and the retaining ring. Place the retaining ring with the open end approximately 1 in. (25mm) from the access hole in the housing.

45. Install the pitman shaft by screwing it into the cover until fully seated.

46. Install the side cover, new gasket and pitman shaft as an assembly.

47. Center the gear by turning the stub shaft.

48. Install the pitman shaft adjuster lock nut and cover bolts. Torque the cover bolts to 44 ft. lbs. (60 Nm).

49. Perform all gear adjustments as previously outlined.

50. Install the power steering gear as previously directed.

51. Connect the negative battery cable.

Power Steering Pump

REMOVAL AND INSTALLATION

1. Remove the hoses at the pump and tape the openings shut to prevent contamination. Position the disconnected lines in a raised position to prevent leakage.

2. Remove the pump belt. Remove the pump pulley, as required

3. Loosen the retaining bolts and any braces, and remove the pump.

4. Install the pump on the engine with the retaining bolt handtight.

5. Connect and tighten the hose fittings.

6. Refill the pump with fluid and bleed by turning the pulley counterclockwise (viewed from the front). Stop the bleeding when air bubbles no longer appear.

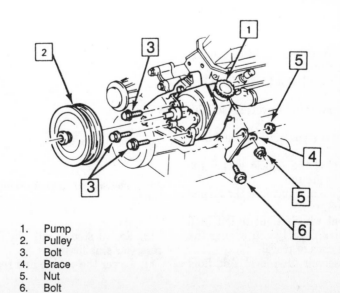

1. Pump
2. Pulley
3. Bolt
4. Brace
5. Nut
6. Bolt

Power steering pump mounting—3.1L engine

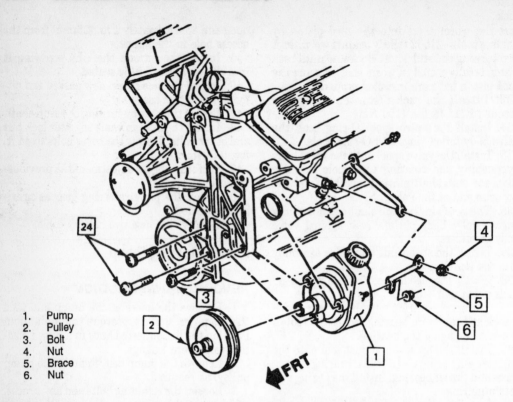

1. Pump
2. Pulley
3. Bolt
4. Nut
5. Brace
6. Nut

Power steering pump mounting—5.0L & 5.7L engine

7. Install the pump belt on the pulley and adjust the tension.

SYSTEM BLEEDING

1. Fill the reservoir with power steering fluid.

NOTE: *The use of automatic transmission fluid in the power steering system is NOT recommended.*

2. Allow the reservoir and fluid to sit undisturbed for a few minutes.
3. Start the engine, allow it to run for a moment, then turn it off.
4. Check the reservoir fluid level and add fluid if necessary.
5. Repeat the above steps until the fluid level stabilizes.
6. Raise the front of the vehicle so that the wheels are off of the ground.
7. Start the engine and increase the engine speed to about 1500 rpm.
8. Turn the front wheels right to left (and back) several times, lightly contacting the wheel stops at the ends of travel.
9. Check the reservoir fluid level. Add fluid as required.

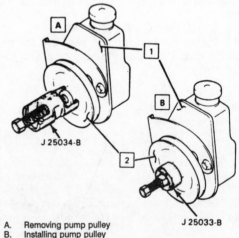

A. Removing pump pulley
B. Installing pump pulley
1. Pump
2. Pulley

Power steering pump pulley removing and installation tools

10. Repeat step 8 until the fluid level in the reservoir stabilizes.
11. Lower the vehicle and repeat steps 8 and 9.

BASIC OPERATING PRINCIPLES

Hydraulic systems are used to actuate the brakes of all automobiles. The system transports the power required to force the frictional surfaces of the braking system together from the pedal to the individual brake units at each wheel. A hydraulic system is used for two reasons.

First, fluid under pressure can be carried to all parts of an automobile by small pipes and flexible hoses without taking up a significant amount of room or posing routing problems.

Second, a great mechanical advantage can be given to the brake pedal end of the system, and the foot pressure required to actuate the brakes can be reduced by making the surface area of the master cylinder pistons smaller than that of any of the pistons in the wheel cylinders or calipers.

The master cylinder consists of a fluid reservoir and a double cylinder and piston assembly. Double type master cylinders are designed to separate the front and rear braking systems hydraulically in case of a leak.

Steel lines carry the brake fluid to a point on the vehicle's frame near each of the vehicle's wheels. The fluid is then carried to the calipers and wheel cylinders by flexible tubes in order to allow for suspension and steering movements.

In drum brake systems, each wheel cylinder contains two pistons, one at either end, which push outward in opposite directions.

In disc brake systems, the cylinders are part of the calipers. One cylinder in each caliper is used to force the brake pads against the disc.

All pistons employ some type of seal, usually made of rubber, to minimize fluid leakage. A rubber dust boot seals the outer end of the cylinder against dust and dirt. The boot fits around the outer end of the piston on disc brake calipers, and around the brake actuating rod on wheel cylinders.

The hydraulic system operates as follows: When at rest, the entire system, from the piston(s) in the master cylinder to those in the wheel cylinders or calipers, is full of brake fluid. Upon application of the brake pedal, fluid trapped in front of the master cylinder piston(s) is forced through the lines to the wheel cylinders. Here, it forces the pistons outward, in the case of drum brakes, and inward toward the disc, in the case of disc brakes. The motion of the pistons is opposed by return springs mounted outside the cylinders in drum brakes, and by spring seals, in disc brakes.

Upon release of the brake pedal, a spring located inside the master cylinder immediately returns the master cylinder pistons to the normal position. The pistons contain check valves and the master cylinder has compensating ports drilled in it. These are uncovered as the pistons reach their normal position. The piston check valves allow fluid to flow toward the wheel cylinders or calipers as the pistons withdraw. Then, as the return springs force the brake pads or shoes into the released position, the excess fluid reservoir through the compensating ports. It is during the time the pedal is in the released position that any fluid that has leaked out of the system will be replaced through the compensating ports.

Dual circuit master cylinders employ two pistons, located one behind the other, in the same cylinder. The primary piston is actuated directly by mechanical linkage from the brake pedal through the power booster. The secondary piston is actuated by fluid trapped between the two pistons. If a leak develops in front of the secondary piston, it moves forward until it bottoms against the front of the master cylinder, and the fluid trapped between the pistons will operate the rear brakes. If the rear brakes develop a leak, the primary piston will move forward until direct contact with the secondary piston takes place, and it will force the secondary piston to actuate the front brakes. In either case, the brake pedal moves farther when the brakes are applied, and less braking power is available.

All dual circuit systems use a switch to warn the driver when only half of the brake system is operational. This switch is located in a valve body which is mounted on the firewall or the frame below the master cylinder. A hydraulic piston receives pressure from both circuits, each circuit's pressure being applied to one end of the piston. When the pressures are in balance, the piston remains stationary. When one circuit has a leak, however, the greater pressure in that circuit during application of the brakes will push the piston to one side, closing the switch and activating the brake warning light.

In disc brake systems, this valve body also contains a metering valve and, in some cases, a proportioning valve. The metering valve keeps pressure from traveling to the disc brakes on the front wheels until the brake shoes on the rear wheels have contacted the drums, ensuring that the front brakes will never be used alone. The proportioning valve controls the pressure to the rear brakes to lessen the chance of rear wheel lock-up during very hard braking.

Warning lights may be tested by depressing the brake pedal and holding it while opening one of the wheel cylinder bleeder screws. If this does not cause the light to go on, substitute a new lamp, make continuity checks, and, finally, replace the switch as necessary.

The hydraulic system may be checked for leaks by applying pressure to the pedal gradually and steadily. If the pedal sinks very slowly to the floor, the system has a leak. This is not to be confused with a springy or spongy feel due to the compression of air within the lines. If the system leaks, there will be a gradual change in the position of the pedal with a constant pressure.

Check for leaks along all lines and at wheel cylinders. If no external leaks are apparent, the problem is inside the master cylinder.

Disc Brakes

BASIC OPERATING PRINCIPLES

Instead of the traditional expanding brakes that press outward against a circular drum, disc brake systems utilize a disc (rotor) with brake pads positioned on either side of it. Braking effect is achieved in a manner similar to the way you would squeeze a spinning phonograph record between your fingers. The disc (rotor) is a casting with cooling fins between the two braking surfaces. This enables air to circulate between the braking surfaces making them less sensitive to heat buildup and more resistant to fade. Dirt and water do not affect braking action since contaminants are thrown off by the centrifugal action of the rotor or scraped off the by the pads. Also, the equal clamping action of the two brake pads tends to ensure uniform, straight line stops. Disc brakes are inherently self-adjusting.

There are three general types of disc brake:
1. A fixed caliper.
2. A floating caliper.
3. A sliding caliper.

The fixed caliper design uses two pistons mounted on either side of the rotor (in each side of the caliper). The caliper is mounted rigidly and does not move.

The sliding and floating designs are quite similar. In fact, these two types are often lumped together. In both designs, the pad on the inside of the rotor is moved into contact with the rotor by hydraulic force. The caliper, which is not held in a fixed position, moves slightly, bringing the outside pad into contact with the rotor. There are various methods of attaching floating calipers. Some pivot at the bottom or top, and some slide on mounting bolts. In any event, the end result is the same.

All the cars covered in this book employ the sliding caliper design.

Drum Brakes

BASIC OPERATING PRINCIPLES

Drum brakes employ two brake shoes mounted on a stationary backing plate. These shoes are positioned inside a circular drum which rotates with the wheel assembly. The shoes are held in place by springs. This allows them to slide toward the drums (when they are applied) while keeping the linings and drums in alignment. The shoes are actuated by a wheel cylinder which is mounted at the top of the backing plate. When the brakes are applied, hydraulic pressure forces the wheel cylinder's actuating links outward. Since these links bear directly against the top of the brake shoes, the tops of the shoes are then forced against the inner side of the drum. This action forces the bottoms of the two shoes to contact the brake drum by rotating the entire assembly slightly (known as servo action). When pressure within the wheel cylinder is relaxed, return springs pull the shoes back away from the drum.

Most modern drum brakes are designed to self-adjust themselves during application when the vehicle is moving in reverse. This motion causes both shoes to rotate very slightly with the drum, rocking an adjusting lever, thereby causing rotation of the adjusting screw.

Power Boosters

Power brakes operate just as non-power brake systems except in the actuation of the master cylinder pistons. A vacuum diaphragm is located on the front of the master cylinder and assists the driver in applying the brakes, reducing both the effort and travel he must put into moving the brake pedal.

The vacuum diaphragm housing is connected to the intake manifold by a vacuum hose. A check valve is placed at the point where the hose enters the diaphragm housing, so that during periods of low manifold vacuum brake assist vacuum will not be lost.

Depressing the brake pedal closes off the vacuum source and allows atmospheric pressure to enter on one side of the diaphragm. This causes the master cylinder pistons to move and apply the brakes. When the brake pedal is released, vacuum is applied to both sides of the diaphragm, and return springs return the diaphragm and master cylinder pistons to the released position. If the vacuum fails, the brake pedal rod will butt against the end of the master cylinder actuating rod, and direct mechanical application will occur as the pedal is depressed.

The hydraulic and mechanical problems that apply to conventional brake systems also apply to power brakes, and should be checked for if the tests below do not reveal the problem.

Testing for System Vacuum Leak

1. Operate the engine at idle without touching the brake pedal for at least one minute.
2. Turn off the engine, and wait one minute.
3. Test for the presence of assist vacuum by depressing the brake pedal and releasing it several times. Light application will produce less and less pedal travel, if vacuum was present. If there is no vacuum, air is leaking into the system somewhere.

Testing System Operation

1. Pump the brake pedal (with engine off) until the supply vacuum is entirely gone.
2. Put a light, steady pressure on the pedal.
3. Start the engine, and operate it at idle. If the system is operating, the brake pedal should fall slightly toward the floor if constant pressure is maintained on the pedal.

Power brake systems may be tested for hydraulic leaks just as ordinary systems are tested.

BRAKE SYSTEM

All vehicles are equipped with independent front and rear brake systems. The systems consist of a power booster, a master cylinder, a combination valve, front disc assemblies and rear disc or drum assemblies.

The master cylinder, mounted on the left firewall or power booster, consists of two fluid reservoirs, a primary (rear) cylinder, a secondary (front) cylinder and springs. The reservoirs, being independent of one another, are contained within the same housing; fluid cannot pass from one to the other. The rear reservoir supplies fluid to the front brakes while the front reservoir supplies fluid to the rear brakes.

During operation, fluid drains from the reservoirs to the master cylinder. When the brake pedal is applied, fluid from the master cylinder is sent to the combination valve (mounted on the left front fender or frame side rail beneath the master cylinder), here it is monitored and proportionally distributed to the front or rear brake systems. Should a loss of pressure occur in one system, the other system will provide enough braking pressure to stop the vehicle. Also, should a loss of pressure in one system occur, the differential warning switch (located on the combination valve) will turn ON the brake warning light (located on the dash board).

As the fluid enters each brake caliper or wheel cylinder, the pistons are forced outward. The outward movement of the pistons force the brake pads against a round flat disc or brake shoes against a round metal drum. The brake lining attached to the pads or shoes comes in contact with the revolving disc or drum causing friction, which brings the wheel to a stop.

In time, the brake linings wear down. If not replaced, their metal support plates (bonded type) or rivet heads (riveted type) will come in contact with the disc or drum; damage to the disc or drum will occur. Never use brake pads or shoes with a lining thickness less than $1/32$ in. (0.8mm).

Most manufacturers provide a wear sensor, a piece of spring steel, attached to the rear edge of the inner brake pad. When the pad wears to the replacement thickness, the sensor will produce a high pitched squeal.

Adjustment

DISC BRAKES

Disc brakes are self-adjusting. No adjustment is possible or necessary. Check fluid level of reservoir, for as brake pads wear, the piston moves out and the piston void must be replaced with brake fluid.

DRUM BRAKES

The drum brakes are designed to self-adjust when applied with the car moving in reverse. However, they can also be adjusted manually.

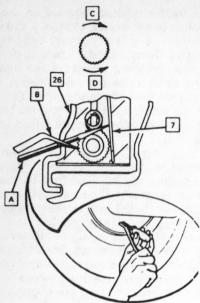

A. Screwdriver used only when backing off adjuster
B. Brake adjusting tool
C. Star wheel rotation to retract brake shoes
D. Star wheel rotation to expand brake shoes
1. Actuator lever
2. Backing plate

Cutaway view of rear brake adjuster

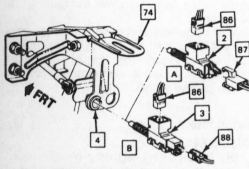

A. Without cruise control
B. With cruise control
1. Switch
2. Switch
3. Retainer
4. Brake pedal bracket
5. Stoplamp connector
6. Transmission converter clutch connector
7. Cruise control connector

Brake light switch—1992 Camaro

This manual adjustment should also be performed whenever the linings are replaced.

1. Use a punch to knock out the lanced area in the brake backing plate. If this is done with the drum installed on the car, the drum must then be removed to clean out all metal pieces. After adjustments are complete, obtain a hole cover to prevent entry of dirt and water into the brakes.

2. Use an adjusting tool especially made for the purpose to turn the brake adjusting screw star wheel. Use a small screwdriver to push the adjusting lever away from star wheel when adjusting brakes. Expand the shoes until the drum can just be turned by hand. The drag should be equal at all the wheel.

3. Back off the adjusting screw 12 notches. If the shoes still are dragging lightly, back off the adjusting screw one or two additional notches. If the brakes still drag, the parking brake adjustment is incorrect or the parking brake is applied. Fix and start over.

4. Install the hole cover into the drum.

5. Check the parking brake adjustment.

Brake Light Switch

REMOVAL AND INSTALLATION

1. Disconnect the wiring harness from the brake light switch.

2. Remove the switch.

3. To install, depress the braked pedal, insert the switch into the tubular clip until the switch body seats on the clip. Clicks should be heard as the threaded portion of the switch are pushed through the clip toward the brake pedal.

4. Pull the brake pedal fully rearward (towards the driver) against the pedal stop, until the click sounds can no longer be heard. The switch will be moved in the tubular clip providing adjustment.

5. Release the brake pedal, and then repeat Step 4, to assure that no click sound remains.

6. Connect the wiring harness to the brake light switch.

Master Cylinder

REMOVAL AND INSTALLATION

1. Disconnect hydraulic lines at master cylinder.

2. Remove the retaining nuts and lockwashers that hold cylinder to firewall or the brake booster. Disconnect pushrod at brake pedal (non-power brakes only).

3. Remove the master cylinder, gasket and rubber boot.

4. On non-power brakes, position master cyl-

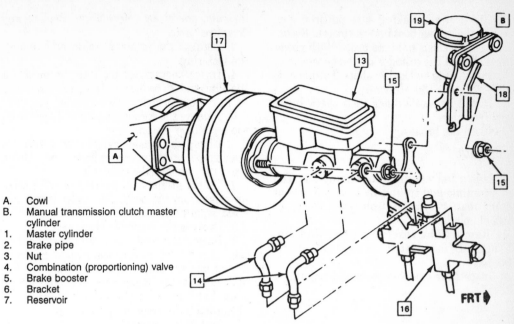

A. Cowl
B. Manual transmission clutch master
   cylinder
1. Master cylinder
2. Brake pipe
3. Nut
4. Combination (proportioning) valve
5. Brake booster
6. Bracket
7. Reservoir

Master cylinder replacement

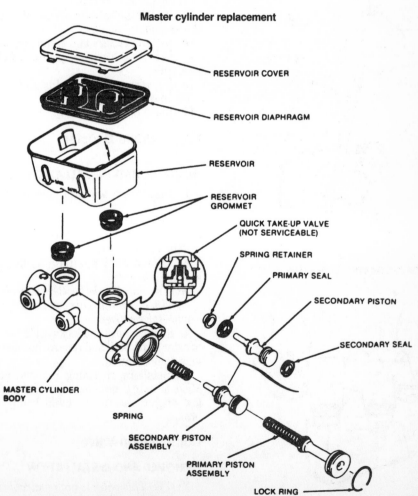

RESERVOIR COVER

RESERVOIR DIAPHRAGM

RESERVOIR

RESERVOIR
GROMMET

QUICK TAKE-UP VALVE
(NOT SERVICEABLE)

SPRING RETAINER

PRIMARY SEAL

SECONDARY PISTON

SECONDARY SEAL

MASTER CYLINDER
BODY

SPRING

SECONDARY PISTON
ASSEMBLY

PRIMARY PISTON
ASSEMBLY

LOCK RING

Master cylinder exploded view

inder on firewall, making sure pushrod goes through the rubber boot into the piston. Reconnect pushrod clevis to brake pedal. With power brakes, install the cylinder on the booster.

5. Install nuts and lockwashers. Torque nuts to 22–30 ft. lbs. (30–45 Nm).

6. Install hydraulic lines then check brake pedal free play.

7. Bleed the brakes.

OVERHAUL

This is a tedious, time-consuming job. You can save time and trouble by buying a new or rebuilt master cylinder from your dealer or parts supply house..

1. Remove the reservoir cover and diaphragm. Discard any brake fluid in the reservoir.

2. Inspect the reservoir cover and diaphragm

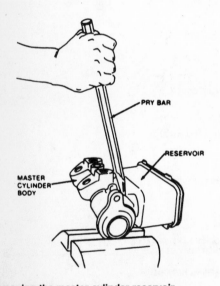

Removing the master cylinder reservoir

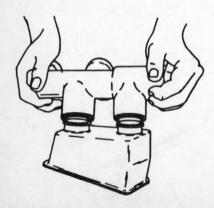

Install the master cylinder-to-reservoir with a rocking motion

for cuts, cracks, or deformation. Replace any defective parts.

3. Depress the primary piston and remove the lock ring.

4. Direct compressed air into the outlet at the blind end of the bore and plug the other outlet to remove primary and secondary piston.

5. Remove the spring retainer and seals from the secondary piston.

6. Clamp the master cylinder in a vise. Do not clamp it on the master cylinder body. Using a pry bar, remove the reservoir.

7. Do not attempt to remove the quick take-up valve from the body. This valve is not serviced separately.

8. Remove the reservoir grommets.

9. Inspect the master cylinder bore for corrosion. If corroded, replace the master cylinder. Do not use any abrasive on the bore.

10. Reassemble, using new seals and grommets. Lubricate all parts with brake fluid.

11. Install the reservoir grommets.

12. Install the reservoir.

13. Install the spring retainer and seals from the secondary piston.

14. Install primary and secondary piston.

15. Depress the primary piston and install the lock ring.

16. Fill with brake fluid. Install the reservoir cover and diaphragm.

17. Bleed brake system.

Power Brake Booster

REMOVAL AND INSTALLATION

1. Disconnect vacuum hose from vacuum check valve.

2. Unbolt the master cylinder and carefully move it aside without disconnecting the hydraulic lines.

3. Disconnect pushrod at brake pedal assembly.

NOTE: *Some brake boosters may also be held on with a sealant. This can be easily removed with tar remover.*

4. Remove nuts and lockwashers that secure booster to firewall and remove booster from engine compartment.

5. Install by reversing removal procedure. Make sure to check operation of stop lights. Allow engine vacuum to build before applying brakes.

Combination Valve

REMOVAL AND INSTALLATION

NOTE: *This valve is not repairable and only serviced as a complete assembly.*

1. Disconnect the hydraulic lines from the

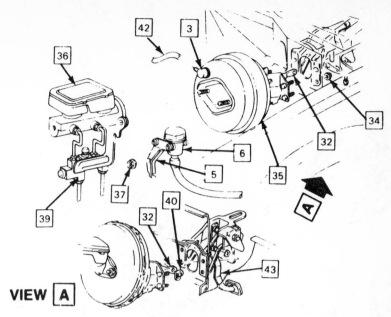

1. Check valve
2. Bracket
3. Reservoir
4. Pushrod
5. Nut
6. Booster
7. Master cylinder
8. Nut
9. Combination (proportioning) valve
10. Retainer
11. Vacuum hose
12. Brake pedal

Removing power brake booster—Note: master cylinder lines are not to be disconnected

valve. Plug the lines to prevent fluid loss and dirt contamination.

2. Disconnect the electrical connection.
3. Remove the valve.
4. To install, position the valve.
5. Connect the electrical connection.
6. Connect the hydraulic lines to the valve.
7. Bleed the brake system.

Brake Hoses

REMOVAL AND INSTALLATION

Front and/or Rear Disc Brake

1. Clean dirt and foreign material from both the hose and fittings.
2. Disconnect the brake pipe from the hose fitting using a backup wrench on the fitting. Be careful not to bend the frame bracket or the brake pipe.
3. Remove the U-clip from the female fitting at the bracket and remove the hose from the bracket.

4. Remove the bolt from the caliper end of the hose. Remove the hose from the caliper and discard the two copper gaskets on either side of the fitting block.
5. To install, use new copper gaskets on both sides of the fitting block. Lubricate the bolt threads with brake fluid. With the fitting flange engaged with the caliper orientation ledge, fasten the hose to the caliper and torque to 32 ft. lbs. (44 Nm).
6. With the weight of the car on the suspension, pass the female fitting through the frame bracket of crossmember. Fitting fits the bracket in only one position. With least amount of twist in the hose, install the fitting in this position. There should be no kinks in the hose.
7. Install the U-clip to the female fitting at the frame bracket.
8. Attach the brake pipe to the hose fitting using a backup wrench on the fitting. Torque to 17 ft. lbs. (24 Nm).
9. Inspect to see that the hose doesn't make contact with any part of the suspension. Check

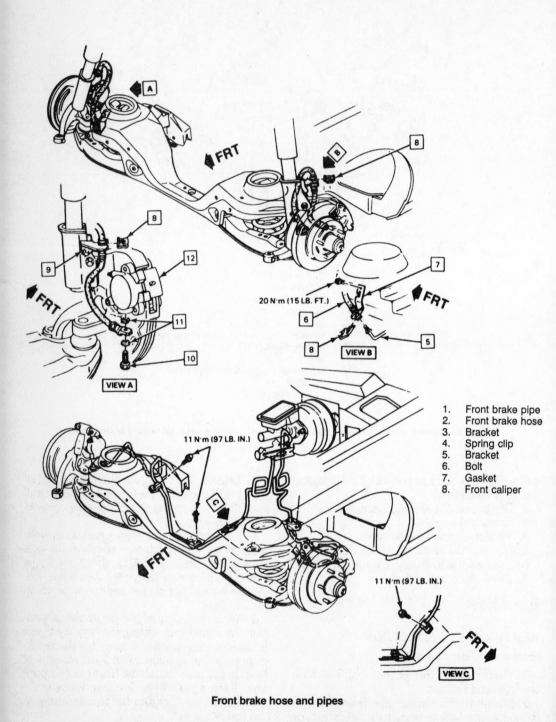

20 N·m (15 LB. FT.)

VIEW B

VIEW A

11 N·m (97 LB. IN.)

11 N·m (97 LB. IN.)

VIEW C

1. Front brake pipe
2. Front brake hose
3. Bracket
4. Spring clip
5. Bracket
6. Bolt
7. Gasket
8. Front caliper

Front brake hose and pipes

1. Center brake hose
2. Bracket
3. Spring clip
4. Left rear brake pipe
5. Right rear brake pipe
6. Bolt
7. Rear axle housing

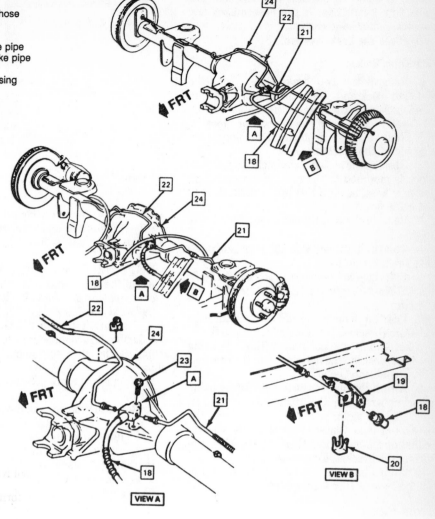

Rear brake hose and pipes

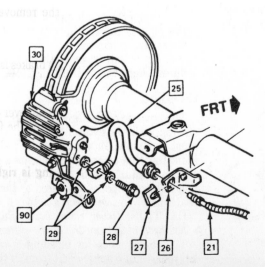

1. Left rear brake pipe
2. Rear disc brake shoe
3. Braket
4. Spring clip
5. Bolt
6. Gasket
7. Rear caliper
8. Vibration dampener

Rear disc brake hose

in the extreme right hand and extreme left hand turn conditions. If the hose makes any contact, remove and correct.

10. Bleed the brake system.

Rear Drum Brakes

1. Remove the two brake pipes from the junction block and , with the use of a backup wrench, remove the hose at the female fitting. Be careful not to bend the bracket or pipes.

2. Remove the U-clip and take the female fitting out of the bracket.

3. Observe the position at which the junction block is mounted to the axle. When installing the new hose, be sure this junction block is in the same position.

4. Remove the bolt attaching junction block to axle.

5. To install, thread both the rear axle pipes into the junction block.

6. Bolt the junction block to the axle to 20 ft. lbs. (27 Nm). Torque the rear pipes to 17 ft. lbs. (24 Nm).

7. Pass the female end of the hose through the frame bracket. The female fitting will fit the bracket in only one position; without twisting the hose, position the female end in the bracket.

8. Install the U-clip.

9. Attach the pipe to the female fitting using a backup wrench on the fitting, torque to 17 ft. lbs. (24 Nm) again be careful not to bend the bracket or pipe. Check to see that the hose installation did not loosen the frame bracket. Retorque the bracket, if necessary.

10. Fill and maintain the brake fluid level in the reservoirs. Bleed the system.

Steel Pipes

When replacing the steel brake pipes, always use steel piping which is designed to withstand high pressure, resist corrosion and is of the same size.

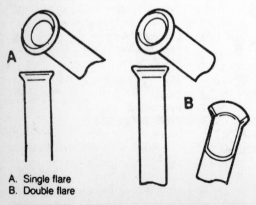

A. Single flare
B. Double flare

Single flare (A) and Double flare (B) ends

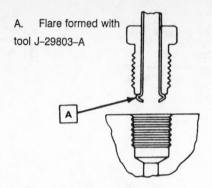

A.   Flare formed with tool J–29803–A

ISO flare

CAUTION: *Never use copper tubing, for it is subject to fatigue, cracking, and/or corrosion, which will result in brake line failure.*

NOTE: *The following procedure requires the use of the GM Tube Cutter tool NO. J–23533 or equivalent, and the GM Flaring tool No. J–29803, J–23530 or equivalent.*

1. Disconnect the steel brake pipe(s) from the flexible hose connections or the rear wheel cylinders, be sure to removal any retaining clips.

2. Remove the steel brake pipe from the vehicle.

3. Repair or replace the pipe as follows:

a. Using new steel pipe (same size) and the GM Tube Cutter tool No. J–23533 or equivalent, cut the pipe to length; be sure to add ⅛ in. (3mm) for each flare.

NOTE: *Be sure to install the correct pipe fittings onto the tube before forming any flares.*

b. Using the Flaring tool NO. J–23530, J–29803 or equivalent, follow the instructions equipped with the tool to form double flares on the end of the pipes.

c. Using the small pipe bending tool, bend the pipe to match the contour of the pipe which was removed.

d. To install, reverse the removal procedures. Bleed the hydraulic system.

Bleeding

The purpose of bleeding the brakes is to expel air trapped in the hydraulic system. The system must be bled whenever the pedal feels spongy, indicating that compressible air has entered the system. It must also be bled whenever the system has been opened, repaired or the fluid appears dirty. You will need a helper for this job.

CAUTION: *Never reuse brake fluid which has been bled from the brake system.*

1. The sequence for bleeding is right rear, left rear, right front and left front. If the car has power brakes, remove the vacuum by applying

the brakes several times. Do not run the engine while bleeding the brakes.

2. Clean all the bleeder screws. You may want to give each one a shot of penetrating solvent to loosen it; seizure is a common problem with bleeder screws, which then break off, sometimes requiring replacement of the part to which they were attached.

3. Fill the master cylinder with good quality brake fluid.

NOTE: *Brake fluid absorbs moisture from the air. Don't leave the master cylinder or the fluid container uncovered any longer than necessary. Be careful handling the fluid; it eats paint. Check the level of the fluid often when bleeding and refill the reservoirs as necessary. Don't let them run dry or you will have to repeat the process.*

4. Attach a length of clear vinyl tubing to the bleeder screw on the wheel cylinder. Insert the other end of the tube into a clear, clean jar half filled with brake fluid.

5. Have your assistant slowly depress the brake pedal. As this is done, open the bleeder screw ¾ of a turn and allow the fluid to run through the tube. Then close the bleeder screw before the pedal reaches the end of its travel. Have your assistant slowly release the pedal. Repeat this process until no air bubbles appear in the expelled fluid.

6. Repeat the procedure on the other three brakes, checking the level of fluid in the master cylinder reservoir often.

7. Upon completion, check the brake pedal for sponginess and the brake warning light for unbalanced pressure. If necessary, repeat the entire bleeding procedure.

FRONT DISC BRAKES

CAUTION: *Brake pads contain asbestos, which has been determined to be a cancer causing agent. Never clean the brake surfaces with compressed air! Avoid inhaling any dust from any brake surface! When cleaning brake surfaces, use a commercially available brake cleaning fluid.*

Brake Pads

INSPECTION

The pad thickness should be inspected every time that the tires are removed for rotation. The outer pad can be checked by looking in each end, which is the point at which the highest rate of wear occurs. The inner pad can be checked by looking down through the inspection hole in the top of the caliper. If the thickness of the pad is worn to within 0.030 in.

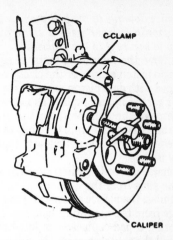

Install a C-clamp and compress the piston into the caliper before removing the assembly

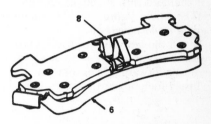

6. Inboard shoe & lining
8. Shoe retainer spring

Install the retaining spring on the inboard (piston side) pad

(0.8mm) of the rivet at either end of the pad, all the pads should be replaced.

NOTE: *Always replace all pads on both front wheels at the same time. Failure to do so will result in uneven braking action and premature wear.*

REMOVAL AND INSTALLATION

1. Siphon ⅔ of the brake fluid from the master cylinder reservoir. Loosen the wheel lug nuts and raise the car. Remove the wheel.

2. Position a C-clamp across the caliper and press on the pads. Tighten it until the caliper piston bottoms in its bore.

NOTE: *If you haven't removed some brake fluid from the master cylinder, it may overflow when the piston is retracted.*

3. Remove the C-clamp.

NOTE: *There are 2 different calipers being used, a single piston or dual piston design. The single piston design uses either an allen head bolt, regular bolt or Torx® head bolt to secure the caliper to the mounting bracket. Do not use an socket in place of the Torx socket, otherwise damage to the bolt may occur. The dual piston caliper uses a slide pin and circlip to secure it to the bracket.*

4. Remove the mounting bolts, if equipped with single piston caliper or the circlip and pin, if equipped with dual piston caliper. Inspect the bolts for corrosion and replace as necessary.

5. Remove the caliper from the steering knuckle and suspend it from the body of the car with a length of wire. Do not allow the caliper to hang by its hose.

6. Remove the pad retaining springs and remove the pads from the caliper.

7. Remove the plastic sleeves and the rubber bushings from the mounting bolt holes.

8. Obtain a pad replacement kit. Lubricate and install the new sleeves and bushings with a light coat of silicone grease.

9. Install the retainer spring on the inboard pad, if equipped with single piston caliper.

NOTE: *A new spring should be included in the pad replacement kit.*

10. Install the new inboard pad into the caliper with the wear sensor at the leading of the shoe during forward wheel rotation.

11. Install the outboard pad into the caliper.

12. Use a large pair of slip joint pliers to bend the outer pad ears down over the caliper, if equipped with the single piston caliper.

13. Install the caliper onto the steering knuckle. Tighten the mounting bolts to 21–35 ft. lbs. (28–47 Nm), if equipped. Install the wheel and lower the car. Fill the master cylinder to its proper level with a good quality brake fluid.

14. Pump the brake pedal slowly and firmly 3 times with the engine running before attempting to move the vehicle; bleed the brakes as required.

Brake Caliper

REMOVAL AND INSTALLATION

CAUTION: *Brake pads contain asbestos, which has been determined to be a cancer causing agent. Never clean the brake surfaces with compressed air! Avoid inhaling any dust from any brake surface! When cleaning brake surfaces, use a commercially available brake cleaning fluid.*

1. Remove ⅔ of the brake fluid from the

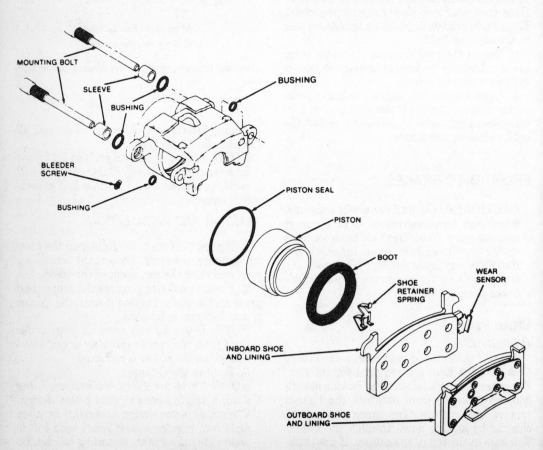

Exploded view of single piston front caliper

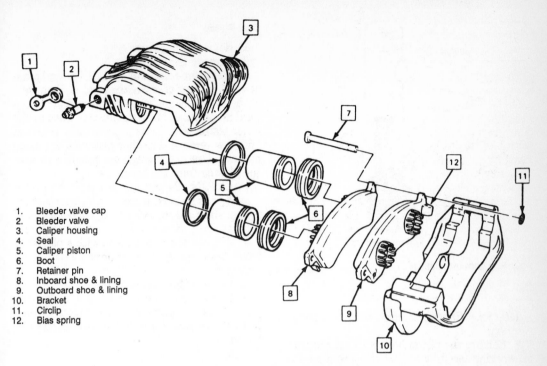

1. Bleeder valve cap
2. Bleeder valve
3. Caliper housing
4. Seal
5. Caliper piston
6. Boot
7. Retainer pin
8. Inboard shoe & lining
9. Outboard shoe & lining
10. Bracket
11. Circlip
12. Bias spring

Exploded view of dual piston front caliper

master cylinder. Raise the vehicle and remove the wheel.

2. Place a C-clamp across the caliper, positioned on the brake pads. Tighten it until the piston is forced into its bore.

3. Remove the C-clamp. Remove the bolt holding the brake hose to the caliper.

4. Remove the allen head caliper mounting bolts. Inspect them for corrosion and replace them if necessary. Remove the caliper.

5. To install, position the caliper with the brake pad installed and install allen head caliper mounting bolts. Mounting bolt torque is 21–35 ft. lbs. (28–47 Nm.) for the caliper.

6. Install the bolt holding the brake hose to

the caliper and tighten to 18–30 ft. lbs. (24–40 Nm.).

7. Fill the master cylinder with brake fluid.

8. Install the wheels and lower the vehicle.

CAUTION: *Before moving the vehicle, pump the brakes several times to seat the brake pad against the rotor.*

OVERHAUL

Single piston

1. Remove the caliper.

2. Remove the pads.

3. Place some cloths or a slat of wood in front of the piston. Remove the piston by applying compressed air to the fluid inlet fitting. Use just enough air pressure to east the piston from the bore.

CAUTION: *Do not try to catch the piston*

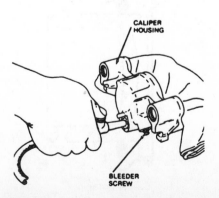

Using compressed air to remove the piston from the caliper bore

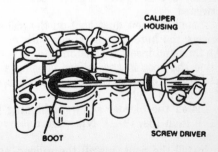

Remove piston boot using an awl

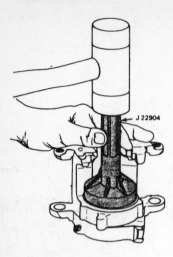

Installing boot into caliper

with your fingers, it can result in serious injury.

4. Remove the piston boot with a screwdriver, working carefully so that the piston bore is not scratched.

5. Remove the bleeder screw.

6. Inspect the piston for scoring, nicks, corrosion, wear, etc., and damaged or worn chrome plating. Replace the piston if any defects are found.

7. Remove the piston seal from the caliper bore groove using a piece of pointed wood or plastic. Do not use a screwdriver, which will damage the bore. Inspect the caliper bore for nicks, corrosion, and wear. Very light wear can be cleaned up with crocus cloth. Use finger pressure to rub the crocus cloth around the circumference of the bore — do not slide it in and out. More extensive wear or corrosion warrants replacement of the part.

8. Clean any parts which are to be reused in denatured alcohol. Dry them with compressed air or allow to air dry. Don't wipe the parts dry with a cloth, which will leave behind bits of lint.

9. Lubricate the new seal, provided in the repair kit, with clean brake fluid. Install the seal in its groove, making sure it is fully seated and not twisted.

10. Install the new dust boot on the piston. Lubricate the bore of the caliper with clean brake fluid and insert the piston into its bore. Position the boot in the caliper housing and seat with a seal driver of the appropriate size, or G.M. tool no. J–26267.

11. Install the bleeder screw, tightening to 80–140 inch lbs. (9–16 Nm). Do not over tighten.

12. Install the pads, install the caliper, and bleed the brakes.

Dual Piston

1. Remove the caliper.

2. Remove the pads.

3. Place some cloths and a 1 in. (25mm) piece of wood in front of one of the pistons. Remove 1 of the piston by applying compressed air to the fluid inlet fitting. Move the piece of wood to the other piston which was just partially removed and now remove the other piston in the same manner. Use just enough air pressure to ease the pistons from the bore.

CAUTION: *Do not try to catch the piston with your fingers, it can result in serious injury. Keep the rag over the assembly to avoid brake fluid from being sprayed everywhere.*

4. Remove the piston boots with a plastic or wood tool, so the seal grooves will not be damaged.

5. Remove the bleeder screw.

6. Inspect the piston for scoring, nicks, corrosion, wear, etc., and damaged or worn chrome plating. Replace the piston if any defects are found.

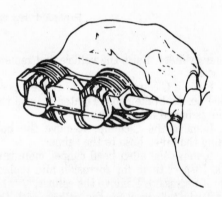

Remove dual caliper pistons with compressed air— one piston at a time

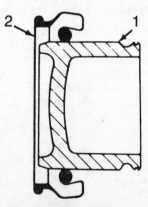

1. Caliper piston
2. Boot

Installing piston boot in proper direction

7. Remove the piston seal from the caliper bore groove using a piece of pointed wood or plastic. Do not use a screwdriver, which will damage the bore. Inspect the caliper bore for nicks, corrosion, and wear. Very light wear can be cleaned up with crocus cloth. Use finger pressure to rub the crocus cloth around the circumference of the bore — do not slide it in and out. More extensive wear or corrosion warrants replacement of the part.

8. Clean any parts which are to be reused in denatured alcohol. Dry them with compressed air or allow to air dry. Don't wipe the parts dry with a cloth, which will leave behind bits of lint.

9. Lubricate the new seals, provided in the repair kit, with clean brake fluid. Install the seals in there grooves, making sure it is fully seated and not twisted.

10. Install the new dust boots on the piston as illustrated with the fold facing outward. Lubricate the bore of the caliper with clean brake fluid and insert the piston into its bore. Position the boot into the caliper groove and slide the caliper piston into the bore. Repeat the procedure for the other piston.

11. Install the bleeder screw, tightening to 80–140 inch lbs. (9–16 Nm.). Do not over tighten.

12. Install the pads, install the caliper, and bleed the brakes.

Brake Disc (Rotor)
REMOVAL AND INSTALLATION

CAUTION: *Brake pads contain asbestos, which has been determined to be a cancer causing agent. Never clean the brake surfaces with compressed air! Avoid inhaling any dust from any brake surface! When cleaning brake surfaces, use a commercially available brake cleaning fluid.*

1. Remove the caliper by following instructions of caliper removal procedure.

2. Remove dust cap, cotter pin, castle nut, thrust washer and outside wheel bearing. Pull the disc/hub assembly from the steering knuckle.

3. To install, position the disc/hub assembly to the spindle/steering knuckle.

4. Install the outside wheel bearing, thrust washer and castle nut. Tighten the castle nut until the bearing is snug. Back off the nut ¼ turn. Refer to Chapter 8 for Wheel Bearing Removal and Installation, and Adjustment.

5. Install the cotter pin and dust cap.

INSPECTION

1. Check the rotor surface for wear, scoring, grooves or rust pitting. Rotor damage can be corrected by refacing, consult your local garage

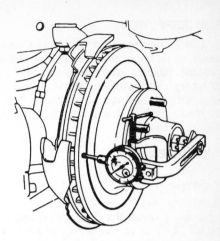

Check the disc rotor runout using a dial indicator

or machine shop. If the damage exceeds the minimum thickness, which is stamped on the rotor, replace the rotor.

2. Check the rotor parallelism at four or more points around the circumference, it must not vary more than 0.0005 in. (0.013mm). Make all measurements at the same distance in from the edge of the rotor. Refinish the rotor if it fails to meet specification.

3. Measure the disc runout with a dial indicator. If runout exceeds 0.004 in. (0.10mm), and the wheel bearings are okay (runout is measured with the disc on the car), the rotor must be refaced or replaced.

REAR DRUM BRAKES

Brake Drums
REMOVAL AND INSTALLATION

CAUTION: *Brake shoes contain asbestos, which has been determined to be a cancer causing agent. Never clean the brake surfaces with compressed air! Avoid inhaling any dust from any brake surface! When cleaning brake surfaces, use a commercially available brake cleaning fluid.*

1. Raise and support the car.

2. Remove the wheel or wheels.

3. Pull the brake drum off. It may be necessary to gently tap the rear edges of the drum to start it off the studs.

4. If extreme resistance to removal is encountered, it will be necessary to retract the adjusting screw. Knock out the access hole in the backing plate and turn the adjuster to retract the linings away from the drum.

5. Install a replacement hole cover before reinstalling drum.

6. Install the drums in the same position on the hub as removed.

DRUM INSPECTION

1. Check the drums for any cracks, scores, grooves, or an out-of-round condition. Replace if cracked. Slight scores can be removed with fine emery cloth while extensive scoring requires turning the drum on a lathe.

2. Never have a drum turned more than 0.060 in. (1.524mm).

Brake Shoes

ADJUSTMENT

Rotate the star wheel adjuster until a slight drag is felt between the shoes and drum, then back off 12 clicks on the adjusting wheel. Put the car in reverse and, while backing up, apply the brakes several times. This will allow the self-adjusters to complete the adjustment.

REMOVAL AND INSTALLATION

CAUTION: *Brake shoes contain asbestos, which has been determined to be a cancer causing agent. Never clean the brake surfaces with compressed air! Avoid inhaling any dust from any brake surface! When cleaning*

brake surfaces, use a commercially available brake cleaning fluid.

1. Raise and safely support the vehicle.
2. Remove the wheel and tire assemblies.
3. Remove the brake drum.
4. Remove the return springs.
5. Remove the hold-down springs and pins. Remove the lever pivot.
6. Remove the actuator link while lifting up on the actuator lever.
7. Remove the actuator lever and lever return spring.
8. Remove the shoe guide, parking brake strut and strut spring.
9. Remove the brake shoes and disconnect the parking brake lever from the shoe.
10. Remove the adjusting screw assembly and spring. Remove the retaining ring, pin from the secondary shoe.

To install:

NOTE: *Any part or spring which may appear worn should be replaced. The short shoe (primary) should be installed to the front of the vehicle and the long shoe (secondary) should be installed to the rear. After complete installation of the brake shoes, a clicking*

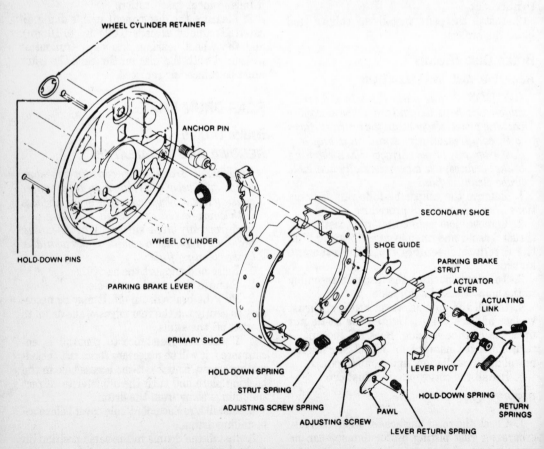

Exploded view of rear drum brakes

sound should be heard when turning the adjusting screw or self-adjuster. Do not switch parts from the left or right brake assembly, the adjusters are designated Left and Right.

11. Clean dirt from all parts and wire brush raised pads on backing plate. Lubricate backing plate pads and adjusting screw with brake grease.

12. Install the parking brake lever on the secondary shoe with the pin and new retaining ring.

13. Install the adjusting screw and spring. Lubricate the adjusting screw with brake (white) grease.

14. Clean and lubricate the contact points of the backing plate. Install the brake shoe assemblies after installing the parking brake cable on the shoe.

15. Install the parking brake strut and strut spring by spreading the shoes apart.

16. Install the shoe guide, actuator lever and lever return spring.

17. Install the hold-down pins, lever pivot and springs. Install the actuator link on the anchor pin.

18. Install the actuator link into the actuator lever while holding up on the lever.

19. Install the shoe return springs. Install the brake drum. Install the wheel and tire assemblies.

20. Adjust the brake and lower the vehicle. Check emergency brake for proper adjustment.

Wheel Cylinders

REMOVAL AND INSTALLATION

CAUTION: *Brake shoes contain asbestos, which has been determined to be a cancer causing agent. Never clean the brake surfaces with compressed air! Avoid inhaling any dust from any brake surface! When cleaning* brake surfaces, use a commercially available brake cleaning fluid.

1. Raise and support the car. Remove the wheel. Remove the brake shoes by following the Brake Shoe Replacement procedure.

2. Remove dirt from around the wheel cylinder inlet and pilot. Disconnect the inlet tube.

3. Using 2 awls, 1/8 in. (3mm) in diameter, or J29839, remove the wheel cylinder retainer. Insert the awls into the access slots between the wheel cylinder pilot and retainer. Simultaneously, bend both tabs away from each other. Remove the wheel cylinder.

4. To install, place wheel cylinder into position and place a block of wood between it and the axle flange. Install a new retainer over the end of the wheel cylinder. Using a 1⅛ in. 12-point socket with an extension, drive the new retainer into position.

5. Connect the inlet tube and torque 120–280 inch lbs. (13.6–20 Nm). Complete installation by reversing the removal procedure. Bleed the brakes.

OVERHAUL

Overhaul kits for wheel cylinders are readily available. When rebuilding and installing wheel

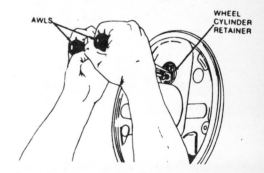

Removing the wheel cylinder retainer using 2 awls

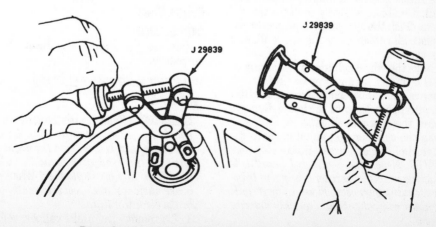

Removing the wheel cylinder retainer using special tool

1. Boot
2. Piston
3. Seal
4. Spring assembly
5. Bleeder valve
6. Cylinder body

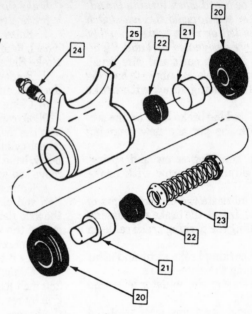

Exploded view of wheel cylinder

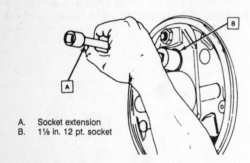

A. Socket extension
B. 1⅛ in. 12 pt. socket

Installing the wheel cylinder retainer

cylinders, avoid getting any contaminants into the system. Always install clean, new high quality brake fluid. If dirty or improper fluid has been used, it will be necessary to drain the entire system, flush the system with proper brake fluid, replace all rubber components, refill, and bleed the system.

1. Remove the wheel cylinder by referring to the Wheel Cylinder Removal procedure.

2. Remove the rubber boots from the cylinder ends with pliers. Discard the boots. Remove and discard the pistons and cups.

3. Wash the cylinder and metal parts in denatured alcohol or clean brake fluid.

CAUTION: *Never use a mineral based solvent such as gasoline, kerosene, or paint thinner for cleaning purposes. These solvents will swell rubber components and quickly deteriorate them.*

4. Allow the parts to air dry or use com-

pressed air. Do not use rags for cleaning since lint will remain in the cylinder bore.

5. Inspect the piston and replace it if it shows scratches.

6. Lubricate the cylinder bore and counterbore with clean brake fluid.

7. Install the seals (flat side out) and then the pistons (flat side in).

8. Insert new boots into the counterbores by hand. Do not lubricate the boots.

9. To install the wheel cylinder refer to the Wheel Cylinder Installation procedure.

REAR DISC BRAKES

Brake Pads

INSPECTION

Refer to the Front Disc Brake Inspection procedure.

REMOVAL AND INSTALLATION

1982–88

CAUTION: *Brake pads contain asbestos, which has been determined to be a cancer causing agent. Never clean the brake surfaces with compressed air! Avoid inhaling any dust from any brake surface! When cleaning brake surfaces, use a commercially available brake cleaning fluid.*

1. To remove the brake caliper, refer to the Rear Caliper Removal procedure.

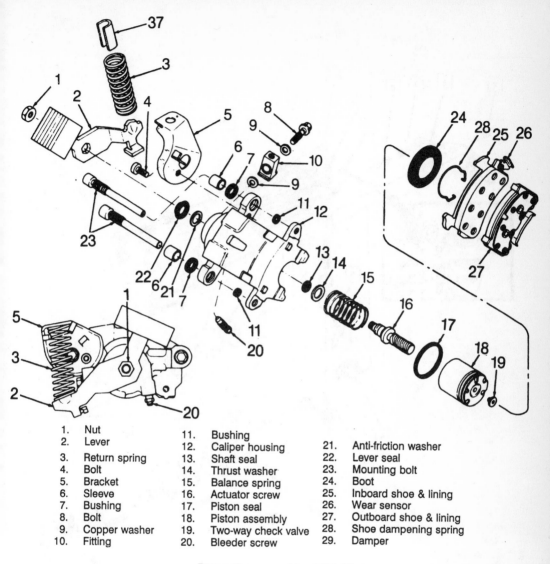

1.	Nut	11.	Bushing			
2.	Lever	12.	Caliper housing	21.	Anti-friction washer
3.	Return spring	13.	Shaft seal	22.	Lever seal
4.	Bolt	14.	Thrust washer	23.	Mounting bolt
5.	Bracket	15.	Balance spring	24.	Boot
6.	Sleeve	16.	Actuator screw	25.	Inboard shoe & lining
7.	Bushing	17.	Piston seal	26.	Wear sensor
8.	Bolt	18.	Piston assembly	27.	Outboard shoe & lining
9.	Copper washer	19.	Two-way check valve	28.	Shoe dampening spring
10.	Fitting	20.	Bleeder screw	29.	Damper

Rear caliper assembly—1982–88

2. Remove the brake pads from the calipers. Remove the sleeves from the mounting bolts and the bushings from the caliper.

3. Using a small screwdriver, remove the 2-way check valve from the end of the piston. Clean and check the valve for leakage.

NOTE: *If leakage is noted, the caliper must be overhauled.*

4. To install, position the brake pads into the caliper. Lubricate and install new bushings, sleeves and check valve.

5. When installing the inner brake pad, make sure that the D-shaped tab of the pad engages with the D-shaped notch of the piston, as illustrated.

6. Upon installation of the inner pad, make sure that the wear sensor of the pad is at the leading edge of the shoe during forward wheel rotation. Slide the metal edge of the pad under the ends of the dampening spring and snap the pad into position against the piston.

7. Install the outer pad and caliper. After installing the caliper, apply the brakes, then bend the ears of the outer pad against the caliper and ensure that there is no excessive clearance.

1989–92

1. Remove ⅔ of the brake fluid from the master cylinder reservoir.

2. Raise and safely support the vehicle.

3. Remove the wheel and tire assembly. Install 2 wheel nuts to retain the rotor.

4. Position a C-clamp and tighten until the piston bottoms in the base of the caliper housing. Make sure 1 end of the C-clamp rests on the

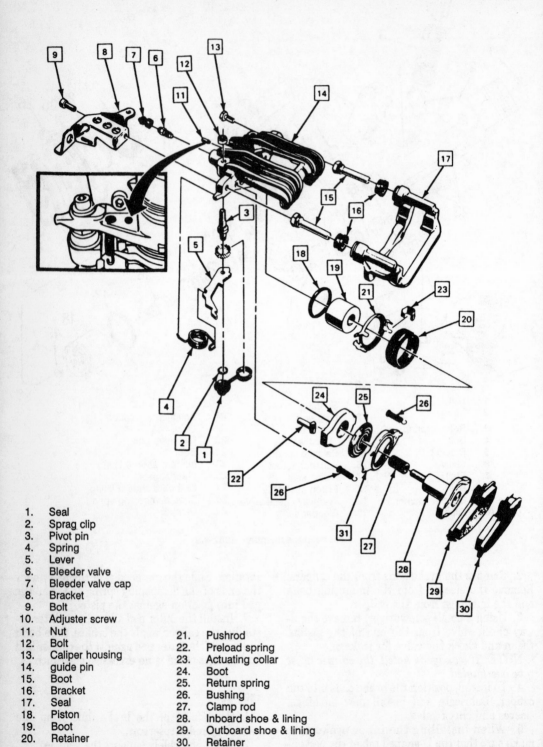

1.   Seal
2.   Sprag clip
3.   Pivot pin
4.   Spring
5.   Lever
6.   Bleeder valve
7.   Bleeder valve cap
8.   Bracket
9.   Bolt
10. Adjuster screw
11. Nut
12. Bolt
13. Caliper housing
14. guide pin
15. Boot
16. Bracket
17. Seal
18. Piston
19. Boot
20. Retainer

21. Pushrod
22. Preload spring
23. Actuating collar
24. Boot
25. Return spring
26. Bushing
27. Clamp rod
28. Inboard shoe & lining
29. Outboard shoe & lining
30. Retainer

Rear caliper assembly—1989–92

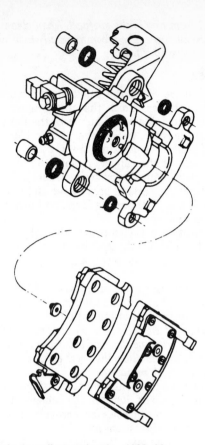

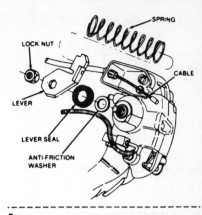

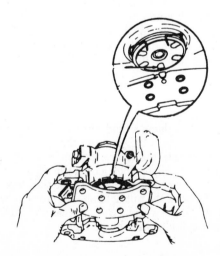

Rear brake caliper and pads—1982-88

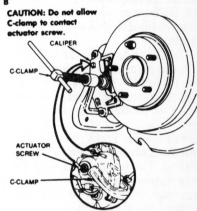

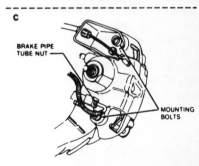

Removing and installing rear caliper—1982-88

Installing inboard shoe correctly—1982-88

inlet fitting bolt and the other against the outboard disc brake pad.

NOTE: *It is not necessary to remove the
parking brake caliper lever return spring to
replace the disc brake pads.*

5. Remove the upper caliper guide pin bolt
and discard.

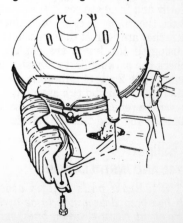

Removing and installing rear disc pads—1989-92

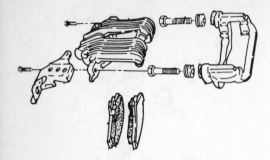

Rear caliper and pads—1989–92

6. Rotate the caliper housing. Be careful not to strain the hose or cable conduit.

7. Remove the disc brake pads.

To install:

8. Clean all residue from the pad guide surfaces on the mounting bracket and caliper housing. Inspect the guide pins for free movement in the mounting bracket. Replace the guide pins or boots, if they are corroded or damaged.

9. Install the disc brake pads. The outboard pad with insulator is installed toward the caliper housing. The inboard pad with the wear sensor is installed nearest the caliper piston. The wear sensor must be in the trailing position with forward wheel rotation.

10. Rotate the caliper housing into it's operating position. The springs on the outboard brake pad must not stick through the inspection hole in the caliper housing. If the springs are sticking through the inspection hole in the caliper housing, lift the caliper housing and make the necessary corrections to the outboard brake pad positions.

11. Install a new upper caliper guide pin bolt and tighten to 26 ft. lbs. (35 Nm). Tighten the lower caliper guide pin bolt to 16 ft. lbs. (22 Nm).

12. With the engine running, pump the brake pedal slowly and firmly to seat the brake pads.

13. Check the caliper parking brake levers to make sure they are against the stops on the caliper housing. If the levers are not on their stops, check the parking brake adjustment.

14. Remove the 2 wheel nuts from the rotor and install the wheel and tire assembly.

15. Lower the vehicle, check the master cylinder fluid level and road test the vehicle.

Brake Caliper

REMOVAL AND INSTALLATION

CAUTION: *Brake pads contain asbestos, which has been determined to be a cancer causing agent. Never clean the brake surfaces with compressed air! Avoid inhaling any* dust from any brake surface! When cleaning brake surfaces, use a commercially available brake cleaning fluid.

1982–88

1. Remove ⅔ of the brake fluid from the master cylinder. Raise the car. Remove the wheel. Reinstall a wheel nut, with the flat side toward the rotor, to hold the rotor in place.

2. Loosen the parking brake cable at the equalizer. At the caliper, remove the parking brake cable, damper and spring from the lever.

3. Hold the parking brake lever and remove the lock nut. Remove the lever, seal and anti-friction washer.

4. Position a C-clamp over the caliper and force the piston into its bore. Remove the C-clamp. Reinstall the lever, seal and nut to the caliper.

5. Loosen the brake tube nut and disconnect the brake tube from the caliper. Plug the tube to prevent the loss of brake fluid.

NOTE: *At the right rear wheel, it may be necessary to remove the rear bolt from the lower control arm to allow the lower caliper mounting bolt to be removed.*

6. Remove the mounting bolts using a ⅜ in. allen head socket. Remove the caliper and inspect the mounting bolts for corrosion. If necessary, replace the mounting bolts.

7. To install, place the caliper onto the rotor and install the mounting bolts. Torque the mounting bolts to 30–45 ft. lbs. (40.7–61 Nm).

8. Install a new anti-friction washer and lubricate the lever with silicone brake lube. Install the lever on the actuator with the lever pointing down. Rotate the lever toward the front of the car and hold while installing the nut. Torque the nut to 30–40 ft. lbs. (40.7–54.2 Nm), then rotate the lever back against the stop on the caliper.

9. Install damper and spring. Connect the parking brake cable. Tighten the cable at the equalizer until the lever starts to move off the stop on the caliper, then loosen the adjustment until the lever moves back against the stop.

10. Remove the nut holding the rotor in place and install the wheel. Lower the car and fill the master cylinder with brake fluid.

1989–92

1. Raise and safely support the vehicle.

2. Loosen the parking brake cable at the equalizer.

3. Remove the wheel and tire assembly. Install 2 wheel nuts to retain the rotor.

4. Remove the bolt, inlet fitting and washers from the caliper housing. Plug the holes in the caliper housing and inlet fitting.

5. Remove the caliper lever return spring

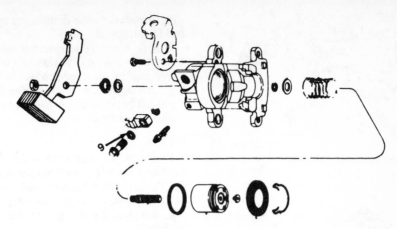

Rear caliper overhaul—1982–88

only if it is defective. Discard the spring if the coils are opened.

6. Disconnect the parking brake cable from the caliper lever and caliper bracket.

7. Remove the 2 caliper guide pin holes.

8. Remove the caliper housing from the rotor and mounting bracket.

To install:

9. Inspect the guide pins and boots and replace if corroded, worn or damaged. Check the inlet fitting bolt for blockage.

10. Install the caliper housing over the rotor and into the mounting bracket. Install the 2 caliper guide pin bolts. Tighten the upper caliper guide pin bolt to 26 ft. lbs. (35 Nm) and the lower guide pin bolt to 16 ft. lbs. (22 Nm).

11. Connect the parking brake cable to the caliper bracket and caliper lever. Install the caliper lever return spring, if removed.

12. Install the inlet fitting, bolt and 2 new washers to the caliper housing. Tighten the bolt to 22 ft. lbs. (30 Nm).

13. Bleed the brake system.

14. Adjust the parking brake free travel if the caliper was overhauled.

15. Lower the vehicle and cycle the parking brake.

16. Raise and safely support the vehicle.

17. Inspect the caliper parking brake levers and ensure they are against the stops on the caliper housing. If the levers are not on their stop, refer to the parking brake adjustment.

18. Remove the 2 nuts securing the rotor and install the wheel and tire assembly. Lower the vehicle.

19. With the engine running, pump the brake pedal slowly and firmly 3 times to seat the disc brake pads. Check the hydraulic system for leaks.

OVERHAUL

1982–88

1. Remove the shoe dampening spring from the end of the piston.

2. Place the caliper in a vise. Move the parking brake lever back and forth to work the piston out of the caliper.

NOTE: *If the piston will not come out, remove the lever and use a wrench to rotate the adjusting screw. Rotate the screw in the direction of brake application. Remove the balance spring.*

3. Remove the nut, lever, lever seal, and anti-friction washer.

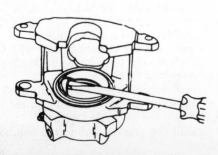

Rear caliper overhaul—1982–88

Installing piston into caliper—1982–88

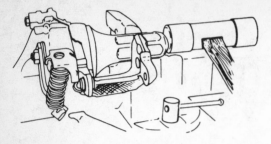

Installing boot into caliper—1982-88

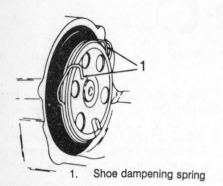

1.   Shoe dampening spring

Installing shoe dampening spring—1982-88

4. Press on the threaded end of the actuator screw to remove it from the housing.

5. Remove the shaft seal and washer.

6. Remove the dust boot. Be careful not to scratch the housing bore.

7. Remove the locator retainer if so equipped. Remove the piston locator if so equipped.

8. Remove the piston seal using a wooden or plastic tool.

9. Remove the bleeder screw, bolt, fitting, and copper washer. Remove the bracket only if it is damaged.

10. Inspect caliper bore for scoring, nicks, corrosion, and wear. Use crocus cloth for light corrosion. Replace caliper if bore will not clean up.

11. To install, replace the bleeder screw, bolt, fitting, and copper washer.

12. Install the piston. Lubricate seals and piston with brake fluid prior to reinstallation.

13. Install the locator retainer if so equipped. Install the piston locator if so equipped.

14. Install the dust boot.

15. Install the shaft seal and washer.

16. Install actuator screw to the housing.

17. Install the nut, lever, lever seal, and anti-friction washer. It may be necessary to rotate the parking brake lever away from the stop to install the nut. Torque the nut 30–40 ft. lbs. (41–54 Nm) and rotate the lever back to the stop.

18. Install the shoe dampening spring to the end of the piston.

NOTE: *It may be necessary to move the parking brake lever off the stop, extending the piston slightly, making the dampening spring groove accessible. If the piston is extended, push it back into the caliper before installing the caliper on the car.*

1989–92

1. Remove the caliper assembly. Remove the 2 collar return springs from the actuating collar. Remove the actuator collar assembly with parts attached out of the housing.

2. Remove the clamp rod and compliance bushing.

3. Remove the boot retainers, 2 boots and pushrod from the compliance bushing. Discard the retainers and boots.

4. Remove the preload spring from the retainer.

5. Using compressed air directed into the brake hose port, carefully extract piston.

CAUTION: *Do not place fingers between piston and brake shoe flange, or personal injury may occur when piston breaks free from bore. Cover caliper assembly with a rage to prevent brake fluid from spraying when piston is extracted.*

6. Inspect and clean piston and bore assembly for cracks or scoring.

7. Remove the piston seal.

8. Remove the bleeder valve.

9. Remove the caliper lever pivot pin seal, sprag clip, spring and lever. Discard the clip.

10. Inspect the caliper lever for worn spots, replace as necessary.

11. Remove the 2 guide pins from the mounting bracket.

12. Clean all parts not included in the rebuild kit in denatured alcohol. Use only dry filtered compressed air to dry parts. Replace the caliper housing if badly scored or corroded.

To install:

13. Lubricate the new piston seal with clean brake fluid. Place the seal into the caliper groove, making sure the seal is not twisted.

14. Install the piston. Lubricate seals and piston with brake fluid prior to reinstallation.

15. Assemble the pushrod, 2 new boots and new retainers to the actuating collar.

16. Lightly coat the actuating collar with the lubricant provided in the rebuild kit. Do not use any other type of lubricant.

17. Install the clamp retainers firmly against the actuating collar. Bend the tabs on the retainer to hold the assembly together.

18. Install the preload spring into the boot retainers.

19. Install the clamp rod to the actuating col-

lar and boot. Lubricate the clamp rod with the lubricant supplied in the kit.

20. Slide the clamp rod through the holes in the boot and actuating collar. The boot must be against the reaction plate on the clamp rod.

21. Lubricate and install the new compliance bushing with the lubricant supplied in the kit.

22. Install the clamp rod with assembled parts into the connecting hole in the caliper piston.

23. Install a new bleeder valve.

24. Install the pivot pin and new nut into the housing, if removed.

25. Install the caliper pivot pin seal, parking brake lever, new sprag clip and spring, in that order. The teeth of the sprag clip must face away from the lever.

26. Install the 2 collar return springs to the retainer. The retainer must enter the return springs at the end of the second coil.

27. Install the adjuster screw into the caliper housing until the actuating collar is parallel to the piston bore face of the caliper housing.

28. Lubricate and install the guide pins and boots. Install the pads and caliper assembly.

29. Bleed the brake system.

Brake Disc (Rotor)

REMOVAL AND INSTALLATION

CAUTION: *Brake pads contain asbestos, which has been determined to be a cancer causing agent. Never clean the brake surfaces with compressed air! Avoid inhaling any dust from any brake surface! When cleaning brake surfaces, use a commercially available brake cleaning fluid.*

1. Raise and support the car. Remove the wheel.

2. Remove the caliper by referring to the Rear Caliper Removal procedure. Pull the brake disc from the axle.

3. To install, place the rotor onto the spindle and install caliper.

4. Install the wheel and lower the car.

INSPECTION

1. Raise and support the car. Remove the wheel. Replace wheel nuts to hold rotor in place.

2. Check the rotor surface for wear, scoring, grooves or rust pitting. Rotor damage can be corrected by refacing, consult your local garage or machine shop. If the damage exceeds the minimum thickness, which is stamped on the rotor, replace the rotor.

3. Using a dial indicator, check the rotor parallelism at several points around the circumference. The difference must not vary more than 0.0005 in. (0.013mm). Make all measurements

at the same distance in from the edge of the rotor.

4. Using the same dial indicator, measure the rotor runout. The runout should not exceed 0.004 in. (0.10mm).

5. If any of these conditions are not met, reface or replace the rotor.

PARKING BRAKE

Cables

REMOVAL AND INSTALLATION

Front Cable

1. Raise the car and support it with jackstands.

2. Remove the adjusting nut at the equalizer.

3. Remove the spring retainer clip from the bracket.

4. Lower the car. Remove the upper console cover and lower console rear screws.

5. Lift the rear of the lower console for access to the cable retainer at the hand lever.

6. Remove the cable retainer pin, cable retainer, then the cable.

7. To install, position the cable retainer pin, cable retainer, then the cable.

8. Install the upper console cover and lower console rear screws. Raise the car and support it with jackstands.

9. Install the spring retainer clip from the bracket.

10. Install the adjusting nut at the equalizer.

11. Adjust the parking brake. Lower the car.

Rear Cable

DRUM BRAKES

CAUTION: *Brake shoes contain asbestos, which has been determined to be a cancer causing agent. Never clean the brake surfaces with compressed air! Avoid inhaling any dust from any brake surface! When cleaning brake surfaces, use a commercially available brake cleaning fluid.*

1. Raise the car and support it with jackstands.

2. Loosen the adjusting nut at the equalizer.

3. Disengage the rear cable at the connector.

4. Remove the wheel assembly and brake drum.

5. Bend the retainer fingers.

6. Disengage the cable at the brake shoe operating lever.

7. To install, engage the cable at the brake shoe operating lever.

8. Bend the retainer fingers.

9. Install the wheel assembly and brake drum.

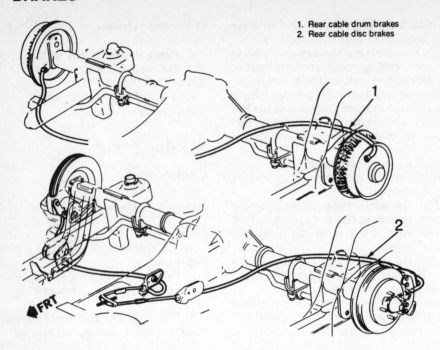

1. Rear cable drum brakes
2. Rear cable disc brakes

Parking brake rear cables

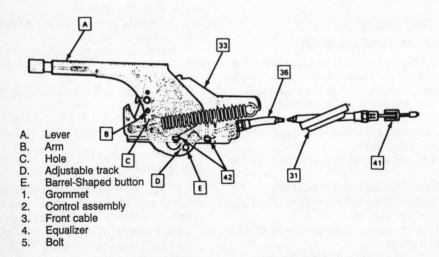

A.   Lever
B.   Arm
C.   Hole
D.   Adjustable track
E.   Barrel-Shaped button
1.   Grommet
2.   Control assembly
3.   Front cable
4.   Equalizer
5.   Bolt

Parking brake lever and front cable—1990–92

10. Engage the rear cable at the connector.
11. Adjust the parking brake by the adjusting nut at the equalizer.
12. Lower the car.

DISC BRAKES

1. Raise the car and support it with jackstands.
2. Loosen the adjusting nut at the equalizer.
3. Disengage the cable at the connector.
4. Push forward on the caliper parking brake apply lever. This allows the cable to be removed from the tang. Then, release the lever.

5. Pull on the caliper parking brake apply lever to engage the cable to the tang.
6. Engage the cable at the connector.
7. Adjust the parking brake cable by the adjusting nut at the equalizer.
8. Apply the parking brake 3 times with heavy pressure and repeat adjustment.
9. Lower the car.

ADJUSTMENT
The parking brake cable is adjustable only on 1982–89 vehicles. 1990–92 vehicles feature a self-adjusting parking brake.

Models With Rear Drum Brakes

1. Depress the parking brake lever exactly two ratchet clicks.

2. Raise the rear of the vehicle and support safely with jackstands.

3. Tighten the brake cable adjusting nut until the left rear wheel can be turned rearward with both hands, but locks when forward rotation is attempted.

4. Release the parking brake lever; both rear wheels must turn freely in either direction without brake drag.

5. Lower the vehicle.

Models With Rear Disc Brakes

1. Apply the brake pedal 3 times with a pedal force of approximately 175 lbs. (778 N). Apply and release the parking brake 3 times.

2. Raise and safely support the vehicle.

3. Check the parking brake lever for full release:

    a. Turn the ignition **ON**.

    b. The brake warning light should be OFF. If the brake warning light is still ON and the parking brake lever is completely released, pull downward on the front parking brake cable to remove slack from the lever assembly.

    c. Turn the ignition switch **OFF**.

4. Remove the rear wheels and tires. Reinstall 2 wheel nuts on each side to retain the brake rotors.

5. Pull the parking lever 4 clicks. The parking brake levers on both calipers should be against the lever stops on the caliper housings. If the levers are not against the stops, check for binding in the rear cables and/or loosen the cables at the equalizer nut until both left and right levers are against their stops.

6. Adjust the equalizer adjusting nut until the parking brake levers on both calipers just begin to move off their stops.

7. Back off the adjuster nut until the levers move back, barely touching their stops.

8. Operate the parking brake lever several times to check adjustment. After cable adjustment, the parking brake lever should travel no more than 14 ratchet clicks. The rear wheels should not turn forward when the parking brake lever is applied 8–16 ratchet clicks.

9. Release the parking brake lever. Both rear wheels must turn freely in both directions. The parking brake levers on both calipers should be resting on their stops.

10. Remove the wheel nuts retaining the rotors. Install the wheel and tire assemblies.

11. Lower the vehicle.

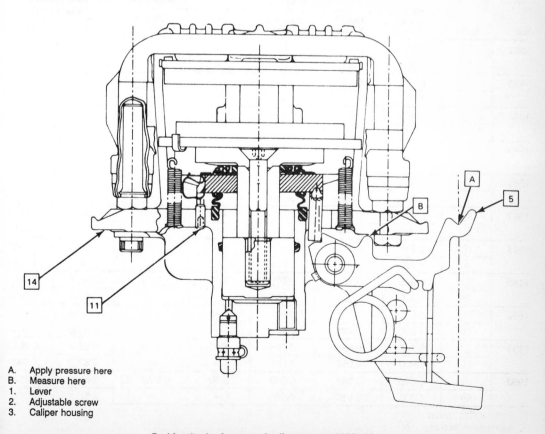

A.   Apply pressure here
B.   Measure here
1.   Lever
2.   Adjustable screw
3.   Caliper housing

Parking brake free travel adjustment—1990–92

Parking Brake Free-Travel
ADJUSTMENT

1989–92

Rear Disc Brakes

NOTE: *Disc brake pads must be new or parallel to within 0.006 in. (0.15mm).*

Parking brake adjustment is not valid with heavily tapered pads and may cause caliper/parking brake binding. Replace tapered brake pads. Parking brake free-travel should only be made if the caliper has been taken apart. This adjustment will not correct a condition where the caliper levers will not return to their stops.

1. Have an assistant apply a light brake ped-

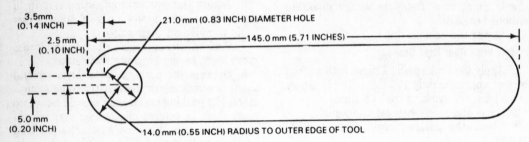

MAKE PARKING BRAKE CABLE RETAINER COMPRESSOR TOOL FROM 28 mm (1.10 INCH) BAR STOCK, 3.2 mm (0.13 INCH) THICK.

Fabricated parking brake cable retainer compressing tool

BRAKE SPECIFICATIONS

Year	Model	Master Cylinder Bore	Brake Disc			Brake Drum	Wheel Cylinder or Caliper Bore Dia.	
			Minimum Thickness	Maximum Runout	Inside Diameter	Maximum Machine O/S	Front	Rear
1982	①	0.945	0.965	0.005	9.50	9.56	2.50	0.748
	②	1.000	0.965	0.005	—	—	2.50	1.890
1983	①	0.945	0.965	0.005	9.50	9.56	2.50	0.748
	②	1.000	0.965	0.005	—	—	2.50	1.890
1984	①	0.945	0.965	0.005	9.50	9.56	2.50	0.748
	②	1.000	0.965	0.005	—	—	2.50	1.890
1985	①	0.945	0.965	0.005	9.50	9.56	2.50	0.748
	②	1.000	0.965	0.005	—	—	2.50	1.890
1986	①	0.945	0.965	0.005	9.50	9.56	2.50	0.750
	②	1.000	0.956	0.005	—	—	2.50	1.870
1987	①	0.945	0.965	0.005	9.50	9.56	2.50	0.750
	②	1.000	0.956	0.005	—	—	2.50	1.870
1988	①	0.945	0.965	0.005	9.50	9.56	2.50	0.750
	②	1.000	0.956	0.005	—	—	2.50	1.870
1989	①	0.945	0.965	0.005	9.50	9.56	2.52③	0.750
	②	1.000	0.724	0.005	—	—	2.52③	1.600
1990	①	0.945	0.965	0.005	9.50	9.56	2.52③	0.750
	②	1.000	0.724	0.005	—	—	2.52③	1.600
1991	①	0.945	0.965	0.005	9.50	9.56	2.52③	0.750
	②	1.000	0.956	0.005	—	—	2.52③	1.600
1992	①	0.945	0.965	0.005	9.50	9.56	2.52③	0.750
	②	1.000	0.956	0.005	—	—	2.52③	1.600

① 2 wheel disc brakes
② 4 wheel disc brakes
③ Heavy duty caliper—1.50 in.

al load, enough to stop the rotor from turning by hand. This takes up all clearances and ensures that components are correctly aligned.

2. Apply light pressure to the caliper lever.

3. Measure the free-travel between the caliper lever and the caliper housing. The free-travel must be 0.0024–0.028 in. (0.6–0.7mm).

4. If the free-travel is incorrect, do the following:

    a. Remove the adjuster screw.

    b. Clean the thread adhesive residue from the threads.

    c. Coat the threads with adhesive.

    d. Screw in the adjuster screw far enough to obtain 0.024–0.028 in. (0.6–0.7mm) free-travel between the caliper lever and the caliper housing.

5. Have an assistant release the brake pedal, then apply the brake pedal firmly 3 times. Recheck the free-travel and adjust as necessary.

Brake Lever

REMOVAL AND INSTALLATION

1982–89

1. Raise and safely support the vehicle.

2. Remove the adjusting nut at the equalizer and remove the front cable from the equalizer and bracket.

3. Lower the vehicle.

4. Remove the upper console and lower console rear screws. Lift the rear of the lower console to gain access to the parking brake control.

5. Remove the pin and retainer from the control assembly and front cable.

6. Remove the cable and casing from the control assembly and bracket and remove the cable and grommet from the vehicle. Remove the parking brake lever mounting bolts and remove the assembly.

7. Installation is the reverse of the removal procedure. Adjust the parking brake.

1990–92

1. Remove the carpet finish molding.

2. Remove the console assembly.

3. With the parking brake lever in the down position, rotate the arm toward the front of the vehicle until a 3mm metal pen can be inserted into the hole. Insert the metal pin into the hole, locking out the self adjuster.

4. Raise and safely support the vehicle.

5. Disconnect the rear cables from the equalizer.

6. Lower the vehicle.

7. Remove the barrel-shaped button from the adjuster track.

8. Remove the parking brake lever mounting bolts.

9. Remove the front cable and casing from the control assembly using a fabricated parking brake cable retainer compressor tool.

10. Installation is the reverse of the removal procedure. Cycle the lever to set the parking lever and cables in there proper location.

Body

![Body 10](door icon) 10

EXTERIOR

Doors

REMOVAL AND INSTALLATION

1. On doors that are equipped with power operated components, do the following:

    a. Remove the door trim panel and inner panel water deflector.

    b. Disconnect the wire harness from all components in the door.

    c. Remove the rubber conduit from the door, then remove the wire harness from the door through the conduit access hole.

2. Tape the area (on the door pillar and body pillar) above the lower hinge with cloth backed body tape.

CAUTION: *Before performing the following step, cover the spring with a shop cloth or rag to prevent the spring from flying and possibly causing personal injury or damage.*

3. Insert a long, flat-blade screwdriver under the pivot point of the hold-open link and over the top of the spring. The screwdriver should be positioned so as not to apply pressure to the hold-open link. Cover the spring with a shop cloth or rag and lift the screwdriver to disengage the spring. The spring can also be removed by using tool J–36604 (or equivalent) door hinge spring compressor tool. The tool is stamped right side and left side. The tool stamped left side is used to service the right-hand hinge spring and vise-a-versa for the tool stamped right side.

4. With the aid of a helper to support the door, remove the lower hinge pin using a soft-headed hammer and locking type pliers. The

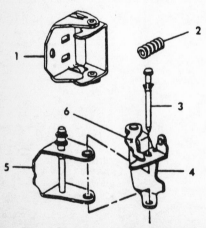

1. Upper hinge assembly
2. Spring
3. Lower hinge pin
4. Door side hinge strap
5. Body side hinge strap
6. Hold open link

Door hinge assembly

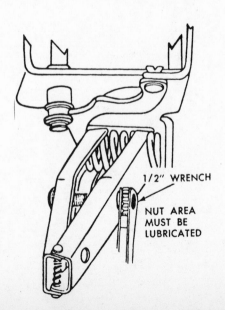

1/2" WRENCH

NUT AREA MUST BE LUBRICATED

Remove door hinge spring using tool J-36604 or flat bladed screwdriver

helper can aid the hinge pin removal by raising and lowering the rear of the door.

5. Insert a bolt into the hole of the lower hinge to maintain the door attachment during upper hinge removal.

6. Using a 13mm socket, remove the upper hinge bolts from the pillar. Remove the bolt from the lower hinge and remove the door from the body.

7. To install, replace the hinge pin clip.

8. With the aid of a helper, position the door and insert the bolt in the hole of the lower hinge.

9. Bolt the upper hinge to the body. The lower hinge pin is installed with the pointed end down.

10. Remove the screw from the lower hinge and install the lower hinge pin. The use of tool J–36604 or equivalent is recommended for installing the hinge spring.

NOTE: *If the spring is installed before installing the lower hinge pin, damage to the hinge bushings may result.*

11. If the spring was removed using a screwdriver, install the spring as follows:

a. Place the spring in tool J–36604 or equivalent.

b. Place the tool and spring in a bench vise.

c. Compress the tool in the vise and install the bolt until the spring is fully compressed.

d. Remove the tool (with the compressed spring) from the vise and install in the proper position in the door lower hinge. A slot in one jaw fits over the hold-open link. The hole on the other jaw fits over the bubble.

e. Remove the bolt from the tool to install the spring.

f. Remove the tool from the door hinge (tool will fall out in three pieces). Cycle the door to check the spring operation.

12. Remove the tape from the door and the body pillars.

13. On doors with power operated components:

a. Install the wire harness to the door through the conduit access hole, then install the rubber conduit to the door.

b. Connect wire harness to all components in the door.

c. Install the inner panel water deflector and door trim panel.

Hood

REMOVAL AND INSTALLATION

1. Open the hood and mark the position of the hood hinge assembly-to-hood by a scribe, caulk or paint.

2. Remove the hood attaching bolts that are towards the front of the hood.

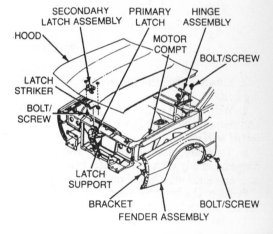

Front end sheet metal

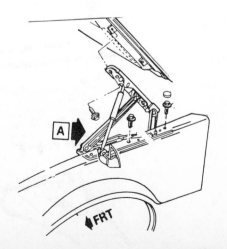

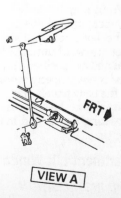

Hood removal

1. Hood
2. Fender
3. Front end fascia

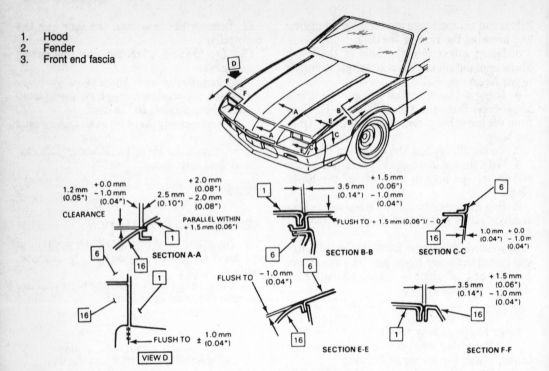

Body panel and hood alignment

3. Slowly loosen the remaining hood attaching bolts.

4. With the aid of a helper, remove the bolts and remove the hood. Place the hood on a protected surface.

5. To install, position the hood over the hood hinge assembly with the aid of a helper and install the hood attaching bolts finger tight.

6. Align the hood to the match marks made earlier and tighten the hood attaching bolts.

7. Close the hood and check align.

ALIGNMENT

Slotted holes are provided at all hood hinge attaching points for proper adjustment — both vertically and fore-and-aft. Vertical adjustments at the front may be made by adjusting the rubber bumpers up and down.

To adjust the hood fore-and-aft move the hood forward or rearward until the hood clearances are equal and as specified in the illustration. If the hood is not properly coming into adjustment then the body panels may also need to be adjusted. To achieve the best results set the hood to any existing marks and make adjustments one at a time.

Rear Compartment Lift Window

REMOVAL AND INSTALLATION

1. Prop the lid open and place a protective covering along the edges of the rear compartment opening to prevent any damage to the painted surfaces.

2. Use a 13mm socket to remove the nuts holding the glass to the hinge.

CAUTION: *Do not attempt to remove or loosen the gas support assembly attachments with the lid in any position other than fully open as personal injury may result.*

3. While a helper supports the glass, disengage the gas supports from the lift window as-

Rear hatch assembly

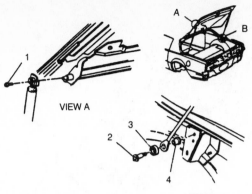

VIEW A

VIEW B

1. Bolt—gas support to rear compartment lift window
2. Bolt—gas support to body
3. Spacer
4. Bushing

Rear hatch gas support removal

sembly and disconnect the harness connector for the electric grid defogger, if equipped.

4. With the aid of a helper, remove the lift window assembly from the body and place it on a protected surface.

5. To install, position the lift window assembly to the body with the aid of a helper. Install the attaching bolts and torque to 11 ft. lbs. (16 Nm).

CAUTION: *Do not over tighten the glass-to-hinge bolts as it could cause the glass to break and possible personal injury. Always wear safety glasses during this operation.*

6. Connect the harness connector for the electric grid defogger, if equipped, and connect the gas supports to the lift window assembly.

7. Lower the lid and check alignment.

ADJUSTMENT

The rear compartment lift window assembly height, fore and aft and side adjustments are controlled at the hinge-to-body location. This area of the body has oversize hinge attaching holes in addition to the hinge-to-body spacers. Adjustments at the hinge location must be made with the gas supports disengaged. Additional height adjustment can also be made at the lower panel by adjusting the rubber bumpers. Bolts holding hinge-to-body should be tightened to 15–20 ft. lbs. (20–28 Nm).

BUMPERS

REMOVAL AND INSTALLATION

Front Fascia

1. Disconnect the negative battery cable.
2. Remove the air cleaner assembly, as required.
3. Remove bumper filler panel.
4. Remove the fascia center bracket at the front end panel reinforcement.
5. Disconnect all electrical equipment, such as headlamps, turn signals, horns, fog lamps, etc.
6. Raise and safely support the vehicle.
7. Remove the front bumper fascia extension.
8. Remove the bolts from the bumper impact bar and radiator lower air baffle, if equipped.

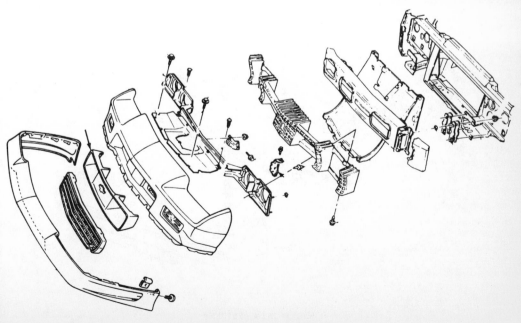

Front bumper assembly

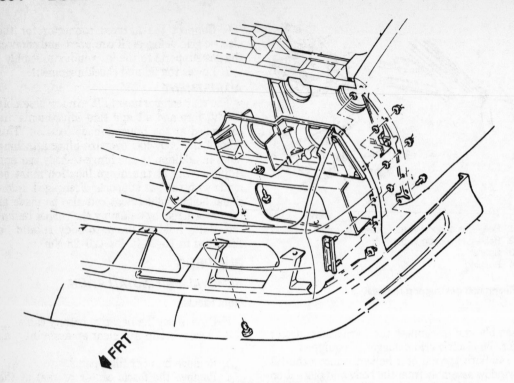

Front bumper fascia removal

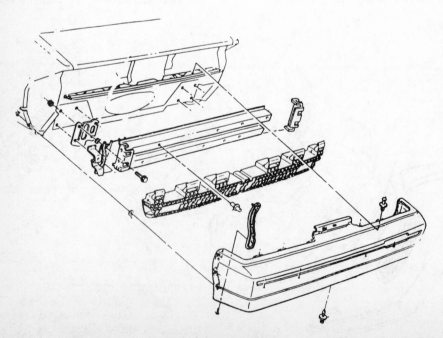

Rear bumper assembly

9. Remove the push-on retainers attaching the bumper fascia to the bumper impact bar.

10. Lower the vehicle and remove the bolts attaching the outer brackets to the front end inner structure.

11. With the aid of an assistant, remove the fascia carefully as not to scratch or damage the assembly.

To install:

12. With the aid of an assistant, install the fascia carefully as not to scratch or damage the assembly.

13. Raise and safely support the vehicle.

14. Install the bolts attaching the outer brackets to the front end inner structure. Torque the bolts to 84 inch lbs. (9.5 Nm).

15. Install the push-on retainers attaching the bumper fascia to the bumper impact bar.

16. Install the bolts at the bumper impact bar and radiator lower air baffle, if equipped.

17. Install the front bumper fascia extension.

18. Connect all electrical equipment, such as headlamps, turn signals, horns, fog lamps, etc.

19. Install the fascia center bracket at the front end panel reinforcement.

20. Install bumper filler panel.

21. Install the air cleaner assembly, as required.

22. Connect the negative battery cable.

Rear

1. Disconnect the negative battery cable.

2. Open the rear compartment hatch.

3. Remove the rear left, right and center trim panel.

4. Remove the spare tire assembly.

5. Remove the left and right side taillamps.

6. Remove the license plate bolts and bracket.

7. Remove the right and left side fascia nuts.

8. Remove the push-on retainers and lower screws.

9. With the aid of an assistant, remove the rear fascia.

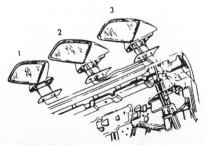

1. Manual mirror
2. Remote control mirror
3. Electirc remote control mirror

Outside mirror assemblies

To install:

10. With the aid of an assistant, install the rear fascia.

11. Install the push-on retainers and lower screws.

12. Install the right and left side fascia nuts.

13. Install the license plate bolts and bracket.

14. Install the left and right side taillamps.

15. Install the spare tire assembly.

16. Install the rear left, right and center trim panel.

17. Close the rear compartment hatch.

18. Connect the negative battery cable.

Outside Mirrors

REMOVAL AND INSTALLATION

Standard Mirrors

1. Remove the door trim panel and detach inner panel water deflector enough to gain access to the mirror retainer nuts.

2. Remove the attaching nuts from the mirror base studs and remove the mirror assembly from the door.

3. To install, position the mirror onto the door making sure the mirror gasket is properly aligned on the door outer panel.

4. Install the attaching nuts to the mirror base studs and tighten.

5. Install the inner panel water deflector and door trim panel.

Remote Control Mirrors

1. Remove the mirror remote control bezel and door trim panel. Detach the inner panel water deflector enough to expose the mirror and cable assembly from the door.

2. Remove the mirror base-to-door outer panel stud nuts, remove the cable from the clip and remove the mirror and cable assembly from the door.

3. To install, position the mirror onto the door making sure the mirror gasket is properly aligned on the door outer panel.

4. Install the cable onto the clip and install the mirror base-to-door outer panel stud nuts. Torque to 72 inch lbs. (8 Nm).

5. Install the inner panel water deflector and door trim panel.

6. Install the mirror remote control bezel.

Power Operated Mirrors

1. Disconnect the negative battery terminal and, from the door trim panel side, remove the remote control mirror bezel, release and remove the door panel.

2. Disconnect wire harness connection from the remote mirror electrical switch.

3. Peel back water deflector enough to de-

tach the harness from the retaining tabs in the door.

4. Remove the mirror base-to-door stud nuts and lift mirror housing and harness assembly from the door.

5. To install, feed the mirror harness through the door along with the mirror assembly. Install the mirror base-to-door stud nuts and tighten.

6. Connect the mirror wire harness and install the water deflector.

7. Connect the wire harness connection to the remote mirror electrical switch.

8. Install the door panel and install the remote control mirror bezel.

9. Connect the negative battery terminal.

Fenders

REMOVAL AND INSTALLATION

1. Disconnect the negative battery cable.
2. Remove the hood.

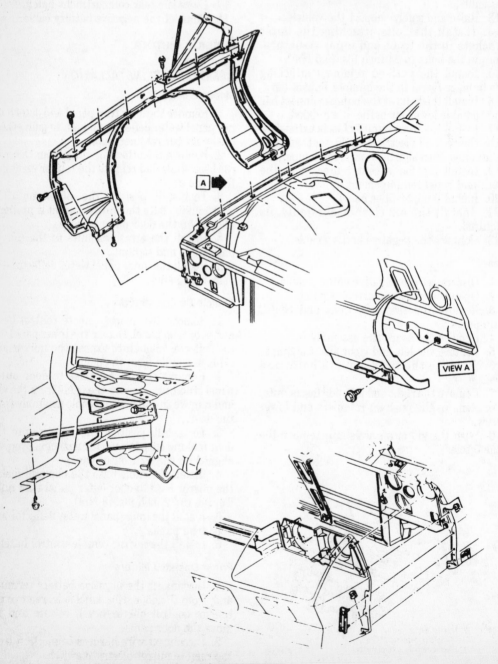

Fender assembly

3. Raise and safely support the vehicle.

4. Remove the lower fender bolts and inner wheel house panel.

5. Remove the rocker panel molding.

6. Remove the lower front end panel deflector-to-fender bolts.

7. Remove the bolt from the support brace.

8. Remove the front end bumper fascia-to-fender nuts and screws.

9. Remove the hood hinge-to-fender bolts.

10. Disconnect all electrical connections from horn, turn signal lamps, etc.

11. Remove the fender by sliding rearward and outward, at rear, with the aid of an assistant. Place an old blanket over the fender as to avoid scratches or dents.

To install:

12. Install the fender with the aid of an assistant. Place an old blanket over the fender as to avoid scratches or dents.

13. Connect all electrical connections to the horn, turn signal lamps, etc.

14. Install the hood hinge-to-fender bolts.

15. Install the front end bumper fascia-to-fender nuts and screws.

16. Install the bolt at the support brace.

17. Install the lower front end panel deflector-to-fender bolts.

18. Install the rocker panel molding.

19. Install the lower fender bolts and inner wheel house panel.

20. Install the hood.

21. Disconnect the negative battery cable. Align the fender and hood as necessary, placing existing shims in original positions.

INTERIOR

Instrument Panel and Pad

REMOVAL AND INSTALLATION

CAUTION: *The 1991–92 vehicles are equipped with an Air Bag system. Proper disarming of the system is necessary before proceeding with any disassembly or repairs to the steering column, dash or electrical system or possible deployment of the air bag might occur. Refer to Chapter 8 — Steering Column Removal for disarming procedure.*

1. Properly disable the SIR air bag system, if equipped. Disconnect the negative battery cable.

2. Remove the center console.

3. Remove the screws attaching the instrument panel pad to the instrument panel.

4. Remove the daytime running light sensor electrical connector, if equipped.

5. Remove the instrument panel pad.

6. Remove the instrument panel sound insulators.

7. Remove the knee bolster and bracket.

8. Remove the instrument panel cluster.

9. Remove the steering column retaining nuts and lower the column.

10. Remove the upper and lower instrument panel to cowl screws.

11. Disconnect and remove the electrical harness at the cowl connector and under dash panel.

12. Remove the instrument panel assembly.

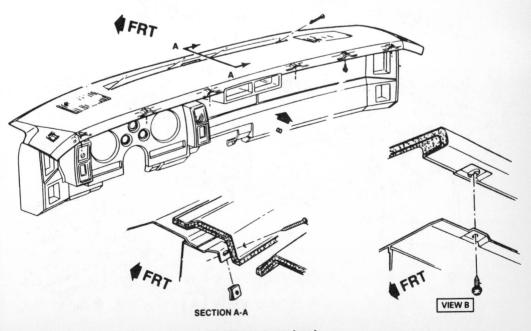

SECTION A-A

Instrument panel pad

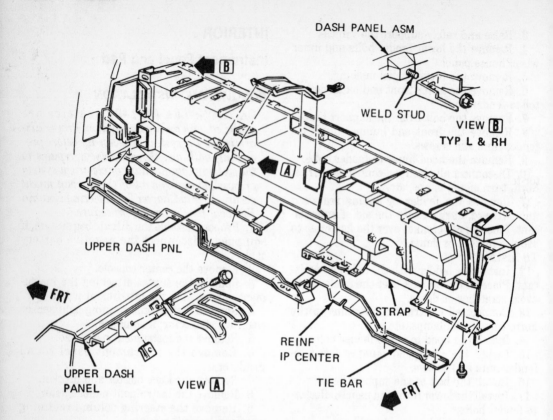

DASH PANEL ASM

WELD STUD

VIEW **B**
TYP L & RH

UPPER DASH PNL

FRT

UPPER DASH
PANEL

VIEW **A**

REINF
IP CENTER

STRAP

TIE BAR

FRT

Instrument panel—1982–90

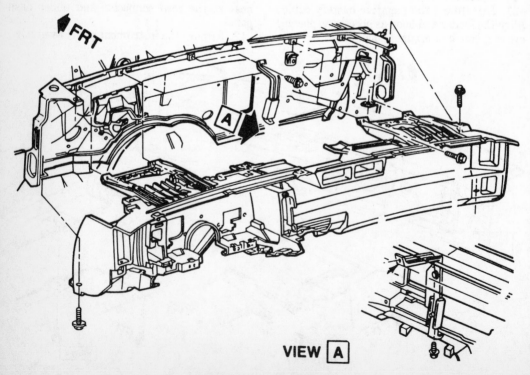

FRT

A

FRT

VIEW A

Instrument panel—1991–92

To install:

13. Install the instrument panel assembly.

14. Install the electrical harness at the cowl connector and under dash panel.

15. Install the upper and lower instrument panel to cowl screws.

16. Install the steering column retaining nuts.

17. Install the instrument panel cluster.

18. Install the knee bolster and bracket.

19. Install the instrument panel sound insulators.

20. Install the instrument panel pad.

21. Install the daytime running light sensor electrical connector, if equipped.

22. Install the screws attaching the instrument panel pad to the instrument panel.

23. Install the center console.

24. Properly disable the SIR air bag system, if equipped. Disconnect the negative battery cable.

Door Panels

REMOVAL AND INSTALLATION

The one-piece trim hangs over the door inner panel across the top and is secured by clips down the sides and across the bottom. It is retained by screws located in the areas of the armrest and pull handle assembly.

1. Remove all the door inside handles.

2. Remove the door inside locking rod knob.

3. Remove the screws inserted through the door armrest and pull the handle assembly into the door inner panel or armrest hanger support bracket.

4. On models with remote control mirror assemblies, remove the control plate from the be-

zel on the trim pad and remove the control from the plate.

5. On models with power door lock controls located in the door trim panel, disconnect the wire harnesses at the switch assemblies.

6. Remove the remote control handle bezel screws.

7. Remove the screws used to hold the armrest to the inner panel.

8. Remove the screws and plastic retainers from the perimeter of the door trim panel using tool BT–7323A or equivalent and a screwdriver. To remove the trim panel, push the trim up-

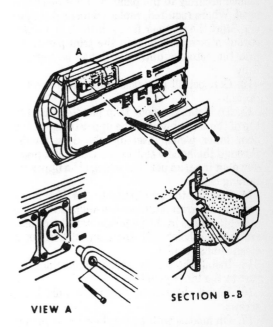

VIEW A   **SECTION B-B**

Door armrest and pull handle attachment

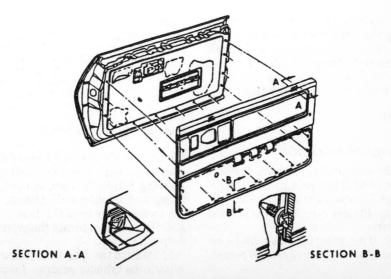

SECTION A-A   SECTION B-B

Door trim panel replacement

ward and outboard to disengage from the door inner panel at the beltline.

9. On models with a water deflector held in place by fasteners, use tool BT–7323A or equivalent to remove the fasteners and water deflector.

10. To install the water deflector, locate the fasteners in the holes in the door inner panel and press in place. Replace all tape which may have been applied to assist in holding the water deflector in place.

11. Before installing the door trim panel, make certain that all the trim retainers are installed securely to the panel and are not damaged. Where required, replace damaged retainers. Start the retainer flange into ¼ in. (6mm) cutout attachment hole in the trim panel, rotate the retainer until the flange is engaged fully.

12. Connect all electrical components where present.

13. To install the door trim panel, locate the top of the assembly over the upper flange of the door inner panel, inserting the door handle through the handle slot in the panel and press down on the trim panel to engage the upper retaining clips.

14. Position the trim panel to the door inner panel so the trim retainers are aligned with the attaching holes in the panel and tap the retainers into the holes with the palm of hand or a clean rubber mallet.

15. Install the screws used to hold the armrest to the inner panel.

16. Install the remote control handle bezel screws.

17. On models with power door lock controls located in the door trim panel, connect the wire harnesses at the switch assemblies.

18. On models with remote control mirror assemblies, install the control to the plate. Install the control plate to the bezel on the trim pad.

19. Install the handle assembly and install the screws inserted through the door armrest.

20. Install the door inside locking rod knob.

21. Install all the door inside handles.

Door Locks

REMOVAL AND INSTALLATION

1. Raise the door window. Remove the door trim panel and detach the inner panel water deflector enough to expose the access hole.

2. Disengage the lock cylinder to the lock rod at the cylinder.

CAUTION: *If removing the lock cylinder retainer by hand, wear gloves to prevent personal injury.*

3. With a screwdriver or similar tool, slide

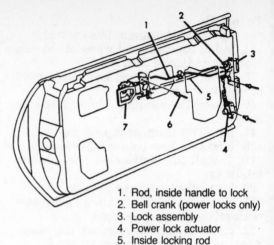

1. Rod, inside handle to lock
2. Bell crank (power locks only)
3. Lock assembly
4. Power lock actuator
5. Inside locking rod
6. Rivet
7. Inside handle

Door locking system (internal)

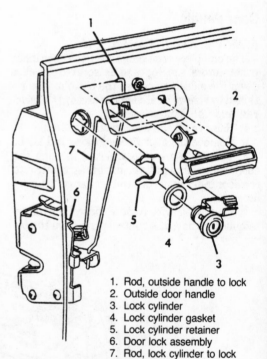

1. Rod, outside handle to lock
2. Outside door handle
3. Lock cylinder
4. Lock cylinder gasket
5. Lock cylinder retainer
6. Door lock assembly
7. Rod, lock cylinder to lock

Door locking system (external)

the lock cylinder retainer forward until it disengages. Retainer can also be removed by hand by grasping anti-theft shield at the top of the retainer and rotating until disengaged. Remove the lock cylinder from the door.

4. To install, lubricate the cylinder with the proper lubricant.

5. Position the cylinder into place and rotate it until the cylinder engages. Install the cylinder retainer.

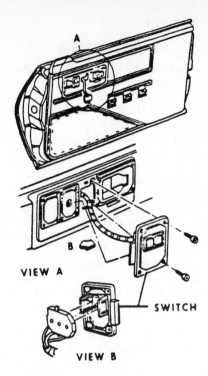

Power door lock switch servicing

6. Engage the lock cylinder to lock rod at the cylinder.

7. Install the inner panel water deflector and door trim panel.

Power Door Lock Actuator

REMOVAL AND INSTALLATION

1. Disconnect the negative battery cable. Remove the door panel.

2. Raise the window fully. Disconnect the electrical connector from the actuator.

3. Drive the rivet center pins out using an ⅛ in. (3mm) punch and hammer, then using a ¼ in. (6mm) drill bit, remove the rivet head.

4. Remove the actuator rod and remove the door lock actuator.

5. Installation is the reverse of the removal procedure.

Rear Liftgate Pull-Down Unit

REMOVAL AND INSTALLATION

1. Open the rear hatch. Disconnect the negative battery cable.

2. Remove the rear trim panel. Disconnect the electrical connector and remove the attaching screws.

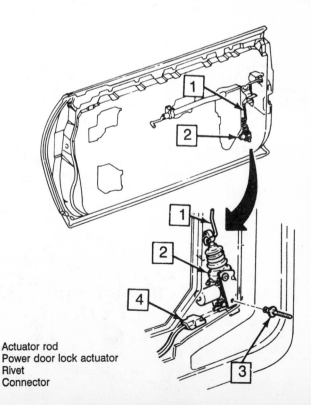

1. Actuator rod
2. Power door lock actuator
3. Rivet
4. Connector

Power door lock actuator

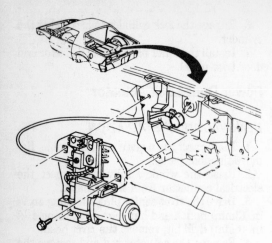

Pull-Down lock unit removal

3. Disconnect the unit lock cable connection from the lock cylinder.

4. Remove the unit.

5. Installation is the reverse of the removal procedure. Torque the screws to 18 ft. lbs. (24 Nm).

ADJUSTMENT

Adjust the unit as necessary for proper lock striker engagement.

Door Window

REMOVAL AND INSTALLATION

1. Remove the door trim panel and the inner panel water deflector.

2. Raise the window to half-up position.

3. Punch out the center pins of the glass to sash channel attaching rivets.

4. Remove the rear guide channel through the rear access hole.

5. Remove the up stop.

6. Using a ¼ in. (6mm) drill bit, drill out the attaching rivets on sash channel.

7. Raise the glass to remove from the sash channel and remove the glass from the door.

8. To install, remove the drilled out rivets and shavings from the door.

9. Check the rivet bushings and retainers on the glass for damage. If necessary, remove the bushings using a flat-bladed tool covered with a cloth body tape. Install by snapping rivet retainer into the bushing.

10. Lower the glass into the door and position on the sash channel so the holes in the sash line up with the holes in the bushings and retainers.

11. Using rivet tool J–29022 or equivalent, install ¼ in. (6mm) peel type rivet (part No. 20184399 or equivalent) to retain the glass to sash channel.

12. Install the rear guide channel.

1. Door glass
2. Lower sash channel
3. Rear guide channel
4. Inner panel cam channel
5. Window regulator
6. Filler assembly
7. Guide stabilizer
8. Support—front up stop

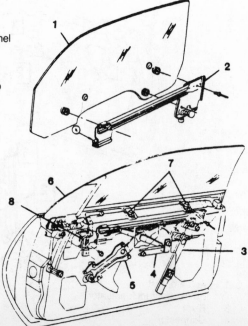

Door glass and regulator assembly.

CHILTON'S
AUTO BODY REPAIR TIPS

EASY STEP-BY-STEP TIPS FROM PROS

Tools and Materials • Step-by-Step Illustrated Procedures
How To Repair Dents, Scratches and Rust Holes
Spray Painting and Refinishing Tips

With a little practice, basic body repair procedures can be mastered by any do-it-yourself mechanic. The step-by-step repairs shown here can be applied to almost any type of auto body repair.

TOOLS & MATERIALS

You may already have basic tools, such as hammers and electric drills. Other tools unique to body repair — body hammers, grinding attachments, sanding blocks, dent puller, half-round plastic file and plastic spreaders — are relatively inexpensive and can be obtained wherever auto parts or auto body repair parts are sold. Portable air compressors and paint spray guns can be purchased or rented.

Auto Body Repair Kits

The best and most often used products are available to the do-it-yourselfer in kit form, from major manufacturers of auto body repair products. The same manufacturers also merchandise the individual products for use by pros.

Kits are available to make a wide variety of repairs, including holes, dents and scratches and fiberglass, and offer the advantage of buying the materials you'll need for the job. There is little waste or chance of materials going bad from not being used. Many kits may also contain basic body-working tools such as body files, sanding blocks and spreaders. Check the contents of the kit before buying your tools.

BODY REPAIR TIPS

Safety

Many of the products associated with auto body repair and refinishing contain toxic chemicals. Read all labels before opening containers and store them in a safe place and manner.

• Wear eye protection (safety goggles) when using power tools or when performing any operation that involves the removal of any type of material.

• Wear lung protection (disposable mask or respirator) when grinding, sanding or painting.

Sanding

1 Sand off paint before using a dent puller. When using a non-adhesive sanding disc, cover the back of the disc with an overlapping layer or two of masking tape and trim the edges. The disc will last considerably longer.

2 Use the circular motion of the sanding disc to grind *into* the edge of the repair. Grinding or sanding away from the jagged edge will only tear the sandpaper.

3 Use the palm of your hand flat on the panel to detect high and low spots. Do not use your fingertips. Slide your hand slowly back and forth.

WORKING WITH BODY FILLER

Mixing The Filler

Cleanliness and proper mixing and application are extremely important. Use a clean piece of plastic or glass or a disposable artist's palette to mix body filler.

1 Allow plenty of time and follow directions. No useful purpose will be served by adding more hardener to make it cure (set-up) faster. Less hardener means more curing time, but the mixture dries harder; more hardener means less curing time but a softer mixture.

2

2 Both the hardener and the filler should be thoroughly kneaded or stirred before mixing. Hardener should be a solid paste and dispense like thin toothpaste. Body filler should be smooth, and free of lumps or thick spots.

Getting the proper amount of hardener in the filler is the trickiest part of preparing the filler. Use the same amount of hardener in cold or warm weather. For contour filler (thick coats), a bead of hardener twice the diameter of the filler is about right. There's about a 15% margin on either side, but, if in doubt use less hardener.

2

2

3 Mix the body filler and hardener by wiping across the mixing surface, picking the mixture up and wiping it again. Colder weather requires longer mixing times. Do not mix in a circular motion; this will trap air bubbles which will become holes in the cured filler.

3

Applying The Filler

1 For best results, filler should not be applied over ¼″ thick.

Apply the filler in several coats. Build it up to above the level of the repair surface so that it can be sanded or grated down.

The first coat of filler must be pressed on with a firm wiping motion.

Apply the filler in one direction only. Working the filler back and forth will either pull it off the metal or trap air bubbles.

REPAIRING DENTS

Before you start, take a few minutes to study the damaged area. Try to visualize the shape of the panel before it was damaged. If the damage is on the left fender, look at the right fender and use it as a guide. If there is access to the panel from behind, you can reshape it with a body hammer. If not, you'll have to use a dent puller. Go slowly and work the metal a little at a time. Get the panel as straight as possible before applying filler.

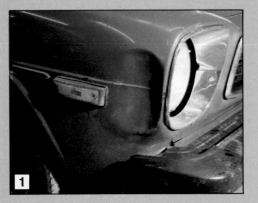

1 This dent is typical of one that can be pulled out or hammered out from behind. Remove the headlight cover, headlight assembly and turn signal housing.

2 Drill a series of holes ½ the size of the end of the dent puller along the stress line. Make some trial pulls and assess the results. If necessary, drill more holes and try again. Do not hurry.

3 If possible, use a body hammer and block to shape the metal back to its original contours. Get the metal back as close to its original shape as possible. Don't depend on body filler to fill dents.

4 Using an 80-grit grinding disc on an electric drill, grind the paint from the surrounding area down to bare metal. Use a new grinding pad to prevent heat buildup that will warp metal.

5 The area should look like this when you're finished grinding. Knock the drill holes in and tape over small openings to keep plastic filler out.

6 Mix the body filler (see Body Repair Tips). Spread the body filler evenly over the entire area (see Body Repair Tips). Be sure to cover the area completely.

7 Let the body filler dry until the surface can just be scratched with your fingernail. Knock the high spots from the body filler with a body file ("Cheesegrater"). Check frequently with the palm of your hand for high and low spots.

8 Check to be sure that trim pieces that will be installed later will fit exactly. Sand the area with 40-grit paper.

9 If you wind up with low spots, you may have to apply another layer of filler.

10 Knock the high spots off with 40-grit paper. When you are satisfied with the contours of the repair, apply a thin coat of filler to cover pin holes and scratches.

11 Block sand the area with 40-grit paper to a smooth finish. Pay particular attention to body lines and ridges that must be well-defined.

12 Sand the area with 400 paper and then finish with a scuff pad. The finished repair is ready for priming and painting (see Painting Tips).

Materials and photos courtesy of Ritt Jones Auto Body, Prospect Park, PA.

REPAIRING RUST HOLES

There are many ways to repair rust holes. The fiberglass cloth kit shown here is one of the most cost efficient for the owner because it provides a strong repair that resists cracking and moisture and is relatively easy to use. It can be used on large and small holes (with or without backing) and can be applied over contoured areas. Remember, however, that short of replacing an entire panel, no repair is a guarantee that the rust will not return.

1 Remove any trim that will be in the way. Clean away all loose debris. Cut away all the rusted metal. But be sure to leave enough metal to retain the contour or body shape.

2 Grind away all traces of rust with a 24-grit grinding disc. Be sure to grind back 3-4 inches from the edge of the hole down to bare metal and be sure all traces of paint, primer and rust are removed.

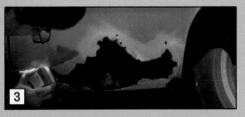

3 Block sand the area with 80 or 100 grit sandpaper to get a clear, shiny surface and feathered paint edge. Tap the edges of the hole inward with a ball peen hammer.

4 If you are going to use release film, cut a piece about 2-3″ larger than the area you have sanded. Place the film over the repair and mark the sanded area on the film. Avoid any unnecessary wrinkling of the film.

5 Cut 2 pieces of fiberglass matte to match the shape of the repair. One piece should be about 1″ smaller than the sanded area and the second piece should be 1″ smaller than the first. Mix enough filler and hardener to saturate the fiberglass material (see Body Repair Tips).

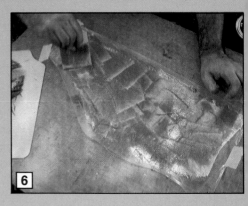

6 Lay the release sheet on a flat surface and spread an even layer of filler, large enough to cover the repair. Lay the smaller piece of fiberglass cloth in the center of the sheet and spread another layer of filler over the fiberglass cloth. Repeat the operation for the larger piece of cloth.

7 Place the repair material over the repair area, with the release film facing outward. Use a spreader and work from the center outward to smooth the material, following the body contours. Be sure to remove all air bubbles.

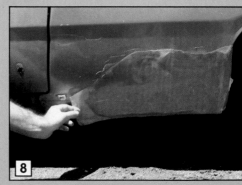

8 Wait until the repair has dried tack-free and peel off the release sheet. The ideal working temperature is 60°-90° F. Cooler or warmer temperatures or high humidity may require additional curing time. Wait longer, if in doubt.

9 Sand and feather-edge the entire area. The initial sanding can be done with a sanding disc on an electric drill if care is used. Finish the sanding with a block sander. Low spots can be filled with body filler; this may require several applications.

10 When the filler can just be scratched with a fingernail, knock the high spots down with a body file and smooth the entire area with 80-grit. Feather the filled areas into the surrounding areas.

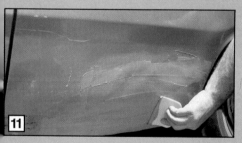

11 When the area is sanded smooth, mix some topcoat and hardener and apply it directly with a spreader. This will give a smooth finish and prevent the glass matte from showing through the paint.

12 Block sand the topcoat smooth with finishing sandpaper (200 grit), and 400 grit. The repair is ready for masking, priming and painting (see Painting Tips).

Materials and photos courtesy Marson Corporation, Chelsea, Massachusetts

PAINTING TIPS

Preparation

1 SANDING — Use a 400 or 600 grit wet or dry sandpaper. Wet-sand the area with a ¼ sheet of sandpaper soaked in clean water. Keep the paper wet while sanding. Sand the area until the repaired area tapers into the original finish.

2 CLEANING — Wash the area to be painted thoroughly with water and a clean rag. Rinse it thoroughly and wipe the surface dry until you're sure it's completely free of dirt, dust, fingerprints, wax, detergent or other foreign matter.

3 MASKING — Protect any areas you don't want to overspray by covering them with masking tape and newspaper. Be careful not get fingerprints on the area to be painted.

4 PRIMING — All exposed metal should be primed before painting. Primer protects the metal and provides an excellent surface for paint adhesion. When the primer is dry, wet-sand the area again with 600 grit wet-sandpaper. Clean the area again after sanding.

Painting Techniques

Paint applied from either a spray gun or a spray can (for small areas) will provide good results. Experiment on an old piece of metal to get the right combination before you begin painting.

SPRAYING VISCOSITY (SPRAY GUN ONLY) — Paint should be thinned to spraying viscosity according to the directions on the can. Use only the recommended thinner or reducer and the same amount of reduction regardless of temperature.

AIR PRESSURE (SPRAY GUN ONLY) — This is extremely important. Be sure you are using the proper recommended pressure.

TEMPERATURE — The surface to be painted should be approximately the same temperature as the surrounding air. Applying warm paint to a cold surface, or vice versa, will completely upset the paint characteristics.

THICKNESS — Spray with smooth strokes. In general, the thicker the coat of paint, the longer the drying time. Apply several thin coats about 30 seconds apart. The paint should remain wet long enough to flow out and no longer; heavier coats will only produce sags or wrinkles. Spray a light (fog) coat, followed by heavier color coats.

DISTANCE — The ideal spraying distance is 8″-12″ from the gun or can to the surface. Shorter distances will produce ripples, while greater distances will result in orange peel, dry film and poor color match and loss of material due to overspray.

OVERLAPPING — The gun or can should be kept at right angles to the surface at all times. Work to a wet edge at an even speed, using a 50% overlap and direct the center of the spray at the lower or nearest edge of the previous stroke.

RUBBING OUT (BLENDING) FRESH PAINT — Let the paint dry thoroughly. Runs or imperfections can be sanded out, primed and repainted.

Don't be in too big a hurry to remove the masking. This only produces paint ridges. When the finish has dried for at least a week, apply a small amount of fine grade rubbing compound with a clean, wet cloth. Use lots of water and blend the new paint with the surrounding area.

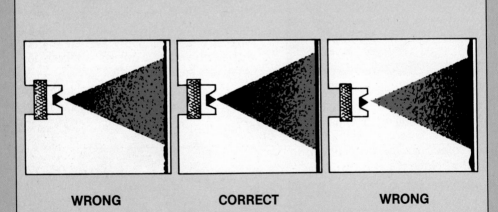

WRONG	CORRECT	WRONG
Thin coat. Stroke too fast, not enough overlap, gun too far away.	*Medium coat. Proper distance, good stroke, proper overlap.*	*Heavy coat. Stroke too slow, too much overlap, gun too close.*

13. Install the front up stop to support on the inner panel.

14. Before installing the trim parts, check the window operation for performance and fit to roof rail weatherstrip.

15. Install the inner panel water deflector and the door trim panel.

Window Regulator and Regulator Motor

REMOVAL AND INSTALLATION

1. Remove the door trim panel and inner panel water deflector.

2. Raise the window to half-up position and hold in place by inserting a rubber wedge door stops at the front and rear of the window between window and inner panel.

3. Remove the rear guide channel and inner panel cam channel.

4. Punch out the center pins of the regulator rivets; then drill out the rivets using a ¼ in. (6mm) drill bit.

5. Move the regulator rearward and disconnect wire harness from the motor (if equipped). Disengage the roller on the regulator lift arm from glass sash channel.

6. Remove the regulator through the rear access hole.

CAUTION: *If electric motor removal from the regulator is required, the sector gear must be locked in position. The regulator lift arm is under tension from the counterbalance spring and could cause personal injury if the sector gear is not locked in position.*

7. Drill a hole through the regulator sector gear and backplate and install a bolt and nut to lock the sector gear in position.

8. Using a ³⁄₁₆ in. (5mm) drill bit, drill out the motor attaching rivets and remove the motor from the regulator.

9. To install the motor to the regulator, use a rivet tool J–29022 or equivalent, and install ³⁄₁₆ in. (5mm) rivets or ³⁄₁₆ in. (5mm) nuts and bolts. Remove bolt and nut used to secure the sector gear in position.

10. Place the regulator through the rear access hole into the door inner panel. If electric regulator is being installed, connect the wire connector to motor prior to installing the regulator to the inner panel.

11. Locate the lift arm roller into the glass sash channel.

12. Using rivet tool J–29022 or equivalent, rivet regulator to the inner panel of the door using ¼ in. (6mm) × ½ in. (13mm) aluminum peel type rivets (part No. 9436175 or equivalent). If rivet tool is not available, use the following nut and bolt method:

a. Install U-clips on the regulator at the at-taching locations. Be sure to install the clips with clinch nuts on the outboard side of the regulator.

b. Locate the regulator in the door inner panel. If the electric regulator is being installed, connect the wire connector to the regulator motor.

c. Locate the lift arm roller in the glass sash channel.

d. Align the regulator with clinch nuts to holes in the inner panel.

e. Attach the regulator (and motor) to the door inner panel with M6.0 × 1 × 13 (¼–20 × ½ in.) screws (part No. 9419723 or equivalent) into ¼ in. (6mm) nuts with integral washers. Tighten the screw to 90–125 inch lbs. (10–14 Nm) torque.

13. Install the inner panel cam channel and rear guide channel.

14. Remove the rubber wedge door stops at the front and rear of the window between window and inner panel.

15. Install the inner panel water deflector and the door trim panel.

Windshield

NOTE: *Bonded windshields require special tools and special removal procedures to be performed to ensure the windshield will be removed without being broken. For this reason we recommend that you refer all removal and installation to a qualified technician.*

CAUTION: *Always wear heavy gloves when handling glass to reduce the risk of injury.*

When replacing a cracked windshield, it is important that the cause of the crack be determined and the condition corrected, before a new glass is installed. The cause of the crack may be an obstruction or a high spot somewhere around the flange of the opening; crack-

Using a hot knife or equivalent to remove the windshield

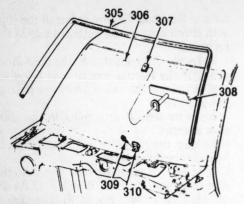

305. Reveal molding
306. Glass
307. Rear view mirror support
308. Rear view mirror
309. Screw
310. Support

Windshield installation

ing may not occur until pressure from the high spot or obstruction becomes particularly high due to winds, extremes of temperature or rough terrain.

When a windshield is broken, the glass may have already have fallen or been removed from the weatherstrip. Often, however, it is necessary to remove a cracked or otherwise imperfect windshield that is still intact. In this case, it is a

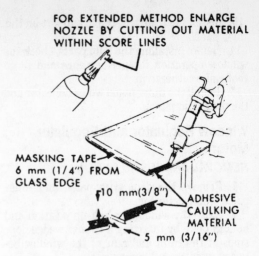

FOR EXTENDED METHOD ENLARGE NOZZLE BY CUTTING OUT MATERIAL WITHIN SCORE LINES

MASKING TAPE 6 mm (1/4") FROM GLASS EDGE

10 mm (3/8")

ADHESIVE CAULKING MATERIAL

5 mm (3/16")

Applying sealant to the glass

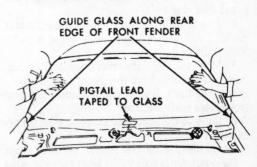

GUIDE GLASS ALONG REAR EDGE OF FRONT FENDER

PIGTAIL LEAD TAPED TO GLASS

Trim the sealant so the reveal molding will fit properly

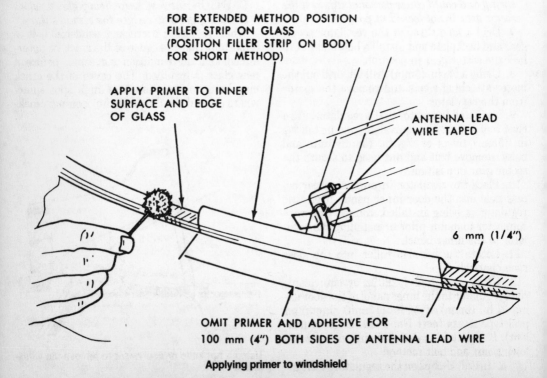

FOR EXTENDED METHOD POSITION FILLER STRIP ON GLASS (POSITION FILLER STRIP ON BODY FOR SHORT METHOD)

APPLY PRIMER TO INNER SURFACE AND EDGE OF GLASS

ANTENNA LEAD WIRE TAPED

6 mm (1/4")

OMIT PRIMER AND ADHESIVE FOR 100 mm (4") BOTH SIDES OF ANTENNA LEAD WIRE

Applying primer to windshield

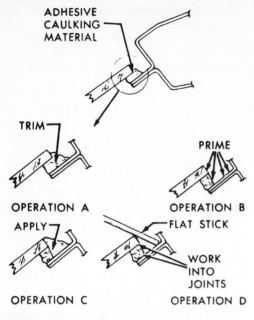

ADHESIVE CAULKING MATERIAL

TRIM

PRIME

OPERATION A

OPERATION B

APPLY

FLAT STICK

WORK INTO JOINTS

OPERATION C

OPERATION D

Installing the windshield

good practice to crisscross the glass with strips of masking tape before removing the it; this will help hold the glass together and minimize the risk of injury.

If a crack extends to the edge of the glass, mark the point where the crack meets the weather strip. (Use a piece of chalk to mark the point on the cab, next to the weatherstrip.) Later, examining the window flange for a cause of the crack which started at the point marked.

The higher the temperature of the work area, the more pliable the weather strip will be. The more pliable the weather strip, the more easily the windshield can be removed.

There are two methods of windshield removal, depending on the method of windshield replacement chosen. When using the short method of installation, it is important to cut the glass from the urethane adhesive as close to the glass as possible. This is due to the fact that the urethane adhesive will be used to provide a base for the replacement windshield.

When using the extended method of windshield replacement, all the urethane adhesive must be removed from the pinchweld flange so, the process of cutting the window from the adhesive is less critical.

REMOVAL AND INSTALLATION

NOTE: *The following procedure requires the use of the Urethane Glass Sealant Remover (hot knife) tool No. J–24709–1 or equivalent, the Glass Sealant Remover Knife tool No. J–24402–A or equivalent.*

1. Place the protective covering around the area where the glass will be removed.

2. Remove the windshield wiper arms, the cowl vent grille, the windshield supports, the rear view mirror and the interior garnish moldings.

NOTE: *If equipped with a radio antennaembedded in the windshield, disconnect the electrical connector from the windshield.*

3. Remove the exterior reveal molding from the urethane adhesive by prying one end of the molding from the adhesive. Pull the free end of the molding away from the windshield or the pinchweld flange until the molding is completely free of the windshield.

4. Using the Urethane Glass Sealant Remover (hot knife) tool No. J–24709–1 or equivalent, and the Glass Sealant Remover Knife tool No. J–24402–A or equivalent, cut the windshield from the urethane adhesive. If the short method of glass replacement is to be used, keep the knife as close to the glass as possible in order to leave a base for the replacement glass.

5. With the help of an assistant, remove the glass.

6. If the original glass is to be reinstalled, place it on a protected bench or a holding or holding fixture. Remove any remaining adhesive with a razor blade or a sharp scraper. Any remaining traces of adhesive material can be removed with denatured alcohol or lacquer thinner.

NOTE: *When cleaning the windshield glass, avoid contacting the edge of the plastic laminate material (on the edge of the glass) with a volatile cleaner. Contact may cause discoloration and deterioration of the plastic laminate. DO NOT use a petroleum based solvent such as gasoline or kerosene; the presence of oil will prevent the adhesion of new material.*

INSPECTION

Inspection of the windshield opening, the weather strip and the glass may reveal the cause of a broken windshield; this can help prevent future breakage. If there is no apparent cause of breakage, the weatherstrip should be removed from the flange and the flange inspected. Look for high weld or solder spots, hardened spot welds sealer, or any other obstruction or irregularity in the flange. Check the weatherstrip for irregularities or obstructions in it.

Check the windshield to be installed to make sure that it does not have chipped edges. Chipped edges can be ground off, restoring a smooth edge to the glass and minimizing concentrations of pressure that cause breakage. Remove no more than necessary, in an effort to maintain the original shape of the glass and the proper clearance between it and the flange of the opening.

INSTALLATION

To replace a urethane adhered windshield, the GM Adhesive Service Kit No. 9636067 contains some of the materials needed and must be used to insure the original integrity of the windshield design. Materials in this kit include:

1. One tube of adhesive material.
2. One dispensing nozzle.
3. Steel music wire.
4. Rubber cleaner.
5. Rubber Primer.
6. Pinchweld primer.
7. Blackout primer.
8. Filler strip (for use on windshield installations of vehicles equipped with an embedded windshield antenna).
9. Primer applicators.

Other materials required for windshield installation which are not included in the service kit, are:

1. GM rubber lubricant No. 1051717.
2. Alcohol for cleaning the edge of the glass.
3. Adhesive dispensing gun No. J–24811 or equivalent.
4. A commercial type razor knife.
5. Two rubber support spacers.

Short Method

1. Using masking tape, apply the tape across the windshield pillar-to-windshield opening, then cut the tape and remove the windshield.
2. Using an alcohol dampened cloth, clean the metal flange surrounding the windshield opening. Allow the alcohol to air dry.
3. Using the pinchweld primer, found in the service kit, apply it to the pinchweld area. DO NOT let any of the primer touch the exposed paint for damage to the finish may occur; allow five minutes for the primer to dry.
4. Cut the tip of the adhesive cartridge approximately $3/16$ in. (5mm) from the end of the tip.
5. Apply the adhesive first in and around the spacer blocks. Apply a smooth continuous bead of adhesive into the gap between the glass edge and the sheet metal. Use a flat bladed tool to paddle the material into position if necessary. Be sure that the adhesive contacts the entire edge of the glass and extends to fill the gap between the glass and the solidified urethane base.
6. With the aid of a helper, position the windshield on the filler strips against the two support spacers.

NOTE: *The vehicle should not be driven and should remain at room temperature for six hours to allow the adhesive to cure.*

7. Spray a mist of water onto the urethane. Water will assist in the curing process. Dry the area where the reveal molding will contact the body and glass.
8. Install new reveal moldings. Remove the protective tape covering the butyl adhesive on the underside of the molding. Push the molding caps onto each end of one of the reveal moldings. Press the lip of the molding into the urethane adhesive while holding it against the edge of the windshield. Take care to seat the molding in the corners. The lip must fully contact the adhesive and the gap must be entirely covered by the crown of the molding. Slide the molding caps onto the adjacent moldings. Use tape to hold the molding in position until the adhesive cures.
9. Install the wiper arms and the interior garnish moldings.

NOTE: *The vehicle should not be driven and should remain at room temperature for six hours to allow the adhesive to cure.*

Extended Method

1. Using the GM Strip Filler No. 20146247 or equivalent, install the sealing strip onto the pinchweld flange. The joint of the molding should be located at the bottom center of the molding.
2. Using masking tape, apply the tape across the windshield pillar-to-windshield opening, then cut the tape and remove the windshield.
3. Using an alcohol dampened cloth, clean the metal flange surrounding the windshield opening. Allow the alcohol to air dry.
4. Using the pinchweld primer, found in the service kit, apply it to the pinchweld area. DO NOT let any of the primer touch the exposed paint for damage to the finish may occur; allow five minutes for the primer to dry.
5. With the aid of an assistant, position the windshield on the filler strips against the two support spacers.
6. Cut the tip of the adhesive cartridge approximately $3/8$ in. (10mm) from the end of the tip.
7. Apply the adhesive first in and around the spacer blocks. Apply a smooth continuous bead of adhesive into the gap between the glass edge and the sheet metal. Use a flat bladed tool to paddle the material into position if necessary. Be sure that the adhesive contacts the entire edge of the glass and extends to fill the gap between the glass and the primed sheet metal.

NOTE: *The vehicle should not be driven and should remain at room temperature for six hours to allow the adhesive to cure.*

8. Spray a mist of warm or hot water onto

the urethane. Water will assist in the curing process. Dry the area where the reveal molding will contact the body and glass.

9. Install the reveal molding onto the windshield and remove the masking tape from the inner surface of the glass.

10. Press the lip of the molding into the urethane adhesive while holding it against the edge of the windshield. Take care to seat the molding in the corners. The lip must fully contact the adhesive and the gap must be entirely covered by the crown of the molding. Use tape to hold the molding in position until the adhesive cures.

11. Install the wiper arms and the interior garnish moldings.

Inside Rear View Mirror

INSTALLATION

The rear view mirror is attached to a support which is secured to the windshield glass. This support is installed by the glass supplier using a plastic-polyvinyl butyl adhesive.

Service replacement windshield glass has the mirror support bonded to the glass assembly. To install a detached mirror support or install a new part, the following items are needed:

• Part No. 1052369, Loctite® Minute-Bond Adhesive 312 two component pack or equivalent

• Original mirror support (prepared per Steps 4 and 5 of the installation procedure) or replacement rear view mirror support

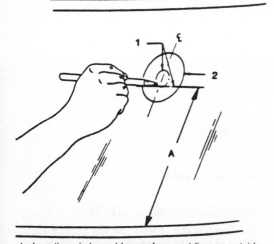

1. Locating circle and base of support line on outside glass surface
2. Circle on outside glass surface indicates area to be cleaned

Locating and marking the bonded support on the windshield

• Wax marking pencil or crayon
• Rubbing alcohol
• Clean paper towels
• Fine grit emery cloth or sandpaper (No. 320 or No. 360)
• Clean toothpick
• Six-lobed socket bit.

1. Determine the rear view mirror support position on the windshield. Support is to be located at the center of the glass 27⅛ in. (69cm) from the base of the glass to the base of the support.

2. Mark the location on the outside of the glass with wax pencil or crayon. also make a larger diameter circle around the mirror support circle on the outside of the glass surface.

3. On the inside of the glass surface, clean the large circle with a paper towel and domestic scouring cleanser, glass cleaning solution or polishing compound. Rub until the area is completely clean and dry. When dry, clean the area with an alcohol saturated paper towel to remove any traces of scouring powder of cleaning solution from this area.

4. With a piece of fine grit (No. 320 or No. 360) emery cloth or sandpaper, sand the bonding surface of the new rear view mirror support or factory installed support. If original rear view mirror support is to be reused, all traces of the factory installed adhesive must be removed prior to reinstallation.

5. Wipe the sanded mirror support with a clean paper towel saturated with alcohol and allow it to dry.

6. Follow the directions on the manufacturer's kit to prepare the rear view mirror support prior to installation on the glass.

7. Properly position the support to its premarked location, with rounded end pointed upward, press the support against the glass for 30–60 seconds, exerting steady pressure against the glass. After five minutes, any excess adhesive may be removed with an alcohol moistened paper towel or glass cleaning solution.

8. Install the mirror.

Seats

REMOVAL AND INSTALLATION

1. Operate the seat to the full-forward position. If six-way power seat is operable, operate seat to the full-forward and up positions. Where necessary to gain access to the adjuster-to-floor pan attaching nuts, remove the adjuster rear foot covers and/or carpet retainers.

2. Remove the track covers where necessary; then remove the adjuster-to-floor pan rear attaching nuts. Operate the seat to the full-rearward position. Remove the adjuster front foot

1. Cover—rear outer adjuster
2. Cover—rear inner adjuster
3. Adjuster—driver
4. Cover—driver's adjuster
5. Adjuster—passenger
6. Cover—passenger's adjuster
7. Nut
8. Auxiliary locking wire

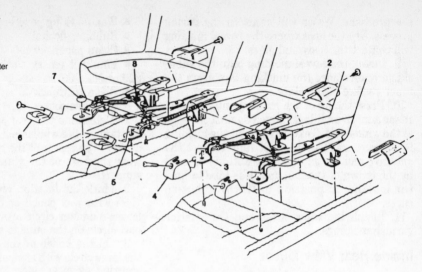

Seat mounting and adjusting mechanism—manual seats

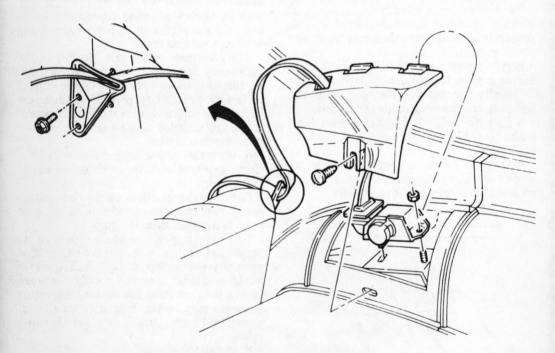

Rear seat belt assembly—coupe

covers; then remove the adjuster-to-floor pan front attaching nuts.

3. Remove the seat assembly from the car.

4. Prior to installing the seat assembly, check that both seat adjusters are parallel and in phase with each other.

5. Install the adjuster-to-floor pan attaching nuts by moving the seat forward and rearward and torque nuts to 15–21 ft. lbs. (20–28 Nm).

6. Check the operation of the seat assembly to full limits of travel.

Seat Belt System

REMOVAL AND INSTALLATION

1. Remove the cover from the anchor plate.

2. Remove the attaching bolt, anchor plate and washer from the door pillar.

3. Remove the bolt cover from the rear of the retractor assembly.

4. Remove the bolt retaining the retractor to the floor panel and remove the retractor.

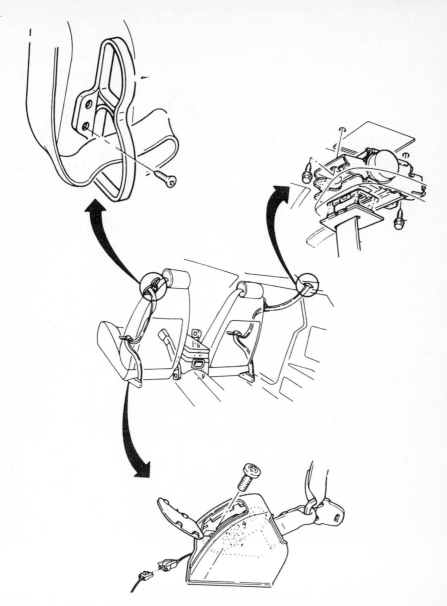

Front seat belt assembly—coupe

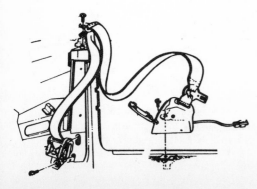

Front seat belt assembly—convertible

5. Remove the buckle assembly from the floor panel.

6. Remove the cap which conceals the buckle assembly bolt and remove the bolt.

7. Remove the seat belt warning wire from the drivers side buckle and remove the buckle assembly from the vehicle.

8. Installation is the reverse of removal. Tighten all bolts to 31 ft. lbs. (43 Nm).

Power Seat Motor

REMOVAL AND INSTALLATION

1. Remove the front seat assembly and place upside down on a clean protected surface.

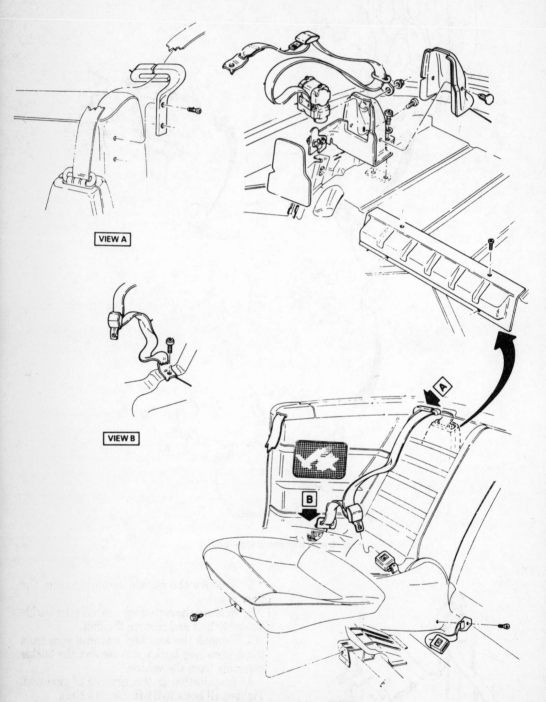

VIEW A

VIEW B

A

B

Rear seat belt assembly—convertible

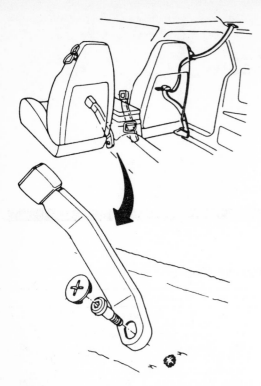

Seat belt attachment

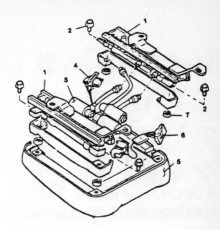

1. Seat adjuster assembly
2. Attaching screw
3. Three motor direct drive
4. Wire harness connector from motor
5. Seat cushion
6. Wire harness connector to seat switch
7. Adjuster to seat spacer

Power seat motor replacement

2. Disconnect the motor feed wires from the motors.

3. Remove the nut securing the front of the motor support bracket to the inboard adjuster and withdraw the assembly from the adjuster and the gearnut drives.

4. Disconnect the drive cables from the motors and complete removal of the support bracket with the motor attached.

5. Grind off the peened over end(s) of the grommet assembly securing the motor to the support and separate the motor(s) as required from the support.

6. Before installation, drill out the top end of the grommet assembly using a $\frac{3}{16}$ in. (5mm) drill.

7. Install the grommet assembly to the motor support bracket and secure the motor to the grommet using $\frac{3}{16}$ in. (5mm) rivet.

8. Install the support bracket with the motor attached and connect the drive cables to the motors.

9. Install the support bracket nuts securing the front of the motor support bracket to the inboard adjuster.

10. Connect the motor feed wires to the motors.

11. Install the front seat assembly.

Mechanic's Data

General Conversion Table

Multiply By	To Convert	To	
	LENGTH		
2.54	Inches	Centimeters	.3937
25.4	Inches	Millimeters	.03937
30.48	Feet	Centimeters	.0328
.304	Feet	Meters	3.28
.914	Yards	Meters	1.094
1.609	Miles	Kilometers	.621
	VOLUME		
.473	Pints	Liters	2.11
.946	Quarts	Liters	1.06
3.785	Gallons	Liters	.264
.016	Cubic inches	Liters	61.02
16.39	Cubic inches	Cubic cms.	.061
28.3	Cubic feet	Liters	.0353
	MASS (Weight)		
28.35	Ounces	Grams	.035
.4536	Pounds	Kilograms	2.20
—	To obtain	From	Multiply by

Multiply By	To Convert	To	
	AREA		
.645	Square inches	Square cms.	.155
.836	Square yds.	Square meters	1.196
	FORCE		
4.448	Pounds	Newtons	.225
.138	Ft./lbs.	Kilogram/meters	7.23
1.36	Ft./lbs.	Newton-meters	.737
.112	In./lbs.	Newton-meters	8.844
	PRESSURE		
.068	Psi	Atmospheres	14.7
6.89	Psi	Kilopascals	.145
	OTHER		
1.104	Horsepower (DIN)	Horsepower (SAE)	.9861
.746	Horsepower (SAE)	Kilowatts (KW)	1.34
1.60	Mph	Km/h	.625
.425	Mpg	Km/1	2.35
—	To obtain	From	Multiply by

Tap Drill Sizes

National Coarse or U.S.S.

Screw & Tap Size	Threads Per Inch	Use Drill Number
No. 5	40	39
No. 6	32	36
No. 8	32	29
No. 10	24	25
No. 12	24	17
1/4	20	8
5/16	18	F
3/8	16	5/16
7/16	14	U
1/2	13	27/64
9/16	12	31/64
5/8	11	17/32
3/4	10	21/32
7/8	9	49/64

National Coarse or U.S.S.

Screw & Tap Size	Threads Per Inch	Use Drill Number
1	8	7/8
1 1/8	7	63/64
1 1/4	7	1 7/54
1 1/2	6	1 11/32

National Fine or S.A.E.

Screw & Tap Size	Threads Per Inch	Use Drill Number
No. 5	44	37
No. 6	40	33
No. 8	36	29
No. 10	32	21

National Fine or S.A.E.

Screw & Tap Size	Threads Per Inch	Use Drill Number
No. 12	28	15
1/4	28	3
6/16	24	1
3/8	24	Q
7/16	20	W
1/2	20	29/64
9/16	18	33/64
5/8	18	37/64
3/4	16	11/16
7/8	14	13/16
1 1/8	12	1 3/64
1 1/4	12	1 11/64
1 1/2	12	1 27/64

Drill Sizes In Decimal Equivalents

Inch	Decimal	Wire	mm
1/64	.0156		.39
	.0157		.4
	.0160	78	
	.0165		.42
	.0173		.44
	.0177		.45
	.0180	77	
	.0181		.46
	.0189		.48
	.0197		.5
	.0200	76	
	.0210	75	
	.0217		.55
	.0225	74	
	.0236		.6
	.0240	73	
	.0250	72	
	.0256		.65
	.0260	71	
	.0276		.7
	.0280	70	
	.0292	69	
	.0295		.75
	.0310	68	
1/32	.0312		.79
	.0315		.8
	.0320	67	
	.0330	66	
	.0335		.85
	.0350	65	
	.0354		.9
	.0360	64	
	.0370	63	
	.0374		.95
	.0380	62	
	.0390	61	
	.0394		1.0
	.0400	60	
	.0410	59	
	.0413		1.05
	.0420	58	
	.0430	57	
	.0433		1.1
	.0453		1.15
	.0465	56	
3/64	.0469		1.19
	.0472		1.2
	.0492		1.25
	.0512		1.3
	.0520	55	
	.0531		1.35
	.0550	54	
	.0551		1.4
	.0571		1.45
	.0591		1.5
	.0595	53	
	.0610		1.55
1/16	.0625		1.59
	.0630		1.6
	.0635	52	
	.0650		1.65
	.0669		1.7
	.0670	51	
	.0689		1.75
	.0700	50	
	.0709		1.8
	.0728		1.85

Inch	Decimal	Wire	mm
	.0730	49	
	.0748		1.9
	.0760	48	
	.0768		1.95
5/64	.0781		1.98
	.0785	47	
	.0787		2.0
	.0807		2.05
	.0810	46	
	.0820	45	
	.0827		2.1
	.0846		2.15
	.0860	44	
	.0866		2.2
	.0886		2.25
	.0890	43	
	.0906		2.3
	.0925		2.35
	.0935	42	
3/32	.0938		2.38
	.0945		2.4
	.0960	41	
	.0965		2.45
	.0980	40	
	.0981		2.5
	.0995	39	
	.1015	38	
	.1024		2.6
	.1040	37	
	.1063		2.7
	.1065	36	
	.1083		2.75
7/64	.1094		2.77
	.1100	35	
	.1102		2.8
	.1110	34	
	.1130	33	
	.1142		2.9
	.1160	32	
	.1181		3.0
	.1200	31	
	.1220		3.1
1/8	.1250		3.17
	.1260		3.2
	.1280		3.25
	.1285	30	
	.1299		3.3
	.1339		3.4
	.1360	29	
	.1378		3.5
	.1405	28	
9/64	.1406		3.57
	.1417		3.6
	.1440	27	
	.1457		3.7
	.1470	26	
	.1476		3.75
	.1495	25	
	.1496		3.8
	.1520	24	
	.1535		3.9
	.1540	23	
5/32	.1562		3.96
	.1570	22	
	.1575		4.0
	.1590	21	
	.1610	20	

Inch	Decimal	Wire & Letter	mm
	.1614		4.1
	.1654		4.2
	.1660	19	
	.1673		4.25
	.1693		4.3
	.1695	18	
11/64	.1719		4.36
	.1730	17	
	.1732		4.4
	.1770	16	
	.1772		4.5
	.1800	15	
	.1811		4.6
	.1820	14	
	.1850	13	
	.1850		4.7
	.1870		4.75
3/16	.1875		4.76
	.1890		4.8
	.1890	12	
	.1910	11	
	.1929		4.9
	.1935	10	
	.1960	9	
	.1969		5.0
	.1990	8	
	.2008		5.1
	.2010	7	
13/64	.2031		5.16
	.2040	6	
	.2047		5.2
	.2055	5	
	.2067		5.25
	.2087		5.3
	.2090	4	
	.2126		5.4
	.2130	3	
	.2165		5.5
7/32	2188		5.55
	.2205		5.6
	.2210	2	
	.2244		5.7
	.2264		5.75
	.2280	1	
	.2283		5.8
	.2323		5.9
	.2340	A	
15/64	.2344		5.95
	.2362		6.0
	.2380	B	
	.2402		6.1
	.2420	C	
	.2441		6.2
	.2460	D	
	.2461		6.25
	.2480		6.3
1/4	.2500	E	6.35
	.2520		6.
	.2559		6.5
	.2570	F	
	.2598		6.6
	.2610	G	
	.2638		6.7
17/64	.2656		6.74
	.2657		6.75
	.2660	H	
	.2677		6.8

Inch	Decimal	Letter	mm
	.2717		6.9
	.2720	I	
	.2756		7.0
	.2770	J	
	.2795		7.1
	.2810	K	
9/32	.2812		7.14
	.2835		7.2
	.2854		7.25
	.2874		7.3
	.2900	L	
	.2913		7.4
	.2950	M	
	.2953		7.5
19/64	.2969		7.54
	.2992		7.6
	.3020	N	
	.3031		7.7
	.3051		7.75
	.3071		7.8
	.3110		7.9
5/16	.3125		7.93
	.3150		8.0
	.3160	O	
	.3189		8.1
	.3228		8.2
	.3230	P	
	.3248		8.25
	.3268		8.3
21/64	.3281		8.33
	.3307		8.4
	.3320	Q	
	.3346		8.5
	.3386		8.6
	.3390	R	
	.3425		8.7
11/32	.3438		8.73
	.3445		8.75
	.3465		8.8
	.3480	S	
	.3504		8.9
	.3543		9.0
	.3580	T	
	.3583		9.1
23/64	.3594		9.12
	.3622		9.2
	.3642		9.25
	.3661		9.3
	.3680	U	
	.3701		9.4
	.3740		9.5
3/8	.3750		9.52
	.3770	V	
	.3780		9.6
	.3819		9.7
	.3839		9.75
	.3858		9.8
	.3860	W	
	.3898		9.9
25/64	.3906		9.92
	.3937		10.0
	.3970	X	
	.4040	Y	
13/32	.4062		10.31
	.4130	Z	
	.4134		10.5
27/64	.4219		10.71

Inch	Decimal	mm
	.4331	11.0
7/16	.4375	11.11
	.4528	11.5
29/64	.4531	11.51
15/32	.4688	11.90
	.4724	12.0
31/64	.4844	12.30
	.4921	12.5
1/2	.5000	12.70
	.5118	13.0
33/64	.5156	13.09
17/32	.5312	13.49
	.5315	13.5
35/64	.5469	13.89
	.5512	14.0
9/16	.5625	14.28
	.5709	14.5
37/64	.5781	14.68
	.5906	15.0
19/32	.5938	15.08
39/64	.6094	15.47
	.6102	15.5
5/8	.6250	15.87
	.6299	16.0
41/64	.6406	16.27
	.6496	16.5
21/32	.6562	16.66
	.6693	17.0
43/64	.6719	17.06
11/16	.6875	17.46
	.6890	17.5
45/64	.7031	17.85
	.7087	18.0
23/32	.7188	18.25
	.7283	18.5
47/64	.7344	18.65
	.7480	19.0
3/4	.7500	19.05
49/64	.7656	19.44
	.7677	19.5
25/32	.7812	19.84
	.7874	20.0
51/64	.7969	20.24
	.8071	20.5
13/16	.8125	20.63
	.8268	21.0
53/64	.8281	21.03
27/32	.8438	21.43
	.8465	21.5
55/64	.8594	21.82
	.8661	22.0
7/8	.8750	22.22
	.8858	22.5
57/64	.8906	22.62
	.9055	23.0
29/32	.9062	23.01
59/64	.9219	23.41
	.9252	23.5
15/16	.9375	23.81
	.9449	24.0
61/64	.9531	24.2
	.9646	24.5
31/32	.9688	24.6
	.9843	25.0
63/64	.9844	25.0
1	1.0000	25.4

GLOSSARY OF TERMS

AIR/FUEL RATIO: The ratio of air to gasoline by weight in the fuel mixture drawn into the engine.

AIR INJECTION: One method of reducing harmful exhaust emissions by injecting air into each of the exhaust ports of an engine. The fresh air entering the hot exhaust manifold causes any remaining fuel to be burned before it can exit the tailpipe.

ALTERNATOR: A device used for converting mechanical energy into electrical energy.

AMMETER: An instrument, calibrated in amperes, used to measure the flow of an electrical current in a circuit. Ammeters are always connected in series with the circuit being tested.

AMPERE: The rate of flow of electrical current present when one volt of electrical pressure is applied against one ohm of electrical resistance.

ANALOG COMPUTER: Any microprocessor that uses similar (analogous) electrical signals to make its calculations.

ARMATURE: A laminated, soft iron core wrapped by a wire that converts electrical energy to mechanical energy as in a motor or relay. When rotated in a magnetic field, it changes mechanical energy into electrical energy as in a generator.

ATMOSPHERIC PRESSURE: The pressure on the Earth's surface caused by the weight of the air in the atmosphere. At sea level, this pressure is 14.7 psi at 32°F (101 kPa at 0°C).

ATOMIZATION: The breaking down of a liquid into a fine mist that can be suspended in air.

AXIAL PLAY: Movement parallel to a shaft or bearing bore.

BACKFIRE: The sudden combustion of gases in the intake or exhaust system that results in a loud explosion.

BACKLASH: The clearance or play between two parts, such as meshed gears.

BACKPRESSURE: Restrictions in the exhaust system that slow the exit of exhaust gases from the combustion chamber.

BAKELITE: A heat resistant, plastic insulator material commonly used in printed circuit boards and transistorized components.

BALL BEARING: A bearing made up of hardened inner and outer races between which hardened steel ball roll.

BALLAST RESISTOR: A resistor in the primary ignition circuit that lowers voltage after the engine is started to reduce wear on ignition components.

BEARING: A friction reducing, supportive device usually located between a stationary part and a moving part.

BIMETAL TEMPERATURE SENSOR: Any sensor or switch made of two dissimilar types of metal that bend when heated or cooled due to the different expansion rates of the alloys. These types of sensors usually function as an on/off switch.

BLOWBY: Combustion gases, composed of water vapor and unburned fuel, that leak past the piston rings into the crankcase during normal engine operation. These gases are removed by the PCV system to prevent the build-up of harmful acids in the crankcase.

BRAKE PAD: A brake shoe and lining assembly used with disc brakes.

BRAKE SHOE: The backing for the brake lining. The term is, however, usually applied to the assembly of the brake backing and lining.

BUSHING: A liner, usually removable, for a bearing; an anti-friction liner used in place of a bearing.

BYPASS: System used to bypass ballast resistor during engine cranking to increase voltage supplied to the coil.

CALIPER: A hydraulically activated device in a disc brake system, which is mounted straddling the brake rotor (disc). The caliper contains at least one piston and two brake pads. Hydraulic pressure on the piston(s) forces the pads against the rotor.

CAMSHAFT: A shaft in the engine on which are the lobes (cams) which operate the valves. The camshaft is driven by the crankshaft, via a belt, chain or gears, at one half the crankshaft speed.

CAPACITOR: A device which stores an electrical charge.

CARBON MONOXIDE (CO): a colorless, odorless gas given off as a normal byproduct of combustion. It is poisonous and extremely dangerous in confined areas, building up slowly to toxic levels without warning if adequate ventilation is not available.

CARBURETOR: A device, usually mounted on the intake manifold of an engine, which mixes the air and fuel in the proper proportion to allow even combustion.

CATALYTIC CONVERTER: A device installed in the exhaust system, like a muffler, that converts harmful byproducts of combustion into carbon dioxide and water vapor by means of a heat-producing chemical reaction.

CENTRIFUGAL ADVANCE: A mechanical method of advancing the spark timing by using flyweights in the distributor that react to centrifugal force generated by the distributor shaft rotation.

CHECK VALVE: Any one-way valve installed to permit the flow of air, fuel or vacuum in one direction only.

CHOKE: A device, usually a moveable valve, placed in the intake path of a carburetor to restrict the flow of air.

CIRCUIT: Any unbroken path through which an electrical current can flow. Also used to describe fuel flow in some instances.

CIRCUIT BREAKER: A switch which protects an electrical circuit from overload by opening the circuit when the current flow exceeds a predetermined level. Some circuit breakers must be reset manually, while other reset automatically

COIL (IGNITION): A transformer in the ignition circuit which steps of the voltage provided to the spark plugs.

COMBINATION MANIFOLD: An assembly which includes both the intake and exhaust manifolds in one casting.

COMBINATION VALVE: A device used in some fuel systems that routes fuel vapors to a charcoal storage canister instead of venting them into the atmosphere. The valve relieves fuel tank pressure and allows fresh air into the tank as fuel level drops to prevent a vapor lock situation.

COMPRESSION RATIO: The comparison of the total volume of the cylinder and combustion chamber with the piston at BDC and the piston at TDC.

CONDENSER: 1. An electrical device which acts to store an electrical charge, preventing voltage surges.
2. A radiator-like device in the air conditioning system in which refrigerant gas condenses into a liquid, giving off heat.

CONDUCTOR: Any material through which an electrical current can be transmitted easily.

CONTINUITY: Continuous or complete circuit. Can be checked with an ohmmeter.

COUNTERSHAFT: An intermediate shaft which is rotated by a mainshaft and transmits, in turn, that rotation to a working part.

CRANKCASE: The lower part of an engine in which the crankshaft and related parts operate.

CRANKSHAFT: The main driving shaft of an engine which receives reciprocating motion from the pistons and converts it to rotary motion.

CYLINDER: In an engine, the round hole in the engine block in which the piston(s) ride.

CYLINDER BLOCK: The main structural member of an engine in which is found the cylinders, crankshaft and other principal parts.

CYLINDER HEAD: The detachable portion of the engine, fastened, usually, to the top of the cylinder block, containing all or most of the combustion chambers. On overhead valve engines, it contains the valves and their operating parts. On overhead cam engines, it contains the camshaft as well.

DEAD CENTER: The extreme top or bottom of the piston stroke.

DETONATION: An unwanted explosion of the air fuel mixture in the combustion chamber caused by excess heat and compression, advanced timing, or an overly lean mixture. Also referred to as "ping".

DIAPHRAGM: A thin, flexible wall separating two cavities, such as in a vacuum advance unit.

DIESELING: A condition in which hot spots in the combustion chamber cause the engine to run on after the key is turned off.

DIFFERENTIAL: A geared assembly which allows the transmission of motion between drive axles, giving one axle the ability to turn faster than the other.

DIODE: An electrical device that will allow current to flow in one direction only.

DISC BRAKE: A hydraulic braking assembly consisting of a brake disc, or rotor, mounted on an axle, and a caliper assembly containing, usually two brake pads which are activated by hydraulic pressure. The pads are forced against the sides of the disc, creating friction which slows the vehicle.

DISTRIBUTOR: A mechanically driven device on an engine which is responsible for electrically firing the spark plug at a predetermined point of the piston stroke.

DOWEL PIN: A pin, inserted in mating holes in two different parts allowing those parts to maintain a fixed relationship.

DRUM BRAKE: A braking system which consists of two brake shoes and one or two wheel cylinders, mounted on a fixed backing plate, and a brake drum, mounted on an axle, which revolves around the assembly. Hydraulic action applied to the wheel cylinders forces the shoes outward against the drum, creating friction and slowing the vehicle.

DWELL: The rate, measured in degrees of shaft rotation, at which an electrical circuit cycles on and off.

ELECTRONIC CONTROL UNIT (ECU): Ignition module, module, amplifier or igniter. See Module for definition.

ELECTRONIC IGNITION: A system in which the timing and firing of the spark plugs is controlled by an electronic control unit, usually called a module. These systems have not points or condenser.

ENDPLAY: The measured amount of axial movement in a shaft.

ENGINE: A device that converts heat into mechanical energy.

EXHAUST MANIFOLD: A set of cast passages or pipes which conduct exhaust gases from the engine.

FEELER GAUGE: A blade, usually metal, of precisely predetermined thickness, used to measure the clearance between two parts. These blades usually are available in sets of assorted thicknesses.

F-Head: An engine configuration in which the intake valves are in the cylinder head, while the camshaft and exhaust valves are located in the cylinder block. The camshaft operates the intake valves via lifters and pushrods, while it operates the exhaust valves directly.

FIRING ORDER: The order in which combustion occurs in the cylinders of an engine. Also the order in which spark is distributed to the plugs by the distributor.

FLATHEAD: An engine configuration in which the camshaft and all the valves are located in the cylinder block.

FLOODING: The presence of too much fuel in the intake manifold and combustion chamber which prevents the air/fuel mixture from firing, thereby causing a no-start situation.

FLYWHEEL: A disc shaped part bolted to the rear end of the crankshaft. Around the outer perimeter is affixed the ring gear. The starter drive engages the ring gear, turning the flywheel, which rotates the crankshaft, imparting the initial starting motion to the engine.

FOOT POUND (ft.lb. or sometimes, ft. lbs.): The amount of energy or work needed to raise an item weighing one pound, a distance of one foot.

FUSE: A protective device in a circuit which prevents circuit overload by breaking the circuit when a specific amperage is present. The device is constructed around a strip or wire of a lower amperage rating than the circuit it is designed to protect. When an amperage higher than that stamped on the fuse is present in the circuit, the strip or wire melts, opening the circuit.

GEAR RATIO: The ratio between the number of teeth on meshing gears.

GENERATOR: A device which converts mechanical energy into electrical energy.

HEAT RANGE: The measure of a spark plug's ability to dissipate heat from its firing end. The higher the heat range, the hotter the plug fires.

HUB: The center part of a wheel or gear.

HYDROCARBON (HC): Any chemical compound made up of hydrogen and carbon. A major pollutant formed by the engine as a byproduct of combustion.

HYDROMETER: An instrument used to measure the specific gravity of a solution.

INCH POUND (in.lb. or sometimes, in. lbs.): One twelfth of a foot pound.

INDUCTION: A means of transferring electrical energy in the form of a magnetic field. Principle used in the ignition coil to increase voltage.

INJECTION PUMP: A device, usually mechanically operated, which meters and delivers fuel under pressure to the fuel injector.

INJECTOR: A device which receives metered fuel under relatively low pressure and is activated to inject the fuel into the engine under relatively high pressure at a predetermined time.

INPUT SHAFT: The shaft to which torque is applied, usually carrying the driving gear or gears.

INTAKE MANIFOLD: A casting of passages or pipes used to conduct air or a fuel/air mixture to the cylinders.

JOURNAL: The bearing surface within which a shaft operates.

KEY: A small block usually fitted in a notch between a shaft and a hub to prevent slippage of the two parts.

MANIFOLD: A casting of passages or set of pipes which connect the cylinders to an inlet or outlet source.

MANIFOLD VACUUM: Low pressure in an engine intake manifold formed just below the throttle plates. Manifold vacuum is highest at idle and drops under acceleration.

MASTER CYLINDER: The primary fluid pressurizing device in a hydraulic system. In automotive use, it is found in brake and hydraulic clutch systems and is pedal activated, either directly or, in a power brake system, through the power booster.

MODULE: Electronic control unit, amplifier or igniter of solid state or integrated design which controls the current flow in the ignition primary circuit based on input from the pickup coil. When the module opens the primary circuit, the high secondary voltage is induced in the coil.

NEEDLE BEARING: A bearing which consists of a number (usually a large number) of long, thin rollers.

OHM: (Ω) The unit used to measure the resistance of conductor to electrical flow. One ohm is the amount of resistance that limits current flow to one ampere in a circuit with one volt of pressure.

OHMMETER: An instrument used for measuring the resistance, in ohms, in an electrical circuit.

OUTPUT SHAFT: The shaft which transmits torque from a device, such as a transmission.

OVERDRIVE: A gear assembly which produces more shaft revolutions than that transmitted to it.

OVERHEAD CAMSHAFT (OHC): An engine configuration in which the camshaft is mounted on top of the cylinder head and operates the valve either directly or by means of rocker arms.

OVERHEAD VALVE (OHV): An engine configuration in which all of the valves are located in the cylinder head and the camshaft is located in the cylinder block. The camshaft operates the valves via lifters and pushrods.

OXIDES OF NITROGEN (NOx): Chemical compounds of nitrogen produced as a byproduct of combustion. They combine with hydrocarbons to produce smog.

OXYGEN SENSOR: Used with the feedback system to sense the presence of oxygen in the exhaust gas and signal the computer which can reference the voltage signal to an air/fuel ratio.

PINION: The smaller of two meshing gears.

PISTON RING: An open ended ring which fits into a groove on the outer diameter of the piston. Its chief function is to form a seal between the piston and cylinder wall. Most automotive pistons have three rings: two for compression sealing; one for oil sealing.

PRELOAD: A predetermined load placed on a bearing during assembly or by adjustment.

PRIMARY CIRCUIT: Is the low voltage side of the ignition system which consists of the ignition switch, ballast resistor or resistance wire, bypass, coil, electronic control unit and pick-up coil as well as the connecting wires and harnesses.

PRESS FIT: The mating of two parts under pressure, due to the inner diameter of one being smaller than the outer diameter of the other, or vice versa; an interference fit.

RACE: The surface on the inner or outer ring of a bearing on which the balls, needles or rollers move.

REGULATOR: A device which maintains the amperage and/or voltage levels of a circuit at predetermined values.

RELAY: A switch which automatically opens and/or closes a circuit.

RESISTANCE: The opposition to the flow of current through a circuit or electrical device, and is measured in ohms. Resistance is equal to the voltage divided by the amperage.

RESISTOR: A device, usually made of wire, which offers a preset amount of resistance in an electrical circuit.

RING GEAR: The name given to a ring-shaped gear attached to a differential case, or affixed to a flywheel or as part a planetary gear set.

ROLLER BEARING: A bearing made up of hardened inner and outer races between which hardened steel rollers move.

ROTOR: 1. The disc-shaped part of a disc brake assembly, upon which the brake pads bear; also called, brake disc.
2. The device mounted atop the distributor shaft, which passes current to the distributor cap tower contacts.

SECONDARY CIRCUIT: The high voltage side of the ignition system, usually above 20,000 volts. The secondary includes the ignition coil, coil wire, distributor cap and rotor, spark plug wires and spark plugs.

SENDING UNIT: A mechanical, electrical, hydraulic or electromagnetic device which transmits information to a gauge.

SENSOR: Any device designed to measure engine operating conditions or ambient pressures and temperatures. Usually electronic in nature and designed to send a voltage signal to an on-board computer, some sensors may operate as a simple on/off switch or they may provide a variable voltage signal (like a potentiometer) as conditions or measured parameters change.

SHIM: Spacers of precise, predetermined thickness used between parts to establish a proper working relationship.

SLAVE CYLINDER: In automotive use, a device in the hydraulic clutch system which is activated by hydraulic force, disengaging the clutch.

SOLENOID: A coil used to produce a magnetic field, the effect of which is produce work.

SPARK PLUG: A device screwed into the combustion chamber of a spark ignition engine. The basic construction is a conductive core inside of a ceramic insulator, mounted in an outer conductive base. An electrical charge from the spark plug wire travels along the conductive core and jumps a preset air gap to a grounding point or points at the end of the conductive base. The resultant spark ignites the fuel/air mixture in the combustion chamber.

SPLINES: Ridges machined or cast onto the outer diameter of a shaft or inner diameter of a bore to enable parts to mate without rotation.

TACHOMETER: A device used to measure the rotary speed of an engine, shaft, gear, etc., usually in rotations per minute.

THERMOSTAT: A valve, located in the cooling system of an engine, which is closed when cold and opens gradually in response to engine heating, controlling the temperature of the coolant and rate of coolant flow.

TOP DEAD CENTER (TDC): The point at which the piston reaches the top of its travel on the compression stroke.

TORQUE: The twisting force applied to an object.

TORQUE CONVERTER: A turbine used to transmit power from a driving member to a driven member via hydraulic action, providing changes in drive ratio and torque. In automotive use, it links the driveplate at the rear of the engine to the automatic transmission.

TRANSDUCER: A device used to change a force into an electrical signal.

TRANSISTOR: A semi-conductor component which can be actuated by a small voltage to perform an electrical switching function.

TUNE-UP: A regular maintenance function, usually associated with the replacement and adjustment of parts and components in the electrical and fuel systems of a vehicle for the purpose of attaining optimum performance.

TURBOCHARGER: An exhaust driven pump which compresses intake air and forces it into the combustion chambers at higher than atmospheric pressures. The increased air pressure allows more fuel to be burned and results in increased horsepower being produced.

VACUUM ADVANCE: A device which advances the ignition timing in response to increased engine vacuum.

VACUUM GAUGE: An instrument used to measure the presence of vacuum in a chamber.

VALVE: A device which control the pressure, direction of flow or rate of flow of a liquid or gas.

VALVE CLEARANCE: The measured gap between the end of the valve stem and the rocker arm, cam lobe or follower that activates the valve.

VISCOSITY: The rating of a liquid's internal resistance to flow.

VOLTMETER: An instrument used for measuring electrical force in units called volts. Voltmeters are always connected parallel with the circuit being tested.

WHEEL CYLINDER: Found in the automotive drum brake assembly, it is a device, actuated by hydraulic pressure, which, through internal pistons, pushes the brake shoes outward against the drums.

ABBREVIATIONS AND SYMBOLS

A: Ampere	F: Farad
AC: Alternating current	pF: Picofarad
A/C: Air conditioning	μF: Microfarad
A-h: Ampere hour	FI: Fuel injection
AT: Automatic transmission	ft.lb., ft. lb., ft. lbs.: foot pound(s)
ATDC: After top dead center	gal: Gallon
μA: Microampere	g: Gram
bbl: Barrel	HC: Hydrocarbon
BDC: Bottom dead center	HEI: High energy ignition
bhp: Brake horsepower	HO: High output
BTDC: Before top dead center	hp: Horsepower
BTU: British thermal unit	Hyd.: Hydraulic
C: Celsius (Centigrade)	Hz: Hertz
CCA: Cold cranking amps	ID: Inside diameter
cd: Candela	in.lb.; in. lb.; in. lbs: inch pound(s)
cm^2: Square centimeter	Int.: Intake
cm^3, cc: Cubic centimeter	K: Kelvin
CO: Carbon monoxide	kg: Kilogram
CO_2: Carbon dioxide	kHz: Kilohertz
cu.in., in^3: Cubic inch	km: Kilometer
CV: Constant velocity	km/h: Kilometers per hour
Cyl.: Cylinder	$k\Omega$: Kilohm
DC: Direct current	kPa: Kilopascal
ECM: Electronic control module	kV: Kilovolt
EFE: Early fuel evaporation	kW: Kilowatt
EFI: Electronic fuel injection	l: Liter
EGR: Exhaust gas recirculation	l/s: Liters per second
Exh.: Exhaust	m: Meter
F: Fahrenheit	mA: Milliampere

mg: Milligram

mHz: Megahertz

mm: Millimeter

mm^2: Square millimeter

m^3: Cubic meter

MΩ: Megohm

m/s: Meters per second

MT: Manual transmission

mV: Millivolt

μm: Micrometer

N: Newton

N-m: Newton meter

NOx: Nitrous oxide

OD: Outside diameter

OHC: Over head camshaft

OHV: Over head valve

Ω: Ohm

PCV: Positive crankcase ventilation

psi: Pounds per square inch

pts: Pints

qts: Quarts

rpm: Rotations per minute

rps: Rotations per second

R-12: A refrigerant gas (Freon)

SAE: Society of Automotive Engineers

SO$_2$: Sulfur dioxide

T: Ton

t: Megagram

TBI: Throttle Body Injection

TPS: Throttle Position Sensor

V: 1. Volt; 2. Venturi

μV: Microvolt

W: Watt

x: Infinity

‹: Less than

›: Greater than

Index

A

Abbreviations and Symbols, 390
Air bag, 316
Air conditioning
    Blower, 258
    Compressor, 260
    Condenser, 23
    Control head, 258
    Refrigerant level checks, 23
    Safety warnings, 21
Air pump, 178
Alternator
    Alternator precautions, 88
    Description, 87
    Removal and installation, 88
    Specifications, 89
    Troubleshooting, 88
Alignment, wheel
    Camber, 311
    Caster, 311
    Toe, 311
Antenna, 263
Automatic transmission
    Adjustments, 287
    Back-up light switch, 289
    Filter change, 30, 286
    Fluid change, 30, 286
    Identification, 286
    Linkage adjustments, 287
    Neutral safety switch, 289
    Operation, 285
    Pan removal, 30, 286
    Removal and installation, 290
Axle
    Rear, 295

B

Back-up light switch
    Automatic transmission, 289
    Manual transmission, 278
Ball joints
    Inspection, 307
    Removal and installation, 307

Battery
    Fluid level and maintenance, 17
    Jump starting, 36
    Removal and installation, 89
Bearings
    Axle, 296
    Engine, 138, 144, 148
    Wheel, 34, 309
Belts, 19
Brakes
    Bleeding, 340
    Brake light switch, 334
    Combination valve, 336
    Disc brakes (Front)
        Caliper, 342
        Operating principles, 332
        Pads, 341
        Rotor (Disc), 345
    Disc brakes (Rear)
        Caliper, 352
        Operating principals, 332
        Pads, 348
        Rotor (Disc), 355
    Drum brakes (Rear)
        Adjustment, 333
        Drum, 345
        Operating principals, 332
        Shoes, 346
        Wheel cylinder, 347
    Fluid level, 32
    Hoses and lines, 337
    Master cylinder, 32, 334
    Parking brake
        Adjustment, 356
        Removal and installation, 355
    Power booster, 336
    Specifications, 358
Bumpers, 363

C

Calipers
    Overhaul, 343, 353
    Removal and installation, 342, 352
Camber, 311

Camshaft and bearings
  Service, 138
  Specifications, 101
Capacities Chart, 37
Carburetor
  Adjustments, 194
  Overhaul, 213
  Removal and Installation, 212
  Specifications, 226
Caster, 311
Catalytic converter, 161
Charging system, 86, 87
Chassis electrical system
  Circuit protection, 273
  Heater and air conditioning, 258, 260
  Instrument cluster, 268
  Instrument panel, 367
  Lighting, 272
  Windshield wipers, 24, 266
Chassis lubrication, 32
Circuit breakers, 275
Circuit protection, 273
Clutch
  Adjustment, 280
  Hydraulic system bleeding, 284
  Master cylinder, 32, 283
  Pedal, 280
  Removal and installation, 283
  Slave cylinder, 284
  Switch, 277
Coil (ignition), 69, 86
Combination valve, 336
Compression testing, 96
Compressor
  Removal and installation, 260
Connecting rods and bearings
  Service, 141-145
  Specifications, 102
Control arm
  Lower, 309, 314
Cooling system, 31
Crankcase ventilation valve, 16, 167
Crankshaft
  Service, 148
  Specifications, 102
  Sprocket, 138
Crankshaft damper, 134
Cylinder head, 124
Cylinders, 146

D

Disc brakes, 341, 348
Distributor
  Removal and installation, 86
  Testing, 66
Door glass, 372
Door locks, 370
Doors
  Glass, 372
  Locks, 370
  Removal and installation, 360

Door trim panel, 369
Drive axle (rear)
  Axle shaft, 296
  Axle shaft bearing, 296
  Fluid recommendations, 31
  Identification, 295
  Lubricant level, 31
  Operation, 295
  Pinion oil seal, 298
  Ratios, 296
  Removal and installation, 299
Driveshaft, 293
Drive Train, 276
Drum brakes, 345

E

EGR valve, 171
Electric cooling fan, 121
Electrical
  Chassis
    Battery, 17, 36, 89
    Circuit breakers, 275
    Fuses, 275
    Fusible links, 273
    Heater and air conditioning, 258-260
    Jump starting, 36
    Spark plug wires, 42, 44
  Engine
    Alternator, 87
    Coil, 69, 86
    Distributor, 66, 86
    Electronic engine controls, 181
    Ignition module, 69, 86
    Starter, 91
Electronic engine controls, 181
Electronic Ignition, 44
Emission controls
  Air pump, 178
  Catalytic Converter, 161
  Early Fuel Evaporation, 180
  Electronic Engine Controls, 181
  Evaporative canister, 16
  Exhaust Gas Recirculation (EGR) system, 171
  Oxygen sensor, 186
  PCV valve, 16, 167
  Thermostatically controlled air cleaner, 177
Engine
  Camshaft, 138
  Compression testing, 96
  Connecting rods and bearings, 141-145
  Crankshaft, 148
  Crankshaft damper, 134
  Cylinder head, 124
  Cylinders, 146
  Electronic controls, 181
  Exhaust manifold, 119
  Fluids and lubricants, 28
  Flywheel, 153
  Freeze plugs, 147
  Front (timing) cover, 135
  Front seal, 137

Identification, 6
Intake manifold, 115
Lifters, 130
Main bearings, 148
Oil pan, 131
Oil pump, 133
Overhaul, 94
Piston pin, 144
Pistons, 141
Rear main seal, 150
Removal and installation, 107
Rings, 141
Rocker arms, 113
Rocker cover, 111
Spark plug wires, 42, 44
Specifications, 97-107
Thermostat, 114
Timing chain and gears, 137
Tools, 94
Valve guides, 130
Valve lifters, 130
Valves, 127
Valve seats, 129
Valve springs, 127
Valve stem oil seals, 129
Water pump, 123
Evaporative canister, 16, 169
Exhaust Manifold, 119
Exhaust pipe, 161
Exhaust system, 153

F

Fan, 121
Fenders, 366
Filters
  Air, 13
  Fuel, 13
  Oil, 29
Firing orders, 43
Flashers, 275
Fluids and lubricants
  Automatic transmission, 30
  Battery, 17
  Chassis greasing, 32
  Coolant, 31
  Drive axle, 31
  Engine oil, 28, 29
  Fuel, 27
  Manual transmission, 29
  Master cylinder
    Brake, 32
    Clutch, 32
  Power steering pump, 32
  Steering gear, 32
Flywheel and ring gear, 153
Front bumper, 363
Front brakes, 341
Front suspension
  Ball joints, 307
  Knuckles, 309
  Lower control arm, 309

Spindles, 309
Springs, 303
Stabilizer bar, 309
Struts, 303
Wheel alignment, 311
Front wheel bearings, 33
Fuel gauge, 243
Fuel injection
  Fuel pump, 225, 236
  Idle air control valve, 230
  Injectors, 231, 240
  Operation, 228, 234
  Relieving fuel system pressure, 225, 236
  Throttle body, 228, 239
  Throttle position sensor, 233
Fuel filter, 13
Fuel pump
  Electric, 225, 236
  Mechanical, 191
Fuel system
  Carbureted, 191
  Gasoline Fuel injection, 225, 234
Fuel tank, 242
Fuses and circuit breakers, 275
Fusible links, 273

G

Gearshift handle, 278
Gearshift linkage
  Adjustment
    Automatic, 288
    Manual, 277
Generator (see alternator)
Glass
  Door, 372
  Lift window, 362
  Windshield, 373
Glossary, 384

H

Hazard flasher, 275
Headlights, 272
Headlight switch, 271
Heater
  Blower, 258
  Control head, 260
  Core, 258
History, 6
Hood, 361
Hoses
  Brake, 337
  Coolant, 21
How to Use This Book, 1

I

Identification
  Axle, 13
  Engine, 6
  Model, 6

Serial number, 6
Transmission
    Automatic, 6
    Manual, 6
Vehicle, 6
Idle speed and mixture adjustment, 72
Ignition
    Coil, 69, 86
    Electronic, 44
    Lock cylinder, 320
    Module, 69, 86
    Switch, 320
    Timing, 70
Injectors, fuel, 231, 240
Instrument cluster, 268
Instrument panel
    Cluster, 268
    Panel removal, 367
    Radio, 260
    Speedometer cable, 271
Intake manifold, 115

J

Jacking points, 37
Jump starting, 36

K

Knuckles, 309

L

Lighting
    Headlights, 272
    Signal and marker lights, 273
Lifters (valve), 130
Lower ball joint, 307
Lower control arm, 309
Lubrication
    Automatic transmission, 30
    Body, 32
    Chassis, 32
    Differential, 31
    Engine, 27
    Manual transmission, 29

M

MacPherson struts, 303
Main bearings, 148
Manifolds
    Intake, 115
    Exhaust, 119
Manual transmission
    Linkage adjustment, 277
    Removal and installation, 278
Marker lights, 273
Master cylinder
    Brake, 32, 334
    Clutch, 283

Mechanic's data, 382
Mirrors, 365, 377
Model identification, 6
Module (ignition), 69, 86
Muffler, 161

N

Neutral safety switch, 289

O

Oil and fuel recommendations, 27, 28
Oil and filter change (engine), 29
Oil level check
    Differential, 31
    Engine, 29
    Transmission
        Automatic, 30
        Manual, 29
Oil pan, 131
Oil pump, 133
Oxygen sensor, 186

P

Parking brake, 356
Piston pin, 144
Pistons, 141
Pitman arm, 323
PCV valve, 16
Power brake booster, 336
Power seat motor, 379
Power steering gear
    Adjustments, 325
    Removal and installation, 328
    Overhaul, 328
    System bleeding, 330
Power steering pump
    Fluid level, 32
    Removal and installation, 329
Power windows, 373
Pushing, 35

R

Radiator, 120
Radiator cap, 23
Radio, 260
Rear axle
    Axle shaft, 296
    Axle shaft bearing, 296
    Fluid recommendations, 31
    Indentification, 295
    Lubricant level, 31
    Operation, 295
    Pinion oil seal, 298
    Ratios, 296
    Removal and installation, 299
Rear brakes, 345
Rear bumper, 364

Rear main oil seal, 150
Rear suspension
   Control arms, 314
   Shock absorbers, 314
   Springs, 312
   Track bar, 314
Rear wheel bearings, 296
Regulator (voltage)
   Removal and installation, 89
Rings, 141
Rocker arms, 113
Rocker cover, 111
Rotor (Brake disc), 345, 355
Routine maintenance, 13

S

Safety notice, 1
Seats, 377
Serial number location, 6
Shock absorbers, 314
Slave cylinder, 284
Spark plugs, 39
Spark plug wires, 42, 44
Special tools, 3
Specifications Charts
   Alternator, 89
   Brakes, 358
   Camshaft, 100
   Capacities, 37
   Carburetor, 226
   Crankshaft and connecting rod, 102
   General engine, 97
   Piston and ring, 104
   Starter, 92
   Torque, 106
   Tune-up, 40
   Valves, 98
   Wheel alignment, 312
Speedometer cable, 271
Spindles, 309
Springs, 303, 312
Stabilizer bar, 309
Starter
   Removal and installation, 91
   Solenoid replacement, 91
   Specifications, 92
Steering column, 320
Steering gear, 325
Steering knuckles, 309
Steering linkage
   Idler arm, 323
   Relay rod, 323
   Pitman arm, 323
   Tie rod ends, 325
Steering wheel, 316
Stripped threads, 95
Struts, 303
Suspension, 303, 312
Switches
   Back-up light, 278, 289
   Blower switch, 260

Brake light switch, 334
Headlight, 271
Ignition switch, 320
Turn signal switch, 317
Windshield wiper, 271

T

Thermostat, 114
Throttle body, 228, 239
Tie rod ends, 325
Timing (ignition), 70
Timing chain and gears, 137
Timing cover, 135
Tires
   Design, 26
   Inflation, 27
   Rotation, 25
   Storage, 27
Toe-in, 311
Tools, 2
Torque specifications, 106
Towing, 35
Track bar, 314
Trailer towing, 34
Transmission
   Automatic, 285
   Manual, 276
   Routine maintenance, 29
Tune-up
   Idle speed, 72
   Ignition timing, 70
   Procedures, 39
   Spark plugs and wires, 39-42
   Specifications, 40
Turn signal flasher, 275
Turn signal switch, 317

U

U-joints, 293
Understanding the manual transmission, 276

V

Valve guides, 130
Valve lash adjustment, 71
Valve lifters, 130
Valve seats, 129
Valve service, 127
Valve specifications, 98
Valve springs, 127
Vehicle identification, 6
Voltage regulator, 89

W

Washer pump, 268
Water pump, 123
Wheel alignment
   Adjustment, 311

Specifications, 312
Wheel bearings
Front wheel, 33, 309
Wheel cylinders, 347
Window regulator, 373
Windshield, 373
Windshield wipers
Arm, 266
Blade, 266

Linkage, 267
Motor, 266, 268
Refills, 24
Windshield wiper switch, 271
Wiring
Spark plug, 42, 44
Trailer, 34
Wiring harnesses, 253
Wiring repair, 255

CHILTON'S REPAIR MANUAL MODEL INDEX
Car and truck model names are listed in alphabetical and numerical order

Part No.	Model	Repair Manual Title
6980	Accord	Honda 1973-88
7747	Aerostar	Ford Aerostar 1986-90
7165	Alliance	Renault 1975-85
7199	AMX	AMC 1975-86
7163	Aries	Chrysler Front Wheel Drive 1981-88
7041	Arrow	Champ/Arrow/Sapporo 1978-83
7032	Arrow Pick-Ups	D-50/Arrow Pick-Up 1979-81
6637	Aspen	Aspen/Volare 1976-80
6935	Astre	GM Subcompact 1971-80
7750	Astro	Chevrolet Astro/GMC Safari 1985-90
6934	A100, 200, 300	Dodge/Plymouth Vans 1967-88
5807	Barracuda	Barracuda/Challenger 1965-72
6844	Bavaria	BMW 1970-88
5796	Beetle	Volkswagen 1949-71
6837	Beetle	Volkswagen 1970-81
7135	Bel Air	Chevrolet 1968-88
5821	Belvedere	Roadrunner/Satellite/Belvedere/GTX 1968-73
7849	Beretta	Chevrolet Corsica and Beretta 1988
7317	Berlinetta	Camaro 1982-88
7135	Biscayne	Chevrolet 1968-88
6931	Blazer	Blazer/Jimmy 1969-82
7383	Blazer	Chevy S-10 Blazer/GMC S-15 Jimmy 1982-87
7027	Bobcat	Pinto/Bobcat 1971-80
7308	Bonneville	Buick/Olds/Pontiac 1975-87
6982	BRAT	Subaru 1970-88
7042	Brava	Fiat 1969-81
7140	Bronco	Ford Bronco 1966-86
7829	Bronco	Ford Pick-Ups and Bronco 1987-88
7408	Bronco II	Ford Ranger/Bronco II 1983-88
7135	Brookwood	Chevrolet 1968-88
6326	Brougham 1975-75	Valiant/Duster 1968-76
6934	B100, 150, 200, 250, 300, 350	Dodge/Plymouth Vans 1967-88
7197	B210	Datsun 1200/210/Nissan Sentra 1973-88
7659	B1600, 1800, 2000, 2200, 2600	Mazda Trucks 1971-89
6840	Caballero	Chevrolet Mid-Size 1964-88
7657	Calais	Calais, Grand Am, Skylark, Somerset 1985-86
6735	Camaro	Camaro 1967-81
7317	Camaro	Camaro 1982-88
7740	Camry	Toyota Camry 1983-88
6695	Capri, Capri II	Capri 1970-77
6963	Capri	Mustang/Capri/Merkur 1979-88
7135	Caprice	Chevrolet 1968-88
7482	Caravan	Dodge Caravan/Plymouth Voyager 1984-89
7163	Caravelle	Chrysler Front Wheel Drive 1981-88
7036	Carina	Toyota Corolla/Carina/Tercel/Starlet 1970-87
7308	Catalina	Buick/Olds/Pontiac 1975-90
7059	Cavalier	Cavalier, Skyhawk, Cimarron, 2000 1982-88
7309	Celebrity	Celebrity, Century, Ciera, 6000 1982-88
7043	Celica	Toyota Celica/Supra 1971-87
8058	Celica	Toyota Celica/Supra 1986-90
7309	Century FWD	Celebrity, Century, Ciera, 6000 1982-88
7307	Century RWD	Century/Regal 1975-87
5807	Challenger 1965-72	Barracuda/Challenger 1965-72
7037	Challenger 1977-83	Colt/Challenger/Vista/Conquest 1971-88
7041	Champ	Champ/Arrow/Sapporo 1978-83
6486	Charger	Dodge Charger 1967-70
6845	Charger 2.2	Omni/Horizon/Rampage 1978-88
6739	Cherokee 1974-83	Jeep Wagoneer, Commando, Cherokee, Truck 1957-86
7939	Cherokee 1984-89	Jeep Wagoneer, Comanche, Cherokee 1984-89
6840	Chevelle	Chevrolet Mid-Size 1964-88
6836	Chevette	Chevette/T-1000 1976-88
6841	Chevy II	Chevy II/Nova 1962-79
7309	Ciera	Celebrity, Century, Ciera, 6000 1982-88
7059	Cimarron	Cavalier, Skyhawk, Cimarron, 2000 1982-88
7049	Citation	GM X-Body 1980-85
6980	Civic	Honda 1973-88
6817	CJ-2A, 3A, 3B, 5, 6, 7	Jeep 1945-87
8034	CJ-5, 6, 7	Jeep 1971-90
6842	Colony Park	Ford/Mercury/Lincoln 1968-88
7037	Colt	Colt/Challenger/Vista/Conquest 1971-88
6634	Comet	Maverick/Comet 1971-77
7939	Comanche	Jeep Wagoneer, Comanche, Cherokee 1984-89
6739	Commando	Jeep Wagoneer, Commando, Cherokee, Truck 1957-86
6842	Commuter	Ford/Mercury/Lincoln 1968-88
7199	Concord	AMC 1975-86
7037	Conquest	Colt/Challenger/Vista/Conquest 1971-88
6696	Continental 1982-85	Ford/Mercury/Lincoln Mid-Size 1971-85
7814	Continental 1982-87	Thunderbird, Cougar, Continental 1980-87
7830	Continental 1988-89	Taurus/Sable/Continental 1986-89
7583	Cordia	Mitsubishi 1983-89
5795	Corolla 1968-70	Toyota 1966-70
7036	Corolla	Toyota Corolla/Carina/Tercel/Starlet 1970-87
5795	Corona	Toyota 1966-70
7004	Corona	Toyota Corona/Crown/Cressida/Mk.II/Van 1970-87
6962	Corrado	VW Front Wheel Drive 1974-90
7849	Corsica	Chevrolet Corsica and Beretta 1988
6576	Corvette	Corvette 1953-62
6843	Corvette	Corvette 1963-86
6542	Cougar	Mustang/Cougar 1965-73
6696	Cougar	Ford/Mercury/Lincoln Mid-Size 1971-85
7814	Cougar	Thunderbird, Cougar, Continental 1980-87
6842	Country Sedan	Ford/Mercury/Lincoln 1968-88
6842	Country Squire	Ford/Mercury/Lincoln 1968-88
6983	Courier	Ford Courier 1972-82
7004	Cressida	Toyota Corona/Crown/Cressida/Mk.II/Van 1970-87
5795	Crown	Toyota 1966-70
7004	Crown	Toyota Corona/Crown/Cressida/Mk.II/Van 1970-87
6842	Crown Victoria	Ford/Mercury/Lincoln 1968-88
6980	CRX	Honda 1973-88
6842	Custom	Ford/Mercury/Lincoln 1968-88
6326	Custom	Valiant/Duster 1968-76
6842	Custom 500	Ford/Mercury/Lincoln 1968-88
7950	Cutlass FWD	Lumina/Grand Prix/Cutlass/Regal 1988-90
6933	Cutlass RWD	Cutlass 1970-87
7309	Cutlass Ciera	Celebrity, Century, Ciera, 6000 1982-88
6936	C-10, 20, 30	Chevrolet/GMC Pick-Ups & Suburban 1970-87

Chilton's Repair Manuals are available at your local retailer or by mailing a check or money order for **$15.95** per book plus **$3.50** for 1st book and **$.50** for each additional book to cover postage and handling to:

Chilton Book Company
Dept. DM
Radnor, PA 19089

NOTE: When ordering be sure to include your name & address, book part No. & title.

CHILTON'S REPAIR MANUAL MODEL INDEX
Car and truck model names are listed in alphabetical and numerical order

Part No.	Model	Repair Manual Title
8055	C-15, 25, 35	Chevrolet/GMC Pick-Ups & Suburban 1988-90
6324	Dart	Dart/Demon 1968-76
6962	Dasher	VW Front Wheel Drive 1974-90
5790	Datsun Pickups	Datsun 1961-72
6816	Datsun Pickups	Datsun Pick-Ups and Pathfinder 1970-89
7163	Daytona	Chrysler Front Wheel Drive 1981-88
6486	Daytona Charger	Dodge Charger 1967-70
6324	Demon	Dart/Demon 1968-76
7462	deVille	Cadillac 1967-89
7587	deVille	GM C-Body 1985
6817	DJ-3B	Jeep 1945-87
7040	DL	Volvo 1970-88
6326	Duster	Valiant/Duster 1968-76
7032	D-50	D-50/Arrow Pick-Ups 1979-81
7459	D100, 150, 200, 250, 300, 350	Dodge/Plymouth Trucks 1967-88
7199	Eagle	AMC 1975-86
7163	E-Class	Chrysler Front Wheel Drive 1981-88
6840	El Camino	Chevrolet Mid-Size 1964-88
7462	Eldorado	Cadillac 1967-89
7308	Electra	Buick/Olds/Pontiac 1975-90
7587	Electra	GM C-Body 1985
6696	Elite	Ford/Mercury/Lincoln Mid-Size 1971-85
7165	Encore	Renault 1975-85
7055	Escort	Ford/Mercury Front Wheel Drive 1981-87
7059	Eurosport	Cavalier, Skyhawk, Cimarron, 2000 1982-88
7760	Excel	Hyundai 1986-90
7163	Executive Sedan	Chrysler Front Wheel Drive 1981-88
7055	EXP	Ford/Mercury Front Wheel Drive 1981-87
6849	E-100, 150, 200, 250, 300, 350	Ford Vans 1961-88
6320	Fairlane	Fairlane/Torino 1962-75
6965	Fairmont	Fairmont/Zephyr 1978-83
5796	Fastback	Volkswagen 1949-71
6837	Fastback	Volkswagen 1970-81
6739	FC-150, 170	Jeep Wagoneer, Commando, Cherokee, Truck 1957-86
6982	FF-1	Subaru 1970-88
7571	Fiero	Pontiac Fiero 1984-88
6846	Fiesta	Fiesta 1978-80
5996	Firebird	Firebird 1967-81
7345	Firebird	Firebird 1982-90
7059	Firenza	Cavalier, Skyhawk, Cimarron, 2000 1982-88
7462	Fleetwood	Cadillac 1967-89
7587	Fleetwood	GM C-Body 1985
7829	F-Super Duty	Ford Pick-Ups and Bronco 1987-88
7165	Fuego	Renault 1975-85
6552	Fury	Plymouth 1968-76
7196	F-10	Datsun/Nissan F-10, 310, Stanza, Pulsar 1976-88
6933	F-85	Cutlass 1970-87
6913	F-100, 150, 200, 250, 300, 350	Ford Pick-Ups 1965-86
7829	F-150, 250, 350	Ford Pick-Ups and Bronco 1987-88
7583	Galant	Mitsubishi 1983-89
6842	Galaxie	Ford/Mercury/Lincoln 1968-88
7040	GL	Volvo 1970-88
6739	Gladiator	Jeep Wagoneer, Commando, Cherokee, Truck 1962-86
6981	GLC	Mazda 1978-89
7040	GLE	Volvo 1970-88
7040	GLT	Volvo 1970-88
7593	Golf	VW Front Wheel Drive 1974-90
7165	Gordini	Renault 1975-85
6937	Granada	Granada/Monarch 1975-82
6552	Gran Coupe	Plymouth 1968-76
6552	Gran Fury	Plymouth 1968-76
6842	Gran Marquis	Ford/Mercury/Lincoln 1968-88
6552	Gran Sedan	Plymouth 1968-76
6696	Gran Torino	Ford/Mercury/Lincoln Mid-Size 1971-85
		1972-76
7346	Grand Am	Pontiac Mid-Size 1974-83
7657	Grand Am	Calais, Grand Am, Skylark, Somerset 1985-86
7346	Grand LeMans	Pontiac Mid-Size 1974-83
7346	Grand Prix	Pontiac Mid-Size 1974-83
7950	Grand Prix FWD	Lumina/Grand Prix/Cutlass/Regal 1988-90
7308	Grand Safari	Buick/Olds/Pontiac 1975-87
7308	Grand Ville	Buick/Olds/Pontiac 1975-87
6739	Grand Wagoneer	Jeep Wagoneer, Commando, Cherokee, Truck 1957-86
7199	Gremlin	AMC 1975-86
6575	GT	Opel 1971-75
7593	GTI	VW Front Wheel Drive 1974-90
5905	GTO 1968-73	Tempest/GTO/LeMans 1968-73
7346	GTO 1974	Pontiac Mid-Size 1974-83
5821	GTX	Roadrunner/Satellite/Belvedere/GTX 1968-73
5910	GT6	Triumph 1969-73
6542	G.T.350, 500	Mustang/Cougar 1965-73
6930	G-10, 20, 30	Chevy/GMC Vans 1967-86
6930	G-1500, 2500, 3500	Chevy/GMC Vans 1967-86
8040	G-10, 20, 30	Chevy/GMC Vans 1987-90
8040	G-1500, 2500, 3500	Chevy/GMC Vans 1987-90
5795	Hi-Lux	Toyota 1966-70
6845	Horizon	Omni/Horizon/Rampage 1978-88
7199	Hornet	AMC 1975-86
7135	Impala	Chevrolet 1968-88
7317	IROC-Z	Camaro 1982-88
6739	Jeepster	Jeep Wagoneer, Commando, Cherokee, Truck 1957-86
7593	Jetta	VW Front Wheel Drive 1974-90
6931	Jimmy	Blazer/Jimmy 1969-82
7383	Jimmy	Chevy S-10 Blazer/GMC S-15 Jimmy 1982-87
6739	J-10, 20	Jeep Wagoneer, Commando, Cherokee, Truck 1957-86
6739	J-100, 200, 300	Jeep Wagoneer, Commando, Cherokee, Truck 1957-86
6575	Kadett	Opel 1971-75
7199	Kammback	AMC 1975-86
5796	Karmann Ghia	Volkswagen 1949-71
6837	Karmann Ghia	Volkswagen 1970-81
7135	Kingswood	Chevrolet 1968-88
6931	K-5	Blazer/Jimmy 1969-82
6936	K-10, 20, 30	Chevy/GMC Pick-Ups & Suburban 1970-87
6936	K-1500, 2500, 3500	Chevy/GMC Pick-Ups & Suburban 1970-87
8055	K-10, 20, 30	Chevy/GMC Pick-Ups & Suburban 1988-90
8055	K-1500, 2500, 3500	Chevy/GMC Pick-Ups & Suburban 1988-90
6840	Laguna	Chevrolet Mid-Size 1964-88
7041	Lancer	Champ/Arrow/Sapporo 1977-83
5795	Land Cruiser	Toyota 1966-70
7035	Land Cruiser	Toyota Trucks 1970-88
7163	Laser	Chrysler Front Wheel Drive 1981-88
7163	LeBaron	Chrysler Front Wheel Drive 1981-88
7165	LeCar	Renault 1975-85

Chilton's Repair Manuals are available at your local retailer or by mailing a check or money order for **$15.95** per book plus **$3.50** for 1st book and **$.50** for each additional book to cover postage and handling to:

Chilton Book Company
Dept. DM
Radnor, PA 19089

NOTE: When ordering be sure to include your name & address, book part No. & title.

CHILTON'S REPAIR MANUAL MODEL INDEX
Car and truck model names are listed in alphabetical and numerical order

Part No.	Model	Repair Manual Title
5905	LeMans	Tempest/GTO/LeMans 1968-73
7346	LeMans	Pontiac Mid-Size 1974-83
7308	LeSabre	Buick/Olds/Pontiac 1975-87
6842	Lincoln	Ford/Mercury/Lincoln 1968-88
7055	LN-7	Ford/Mercury Front Wheel Drive 1981-87
6842	LTD	Ford/Mercury/Lincoln 1968-88
6696	LTD II	Ford/Mercury/Lincoln Mid-Size 1971-85
7950	Lumina	Lumina/Grand Prix/Cutlass/Regal 1988-90
6815	LUV	Chevrolet LUV 1972-81
6575	Luxus	Opel 1971-75
7055	Lynx	Ford/Mercury Front Wheel Drive 1981-87
6844	L6	BMW 1970-88
6344	L7	BMW 1970-88
6542	Mach I	Mustang/Cougar 1965-73
6812	Mach I Ghia	Mustang II 1974-78
6840	Malibu	Chevrolet Mid-Size 1964-88
6575	Manta	Opel 1971-75
6696	Mark IV, V, VI, VII	Ford/Mercury/Lincoln Mid-Size 1971-85
7814	Mark VII	Thunderbird, Cougar, Continental 1980-87
6842	Marquis	Ford/Mercury/Lincoln 1968-88
6696	Marquis	Ford/Mercury/Lincoln Mid-Size 1971-85
7199	Matador	AMC 1975-86
6634	Maverick	Maverick/Comet 1970-77
6817	Maverick	Jeep 1945-87
7170	Maxima	Nissan 200SX, 240SX, 510, 610, 710, 810, Maxima 1973-88
6842	Mercury	Ford/Mercury/Lincoln 1968-88
6963	Merkur	Mustang/Capri/Merkur 1979-88
6780	MGB, MGB-GT, MGC-GT	MG 1961-81
6780	Midget	MG 1961-81
7583	Mighty Max	Mitsubishi 1983-89
7583	Mirage	Mitsubishi 1983-89
5795	Mk.II 1969-70	Toyota 1966-70
7004	Mk.II 1970-76	Toyota Corona/Crown/Cressida/Mk.II/Van 1970-87
6554	Monaco	Dodge 1968-77
6937	Monarch	Granada/Monarch 1975-82
6840	Monte Carlo	Chevrolet Mid-Size 1964-88
6696	Montego	Ford/Mercury/Lincoln Mid-Size 1971-85
6842	Monterey	Ford/Mercury/Lincoln 1968-88
7583	Montero	Mitsubishi 1983-89
6935	Monza 1975-80	GM Subcompact 1971-80
6981	MPV	Mazda 1978-89
6542	Mustang	Mustang/Cougar 1965-73
6963	Mustang	Mustang/Capri/Merkur 1979-88
6812	Mustang II	Mustang II 1974-78
6981	MX6	Mazda 1978-89
6844	M3, M6	BMW 1970-88
7163	New Yorker	Chrysler Front Wheel Drive 1981-88
6841	Nova	Chevy II/Nova 1962-79
7658	Nova	Chevrolet Nova/GEO Prizm 1985-89
7049	Omega	GM X-Body 1980-85
6845	Omni	Omni/Horizon/Rampage 1978-88
6575	Opel	Opel 1971-75
7199	Pacer	AMC 1975-86
7587	Park Avenue	GM C-Body 1985
6842	Park Lane	Ford/Mercury/Lincoln 1968-88
6962	Passat	VW Front Wheel Drive 1974-90
6816	Pathfinder	Datsun/Nissan Pick-Ups and Pathfinder 1970-89
5790	Patrol	Datsun 1961-72
6934	PB100, 150, 200, 250, 300, 350	Dodge/Plymouth Vans 1967-88
5982	Peugeot	Peugeot 1970-74
7049	Phoenix	GM X-Body 1980-85
7027	Pinto	Pinto/Bobcat 1971-80
6554	Polara	Dodge 1968-77
7583	Precis	Mitsubishi 1983-89
6980	Prelude	Honda 1973-88
7658	Prizm	Chevrolet Nova/GEO Prizm 1985-89
8012	Probe	Ford Probe 1989
7660	Pulsar	Datsun/Nissan F-10, 310, Stanza, Pulsar 1976-88
6529	PV-444	Volvo 1956-69
6529	PV-544	Volvo 1956-69
6529	P-1800	Volvo 1956-69
7593	Quantum	VW Front Wheel Drive 1974-87
7593	Rabbit	VW Front Wheel Drive 1974-87
7593	Rabbit Pickup	VW Front Wheel Drive 1974-87
6575	Rallye	Opel 1971-75
7459	Ramcharger	Dodge/Plymouth Trucks 1967-88
6845	Rampage	Omni/Horizon/Rampage 1978-88
6320	Ranchero	Fairlane/Torino 1962-70
6696	Ranchero	Ford/Mercury/Lincoln Mid-Size 1971-85
6842	Ranch Wagon	Ford/Mercury/Lincoln 1968-88
7338	Ranger Pickup	Ford Ranger/Bronco II 1983-88
7307	Regal RWD	Century/Regal 1975-87
7950	Regal FWD 1988-90	Lumina/Grand Prix/Cutlass/Regal 1988-90
7163	Reliant	Chrysler Front Wheel Drive 1981-88
5821	Roadrunner	Roadrunner/Satellite/Belvedere/GTX 1968-73
7659	Rotary Pick-Up	Mazda Trucks 1971-89
6981	RX-7	Mazda 1978-89
7165	R-12, 15, 17, 18, 18i	Renault 1975-85
7830	Sable	Taurus/Sable/Continental 1986-89
7750	Safari	Chevrolet Astro/GMC Safari 1985-90
7041	Sapporo	Champ/Arrow/Sapporo 1978-83
5821	Satellite	Roadrunner/Satellite/Belvedere/GTX 1968-73
6326	Scamp	Valiant/Duster 1968-76
6845	Scamp	Omni/Horizon/Rampage 1978-88
6962	Scirocco	VW Front Wheel Drive 1974-90
6936	Scottsdale	Chevrolet/GMC Pick-Ups & Suburban 1970-87
8055	Scottsdale	Chevrolet/GMC Pick-Ups & Suburban 1988-90
5912	Scout	International Scout 1967-73
8034	Scrambler	Jeep 1971-90
7197	Sentra	Datsun 1200, 210, Nissan Sentra 1973-88
7462	Seville	Cadillac 1967-89
7163	Shadow	Chrysler Front Wheel Drive 1981-88
6936	Siera	Chevrolet/GMC Pick-Ups & Suburban 1970-87
8055	Siera	Chevrolet/GMC Pick-Ups & Suburban 1988-90
7583	Sigma	Mitsubishi 1983-89
6326	Signet	Valiant/Duster 1968-76
6936	Silverado	Chevrolet/GMC Pick-Ups & Suburban 1970-87
8055	Silverado	Chevrolet/GMC Pick-Ups & Suburban 1988-90
6935	Skyhawk	GM Subcompact 1971-80
7059	Skyhawk	Cavalier, Skyhawk, Cimarron, 2000 1982-88
7049	Skylark	GM X-Body 1980-85

Chilton's Repair Manuals are available at your local retailer or by mailing a check or money order for **$15.95** per book plus **$3.50** for 1st book and **$.50** for each additional book to cover postage and handling to:

Chilton Book Company
Dept. DM
Radnor, PA 19089

NOTE: When ordering be sure to include your name & address, book part No. & title.

CHILTON'S REPAIR MANUAL MODEL INDEX
Car and truck model names are listed in alphabetical and numerical order

Part No.	Model	Repair Manual Title
7675	Skylark	Calais, Grand Am, Skylark, Somerset 1985-86
7657	Somerset	Calais, Grand Am, Skylark, Somerset 1985-86
7042	Spider 2000	Fiat 1969-81
7199	Spirit	AMC 1975-86
6552	Sport Fury	Plymouth 1968–76
7165	Sport Wagon	Renault 1975-85
5796	Squareback	Volkswagen 1949-71
6837	Squareback	Volkswagen 1970-81
7196	Stanza	Datsun/Nissan F-10, 310, Stanza, Pulsar 1976-88
6935	Starfire	GM Subcompact 1971-80
7583	Starion	Mitsubishi 1983-89
7036	Starlet	Toyota Corolla/Carina/Tercel/Starlet 1970-87
7059	STE	Cavalier, Skyhawk, Cimarron, 2000 1982-88
5795	Stout	Toyota 1966-70
7042	Strada	Fiat 1969-81
6552	Suburban	Plymouth 1968-76
6936	Suburban	Chevy/GMC Pick-Ups & Suburban 1970-87
8055	Suburban	Chevy/GMC Pick-Ups & Suburban 1988-90
6935	Sunbird	GM Subcompact 1971-80
7059	Sunbird	Cavalier, Skyhawk, Cimarron, 2000 1982-88
7163	Sundance	Chrysler Front Wheel Drive 1981-88
7043	Supra	Toyota Celica/Supra 1971-87
8058	Supra	Toyota Celica/Supra 1986-90
6837	Super Beetle	Volkswagen 1970-81
7199	SX-4	AMC 1975-86
7383	S-10 Blazer	Chevy S-10 Blazer/GMC S-15 Jimmy 1982-87
7310	S-10 Pick-Up	Chevy S-10/GMC S-15 Pick-Ups 1982-87
7383	S-15 Jimmy	Chevy S-10 Blazer/GMC S-15 Jimmy 1982-87
7310	S-15 Pick-Up	Chevy S-10/GMC S-15 Pick-Ups 1982-87
7830	Taurus	Taurus/Sable/Continental 1986-89
6845	TC-3	Omni/Horizon/Rampage 1978-88
5905	Tempest	Tempest/GTO/LeMans 1968-73
7055	Tempo	Ford/Mercury Front Wheel Drive 1981-87
7036	Tercel	Toyota Corolla/Carina/Tercel/Starlet 1970-87
7081	Thing	Volkswagen 1970-81
6696	Thunderbird	Ford/Mercury/Lincoln Mid-Size 1971-85
7814	Thunderbird	Thunderbird, Cougar, Continental 1980-87
7055	Topaz	Ford/Mercury Front Wheel Drive 1981-87
6320	Torino	Fairlane/Torino 1962-75
6696	Torino	Ford/Mercury/Lincoln Mid-Size 1971-85
7163	Town & Country	Chrysler Front Wheel Drive 1981-88
6842	Town Car	Ford/Mercury/Lincoln 1968-88
7135	Townsman	Chevrolet 1968-88
5795	Toyota Pickups	Toyota 1966-70
7035	Toyota Pickups	Toyota Trucks 1970-88
7004	Toyota Van	Toyota Corona/Crown/Cressida/Mk.II/Van 1970-87
7459	Trail Duster	Dodge/Plymouth Trucks 1967-88
7046	Trans Am	Firebird 1967-81
7345	Trans Am	Firebird 1982-90
7583	Tredia	Mitsubishi 1983-89
7040	Turbo	Volvo 1970-88
5796	Type 1 Sedan 1949-71	Volkswagen 1949-71
6837	Type 1 Sedan 1970-80	Volkswagen 1970-81
5796	Type 1 Karmann Ghia 1960-71	Volkswagen 1949-71
6837	Type 1 Karmann Ghia 1970-74	Volkswagen 1970-81
5796	Type 1 Convertible 1964-71	Volkswagen 1949-71
6837	Type 1 Convertible 1970-80	Volkswagen 1970-81
5796	Type 1 Super Beetle 1971	Volkswagen 1949-71
6837	Type 1 Super Beetle 1971-75	Volkswagen 1970-81
5796	Type 2 Bus 1953-71	Volkswagen 1949-71
6837	Type 2 Bus 1970-80	Volkswagen 1970-81
5796	Type 2 Kombi 1954-71	Volkswagen 1949-71
6837	Type 2 Kombi 1970-73	Volkswagen 1970-81
6837	Type 2 Vanagon 1981	Volkswagen 1970-81
5796	Type 3 Fastback & Squareback 1961-71	Volkswagen 1949-71
7081	Type 3 Fastback & Squareback 1970-73	Volkswagen 1970-70
5796	Type 4 411 1971	Volkswagen 1949-71
6837	Type 4 411 1971-72	Volkswagen 1970-81
5796	Type 4 412 1971	Volkswagen 1949-71
6845	Turismo	Omni/Horizon/Rampage 1978-88
5905	T-37	Tempest/GTO/LeMans 1968-73
6836	T-1000	Chevette/T-1000 1976-88
6935	Vega	GM Subcompact 1971-80
7346	Ventura	Pontiac Mid-Size 1974-83
6696	Versailles	Ford/Mercury/Lincoln Mid-Size 1971-85
6552	VIP	Plymouth 1968-76
7037	Vista	Colt/Challenger/Vista/Conquest 1971-88
6933	Vista Cruiser	Cutlass 1970-87
6637	Volare	Aspen/Volare 1976-80
7482	Voyager	Dodge Caravan/Plymouth Voyager 1984-88
6326	V-100	Valiant/Duster 1968-76
6739	Wagoneer 1962-83	Jeep Wagoneer, Commando, Cherokee, Truck 1957-86
7939	Wagoneer 1984-89	Jeep Wagoneer, Comanche, Cherokee 1984-89
8034	Wrangler	Jeep 1971-90
7459	W100, 150, 200, 250, 300, 350	Dodge/Plymouth Trucks 1967-88
7459	WM300	Dodge/Plymouth Trucks 1967-88
6842	XL	Ford/Mercury/Lincoln 1968-88
6963	XR4Ti	Mustang/Capri/Merkur 1979-88
6696	XR-7	Ford/Mercury/Lincoln Mid-Size 1971-85
6982	XT Coupe	Subaru 1970-88
7042	X1/9	Fiat 1969-81
6965	Zephyr	Fairmont/Zephyr 1978-83
7059	Z-24	Cavalier, Skyhawk, Cimarron, 2000 1982-88
6735	Z-28	Camaro 1967-81
7318	Z-28	Camaro 1982-88
6845	024	Omni/Horizon/Rampage 1978-88
6844	3.0S, 3.0Si, 3.0CS	BMW 1970-88
6817	4-63	Jeep 1981-87

Chilton's Repair Manuals are available at your local retailer or by mailing a check or money order for **$15.95** per book plus **$3.50** for 1st book and **$.50** for each additional book to cover postage and handling to:

Chilton Book Company
Dept. DM
Radnor, PA 19089

NOTE: When ordering be sure to include your name & address, book part No. & title.

CHILTON'S REPAIR MANUAL MODEL INDEX
Car and truck model names are listed in alphabetical and numerical order

Part No.	Model	Repair Manual Title
6817	4×4-63	Jeep 1981-87
6817	4-73	Jeep 1981-87
6817	4×4-73	Jeep 1981-87
6817	4-75	Jeep 1981-87
7035	4Runner	Toyota Trucks 1970-88
6982	4wd Wagon	Subaru 1970-88
6982	4wd Coupe	Subaru 1970-88
6933	4-4-2 1970-80	Cutlass 1970-87
6817	6-63	Jeep 1981-87
6809	6.9	Mercedes-Benz 1974-84
7308	88	Buick/Olds/Pontiac 1975-90
7308	98	Buick/Olds/Pontiac 1975-90
7587	98 Regency	GM C-Body 1985
5902	100LS, 100GL	Audi 1970-73
6529	122, 122S	Volvo 1956-69
7042	124	Fiat 1969-81
7042	128	Fiat 1969-81
7042	131	Fiat 1969-81
6529	142	Volvo 1956-69
7040	142	Volvo 1970-88
6529	144	Volvo 1956-69
7040	144	Volvo 1970-88
6529	145	Volvo 1956-69
7040	145	Volvo 1970-88
6529	164	Volvo 1956-69
7040	164	Volvo 1970-88
6065	190C	Mercedes-Benz 1959-70
6809	190D	Mercedes-Benz 1974-84
6065	190DC	Mercedes-Benz 1959-70
6809	190E	Mercedes-Benz 1974-84
6065	200, 200D	Mercedes-Benz 1959-70
7170	200SX	Nissan 200SX, 240SX, 510, 610, 710, 810, Maxima 1973-88
7197	210	Datsun 1200, 210, Nissan Sentra 1971-88
6065	220B, 220D, 220Sb, 220SEb	Mercedes-Benz 1959-70
5907	220/8 1968-73	Mercedes-Benz 1968-73
6809	230 1974-78	Mercedes-Benz 1974-84
6065	230S, 230SL	Mercedes-Benz 1959-70
5907	230/8	Mercedes-Benz 1968-73
6809	240D	Mercedes-Benz 1974-84
7170	240SX	Nissan 200SX, 240SX, 510, 610, 710, 810, Maxima 1973-88
6932	240Z	Datsun Z & ZX 1970-87
7040	242, 244, 245	Volvo 1970-88
5907	250C	Mercedes-Benz 1968-73
6065	250S, 250SE, 250SL	Mercedes-Benz 1959-70
5907	250/8	Mercedes-Benz 1968-73
6932	260Z	Datsun Z & ZX 1970-87
7040	262, 264, 265	Volvo 1970-88
5907	280	Mercedes-Benz 1968-73
6809	280	Mercedes-Benz 1974-84
5907	280C	Mercedes-Benz 1968-73
6809	280C, 280CE, 280E	Mercedes-Benz 1974-84
6065	280S, 280SE	Mercedes-Benz 1959-70
5907	280SE, 280S/8, 280SE/8	Mercedes-Benz 1968-73
6809	280SEL, 280SEL/8, 280SL	Mercedes-Benz 1974-84
6932	280Z, 280ZX	Datsun Z & ZX 1970-87
6065	300CD, 300D, 300SD, 300SE	Mercedes-Benz 1959-70
5907	300SEL 3.5, 300SEL 4.5	Mercedes-Benz 1968-73
5907	300SEL 6.3, 300SEL/8	Mercedes-Benz 1968-73
6809	300TD	Mercedes-Benz 1974-84
6932	300ZX	Datsun Z & ZX 1970-87
5982	304	Peugeot 1970-74
5790	310	Datsun 1961-72
7196	310	Datsun/Nissan F-10, 310, Stanza, Pulsar 1977-88
5790	311	Datsun 1961-72
6844	318i, 320i	BMW 1970-88
6981	323	Mazda 1978-89
6844	325E, 325ES, 325i, 325iS, 325iX	BMW 1970-88
6809	380SEC, 380SEL, 380SL, 380SLC	Mercedes-Benz 1974-84
5907	350SL	Mercedes-Benz 1968-73
7163	400	Chrysler Front Wheel Drive 1981-88
5790	410	Datsun 1961-72
5790	411	Datsun 1961-72
7081	411, 412	Volkswagen 1970-81
6809	450SE, 450SEL, 450 SEL 6.9	Mercedes-Benz 1974-84
6809	450SL, 450SLC	Mercedes-Benz 1974-84
5907	450SLC	Mercedes-Benz 1968-73
6809	500SEC, 500SEL	Mercedes-Benz 1974-84
5982	504	Peugeot 1970-74
5790	510	Datsun 1961-72
7170	510	Nissan 200SX, 240SX, 510, 610, 710, 810, Maxima 1973-88
6816	520	Datsun/Nissan Pick-Ups and Pathfinder 1970-89
6844	524TD	BMW 1970-88
6844	525i	BMW 1970-88
6844	528e	BMW 1970-88
6844	528i	BMW 1970-88
6844	530i	BMW 1970-88
6844	533i	BMW 1970-88
6844	535i, 535iS	BMW 1970-88
6980	600	Honda 1973-88
7163	600	Chrysler Front Wheel Drive 1981-88
7170	610	Nissan 200SX, 240SX, 510, 610, 710, 810, Maxima 1973-88
6816	620	Datsun/Nissan Pick-Ups and Pathfinder 1970-89
6981	626	Mazda 1978-89
6844	630 CSi	BMW 1970-88
6844	633 CSi	BMW 1970-88
6844	635CSi	BMW 1970-88
7170	710	Nissan 200SX, 240SX, 510, 610, 710, 810, Maxima 1973-88
6816	720	Datsun/Nissan Pick-Ups and Pathfinder 1970-89
6844	733i	BMW 1970-88
6844	735i	BMW 1970-88
7040	760, 760GLE	Volvo 1970-88
7040	780	Volvo 1970-88
6981	808	Mazda 1978-89
7170	810	Nissan 200SX, 240SX, 510, 610, 710, 810, Maxima 1973-88
7042	850	Fiat 1969-81
7572	900, 900 Turbo	SAAB 900 1976-85
7048	924	Porsche 924/928 1976-81
7048	928	Porsche 924/928 1976-81
6981	929	Mazda 1978-89
6836	1000	Chevette/1000 1976-88
6780	1100	MG 1961-81
5790	1200	Datsun 1961-72
7197	1200	Datsun 1200, 210, Nissan Sentra 1973-88
6982	1400GL, 1400DL, 1400GF	Subaru 1970-88
5790	1500	Datsun 1961-72

Chilton's Repair Manuals are available at your local retailer or by mailing a check or money order for **$15.95** per book plus **$3.50** for 1st book and **$.50** for each additional book to cover postage and handling to:

Chilton Book Company
Dept. DM
Radnor, PA 19089

NOTE: When ordering be sure to include your name & address, book part No. & title.

CHILTON'S REPAIR MANUAL MODEL INDEX
Car and truck model names are listed in alphabetical and numerical order

Part No.	Model	Repair Manual Title	Part No.	Model	Repair Manual Title
6844	1500	DMW 1970-88	6844	2000	BMW 1970-88
6936	1500	Chevy/GMC Pick-Ups & Suburban 1970-87	6844	2002, 2002Ti, 2002Tii	BMW 1970-88
8055	1500	Chevy/GMC Pick-Ups & Suburban 1988-90	6936	2500	Chevy/GMC Pick-Ups & Suburban 1970-87
6844	1600	BMW 1970-88	8055	2500	Chevy/GMC Pick-Ups & Suburban 1988-90
5790	1600	Datsun 1961-72	6844	2500	BMW 1970-88
6982	1600DL, 1600GL, 1600GLF	Subaru 1970-88	6844	2800	BMW 1970-88
6844	1600-2	BMW 1970-88	6936	3500	Chevy/GMC Pick-Ups & Suburban 1970-87
6844	1800	BMW 1970-88	8055	3500	Chevy/GMC Pick-Ups & Suburban 1988-90
6982	1800DL, 1800GL, 1800GLF	Subaru 1970-88	7028	4000	Audi 4000/5000 1978-81
6529	1800, 1800S	Volvo 1956-69	7028	5000	Audi 4000/5000 1978-81
7040	1800E, 1800ES	Volvo 1970-88	7309	6000	Celebrity, Century, Ciera, 6000 1982-88
5790	2000	Datsun 1961-72			
7059	2000	Cavalier, Skyhawk, Cimarron, 2000 1982-88			

Chilton's Repair Manuals are available at your local retailer or by mailing a check or money order for **$15.95** per book plus **$3.50** for 1st book and **$.50** for each additional book to cover postage and handling to:

Chilton Book Company
Dept. DM
Radnor, PA 19089

NOTE: When ordering be sure to include your name & address, book part No. & title.